Two year olds of 2010

STEVE TAPLIN

Raceform

Published in 2010 by Raceform
Compton, Newbury, Berkshire, RG20 6NL

Copyright © Steve Taplin 2010

The right of Steve Taplin to be identified as the author of this work has been asserted by him in accordance with the Copyright, Designs and Patents Act 1988.

All rights reserved. No part of this publication may be reproduced, stored in a retrieval system, or transmitted in any form or by any means, electronic, mechanical, photocopying, recording, or otherwise, without the prior written permission of the publishers.

A catalogue record for this book is available from the British Library.

ISBN 978-1-906820-47-3

Designed by Fiona Pike

Printed in the UK by CPI William Clowes Beccles NR34 7TL

Contents

Foreword by John Oxx	4
Introduction	5
Fifty to Follow	7
Ten to Follow in Ireland	10
Star Two-Year-Olds	11
The Bloodstock Experts Mark Your Card	12
Trainers' Bargain Buys	20
Two-Year-Olds	22
Stallion Reference	325
Stallion Index	344
Racing Trends	347
Index to Horses	353
Index to Dams	360

Foreword

If you're reading this after waiting eagerly throughout the spring for the book to be published, then you're in good company. I'm always pleased to help Steve with comments on the young horses in my care and I'm equally keen to see what other trainers think of their 'swans'!

Not that I usually feel confident about my two-year-olds so early in the year. Most of you will know that my owners tend to favour later maturing horses and Steve and I often laugh when he asks me questions like 'what about the Aga Khan's Sadler's Wells colt out of the Darshaan mare?' Steve knows the answer to that before I say a word! But nevertheless between us we manage to unearth a few nuggets I expect will be competitive in the Group races from mid-summer onwards. A case in point of course was Sea The Stars. The champion racehorse of 2009 took my eye as soon as I saw him – and he never let anyone down. Glancing back at Steve's book *Two-Year-Olds of 2008* I see my comment on Sea The Stars was – 'A very nice horse, really good-looking and a very fluent mover. Despite the fact he's quite well grown he looks as if he'll show something as a 2-y-o because he's not backward at all. Seven furlongs in early July should suit him to start with. You'd have to like him, he's a real good sort'. Considering his debut was over three months away I don't think that was at all bad! Steve was so impressed that he gave Sea The Stars a maximum five star rating, so I must have sounded very enthusiastic!

If you've bought any of the previous editions of *Two-Year-Olds* you'll be well aware it's not a book to be glanced at once and then stored away. You'll want to weave your way through the pages regularly to see which of that day's runners have been mentioned favourably by the trainer – and maybe even allotted five stars by the author. Steve gets as many comments from trainers as possible and it's nice to see that most people are very co-operative.

I can wholeheartedly recommend *Two-Year-Olds of 2010* both as a work of reference and for anyone searching for winners to help beat the bookies at their own game.

JOHN OXX

Introduction

A warm welcome to *Two-Year-Olds* whether this is the first edition you've seen or if you've stuck by me over the years.

It's a real privilege for me to have John Oxx endorsing my book this year. What a wonderful season he had in 2009 with Sea The Stars – as near the perfect racehorse as many of us have seen. John has been kind enough to give me his incisive comments on his two-year-olds for many years and it's always a pleasure to chat with him.

The first three weeks of April sees me out and about interviewing trainers for the book and hopefully improving on the previous season's tally. This year I've interviewed 66 trainers and their thoughts are printed here for you to dissect.

In late March Godolphin confirmed that they would be using a second trainer in England. Both Saeed Bin Suroor and Mahmoud Al Zarooni will be based in Newmarket and both will train for the Maktoum family. Given the terrific season Godolphin had with their juveniles in 2009 it will be fascinating to see how they fare with their blue bloods this year.

The trainers who are new to the book this year are George Baker, David Brown, Jo Crowley, Richard Fahey, Michael Halford, Ben Haslam and Chris Wall. No doubt you'll be wondering why at least a couple of them haven't been involved before – and so am I!

I tend to visit half the trainers personally and telephone the other half to save time. I don't always get a warm welcome however. On one occasion this year I telephoned one Yorkshire trainer – who shall remain nameless – and he asked me to hang on for a minute, only for the phone to go dead two minutes later! He never did ring back, but maybe he knows I'm a Lancastrian.

Each year it's hard not to mention in the Introduction at least a couple of trainers I enjoyed visiting in April. Jamie Osborne is getting stuck in at his new yard in Lambourn and he surely deserves to make it back to the Premier League – particularly if his persistence and optimism is any guide.

Last year George Margarson was down to single figures in terms of the horses in his care, but it's great to see that this year that figure has quadrupled. It's such a pleasure talking to people like Jamie and George. They're always prepared to give you plenty of their time – and their enthusiasm is infectious.

It was a pleasure for me to accompany Richard Hannon on the gallops on a beautiful sunny morning in early April – especially as owners Julie and Chris Wood were there as well. Julie proved a particularly good assistant for me with the digital recorder as she sat next to Richard in the Land Rover!

My own Racing Partnership had two horses last year and we still didn't manage to get a runner, but in an effort to turn things around we started with three horses this season and managed to have a winner in March – what a thrilling night!

As an indication as to how pathetic the returns are for racing owners (including partnership and syndicate members), our recent winner managed to swell the bank balance by just £1400 when you take into account transport costs, the trainers' and jockey's percentages and goodness know what else. In other words it hardly paid for a month's training fees! No wonder places like Lambourn are struggling and are about 30 to 40 per cent down on horses. A Tote monopoly surely can't come soon enough for everyone except rich bookies and addicted punters.

Oh well, having got that gripe out of the way let's look at what you can expect to find in this book! The following is a rough guide to my description of the ability of family members mentioned in the pedigree assessment of every two-year-old, based upon professional ratings. Please note that these descriptions are standard throughout the book in the vast majority of cases, but there are instances where I rely upon my own judgement of each horse's rating.

Below 60 = moderate
60 – 69 = modest
70 – 79 = fair
80 – 89 = quite useful
90 – 99 = fairly useful
100 – 107 = useful

108 – 112 = very useful
113 – 117 = smart
118 – 122 = very smart
123 – 127 = high-class
128 – 134 = top-class
135 and above = outstanding

The two-year-olds in this book are listed under their trainers and I have carefully selected those horses most likely to be winners. There are several horses to follow lists, such as the sections 'Fifty To Follow' and 'Star Two-Year-Olds'. These are always useful for those who want to follow a select number of horses. The 'Bloodstock Experts Mark Your Card' is a particularly fruitful section for pinpointing winners and note also that many trainers suggest their 'Bargain Buy'. My only stipulation is that the horse cannot have cost more than 25,000 guineas at the yearling sales (a slight reduction from last year). It's always a bit of a problem as to what price I should set. Many trainers won't have a single horse costing that amount, whilst others don't have any below it!

To make it easier to find any specific horse the book is comprehensively indexed. So you'll find an index of the horses, of their dams and their sires (in the stallion reference section).

The book is divided into the following sections:

- Fifty To Follow.
- Ten to Follow in Ireland.
- Star Two-Year-Olds. This system gives an instant appraisal of the regard in which a horse is held. Those horses awarded five stars are listed here.
- The Bloodstock Experts Mark Your Card. Bloodstock agents and stud managers suggest potentially smart two-year-olds bought or raised by them.
- Bargain Buys. A list of cheaply bought two-year-olds the trainers feel will turn out to be good deals.
- Two-Year-Olds of 2010. The main section of the book, with each two-year-old listed under the trainer. *Trainers' comments (when given) are in italics after the pedigree assessments*. Readers should bear in mind that all the trainers' comments come from my interviews, which took part in early April.
- Stallion Reference, detailing the racing and stud careers of the vast majority of sires with two-year-olds in the book. Included is the stallion index – back by popular demand!
- Racing Trends. An analysis of some juvenile events that regularly highlight the stars of the future. It includes a list of three-year-olds to follow this season.
- Index of Two-Year-Olds.
- Index of Dams.

There are inevitably some unnamed horses in the book, but please access my website www.stevetaplin.co.uk throughout the season for updates on those horses named after the book was published.

The help I've had from my friend Hilda Marshal over the past few weeks has taken the pressure off and ensured the book is ready on time. So I must say a big thank you to her, also to the racing and stud secretaries for their assistance and of course the trainers for being so generous with their time once again.

Researched and compiled
by Steve Taplin BA (Hons)

Fifty to Follow

A choice selection of two-year-olds from the book for you to follow.

ARABIAN STAR (IRE) *"A lovely horse and he'll be a two-year-old from the end of May onwards. A smashing horse, being out of a Galileo mare might make stretch him to seven furlongs but I don't think that matters too much. I like him and he's one to follow."* Mick Channon.

ASKER (IRE) *"He's in full work – and you wouldn't expect that because on pedigree you'd think he'd be one for seven furlongs and a mile... He's done very well, we're very happy with him, his work is nice and I think he's a really nice colt by a very good stallion. He has a very good action, a good temperament and he could be anything. He certainly looks the part to me."* Marcus Tregoning

AWAROA (IRE) *"I'm really excited by her, she's very nice, has a typical 'Cape Cross' head and I'm very pleased with her...she has plenty of speed and looks well forward...she has a brilliant temperament, not over-big but she's going to grow a bit. I really do like her."* Marcus Tregoning

BURJ HATTA (USA) *"We like this horse, he's a very athletic, straightforward colt with plenty of quality and a seven furlong type for mid-summer."* Saeed bin Suroor.

BYRONY (IRE) ch.f. Byron – Saphire (College Chapel). *"She'd be one of my picks – a very nice filly and she's going to be sharp. A strong, good-moving sort with a big backside on her."* Richard Hannon

CADORE (IRE) *"A big colt that's going to take quite a bit of time, but he moves well and goes along really nicely. He'd probably be the pick of my two-year-olds but I don't see him being out until August time over seven furlongs or a mile. A horse I like a lot."* Peter Chapple-Hyam.

CLINICAL *"The family have done me jolly well and they normally come at two, so I would think she'd run in mid-season over six/seven furlongs. Despite being by Motivator, there are plenty of quick ones in the family."* Sir Mark Prescott.

CODEMASTER *"I think this is the most eye-catching of my two-year-olds cantering. He's a tremendous mover, very well-balanced and very athletic ...you would think that by June time he'd be able to go racing. He'll be a five furlong type and I think he'd get six."* Henry Candy.

COUNTESS ELLEN (IRE) *"A really beautiful filly, she could be one of the nicest of those likely to be at their best as two-year-olds. If you had to push me now, I would say she'd be our Queen Mary type two-year-old and I like her a lot."* Tom Dascombe.

DEAN SWIFT *"A high quality colt, he looks very nice and I can see him doing well over seven furlongs in July."* Brian Meehan.

DEFENCE OF DURESS (IRE) *"A nice-moving, staying type of horse who will mature into a nice three-year-old but nevertheless he should be running in the second half of the season. A very nice, good-sized, quality horse."* Tom Tate.

DUBAI AFFAIR *"She'll probably take a similar sort of route as her half-sister Queen's Grace... she's quite sharp looking and won't take long to get ready. She's maybe a bit better looking than Queen's Grace, so I'd have to be hopeful."* Hughie Morrison.

DYSIOS (IRE) *"A really nice horse, very good-looking and moves well. He'll be a July type two-year-old starting at six furlongs and he should get seven."* Luca Cumani.

EBONY SONG (USA) *"A nice, big scopey horse and a good mover, with a bit of luck he should be a June type two-year-old. Songandaprayer is a good sire of two-year-olds and this is a nice, solid horse who I think will win races at six and seven furlongs this year."* Jeremy Noseda.

ELZAAM (AUS) *"He's Australian-bred and they tell me he's typical of the sire. A very nice colt, he's a precocious two-year-old and he's one we*

could start off at five furlongs, so we'll be getting on with him now." Michael Jarvis.

ENJOY TODAY (USA) "He looks very nice. A quality colt for around July over seven furlongs." Brian Meehan.

EXCELEBRATION (IRE) "A nice colt, he's done well since we bought him. He was quite narrow at the sales but he's filled out and turned into a nice horse...He's shown speed and is a promising colt." Marco Botti.

FACE THE PROBLEM (IRE) "He's just arrived on the radar – and all the boys who ride him say he goes well. He's ready to run now and he may have won before your book comes out. One to follow." Barry Hills.

FIFTH ESTATE "I'm going to firmly predict right now that I've got a Needwood Blade that can run!...He's jet black and looks just like Polar Falcon...I just think he's a lovely horse...I love him." Jamie Osborne.

FURY "Fury has always gone well, he's very good-natured, strong and a mid-season type two-year-old. He's a nice colt and I like him." William Haggas.

HONEYMEAD (IRE) "A lovely filly, I like her and she's one of my nicest. She's got natural ability, she's breezed well and worked a couple of times, so despite being by Pivotal she could be out sooner than you'd think. She's very nice and if I have a really good two-year-old this could be the one." Richard Fahey.

INIMITABLE ROMANEE (USA) "An absolutely beautiful filly...I would think that as she's a big filly she'll be suited by a mile later in the season and I'd have to say she's every TRAINERS' dream." Amanda Perrett.

LIBERTY CAP (USA) "A sweet little horse, he was on the Al Bahathri gallop this morning and he has a good attitude. Not very big, but a real nice two-year-old type...I hope to have him out in May over six furlongs." John Gosden.

LOVE NEST "A smart looking colt that's bred for speed." John Dunlop.

MAQAASID "I like her, she's strong and did some upsides work on the Al Bahathri gallop this morning. She did it well, looks like a six furlong two-year-old and is a good filly. One to watch out for." John Gosden.

MARAHEB "An attractive and powerful son of the outstanding top Australian sire. He has plenty of scope and a lot to like about him. One for the second part of the season." John Dunlop.

MEINAAWI (USA) "He's showing up well, he should start off at six furlongs in mid-May and he'll be a very nice six/seven furlong horse in the future. He goes well, he's a very likeable, scopey horse and it's a family that does surprisingly well at two." David Simcock.

MI REGALO "He goes well and we might start him off in April. A nice, sharp, two-year-old type with a bit of class, he'll start off at five furlongs but he'll stay six." Andrew Balding.

MRS DEE BEE (IRE) "She's going to take a bit of time because she's growing like hell at the minute, but the Boss really likes her. Barathea's need a bit of cut in the ground normally and I don't think she'll be rushed. One for a bit later on, but she might be worth watching out for." Barry Hills

MUJRAYAAT (IRE) "He's well-grown and a good mover with good conformation. We're thinking of him being one of our two-year-old types. He's a good actioned horse, so we'll get on with him and he should be out in late May over six furlongs." Michael Jarvis.

MUSHARAKAAT (IRE) "Nice. She's a very good-looking filly with scope, size and a good temperament. Goes nicely and we'll probably wait for the six furlong races." Ed Dunlop.

OLD MASTER EXPERT "One of our sharper ones, I trained the dam and she was very useful and would have got black type but she hurt herself. This is quite a promising colt and he should be able to start over five or six furlongs. A possible Royal Ascot two-year-old." Michael Bell.

ORIENTALIST "He's a lovely horse...Really

strong and compact, everything is in the right place and he looks a million dollars." Eve Johnson-Houghton.

PABUSAR *"He's a forward sort, his mother was a two-year-old, he's really strengthened over the winter and he was a January foal. So we'll be stepping him up over the next month or so and it looks like he'll want quickish ground...he's showing us plenty without us having asked him anything."* Ralph Beckett.

PALITANA (USA) *"A good-looking filly, strong with a good action. She has the attitude of a colt – she's aggressive. Very likeable, I would have thought she'd be out in mid-season and she has the power to start at six furlongs."* John Gosden.

RED LOVER *"This is a very nice horse, he's strong, looks to have a good attitude, moves well and has quite a lot of speed. I like this colt – he's nice."* Ed Dunlop

RED PRESENCE (IRE) *"A beautiful moving horse with a lot of quality, he was bought for the owners as a replacement for Orpen Grey... Both the way he moves and his attitude to his work suggests he'll be an above average two-year-old."* Tom Dascombe.

ROBIN HOOD USA (USA) *"He's a lovely horse that goes very nicely. We'll probably wait for six furlongs and I think he could be a nice two-year-old. He goes along real well."* Andrew Balding.

SADAFIYA b.f. Oasis Dream – Nidhaal (Observatory). *"The dam was small and won a listed race for us. This filly is small, racy and neat. She'll be early and is an active, powerful two-year-old."* Ed Dunlop.

SILCA CONEGLIANO (IRE) *"What's the race at Ascot we normally win? Oh yes ... the Albany Stakes! She's very nice and a two-year-old that's very correct and has a good attitude. I think she's one of the better ones."* Mick Channon.

SILVER SHINE (IRE) *"He'll be sharp and I think he'll be a tough, six furlong two-year-old from May onwards. If he's any good he'll go to Ascot. One of my sharper ones."* William Haggas.

SLEEPING WOLF *"This is a nice colt and I like him a lot. He'll be early and could go five or six furlongs. A nice, strong type of horse, he goes well."* Richard Hannon.

STRONG SUIT (USA) *"A fine horse, he's strong and a lovely mover that won't take long. Should be one to look out for over six furlongs."* Richard Hannon

SWEETIE TIME *"Quite sharp and very willing, I'm sure she'll be seen to good effect in the first half of the season."* Michael Bell.

SWISS DREAM *"This could be a Royal Ascot filly if all goes right for her. She does everything nicely, the other foals out of the dam have been fast and I'd be disappointed if she didn't deliver at a fairly high standard as a two-year-old."* David Elsworth.

TEMPLE MEADS *"He's a proper two-year-old type, very well-made with plenty of size and scope. He'll be going places this year."* Ed McMahon.

TIBERIUS CLAUDIUS (IRE) *"The apple of my eye at the moment – he's the one that you wait for...No matter what I've worked him with he's never been off the bridle and all I'm training now is the brain because he's such a laid-back character...if he's as good as I think he is he could be a Royal Ascot horse."* George Margarson.

TOTHEENDOFTHEEARTH *"A lovely, good-sized filly, she'll be early enough despite being by Hurricane Run and she's well-balanced. She has enough speed but I'll hang on to her a bit longer. One to watch out for."* Sylvester Kirk.

TRAFFIC'S SISTER (USA) *"A very big filly that should be suited by seven furlongs and seems to have a lot of class about her. She goes real good."* Stan Moore.

TULLIUS *"He was quite a late foal but he's a very athletic individual...and although you won't see him until May he's one of the most forward I've got, despite his foaling date. He'll definitely win races."* Peter Winkworth.

Ten to Follow in Ireland

ASHEERAH (IRE) *"We like her a lot, she's a bigger and stronger filly than her half-sister of last year, the sire is very good and I'd say this filly will start her at six before we move her up in trip."* Kevin Prendergast.

CLONDINERRY (IRE) *"A nice colt that ran really well from a bad draw and in bad ground at the Curragh. He'll improve a tremendous amount for that, he'll definitely win his maiden and hopefully he'll be a good bit better than that. A gorgeous looking horse – he's very eye-catching and I think he's smart."* Ger Lyons.

DANCE SECRETARY *"A really nice filly, I've had a few of her sisters who were all by Sadler's Wells but she's more precocious than they were. She wouldn't be far off starting some fast work, I like her and she should show us something from mid-summer onwards."* John Oxx.

HIGH AWARD (IRE) *"He won the first two-year-old race of the season, at the Curragh in mid-March, he'll go to Cork next, then the Marble Hill and hopefully Royal Ascot after that. He has plenty of speed, he isn't over-big but I suppose that's the sire's influence. A good, strong, tough horse."* Tommy Stack.

MORE THAN A LOT (IRE) *"She should be running by the end of May and she's a good, strong filly, well-balanced with a good attitude."* Michael Halford.

OBLIGADA (IRE) *"A very nice filly, she's goes really well and we like her a lot. Six furlongs plus at the end of May or early June should be fine for her."* Kevin Prendergast.

TRANS CITY (IRE) *"He'll be every bit as good as his brother Bond City. He's a lovely horse that covers some ground and I did everything I could not to buy him because he's a Trans Island. But he is a cracker, he's probably got the biggest stride in the yard and he's 'on the leg' at the moment and will probably be a six/seven furlong horse later on."* Ger Lyons.

VALESGO (IRE) *"He's a very nice colt, there's nothing wrong with him, he's correct and a good mover with a good temperament. He's coming along on well, I like him and he's a very nice horse. He should be doing some fast work soon and he'll be a two-year-old in the middle-to-second half of the season. A good sort."* John Oxx.

WAVE OF APPLAUSE *"She's a very good mover, she's been going nicely...she's a big, strong, very mature filly with plenty of size and scope and we're very happy with her progress."* Tommy Stack.

ZOFFANY (IRE) This colt won on his debut at Leopardstown in mid-April and was described previously as a grand colt that was working well at home. Aidan O'Brien.

Star Two-year-olds

Potential superstars to look out for!

The stars placed alongside the names of each two-year-old in the main section of the book give the reader an instant appraisal of the regard in which each horse is held. The highest rating a horse can attain is five stars.

All the five star two-year-olds of 2010 are listed below for quick reference.

AULD BURNS	Richard Hannon
BEDEVILMENT	Saeed bin Suroor
CENSUS	Richard Hannon
DESERT LAW (IRE)	Andrew Balding
GOLDEN SHINE	Mick Channon
HAPPY TODAY	Brian Meehan
LIGHT WELL	John Gosden
LORDOFTHEHOUSE (IRE)	William Haggas
MAP OF HEAVEN	William Haggas
MILLENNIUM STAR	Tom Dascombe
MISS TOPSY TURVY (IRE)	John Dunlop
RAASEKHA	Barry Hills
SUHAILI	Michael Jarvis
TASHQEEL	Kevin Prendergast
TRADE COMMISIONER	John Gosden
b.br.c. Kingmambo – Because	Michael Bell
b.br.f. Dansili – Clepsydra	Henry Cecil
b.c. Montjeu – Waldmark	John Gosden

The Bloodstock Experts Mark your Card

Last year's picks from this section weren't able to reach the dizzy heights of those in the 2008 edition (28 winners of 44 races), but nonetheless our experts still managed to pick out 23 individual two-year-old winners of 28 races – still a pretty good result.

Top billing last year was hotly contested by Peter Doyle, Angus Gold, Harry Herbert and Johnny McKeever. Peter's first choice was none other than the impressive Coventry Stakes winner Canford Cliffs and with Sabii Sands in a supporting role he ended up with two winners from his four selections. Angus again did remarkably well. Hot on the heels of his excellent four from five in 2008, he repeated that performance and had a Group 3 winner to boot (Habaayib in the Albany Stakes). To rub it in, he even told us that the filly might be Royal Ascot material. Harry had four selections and three of them entered the winner's enclosure – a fine effort indeed, whilst Johnny did even better. His netted four winners from five, including the Group 2 Lowther Stakes second Beyond Desire and the listed-placed Never The Waiter.

I must also give gold stars to Ross Doyle (only one winner from four selections, but that was the Goffs Million Sprint hero Lucky General who won three races in total), David McGreavy (two winners from three selections), Amanda Skiffington (also two out of three), David Redvers (two from four), Luke Lillingston (two from five) and both Robin Sharp and Will Edmeades with one winner apiece.

So who got the top marks? Well, both Angus Gold and Johnny McKeever picked four winners out of five and had Group performers, so surely it's only fair for them to share top spot on the podium.

Thank you to all the experts who have had a go at selecting potential winners once again – now let's see if you can beat the 2008 figure! Remember that most of the two-year-old selected here can be found in the main section of the book listed under their trainers and highlighted by the symbol ♠

JAMES DELAHOOKE
AROUND THE CLOCK (USA)
b.br.c. Bernardini – Plenty Of Light (Colony Light).
An impressive Bernardini colt I short-listed for Amanda Perrett at Keeneland September. Bought for Alan Spence, he moved very fluently at Amanda's recent open day. Trained by Amanda Perrett.

ELFINE (IRE)
b.f. Invincible Spirit – Donnelly's Hollow (Docksider).
Purchased as a foal for Lawn Stud, this filly failed to thrive all her yearling summer at Wakefield. Ralph Beckett had first choice of the three yearling fillies on the stud and chose the other two. Good luck, Harry! Trained by Harry Dunlop.

GLENAVON
b.c. Nayef – Corndavon (Sheikh Albadou).
Two of my most loyal and long-standing clients, John Bodie and Julian Richmond-Watson, asked me to buy a colt in Tattersalls Part One to win one of the sales races. Here he is! Trained by Amanda Perrett.

PETER DOYLE
OMNIPOTENT (IRE)
b.c. Tagula – Bobbydazzle (Rock Hopper).
A lovely, mature colt by Tagula, the sire of Canford Cliffs. Tagula has been good to us over the years. Richard and I were also under bidders for him as a yearling. Trained by Richard Hannon.

ENABLING
b.c. High Chaparral – Joyful (Green Desert).
Has always been an eyecatcher and oozes quality, fingers crossed. Trained by Richard Hannon.

KORNGOLD
b.c. Dansili – Eve (Rainbow Quest).

A horse of quality, great size and a good outlook. Trained by John Dunlop.

UNNAMED
b.f. Montjeu – Quiet Waters (Quiet American).
One of the nicest fillies we bought in 2009, could be anything. Trained by Richard Hannon.

ROSS DOYLE
RECKLESS REWARD (IRE)
ch.c. Choisir – Champagne Toni.
This colt has great presence, attitude and walked for fun at the Doncaster St Leger Yearling Sale. We have been very lucky with the sires offspring such as Fat Boy & Sir Parky and this colt comes from a fast family that has been good to the Doyle and Hannon team in the past. Trained by Richard Hannon.

REE'S RASCAL (IRE)
gr.c. Verglas – Night Scent.
A very strong and well balanced horse that looks like he would not take to long to come to hand. His sire is capable of getting a very good horse and there is plenty of speed on the dam's side. Trained by Jim Boyle.

TALE UNTOLD (USA)
ch.f. Tale Of The Cat – Bank On Her.
This filly took the eye walking around the pre-sales ring at Tattersalls. She is a very sharp looking filly for a May foal by a stallion that is capable of getting very good horses and hopefully this filly is the next. Trained by Richard Hannon.

DATE WITH DESTINY (IRE)
b.f George Washington – Flawlessly.
A special filly for a lot of reasons, she is a beautiful filly to look at and moves like a real athlete. Her dam's best progeny have all been fillies to date and her ill-fated father was a special horse in his own right. This filly looks like she could be a mid season type and hopefully this is only the beginning of the story! Trained by Richard Hannon.

WILL EDMEADES
ANOTHER WHISPER
b.f. Montjeu – Heavenly Whisper.
A very nice well bred filly with a presence, whom I bought for Bunny Roberts. Montjeu on

Halling on Slip Anchor does not exactly shout two-year-old, but she looks sharp enough physically to be out mid summer. In training with Barry Hills.

KING FERDINAND
b.c. Tobougg – Spanish Gold.
Although a May foal, this colt looks pretty sharp. He was bought at Doncaster for Thurloe Thoroughbreds, and Andrew Balding, who knows the family well, was the under bidder. It was therefore logical to send him to Kingsclere, as a replacement for Brief Encounter who was another successful Doncaster graduate for the same team. In training with Andrew Balding.

MI REGALO
b.c. Cadeaux Genereux – Lloc.
A tough, good-looking colt who is out of a half-sister to Compton Place. Bought as a foal, he was raised and prepped here at Fair Winter Farm. He turned out to be a successful pinhook when purchased by Andrew Balding, who reports him to have ability. He should be out pretty early too. In training with Andrew Balding.

SLEEPING WOLF
ch.c Sleeping Indian – Sound Of Sleat.
Another Doncaster graduate for Thurloe Thoroughbreds, in training with Richard Hannon and another who should be out early. This was a taking yearling with a great outlook from one of Whatton Manor Stud's prolific winning families. Vibes are good so far – from a yard where it is not easy to stand out from the crowd!

TOM GOFF
FOGHORN LEGHORN
ch.c. Medicean – Dance Away.
This is a quality but straightforward colt I bought for Peter Chapple-Hyam at the Doncaster St Leger Yearling Sale from Mark Dwyer, who sold us Winker Watson. He was always a good mover that I felt was very much in the Dutch Art mould and he's from a good family that includes Lowther Stakes winner Dance Sequence. He is owned by The Comic Strip Heroes who are as good a bunch of owners as you could hope to find in Racing so it would fantastic if he turns out to

be half decent. Pete is happy enough at this early stage and he thinks he could be quite precocious. Fingers crossed that the Medicean magic can strike again for us. Trained by Peter Chapple-Hyam.

WOLF SLAYER
b.br.f. Diktat – Bolsensa.
This is a really attractive and racy brown filly owned by Andrew Black and Michael Owen and trained by Tom Dascombe. Mr Black picked her out on pedigree during the sale. I went to see her and liked her plenty; she cost 20,000gns at Tattersalls October Part 2 last year from Langton Stud. Her second dam, Waya, was a really outstanding racemare in France and the USA and it's certainly a very interesting pedigree. Tom has obviously assembled a very good group of two-year-olds for this year but he says this filly is not out of place so I very much hope she can do the business both for her owners and her trainer at his new base in Cheshire. Trained by Tom Dascombe.

UNNAMED
b.f. Holy Roman Emperor – Dabiliya.
This is a really nice filly I bought for €150,000 from Haras d'Etreham at Arqana August Sale for Lawrie Inman. I was very taken with Holy Roman Emperor's yearlings as they were very racy and athletic. This filly has the advantage of coming from a great Aga Khan family as her second dam, Delsy, is the dam of Darshaan. She's been bought to breed from in the end but she's racy enough to be successful on the track. If she runs as fast as she looked as a yearling, then we'll hopefully be in business. Trained by Peter Chapple-Hyam.

UNNAMED
b.f. Ivan Denisovitvh – Top Of The Form.
A weet, racy filly I bought for Byculla Thoroughbreds from Ballyphilip Stud, Ireland. She cost 10,000gns at Tattersalls Part 3 and has gone to Ed Dunlop. It's early days but she goes up Warren Hill well and we like her. She'll hopefully be precocious and maybe lucky. It's a very sharp family so we just need a little luck. Trained by Ed Dunlop.

ANGUS GOLD
EL MUQBIL (IRE)
br.c. Medicean – Tariysha.
He is a Medicean half brother to Arcano who was a beautiful yearling. He has a tremendous action and a very good temperament and again if he is half as good as his older brother he will be ok. Trained by Brian Meehan.

ELZAAM (AUS)
b.c. Redoute's Choice – Mambo in Freeport.
He is from the first proper crop of Redoute's Choice two year olds in this hemisphere and it will be very interesting to see how they get on up here. This horse is a January foal and looked sharp at the sales and I wouldn't be surprised if he was early. Trained by Michael Jarvis.

MUSHARAKAAT (IRE)
b.f. Iffraaj – Gift of Spring.
This is a tough, hardy looking filly, bought at the Newmarket Sales. The TRAINERS' wife has been riding her recently and seems very keen on her, so I hope she is a good judge! Trained by Ed Dunlop.

RAASEKHA
b.f. Pivotal – Tahrir.
This is a very nice individual who is a sister to a nice three year old of this year called Tamaathul – she was one of our nicer homebred yearlings last year, and hopefully will be seen to good effect later in the year. Trained by B W Hills.

TASFEYA
b.c. Haafhd – Nufoos.
He is a half brother to Awzaan and his trainer seems to like him so far – I hope he does half as well as his three quarter brother. Trained by M Johnston.

CHARLIE GORDON-WATSON
RED LOVER
b.c. Azamour – Love Me Tender (Green Desert).
A colt bought from Willie Carson, he's more forward than would be expected which is a good sign. Will be out sooner rather than later. Trained by Ed Dunlop.

FREEDOM
b.c. Hurricane Run – Cute Cait (Cadeaux Genereux).
By my favourite first season sire Hurricane Run, this colt has speed on his dam's side and reports are encouraging. Trained by A P O'Brien.

SUHAILI
b.c. Shirocco – Mezzogiorno (Unfuwain).
By my second favourite first season sire Shirocco, definitely more of a three year old type in the right hands but would like to see him do well at two. Trained by Michael Jarvis.

UNNAMED
b.c. Cape Cross – Harda Arda (Nureyev).
Fine, well grown, scopey horse for later on but sure to make a mark this year. Trained by Michael Jarvis.

TREVOR HARRIS
AGADIR SUMMER
b.f. Cape Cross – Easy To Love.
The dam is a full sister to the Oaks winner Love Divine. This filly sold for 30,000 guineas at Tattersalls October Part 1. She has a lovely attitude, is a very good mover and has a long flowing stride. She should be out when the seven furlong races start and is much admired by her trainer David Simcock.

EARTH TOUR
b.c. Dansili – Moonshadow.
The dam is another full sister to Oaks winner Love Divine. He sold for 150,000 guineas at Tattersalls October Part 1 to John Ferguson. He is going well and should be on the racecourse around mid summer. Trainer: Saeed Bin Suroor.

SWEETIE TIME
b.f. Invincible Spirit – Blessing.
A racy looking filly by Invincible Spirit and the first foal out of Blessing, a Dubai Millennium mare out of Group 2 Prix D'Astarte winner Hydro Calido. She is going well, is among her trainers early group and could be a bright prospect. Trainer: Michael Bell.

SWISS DREAM
b.f. Oasis Dream – Swiss Lake.
An Oasis Dream filly out of the speedy Swiss Lake and therefore a half to Coventry runner-up Swiss Franc and listed placed Swiss Diva. She looks sharp and early and could be out by early May and is one to look forward to. Trainer: David Elsworth.

HARRY HERBERT
CENSUS
b.c. Cacique – Slieve.
This is a really stunning colt who has strengthened up much more quickly than I would have anticipated. He has a very easy way of going and Richard Hughes has already staked his claim to ride him! I would expect him to be on the racecourse sometime in June or early July. Trained by Richard Hannon.

DENY
ch.c. Mr Greeley – Sulk.
An imposing son of Mr Greeley out of the champion two year old "Sulk." This horse has the looks and pedigree to be a bit special. He is currently doing two canters up Warren Hill very easily and is a particularly eye-catching horse to watch on the move. He could be on the racecourse towards the end of July or beginning of August. Trained by Sir Michael Stoute.

GUARDS CHAPEL
b.c. Motivator – Intaaj.
This colt is more one for the back end of the season, but is certainly one to put in the notebook for the future. He is extremely athletic and for a more backward individual, finds it all very easy when going up Warren Hill. Hopefully he will be mature enough to make an impact towards the end of this season and be a Derby prospect for next year. Trained by Luca Cumani.

NUMERAL
b.c. Holy Roman Emperor – Savieres.
This is a very precocious colt who is likely to be Highclere's first two year old runner. He is finding it all very easy at the moment and looks to be a Royal Ascot prospect. Trained by Richard Hannon.

PLEA
b.c. Motivator – Request.
This is a stunning son of Motivator and is a half brother to the Coronation Cup Winner "Ask."
He is a neat, strong and generally very mature colt who, despite his pedigree, should be ready to run in late May over 6 furlongs before hopefully being good enough to be aimed at the Chesham at Royal Ascot. Trained by John Gosden.

DAVID MCGREAVY
GREAT ACCLAIM
b.c. Acclamation – Pearl Bright.
I bought the mare originally carrying a full brother to this colt (Berbice). This fellow looked a better model at the sales. Trained by James Fanshawe.

UNNAMED
b.c. Piccolo – Alhufoof.
He was a smasher as a foal when I was lucky to buy him for a client. He realised 90,000gns as a yearling and was bought by a very good judge John O'Byrne to race in Ireland. Trained by Tommy Stack.

UNNAMED
b.f. Noverre – Lady Miletrian.
A really sweet filly who was purchased at the Kempton Breeze Up. She floated along and will try and emulate Langs Lash (by Noverre) for the same stable. Trained by Mick Quinlan.

JOHNNY MCKEEVER
TALK TALK (IRE)
b.c. Oratorio – Sybella (In The Wings).
Bought for my luckiest owners Carmen Burrell and Jonathan Harvey (of Crowded House and Radiohead fame) from Doncaster. Trained by Brian Meehan.

BLACK MOTH (IRE)
b.c. Invincible Spirit – Tshusick (Dancing Brave).
I had a bit of luck for Harry Findlay last year with Hold Your Colour and the same syndicate bought this colt. He seems sharp. Trained by Brian Meehan.

WEB OF DREAMS (IRE)
b.c. Oasis Dream – Web Of Intrigue (Machiavellian).
After Arcano, we had to buy another Oasis Dream so I ought to mention this one. He's owned by the same Sangster team. Trained by Brian Meehan.

UNNAMED
br.f. Cape Cross – Jazz Princess (Bahhare).
I loved this filly we bought at Goffs for Joey Barton. The trainer did so well with Electric Feel last year. Trained by Marco Botti.

UNNAMED
b.c. Arch – La Reine Mambo (High Yield).
Another colt I loved at the Sales, we got him from Goffs. Trained by Brian Meehan.

KIRSTEN RAUSING
(All these are all Lanwades-bred and/or raised, and sold under our Staffordstown banner)

ALBERT BRIDGE
gr.c. Hernando – Alvarita.
The second foal of a stakes-winning daughter of World Champion 3-y-o filly, Alborada. This colt's year-older half-sister Almiranta was injured last year, when showing much promise in training. Albert Bridge, though not over-big, always had great presence, even as a foal and yearling. Whilst his main aim would be his 3-y-o career, it would not be wholly improbable to see him to advantage from Sept onwards this year. He was a 60,000 gns yearling, purchased by David Redvers. Trained by Ralph Beckett.

MISS VILLEFRANCHE
b.f. Danehill Dancer – Miss Corniche.
Owner/bred (as were her dam and grandam) by Mr J.L.C. Pearce at Lanwades Stud. This filly's dam was a useful Listed winner for Geoff Wragg; she is an own sister to another Listed winner (Miss Riviera Golf) and her first two foals have both won in good company. Miss Villefranche looks a tough and willing sort, and could be seen in public from about mid-summer, if all goes to plan. Trained by Michael Bell.

STATE SENATOR (USA)
b.c. Mr Greeley – Summer Night.
Foaled in Kentucky, but bred and raised, as were his dam and granddam, at Lanwades Stud. Half-brother to 5 winners (the mare's first 5 foals), 4 of whom were Group or Stakes winners. The dam was a useful winner and her dam, a Group-placed dual winner at 2, was a half-sister to Lanwades-bred "King George VI" winner PETOSKI. A sturdy, strong colt, he looks a thorough professional, and should be seen out probably from August onwards. Purchased for 70,000 gns at Tatts Oct Sales Book 1. Trained by Sir Mark Prescott.

STRATEGIC BID
b.c. Selkirk – Eminencia.
This colt is the first foal of a mare who showed much talent when trained by Geoff Wragg. Unfortunately she was injured in training and never ran. Her dam, My Emma, won the Group 1 Yorkshire Oaks and Prix Vermeille, and is a half-sister to another dual Group 1 winner, Classic Cliche (St Leger, Ascot Gold Cup). The colt was the joint sales-topper (260,000gns) at Tattersalls Oct Sales Book 2. Bred to get 12f at 3 years, he is a big, strong, but extremely well-balanced colt. We hope he'll be a force to reckon with in the latter half of the 2010 season. Trained by Paul Cole.

BRUCE RAYMOND
GOLDEN SHINE
b.f. Royal Applause – Branston Jewel.
Looks another great buy from Gill Richardson from Doncaster. Already showing natural speed, I expect her to have a good season. Trained by Mick Channon.

PLANET WAVES
b.c. Red Ransom – Rock Salt (Selkirk).
From Tattersalls December. A good looking colt with a very bright future. Trained by Clive Brittain.

SHAFGAAN
b.c. Oasis Dream – Night Haven.
Good bodied, strong, has great speed and will be better suited to 6f. Trained by Clive Brittain.

YAHROOH
b.f. Medaglia d'Oro – Country Maiden.
Bought at Keeneland for $100,000, she is already showing a lot of quality. She will of course be better over 6f+. Trained by Clive Brittain. n.b. They will all win for sure!

DAVID REDVERS
COEUS
gr.c. Ishiguru – Lady Georgia.
Bred and raised at Tweenhills and always the Alpha male of the colts here. Now owned by two of my best clients Richard Pegum and William Charnley and trained by Sir Mark who had been complaining that no one ever sends him sharp colts any more. He is sharp and will be out before Ascot barring problems. Trained by Sir Mark Prescott.

PEAHEN
b.f. Ishiguru – Ulysees Daughter.
I bought this filly from her breeder as a foal when the mare was visiting Ishiguru at Tweenhills and have always liked her. We sent her to the St Leger Sales but she was in the middle of a growth spurt and was dismissed by the market as being too big and it is rare that I am happy not to sell one. Ger and I enjoyed great success with PASAR SILBANO and I promised him another nice filly. So far so good. Trained by Ger Lyons.

RIGHTSAIDFRED (IRE)
b.c. Holy Roman Emperor – Tender is The Night.
Described by Ralph as a 'Dinger', which is his code for 'a very nice little horse that I like a lot because it appears to have a good tough attitude and bounces along well and should ring the bell'. A likeable horse. Trained by Ralph Beckett.

SLEEPING WOLF
ch.c. Sleeping Indian – Sound of Sleat.
By our first season sire and a very smart colt Ralph and I were under bidder on at Doncaster. I hear good things from Hannon's, not least that they like him more than Takeaway who was the stallion's first winner on the first day of the season. Trained by Richard Hannon.

TULLIUS
ch.c. *Le Vie Dei Colori – Whipped Queen.*
A very sharp colt of Kennet Valley's with Peter Winkworth that I bought to replace their good two year old last year Marcus Cicero. I am confident the sire is a huge loss and that this colt will further advertise the fact. Trained by Peter Winkworth.

CHRIS RICHARDSON
APACE
b.f. *Oasis Dream – Much Faster.*
Purchased at the Tattersalls Book 1 yearling sale for 350,000 Guineas from Watership Down Stud. This beautifully bred filly is a full sister to the Listed winner and Group placed, Sugar Free. Trained by Sir Michael Stoute.

CHILLED
b.c. *Iceman – Irresistible* – homebred – a precious looking half brother to the Leslie Harrison Memorial Nell Gwyn Stakes winner and duel Group 1 placed, Infallible. Trained by Sir Michael Stoute.

FURY
gr.f. *Invincible Spirit – Courting.*
A homebred daughter of the four time two year-old winner and duel Listed winner, from the family of Cassandra Go, Verglas and Halfway To Heaven. Trained by William Haggas.

REGAL HEIRESS
b.f. *Pivotal – Regal Rose.*
A homebred daughter of a Group 1 Cheveley Park Stakes winner, who very much looks her mother's daughter. Trained by Sir Michael Stoute.

GILL RICHARDSON
CHISWICK BEY (IRE)
b.c. *Elusive City-Victoria Lodge.*
He was my pick of the yearlings at the Doncaster St Leger Sale and cost 90,000 from Egmont Stud. He won the Brocklesby nicely and hopefully will appreciate further and go on to good things. He is owned by Norman & Helen Steel. Trained by Richard Fahey.

GOLDEN SHINE
b.f. *Royal Applause-Branston Jewel.*
She is bred to run being from the fast family of Branston Abby. She shows natural speed. She is owned by Jaber Abdullah and cost 28,000 from Mickley Stud. Trained by Mick Channon.

EXTRA POWER (IRE)
b.c. *Acclamation – Vintage Escape.*
He cost 37,000 gns from Edmond Kent's Ballyhampshire Stud. He is from the family of Vintage Crop and will be a two year old for later in the season. He is showing the right signs at the moment but has a way to go. When we bought him he was knocked down to "Gill Richardson in Cambridge" as we were stood that far out of the ring. We had a lot of fun buying him so let's hope he gives us as much fun on the track! Trained by Mick Channon.

SILCA CONEGLIANO (IRE)
b.f. *Alhaarth – Sarah Stokes.*
She is a very attractive filly owned by Eddie and Carmel Aldridge who owned Golden Silca. She is showing speed at home and hopefully will contest some of the nicer fillies races later in the season. She is from the family of Al Bahathri and is bred to run. We bought her from Flash Conroy's Glenvale Stud for 55,000. Trained by Mick Channon.

ROBIN SHARP
BOOGIE SHOES
b.c. *Bertolini – Space Time.*
I couldn't believe he was sold so cheap. A really athletic colt with a great stride bought by one of the best in Michael Jarvis.

PLENTY POWER
b.c. *Acclamation – Maugwenna.*
A really smart, early two-year-old we sold for 60.000 at Tattersalls October 2. I loved his attitude and he's sure to win. Trained by Mick Channon.

MAJOR DUDE
ch.c. *Sakhee – Diliza.*
A good moving, flashy colt who always wanted to please, bought by the right man in Richard Hannon.

AMANDA SKIFFINGTON

It looks like Amanda is determined to get the most individual winners this year!

CULT CLASSIC
ch.c. Choisir – Fashion Guide.
A really lovely colt by my favourite sire, Choisir. He is racing for a new syndicate of people from Jersey and the hopes are really high. Trained by Richard Hannon.

MAP OF HEAVEN
b.f. Pivotal – Superstar Leo
I do the matings for the owners and this filly has always looked a star. Trained by William Haggas.

PURIFICATION (IRE)
b.c. Hurricane Run – Ceanothus.
He might not be early but he looks nice. Trained by John Gosden.

SERGEANT TROY
br.c. Aussie Rules – Et Dona Ferentes.
A colt by Aussie Rules who I overspent on, so he'd better be good – he certainly looks the part. Trained by Roger Charlton.

LARRY STRATTON

COMETH
b.f. Iceman – Ennobling.
A racy first foal by Iceman, bred by me. She should be out pretty early in the hope of getting her dam off the mark with a 2-y-o winner. Trained by Nick Littmoden.

RIOCHAS
b.f. Val Royal – Dark Indian.
A Val Royal full-sister to the high-class Valbenny. A filly with plenty of size and scope and a lot of class. Trained by Jim Bolger.

UP IN TIME
ch.f. Noverre – Up At Dawn.
A strong, athletic sort, she is a first foal by Noverre from the good Whatton Manor Upend family which is really happening at the moment, with Overdose and Summer Fete among plenty of recent winners. Trained by William Knight.

ZENELLA
b.f. Kyllachy – West One.
A filly by Kyllachy from a good family. A lovely strong-bodied, sharp sort, just the type to make a 2yo. Trained by Ann Duffield.

ANTHONY STROUD

UNNAMED
ch.c. Danehill Dancer – Ho Hi The Moon.
A very nice, athletic colt. An extremely well-balanced colt, he has a good way of going about him. By a very good stallion. Trained by Mikael Magnusson.

UNNAMED
b.f. Royal Applause – Tychy.
She was a very sharp sort from a mare that won a number of races and was quite tough. She looked like she would come to hand quite early. Trained by James Henderson.

UNNAMED
b.f. Invincible Spirit – Honour Bright.
A very well balanced filly. She lacked a little size, but was very reminiscent of Fleeting Spirit, very athletic and light on her feet. Obviously, Invincible Spirit has done very well. Trained by Clive Brittain.

UNNAMED
br.c. Marju – Unreal.
A very well balanced horse with a good way of going. He is not going to come to hand early, but he should be a nice horse. Trained by James Given.

Trainers' Bargain Buys

How good are the trainers at spotting good value for money? Check these two-year-olds out because their handlers have recommended them as being bargains from the yearling sales. They cost 25,000 Guineas or less and some were most at the lower end of the scale in terms of purchase price. If your favourite trainer isn't on this list, he/she either doesn't have a horse as cheap as 25 grand, or I simply forgot to ask! If you look at the prices you'll see that one trainer cheated a little bit – but we'll let her off! You may also notice that Sylvester Kirk insisted on having two cracks at it, but as both horses were dirt-cheap I'm fascinated to see how they go on.

Horse	Price	Trainer
DAMSON VODKA	€5,500	George Baker
SOVIET SPRING	£3,000	Andrew Balding
MOONE'S MY NAME	£11,000	Ralph Beckett
KING'S FORTUNE	£13,000	Michael Bell
MINISTRY	15,000 Gns	John Best
BRADBURY	9,500 Gns	James Bethell
MEDIPLOMAT	23,000 Gns	Marco Botti
MOTHER JONES	£10,000	David Brown
SLUGGSY MORANT	£3000	Henry Candy
SAUCY BUCK	£24,000	Mick Channon
MISS EXHIBITIONIST	3,700 Gns	Peter Chapple-Hyam
PRINCESS ICICLE	15,000 Gns	Jo Crowley
PICENO	13,000 Gns	Luca Cumani
BALLISTA	€11,000	Tom Dascombe
TOM BOWLER	£7,000	Ann Duffield
YA HAFED	3,000 Gns	Ed Dunlop
VIKING STORM	24,000 Gns	Harry Dunlop
b.c. Avonbridge – Feeling Blue	£11,000	Pat Eddery
TENBA	16,000 Gns	James Eustace
ABOVE THE STARS	£11,000	Richard Fahey
PALINDRAMIC	11,000 Gns	Jeremy Gask
CHASING PIRATES	4,000 Gns	Rae Guest
AROWANA	17,000 Gns	William Haggas
KINLOCHRANNOCH	6,500 Gns	Ben Haslam
CAPAL LIATH	£7,000	Barry Hills
WHAT ABOUT NOW	£20,000	John Hills
BOOGIE SHOES	20,000 Gns	Michael Jarvis
ORIENTALIST	14,000 Gns	Eve Johnson Houghton
DRESS UP	€1,000	Sylvester Kirk
SILLY BILLY	€1,000	Sylvester Kirk
BLOODSWEATANDTEARS	£16,000	William Knight
b.c. Dubai Destination – Rah Wa	1,200 Gns	David Lanigan
TIBERIUS CLAUDIUS	21,000 Gns	George Margarson
GEORGINA BAILEY	£3,000	Alan McCabe
TEMPLE MEADS	£16,000	Ed McMahon
INDIGO WAY	20,000 Gns	Brian Meehan
BASILICA	£7,000	Rod Millman
SLIM SHADEY	£1,000	Stan Moore
EXPERIMENTALIST	22,000 Gns	Hughie Morrison
THE GURU OF GLOOM	15,000 Gns	Willie Muir

TWIST OF SILVER	$30,000	Jeremy Noseda
DUBAI CELEBRATION	£17,000	Jedd O'Keeffe
FIFTH ESTATE	12,000 Gns	Jamie Osborne
DARE TO BARE	26,000 Gns	Amanda Perrett
b.c. Balmont – Presently	£3,000	Jon Portman
ALEMARATIYA	10,000 Gns	David Simcock
WAVE OF APPLAUSE	£19,000	Tommy Stack
b.c. Librettist – Fiveofive	15,500 Gns	Tom Tate
COMRADE BOND	3,500 Gns	Mark Tompkins
CHATTERER	€24,000	Marcus Tregoning
PRECOCIOUS KID	13,000 Gns	Chris Wall
TULLIUS	20,000 Gns	Peter Winkworth

Two-year-olds

GEORGE BAKER

1. CERTRAL ★★★
b.f. Iffraaj – Craigmill (Slip Anchor).
April 6. Twelfth foal. 27,000Y. Tattersalls October Book 2. Angie Sykes. Half-sister to the smart 1m winner and listed-placed Castleton, the fairly useful dual 10f winner Craigstown (both by Cape Cross), the German listed winner and Group 3 placed Fleurie Domaine (by Unfuwain), the fairly useful 12f and 2m winner Astyanax (by Hector Protector), the quite useful 2-y-o 1m winner Stirling Castle (by Dubai Destination), the quite useful 10.5f winner Heather Mix (by Linamix), the quite useful 9.5f all-weather winner Oscillator (by Pivotal) and the German 2-y-o winner Global Champion (by Elnadim). The dam, a fair 2-y-o 7f winner, is a half-sister to 6 winners including the Group 3 Park Hill Stakes winner Coigach and the Park Hill Stakes second and smart broodmare Applecross. The second dam, Rynechra (by Blakeney), was a useful 12f winner and a half-sister to 6 winners. (Mrs M Findlay). *"A nice filly, she'll be racing in mid-summer over seven furlongs. She's grown through the winter, I'm very pleased with her and she's a horse with enough scope to go on"*

2. DAMSON VODKA ★★
ch.f. Kheleyf – Amsicora (Cadeaux Genereux).
April 12. €5,500Y. Tattersalls Ireland. Tom Malone. Closely related to the minor Italian winner Efisina (by Agnes World) and half-sister to the fairly useful 2-y-o 5f winner and Group 3 6f Princess Margaret Stakes third Excellerator (by Exceed And Excel), the fairly useful 2-y-o 6f and 7f winner Go Bananas (by Primo Dominie) and a winner in Spain by Diktat. The dam is an unraced half-sister to 3 winners. The second dam, Santi Sana (by Formidable), a quite useful 3-y-o 7f winner, is a sister to the very smart Group 1 Premio Emilio Turati winner and good sire Efisio and a half-sister to 5 winners including the Grade 1 Santa Barbara Handicap winner Mountain Bear and the unraced dam of the dual US Grade 1 winner Timboroa. *"She's a half-sister to a black-type filly we have called Excellerator who will hopefully continue to do well on the track this year. If so, she'll enhance this filly's pedigree. Her conformation isn't fantastic, but if she has even a modicum of the ability that Excellerator has and can win a small race, then we'll be happy. She's stocky, tough, not over-big but well put-together."* TRAINERS' BARGAIN BUY

3. IN SPIRIT BAR (IRE) ★★★
b.f. Invincible Spirit – Barnabas (Slip Anchor).
February 2. Eighth foal. 25,000Y. Tattersalls October Book 1. Angie Sykes. Half-sister to Carimo (by Fasliyev), a winner of 5 races in France including over a mile at 2 yrs, to the quite useful 2-y-o 7f and subsequent US stakes-placed winner Mighty Empire (by Second Empire) and a minor winner in the USA by Statue Of Liberty. The dam is an unraced half-sister to 7 winners including three Japanese stakes winners. The second dam, Bubble Prospector (by Miswaki), won at 3 yrs and is a half-sister to 5 winners including the Group 1 Criterium de Saint Cloud winner Intimiste. (Mr Peter Robinson & Partners). *"We thought she was relatively cheap for an Invincible Spirit in Book 1, she's progressed well over the winter and has done everything well during the spring. She'll start off in late May/early June and is a nice, solid, compact two-year-old for five and six furlongs. She's not particularly scopey, so you'd imagine this would be her year."*

4. MISS NIMBUS (USA) ★★★
ch.f. Thunder Gulch – Oak Tree Miss (Woodman).
January 16. The dam, a US 2-y-o winner, is a half-sister to numerous winners including the French listed winner and Group 2 Criterium de Maisons-Laffitte second Black Escort and the French Group 3 placed Contexte. The second dam, Company (by Nureyev), won once as a 2-y-o at Longchamp, was third in the listed Prix Zeddaan and fourth in the Group 3 5f Prix d'Arenburg. She is a sister to the very useful sprinter King's Signet, is closely related to the good sprinter Sicyos and a half-sister to the 2-y-o Group 3 6.5f Prix Eclipse winner Radjhasi. (The Seaton Partnership). *"It's early days for her, but she's progressing nicely and I*

guess she'll be racing in June, over six furlongs to start with."

ANDREW BALDING

5. ALLUMEUSE (USA) ★★★
gr.f. Rockport Harbor – Atlantic Frost (Stormy Atlantic).
January 23. First foal. $130,000Y. Saratoga August. Andrew Balding. The dam, a stakes winner of 7 races in the USA, is a sister to another minor US stakes winner, Snow Lass. The second dam, Keri's Snowman (by Frosty The Snowman), is an unraced half-sister to 4 winners including the US Grade 3 winner Palliser Bay. (E N Kronfeld). *"A nice, tall, rangy filly that's going to be an autumn type. The sire is a bit of an unknown in Europe but she's lovely, has some class and she moves nicely. I'd say she'd make a two-year-old at some stage although we won't be in a hurry with her."*

6. AUSSIE DOLLAR ★★
b.c. Dansili – Spectacular Show (Spectrum).
March 8. First foal. 90,000Y. Tattersalls October Book 1. N Botica. The dam, a quite useful 2-y-o 5f winner, is a half-sister to the Group 3 7f Sweet Solera Stakes winner and Group 1 Fillies' Mile third English Ballet. The second dam, Stage Presence (by Selkirk), a 7f and 1m 3-y-o winner, is a half-sister to 6 winners including the 6f (at 2 yrs) and Group 3 7f Ballycorus Stakes winner Rum Charger. (Mr N Botica). *"A big, backward colt for the mile maidens at the back-end of the season."*

7. BARACHIEL ★★★
b.c. Pivotal – Coveted (Sinndar).
January 31. Second foal. 65,000Y. Tattersalls October Book 1. A Balding. The dam is an unraced half-sister to 5 winners including the Group 1 1m St James's Palace Stakes and Group 2 6f Mill Reef Stakes winner Excellent Art. The second dam, Obsessive (by Seeking The Gold), a useful 2-y-o 6f winner and third in the Group 3 10.4f Musidora Stakes, is a half-sister to 7 winners. (Mick & Janice Mariscotti). *"He's a nice, tall, rangy horse and he's a dead ringer for a good Pivotal horse we had called Bourgainville, but he has rather open knees and he's done a lot of growing since the sales so we'll take our time with him. One for the second half of the season over seven furlongs."*

8. BLACK CADILLAC (IRE) ★★★★
br.c. Kheleyf – Desert Design (Desert King).
March 7. Second foal. 26,000Y. Tattersalls October Book 2. Neven Botica. Half-brother to the modest 2010 10f and 12f winner Desert Recluse (by Redback). The dam is an unraced half-sister to 5 winners here and abroad. The second dam, Shapely (by Alleged), a quite useful 2-y-o 7f winner, is a full or half-sister to 10 winners including the Group 3 6f July Stakes winner Wharf and the dams of Rail Link (Prix de l'Arc de Triomphe) and Linda's Lad (Criterium de Saint-Cloud). (Mrs N Botica). *"He's quite nice, he goes very well and is fairly precocious. I'd be surprised if he couldn't win race early on because he has plenty of speed."*

9. BUDDY MIRACLE ★★
ch.f. Reel Buddy – Sukuma (Highest Honor).
March 17. Third foal. 400Y. Ascot December. Not sold. Half-sister to the fair 2009 2-y-o 1m winner Flaming Miracle (by Firebreak). The dam was a moderate 1m placed 3-y-o. The second dam, Selva (by Darshaan), is an unplaced half-sister to numerous winner. (M A L Evans). *"A home-bred and a half-sister to a winner we had last year called Flaming Miracle. She goes quite well and looks like having the speed for six furlongs. I like her and she's a good mover."*

10. BUMBLING BERTIE ★★★
b.c. Bertolini – Putuna (Generous).
March 15. Seventh foal. Half-brother to the fairly useful 1m to 10f winner of 6 races winner Kingsholm (by Selkirk) and to the quite useful dual 10f winner My Aunt Fanny (by Nayef). The dam, a useful listed 8.5f and listed 10f winner, is a half-sister to the useful sprinter Lochonica, the fairly useful listed 2-y-o 6f winner Ivory Bride and the fairly useful 7f (at 2 yrs) and 12f Bessborough Handicap winner Tykeyvor. The second dam, Ivoronica (by Targowice), a fairly useful 2-y-o 5f winner, is a half-sister to 3 winners. (J C & S R Hitchins). *"He's going to take a bit of time. He's out of a Generous mare we had called Putuna and in fact we've had a few from the family. He's very straightforward and a very good-looking horse for the second half of the season."*

11. DESERT LAW (IRE) ★★★★★
b.c. Oasis Dream – Speed Cop (Cadeaux Genereux).
January 22. The dam, a useful 2-y-o listed 5.2f winner and third in the Group 2 Flying Childers Stakes, is a sister to the fairly useful triple 5f winner (including at 2 yrs) and listed-placed Siren's Gift and a half-sister to the fair 6f winner Indiana Blues. The second dam, Blue Siren (by Bluebird), a very useful winner of three races from 5f to 7f, was disqualified from first place in two more, notably the Group 1 5f Nunthorpe Stakes (the winner on merit) and is a half-sister to several winners including the quite useful 9f winner Northern Habit. (J C Smith). *"Yes, he's a nice horse He's had a few niggling issues that have stopped us pressing on with him but he's a very good mover and he goes nicely. As the pedigree would suggest he's potentially a very nice horse and definitely one of my nicest two-year-olds."*

12. DISCOTECA ★★★★
b.c. Nayef – Blaenavon (Cadeaux Genereux).
February 26. Second foal. 35,000Y. Tattersalls October Book 1. A Balding. The dam is an unplaced half-sister to 2 winners. The second dam, One Of The Family (by Alzao), a fair 1m placed 4-y-o, is a sister to the Rockfel Stakes winner Relatively Special and a half-sister to 7 winners including the Dante Stakes and Craven Stakes winner Alnasr Alwasheek and to the Juddmonte International Stakes winner One So Wonderful. (D E Brownlow). *"He's nice and it's the same Nayef-Cadeaux Genereux cross that produced a smart colt called Top Lock we had two years ago. He's very similar in make and shape, a good mover and he could be the sort to start making a name for himself when the seven furlong races start."*

13. ENCORE VIEW ★★★
b.f. Oasis Dream – Aricia (Nashwan).
February 20. Second foal. The dam, a fairly useful 3-y-o 7f winner, is a half-sister to 7 winners including the Group 2 5f Kings Stand Stakes winner Cassandra Go (herself dam of the Irish 1,000 Guineas winner Halfway To Heaven) and the smart Group 3 6f Coventry Stakes winner and Irish 2,000 Guineas second Verglas. The second dam, Rahaam (by Secreto), a fairly useful 3-y-o 7f winner, is a half-sister to 8 winners including the French 2,000 Guineas third Glory Forever. (George Strawbridge). *"She hasn't come in and I haven't seen her, but apparently she's quite nice. I'm not aware why she's so late but it's not that unusual and she'll have been in pre-training."*

14. GUIDED MISSILE (IRE) ★★★
b.f. Night Shift – Exorcet (Selkirk).
February 8. Sister to the very useful 6f winner of 4 races and Group 2 6f Diadem Stakes second Dark Missile and to the fair dual 6f winner Night Rocket and half-sister to the fair 2009 1m placed 2-y-o Breakheart (by Sakhee). The dam, a fair 3-y-o 6f winner, is a half-sister to 2 winners including the useful UAE 7f and 1m winner Rock Music. The second dam, Stack Rock (by Ballad Rock), was a very useful winner of 9 races from 5f to 1m including the listed Hopeful Stakes and was second in the Group 1 Prix de l'Abbaye. (J C Smith). *"A nice filly and more precocious than either of the siblings we've had here, Dark Missile or Breakheart, she's probably one for six furlongs in June."*

15. HIDDEN VALLEY ★★★
b.f. Haafhd – Spurned (Robellino).
May 18. Half-sister to the very smart Group 2 1m Oettingen-Rennen and Group 3 8.5f Diomed Stakes winner Passing Glance (by Polar Falcon), to the smart Group 3 7f Prix de Palais-Royal and European Free Handicap winner Hidden Meadow, the smart listed 11f winner Scorned (both by Selkirk), the useful 6f (at 2 yrs) and listed 1m winner Kingsclere (by Fairy King), the fairly useful sprinter Overbrook (by Storm Cat), the fairly useful 12f winners Inhibition (by Nayef) and Casual Glance (by Sinndar), the quite useful dual 14f winner Victoria Montoya (by High Chaparral) and the modest 9.7f winner Jona Holley (by Sharpo). The dam, a fairly useful 2-y-o 7f winner, later stayed 10f. The second dam, Refill (by Mill Reef), was placed over 6f here before winning over 11f in the USA. (Kingsclere Racing Club). *"She out of Spurned who's been very good to us. A lovely filly with a lot of quality, she's probably got more quality than any of the other fillies we've had out the dam. Light on her feet and athletic, I'd hope to see her out over seven furlongs in June. Most of the dam's previous foals have been big and needed time, but this filly is much neater."*

16. HOLLOW TREE ★★
b.c. Beat Hollow – Hesperia (Slip Anchor).
February 19. Eighth foal. 20,000Y. Tattersalls October Book 2. A Balding. Half-brother to the fairly useful 2-y-o 7f winner and listed-placed Lucky Date (by Halling), to the fairly useful 1m winner Namroc (by Indian Ridge), the modest 11f and 12f winner Western Point (by Pivotal) and a minor 3-y-o winner in Germany by Acatenango. The dam, a winner over 11f and 12f including a listed event in Italy, is a half-sister to the French listed winners Wavey and Rebuff . The second dam, Throw Away Line (by Assert), won once in the USA at 4 yrs and is a half-sister to 9 winners including Go For Wand (a winner of seven Grade 1 events in the USA) and the US Grade 2 winners Dance Spell and Discorama. (Friends of Saunton Sands). *"He's a nice horse but he's a back-end type and much more of a middle-distance horse. An athletic, well-made individual, however."*

17. KING FERDINAND ★★★♠
b.c. Tobougg – Spanish Gold (Vettori).
May 6. Third foal. £40,000Y. Doncaster St Leger. Will Edmeades. Half-brother to the 2009 5f placed 2-y-o Spanish Acclaim (by Acclamation) and to the fairly useful triple 6f winner (including at 2 yrs) and listed-placed Spanish Bounty (by Bahamian Bounty). The dam, an 8.5f winner, is a half-sister to 4 winners including the useful 1m Victoria Cup winner Bold King and the Group 2 Railway Stakes second Spanish Ace. The second dam, Spanish Heart (by King Of Spain), a quite useful winner of 4 races over 7f and 1m, is a half-sister to 7 winners. (Thurloe Thoroughbreds XXVII). *"He's a May foal but he isn't necessarily that backward, we're just starting to press a few buttons with him now."*

18. LAY TIME ★★
b.f. Galileo – Time Saved (Green Desert).
April 25. Sixth foal. Half-sister to the useful 2009 listed 6f winner Jira (by Medicean), to the quite useful 6f (at 2 yrs) and 1m winner Emirates Sports (by King's Best), to the smart 7f (at 2 yrs) and Group 2 12f King Edward VII Stakes winner Plea Bargain (by Machiavellian), the useful 2-y-o 7f winner and Group 3 1m Prix des Chenes second Dubai Time (by Dubai Destination) and the modest 1m winner Tipsy Me (by Selkirk). The dam, a fairly useful 10f winner, is a sister to the useful 1m winner Illusion and a half-sister to 5 winners including Zinaad and Time Allowed, both winners of the Group 2 12f Jockey Club Stakes and the dams of the Group winners Anton Chekhov, First Charter, Plea Bargain and Time Away. The second dam, Time Charter (by Saritamer), was an exceptional filly and winner of the Oaks, the King George VI and Queen Elizabeth Diamond Stakes, the Champion Stakes, Coronation Cup, Prix Foy and Sun Chariot Stakes. (R Barnett). *"She's isn't a forward two-year-old, but she's a quality, attractive filly that will want some time and a trip."*

19. MAGIC MINSTREL ★★★
b.c. Norse Dancer – Lochsong (Song).
March 2. Half-brother to the smart listed 6f winner of 5 races Lochridge (by Indian Ridge), to the useful listed 5f winner Loch Verdi (by Green Desert), the quite useful dual 6f winner Rapid Water and the quite useful 5f and 6f winner Lochstar (both by Anabaa). The dam, a champion sprinter and winner of the Prix de l'Abbaye (twice), the Kings Stand Stakes and the Nunthorpe Stakes, is a half-sister to the Nunthorpe Stakes winner Lochangel. The second dam, Peckitts Well (by Lochnager), was a fairly useful winner of five races at 2 and 3 yrs from 5f to 6f. (J C Smith). *"He's had a setback but he's a good-looking horse and is more forward-looking than any of the siblings we've had. He's having a break but he's a nice horse to look forward to later in the season."*

20. MI REGALO ★★★★♠
b.c. Cadeaux Genereux – Lloc (Absalom).
March 13. Tenth foal. 55,000Y. Tattersalls October Book 1. A Balding. Half-brother to the quite useful 5f and 6f winner of 5 races (including at 2 yrs) Luscivious (by Kyllachy), to the quite useful 5f to 1m winner of 3 races at 2 and 3 yrs Aimee's Delight (by Robellino), the modest 10f and hurdles winner Gulf Coast (by Dubai Destination) and the modest triple 6f winner Cape Of Storms (by Cape Cross). The dam, a fair 5f winner at 2 and 4 yrs, is a half-sister to 5 winners including the Grade 1 6f July Cup winner and sire Compton Place and the US Grade 3 winner Mantles Star.

The second dam, Nosey (by Nebbiolo), a fairly useful Irish 2-y-o 5f and 6f winner, was listed-placed and is a half-sister to 7 minor winners. (Mick & Janice Mariscotti). *"He goes well and we might start him off in April. A nice, sharp, two-year-old type with a bit of class, he'll start off at five furlongs but he'll stay six."*

21. MOMENT OF TIME ★★
b.f. Rainbow Quest – Not Before Time (Polish Precedent).
May 11. Closely related to the 10f winner and Group 1 French Oaks second Time Ahead (by Spectrum) and half-sister to the Group 3 10.4f Musidora Stakes winner and Group 1 Prix de Diane third Time Away (by Darshaan), the useful dual 1m winner Duntulm (by Sakhee), the fairly useful 10f and 12.4f winner Original Spin (by Machiavellian), the quite useful 10f winners Ringing Hill (by Charnwood Forest) and Time Loss (by Kenmare) and the fair 1m winner Time Over (by Mark Of Esteem). The dam is an unraced half-sister to the Group 3 12f Jockey Club Stakes winner Zinaad and to the Group 3 12f Princess Royal Stakes winner Time Allowed. The second dam, Time Charter (by Saritamer), won the Oaks, the King George VI and Queen Elizabeth Diamond Stakes, the Champion Stakes, the Coronation Cup, the Prix Foy and the Sun Chariot Stakes. (R Barnett). *"She's very nice, a quality filly and a nice mover but a family like hers can't be rushed and we have a lot to look forward to in the future."*

22. PERFECT MISSION ★★★
b.c. Bertolini – Sharp Secret (College Chapel).
March 13. Half-sister to the modest 2009 7f placed 2-y-o Perfect Secret (by Spinning World). The dam, a modest winner of 6 races from 6f to 1m, is a half-sister to numerous winners. The second dam, State Treasure (by Secretariat), won in the USA and is a half-sister to a Group 3 winner. (Mildmay Bloodstock). *"He goes well but he's just on a bit of a growing spell at the moment. I have the half-sister who is still a maiden but she would have won by now if she hadn't had problems. This colt is straightforward, a good mover and I like him."*

23. QUEEN O' THE DESERT (IRE) ★★★
b.f. Green Desert – Al Dhahab (Seeking The Gold).
February 4. First foal. 50,000Y. Tattersalls October Book 1. Neven Botica. The dam, placed fourth once over 7f at 2 yrs, is a half-sister to 2 minor winners. The second dam, South Of Saturn (by Seattle Slew), a minor French 2-y-o 6f winner, is a half-sister to 11 winners including the Group 1 6f Cheveley Park Stakes winner Gay Gallanta (herself dam of the Group 2 winner Byron). (Mr N Botica). *"A well-made filly and a good mover, she looks like making up into a nice filly by mid-summer. She'll probably start off at six furlongs."*

24. RAWAKI (IRE) ★★★
b.c. Phoenix Reach – Averami (Averti).
March 18. Third foal. Half-brother to the fairly useful 2009 2-y-o 6f winner Side Glance and to the fair 2-y-o 7f winner Advertise (both by Passing Glance). The dam, a moderate 7f winner, is a sister to 2 winners. The second dam, Friend For Life (by Lahib), was unplaced. (Kingsclere Racing Club). *"He's a nice horse, I've got a few by this sire and they're all similar. They're just starting to do well physically and they all look just as he did at this stage. Phoenix Reach would have won as a two-year-old but he split a pastern. This colt is a good mover and he'll be a mid-summer two-year-old."*

25. ROBIN HOOD USA (USA) ★★★★
ch.c. Mr Greeley – Fashion Cat (Forest Wildcat).
February 17. Third foal. $200,000Y. Saratoga August. Andrew Balding. The dam, a minor winner at 3 yrs in the USA, is a half-sister to 4 winners including the triple US Grade 1 winner Peace Rules (by Jules) and the minor US stakes winner Wild Fashion (by Once Wild). The second dam, Hold To Fashion (by Hold Your Peace), a minor winner of 2 races at 3 yrs in the USA, is a half-sister to 6 minor winners. (E N Kronfeld). *"He's a lovely horse that goes very nicely. We'll probably wait for six furlongs and I think he could be a nice two-year-old. He goes along real well."*

26. ROJO BOY ★★★★
gr.c. Red Ransom – Way To The Stars (Dansili).
February 7. First foal. 20,000Y. Tattersalls October Book 1. A Balding. The dam is a placed half-sister to 6 winners including to the

South African multiple Group 1 winner Dancer's Daughter and the 2-y-o Group 3 7f Somerville Tattersall Stakes winner Diktatorial. The second dam, Reason To Dance (by Damister), a useful 2-y-o 5f and 5.8f winner, was third in the Group 2 1m Falmouth Stakes and is a half-sister to 4 minor winners. (D E Brownlow). *"He's definitely an early two-year-old. I trained the dam who didn't win but she was alright and this colt is forward, he's pretty smart and he moves well. He has a good attitude and he's owned by the same Partnership that owned Stargaze last year and he looks a very similar type – a nice, precocious two-year-old."*

27. SHAMAN DANCER (GER) ★★
b.c. Oasis Dream – Square The Circle (Second Empire).
March 14. Second foal. 30,000Y. Tattersalls October Book 1. A Balding. The dam, placed once at 3 yrs in Germany, is a half-sister to 5 winners including the US Grade 3 placed Add The Gold. The second dam, Sum (by Spectacular Bid), won the Grade 3 Pucker Up Stakes and is a half-sister to 9 stakes winners including the Group 1 William Hill Futurity winner Bakharoff and the Group 2 Lockinge Stakes winner Emperor Jones. (Mick & Janice Mariscotti). *"He's going to take a bit of time, he has a bit of scope but he had a bit of a setback and I had to back of him. I'm chuffed to bits with him though and he's a nice colt that should make a two-year-old later on."*

28. SIRIUS SUPERSTAR ★★
b.c. Galileo – Brightest (Rainbow Quest).
April 16. Fourth foal. 20,000Y. Tattersalls October. Norris/Huntingdon. Half-brother to the useful Irish 1m (including at 2 yrs) and Group 3 7f Brownstown Stakes winner Glowing (by Dansili). The dam is a placed half-sister to 4 winners including the 1m (at 2 yrs) and Group 1 10f Grand Prix de Paris winner Beat Hollow and the US Grade 3 winner Yaralino. The second dam, Wemyss Bight (by Dancing Brave), a very smart filly, won 5 races including the Group 1 12f Irish Oaks and the Group 2 12f Prix de Malleret. (J Pearce). *"Probably the cheapest Galileo to have gone through the ring, he has a wonderful pedigree but his conformation let him down at the Sales. But he's actually light on his feet, a really good mover and I like him.*

His bad forelegs don't seem to stop him moving forward in a reasonably balanced manner!."

29. SONG OF THE SIREN ★★
ch.f. With Approval – Sulitelma (The Minstrel).
April 11. €800Y. Goffs Open. Not sold. Half-sister to the quite useful 2-y-o 5f winner Ice Mountain (by Kyllachy), to the quite useful 10f to 12f winner Tromp, the fair 7f and 1m winner Robinzal (both by Zilzal), the fair 2-y-o 1m winner Min Mirri, the modest 6f and 1m winner Border Glen (both by Selkirk), the fair Irish 5f winner Neeze (by Cadeaux Genereux), the modest 2-y-o 6f winner Seta Pura (by Domedriver) and the modest 9.4f all-weather winner Semiramis (by Darshaan). The dam, a modest 2-y-o 5f all-weather winner, is a half-sister to 3 winners including the German listed winner El Supremo. The second dam, Sharmila (by Blakeney), ran once unplaced and is a half-sister to the King George VI and Queen Elizabeth Diamond Stakes winner Petoski. (Kirsten Rausing). *"She's looks as though she should be running and hopefully winning this year."*

30. SOVIET SPRING ★★★
b.g. Soviet Star – Spring Will Come (Desert Prince).
March 2. First foal. £3,000Y. Doncaster St Leger Festival. Andrew Balding. The dam is an unraced half-sister to 3 winners here and abroad. The second dam, Shauna's Honey (by Danehill), a quite useful 7f winner at Leopardstown, is a half-sister to 5 winners including the smart Ahohoney, a winner over 6f and 1m here at 2 yrs and the Group 3 10.5f Prix Fille de l'Aire. (Kingsclere Racing Club). *"He goes well and he looks nice enough. Hopefully he'll have the speed for six furlongs and we're pretty pleased with him."* TRAINERS' BARGAIN BUY

31. STAGE ATTRACTION (IRE) ★★★
b.c. Royal Applause – Mona Em (Catrail).
March 14. Fifth foal. £32,000Y. Doncaster St Leger. Bobby O'Ryan. Brother to the French listed 10f winner of 9 races Nice Applause (by Royal Applause) and half-brother to the fair 2-y-o 5f winner Monalini (by Bertolini) and the minor French 2-y-o winner Monatora (by Hector Protector). The

dam, a French listed sprint winner, is a half-sister to 4 winners including the Irish 2,000 Guineas fourth Maumee. The second dam, Moy Water (by Tirol), an Irish 1m (at 2 yrs) and 9f winner, is a half-sister to 8 winners including the very useful listed sprint winners Bufalino and Maledetto. (Miss A V Hill). *"A nice little horse, he'll be forward enough, he'll hopefully have enough speed for five furlongs and he's an attractive colt that goes well enough. He should win races."*

32. SUNPEARL ★★★
ch.f. Compton Place – Star Tulip (Night Shift).
April 9. Half-sister to the fairly useful 2009 2-y-o 5f winner Swan Wings, to the fair dual 5f winner Spring Green, the modest 2-y-o 7f winner Kamal (both by Bahamian Bounty), the smart and consistent sprint winner of 15 races Texas Gold (by Cadeaux Genereux), to the fair 6f (at 2 yrs) to 11f and hurdles winner Indian Sun (by Indian Ridge), the fair 6f winner Kansas Gold (by Alhaarth), the modest dual 10f winner Choristar (by Inchinor) and a 4-y-o winner in Germany by Hector Protector. The dam was a useful winner of 3 races over 6f including the listed Sandy Lane Stakes and is a half-sister to 4 minor winners. The second dam, Silk Petal (by Petorius), a useful winner of 3 races over 7f including a German listed event, was third in the Group 3 Prix de Flore and is a half-sister to 5 winners. (N Jones). *"She has a big backside on her, very much a sprinter type on looks and she could be fast. I haven't done enough with her yet but I'd guess that she could be a nice, mid-summer type two-year-old."*

33. TWIN SOUL (IRE) ★★★
b.f. Singspiel – Kirk Wynd (Selkirk).
February 4. Third foal. 70,000Y. Tattersalls October Book 1. Neven Botica. Half-sister to the fair 12f winner Uncle Eric (by Alhaarth). The dam, a quite useful 10.2f winner, is a half-sister to the 7f (at 2 yrs) and Group 1 9f Dubai Duty Free Stakes winner Right Approach, to the 9f and 10f winner New Assembly, the 1m winners Benedict and Celtic Cross and the stayer Temple Way – all useful. The second dam, Abbey Strand (by Shadeed), a fair Irish 10f winner, is a half-sister to 13 winners including the 2-y-o Group 3 winners Grand Chelem and Splendid Moment. (Mr N Botica). *"A nice filly, she's light, neat and she goes well. I think she'll have enough speed to start at seven furlongs."*

34. TIME TO WORK (IRE) ★★
b.c. Hurricane Run – Viscoumtess Brave (Law Society).
March 25. Seventh foal. 38,000Y. Tattersalls October Book 1. A Balding. Half-brother to 2 minor winners abroad by Desert King and Namid. The dam won 4 races at 2 and 4 yrs in Italy and was listed-placed and is a half-sister to 4 winners. The second dam, Vadrouille (by Foolish Pleasure), won twice at 3 yrs. (Another Bottle Racing). *"He goes quite nicely and I should think seven furlongs around June time would be alright for him. It's the first crop of Hurricane Run and this colt is the only one we have by him. He hasn't put me off getting another one."*

35. WHIPLASH WILLIE ★★★
ch.c. Phoenix Reach – Santa Isobel (Nashwan).
March 27. Half-brother to the fair 15f and 2m winner Isabelonabicycle (by Helissio). The dam, a fairly useful listed 10f winner, is a half-sister to 3 winners. The second dam, Atlantic Record (by Slip Anchor), is an unraced half-sister to 4 winners including the useful 2-y-o 8.2f winner Fascinating Rhythm and the useful 10f and 10.3f winner Migwar. (J C & S R Hitchins). *"He's going through a bit of a growing spell but he's a good mover and he's just beginning to do well. It's not really a two-year-old pedigree but I'd be disappointed if he couldn't do something this year."*

36. WINGED DIVA (IRE) ★★
b.f. Hawk Wing – Opera Glass (Barathea).
April 10. Second foal. Half-sister to the fair 2009 7f placed 2-y-o Opera Gal (by Galileo). The dam, a quite useful 8.5f winner, is a sister to the very smart 2-y-o Group 3 7f Solario Stakes winner and Group 1 Dewhurst Stakes third Opera Cape and a half-sister to the high-class stayer Grey Shot and the smart sprint winner of 4 races Night Shot. The second dam, Optaria (by Song), was a quite useful 2-y-o 5f winner. (J C Smith). *"We haven't done much with her, she's only cantering but she moves well. I couldn't tell you much about her yet."*

37. WITH A FLOWER ★★★★
b.f. *Shirocco – Amaryllis (Sadler's Wells).*
April 10. Half-sister to the fairly useful 2009 2-y-o 7f winner and listed-placed Pipette (by Pivotal), to the French 10f and 12f winner and Group 2 10.5f Prix Greffuhle second Day Or Night (by Daylami) and the French 12f and 14f winner According (by Dalakhani). The dam, a fair 7f all-weather winner at 2 yrs, is closely related to the smart French/US 1m/9f winner Corrazona and a half-sister to the Breeders Cup Classic third Thirty Six Red. The second dam, Heartbreak (by Stage Door Johnny), won at up to 9f in the USA. (George Strawbridge). *"She's done well since she came in and she's very different to her sister Pipette in that she's more highly strung and active. A very good mover, she looks like she might be a very nice filly. I should think we'll start her at seven furlongs and step up from there."*

38. UNNAMED ★★★
ch.c. *Shirocco – Black Opal (Machiavellian).*
March 10. First foal. £21,000Y. Doncaster St Leger. I Balding. The dam, placed four times in France at 2 and 3 yrs, is a daughter of the French listed winner Gold Field (by Unfuwain), herself a half-sister to 4 winners. (J Dwyer). *"He's a lovely horse, looks like being a middle-distance horse in time but he has a lovely attitude, he's a nice mover. He's nice enough."*

39. UNNAMED ★★★★
b.f. *Cape Cross – Garanciere (Anabaa).*
February 4. First foal. 45,000Y. Tattersalls October Book 1. Neven Botica. The dam, a minor 3-y-o winner in France, is a half-sister to 7 winners including the Group 1 Fillies' Mile winner Gloriosa. The second dam, Golden Sea (by Saint Cyrien), won 4 races at 2 and 4 yrs in France and is a half-sister to 8 winners including the French Group 2 winner Glity. (Mr N Botica). *"A real quality individual. She moves very well, has a lovely attitude and I couldn't be happier with her. She'll be out in mid-summer and she's one of the nicest fillies we've got."*

40. UNNAMED ★★★
b.c. *Singspiel – Rada (Danehill).*
February 27. First foal. 46,000Y. Tattersalls October Book 2. A Balding. The dam is an unplaced half-sister to 9 winners including the high-class Group 1 6f July Cup winner Owington. The second dam, Old Domesday Book (by High Top), a fairly useful 3-y-o 10.4f winner, was listed placed. (A Burdett). *"We've had to give him a break because his knees were a bit immature but for a Singspiel he looks like he'll certainly make up into a two-year-old at some point. A racy-looking type, he's a sort of neat middle-distance horse."*

RALPH BECKETT

41. ABACIST (IRE) ★★★
b.c. *Desert Style – Trishay (Petong).*
April 16. Second foal. £42,000Y. Doncaster St Leger. David Redvers. The dam, a modest 5f placed 2-y-o, is a sister to 3 winners and a half-sister to the 2-y-o Group 3 6f Princess Margaret Stakes winner Mixed Blessing. The second dam, Marjorie's Memory (by Fairy King), a fair 5f winner at 2 and 3 yrs, is a half-sister to 5 winners. (Mr R J Roberts). *"I don't think we'll see him until the second half of the summer. The sire slips under the radar in a way – he's not just the sire of Paco Boy, he gets lots of other decent winners. This colt is all speed but I won't crack on with him yet. A nice sort with a good temperament, he should be worth waiting for."*

42. ALBERT BRIDGE ★★★★♣
gr.c. *Hernando – Alvarita (Selkirk).*
February 28. Second foal. 60,000Y. Tattersalls October Book 1. David Redvers. The dam was a French listed 10.5f winner. The second dam, Alborada (by Alzao), was a high-class winner of the Champion Stakes (twice), Nassau Stakes and Pretty Polly Stakes and is a sister to the smart listed 10.2f winner Albanova and a half-sister to 6 winners. (The Cheyne Walkers). *"I don't need to tell you how good the pedigree is. I wasn't mad on him when I first saw him at the Sales, but when he got up to the collecting ring he just seemed to grow half an inch and looked a different horse. He's still that way because in the box he doesn't grab you, but he does when he's out exercising. He won't appear until September and I doubt him having more than a couple of starts. I like him a lot, his attitude shines through and he makes great use of himself."*

43. CAROUSEL ★★
b.f. Pivotal – Supereva (Sadler's Wells).
January 17. Half-sister to the fair 1m winner Royal Superlative (by King's Best). The dam, an Italian winner of 5 races, is a half-sister to several winners. The second dam, Final Farewell (by Proud Truth), ran once unplaced and is a half-sister to 3 winners and to the dam of Danehill. *"She had three months with us before going back to the Royal Studs for a break. She won't have too much of a career this season and it'll be next year before we see the best of her."*

44. CONTROL CHIEF ★★★
b.c. Medicean – Sahara Rose (Green Desert).
March 18. Fifth foal. 46,000Y. Tattersalls October Book 1. David Redvers. Half-brother to Mighty Aphrodite (by Observatory), unplaced in one start at 2 yrs in 2009, to the quite useful 1m and 10f winner of 3 races Nelsons Column (by Benny The Dip), the fair 2-y-o 6f winner Oriental Rose (by Dr Fong) and a minor 9f winner abroad by Xaar. The dam ran once unplaced and is a half-sister to 9 winners including the Group 1 6f Cheveley Park Stakes winner Regal Rose. The second dam, Ruthless Rose (by Conquistador Cielo), ran twice unplaced and is a half-sister to 9 winners including the high-class miler Shaadi. (P Hickey). *"A good-looking horse. His owner was looking for something that would go middle distances and maybe become a dual purpose horse if he went that way. I actually think he's showing quite a lot for that brief and I think he'll be competitive over seven later on this year. He's a big, solid, scopey horse and he'll do well."*

45. DAYS OF SUMMER (IRE) ★★★★
b.f. Bachelor Duke – Pharaoh's Delight (Fairy King).
February 24. Twelfth foal. €76,000Y. Goffs Orby. Steve Parkin. Half-sister to the Irish 2-y-o listed 6f winner Pharmacist (herself dam of the Breeders Cup Turf winner Red Rocks), to the minor French 9f winner Conspirator (both by Machiavellian), the Irish 2-y-o 7f winner Phariseek, the fair 4-y-o 7f winner Mutamarkiz (both by Rainbow Quest) and a winner in Japan by Caerleon. The dam won the Group 1 5f Heinz "57" Phoenix Stakes, was Group 1 placed four times and is a half-sister to 8 winners. The second dam, Ridge The Times (by Riva Ridge), a fair 2-y-o 5f winner, is a half-sister to 6 winners in the USA. (Clipper Group Holdings Ltd). *"She's a forward filly although she's still slightly in two halves, being quite long backed and still having a bit of levelling off to do. But she's telling us she's ready to step up and hopefully she'll be an April/May two-year-old that will give her owner the chance to see her in some nice races. She's showing plenty and I haven't really asked her any questions yet."*

46. ECHO RIDGE (IRE) ★★
b.f. Oratorio – Lochridge (Indian Ridge).
April 9. The dam, a smart listed 6f winner of 5 races, is closely related to the useful listed 5f winner Loch Verdi. The second dam, Lochsong (by Song), a champion sprinter and winner of the Prix de l'Abbaye (twice), the Kings Stand Stakes and the Nunthorpe Stakes, is a half-sister to the Nunthorpe Stakes winner Lochangel. (J C Smith). *"She's had a few problems in that she's been a bit sick and she has a bit of growing to do, so I haven't got on with her yet. She has the make and shape of a two-year-old and her time will come, but she needs to grow and I don't think I can get going with her for another month or so."*

47. ENCORE UNE ANNEE ★★
ch.f. Hernando – Eternelle (Green Desert).
February 10. Fourth foal. Sister to the moderate 11f winner Eloise and to the Spanish 7.5f winner Sassicaia. The dam, a quite useful 9.4f all-weather winner, is a sister to the useful winner of 11 races at up to 7f Everset and a half-sister to the champion German horse and dual Group 1 middle-distance winner Caitano and to the US Grade 3 1m winner Lady Lodger. The second dam, Eversince (by Foolish Pleasure), won over 5.5f and 1m in France and is a half-sister to the Group 3 Premio Ellington winner and Italian Derby second Artic Envoy. (Miss K Rausing). *"A nice filly that was a very weak yearling, but she's done very well over the winter. Hernando can get two-year-old winners and it'll be the autumn before we see the best of her, but I like her."*

48. FARLOW (IRE) ★★★
ch.c. Exceed And Excel – Emly Express (High Estate).
April 5. Sixth foal. 25,000Y. Tattersalls October Book 2. David Redvers. Half-brother to the quite useful 2009 2-y-o 6f winner Amitola (by Choisir), to the useful 6f and 7f winner and listed-placed Damika (by Namid), the quite useful 10f to 12f and hurdles winner Quai Du Roi (by Desert King) and a minor winner in Italy by Intikhab. The dam won once over 11f at 4 yrs in France and is a half-sister to 6 winners including the Irish Group 3 winner Rainbows For All. The second dam, Maura's Guest (by Be My Guest), is an unraced half-sister to 7 winners including Bold Apparel (Group 2 Premio Umbria). (Lawrence, Deal & Carolyn Thornton). *"He's a horse that's done very well over the winter, but he's still quite immature both physically and mentally. I saw the half-sister, David Barron's Amitola, win impressively last year and that helped me make up my mind to buy this horse. He looks all speed, I like the horse and he'll start at five furlongs before moving up to six. He should be able to win an auction race."*

49. FAVORITE GIRL (GER) ★★
b.f. Shirocco – Favorite (Montjeu).
March 25. First foal. €100,000Y. Arqana Deauville August. David Redvers. The dam, a minor German 3-y-o winner, is a half-sister to 5 winners including the dam of the Group 1 Premio Lydia Tesio winner Floriot. The second dam, Fluid Dancer (by Irish River), was a listed stakes winner in the USA. (M C Denmark). *"She's a very backward filly and she'll need plenty of time. She's tall she hasn't filled her frame yet, so it'll be a while before we do anything with her."*

50. FLORESTAN MATCH ★★★
ch.f. Medicean – Fidelio's Miracle (Mountain Cat).
March 24. Fourth foal. £28,000Y. Doncaster St Leger. Not sold. Half-sister to the fair 2009 1m placed 2-y-o Philander (by Red Ransom). The dam won 3 races from 7f to 10f including a French listed 7f event, was second in the Group 3 Prix de la Grotte and is a half-sister to 2 winners. The second dam, Flurry (by Groom Dancer), a winner in France and the USA and listed-placed twice, is a half-sister to 6 winners and to the dams of the Group/Grade 1 winners Myboycharlie and Snowland. (Mrs J Jacobs). *"She's forward and looks like appearing in April or May. She shows a bit of speed and we like her. On pedigree you wouldn't think she'd be a five furlong filly, but she has plenty of boot. She's medium-sized, so she has a bit of scope about her."*

51. LUPA MONTANA (USA) ★★
ch.f. Giant's Causeway – Louve Royale (Peintre Celebre).
February 29. First foal. $80,000Y. Keeneland September. Not sold. The dam won over 11f in France and was Grade 3 placed four times in the USA and is a half-sister to the Group 2 10f Prix d'Harcourt and US Grade 2 10f winner Loup Breton and two listed-placed winners in France. The second dam, Louve (by Irish River), winner of the Group 3 10.5f Prix de Flore, is closely related to the very smart Group 3 10f Prix du Prince d'Orange winner and Irish Derby third Loup Sauvage and a half-sister to the Group 1 1m Grand Criterium winner and Group 1 10.5f Prix Lupin second Loup Solitaire. (J L Rowsell). *"A light-framed filly, it'll be a while before we see her and she might go home shortly for a break."*

52. MEGA MOUNT (IRE) ★★
b.c. Acclamation – Changing Partners (Rainbow Quest).
March 28. Eighth foal. €34,000Y. Tattersalls Ireland. David Redvers. Half-brother to the useful 7f and dual 1m winner Swop (by Shinko Forest), to the fair 8.2f winner Love Affair (by Tagula), the Italian 2-y-o and 3-y-o winner Royal Partners (by Ali-Royal) and the German 2-y-o and 3-y-o winner Glockenbach (by Doyoun). The dam, a modest 12f all-weather winner, is a half-sister to 5 winners including the Group 1 Prix Maurice de Gheest winner May Ball. The second dam, Minute Waltz (by Sadler's Wells), is an unraced full or half-sister to 7 winners including the Lincoln Handicap winner King's Glory. (Mr R J Roberts). *"Not a very big horse and I haven't done much with him yet. I would think he'll be a six furlong horse to start with, I like him, he has a good temperament but I just hoped he'd do a bit better over the winter. He's just started to improve now."*

53. MISS DIAGNOSIS (IRE) ★★
b.f. Medicean – Changeable (Dansili).
January 18. First foal. 40,000foal. Tattersalls December. Lawn Stud. The dam, a French 10.5f winner, was listed-placed over 9f and 10f and is a half-sister to 3 winners. The second dam, High And Low (by Rainbow Quest) won the Cheshire Oaks, was second in the Yorkshire Oaks and the St Leger and is a half-sister to the very useful 12f to 14.6f winner Corradini. (J H Richmond-Watson). *"A big, strong, decent filly with a staying pedigree, she'll be one for the second half of the year and she's just about to go back to the stud for a break. I like her though and I had to pick two out of the three that the owner offered me. Although she wasn't the obvious one I'm glad I picked her. She's done really well and she doesn't look weak although she has a staying pedigree. We'll get her a run or two at the back-end and next season will be her year."*

54. MOONE'S MY NAME ★★★
gr.f. Intikhab – The Manx Touch (Petardia).
February 28. £11,000Y. Doncaster St Leger. David Redvers. Half-sister to the fairly useful 5f (at 2 yrs) and listed 6f winner and Group 2 Criterium de Masons Laffitte second Baby Strange, to the modest 7f, 1m and hurdles winner Mambo Sun (both by Superior Premium) and the modest 6f winner Ride A White Swan (by Baryshnikov). The dam, a moderate 7f and 1m winner at 3 yrs, is a half-sister to 2 winners. The second dam, Chapter And Verse (by Dancer's Image), is an unraced daughter of the 1,000 Guineas and Oaks winner Altesse Royale. (McDonagh, Murphy and Dixon). *"She took all winter to really look like she was going to be a two-year-old but I'd be surprised if she wasn't up to winning in the second half of the season."* TRAINERS' BARGAIN BUY

55. NORSE WING ★★★
ch.f. Norse Dancer – Angel Wing (Barathea).
February 3. Second foal. Half-sister to the modest 2009 6f placed 2-y-o Wing Of Faith (by Kirkwall). The dam is an unraced half-sister to one winner. The second dam, Lochangel (by Night Shift), a very smart winner of the Group 1 5f Nunthorpe Stakes, is a half-sister to the champion sprinter Lochsong. (J C Smith). *"She's sharp, not very big and forward. I'll be looking towards getting her out early so that perhaps we can get the first season sire Norse Dancer some profile.*

56. PABUSAR ★★★★
b.c. Oasis Dream – Autumn Pearl (Orpen).
January 27. Second foal. 62,000Y. Tattersalls October Book 1. Not sold. Half-brother to the modest 2009 7f placed 2-y-o Thaliwarru (by Barathea). The dam, a winner of 3 races over 5f and 6f at 2 and 3 yrs, was second in the Group 2 Temple Stakes and is a half-sister to 2 winners abroad. The second dam, Cyclone Flyer (by College Chapel), won once at 3 yrs and is a half-sister to 8 winners including the Group 2 King's Stand Stakes winner Bolshoi. (Mr & Mrs Kevan Watts). *"He's a forward sort, his mother was a two-year-old, he's really strengthened over the winter and he was a January foal. So we'll be stepping him up over the next month or so and it looks like he'll want quickish ground. He hasn't got a great walk on him, which is why I suspect he didn't take the eye as a yearling, but he's showing us plenty without us having asked him anything."*

57. RAFELLA (IRE) ★★★
b.f. Iffraaj – Cappella (College Chapel).
March 25. Seventh foal. £18,000Y. Doncaster St Leger Festival. David Redvers. Half-sister to the useful 2-y-o 6f and 7f winner Dickensian (by Xaar), to the quite useful 10f winner Red Birr (by Bahhare), the moderate triple 6f winner (including a 2-y-o seller) Azuree (by Almutawakel) and a winner in Cyprus by Noverre. The dam, a fair dual 5f winner at 2 yrs, is a full or half-sister to 5 winners including the fairly useful 5f (at 2 yrs) and 7f winner and Group 2 placed Queenfisher. The second dam, Mavahra (by Mummy's Pet), a fairly useful 5f and 6f winner, is a half-sister to 5 winners. (Favourites Racing IX). *"She was bought to be forward and she looks that way. Her sire was a good racehorse and he's a son of a great sire of sires in Green Desert. We'll see how we go, but she's done a couple of bits of fast work and she'll be racing in April or May. It's a fast family and I should think she'd want fast ground."*

58. RHODESIAN MOON (IRE) ★★★
b.br.f. Holy Roman Emperor – Moon Drop (Dominion).

May 11. Fourteenth foal. €38,000Y. Goffs Orby. Not sold. Closely related to the useful 2-y-o 5f winner and Group 2 6f Railway Stakes second South Dakota (by Danehill Dancer), to the very useful dual 6f winner and Group 3 Greenlands Stakes second Abraham Lincoln and the useful Irish 5f winner and Group 2 7f Vintage Stakes third Devil Moon (both by Danehill) and half-sister to the useful sprint winner Dancing Drop (by Green Desert and herself dam of the Cherry Hinton Stakes winner Jewel In The Sand), the useful sprinters Wisam (by Shaadi), Moon King (by Cadeaux Genereux) and Mithl Al Hawa (by Salse), the fairly useful 7f to 8.5f winner Lake Sunbeam (by Nashwan) and the Irish 2-y-o 7f winner Elbader (by Machiavellian). The dam, a useful winner of 3 races over 5f and 6f, is a half-sister to 7 winners including the very useful 7f and 12f winner Beldale Star. The second dam, Little White Star (by Mill Reef), showed no form but is out of a half-sister to the high-class miler Saintly Song. (Mrs I M Beckett). *"Not a big filly – she's very much like her sire in that respect. She's a late foal too with some growing to do, so I haven't done a lot with her yet. We'll be able to bash on with her in the second half of the season."*

59. RIGHT SAID FRED (IRE) ★★★♣
b.g. Holy Roman Emperor – Tender Is Thenight (Barathea).
April 29. Eighth foal. 42,000Y. Tattersalls October Book 2. David Redvers. Half-brother to the French 1,000 Guineas winner Tie Black (by Machiavellian), to the modest 1m winner Zaarmit and the minor Irish 7f winner Midnight Folk (both by Xaar). The dam won once at 3 yrs in France and is a half-sister to 10 winners including the Breeders Cup Mile and William Hill Sprint Championship winner Last Tycoon, the Group 2 6f Premio Melton and Group 3 6f Goldene Peitsche winner Astronef and the French winner Save Me The Waltz (herself dam of the Group 1 winners Sense Of Style and Valentine Waltz). The second dam, Mill Princess (by Mill Reef), won over 10f at 2 yrs in France and is a half-sister to the Irish Derby winner Irish Ball and the top-class broodmare Irish Bird (dam of the classic winners Assert, Bikala and Eurobird). (Mr R J Roberts). *"Again,* he's much like his sire in that he's not very big. I thought he was good value, given that he's a half-brother to a French Guineas winner. He's forward and if he wasn't nearly a May foal I'd have done a bit with him now. As it turns out we felt he was over-revving slightly at home, so we gelded him. There wasn't a problem with his attitude, he was just doing too much for his own good."

60. RINGSTEAD BAY (FR) ★★★
b.c. Intikhab – Praia Grande (Lagunas).
April 8. Fourth foal. €24,000Y. Arqana Deauville October. David Redvers. Half-brother to 2 minor winners in Germany by Kornado. The dam, a minor winner in Germany, is a half-sister to 6 winners including the listed winner Prada (dam of the Group 1 Criterium de Saint-Cloud winner Paita and the Group 2 German Oaks winner Puntilla). The second dam, Pradera (by Abary), won 3 races including a listed event in Germany and is a half-sister to 6 winners. (Lawrence, Wilkinson & Deal). *"We've had a lot of luck with the stallion although he isn't everyone's cup of tea. This colt has changed shape completely since arriving. He was quite a neat, 'set' yearling but now he looks quite leggy and tall. A good-moving sort of horse with a very good attitude to his work, I can see him doing a job for us in the second half of the year. He has a slightly rounded action, so he may want a bit of give in the ground."*

61. ROCKY REBEL ★★
b.c. Norse Dancer – Gulchina (Gulch).
May 1. Second foal. Half-brother to the unplaced 2009 2-y-o Mahjong Girl (by Kirkwall). The dam, a fair 7f placed maiden (including at 2 yrs), is a half-sister to several winners. The second dam, Harda Arda (by Nureyev), a minor Irish 3-y-o 9f winner, is a half-sister to 8 winners including the Group 2 10f Derrinstown Stud Derby Trial and dual US Grade 2 winner Phantom Breeze. (J C Smith). *"A really good-looking two-year-old, he's really athletic and although his half-sister was temperamentally unsuited to being a racehorse he's completely the opposite! A straightforward colt but a May foal, it'll be a while before he appears."*

62. RUBY ALEXANDER (IRE) ★★
ch.f. Redback – Alexander Eliott (Night Shift).
February 17. €4,000Y. Tattersalls Ireland. R Beckett. Half-sister to the quite useful 5f (at 2 yrs) and 6f winner of 6 races Artistic License (by Chevalier) and to the fair 5f (including at 2 yrs) and 6f winner of 7 races Brandywell Boy (by Danetime). The dam, an Irish maiden, was placed at up to 10f and is a half-sister to one winner. The second dam, Olivia (by Ela-Mana-Mou), won over 10f in Ireland and is a half-sister to 4 winners. (The Millennium Madness Partnership). *"It looks like she'll take in plenty of graft and I imagine I'll be able to slot her in somewhere."*

63. RUBY BROOK ★★★
b.g. Sakhee – Highbrook (Alphabatim).
March 9. Seventh foal. £26,000Y. Doncaster St Leger. David Redvers. Half-brother to the fairly useful 9f winner Ted Spread (by Beat Hollow), to the quite useful 6f (at 2 yrs) to 10f and hurdles winner Niagara (by Rainbows For Life) and the fair 2-y-o 6f winner Pink Sapphire (by Bluebird). The dam, a quite useful 10f to 13f and hurdles winner, is a half-sister to 5 minor winners in the USA. The second dam, Tellspot (by Tell), is a placed half-sister to 10 winners. (Mr A E Frost & Mr A R Adams). *"He was 'bit of a lad' to put it mildly and giving us a hard time, so we gelded him. I've had a few Sakhee's like that. But the form of his half-brother Ted Spread is good and this is a good-looking horse. I like him and he's done nothing but improve since we gelded him."*

64. SYLVESTRIS (IRE) ★★★
b.f. Arch – Woodmaven (Woodman).
March 21. Fourth foal. 75,000foal. Tattersalls December. BBA (Ire). Half-sister to the fairly useful 2-y-o 5f winner and listed-placed Roof Fiddle (by Cat Thief). The dam, placed once at 3 yrs in the USA, is a half-sister to 2 winners including the dual Group 3 winner and 1,000 Guineas second Arch Swing. The second dam, Gold Pattern (by Slew O'Gold), a minor US winner of 4 races, is a half-sister to 5 winners. (Mrs & Mrs David Aykroyd). *"She has a good pedigree, being a three-parts sister to Arch Swing, and she was quite an expensive foal purchase. Quite a long-backed filly that'll need a bit of time, she has a bit of growing up to do mentally but there are two-year-old winners on the page and she doesn't find it a struggle. She'll have a campaign this year because physically it looks like she'll be able to do it. A good sort."*

65. THIRTY PIECES (IRE) ★★★
ch.g. Choisir – Silver Bandana (Silver Buck).
April 3. Fifth foal. 31,000Y. Tattersalls October Book 2. Anthony Stroud. Half-brother to the quite useful dual 7f winner (including at 2 yrs) Silver Dip (by Gulch) and to the modest 7f winner Blue Bamboo (by Green Desert). The dam, a US stakes winner of 6 races at 3 to 5 yrs and Grade 3 placed twice, is a half-sister to 5 winners. The second dam, Datum Line (by High Line), is an unraced sister to the Group 2 winners Ancholia and Quay Line and to the dam of the Group 1 Locking Stakes winner Soviet Line. (Mrs E Kennedy). *"We bought him to be a two-year-old, but he was getting a bit top heavy so we gelded him. It didn't appear to take too much out of him and he's come back on the road again quite quickly. A big, tall horse and when he fills his frame he'll be quite a nice individual. He has a bit of a way to go yet, but I think he'll make a two-year-old for sure."*

66. UNNAMED ★★★
ch.f. Medicean – Australian Dreams (Magic Ring).
March 6. Fourth foal. 55,000Y. Tattersalls October Book 2. David Redvers. The dam, a listed winner of 7 races at 3 and 4 yrs in Germany, is a half-sister to 6 winners including the smart Group 3 5f Palace House Stakes and subsequent US Grade 3 9f winner Needwood Blade and the US Grade 3 winner Islay Mist. The second dam, Finlaggan (by Be My Chief), a quite useful 11f to 2m winner, is a half-sister to 7 winners. (N H T Wrigley). *"A very attractive filly, a good walker and a good mover that's come 'up behind' so she needs to level off. She'll make a two-year-old in the second half of the season over seven furlongs."*

67. UNNAMED ★★★
b.c. Footstepsinthesand – Border Minstral (Sri Pekan).
April 29. Fourth foal. 27,000Y. Tattersalls October Book 2. R Frisby. Half-brother to the

fair 2009 2-y-o 5f winner Felsham (by Kyllachy) and to the useful 5f winner of 4 races at 2 and 4 yrs Oldjoesaid (by Royal Applause). The dam, a fair 2-y-o 6f winner, is a sister to one winner and a half-sister to 6 winners including the Group 2 Cherry Hinton Stakes winner Please Sing and the very useful 7f (at 2 yrs) to 10f winner and Group 1 National Stakes third Mountain Song. The second dam, Persian Song (by Persian Bold), is an unplaced sister to the Solario Stakes winner Bold Arrangement (placed in seven Group/Grade 1 races including the Kentucky Derby). (G B Partnership). *"A tall, leggy, quite narrow horse but I suspect that's to do with the stallion because they seem to be made that way. Quite a late foal, so he'll be one for the second half of the year, but he looks to have a terrific attitude, he's done a lot of growing and although he went through an 'ugly duckling' stage he's come out of that now. He'll make a two-year-old in July or August. His breeders, the Peacocks, are very good at their job and this colt's half-brother Oldjoesaid is partly what attracted him to me."*

68. UNNAMED ★★★
b.f. Haafhd – Clare Hills (Orpen).
January 26. First foal. The dam won the 2-y-o listed 5f Hilary Needler Trophy and is a half-sister to 2 winners. The second dam, Morale (by Bluebird), is an unraced sister to the Scandinavian listed winner Bluebeard and a half-sister to 3 winners including the useful 1m and 10f winner Sheba Spring. (P K Gardner T/A Springcombe Park Stud). *"She came in quite late and was one of the last to be broken in, so I don't know where we'll be with her yet. Physically she's changed a lot since she arrived but the mare was very quick and hopefully she will be too."*

69. UNNAMED ★★★
br.c. Ishiguru – Cradle Brief (Brief Truce).
March 5. Sixth foal. €55,000Y. Goffs Orby. David Redvers. Half-brother to the useful 2-y-o listed 6f winner and Group 2 6f Mill Reef Stakes second Sir Xaar (by Xaar), to the useful Irish 1m to 9.5f winner Fuerta Ventura (by Desert Sun) and the quite useful 13f and hurdles winner Mamlook (by Key Of Luck). The dam is an unraced half-sister to the Group 3 6f Greenlands Stakes winner Tiger Royal. The second dam, Lady Redford (by Bold Lad), ran once unplaced and is a half-sister to 5 winners. (R A Pegum). *"A big, solid sort of horse, he was bought to be a two-year-old and we like him but we haven't really stepped him up yet. He's been coughing but I think he's finished growing so as so as he's healthy we'll move him up. He should be a five furlong type because he's built like that"*

70. UNNAMED ★★★★
b.f. Hurricane Run – Dance Lively (Kingmambo).
April 29. Fourth foal. 43,000Y. Tattersalls October Book 2. David Redvers. Half-sister to the Japanese 1m stakes winner Live Concert (by Singspiel) and a winner in Greece by High Chaparral. The dam is an unraced half-sister to 7 winners including 3 stakes winners in the USA. The second dam, Tivli (by Mt Livermore), a US stakes winner of 7 races, is a half-sister to a stakes winner. (R A Pegum). *"A really cracking sort of filly. She wouldn't necessarily stand out when she's walking around with her age group, but she does when she starts cantering. We like her, she probably won't appear for a while yet and she's very nice."*

71. UNNAMED ★★★★
b.c. Cadeaux Genereux – Gloved Hand (Royal Applause).
March 11. First foal. €65,000Y. Goffs Orby. David Redvers. The dam, a useful 5f (at 2 yrs) to 7f winner of 4 races and second in the Group 3 Summer Stakes, is a half-sister to 3 winners. The second dam, Fudge (by Polar Falcon), is an unraced half-sister to 7 winners including the quite useful 1m to 10f winner Summer Fashion (herself dam of the Group winners Definite Article, Salford City and Salford Express). (M C Denmark). *"He's a lovely horse and I actually trained him 'in utero' because I had the mother when she was second in the Summer Stakes. She improved hugely for being in foal, because she wasn't an easy filly to train at all – she had a stalls aversion and all sorts. But about a month after being in foal it was as if someone had flicked a switch, she completely changed and really showed her true colours. I like this colt, but he's had a few issues with coughing, spots and so on. When he's healthy I'm sure he'll come forward. A sprinting type two-year-old."*

72. UNNAMED ★★★★
b.c. Seeking The Gold – Oyster Bay (Saint Ballado).
March 2. Fourth foal. $180,000Y. Keeneland September. BBA (Ire). Brother to the minor US winner 4-y-o Hidden Bay and half-brother to 2 minor winners in the USA by Storm Cat and Cape Canaveral. The dam was placed at 2 and 3 yrs in the USA and is a half-sister to one winner. The second dam, Clamorosa (by Seattle Dancer), won 5 races in the USA including a Grade 3 event and is a half-sister to numerous winners. (Mr M Gittins). *"He has quite a speedy pedigree and he's a sharp, forward sort of horse so I'll be looking to move him up and get on with him early. A five/six furlong colt for fast ground – he takes everything in his stride."*

73. UNNAMED ★★★★
b.f. Arch – Promptly (Lead On Time).
April 13. Ninth foal. 250,000Y. Tattersalls October Book 1. R Frisby. Half-sister to the 2-y-o Group 3 Autumn Stakes winner and Group 1 Racing Post Trophy second Fantastic View (by Distant View), to the useful 2-y-o winner and Group 2 Superlative Stakes second Weald Park, the quite useful 2-y-o 6f and 7f winner To The Rescue (both by Cozzene), the quite useful 8.5f winner Escape Clause (by Red Ransom), the fair 6f to 9f winner Dart Along (by Bahri) and the fair 1m winner Expedience (by With Approval). The dam, a quite useful 6f winner here, subsequently won a minor stakes event over 1m in the USA and is a half-sister to 6 winners. The second dam, Ghariba (by Final Straw), won the Group 3 Nell Gwyn Stakes and is a half-sister to the Group 1 Prix Royal Oak winner Braashee. (GB Partnership). *"Definitely the most expensive yearling we've ever trained – by about a hundred grand! She's had a hold-up with a splint but she's a real athlete, she moves really well and I think she's a very nice filly. The owner kindly sent her to us because we had a bit of luck with a horse for him last year. Quite a tall, leggy filly, she should make a two-year-old in the second half of the season."*

MICHAEL BELL

74. BEDJAT ★★
ch.c. Dr Fong – Welsh Valley (Irish River).
February 13. Fourth foal. 24,000Y. Tattersalls October Book 3. Kern/Lillingston. Half-brother to the fairly useful 2-y-o 7f winner Brecon (by Unfuwain) and the fair 4-y-o 9.5f and 10f winner Man Of Gwent (by In The Wings). The dam, a modest 6f placed maiden, is a half-sister to 8 winners including the Group 2 6f Gimcrack Stakes winner Chilly Billy and the US Grade 3 placed Mister Approval. The second dam, Sweet Snow (by Lyphard), won over an extended 10f in France and is a half-sister to 9 winners including the US stakes winners Windansea and Sing And Swing. (Mr Colin Gerchinson). *"He's quite big and backward and I imagine we won't see him until the second half of the season."*

75. BIARAAFA (IRE) ★★★★
b.f. Araafa – Bianca Nera (Salse).
March 27. Half-sister to the Irish 2-y-o 7f winner and listed placed Pietra Dura (by Cadeaux Genereux), to the fair 12f winner Ever Rigg (by Dubai Destination) and the fair 5f to 7f winner of 5 races Glencairn Star (by Selkirk). The dam, a smart 2-y-o winner of the Group 1 7f Moyglare Stud Stakes and the Group 2 6f Lowther Stakes, is half-sister to 4 winners including the very useful Group 1 Moyglare Stud Stakes second Hotelgenie Dot Com (herself dam of the dual Group 1 winner Simply Perfect). The second dam, Birch Creek (by Carwhite), was placed five times including when third in the Group 3 1m Premio Royal Mares and is a half-sister to 7 winners. (Mr R Frisby). *"She looks very promising and she has plenty of natural speed, so she's in my 'A team'. We haven't worked any of them yet, but she looks quick."*

76. BLINK OF AN EYE ★★★
ch.c. Compton Place – Wink (Salse).
March 3. Fourth foal. 58,000Y. Tattersalls October Book 1. Kern/Lillingston. Half-brother to the useful 7f (at 2 yrs) and 1m winner Secrecy (by King's Best) and to the minor French winner Knowing Look (by Daylami). The dam, a French 2-y-o 6f winner, was listed-placed and is a half-sister to 7 winners. The second dam, Blink Naskra (by Naskra), won twice at 2 and 3 yrs in the USA and is a half-sister to 8 winners including the dam of the high-class Bakharoff and the very smart Emperor Jones. (Mr Billy Maguire). *"A nice, big, scopey horse with plenty of size about him. He looks*

promising but I won't be rushing him because he looks slightly 'on the leg' at the moment. A good-looking horse."

77. COMMUNICATOR ★★★★
b.c. Motivator – Goodie Twosues (Fraam).
January 26. Third foal. Half-brother to the quite useful 2-y-o 9f winner Goodie Twosues (by Dr Fong). The dam, a fairly useful dual 6f winner, is a half-sister to 3 winners. The second dam, Aliuska (by Fijar Tango), a minor dual 5f winner in Ireland at 2 yrs, is a half-sister to 3 minor winners including one in Germany. (Lady Sue Davis). "A very good advertisement for his sire, he's a very good mover with plenty of size and scope and he's a horse I like a lot for the second half of the season over seven furlongs plus. A nice colt."

78. COMPASSION ★★
b.f. Tiger Hill – Windmill (Ezzoud).
February 2. Fifth living foal. 70,000Y. Tattersalls October Book 2. John Warren. Closely related to the quite useful 2-y-o 6f winner and subsequent US and Canadian winner Winds Of Time (by Danehill) and to the fair 9f winner Inis Boffin (by Danehill Dancer) and half-sister to a winner abroad by Mark Of Esteem. The dam, a fair 13.8f winner, is a half-sister to 8 winners including the very smart Group 2 12f Ribblesdale Stakes winner Gull Nook (herself dam of the top-class colt Pentire), the equally smart Group 3 12f Princess Royal Stakes winner Banket and the useful Group 3 Ormonde Stakes winner Mr Pintips. The second dam, Bempton (by Blakeney), was placed three times at up to 11f and is a half-sister to Shirley Heights. (Highclere Thoroughbred Racing, Isinglass). "A filly with has a nice middle-distance pedigree and so she's being trained with her three-year-old career in mind. She's just gone back to the stud for some spring grass, but she's got a great temperament and she moves well, but realistically she'll want one or two runs at the back end of the season."

79. CRÈME ANGLAISE ★★
b.f. Motivator – Reading Habit (Half A Year).
February 15. Sixth foal. 26,000Y. Tattersalls October Book 2. Kern/Lillingston. Half-brother to the Scandinavian listed winner Grafitti (by Dansili), to the fairly useful 2-y-o 7f winner Read Federica (by Fusaichi Pegasus) and a minor winner abroad by Selkirk. The dam, a 5f (at 2 yrs) to 6f minor stakes winner in the USA, is a half-sister to 7 winners. The second dam, Paperback Habit (by Habitony), a minor US stakes winner of 3 races, is a half-sister to 6 winners and to the dam of the multiple US Grade 1 winner Best Pal. (Mrs G Rowland-Clark). "She's a very athletic filly who was given a break in the new year, basically to give her plenty of time. The time she was given will benefit her later on, she's a very good mover with a great temperament and I liked what I saw when we were breaking her in."

80. EMPRESS CHARLOTTE ★★★★
b.f. Holy Roman Emperor – Charlotte O'Fraise (Beat Hollow).
March 18. First foal. The dam, a French 2-y-o 6f and Group 3 7f Prix du Calvados winner, is a half-sister to numerous winners including the smart 2-y-o 6f, 7f and subsequent US stakes winner and Group 2 6f Coventry Stakes third Luck Money. The second dam, Dundel (by Machiavellian), a quite useful 7f winner, is a half-sister to 6 winners including the Group 3 6f Prix de Seine-et-Oise winner Seltitude. (Lord Derby). "Quite a spunky filly with a bit of an attitude which isn't always a bad thing. A good mover, she looks quite sharp and will be one of our earlier two-year-olds."

81. GRUMETI ★★★
b.c. Sakhee – Tetravella (Groom Dancer).
March 3. Seventh foal. 42,000Y. Tattersalls October Book 2. Will Edmeades. Half-brother to the fairly useful 10f to 12f winner Island Odyssey (by Dansili), to the fair 7f (at 2 yrs) and 12f winner Mizooka (by Tobougg), the fair 12f and hurdles winner Ellerslie Tom (by Octagonal), the minor Italian 2-y-o winner King Beat (by Beat Hollow) and the minor French winner of 3 races at 4 yrs Berissimo (by Bering). The dam, a French 12f and 15f winner, is a half-sister to 5 winners. The second dam, Vanya (by Busted), won the listed Prix d'Automne and is a full or half-sister to 7 winners including the French Group 3 winner Muroto. (Thurloe Thoroughbreds XXVIII). "A big, strong horse, he's very much a two year project but he looks like he can do himself justice in the second

half of the season. There's plenty of size about him and plenty of bone, so he's an attractive colt. The name Grumeti comes from a game reserve in Tanzania."

82. HANDEL'S MESSIAH ★★
gr.c. Oratorio – Silver Pursuit (Rainbow Quest).
March 27. Seventh foal. 45,000Y. Tattersalls October Book 2. Kern/Lillingston. Half-brother to the French 1m (at 2 yrs) to 10.5f winner and listed placed Strive (by Dr Fong), subsequently a winner in Saudi Arabia, to the minor Italian 4-y-o winner Sand Seeker (by Desert King) and a bumper winner by In The Wings. The dam is an unraced sister to the Group 3 Rose Of Lancaster Stakes and subsequent Grade 1 Santa Anita Handicap winner Urgent Request and a half-sister to 5 winners including the Ebor Handicap winner Sanmartino. The second dam, Oscura (by Caro), won at 3 yrs in England and is a half-sister to 8 winners including the Grade 1 Washington D.C. International winner Johnny D and to the US Grade 2 winner Stardusk. (Sir Alex Ferguson & Mr Mike Dawson). *"He looks as though he's going to appreciate a distance of ground. He's a well-made horse with a good temperament and he's a good mover. It's a nice middle-distance pedigree so we won't be pressing any buttons for a while yet."*

83. HISTORY REPEATING ★★★
b.f. Singspiel – Annapurna (Brief Truce).
February 1. Sixth foal. 30,000Y. Tattersalls October Book 1. Not sold. Sister to the quite useful dual 10f and subsequent US stakes winner and Grade 2 second Solva and half-sister to the quite useful 2-y-o 7f winner Anthology (by Haafhd) and the fair 6f (at 2 yrs) and 1m winner Aberdovey (by Mister Baileys). The dam, a useful 7f winner (at 2 yrs) and listed-placed twice, is a half-sister to 4 winners including the very useful 2-y-o Group 3 7f Rockfel Stakes winner Name Of Love. The second dam, National Ballet (by Shareef Dancer), is an unraced half-sister to 7 winners including the listed winners Broken Wave, Guarde Royale, Clifton Chapel and Saxon Maid. (Mr Chris Wright and The Hon Mrs J M Corbett). *"A nicely bred filly, not over-big and quite sharp, so we'll be cracking on with her."*

84. JOE STRUMMER (IRE) ★★★★
b.c. Librettist – Post Modern (Nureyev).
March 5. Seventh living foal. 44,000Y. Tattersalls October Book 1. Kern/Lillingston. Half-brother to the useful 3-y-o 1m winner and Group 3 Chester Vase third Risk Taker (by Rainbow Quest), to the French listed 1m winner of 4 races Chasing Stars (by Observatory) and the modest 1m, 9f and hurdles winner Postmaster (by Dansili). The dam is an unraced sister to Reams of Verse, winner of the Oaks and the Group 1 Fillies Mile and a half-sister to the Group 1 10f Coral Eclipse Stakes and Group 1 10f Phoenix Champion Stakes winner Elmaamul. The second dam, Modena (by Roberto), is an unraced half-sister to the smart 2-y-o 7f winner and Queen Elizabeth II Stakes third Zaizafon – herself dam of Zafonic. (Mr Edward Ware). *"A good advertisement for his sire, he's very well-bred and a nice colt for the second half of the season."*

85. KINGS FORTUNE ★★★
b.c. Tobougg – Polished Up (Polish Precedent).
March 13. £13,000Y. Doncaster St Leger. Highflyer/Shefford. Half-brother to the fairly useful 2-y-o 6f winner Love Thirty (by Mister Baileys). The dam, a modest 10f placed 3-y-o, is a half-sister to 9 winners including the champion sprinter and high-class sire Cadeaux Genereux and the dam of the listed winning sprinters Ya Malak and Dominio. The second dam, Smarten Up (by Sharpen Up), won the Group 3 Temple Stakes and is a half-sister to 4 winners. (Mr W H Ponsonby). *"He has a great temperament and he's good mover from a fast family. We're pressing on with him and I think he'll be one of our earlier colts. He was well-bought, I think."* TRAINERS' BARGAIN BUY

86. METTAL ★★
b.f. Singspiel – Local Spirit (Lion Cavern).
February 29. First foal. The dam, a useful 10f winner, was second in the Group 2 12f Lancashire Oaks and is a sister to the high-class Irish 1,000 Guineas, Coronation Stakes and Nassau Stakes winner Crimplene and a half-sister to the smart Group 3 12.3f Chester Vase winner Dutch Gold. The second dam, Crimson Conquest (by Diesis), a quite useful 2-y-o 6f winner, is a half-sister to the US stakes winner at around 1m Sword Blade. (Marwan

Al Maktoum). *"The dam was a middle-distance performer and this filly won't be early but she moves well and is doing everything easily. No buttons pressed yet."*

87. MISS VILLEFRANCHE ★★★♠
b.f. Danehill Dancer – Miss Corniche (Hernando).
March 8. Fourth foal. Sister to the quite useful 2-y-o 6f winner Miss Eze and half-sister to the very useful 1m winner and listed-placed Moyenne Corniche (by Selkirk). The dam, a 7f (at 2 yrs) and listed 10f winner, is a sister to 2 winners and a half-sister to numerous winners including the listed 1m winner Miss Riviera Golf. The second dam, Miss Beaulieu (by Northfields), was a useful 6f and 10f winner. (J L C Pierce). *"A big, strong filly but I would imagine she's one for the second half of the season. We've had a few out of this mare."*

88. MOHEDIAN LADY (IRE) ★★★★
b.f. Hurricane Run – Amathia (Darshaan).
April 10. Third foal. 240,000Y. Tattersalls October Book 1. Kern/Lillingston. Half-sister to the 7f (at 2 yrs) and dual 10f winner and listed-placed Distant Memories (by Falbrav). The dam, a listed 9f winner in France and Group 3 placed twice, is a half-sister to 7 winners including the 1,000 Guineas third Hathrah, the smart Group 2 12f Premio Ellington winner Ivan Luis, the UAE Group 3 winner Stagelight and the German listed winner Zero Problemo. The second dam, Zivania (by Shernazar), a useful Irish winner of 4 races from 1m to 9.5f, is a half-sister to 7 winners including the Group 3 Prix Gontaut Biron winner Muroto. (Mrs Olivia Hoare). *"A lovely, easy-mover with plenty of scope, she floats up Warren Hill and I like her a lot. A middle-distance filly in the making, she's just doing ordinary canters but she looks very high-class."*

89. MOKALIF ★★★★
b.c. Halling – Velvet Waters (Unfuwain).
March 20. Second foal. 48,000Y. Tattersalls October Book 2. Rabbah Bloodstock. Half-brother to Torran Sound (by Tobougg) unplaced in two starts at 2 yrs in 2009. The dam, a fair 12f winner, is a half-sister to 7 winners including the 10f, 12f and subsequent UAE Group 3 12f winner Gower Song. The second dam, Gleaming Water (by Kalaglow), a quite useful 2-y-o 6f winner, is a sister to the Group 3 Solario Stakes winner Shining Water (herself dam of the Group 1 Grand Criterium winner Tenby) and a half-sister to 8 winners. (Ahmed Ali). *"A second half of the season job, he has slightly sore shins at the moment but he moves well and shows plenty in his canters. He's one I have high hopes for."*

90. NEYTIRI ★★
ch.f. Sleeping Indian – Science Fiction (Starborough).
March 11. 400Y. Ascot Sales. Whitsbury Manor Stables. Half-brother to the moderate 1m winner Space Pirate (by Bahamian Bounty). The dam is an unraced half-sister to the useful 6f winners Polar Kingdom and Goodwood Prince. The second dam, Scarlet Lake (by Reprimand), is an unplaced half-sister to 6 winners and to the dams of the US Grade 1 winner Stroll and the Group 2 Sun Chariot Stakes winner Lady In Waiting. (Mr W Fox, Mr R Frisby and Mr S Frisby). *"A sharp little filly and obviously very inexpensive! But we should still be able to get the job done."*

91. OLD MASTER EXPERT ★★★★
b.c. Royal Applause – Leonica (Lion Cavern).
April 25. Second living foal. £50,000Y. Doncaster St Leger. M Bell. Half-brother to the quite useful 2009 2-y-o 6f winner Rodrigo de Torres (by Bahamian Bounty). The dam, a fairly useful 1m winner, is a half-sister to 5 minor winners including the listed Prix de Saint-Cyr winner South Rock. The second dam, South Shore (by Caerleon), was a useful winner of 4 races at up to 12f and is a half-sister to 4 winners including the Lockinge Stakes winner Soviet Line. (Richard Green). *"One of our sharper ones, I trained the dam and she was very useful and would have got black type but she hurt herself. This is quite a promising colt and he should be able to start over five or six furlongs. A possible Royal Ascot two-year-old."*

92. PURE LUCK (IRE) ★★
b.f. Galileo – Birdie (Alhaarth).
April 24. Fourth foal. 120,000Y. Tattersalls October Book 1. John Magnier. Half-sister to Salvation (by Montjeu), unplaced in one start

at 2 yrs in 2009. The dam, a 1m and listed 11.5f winner, is a half-sister to 7 winners including the French middle-distance winner of 10 races (including 4 listed events) Faru and the listed winner Fickle (herself dam of the Group 3 winner Tarfah). The second dam, Fade (by Persepolis), is an unraced half-sister to Tom Seymour, a winner of five Group 3 events in Italy. (John Magnier, Derek Smith & Michael Tabor). *"An attractive filly and I've trained a lot of the family. As her pedigree suggests, she won't be early but she's a nice, easy mover with a good temperament. I trained her mother who peaked as a three-year-old and Galileo's also get better with age, so we're just giving her plenty of time."*

93. RED COPPER ★★
b.f. Cape Cross – Red Conquest (Lycius).
February 4. Sister to the quite useful 7f (at 2 yrs) and 1m winner Karoo Blue and to the fair 12f winner Red Linnet. The dam, a moderate 7f placed 3-y-o, is a half-sister to 5 winners including the high-class Irish 1,000 Guineas, Coronation Stakes and Nassau Stakes winner Crimplene and the smart Group 3 12.3f Chester Vase winner Dutch Gold. The second dam, Crimson Conquest (by Sweet Ramblin Rose), a quite useful 2-y-o 6f winner, is a half-sister to the US stakes winner at around 1m Sword Blade. (Marwan Al Maktoum). *"A big, heavy-topped filly and quite backward, but we're waiting on a fitness regime at the moment because we can't get any weight off her. When she gets fitter and stronger she'll hopefully show a bit more."*

94. RISHIKESH ★★
b.c. Cape Cross – Maycocks Bay (Muhtarram).
April 28. Sixth foal. Half-brother to the 7f (at 2 yrs), Epsom Oaks and Irish Oaks winner Sariska (by Pivotal) and to the 8.7f (at 2 yrs), 10f and listed 14f winner Gull Wing (by In The Wings). The dam, a useful 14f listed winner, is a half-sister to several winners including the useful 7f and 1m winner (at 2 yrs) and listed 10.3f placed 3-y-o Indian Light. The second dam, Beacon (by High Top), is an unraced half-sister to 6 winners including the Group 3 10f Gordon Richards Stakes winner Compton Ace. (Lady Bamford). *"He's not here yet because he's big and backward. The produce of this dam don't usually make it until they're older, so he's one for next year."*

95. RIVIERA STARS ★★★
b.c. Galileo – Miss Riviera Golf (Hernando).
February 23. Half-brother to the fairly useful 2009 2-y-o 1m winner Mont Agel (by Danehill Dancer), to the listed 7f winner Hotel Du Cap, the fairly useful 10f and 12f winner The Carlton Cannes (both by Grand Lodge) and the fair 7f and 1m winner Gassin (by Selkirk). The dam won a listed event over 1m in France at 3 yrs and is a half-sister to several winners including the useful 2-y-o 6f winner and listed-placed Miss Riviera. The second dam, Miss Beaulieu (by Northfields), was a useful 6f and 10f winner. (Mr J L Pearce). *"He had a nasty injury as a foal but it doesn't affect him at all, he's doing routine canters and I really like him. He's got a good attitude, he's a good mover and wants to be a racehorse."*

96. ROSA MIDNIGHT (USA) ★★★
b.f. Lemon Drop Kid – Christmas Player (Theatrical).
February 25. First foal. $75,000Y. Keeneland September. BBA (Ire). The dam, a fair 9f winner here, is a half-sister to the US Grade 1 Ashland Stakes winner Christmas Kid. The second dam, Christmas Gift (by Green Desert), won the Grade 3 Beaugay Handicap and the Grade 3 Rockingham Handicap in the USA and is a full or half-sister to 10 winners in the USA including the dam of the US Grade 1 winner Grand Slam. (Mr Colin Bryce). *"A nice, easy moving filly, she won't be rushed but she has a good temperament and were just taking our time with her."*

97. ROYAL LIAISON ★★★
b.f. Ad Valorem – Royal Mistress (Fasliyev).
February 10. Second foal. £33,000Y. Doncaster St Leger. Kern/Lillingston. Half-sister to the fair dual 6f winner Hysterical Lady (by Choisir). The dam, a 2-y-o 6f winner and listed-placed in France, is a half-sister to 5 winners including the dam of the US Grade 2 winner Friendly Island. The second dam, Regal Peace (by Known Fact), a fairly useful 2-y-o listed 5f winner and third in the Group 3 Phoenix Flying Five, subsequently won in the USA and was stakes placed. She is a half-sister

to 4 winners including the Group 1 6f Middle Park Stakes winner Stalker. (Mrs P D Gray, Mr J Law and Mr P Morrison). *"A sharp filly, as her pedigree suggests. She's just held up by sore shins at present but I look at her as being one of those to be getting on with. Looks to go nicely."*

98. SCREENPRINT ★★★
ch.c. Shamardal – Painted Moon (Gone West).
March 26. Third foal. Brother to the fair 2009 2-y-o 1m winner Pastel Blue. The dam is an unplaced half-sister to numerous winners including the high-class Irish 1,000 Guineas, Coronation Stakes and Nassau Stakes winner Crimplene and the smart Group 3 12.3f Chester Vase winner Dutch Gold. The second dam, Crimson Conquest (by Diesis), a quite useful 2-y-o 6f winner, is a half-sister to the US stakes winner at around 1m Sword Blade. (Marwan Al Maktoum). *"Quite a sharp, well-made horse. He looks as if he could start at six furlongs and go on to be another good representative of the sire."*

99. SET TO MUSIC (IRE) ★★★★
b.f. Danehill Dancer – Zarabaya (Doyoun).
February 18. Half-sister to the fairly useful Irish 10f winner and listed-placed Zarafsha (by Alzao) and to the French 10f and 12f winner Zaranal (by Sinndar). The dam is an unraced half-sister to the Irish listed winner Zafadola out of Zarafa (by Blushing Groom). (The Queen). *"This is a nice filly, she's been going well and is a good mover. Like a lot by this sire she's quite feisty but she's pleasing me at home and she looks quite sharp."*

100. SWEETIE TIME ★★★★♠
b.f. Invincible Spirit – Blessing (Dubai Millennium).
March 18. First foal. The dam is an unraced half-sister to the French listed 7f winner Esperero. The second dam, Hydro Calido (by Nureyev), a very useful filly and winner of the Group 2 1m Prix d'Astarte, was second in the French 1,000 Guineas and is a half-sister to the champion European 2-y-o and 2,000 Guineas second Machiavellian, to the smart Group 1 Prix Morny and Group 1 Prix de la Salamandre winner and 1,000 Guineas third Coup de Genie and the very smart Group 1 Prix Jacques le Marois winner Exit to Nowhere (by Irish River). (Lordship Stud). *"Quite sharp and very willing, I'm sure she'll be seen to good effect in the first half of the season."*

101. TREND ★★
b.c. Marju – Fashion (Bin Ajwaad).
March 14. Sixth foal. 60,000Y. Tattersalls October Book 2. John Warren. Half-brother to Fashionable Gal (by Galileo), unplaced in one start at 2 yrs in 2009, to the fair 1m and hurdles winner Scot Love (by Dansili) and the modest 2-y-o 7f seller winner Disco Queen (by Night Shift). The dam, a quite useful 1m (at 2 yrs) to 10f winner, is closely related to the Italian Oaks winner and Moyglare Stud Stakes second Bright Generation and a half-sister to 4 winners. The second dam, New Generation (by Young Generation), a fairly useful winner 6f (at 2 yrs) to 1m winner, is a half-sister to 7 winners. (Highclere Thoroughbred Racing, Beeswing). *"He's bred to come into his own as a three-year-old, but he's a handsome, good-moving colt."*

102. TWINKLED ★★★
ch.c. Bahamian Bounty – Panic Stations (Singspiel).
January 30. First foal. 36,000Y. Tattersalls October Book 3. R Frisby. The dam, a modest 8.5f winner at 3 yrs, is a half-sister to 2 winners. The second dam, Fiddle-Dee-Dee (by Mujtahid), is an unraced half-sister to 5 winners including the listed Ulster Harp Derby winner Sir Simon and the Sun Chariot Stakes second Dartrey. (D W & L Y Payne). *"He's quite a sharp, well-bodied individual, but his knees are still open so that's holding us up. We'll have some fun with him this year."*

103. UNIVERSE ★★
b.f. Cape Cross – Rachelle (Mark Of Esteem).
March 23. Half-sister to the Group 1 Middle Park Stakes, Group 2 Duke Of York Stakes and Group 2 Gimcrack Stakes winner Amadeus Wolf (by Mozart), to the fairly useful 10f winner Benedicte (by Galileo) and the quite useful 7f and 1m winner Always A Rock (by Rock Of Gibraltar). The dam, a minor winner in Italy at around 1m, is a half-sister to one winner. The second dam, Rose Violet (by Alleged), won a listed event in Italy and was third in the Group

1 Italian Oaks and is a half-sister to 4 winners including the US Grade 3 winner Storm Creek. (The Queen). *"Obviously she's a nicely bred filly but like a lot by this sire she's not precocious and will benefit for time, so she's just gone back to the Royal Studs for a break. She'll be a middle-distance filly next year."*

104. WARM WELCOME ★★
b.f. Motivator – Arutua (Riverman).
February 15. Half-sister to the 7f (at 2 yrs) and listed 12f winner Juliette (by Sadler's Wells), to the useful Irish 6f (at 2 yrs) and 1m winner and subsequent US Grade 2 placed Plato (by Lure), the fairly useful 6f winner (including at 2 yrs) Farha (by Nureyev), the quite useful 2-y-o 7.5f winner Lost In Wonder (by Galileo) and the fair 2-y-o 7f winner Naval Review (by Storm Cat). The dam is an unraced half-sister to the Group 2 Prix Greffuhle Stakes winner Along All and the French Group 3 placed Arnaqueur. The second dam, All Along (by Targowice), was a top-class middle-distance filly and winner of the Prix de l'Arc de Triomphe, Prix Vermeille, Turf Classic, Washington D C International and Rothmans International (all Group or Grade 1 events). (The Queen). *"She's a nice, well-made filly and a good mover but she'll take a bit of time, as her pedigree suggests."*

105. UNNAMED ★★★★★
b.br.c. Kingmambo – Because (Sadler's Wells).
February 19. Third foal. Brother to the fairly useful 2009 2-y-o 1m winner Anhar. The dam is an unraced sister to the Irish 1,000 Guineas winner Yesterday and to the Group 1 7f Moyglare Stud Stakes winner and Irish 1,000 Guineas, Oaks and Irish Oaks placed Quarter Moon. The second dam, Jude (by Darshaan), a moderate 10f placed maiden, is a sister to the very useful Irish listed 14f winner and Irish Oaks third Arrikala and to the useful Irish 12f listed winner Alouette (herself dam of the Champion Stakes winner Alborada) and a half-sister to the very smart Group 2 10f Nassau Stakes and Sun Chariot Stakes winner Last Second. (Lady Bamford). *"A lovely, big, strong colt. He has a lovely pedigree and he's impressive to look at. Whoever rides him likes him and he's a good mover but we haven't pressed any buttons yet. He ticks all the boxes and we should see him out in August over seven furlongs."*

106. UNNAMED ★★★
b.f. Iffraaj – Congressional (Grand Lodge).
February 19. First foal. 50,000Y. Tattersalls October Book 2. Not sold. The dam, a quite useful 2-y-o 8.3f winner, is a half-sister to 2 winners. The second dam, Gilah (by Sadler's Hall), is an unraced half-sister to 7 winners including the very useful 10.2f winner Cocotte (the dam of 6 stakes winners including the top-class colt Pilsudski). (Saif Ali & Saeed H Altayer). *"A big, strong filly, I think she'll certainly make a mid-season two-year-old, but although she might be alright over six furlongs she has a lot of size and scope, so I should think seven would suit her.*

107. UNNAMED ★★
ch.f. Medicean – Coyote (Indian Ridge).
May 1. Sixth foal. 105,000Y. Tattersalls October Book 1. Rabbah Bloodstock. Sister to the useful listed 12f winner and Group 3 Prix Gontaut-Biron third Eradicate and closely related to the 1m (at 2 yrs) and Group 2 Park Express Stakes winner and Irish 1,000 Guineas third Oh Goodness Me (by Galileo). The dam, a fairly useful 1m winner, was listed-placed and is a half-sister to one winner. The second dam, Caramba (by Belmez), winner of the Group 2 1m Falmouth Stakes and the Group 2 10f Nassau Stakes, is a half-sister to 7 winners including the Moyglare Stud Stakes and Falmouth Stakes winner Lemon Souffle. (Dr Ali Ridha). *"She's a nice, scopey filly and one for the second half of the season, so we're just slightly on hold at the moment, just ticking her along."*

108. UNNAMED ★★★
ch.c. Dubawi – Dubai Surprise (King's Best).
March 13. Second foal. Half-brother to the quite useful 2009 2-y-o 6f winner Sand Skier (by Shamardal). The dam, a winner of 4 races here and in Italy including the Group 1 Premio Lydia Tesio and the Group 3 Prestige Stakes, was second in the Group 1 Criterium de Saint-Cloud and is a half-sister to 2 winners. The second dam, Toujours Irish (by Irish River), is an unraced half-sister to 7 winners including the French multiple Group winner Athyka. (Dr Ali Ridha). *"I would hope that he's going to be one of our earlier colts as he's very strong and mature. The dam was a Group 1 winner, so hopefully he'll be a two-year-old to be going to*

war with from June onwards."

109. UNNAMED ★★★★
ch.f. Exceed And Excel – Farrfesheena (Rahy).
March 21. Half-sister to the fair 2009 1m placed 2-y-o Dr Finley (by Dr Fong), to the fair 8.7f winner House Of Lords (by Doneraile Court) and the modest 6f and 7f winner Blackmalkin (by Forest Wildcat). The dam, a fairly useful 1m placed maiden, is a sister to 2 winners including the fairly useful 12f winner Heavenly Bay and a half-sister 2 winners. The second dam, Bevel (by Mr Prospector), a French 1m winner, is out of a half-sister to Ajdal, Formidable and the dam of Arazi. (Marwan Al Maktoum). *"A really nice filly, she has a good temperament and plenty of pace, so I think she'll be one of our earlier fillies."*

110. UNNAMED ★★
ch.c. Pivotal – Hidden Hope (Daylami).
February 7. First foal. 100,000Y. Tattersalls October Book 1. Rabbah Bloodstock. The dam, a useful listed 11.4f Cheshire Oaks winner, is a half-sister to 9 winners including the Group 1 1m Coronation Stakes winner Rebecca Sharp and the Group 3 11.5f Lingfield Derby Trial winner Mystic Knight. The second dam, Nuryana (by Nureyev), was a useful winner of the listed 1m Grand Metropolitan Stakes and is a half-sister to 5 winners. (Saif Ali & Saeed H Altayer). *"He's not over-big and he looks quite sharp, but his pedigree suggests otherwise so I think it's deceptive and I'm going to back off him."*

111. UNNAMED ★★★
b.br.f. Kingmambo – Kamarinskaya (Storm Cat).
January 25. First foal. $575,000Y. Saratoga August. Not sold. The dam won the Irish 1,000 Guineas Trial winner and is a half-sister to the champion 2-y-o colt Fasliyev and to the winner and Group 3 Greenham Stakes third Chinook. The second dam, Mr P's Princess (by Mr Prospector), is an unraced half-sister to the US Grade 1 winners Menifee and Desert Wine. (My Meadowview LLC). *"She's only just arrived. I saw her at Saratoga and she's done very well physically in the interim. She's obviously something to look forward to but as she's literally just got off the plane I don't know anything about her yet."*

112. UNNAMED ★★
b.f. Cape Cross – Karla June (Unfuwain).
May 18. Fifth foal. 25,000Y. Tattersalls October Book 1. Rabbah Bloodstock. Half-sister to the quite useful 1m and 10f winner Uncle Fred (by Royal Applause) and the fair 2-y-o 7f winner Little Eskimo (by Johannesburg). The dam, a US stakes-placed winner, is a sister to the listed 15f winner of 10 races Sweetness Herself and the US listed winner Unrivalled and a half-sister to numerous winners. The second dam, No Sugar Baby (by Crystal Glitters), was placed 8 times at 2 and 3 yrs in France and is a half-sister to 11 winners including three French listed winners. (Dr Ali Ridha). *"As a physical specimen she's probably done best of all the horses over the winter. She was relatively inexpensive, a late foal and we'll give her plenty of time. One for the second half of the season but she looks well-bought."*

113. UNNAMED ★★★★
b.f. Kheleyf – Sanpala (Sanglamore).
April 9. Seventh foal. 60,000Y. Tattersalls October Book 1. Rabbah Bloodstock. Half-sister to the Group 3 7f Criterion Stakes and listed 7f winner and Group 1 Prix Maurice de Gheest third Silver Touch (by Dansili), to the quite useful 7f to 9f winner of 4 races Desire To Excel (by Desert Style) and the minor French 7.5f winner HMS Pinafore (by Singspiel). The dam ran once unplaced in France and is a half-sister to 7 winners including the Group 3 winners Danefair, Prove and Vortex and the dam of the dual Grade 1 winner Ventura. The second dam, Roupala (by Vaguely Noble), a fair 3-y-o 1m winner, is a half-sister to 5 winners and to the dams of the Group/Graded stakes winners Bad Bertrich Again, Prolix and Daros. (Saif Ali & Saeed H Altayer). *"This is a nice filly, the sire gets plenty of two-year-old winners, there's a bit of speed in the family and she's going to be one our earlier two-year-olds. She skips along nicely and certainly should have the speed for six furlongs."*

114. UNNAMED ★★★
b.f. Green Desert – Star Express (Sadler's Wells).
March 8. Fourth foal. 55,000Y. Tattersalls October Book 1. M Bell. Half-sister to the

moderate 2009 7f fourth placed 2-y-o Star Twilight and to the moderate 6f winner Haedi (both by King's Best). The dam, a minor 12f winner in France, is a sister to the Group 3 7f Greenham Stakes winner and Irish 2,000 Guineas fourth Yalaietanee and a half-sister to 5 winners including the Group 3 5f Molecomb Stakes winner Sahara Star (herself dam of the Group 2 5f Flying Childers Stakes winner Land Of Dreams). The second dam, Vaigly Star (by Star Appeal), a smart sprint winner of 3 races, was second in the Group 1 July Cup and a half-sister to 6 winners including the high-class sprinter Vaigly Great. (Dr Ali Ridha). *"This filly looks quite sharp, the sire gets plenty of early two-year-olds and I've put her in the early bunch, so we'll see how we get on. So far so good."*

115. UNNAMED ★★★★
gr.f. Verglas – Up And About (Barathea).
April 18. Eighth foal. 44,000Y. Tattersalls October Book 1. Kern/Lillingston. Half-sister to the fairly useful 2009 2-y-o 6f and 10f winner Take It To The Max (by Bahamian Bounty), to the fairly useful 2-y-o 8.3f and UAE 3-y-o winner Tamarillo (by Daylami), the fair 6f winner Wake Up Call (by Noverre), the modest 2-y-o 9f winner Tiger Spice (by Royal Applause) and the moderate 12f and hurdles winner Park's Prodigy (by Desert Prince). The dam, a fair all-weather 14.8f winner, is a half-sister to 7 winners including the listed winner and Group 1 placed Musicanna. The second dam, Upend (by Main Reef), a smart winner of 3 races from 10f to 12f including the Group 3 St Simon Stakes and the listed Galtres Stakes, is a half-sister to 6 winners including the dam of the high-class stayer and champion hurdler Royal Gait. (GKM Partnership). *"Since we bought this filly the mare has kept spitting out winners. She's a nice filly and will be a mid-summer two-year-old. A good mover and over six or seven furlongs come June or July time you'll see her in action. Could be quite nice."*

116. UNNAMED ★★★
gr.c. El Prado – Warsaw Girl (Polish Precedent).
March 10. Third foal. $185,000Y. Saratoga August. Rabbah Bloodstock. Half-brother to the fair 1m and 9f winner McConnell (by Petionville) and a winner in France by Malabar Gold. The dam, a minor US 4-y-o winner, is a half-sister to the Epsom Derby winner Motivator and the Group 2 Hardwicke Stakes winner Macarthur. The second dam, Out West (by Gone West), a useful 7.5f (at 2 yrs) and 1m listed winner, is a half-sister to 3 winners. (Ali Saeed). *"This is a nice filly and is related to Motivator, which is a plus point. The few El Prado horses I've had have done well and this looks a nice filly for the second half of the season."*

117. UNNAMED ★★
ch.f. Kingmambo – Winds Of March (Sadler's Wells).
February 4. Second foal. The dam, a fairly useful 10f winner, was fourth in a listed event on her only other outing and is a half-sister to the Sussex Stakes winner Ali Royal, the 1,000 Guineas winner Sleepytime and the Group 1 12f Europa Preis and Group 1 10f Premio Roma winner Taipan. The second dam, Alidiva (by Chief Singer), a useful listed winner of 3 races from 6f to 1m, is a half-sister to 6 winners including the dual Group 1 winner Croco Rouge. (My Meadowview LLC). *"A big, backward filly with a good temperament and plenty of size and scope, but she'll be a late season two-year-old and a middle-distance filly next year."*

118. UNNAMED ★★★
b.f. Dansili – Zither (Zafonic).
February 9. Fifth foal. Half-sister to the fair 8.5f winner Themwerethedays (by Olden Times). The dam, a fairly useful 6f (at 2 yrs) and 7f winner, is a half-sister to the useful 2-y-o listed 6f winner Dowager and the useful 1m (at 2 yrs) and 10f winner Dower House. The second dam, Rose Noble (by Vaguely Noble), a modest 3-y-o 11.5f winner, is a half-sister to 6 winners including the champion two-year-old and high-class sire Grand Lodge, winner of the Dewhurst Stakes and the St James's Palace Stakes. (Luke Lillingston, Bryan Burrough, John Root). *"This filly hasn't arrived yet but she's a big, strong, scopey filly. Unfortunately she only has one eye, but I've only had one horse like that and it won lots of races. She's very good-looking and the sire is more than useful."*

JOHN BEST

119. MANCUNIAN (IRE) ★★★
b.c. Motivator – Winesong (Giant's Causeway).
January 23. First foal. 18,000Y. Tattersalls October Book 2. Not sold. The dam, placed third over 10f in Ireland on her only start, is a half-sister to numerous winners the 2-y-o Group 1 6f Cheveley Park Stakes winner Seazun and the 2-y-o 7f winner and listed-placed Mahogany. The dam, a minor Irish 12f winner, is a sister to the Group 3 Prix Foy winner Beeshi and a half-sister to 8 winners including the John Smiths Magnet Cup winner Chaumiere and the dam of the high-class 10f colt Insatiable. The second dam, Cafe Au Lait (by Espresso), was a fairly useful winner of 3 races and stayed middle-distances. (Mr S D Malcolm). *"I thought Motivator had a great season last year with his two-year-olds because you would have thought they'd be later types. This lad looks just like a proper two-year-old and he should be reasonably early. He's doing it all quite nicely and sensibly and I'm really not in a panic with him. The penny hasn't quite dropped yet, but I think he'll make a proper two-year-old."*

120. MINISTRY ★★★
b.c. Iceman – Choirgirl (Unfuwain).
March 3. Sixth foal. 15,000Y. Tattersalls October Book 2. John Best. Closely related to the quite useful dual 12f winner Chord and to the fair 12f winner Choral Festival (both by Pivotal). The dam, a very useful 2-y-o 7f winner and second in the Group 3 7f Prestige Stakes, was listed-placed twice over 10f and is a half-sister to numerous winners including the Group 1 10f Curragh Pretty Polly Stakes winner Chorist. The second dam, Choir Mistress (by Chief Singer), is an unraced half-sister to 6 winners including the smart Group 2 11.9f Great Voltigeur Stakes winner Sacrament. *"I loved him at the Sales and I think we got him at a bargain price. He was recommended by Chris Richardson and John Marsh from Iceman's base at Cheveley Park Stud. A big, strong, impressive looking horse, we had his knees x-rayed and they were perfect. He had a little setback but he'll be fine and he'll be one of my nicer ones, probably over seven furlongs plus."* TRAINERS' BARGAIN BUY

121. ST AUGUSTINE (IRE) ★★★
b.c. Holy Roman Emperor – Najiya (Nashwan).
May 11. Eighth foal. £20,000Y. Doncaster St Leger. John Best. Half-brother to Beat Baby (by Johannesburg), unplaced in 2 starts at 2 yrs in 2009 and to the minor US winner of 3 races in the USA at 3 and 4 yrs Alwajd (by Deputy Minister). The dam, a useful 2-y-o 6f winner and second in the Group 1 Cheveley Park Stakes, is a sister to the very smart middle-distance colt Rabah. The second dam, The Perfect Life (by Try My Best), won the Group 3 5f Prix du Bois and the listed 7f Prix Imprudence, was second in the Group 2 6f Prix Robert Papin and is a full sister to the Breeders Cup Mile, Kings Stand Stakes and William Hill Sprint Championship winner Last Tycoon. (Pattern Racing UK Ltd). *"He's not over-big but he reminds me very much of Flashmans Papers – a Royal Ascot winning two-year-old we trained. He looks like he should be OK but his knees are not mature enough yet. If he'd been a bit bigger I think he'd have been too expensive for us."*

122. STREWTH (IRE) ★★
ch.c. Encosta De Lago – Alpine Park (Barathea).
May 10. €11,000Y. Goffs Orby. J Best. Half-brother to the quite useful Irish 1m winner Leo's Pride (by Medicean) and to the fair 7f and 1m winner of 6 races Swiss Art (by One Cool Cat). The dam, a quite useful 2-y-o dual 6f winner, is a half-sister to 4 winners including the 6f (at 2 yrs) and Group 3 7f Ballycorus Stakes winner Rum Charger and the very useful 2-y-o 6f winner and dual Group 3 placed Pakhoes. The second dam, Park Charger (by Tirol), a useful winner over 1m and 10f at 3 yrs in Ireland, was listed-placed several times and is a half-sister to 9 winners. (Simon Malcolm & John Foulger). *"Because my orders were a lot less than in previous years I was being a lot more picky at the Sales and we were shocked to get him for the price that we did. He was from a Vendor that had just one horse to sell, so I think a lot of the bigger buyers ignored him. So I think this colt slipped through the net. He doesn't look like an early type, but he's a very good moving horse and mentally he's holding up very well."*

123. UNNAMED ★★
b.c. Diamond Green – Baileys On Line (Shareef Dancer).
April 5. Sixth foal. £6,000Y. Doncaster St Leger Festival. Half-brother to the French 11f winner and Prix Greffulhe second Onerous (by Groom Dancer) and the modest 9f winner of 4 races Prince Noel (by Dr Fong). The dam is a placed half-sister to 8 winners including the very smart Group 1 12f Irish Oaks and Group 2 12f Ribblesdale Stakes winner Bolas. The second dam, Three Stars (by Star Appeal), a fairly useful 3-y-o dual 12f winner, is a half-sister to the Ascot Gold Cup, Goodwood Cup and Doncaster Cup winner Longboat and to the useful middle-distance colt Sailor's Dance. "He's heading in the right direction, he moves beautifully and he's a decent size. Everyone is saying good things about Diamond Green, this colt is doing everything right at the moment and I'm genuinely excited about him. He's still for sale and anyone who came to see him would love him, I know."

124. UNNAMED ★★
ch.c. Officer – Drawing A Blank (El Prado).
February 27. Fourth foal. £30,000Y. Doncaster St Leger. J Best. Half-brother to the minor US winner at 2 and 3 yrs Toothache (by Sunday Break). The dam won 5 minor races in the USA and is a full or half-sister to 7 winners including the US Grade 3 winner Miss Matched. The second dam, Ivory Princess (by Cure The Blues), a listed winner of 8 races, is a half-sister to 13 winners. (Splinter Group). "He's shown he's going to need time, but he's a nice horse and a good mover. Quite heavy topped, if we got him out in July I'd be happy with that."

125. UNNAMED ★★★
br.c. Pastoral Pursuits – Fizzy Treat (Efisio).
March 20. Fifth foal. 12,000Y. Tattersalls October Book 2. J Best. Half-brother to the modest 9f to 12f winner Formidable Guest (by Dilshaan). The dam, a fair 5f and 6f winner at 4 yrs, is a sister to the useful 2-y-o 5f and 6f winner and Group 3 placed Hoh Chi Min and a half-sister to 7 winners including the listed 7f winner Cragganmore. The second dam, Special Guest (by Be My Guest), a modest 2-y-o 7f winner, is a half-sister to 3 minor winners. (Hucking Horses). "I like this colt, he's progressing really nicely and he could probably be one of the earlier types. He's showing a very willing attitude, he's heading in the right direction and looks like making a two-year-old although he looks like he'll be progressive and will develop as the season goes on. He'll probably be out in June."

126. UNNAMED ★★★
ch.c. Johannesburg – Lady Of Talent (Siphon).
April 26. Fifth foal. £16,000Y. Doncaster St Leger. Not sold. Half-brother to the minor French 2-y-o winner Niska (by Smart Strike) and to the minor US 2-y-o winner Giant Talent (by Giant's Causeway). The dam is a placed half-sister to 10 winners including the US Grade 2 winner She's Tops (herself dam of the US dual Grade 1 winner and sire Dixie Union). The second dam, She's A Talent (by Mr Prospector), a minor winner in the USA, is a half-sister to 4 winners. (Hucking Horse). "Johannesburg's tend to be a bit hot but this colt has a very good temperament. He's a decent size, he's filling out and progressing quite nicely and doing everything I want him to do."

JAMES BETHELL

127. BASH ON (IRE) ★★
b.c. High Chaparral – Withorwithoutyou (Danehill).
April 6. Third foal. 38,000Y. Tattersalls October Book 2. J Bethell. Half-brother to the Group 1 6f Golden Jubilee Stakes and Group 2 6f Coventry Stakes winner and Group 1 6f Phoenix Stakes second Art Connoisseur (by Lucky Story). The dam, a quite useful 2-y-o 7f winner, is a half-sister to one winner. The second dam, Morningsuprice (by Future Storm), is an unraced half-sister to 5 winners including the high-class broodmare Morning Devotion (dam of the Oaks and Irish Derby winner Balanchine and the Group 2 winners Romanov and Red Slippers). (Clarendon Thoroughbred Racing). "He's very small, but he's grown two inches since we had him and he's 15.1 hands now. The sire normally gets quite rangy horses and this colt is quite backward but he'll be alright in time. I might well start him off at six furlongs around July time, but personally I think he'll take after the sire rather than the dam in terms of distance requirements."

128. BRADBURY (IRE) ★★★
ch.c. Redback – Simonaventura (Dr Devious).
March 7. Third foal. 9,500Y. Tattersalls October 3. J Bethell. Half-brother to Make Your Choice (by Spartacus), a winner of 2 races at 2 and 3 yrs in Italy. The dam is an unraced half-sister to the smart 6f (at 2 yrs), 1m and subsequent US Grade 1 placed Lucayan Indian. The second dam, Eleanor Antoinette (by Double Schwartz), is an unraced half-sister to 7 winners including the 2-y-o listed 6f winner (stayed 12f) Lifewatch Vision. (Clarendon Thoroughbred Racing). *"He looks quite sharp, he's really thrived and should be racing by the end of April. Quite a nice horse that should get six or seven furlongs later on, he's very well put-together, very strong and the most forward of my two-year-olds. He reminds me very much of a horse we had called Healey who was also out of a Dr Devious mare."* TRAINERS' BARGAIN BUY

129. DAMASCUS SYMPHONY ★★★
b.f. Pastoral Pursuits – Syrian Queen (Slip Anchor).
February 4. Eighth foal. 26,000Y. Tattersalls October Book 2. J Bethell. Half-sister to the fairly useful triple 6f winner (including at 2 yrs) Dark Mischief (by Namid), to the modest 9f winner Sham Sharif (by Be My Chief) and two minor French winners by Oscar and Croco Rouge. The dam, a quite useful 10f winner, is a half-sister to 8 winners including the Cherry Hinton Stakes winner and 1,000 Guineas second Kerrera and the Coventry, July, Gimcrack, Greenham and Criterion Stakes winner Rock City. The second dam, Rimosa's Pet (by Petingo), won the Group 3 8.5f Princess Elizabeth Stakes (at 2 yrs) and the Group 3 10.5f Musidora Stakes and is a half-sister to 5 winners. (J D Bethell). *"She's very nice and I'm still waiting for someone to buy a share in her. I'm just about to start working her, I think she ought to be racing in early May and she could start at five furlongs because she's quite sharp and definitely a sprint type."*

130. PINTRADA ★★
b.c. Tiger Hill – Ballymore Celebre (Peintre Celebre).
March 22. Fourth foal. 25,000Y. Tattersalls October Book 2. Not sold. Half-brother to Sweet Secret (by Singspiel), unplaced in two starts at 2 yrs in 2009. The dam won twice at 3 yrs in France and is a half-sister to 10 winners including the Irish triple Group 3 winner Nysaean. The second dam, Irish Arms (by Irish River), won once in France and is a half-sister to 9 winners including the US Grade 2 winner Morold. (Scot York Partnership). *"One for much later in the season, probably August/September and he'll be suited by seven furlongs and a mile. He was neat when we bought him but he's growing now and he's rangy and quite scopey. A very good mover, I like him and he's doing nicely."*

131. SPEY SONG (IRE) ★★★
b.f. Singspiel – All Embracing (Night Shift).
March 5. Third foal. 31,000Y. Tattersalls October Book 2. J Bethell. Half-sister to Engulf (by Danehill Dancer), unplaced in one start at 2 yrs in 2009. The dam, a quite useful 7f winner, is a half-sister to 6 winners including the very smart 6f and 7f (at 2 yrs) and Group 2 10f Prix Guillaume d'Ornano winner Highdown and the Group 2 12f King Edward VII Stakes second Elshadi. The second dam, Rispoto (by Mtoto), a modest 12f winner, is a half-sister to 7 winners including the Group 3 10f Royal Whip Stakes winner Jahafil. (Clarendon Thoroughbred Racing). *"A big filly – probably the biggest two-year-old I've got, she's very nice and a very, very good mover. One for August/September over seven furlongs and a mile. I'm quite impressed with her."*

JIM BOLGER

132. BANIMPIRE (IRE) ★★★
b.f. Holy Roman Emperor – My Renee (Kris S).
May 3. Third foal. €52,000Y. Goffs Orby. J Bolger. The dam, a very useful listed 12f winner, was second in the Group 3 Princess Royal Stake and is a half-sister to 4 winners including the useful 2-y-o 6f to 7f winner of 3 races Sutter's Fort. The second dam, Mayenne (by Nureyev), is an unraced three-parts sister to the Prix de l'Arc de Triomphe winner Carnegie and to the smart Group 2 10f Prix Guillaume d'Ornano winner Antisaar. (Mrs J S Bolger).

133. BEART (IRE) ★★★
b.c. Invincible Spirit – Bronntanas (Spectrum).
May 30. First foal. The dam, a quite useful Irish

2-y-o 7f winner, is a half-sister to one winner. The second dam, Scarpetta (by Seattle Dancer), a fair 7f to 10f placed maiden, is closely related to the Irish listed middle-distance winner Classic Sport and a half-sister to the very smart Group 2 1m Berlin Brandenburg Trophy and Group 2 Hong Kong International Mile winner Docksider. (Mrs J S Bolger).

134. BUILLE CLISTE (IRE) ★★★
ch.f. Smart Strike – Crystal Ballet
(Royal Academy).
March 23. Fifth foal. The dam ran once unplaced and is a half-sister to numerous winners including the top-class colt Rodrigo de Triano (winner of the Group 1 6f Middle Park Stakes (at 2 yrs), the 2,000 Guineas, the Irish 2,000 Guineas, the Juddmonte International Stakes and the Dubai Champion Stakes) and to the Group 3 7f Tetrarch Stakes winner Modigliani. The second dam, Hot Princess (by Hot Spark), was a useful winner over 5f and 6f at 2 yrs, the 7f Ballycorus Stakes at 3 yrs and three races in the USA from 8.5f to 9f as a four year old. (Mrs J S Bolger).

135. BURN THE FLOOR (IRE) ★★★
b.f. Indian Haven – Dance Time
(Sadler's Wells).
April 28. Fourth foal. €95,000Y. Goffs Orby. J Bolger. Half-sister to the US stakes winner and Grade 3 placed Dancing Master (by Nashwan). The dam is an unraced sister to the very useful filly Dancing Bloom, a winner over 6f (at 2 yrs) and the Group 3 12f Princess Royal Stakes (at 4 yrs) and second twice in the Group 1 Yorkshire Oaks and a half-sister to the French 2-y-o 5f winner and 1,000 Guineas third River Dancer (herself dam of the Champion Stakes winner Spectrum) and the dam of the St Leger winner Millenary. The second dam, Dancing Shadow (by Dancer's Image), a very useful winner over 1m and 10f, was third in the Group 2 Nassau Stakes and is a half-sister to the top-class Oaks winner Sun Princess and the high-class middle-distance colt Saddlers Hall. (Mrs J S Bolger).

136. CHABELLE ★★★★
b.f. Shirocco – Vagary (Zafonic).
February 9. Second foal. Half-sister to the smart 2009 Irish 2-y-o 7f winner and Group 1 7f National Stakes second Chabal (by Galileo). The dam is an unraced half-sister to the quite useful 2-y-o 7f winner and listed-placed Global Genius. The second dam, Vadsagreya (by Linamix), a French 7f (at 2 yrs) and 1m winner, was listed-placed and is a half-sister to 12 winners including the dams of the French 1,000 Guineas winner Vahorimix and the Breeders Cup Mile winner Val Royal. (Lady O'Reilly).

137. CISTE NAISIUNTA (IRE) ★★
b.f. Galileo – National Swagger
(Giant's Causeway).
April 4. Half-sister to the unplaced 2009 2-y-o Cre Na Coille (by Rock Of Gibraltar). The dam, a fairly useful Irish 7f winner, was fourth in the 2-y-o Group 2 7f Debutante Stakes and is a half-sister to one winner. The second dam, Eva Luna (by Double Schwartz), a very useful winner of 5 races at up to 6f at 2 yrs including the Group 1 Heinz 57 Phoenix Stakes and the Group 3 6f Railway Stakes, is a sister to the Group 3 1m Futurity Stakes winner Cois Na Tine. (Mrs J S Bolger).

138. CISTEOIR (USA) ★★
gr.f. D'Wildcat – Unbridled Treasure
(Unbridled's Song).
February 29. Fourth foal. €30,000Y. Tattersalls Ireland. BBA (Ire). Half-sister to a minor 3-y-o winner in the USA by Posse. The dam is an unraced half-sister to the Group 1 Moyglare Stud Stakes and Group 1 Phoenix Stakes winner Saoirse Abu. The second dam, Out Too Late (by Future Storm), is an unraced half-sister to the dam of the Oaks and Irish Derby winner Balanchine. (Mrs J S Bolger).

139. CLAIOMH SOLAIS (IRE) ★★★★
ch.f. Galileo – Scribonia (Danehill).
May 5. Third foal. Sister to the 2009 Irish 2-y-o 7f winner Gile Na Greine and to the very useful 2-y-o dual Group 3 6f winner Cuis Ghaire. The dam is an unraced half-sister to 6 winners including the very useful 2-y-o listed 6f winner and dual Group 1 placed Luminata and the very useful dual 6f winner (including at 2 yrs) and Group 3 placed Aretha. The second dam, Smaoineamh (by Tap On Wood), an Irish 6f winner at 2 yrs and useful at up to 14f, is a half-sister to the champion sprinter Double

Form and the Lupe Stakes winner Scimitarra. (Mrs J S Bolger).

140. DANCING ON TURF (IRE) ★★★
b.f. *Dalakhani – Irish Question (Giant's Causeway).*
February 21. Second foal. Half-sister to the quite useful 2009 Irish 2-y-o 5f winner Eireannach (by Rock Of Gibraltar). The dam, a fair Irish 1m winner, is a half-sister to 2 winners. The second dam, Key To Coolcullen (Royal Academy), is an unraced half-sister to numerous winners including the Group 1 6f Phoenix Stakes winner Eva Luna and the Group 3 1m Futurity Stakes winner Cois Na Tine. (Mrs J S Bolger).

141. DO THE BOSANOVA (IRE) ★★
ch.f. *Galileo – Sateen (Barathea).*
April 30. Fourth foal. €50,000Y. Goffs Orby. Pat Neary. Half-sister to the minor French 1m winner Sendora (by Kendor). The dam, a fairly useful 6f winner, is a half-sister to 10 winners including the listed 12f winner Puce (herself dam of the Group 2 Lancashire Oaks winner Pongee) and the minor winner Shouk (dam of the Oaks, Irish Oaks and Yorkshire Oaks winner Alexandrova and the Cheveley Park Stakes winner Magical Romance). The second dam, Souk (by Ahonoora), a fairly useful 7f winner, was listed placed over 1m and is a half-sister to 3 winners. (Mrs J S Bolger).

142. FLEA CHEOIL (IRE) ★★
b.f. *Galileo – Manger Square (Danehill).*
February 21. Fifth foal. Sister to the useful Irish dual 12f winner and listed-placed Via Galilei. The dam is an unraced sister to the Irish listed 1m winner Speirbhean – herself dam of the champion 2-y-o colt Teofilo (by Galileo) – and a half-sister to numerous winners including the Irish listed 9f winner Graduated. The second dam, Saviour (by Majestic Light), won 3 races at 2 and 3 yrs and is a half-sister to 5 winners including the triple US Grade 1 winner Judge Angelucci and the US Grade 1 winners Peace and War. (Mrs J S Bolger).

143. FLEISCIN (IRE) ★★★
b.f. *Invincible Spirit – Ceirseach (Don't Forget Me).*
May 30. Sixth foal. Half-sister to the fairly useful 2-y-o 5f winner and Group 3 7f Killavullan Stakes third Clash Of The Ash (by King Of Kings), to the 2-y-o 7f winner New Currency (by Touch Gold) and the Irish 7.5f (at 2 yrs) and 9.6f winner Laoch Na Mara (by Sea Hero) – both quite useful. The dam, a useful 7f (at 2 yrs) and 9.6f winner, is a half-sister to 5 winners including the smart listed 7f Tyros Stakes (at 2 yrs) and Group 2 10f Gallinule Stakes winner Project Manager. The second dam, Beparoejojo (by Lord Gayle), a useful Irish middle-distance performer, was also a leading juvenile hurdler. (Mrs J Bolger).

144. GRADAM CEOIL (USA) ★★★
ch.f. *Congaree – St Clair Ridge (Indian Ridge).*
May 4. Sixth foal. $65,000foal. Keeneland November. Tom Gentry. Half-sister to the Irish 7f and 1m winner and subsequent US Grade 2 winner Cat By The Tail (by Tale Of The Cat). The dam won the 2-y-o Group 3 7f Curragh Futurity Stakes and is a half-sister to numerous winners. The second dam, St Clair Star (by Sallust), a winner in Canada, is a half-sister to 7 winners including the Flying Childers Stakes winner Superlative. (Mrs J S Bolger).

145. HEAD SPACE (IRE) ★★★
b.c. *Invincible Spirit – Danzelline (Danzero).*
January 29. Second foal. €130,000Y. Goffs Orby. J Bolger. Half-brother to the fair 2009 Irish 2-y-o 6f winner Diva Dolce (by Domedriver). The dam, a fair Irish 1m and 10f winner, is a half-sister to 4 winners including the high-class Group 1 10.5f Tattersalls Gold Cup and Group 2 10f Pretty Polly Stakes winner Rebelline, the Group 2 Blandford Stakes and Group 3 Gallinule Stakes winner Quws and the useful 2-y-o 6f and 7f winner and listed-placed Moonlight Man. The second dam, Fleeting Rainbow (by Rainbow Quest), a modest 10f placed 3-y-o, is a half-sister to 3 winners. (Mrs J S Bolger).

146. HURRICANE HAVOC (IRE) ★★
b.f. *Hurricane Run – Cheeky Madam (Night Shift).*
March 11. Third foal. €95,000Y. Goffs Orby. J Bolger. The dam was placed at 3 yrs in France and is a half-sister to 5 winners including the Group 1 Criterium de Saint-Cloud winner Linda's Lad. The second dam, Colza (by

Alleged), a quite useful 2-y-o 1m winner, is a half-sister to 10 winners including the Group 3 6f July Stakes winner Wharf and the top-class broodmare Docklands (dam of the Arc winner Rail Link). (Mrs June Judd).

147. IMEALL NA SPEIRE (USA) ★★★
b.f. *Galileo – Altana (Mountain Cat).*
May 2. $725,000foal. Keeneland November. Not sold. Sister to the Group 3 10f Blue Wind Stakes winner Galatee. The dam is a half-sister to the top-class Grade 1 10f Breeders Cup Classic, Group 1 9f Prix d'Ispahan and Group 2 10f Prix Eugene Adam winner Arcangues and the very useful Group 3 10f Prix de Psyche winner and French 1,000 Guineas and Prix de Diane placed Agathe. The second dam, Albertine (by Irish River), won twice in France, was third in the Group 2 9.2f Prix de l'Opera and is a half-sister to the high-class middle-distance stayer Ashmore and the smart middle distance filly Acoma. (Mrs J S Bolger).

148. ISLAND COMMANDER (USA) ★★
ch.c. *Giant's Causeway – Island Escape (Petionville).*
February 8. First foal. 170,000Y. Tattersalls October Book 1. BBA (Ire). The dam won 4 races including a stakes event in the USA and is a half-sister to 6 winners. The second dam, Royal Deception (by Sovereign Dancer), is an unplaced half-sister to 5 winners including the US Grade 1 winner All Fired Up. (Mrs June Judd).

149. LISA GHERARDINI (IRE) ★★★
ch.f. *Barathea – Petite Spectre (Spectrum).*
February 7. Second foal. 155,000Y. Tattersalls October Book 1. BBA (Ire). Half-sister to the 2009 2-y-o 5.7f winner and Group 2 6f Coventry Stakes third Rakaan (by Bahamian Bounty). The dam, a fair 2-y-o 6f all-weather winner, is a half-sister to 7 winners including the useful 2-y-o Group 3 7f C L Weld Park Stakes winner Rag Top. The second dam, Petite Epaulette (by Night Shift), a fair 5f winner at 2 yrs, is a full or half-sister to 3 winners. (Mrs J S Bolger).

150. MALIBU BEACH (IRE) ★★★
b.c. *Shamardal – Ramona (Desert King).*
March 12. Sixth foal. 90,000Y. Tattersalls October Book 1. John Ferguson. Half-brother to the useful Group 3 7f Athasi Stakes winner Prima Luce (by Galileo), to the fairly useful 3-y-o 1m winner Toraidhe (by High Chaparral), the fair Irish 10f winner Home You Stroll (by Selkirk) and the modest Irish 6f winner Sheer Silk (by Fasliyev). The dam is an unraced half-sister to 9 winners including the Group 2 5f Kings Stand Stakes winner Cassandra Go (herself dam of the Irish 1,000 Guineas winner Halfway To Heaven) and the smart Group 3 6f Coventry Stakes winner and Irish 2,000 Guineas second Verglas. The second dam, Rahaam (by Secreto), a fairly useful 3-y-o 7f winner, is a half-sister to 8 winners including the French 2,000 Guineas third Glory Forever. (Sheikh Mohammed).

151. MUSIC IN THE RAIN (IRE) ★★
b.c. *Invincible Spirit – Greek Symphony (Mozart).*
February 1. First foal. 80,000Y. Tattersalls October Book 1. BBA (Ire). The dam was placed once over 7f in Ireland, is a half-sister to 3 winners including the Irish dual Group 3 winner Marionnaud. The second dam, Raghida (by Nordico), a fairly useful Irish 2-y-o dual 5f winner, was second in the Group 3 5f Curragh Stakes and the Group 3 Molecomb Stakes and is a full or half-sister to 8 winners including the Group 1 Gran Criterium winner Sholokhov and the dam of the Irish Derby winner Soldier Of Fortune. (Mrs June Judd).

152. RIOCHAS (IRE) ★★★♠
b.f. *Val Royal – Dark Indian (Indian Ridge).*
March 2. Sixth foal. 95,000Y. Tattersalls October Book 2. BBA (Ire). Sister to the US Grade 2 Honeymoon Breeders Cup Handicap and Grade 3 Senorita Stakes winner Valbenny and half-sister to the minor Italian winner of 6 races at 3 and 4 yrs Rosso Dark (by Entrepreneur). The dam, an Italian listed-placed winner, is a half-sister to 3 minor winners. The second dam, Dark Hyacinth (by Darshaan), was placed at up to 1m 5f in Ireland at 3 yrs and is a half-sister to 6 minor winners. (Mrs J S Bolger).

153. SHOP LOCAL (IRE) ★★★
b.c. *Whipper – Majinskaya (Marignan).*
May 22. Tenth foal. €45,000Y. Goffs Orby. J Bolger. Half-brother to the useful triple listed

7f winner (including at 2 yrs) and Cheveley Park Stakes fourth Modeeroch (by Mozart), to the useful Irish 2-y-o 6f winner and Group 1 6f Cheveley Park Stakes third Danaskaya (by Danehill), the Irish 2-y-o 7f winner Maidin Maith, the Irish 2-y-o 8.5f winner and Group 1 1m Gran Criterium third Chinese Whisper (both by Montjeu), the fairly useful 8.3f and 9f winner Prime Number (by King's Best), the Irish 2-y-o 5f winner Maskaya (by Machiavellian) and the French 13f winner Major Wing (by Hawk Wing). The dam, winner of the listed 12f Prix des Tuileries, is a half-sister to 6 winners including the dam of the Group 1 5f Prix de l'Abbaye winner Kistena. The second dam, Makarova (by Nijinsky), a middle-distance winner of 3 races in France, is a half-sister to 6 winners including the dam of the Group winners Mujadil and Fruits Of Love. (Mrs J S Bolger).

154. SINGE THE TURF (IRE) ★★★
ch.c. Galileo – Affianced (Erins Isle).
May 30. Sixth foal. Brother to the 1m (at 2 yrs) and Group 1 Irish Derby, Group 1 Coronation Cup, Group 2 Prix Niel and Group 2 Prix Noailles winner Soldier Of Fortune and to the smart 7f (at 2 yrs) and Group 3 10f Meld Stakes winner Heliostatic and half-brother to the quite useful Irish dual 10f winner Ard Fheis (by Lil's Boy). The dam, a useful 7f listed (at 2 yrs) and 10f winner in Ireland, is a half-sister to the Group 1 1m Gran Criterium winner Sholokhov and to 4 other stakes horses. The second dam, La Meillure (by Lord Gayle), a listed winner and Group 3 placed in Ireland, is a half-sister to 8 winners. (Mrs J S Bolger).

155. SOLAR EVENT ★★
b.f. Galileo – Time Away (Darshaan).
March 9. Fifth foal. 150,000Y. Tattersalls October Book 1. BBA (Ire). Closely related to the Group 2 Prix de Malleret and listed Cheshire Oaks winner Time On and to the quite useful 10f winner Time Control (both by Sadler's Wells). The dam won the Group 3 10.4f Musidora Stakes, was third in the Group 1 Prix de Diane and the Group 1 Nassau Stakes and is a half-sister to 6 winners including the 10f winner and Prix de Diane second Time Ahead. The second dam, Not Before Time (by Polish Precedent), is an unraced half-sister to 7 winners including the Group 2 winners Zinaad and Time Allowed. (Mrs J S Bolger/J Corcoran/Ennistown Stud).

156. STYLISH ONE (IRE) ★★★
b.f. Invincible Spirit – Great Hope (Halling).
February 27. First foal. 85,000Y. Tattersalls October Book 1. BBA (Ire). The dam, a quite useful Irish dual 1m winner, is a half-sister to 5 winners including the Irish 2-y-o 7f winner and dual Group 3 placed Chivalrous. The second dam, Aspiration (by Sadler's Wells), a 10f winner in Ireland, is a sister to the Group 1 1m Gran Criterium winner Sholokhov and a half-sister to 7 winners including the listed winners Zavaleta, Napper Tandy and Affianced (herself dam of the Irish Derby winner Soldier Of Fortune). (Mrs J S Bolger).

157. TEO'S SISTER (IRE) ★★★★
b.f. Galileo – Speirbhean (Danehill).
March 2. Fifth foal. Sister to the champion 2-y-o colt and Group 1 Dewhurst Stakes and Group 1 National Stakes winner Teofilo and to the fairly useful Irish 10f winner Senora Galilei. The dam, an Irish listed 1m winner, is a half-sister to numerous winners including the Irish listed 9f winner Graduated. The second dam, Saviour (by Majestic Light), won 3 races at 2 and 3 yrs and is a half-sister to 5 winners including the triple US Grade 1 winner Judge Angelucci and the US Grade 1 winners Peace and War. (Mrs J S Bolger).

158. TOBAR NA GAOISE (IRE) ★★★
b.c. Whipper – Starchy (Cadeaux Genereux).
March 25. Second foal. €35,000Y. Goffs Orby. Pat Neary. The dam, a fair 2-y-o 6f winner, is a sister to the smart Group 2 5f Flying Childers Stakes and Group 3 5f King George V Stakes winner Land Of Dreams (herself dam of the dual listed winner Into The Dark) and a half-sister to 4 winners. The second dam, Sahara Star (by Green Desert), winner of the Group 3 5f Molecomb Stakes, was third in the Lowther Stakes and is a half-sister to the Group 3 7f Greenham Stakes winner and Irish 2,000 Guineas fourth Yalaietanee. (Mrs J S Bolger).

159. VENCEDOR (IRE) ★★
b.c. Gone West – Honey Gold (Indian Ridge).
March 20. Second foal. €150,000Y. Goffs

Orby. J Bolger. The dam is an unplaced half-sister to 2 minor winners. The second dam, Half-Hitch (by Diesis), a quite useful 2-y-o 6f winner, is a half-sister to 4 winners including the listed winner and Group 3 Duke Of York Stakes second Mugharreb. (International Equities PLC).

160. VESTITAS (IRE) ★★
b.f. Green Desert – Kahira (King's Best).
March 13. Second foal. 105,000Y. Tattersalls October Book 1. BBA (Ire). Half-sister to the fair 2009 7f placed 2-y-o Poor Prince (by Royal Applause). The dam, a fair 2-y-o 7f placed maiden, is a half-sister to the Group 1 6f Haydock Park Sprint Cup winner Tamarisk. The second dam, Sine Labe (by Vaguely Noble), is an unplaced half-sister to the Group 1 Prix Saint-Alary winner Treble. (Mrs J S Bolger).

161. WHAT IS THE STARS (IRE) ★★★
b.c. Galileo – Key To Coolcullen (Royal Academy).
March 13. Brother to the fairly useful Irish 2-y-o 7f winner Solas Na Greine and half-brother to the fairly useful Irish 1m to 11f winner Coolcullen Times (by Rock Of Gibraltar) and the fair Irish 1m winner Irish Question (by Giant's Causeway). The dam is an unraced half-sister to numerous winners including the Group 1 6f Phoenix Stakes winner Eva Luna and the Group 3 1m Futurity Stakes winner Cois Na Tine. The second dam, Guess Again (by Stradavinsky), won over 1m at 3 yrs and is out of the Molecomb Stakes third Galka (by Deep Diver), herself a half-sister to the high-class sprinter Double Form and the Lupe Stakes winner Scimitarra. (Mrs J S Bolger).

162. WHIPLESS (IRE) ★★★
b.c. Whipper – Kimola (King's Theatre).
March 10. Third foal. €77,000Y. Goffs Orby. J Bolger. Half-brother to the fairly useful Irish 2-y-o dual 6f winner Tomas An Tsioada (by Bachelor Duke). The dam won 9 races in Scandinavia including 2 listed events and is a half-sister to 4 winners. The second dam, La Mortola (by Bold Lad), is an unraced half-sister to 5 winners including the Irish 1,000 Guineas winner Katies. (Mrs J S Bolger).

163. ZIPPY ZITTER (IRE) ★★
b.f. Galileo – Ezilla (Darshaan).
April 28. Eighth foal. €150,000Y. Goffs Orby. J Bolger. Closely related to the smart 1m, listed 10f and listed 12f winner Ezima and the fairly useful Irish 12f winner Gentle On My Mind (by Sadler's Wells). The dam is an unraced sister to 5 winners including the top-class broodmare Ebaziya, a triple listed winner from winner from 7f (at 2 yrs) to 12f in Ireland (herself dam of the Group 1 winners Edabiya, Ebadiyla and Enzeli) and a half-sister to 7 winners. The second dam, Ezana (by Ela-Mana-Mou), a winner in France at 3 yrs over 11.5f, is a half-sister to 5 winners including the Group 3 10.5f Prix de Flore and Group 3 10.5f Prix Penelope winner Demia. (Mrs June Judd).

164. UNNAMED ★★
b.f. Hurricane Run – Dance Troupe (Rainbow Quest).
April 6. Second foal. €100,000Y. Goffs Orby. J Bolger. Half-sister to the quite useful 2009 Irish 2-y-o dual 1m winner Puncher Clynch (by Azamour). The dam is a placed half-sister to 5 winners including the French listed winner and multiple Group-placed Self Defense. The second dam, Dansara (by Dancing Brave), is an unraced half-sister to 10 winners including the Irish Oaks winner Princess Pati and the Great Voltigeur Stakes winner Seymour Hicks. (Mrs J S Bolger).

165. UNNAMED ★★★
b.f. Invincible Spirit – Recite (Forty Niner).
January 29. First foal. €100,000Y. Tattersalls Ireland. J Bolger. The dam, a fair Irish 2-y-o 1m winner, is a half-sister to 4 winners including the Group 1 Haydock Park Sprint Cup and Group 1 Prix Maurice de Gheest winner Diktat. The second dam, Arvola (by Sadler's Wells), a fair 3-y-o 8.2f winner, is a sister to the 12.5f listed placed Lord of Appeal and a full or half-sister to 8 winners including the Group 1 Lockinge Stakes winner and high-class sire Cape Cross. (A H Marshall).

MARCO BOTTI
166. ARMOISE ★★
b.f. Sadler's Wells – Di Moi Oui (Warning).
February 23. Fifth foal. 45,000Y. Tattersalls

October Book 1. Not sold. Half-sister to the Italian 3-y-o winner and Group 2 Italian Oaks second Moi Non Plus (by Singspiel) and to the minor Italian 4-y-o winner Coup De Foudre (by Fantastic Light). The dam won the Group 3 Prix Chloe and the Group 3 Prix de la Nonette and is a half-sister to 4 winners. The second dam, Biosphere (by Pharly), won 3 races in Italy and was listed placed and is a full or half-sister to 4 winners. (Grundy Bloodstock Ltd). *"She's a big filly and she looks smart. Obviously she's bred to go a mile and a quarter next year so we're not rushing her, but so far she's shown that she's a good mover and has a good temperament. One for the mid-summer onwards over seven furlongs and a mile."*

167. CARESSE ★★
b.f. Hernando – Carenage (Alzao).
January 27. Fourth foal. Sister to the fair 3-y-o 9.5f winner Caribana. The dam, a quite useful 12f winner, is a half-sister to 4 winners. The second dam, Key Change (by Darshaan), won the Yorkshire Oaks and is a half-sister to 7 winners. (Miss K Rausing). *"Quite a small filly but she's stocky, so physically she looks a two-year-old but the pedigree suggests she wants time. Right now she's just ticking over and I doubt her being sharp enough for six furlongs. We'll probably aim to get her on the racecourse from July onwards."*

168. EXCELEBRATION (IRE) ★★★★
b.c. Exceed And Excel – Sun Shower (Indian Ridge).
April 13. Third foal. £20,000Y. Doncaster St Leger. Marco Botti. Half-brother to the fair 2009 7f and 1m placed 2-y-o Tashzara (by Intikhab) and to the fairly useful 7f and 1m winner Mull Of Killough (by Mull Of Kintyre). The dam is a placed half-sister to 2 minor winners in France. The second dam, Miss Kemble (by Warning), ran once unplaced and is a full or half-sister to 10 winners including the high-class Irish Oaks winner Princess Pati and to the Great Voltigeur Stakes winner Seymour Hicks. (G Manfredini). *"A nice colt, he's done well since we bought him. He was quite narrow at the sales but he's filled out and turned into a nice horse. We could probably push him a bit more than the others and get him ready for mid-May over six furlongs although he'll definitely stay further. He's shown speed and is a promising colt."*

169. MEDIPLOMAT ★★★★
b.c. Medicean – Upskittled (Diktat).
March 16. First foal. 23,000Y. Tattersalls October Book 2. Marco Botti. The dam, placed twice at 3 yrs in France is a half-sister to 8 winners including the listed winner and dual Group 1 third Musicanna. The second dam, Upend (by Main Reef), won 3 races from 10f to 12f including the Group 3 St Simon Stakes and the listed Galtres Stakes, was second in the Group 3 Princess Royal Stakes and is a half-sister to 6 winners including the dam of the high-class stayer and champion hurdler Royal Gait. *"A very smart colt with a good attitude – we like him a lot. He's bred to go seven furlongs plus but he's quite forward, so I wouldn't be surprised if he started off in June over six. When we bought him everyone said they thought he was a bargain."* TRAINERS' BARGAIN BUY

170. ORATOUCH (IRE) ★★★
b.f. Oratorio – Ravish (Efisio).
March 20. First foal. £20,000Y. Doncaster St Leger. Marco Botti. The dam, a moderate 1m placed maiden, is a half-sister to 5 winners including the quite useful 2-y-o 5f winner and listed Firth of Clyde Stakes second Yakin and the French listed 7f winner Special Discount. The second dam, Looks Sensational (by Majestic Light), is an unplaced half-sister to the dual US Grade 1 winner Awe Inspiring and the US Grade 2 winner Recognizable. (G Manfredini). *"We thought she was going to be an early type but she started growing and changing and her knees are still a bit open. So I would imagine she's going to be a mid-summer type over seven furlongs. We like her, she has a good attitude and is a good mover, so she just needs a bit of time."*

171. ROSE BUSH (IRE) ★★★
b.f. Pivotal – Centifolia (Kendor).
March 10. Second foal. €160,000Y. Arqana Deauville August. Chantilly Bloodstock. The dam won 4 races at 2 yrs in France including the Group 2 Criterium de Maisons-Laffitte and is a half-sister to one winner. The second dam, Djayapura (by Fabulous Dancer), won once at

3 yrs in France and is a half-sister to 4 winners. (Grundy Bloodstock Ltd). *"A well-bred filly, the dam was quite fast and she was bought by the owner with the intention of having a sharp two-year-old, but actually she's growing a lot and changing. She's still in light work and we like her but it might time before she's ready."*

172. SCIAMPIN ★★★
b.c. Invincible Spirit – Gracious (Grand Lodge).
April 22. Second foal. 50,000Y. Tattersalls October Book 3. Marco Botti. The dam is an unraced half-sister to 4 winners including the smart 2-y-o 6f winner and Group 1 1m Racing Post Trophy third Henrik. The second dam, Clincher Club (by Polish Patriot), a fair 5f (at 2 yrs) and 7.5f winner, is a half-sister to 9 winners. (Scuderia Rencati Srl). *"He's probably our biggest two-year-old. In January it looked like he was going to be an early two-year-old but he's grown a lot since then. He should still be out in mid-summer, probably over seven furlongs or a mile. A nice mover and a nice type."*

173. TIMOTHY T ★★★
bl.g. Pastoral Pursuits – Point Perfect (Dansili).
January 24. First foal. 27,000Y. Tattersalls October Book 3. Marco Botti. The dam ran twice unplaced and is a half-sister to a winner over hurdles. The second dam, Supersonic (by Shirley Heights), was placed 7 times and stayed 10.5f and is a sister to the listed 2-y-o 10f Zetland Stakes and listed 2 mile George Stubbs Stakes winner Upper Strata (herself dam of the Prix de la Salamandre winner Lord Of Men and the French Oaks second Her Ladyship) and a half-sister to 5 winners. (Op Center). *"He was a cheeky two-year-old so we had to geld him and he's settled down a lot now and is doing his job properly. He's stocky and compact and he's bred to be sharp, so we'd like to start him over five furlongs in April or May."*

174. YAKAMOZ ★★
b.f. Tiger Hill – Kelang (Kris).
April 26. Ninth foal. Half-sister to the quite useful 2009 2-y-o 1m winner Kavak (by Dubawi), to the Italian listed winner Bukat Timah (by Inchinor), the Italian listed-placed winner Daylang (by Daylami), the quite useful Italian 9f winner Kayak (by Singspiel) and two minor winners in Italy by Dansili and Dr Fong. The second dam, Ebbing Tide (by His Majesty), is an unplaced half-sister to 5 winners including the dam of Oh So Sharp. (Grundy Bloodstock Ltd). *"She's nice but she'll need time. The half-brother won a maiden for us last year before being sold to Hong Kong, but this filly will take longer than him. She's more backward, but she's doing nothing wrong and is a good mover."*

175. UNNAMED ★★♠
br.f. Cape Cross – Jazz Princess (Bahhare).
April 7. First foal. €110,000Y. Goffs Orby. McKeever St Lawrence. The dam, a smart 2-y-o winner of the Group 3 7f C L Weld Park Stakes and the Group 3 7f Athasi Stakes, was second in the Group 2 Ridgewood Pearl Stakes and is a half-sister to one winner. The second dam, Jazz Up (by Cadeaux Genereux), is an unraced half-sister to 5 winners including the dual Italian listed winner Mister Cavern. (J Barton). *"Still in pre-training and I know she's been cantering but I don't really know much about her yet. She was quite small at the sales and she needed to grow. Being by Cape Cross it suggests she'll want seven furlongs or more."*

176. UNNAMED ★★
b.f. Refuse To Bend – Mureefa (Bahri).
May 12. Fifth foal. Half-sister to the fairly useful 1m to 8.5f (at 2 yrs) and 10f winner and Group 3 placed Habalwatan (by In The Wings). The dam is a placed half-sister to several winners including the French listed 2-y-o 1m winner River Cara. The second dam, Mata Cara (by Storm Bird), a useful triple 7f winner, is a half-sister to several winners. (Rabbah Bloodstock). *"I like her a lot, despite being by Refuse To Bend who isn't everyone's favourite sire. She's a very easy filly to train and has a good, straightforward attitude. She's probably still a bit immature and has slightly open knees so I just need to let her strengthen up a bit, but I would say that she could make a two-year-old from June onwards."*

177. UNNAMED ★★★
b.f. Barathea – Rasana (Royal Academy).
March 23. Fourth foal. 40,000Y. Tattersalls December. Not sold. Half-sister to the quite useful 5f and 6f winner of 7 races Rasaman

(by Namid), to the quite useful 10f winner Everynight (by Rock Of Gibraltar) and the 2010 3-y-o 1m winner Aldovrandi (by Cape Cross). The dam is an unplaced half-sister to the top-class colt Rakti, a winner of six Group 1 events including the Champion Stakes, the Eclipse Stakes and the Queen Elizabeth II Stakes. The second dam, Ragera (by Rainbow Quest), was placed in Italy and is a half-sister to 8 winners. "We've had two of the mares foals and they both won but needed time. This filly surprises me because she's more straightforward than the other two and I think she'll be earlier than they were. I wouldn't be surprised if she made a mid-season two-year-old."

CLIVE BRITTAIN

178. ABJER (FR) ★★
b.c. Singspiel – Fine And Mellow (Lando).
March 24. Fifth foal. 28,000Y. Tattersalls October Book 1. Rabbah Bloodstock. Brother to the minor French winner For Joy and half-brother to another minor French winner by Soviet Star. The dam, a listed winner of 4 races in France, is a half-sister to 7 winners. The second dam, Mika Red (by Red Steps), won two Group 1 races in Belgium. (Mr M Al Shafar).

179. AFKAR (IRE) ★★
b.c. Invincible Spirit – Indienne (Indian Ridge).
April 2. Second foal. 70,000Y. Tattersalls December. Rabbah Bloodstock. Brother to the moderate 5f winner Brown Lentic. The dam, placed once over 7f in Ireland, is a sister to the 2-y-o Group 3 7f Curragh Futurity Stakes winner St Clair Ridge and a half-sister to 8 winners. The second dam, St Clair Star (by Sallust), a winner in Canada, is a half-sister to 7 winners including the Flying Childers Stakes winner Superlative. (S Manana).

180. DFFAR (USA) ★★★★
b.c. Shamardal – Deveron (Cozzene).
March 27. First foal. 50,000Y. Tattersalls October Book 1. David Lanigan. The dam, a very useful 2-y-o 7f winner, was third in the Group 1 1m Prix Marcel Boussac and is a sister to the Canadian stakes winner and Grade 2 placed Windward Islands and a half-sister to 5 winners including the minor US stakes winner Hunter Cruise. The second dam, Cruisie

(by Assert), won 3 minor races at 3 yrs in the USA and is a half-sister to 4 stakes winners including the dam of the US Grade 1 winner Capote Belle. (S Ali).

181. DFFRA (IRE) ★★★★
b.f. Refuse To Bend – Sonachan (Darshaan).
January 31. Fourth foal. 50,000Y. Tattersalls October Book 1. Not sold. Half-sister to the Group 3 7f Sweet Solera Stakes winner Albabilia (by King's Best) and to the quite useful 2-y-o 1m winner Brainy Benny (by Barathea). The dam, a minor Irish 14f winner, is a half-sister to the listed 1m Brownstown Stud Stakes and US stakes winner Inchacooley. The second dam, Blue Cashmere (by Secreto), is an unraced half-sister to 10 winners including the US Grade 2 placed Receiver and Phone Bird. (S Ali).

182. DIPLOMASI ★★★
b.c. Iceman – Piper's Ash (Royal Academy).
April 14. Second foal. 24,000Y. Tattersalls December. Rabbah Bloodstock. Half-brother to the fair 2-y-o 5f winner Avonvalley (by Avonbridge). The dam, a quite useful 2-y-o 5f winner, is a half-sister to 4 winners. The second dam, Merida (by Warning), a 1m winner in France and the USA, is a full or half-sister to 8 winners including the dual US Grade 2 1m winner Tychonic. (S Manana).

183. EL WASMI ★★★★
b.c. Oasis Dream – Wendylina (In The Wings).
March 5. Fifth foal. 150,000Y. Tattersalls October Book 1. Rabbah Bloodstock. Brother to the very smart 2-y-o Group 3 Solario Stakes and 3-y-o Group 2 10f Prix Guillaume d'Ornano winner Sri Putra and half-brother to the fairly useful 11f and hurdles winner Duty (by Rainbow Quest). The dam is an unraced half-sister to 9 winners including the Group 1 10.5f Prix de Diane winner Caerlina. The second dam, Dinalina (by Top Ville), a French 2-y-o 10f winner, is a half-sister to 8 winners including the Doncaster Cup winner Karadar and the dams of the Group 1 winners Kartajana and Khariyda. (S Manana).

184. JIBOUTI ★★★
b.c. Exceed And Excel – Treble Seven (Fusaichi Pegasus).
January 17. Second foal. Half-brother to the

unplaced 2009 2-y-o Stadium Of Light (by Fantastic Light). The dam, placed once over 1m, is a half-sister to the very smart filly Lovers Knot, winner of the Group 2 1m Falmouth Stakes and the US Grade 3 De La Rose Handicap and to the very useful 1m (at 2 yrs) and 9f winner and listed-placed Foodbroker Founder. The second dam, Nemea (by The Minstrel), a fairly useful 10f winner, stayed 2m and is a half-sister to 8 winners including the useful 12f winners Topsider Man and Bryan Station and the useful stayer Muir Station. (S Manana).

185. MAYHAB ★★★
ch.c. Cadeaux Genereux – Amazed (Clantime).
February 19. Sixth foal. 80,000Y. Tattersalls October 1. Rabbah Bloodstock. Half-brother to the useful 2-y-o listed 6f and 3-y-o listed 5f winner Dazed And Amazed (by Averti) and to the quite useful dual 5f winner (including at 2 yrs) Nawaaff (by Compton Place). The dam, a modest 5f placed 3-y-o, is a sister to the Group 3 Prix du Petit Couvert winner Bishops Court and a half-sister to 5 winners including the listed winning sprinter Astonished. The second dam, Indigo (by Primo Dominie), a quite useful 2-y-o 5f winner, is a half-sister to 5 winners.

186. MEEJANAH ★★★
b.f. Diktat – Aberdovey (Mister Baileys).
January 31. Second foal. 20,000Y. Tattersalls October Book 2. Rabbah Bloodstock. Half-sister to the unplaced 2009 2-y-o Stormglass (by Galileo). The dam, a fair 6f (at 2 yrs) and 1m winner, is a half-sister to 2 winners including the dual 10f and subsequent US stakes winner and Grade 2 placed Solva. The second dam, Annapurna (by Brief Truce), a useful 7f winner (at 2 yrs) and 9f listed placed, is a half-sister to 4 winners including the 2-y-o Group 3 7f Rockfel Stakes and listed 7f winner Name Of Love. (S Manana).

187. MISHTAAG ★★★
b.c. Bertolini – Raze (Halling).
February 22. Second foal. 26,000Y. Tattersalls October Book 2. Rabbah Bloodstock. The dam, a fair 10f winner, is a half-sister to 5 winners including the Group 3 placed Queen's Vase. The second dam, Rive (by Riverman), won once at 2 yrs in France and is a half-sister to 10 winners. (S Manana).

188. MURJAAN ★★★
b.c. Iceman – Entrap (Phone Trick).
March 24. Second foal. 70,000Y. Tattersalls October 2. Rabbah Bloodstock. Half-brother to the fair 1m and 9f winner Ensnare (by Pivotal). The dam, a useful listed-placed 6f winner of 3 races (including on her 2-y-o debut), is a half-sister to 3 winners. The second dam, Mystic Lure (by Green Desert), a fair 5f and 6f placed 2-y-o, is a half-sister to 5 winners including the Grade 1 Hollywood Derby and Group 3 Prix Daphnis winner Thrill Show and the Grade 3 Pilgrim Stakes winner David's Bird. (S Manana).

189. PLANET WAVES (IRE) ★★★
b.c. Red Ransom – Rock Salt (Selkirk).
February 19. Third foal. 100,000Y. Tattersalls December. Rabbah Bloodstock. Half-brother to the Group 1 7f Moyglare Stud Stakes winner Termagant (by Powerscourt) and to the fairly useful 1m (at 2 yrs) to 10f winner of 4 races Splinter Cell (by Johannesburg). The dam, placed twice at 3 yrs in France, is a sister to the very smart Group 2 10f Prix Eugene Adam and Group 3 9f Prix de Guiche winner Kirkwall and a half-sister to 3 winners. The second dam, Kamkova (by Northern Dancer), a placed middle-distance stayer, is a half-sister to 10 winners including the top-class US middle-distance colt Vanlandingham and to the dams of the Group/Grade 1 winners Distant Music and Funny Moon. (S Manana).

190. SHAFGAAN ★★★★♠
b.c. Oasis Dream – Night Haven (Night Shift).
February 7. Sixth foal. 17,000Y. Tattersalls October. Rabbah Bloodstock. Half-brother to the useful 2-y-o 7f and listed 10f winner Rosa Grace (by Lomitas), the fairly useful 5f and all-weather 6f winner and listed-placed Secret Night (by Dansili) and the moderate dual 5f winner Duke Of Rainford (by Bahamian Bounty). The dam, a fairly useful 5f (at 2 yrs) and 6f winner and 6f listed-placed, is a sister to 3 winners including the French 2-y-o listed 5f and subsequent UAE winner Shoalhaven. The second dam, Noble Haven (by Indian King), won once at 2 yrs and is a half-sister to 6 winners. (S Manana). This colt ran well first time out at Newbury.

191. SIKEEB (USA) ★★★
b.c. Alhaarth – Erstwhile (Desert Prince).
February 28. Second foal. 66,000Y. Tattersalls December. Rabbah Bloodstock. Half-brother to the fair 2009 2-y-o 5f winner Gypsie Queen (by Xaar). The dam won once at 5 yrs in France and is a half-sister to 7 winners. The second dam, Urmia (by Persian Bold), a listed-placed winner of 3 races in France, is a half-sister to 10 winners including Gunboat Diplomacy (Group 2 Prix Noailles). (S Manana).

192. YAROOH (USA) ★★★
b.f. Medaglia d'Oro – Country Maiden (Forest Camp).
February 12. First foal. $100,000Y. Keeneland September. Rabbah Bloodstock. The dam, a minor US winner of 4 races, is a half-sister to the US stakes winner and Grade 3 placed Motovato. The second dam, Buffalo Bird Woman (by Slew City Slew), a US stakes-placed winner of 4 races, is a half-sister to 12 winners. (Mr M Al Shafar).

193. ZAIDAN (USA) ★★★★
b.br.c. Street Cry – Element Of Truth (Atticus).
May 8. Second foal. $200,000Y. Keeneland September. Anthony Stroud. The dam, a fairly useful 1m winner, was listed-placed and is a half-sister to 5 winners including the smart Group 3 Criterion Stakes and Group 3 1m Minstrel Stakes winner Ramooz and the useful 7f (at 2 yrs) and 1m winner and Group 1 Fillies Mile third My Hansel. The second dam, My Shafy (by Rousillon), a fairly useful dual 1m winner, is a half-sister to 3 minor winners. (S Manana).

194. UNNAMED ★★★
b.c. Street Cry – Agata (Poliglote).
March 14. First foal. 90,000Y. Tattersalls October Book 1. John Ferguson. The dam, a minor US dual winner at 4 yrs, was third in the Group 1 Prix Saint-Alary and is a half-sister to 5 minor winners. The second dam, Ambri Piotta (Caerwent), a French listed winner of 11 races, is a half-sister to 8 winners. (S Manana).

195. UNNAMED ★★★
b.f. Dansili – Anbella (Common Grounds).
February 11. Third foal. 140,000Y. Tattersalls October Book 1. Rabbah Bloodstock. Sister to the fair 6f winner Anacreon and half-sister to the minor French winner Reasons (by Malabar Gold). The dam, a French 2-y-o listed 7f winner, is a half-sister to 8 winners including the Group 1 Criterium de Saint-Cloud winner Spadoun and the dual Group 1 Prix de l'Opera winner Satwa Queen. The second dam, Tolga (by Irish River), is a placed half-sister to 6 winners including the dam of the Group 2 winner and Group 1 placed Signe Divin. (S Manana).

196. UNNAMED ★★★
b.c. Red Ransom – Chelsea Rose (Desert King).
January 26. First foal. 55,000Y. Tattersalls October Book 1. Rabbah Bloodstock. The dam, winner of the Group 1 7f Moyglare Stud Stakes, is a half-sister to 4 winners including the Irish 6f (at 2 yrs), listed 1m and subsequent US winner and Grade 2 placed European. The second dam, Cinnamon Rose (by Trempolino), an Irish 10f winner, is a half-sister to 6 winners including the Group 2 Prix Eugene Adam winner River Warden and the US Grade 3 winner Sweettuc. (S Manana).

197. UNNAMED ★★★
b.f. Cadeaux Genereux – Eternal Beauty (Zafonic).
April 12. Fourth foal. 95,000Y. Tattersalls October Book 2. Rabbah Bloodstock. Half-sister to the 2009 German 2-y-o winner and Group 3 7f third Eternal Power (by Tiger Hill), to the fair French (over 6f at 2 yrs) and German winner Eternal Flash (by One Cool Cat) and the fair 2-y-o triple 5f winner Artdeal (by Fasliyev). The dam was unplaced in France and is a half-sister to one winner. The second dam, Strawberry Roan (by Sadler's Wells), an Irish 7f and 1m listed winner, was second in the Irish 1,000 Guineas and is a sister to the Oaks and Irish 1,000 Guineas winner Imagine and a half-sister to the top-class colt Generous and the dual Group 1 winner Imagine. (S Manana).

198. UNNAMED ★★★
b.f. Acclamation – Express Logic (Air Express).
March 23. Second foal. 85,000Y. Tattersalls October Book 1. Rabbah Bloodstock. Half-sister to the listed Easter Stakes winner and Group 3 Craven Stakes third Pure Poetry (by Tagula). The dam ran once unplaced and is

a half-sister to one winner. The second dam, Hazarama (by Kahyasi), won over 13f and is a half-sister to 5 winners including the Group 3 winners Hazariya and Hazarista. (S Manana).

199. UNNAMED ★★★♣
b.f. Invincible Spirit – Honour Bright (Danehill).
March 9. First foal. €105,000Y. Goffs Orby. Anthony Stroud. The dam is an unraced half-sister to 4 winners including the listed 10f Ballyroan Stakes winner Dabtiya and the 10f winner and listed-placed Dabaya. The second dam, Dabiliya (by Vayrann), is an unraced half-sister to 12 winners including the top-class French Derby winner and sire Darshaan, the top-class Prix Vermeille winner Darara (dam of the Group 1 winners Diaghilev, Dar Re Mi and Darazari) and the Prix de Royallieu winner Dalara (dam of the Coronation Cup winner Daliapour). (S Manana).

200. UNNAMED ★★★
ch.f. Cadeaux Genereux – Isis (Royal Academy).
March 11. First foal. 60,000Y. Tattersalls October Book 2. Rabbah Bloodstock. The dam, placed once over 6f from 2 starts at 2 yrs, is a half-sister to 3 winners including the Group 2 6f Gimcrack Stakes winner Sir Gerry. The second dam, Incredulous (by Indian Ridge), a useful 3-y-o 1m winner, is a half-sister to 6 winners. (S Manana).

201. UNNAMED ★★★
b.c. Oasis Dream – Lady In Waiting (Kylian).
May 16. Sixth foal. 150,000Y. Tattersalls October Book 1. Rabbah Bloodstock. Brother to the quite useful 2-y-o 6.5f winner Dream In Waiting and half-brother to the 2009 9f placed 2-y-o Red Courtier (by Red Ransom), the quite useful 2-y-o 7f winner Wait For The Light (by Fantastic Light) and the minor German winner of 2 races at 5 yrs Macabre (by Machiavellian). The dam won 6 races including the listed 6f Empress Stakes (at 2 yrs) and the Group 2 10f Sun Chariot Stakes and was Group placed four times. She is closely related to the 7f (at 2 yrs) and Group 3 15f Prix du Lutece winner Savannah Bay and a half-sister to 6 winners. The second dam, High Savannah (by Rousillon), a fair middle-distance placed maiden, is a half-sister to 6 winners including the useful sprinters Maid For The Hills and Maid For Walking (herself dam of the US Grade 1 winner Stroll). (S Manana).

202. UNNAMED ★★★
ch.f. Pivotal – Our Queen Of Kings (Arazi).
March 13. Seventh foal. 130,000Y. Tattersalls October Book 1. Rabbah Bloodstock. Half-sister to the fair 2009 2-y-o 6f winner Our Dream Queen (by Oasis Dream), to the Group 3 Brownstown Stakes winner and Group 2 Cherry Hinton Stakes third Spinning Queen (by Spinning World), the useful 10f and 12f winner and 2-y-o 7f listed-placed Shannon Springs (by Darshaan), the fairly useful dual 7f winner Amber Queen (by Cadeaux Genereux) the quite useful 2-y-o 5f, 7f and 10f winner Changing The Guard (by King's Best) and the Italian winner of 4 races Jekill (by Royal Academy). The dam is an unraced half-sister to 7 winners including the Grade 1 9f Hollywood Derby winner Labeeb, the Grade 2 Arlington Handicap winner Fanmore and the Group 2 9f Budweiser International Stakes winner Alrassam. The second dam, Lady Blackfoot (Prince Tenderfoot), a very useful Irish listed winning sprinter, is a half-sister to 3 winners. (S Manana).

203. UNNAMED ★★
b.c. Rahy – Plenty Of Grace (Roberto).
February 6. Tenth foal. $130,000Y. Keeneland September. Rabbah Bloodstock. Half-brother to 4 minor winners, including two in the USA by Storm Cat and Deputy Minister and to the placed dam of the US Grade 2 winner Diabolical. The dam won the Grade 1 Yellow Ribbon Invitational and four Grade 2 events in the USA and is a half-sister to 7 winners including the US dual Grade 1 winner Soaring Softly. The second dam, Wings Of Grace (by Key To The Mint), won 6 races in the USA including the Grade 3 Boiling Springs Handicap. (S Manana).

204. UNNAMED ★★★
br.f. Cadeaux Genereux – Prancing (Prince Sabo).
March 29. Ninth foal. 90,000Y. Tattersalls October Book 2. Rabbah Bloodstock. Half-sister to the very useful 6f (at 2 yrs) and 7f listed winner Levera (by Groom Dancer), to the fairly useful 3-y-o 5f and 6f winner Catherine

Wheel, the fair 5f and 6f winner of 6 races Firework (both by Primo Dominie), the fair 7f and 1m winner Kiss A Prince (by Fraam) and the Scandinavian winner of 9 races Cavorting (by Polar Falcon). The dam, a useful 2-y-o 5f winner, stayed 1m and is a full or half-sister to 4 winners including the Group 1 6f Middle Park Stakes winner First Trump. The second dam, Valika (by Valiyar), was placed three times from 1m to 12f at 3 yrs and is a half-sister to 6 winners including the high-class sprinter Mr Brooks. (S Manana).

205. UNNAMED ★★★
b.f. *Dansili – Sauterne (Rainbow Quest).*
February 12. Fifth foal. 38,000Y. Tattersalls October Book 1. Rabbah Bloodstock. Half-brother to the fair 2-y-o 7f winner Determined Stand (by Elusive Quality). The dam, a listed winner of 3 races from 7f to 10f, is a half-sister to 5 winners including the smart 2-y-o Group 2 6f Cherry Hinton Stakes winner Applaud. The second dam, Band (by Northern Dancer), is a placed half-sister to 5 winners including the US Grade 3 9f New Orleans Handicap winner Festive. (S Manana).

206. UNNAMED ★★★
br.f. *Songandaprayer – Think (Marchand De Sable).*
February 20. First foal. 30,000Y. Tattersalls October Book 2. Rabbah Bloodstock. The dam, a 2-y-o winner in France, was third in the Group 3 Prix Du Bois and is a half-sister to 7 winners. The second dam, Montagne Bleue (by Legend Of France), is a placed half-sister to 5 winners. (S Manana).

207. UNNAMED ★★★
b.f. *Oasis Dream – Triennial (Giant's Causeway).*
April 6. Second foal. 70,000Y. Tattersalls October Book 1. Rabbah Bloodstock. The dam is an unraced half-sister to 4 winners including the smart 7f (at 2 yrs) and listed 1m winner Flat Spin. The second dam, Trois Graces (by Alysheba), won once over 1m at 3 yrs in France and is a half-sister to 5 winners including Rami (Group 3 Concorde Stakes), Crack Regiment (Group 3 Prix Eclipse) and La Grand Epoque (second in the Group 1 Prix de l'Abbaye). (S Manana).

208. UNNAMED ★★★
b.f. *Noverre – Very Nice (Daylami).*
April 22. Third foal. 38,000Y. Tattersalls October Book 2. Rabbah Bloodstock. Half-sister to the fair 2-y-o 7f winner Dream Number (by Fath) and to the fairly useful triple 7f winner Seek N' Destroy (by Exceed And Excel). The dam is an unraced half-sister to 2 winners. The second dam, All Time Great (by Night Shift), a fairly useful 2-y-o 6f winner and fourth in the 7.3f Fred Darling Stakes, is closely related to the Dante Stakes and Craven Stakes winner Alnasr Alwasheek and a half-sister to 6 winners including the Juddmonte International Stakes winner One So Wonderful and the Rockfel Stakes winner Relatively Special. (S Manana).

209. UNNAMED ★★★
b.f. *Dansili – Woodlass (Woodman).*
April 20. Third foal. 50,000Y. Tattersalls October Book 1. Rabbah Bloodstock. Half-sister to the 2009 6f placed 2-y-o (on only start) Always Dazzling (by Cadeaux Genereux) and to the French 2-y-o 7f and subsequent US listed stakes winner and Grade 3 placed Duke Of Homberg (by Dynaformer). The dam won 3 races in France and the USA, was stakes-placed and is a half-sister to 8 winners including the 2-y-o listed Prix Herod winner Vitaba. The second dam, Vitola (by Sallust), won 3 races in France and was Grade 2 placed in the USA and is a half-sister to 5 winners. (S Manana).

DAVID BROWN

210. CLARA ZETKIN ★★★
b.f. *Elusive City – Pantita (Polish Precedent).*
February 9. Third foal. £9,000Y. Doncaster St Leger Festival. D Brown. Half-sister to the fair 2009 2-y-o 6f winner La Pantera (by Captain Rio). The dam, a fair 1m and 10f placed maiden, is a half-sister to 5 winners abroad. The second dam, Dedara (by Head For Heights), won once at 3 yrs and is a half-sister to 6 winners. (Norton Common Farm Racing Ltd). *"She's certainly got a big future, she'll be racing by mid-season and she's a very strong, medium-sized filly."* She gets her name from an influential socialist German politician and fighter for women's rights.

211. EASY TICKET (IRE) ★★
ch.c. Kheleyf – Lady Joshua (Royal Academy).
March 28. Ninth foal. 26,000Y. Tattersalls October 1. J Fretwell. Half-brother to the smart listed 7f Tyros Stakes and listed 1m Easter Stakes winner Privy Seal, to the quite useful 6f and 7f winner of 10 races (including at 2 yrs) Super Frank (both by Cape Cross), the fairly useful winner of 2 races at up to 14.4f Lord Joshua (by King's Theatre), the fair 14f winner Master Cobbler and a winner in Australia (both by Alhaarth). The dam, a fairly useful 7f (at 2 yrs) to 12f placed maiden, is a half-sister to 8 winners including the high-class Group 2 12f Jockey Club Stakes winner Sapience. The second dam, Claretta (by Roberto), a quite useful 2-y-o 7f winner, is a half-sister to 7 winners including the Italian 1,000 Guineas winner Rosananti. (J Fretwell). *"This colt is one for later in the year. He's a nice, big horse but seven furlongs will be his trip this season."*

212. GOOD TIMIN ★★★
b.c. Royal Applause – Record Time (Clantime).
February 15. Sixth foal. Half-brother to the smart dual Group 3 5f winner Moorhouse Lad (by Bertolini), to the useful 5f (including at 2 yrs) and 6f winner of 5 races Off The Record (by Desert Style) and the modest 2-y-o 5f winner Pro Tempore (by Fraam). The dam, a fair 5f winner at 3 and 4 yrs, is a sister to the listed winning sprinter Lago Di Varano and a half-sister to 3 winners. The second dam, On The Record (by Record Token), a fair dual sprint winner at 2 and 4 yrs, is a half-sister to 3 winners. (R Hull & P Onslow). *"He's one for the middle of the season, he's big and strong and will be suited by five and six furlongs this season. A longer term prospect as well as a two-year-old."*

213. MOTHER JONES ★★★
b.f. Sleeping Indian – Bella Chica (Bigstone).
March 22. Fifth foal. £10,000Y. Doncaster St Leger Festival Sales. D Brown. Half-sister to the modest 5f and 6f winner of 5 races Fast Freddie (by Agnes World). The dam, a fairly useful 2-y-o winner of 3 races from 5f to 6f, is a half-sister to two winners. The second dam, Just Like Annie (by Mujadil), a minor Irish 3-y-o 5f winner, is a half-sister to 6 winners including the very smart Group 3 7f Criterion Stakes winner Pipe Major (by Tirol). (Norton Common Farm Racing Ltd). *"This is certainly a lovely filly, she'll be out early and she's one to watch out for. I can see her improving as the year goes on and as she fills out more. Well put-together and compact, she'll start off at five furlongs but I should think she'll go seven later on."* The filly is named after a prominent American labour and community organiser who helped co-ordinate major strikes. TRAINERS' BARGAIN BUY

214. ONELADYOWNER ★★★
b.c. Auction House – Inya Lake (Whittingham).
April 28. £14,000Y. Doncaster October. D H Brown. Half-brother to the useful 6f winner of 5 races Jimmy Styles (by Inchinor), to the fair 2-y-o dual 5f winner Lake Hero (by Arkadian Hero) and the modest triple 5f winner Special Gold (by Josr Algarhoud). The dam, a useful 2-y-o winner of 4 races over 5f including the Group 3 Molecomb Stakes, subsequently won a listed 5f event at 3 yrs and is a half-sister to one winner. The second dam, Special One (by Aragon), was a modest 2-y-o 5f winner and a half-sister to 7 winners. (S Bolland and Partnership). *"He just needs a bit of time, but he'll be racing in June and he's a really nice colt for the future. He'll be a two-year-old over five furlongs to start with but I think he'll be better over six. A nice, medium-sized horse and well put-together."*

HENRY CANDY

215. ARDLUI (IRE) ★★★★
b.c. Galileo – Epping (Charnwood Forest).
January 21. Fifth foal. 360,000Y. Tattersalls October Book 1. M H Goodbody. Brother to the 2009 Irish 2-y-o 7f winner Nebula Storm and to the smart 10f winner and Group 1 St Leger second The Last Drop and half-brother to the winner Cherry Orchard (by King's Best). The dam, a quite useful 3-y-o 7f winner, is a half-sister to 4 winners including the French listed winner and multiple Group-placed Self Defense. The second dam, Dansara (by Dancing Brave), is an unraced half-sister to 10 winners including the Irish Oaks winner Princess Pati and the Great Voltigeur Stakes winner Seymour Hicks. (Thomas Barr). *"Ardlui is a place just above Loch Lomond. This colt is a great big, strong bull of a horse. John Oxx

trained his half-brother Nebula Storm to win at the second attempt last year. He had to take 20 kgs off him between runs and this horse would be the same – very gross, very greedy, very laid-back but very nice. He'd want a minimum of seven furlongs this year."

216. BEAUCHAMP ZORRO ★★
ch.c. Zamindar – Aquarelle (Kenmare).
February 8. Half-brother to the fairly useful 9f and hurdles winner Aqualung (by Desert King), to the quite useful 1m and 9f winner Skyscape (by Zafonic), the fair 2-y-o 7f winner Emulate (by Alhaarth) and the French 6f to 1m (including at 2 yrs) winner Coastline (by Night Shift). The dam, a useful French 2-y-o 1m winner, is a half-sister to the useful 9f and listed 12f winner Marani. The second dam, Aquamarine (by Shardari), won the listed Cheshire Oaks and is a half-sister to the St Leger winner Toulon. (E Penser). *"He's a real giant, but a lovely horse that carries himself very well for his size. I wouldn't dare do anything with him until September, but he's very attractive and he'd probably want a mile this year."*

217. BLESS YOU ★★★★
b.f. Bahamian Bounty – Follow Flanders (Pursuit Of Love).
May 2. Third foal. Half-sister to Hallucinating (by Oasis Dream), unplaced in one start at 2 yrs in 2009, to the quite useful dual 10f winner Fever (by Dr Fong) and the fair 1m winner Sir Billy Nick. The dam, a fairly useful dual 5f winner, is a half-sister to 9 winners including the top-class Group 1 5f Nunthorpe Stakes winner Kyllachy. The second dam, Pretty Poppy (by Song), a modest 2-y-o 5f winner, stayed 7.6f and is a half-sister to 4 winners. (T A F Frost). *"The opposite end of the spectrum to Beauchamp Zorro, she's very robust with great quarters and great shoulders on her. I had her knees x-rayed in late March and she's quite a way off being mature enough yet and also still looks fairly woolly. She looks a real sprinter, so you'd hope that by June time she'd be ready to do something."*

218. CAPE RAMBLER ★★★
ch.c. Pastoral Pursuits – Cape Charlotte (Mon Tresor).
April 14. Third foal. **£8,000Y. Doncaster St Leger Festival. H Candy.** Half-brother to the fair 6f winner Cape Melody (by Piccolo). The dam is an unraced half-sister to the dam of the Group 1 Golden Jubilee Stakes winner Cape Of Good Hope. The second dam, Laena (by Roman Warrior), was placed once at 2 yrs and is a half-sister to one winner. (Simon Broke & Partners II). *"A relation of a family we've had a lot of fun with. I bought him as a foal for 6.2k and he was about the size of a Labrador but because of his pedigree he attracted a fair bit of attention. I tried to sell him on as a yearling but without success. He's really developed since then and turned into a lovely looking horse – quite rangy. With his pedigree I suppose he has to be a sprinter and he's a nice, big strong horse."*

219. CODEMASTER ★★★★
b.c. Choisir – Verbal Intrigue (Dahar).
April 14. £16,000Y. Doncaster St Leger. Not sold. Half-brother to the US Grade 2 winner Monkey Puzzle (by Country Pine), to the fair 10f winner Sainglend (by Galileo) and four minor winners in the USA by Dr Caton, Bates Motel, Saint Ballado and Pleasant Tap. The dam, a minor US 3-y-o winner, is a half-sister to 6 winners including the US Grade 1 placed Verbasle. The second dam, Verbality (by Verbatim), a stakes winner and Grade 2 placed in the USA, is a half-sister to 2 winners. (John Joseph Byrne). *"I think this is the most eye-catching of the two-year-olds cantering. He's a tremendous mover, very well-balanced and very athletic. I think it's such a shame that Choisir isn't coming back from Australia because he's a good sire. This colt looks a proper little athlete, his knees aren't mature yet but you would think that by June time he'd be able to go racing. He'll be a five furlong type and I think he'd get six."*

220. DINKUM DIAMOND (IRE) ★★★
b.c. Aussie Rules – Moving Diamonds (Lomitas).
February 24. First foal. The dam, a fair Irish 5f winner at 3 yrs, is a half-sister to 2 winners. The second dam, a dual 2-y-o stakes winner in the USA, was placed in two Grade 1 events and is a half-sister to 3 minor winners out of Euro Empire (by Bartok). *"He'll be the first of my two-year-olds to go into work, so he may*

be my first runner. He looks a proper sharp little two-year-old and five/six furlongs will be his trip."

221. HARRY LUCK (IRE) ★★★
b.c. Red Ransom – Tara Gold (Royal Academy).
April 14. Fourth foal. 30,000Y. Tattersalls October 2. H Candy. Half-brother to the quite useful Irish dual 10f winner Tarrsille (by Dansili) and to the quite useful Irish dual 11f winner Timoca (by Marju). The dam, a quite useful 10f winner, subsequently won once at 4 yrs in the USA and is a sister to the smart listed 9f Strensall Stakes winner and dual Group 1 third Gold Academy and a half-sister to 2 winners. The second dam, Soha (by Dancing Brave), a modest 12f placed 3-y-o, is a half-sister to one winner. (Six Too Many). *"A big horse and he's going to take a bit of time because of that, but he's very strong and very well-balanced. He looks as if he could cope with six furlongs the way he goes at the moment and he'll get a mile in time. Looks a nice horse for the second half of the year."*

222. L'AMI LOUIS (IRE) ★★★★
b.c. Elusive City – Princess Electra (Lake Coniston).
February 16. Fourth foal. 35,000Y. Tattersalls October 1. H Candy. The dam, a modest 2-y-o 5.6f winner, is a half-sister to 8 winners including the US Grade 3 winner Aquaba (herself dam of the dual Group 3 winner Millstream). The second dam, Elect (by Vaguely Noble), a very useful winner of 3 races from 10f to 12.3f, was third in the Sun Chariot Stakes and is a half-sister to the dams of the Group 1 winners Sadeem and Too Chic. (First Of Many Partnership). *"The name comes from a much-enjoyed restaurant in Paris – so his owners tell me! He's grown a shade too much and I've just had to stop with him over the last few weeks, but he's a wonderfully good-topped horse with a great head and a great outlook. I would think six furlongs in July time would suit and he looks a nice horse."*

223. NO LARKING (IRE) ★★★
b.c. Refuse To Bend – Dawn Chorus (Mukaddamah).
April 19. Eighth foal. £20,000Y. Doncaster St Leger. H Candy. Half-brother to the Irish 7f (at 2 yrs) to 10f and subsequent Hong Kong stakes winner Solid Approach (by Definite Article), to the useful Irish 7f winner and listed-placed Dangle (by Desert Style), the quite useful 2009 2-y-o 6f winner Bahati (by Intikhab), the Irish 5f winner Divert (by Averti), the Irish 7f winner Devious Diva (by Dr Devious), the 6f winner Zero Money (by Bachelor Duke) and the 2-y-o dual 6f winner La Campanella (by Tagula) – all five quite useful. The dam is an unraced half-sister to 6 winners including Barrier Reef, a winner of 8 races and second in the Group 3 Beresford Stakes. The second dam, Singing Millie (by Millfontaine), won twice in Ireland at 3 yrs and is a half-sister to 7 winners. (Simon Broke & Partners). *"I know what they say about the sire but he was a very good racehorse and he's bound to get some nice horses. This is out of a mare that hasn't bred a loser yet in seven attempts and he's turned into a very classy looking horse. A big, strong colt that's bred to get ten furlongs next year."*

224. SCHISM ★★
ch.f. Shirocco – Alla Prima (In The Wings).
March 3. Third foal. 100,000Y. Tattersalls October Book 1. H Candy. Half-sister to the German 2-y-o winner and listed 10f placed All Annalena (by Dubai Destination). The dam is an unplaced half-sister to 6 winners including the smart French 2-y-o Group 3 1m Prix d'Aumale winner and smart broodmare Anna Palariva. The second dam, Anna Of Saxony (by Ela-Mana-Mou), a very useful winner of the Group 2 14.6f Park Hill Stakes, is a half-sister to 9 winners including the Group 2 winners Annaba and Pozarica. (Major M G Wyatt). *"A big filly – she was that way when I bought her, but she's a tremendous mover and really handles herself well. She's bred to get a serious trip so I would think she'll just have a couple of runs in the autumn. Everyone who rides her likes her."*

225. SEAL ROCK ★★★
b.c. Ishiguru – Satin Doll (Diktat).
March 12. First foal. £6,000Y. Doncaster St Leger Festival. H Candy. The dam is an unplaced half-sister to 3 winners including the useful 5f and 6f winner of 7 races (including at 2 yrs) First Order. The second dam, Unconditional Love (by Polish Patriot), a useful

5f (at 2 yrs) and 10f winner, was third in the Group 3 Hungerford Stakes and is a half-sister to 5 winners. (P A Deal). *"A bit heavy-topped at the moment, but he'll make a two-year-old once his bones have hardened up a bit. He'd be the strongest of the two-year-olds – he's a massive horse and a great mover but just a bit too enthusiastic for his own good at the moment. An out-and-out sprinter."*

226. SLUGGSY MORANT ★★★
b.g. Monsieur Bond – Breezy Louise (Dilum).
March 8. £3,000Y. Doncaster St Leger Festival. H Candy. Half-brother to the quite useful Irish 7f winner of 3 races Rockie (by Bertolini). The dam, a 5f seller winner, is a half-sister to several winners abroad. The second dam, Louise Moillon (by Mansingh), a quite useful 2-y-o 5f winner, subsequently won over the jumps in France and is a half-sister to 8 winners including the Group 2 6f Coventry Stakes winner Whip It Quick and the dam of the Group 2 12f Ribblesdale Stakes winner Miss Boniface. (Mr H Candy & Partners). *"Sluggsy Morant was a baddie in a James Bond film! I bought him quite cheaply as a foal along with two others. I thought I'd make some money on them all and didn't, but I'm pleased now though. He's a very, very easy goer and a nice, big strong horse that enjoys life. He'll be running in June and I can see him possible starting at five but I think he'll be a six furlong horse."* TRAINERS' BARGAIN BUY

HENRY CECIL
227. BAISSE ★★★
b.f. High Chaparral – Best Side (King's Best).
April 12. Second foal. 48,000Y. Tattersalls October Book 2. C de Moubray. Half-sister to the useful 2009 2-y-o listed 7f winner Azmeel (by Azamour). The dam, an Irish 7f (at 2 yrs) and 1m winner, was listed-placed and is a half-sister to 5 winners including the Irish Group 3 winner Grand Ducal and the useful 2-y-o 6f winner and listed placed Hurricane Floyd. The second dam, Mood Swings (by Shirley Heights), a fair 2-y-o 6f winner, is a sister to the listed 2-y-o Sweet Solera Stakes winner Catwalk and a half-sister to 5 winners. (Mr G Schoeningh). *"Tall and immature, but she's likeable and she moves nicely."*

228. BRIDE UNBRIDLED (IRE) ★★★
b.f. Hurricane Run – Se La Vie (Highest Honor).
February 3. First foal. 80,000Y. Tattersalls October 1. Not sold. The dam won 2 minor races at 2 and 3 yrs in France and is a half-sister to 4 winners including the Canadian stakes winner and Grade 2 placed Daylight Come. The second dam, Lady Winner (by Fabulous Dancer), won the Group 2 Prix d'Astarte and the Grade 3 Chrysanthemum Handicap and is a half-sister to 4 winners. (HE Sheikh Sultan bin Khalifa Al Nahyan). *"This filly will need time, but she moves nicely."*

229. DISCO DANCING ★★★
b.f. Singspiel – Disco Ball (Fantastic Light).
February 2. The dam, a fair 6f and 7f placed maiden, is a half-sister to the French listed 9f winner Rainbow Dancing (by Rainbow Quest). The second dam, Danceabout (Shareef Dancer), won the Group 2 Sun Chariot Stakes and the listed 7f Oak Tree Stakes and is a half-sister to 4 winners including the Group 3 6f Prix de Meautry winner Pole Position. (Bloomsbury Stud). *"She's a medium-sized filly that should make a two-year-old."*

230. DURANTE ALIGHIERI ★★★
b.c. Galileo – Puce (Darshaan).
March 4. Ninth foal. 475,000Y. Tattersalls October Book 1. Blandford Bloodstock. Closely related to the dual listed winner and Group 3 placed Lion Sands (by Montjeu), to the very useful 10f (at 2 yrs) and 11f winner and listed-placed Pukka (by Sadler's Wells) and the very useful Group 2 12f Lancashire Oaks winner Pongee (by Barathea) and half-brother to the quite useful 10f winner Celt (by Selkirk) and the 12f seller winner Garhoud (by Grand Lodge). The dam, a very useful listed 12f winner, is a half-sister to 10 winners including the dam of the Group 1 winners Alexandrova and Magical Romance. The second dam, Souk (by Ahonoora), a fairly useful 7f winner, was listed placed over 1m and is a half-sister to 3 winners. (HE Sheikh Sultan bin Khalifa Al Nahyan). *"This colt has grown over the winter so he's going to take time, but he's very likeable."*

231. FLASH OF INTUITION (IRE) ★★★
b.c. Mingun – Insight (Sadler's Wells).
February 14. Closely related to the French dual 10f winner Izanagi (by A P Indy) and half-brother to the French 7f (at 2 yrs) and 1m winner and Group 1 Prix Jean Prat third Ershaad (by Kingmambo). The dam, winner of the Grade 1 E P Taylor Stakes, is a sister to the Irish 2,000 Guineas winner Saffron Walden and a half-sister to the Group 1 7f Prix de la Foret, Group 2 6.5f Prix Maurice de Gheest and Group 3 6f Prix de Seine-et-Oise winner Dolphin Street. The second dam, Or Vision (by Irish River), won over 5.5f and 7f at 2 yrs and the listed 7f Prix de l'Obelisque at 3 yrs and is a half-sister to the US stakes winners Dixie Fine and Nijinsky's Lover (herself dam of 2 US Graded stakes winners) and to the dam of the Moyglare Stud Stakes winner Sequoyah. (Niarchos Family). *"A tall colt, he's a good mover and likeable."*

232. GLOBAL DANCE (IRE) ★★★
b.f. Sadler's Wells – Solo De Lune (Law Society).
March 27. Sister to the fairly useful dual 14f winner Moon Indigo and half-sister to the 1m (at 2 yrs) and Group 1 10f Prix Saint-Alary winner Cerulean Sky, the smart 10f winner Qaatef, the listed 12f winner and Breeders Cup Filly & Mare second L'Ancresse (all by Darshaan) and the useful French 2-y-o listed 7f winner Diner de Lune (by Be My Guest). The dam, a French 11f winner, is a half-sister to the Grade 2 E P Taylor Stakes winner Truly A Dream and the French Group 2 winner Wareed. The second dam, Truly Special (by Caerleon), won the Group 3 10.5f Prix de Royaumont, was placed in five other Group events in France and is a half-sister to the French Group 2 winners Modhish and Russian Snows. (John & Fu Mei). *"A nice filly who has done everything right so far, but she'll obviously need time and looks like a mile and a half prospect."*

233. LADY MAGDALENA (IRE) ★★
b.f. Invincible Spirit – Stylist (Sadler's Wells).
March 23. Second foal. €74,000Y. Goffs Orby. BBA (Ire). Half-sister to the modest 2009 5f placed 2-y-o Mount Juliet (by Danehill Dancer). The dam, a fair 8.5f winner, is a sister to French Ballerina (winner of four listed events in Ireland from 1m to 2m) and a half-sister to 4 winners including the Group 1 Fillies Mile winner and Irish Oaks second Sunspangled. The second dam, Filia Ardross (by Ardross), a very smart filly, won three Group 2 events in Germany and the Group 3 10f Select Stakes at Goodwood. (Niarchos Family). *"A nice mover, she's doing everything right but she'll need time."*

234. LATE TELEGRAPH (IRE) ★★
b.c. Montjeu – Bywayofthestars (Danehill).
February 12. Second foal. 320,000Y. Tattersalls October Book 1. M H Goodbody. The dam was listed-placed over 1m in Ireland and is a half-sister to 9 winners including the Group 1 Irish Oaks winner Moonstone, the Group 1 10f Prix Saint-Alary winner Cerulean Sky (herself dam of the Group 2 Doncaster Cup winner Honolulu) and the Breeders Cup second L'Ancresse. The second dam, Solo de Lune (by Law Society), a French 11f winner, is a half-sister to 7 winners including the Grade 2 E P Taylor Stakes winner Truly A Dream and the French Group 2 winner Wareed. (T Barr). *"He's grown a lot and will need time. He's a good mover and likeable, but more of a three-year-old type."*

235. MAHOYOGIN (IRE) ★★★
b.br.c. Dixie Union – Shiva (Hector Protector).
April 18. The dam, a high-class winner of the Group 2 10.5f Tattersalls Gold Cup and the Group 3 10f Brigadier Gerard Stakes, is a sister to the high-class Group 2 12f Prix Jean de Chaudennay and Group 3 12f Prix Foy winner Limnos and a half-sister to the useful 7f and listed 1m winner Burning Sunset. The second dam, Lingerie (by Shirley Heights), placed 7 times in France, is a half-sister to 4 winners including the French listed placed Evocatrice. (Niarchos Family). *"He's a big colt and he needs time but he's very likeable."*

236. NEUTRAFA (IRE) ★★★
ch.f. Araafa – Neutrina (Hector Protector).
March 6. Third foal. €75,000Y. Goffs Orby. David Howard. Half-sister to the minor French dual 12f winner Pure Will (by Dream Well). The dam is an unplaced half-sister to 5 winners including the Grade 1 Breeders Cup Mile winner Domedriver, the French Group 3 winner Tau Ceti and the dam of the Group 2

winner Freedonia. The second dam, Napoli (by Baillamont), won 3 listed races in France and is a sister to the French Group 3 winner D'Arros. (Tony Ashley). *"A medium-sized filly, she moves nicely, she's tough and has some character."*

237. NIGHT AND DANCE ★★★
b.f. Danehill Dancer – Evensong
(Waky Nao).
February 29. First foal. 350,000Y. Tattersalls October Book 1. Blandford Bloodstock. The dam won 4 races in France and Germany including a French listed event over 9f and is a half-sister to the Italian and German Group 2 winner Eagle Rise and the French listed winner Echoes Rock. The second dam, Evening Breeze (by Surumu), a German listed winner of 6 races, is a half-sister to the Singapore Group 1 winner Epalo and the French Group 2 winner Elopa. (HE Sheikh Sultan bin Khalifa Al Nahyan). *"Has had a setback but a nice filly in the making."*

238. RAVINDRA ★★★
b.c. Red Ransom – Young And Daring
(Woodman).
February 26. Brother to the useful 2-y-o 6f winner and listed 10f and 12f placed Daring Ransom. The dam, a stakes winner in the USA, is a half-sister to 8 winners including two other US stakes winners. (HE Sheikh Sultan bin Khalifa Al Nahyan). *"This colt needs time but he moves nicely. More likely to be best as a three-year-old."*

239. REAL SENSE (IRE) ★★★
b.f. Galileo – Remote Romance (Irish River).
April 5. Closely related to Saddex (by Sadler's Wells), a winner of two Group 1 12f races in Italy and Germany. The dam is an unplaced half-sister to the multiple US Grade 1 winner Denon, to the listed 6f winner and Group 1 6f Cheveley Park Stakes second Imperfect Circle (herself dam of the top-class miler Spinning World) and the very smart Moyglare Stud Stakes, Coronation Stakes, Child Stakes and Cherry Hinton Stakes winner Chimes of Freedom (dam of the multiple US Grade 1 winner Aldebaran). The second dam, Aviance (by Northfields), won the 6f Heinz "57" Phoenix Stakes at 2 yrs. (Niarchos Family). *"She'll obviously need time, but she may come to herself later this season."*

240. ROYAL PECULIAR ★★★
b.c. Galileo – Distinctive Look (Danehill).
April 24. First foal. 100,000Y. Tattersalls October 1. Not sold. The dam, a quite useful 9f winner, is a half-sister to 6 winners including the Group 1 Fillies' Mile, Group 2 Lancashire Oaks and Group 2 May Hill Stakes winner Playful Act, the Group 2 Yorkshire Cup winner Percussionist and the Group 2 Sun Chariot Stakes and Group 2 Park Hill Stakes winner Echoes In Eternity. The second dam, Magnificient Style (by Silver Hawk), won the Group 3 10.5f Musidora Stakes and is a half-sister to the Grade 1 10f Charles H Strub Stakes winner Siberian Summer. (De La Warr Racing & Newsells Park Stud). *"A nice, big colt and a good mover."*

241. SEARING HEAT (USA) ★★★
b.br.c. Empire Maker – Valentine Band
(Dixieland Band).
March 19. Half-brother to the 2009 Irish 2-y-o 1m winner Await The Dawn (by Giant's Causeway), to the French 1m, 10f (both at 2 yrs) and listed 9f winner Putney Bridge (by Mizzen Mast) and the quite useful 11f to 13f winner Spruce (by Maria's Mon). The dam, the very useful 10f winner, is a half-sister to the French 7f (at 2 yrs) and listed 1m winner Multiplex, to the very useful 10f and Irish Group 3 14f winner Memorise, the useful 7.5f winner and listed 1m placed Sparkling Water and the useful 2-y-o 7f winner Fully Invested. The second dam, Shirley Valentine (by Shirley Heights), a useful 12f winner, was fourth in the Park Hill Stakes and the Lancashire Oaks and is a sister to the high class Irish Derby second Deploy and a half-sister to the Derby and Irish Derby winner Commander in Chief, the champion 2-y-o and miler Warning and the Grade 1 10f Flower Bowl Invitational Handicap winner Yashmak. (Khalid Abdulla). *"A good mover and very likeable. Hopefully he'll be strong and forward enough by July to give a good account of himself, but he looks a three-year-old prospect."*

242. SINNFONIA (IRE) ★★★
b.f. Sinndar – Kalimanta (Lake Coniston).
February 22. Fifth foal. €80,000Y. Goffs Orby. Elite Racing Ltd/M Budden. Half-sister to the useful 7f (at 2 yrs) and 1m winner and

Group 3 Brownstown Stakes third Kalidaha (by Cadeaux Genereux) and to the quite useful Irish 11f and 12f winner Kallithea (by Dr Fong). The dam ran twice unplaced and is a half-sister to 5 winners including the top-class Champion Stakes and Breeders Cup Turf winner Kalanisi and the high-class 1m listed winner and Group 1 St James's Palace Stakes second Kalaman. The second dam, Kalamba (by Green Dancer), was placed over 9f and 10f and is a full or half-sister to 3 winners. (Elite Racing Club). *"A nice looking filly that moves well."*

243. SUKHOTHAI ★★★
gr.f. *Maria's Mon – Succession (Groom Dancer)*.
February 1. The dam, a fairly useful 7f and 1m (including at 2 yrs) and German listed 1m winner, is a half-sister to the useful 3-y-o listed 10f winner Succinct. The second dam, Pitcroy (by Unfuwain), a useful 10f winner, is a half-sister to 8 winners including the very useful Group 3 7f Jersey Stakes winner Ardkinglass. (Dr Catherine Wills). *"An active filly, she doesn't have the best conformation but she could make a two-year-old."*

244. SPECIFIC GRAVITY (FR) ★★★★
b.c. *Dansili – Colza (Alleged)*.
Half-brother to the 2-y-o Group 1 10f Criterium de Saint-Cloud winner Linda's Lad (by Sadler's Wells), to the useful French dual 1m winner and Group 3 placed Ulterior Motives (by Selkirk) and the minor French 1m winner Volantis (by Bluebird). The dam, a quite useful 2-y-o 1m winner, is a full or half-sister to 9 winners including the very useful Group 3 6f July Stakes and listed 3-y-o 9f winner Wharf. The second dam, Dockage (by Riverman), a winner over 1m at 2 yrs and a 9f listed event at 3 yrs in France, is a half-sister to 3 winners. (Niarchos Family). *"He moves nicely and is a colt for the second half of the season."*

245. TIGER WEBB ★★★
b.c. *Hurricane Run – Wonderful Desert (Green Desert)*.
February 1. First foal. 65,000Y. Tattersalls October Book 2. Henry Cecil. The dam is an unplaced half-sister to the US Grade 2 8.5f winner Sun Boat. The second dam, One So Wonderful (by Nashwan), won the Group 1 Juddmonte International Stakes and the Group 2 Sun Chariot Stakes and is a half-sister to 7 winners including the Rockfel Stakes winner Relatively Special and the Dante Stakes and Craven Stakes winner Alnasr Alwasheek. (R A H Evans). *"A good mover, he's not over big and he could run from July onwards."*

246. WILD COCO (GER) ★★
ch.f. *Shirocco – Wild Side (Sternkoenig)*.
January 31. Fourth foal. 60,000Y. Tattersalls October Book 1. Not sold. Half-sister to two minor winners in France and Germany by Definite Article and Night Shift. The dam, a German Group 2 winner, is a half-sister to the 2-y- Group 3 7f Prix Miesque winner and German 1,000 Guineas and German Oaks second White Rose and the Group 2 German St Leger winner Win For Us. The second dam, Wild Romance (by Alkalde), a champion 2-y-o filly in Germany, is a half-sister to 4 winners. (Gestut Rottgen). *"A big filly who moves nicely but will need plenty of time."*

247. UNNAMED ★★★
ch.f. *North Light – Blush Damask (Green Dancer)*.
April 5. Half-sister to the quite useful French triple 6f winner (including at 2 yrs) and Group 3 fourth Blue Damask (by Rahy), to the useful 10f winner Blizzard Blues (by Mr Greeley) and the fair French 7f winner Brass Damask (by Lemon Drop Kid). The dam was placed in a Group 3 11f event in Germany and is a half-sister to the Italian listed 1m winner Bog Wild. (Gestut Ammerland). *"A good-sized, strong filly, she moves nicely and could make a two-year-old."*

248. UNNAMED ★★★★★
b.br.f. *Dansili – Clepsydra (Sadler's Wells)*.
January 31. Seventh foal. Sister to the very smart Group 1 10f Criterium de Saint-Cloud (at 2 yrs) and Group 3 10.3f Musidora Stakes winner Passage Of Time and to the 6f (at 2 yrs) and Group 2 12f King Edward VI Stakes winner Father Time and half-sister to the useful 2-y-o listed 1m winner Timepiece (by Zamindar), the fairly useful 10f winner Sandglass (by Zafonic) and the quite useful 1m and 10f winner Timetable (by Observatory). The dam, a quite useful 12f winner, is a half-sister to several winners including the useful listed 10.5f winner

Double Crossed. The second dam, Quandary (by Blushing Groom), a useful winner of 4 races from 9f to 10f including the listed James Seymour Stakes at Newmarket, is a half-sister to the Group 1 Prix du Moulin winner All At Sea. (Khalid Abdulla). *"A very nice filly, she's a good mover and we're hopeful for her in the second half of this season. At this stage she's as promising as any of the family that I have trained."*

249. UNNAMED ★★★★
b.c. Dansili – Emplane (Irish River).
March 16. Brother to Aviate, a winner over 1m on his only start at 2 yrs in 2009, to the very useful 2-y-o dual 7f winner Wingwalker and the 2-y-o Group 3 7f Prix la Rochette winner and Group 1 placed Early March and half-brother to the fairly useful French 10f winner Itinerary (by Dr Fong), the quite useful 7f winner Painted Sky (by Rainbow Quest) and the minor French 11f winner Coach Lane (by Barathea). The dam, a useful 3-y-o 1m winner, is a sister to the useful 2-y-o 1m winner Boatman and a half-sister to the quite useful 2-y-o 7f winner Palisade. The second dam, Peplum (by Nijinsky), a useful winner of the listed 11.3f Cheshire Oaks, is a half-sister to the top class filly Al Bahathri, winner of the 1,000 Guineas and the Coronation Stakes. (K Abdulla). *"He's a very big colt that will need time but he's a nice mover and very likeable."*

250. UNNAMED ★★★
b.f. Hurricane Run – Half Glance (Danehill).
February 24. Half-sister to the quite useful dual 12f winner Brief Look (by Sadler's Wells). The dam won 3 races including the 2-y-o Group 3 1m May Hill Stakes and is a half-sister to the Irish Derby, St Leger and Turf Classic placed Tycoon. The second dam, Fleeting Glimpse (by Rainbow Quest), a 10f winner in France, was second in the Group 1 10f Prix Saint-Alary and is a half-sister to the 1,000 Guineas winner Wince (herself dam of the Group 1 Yorkshire Oaks winner Quiff). (K Abdulla). *"A nice filly who will need time."*

251. UNNAMED ★★★
b.br.f. Storm Cat – High Walden (El Gran Senor).
March 28. Half-sister to the quite useful dual 7f winner Portodora (by Kingmambo) and to the fair 1m winner Heather Moor (by Diesis). The dam, a smart 2-y-o 1m winner, was Group-placed and is closely related to the Oaks, Fillies Mile, Musidora Stakes and May Hill Stakes winner Reams of Verse and a half-sister to the Group 1 10f Coral Eclipse Stakes and Group 1 10f Phoenix Champion Stakes winner Elmaamul (by Diesis). The second dam, Modena (by Roberto), is an unraced half-sister to the smart 2-y-o 7f winner and Queen Elizabeth II Stakes third Zaizafon – herself the dam of Zafonic. (Khalid Abdulla). *"Not over big, but she moves nicely and she could make a two-year-old."*

252. UNNAMED ★★★
b.c. Galileo – Kind (Danehill).
February 11. Second foal. Closely related to Bullet Train (by Sadler's Wells), a fair 1m winner on his only start at 2 yrs in 2009. The dam, a dual listed winner over 5f and 6f, was Group 3 placed and is a half-sister to the Arlington Million and Tattersalls Rogers Gold Cup winner Powerscourt (by Sadler's Wells) and to the smart 14f winner of 3 races Brimming. The second dam, Rainbow Lake (by Rainbow Quest), a smart winner of 3 races including the Group 3 12f Lancashire Oaks and the listed 10f Ballymacoll Stud Stakes, is a half-sister to several winners including the useful middle-distance winner Vertex. (Khalid Abdulla). *"A nice colt who will need time, but he has plenty of size and scope."*

253. UNNAMED ★★★
ch.c. Galileo – La Sky (Law Society).
May 16. Twelfth foal. 80,000Y. Tattersalls October Book 1. Not sold. Half-brother to the Group 1 12f Oaks winner Love Divine (herself dam of the St Leger winner Sixties Icon), to the quite useful 11.5f winner Easy To Love (both by Diesis), the useful listed 12f winner Floreeda (by Linamix), the French 12f winner Laurentine and the US winner and Grade 1 fourth Security Code (both by Private Account). The dam, a useful 10f winner and second in the Lancashire Oaks, is closely related to the Champion Stakes winner Legal Case and a half-sister to 4 winners. The second dam, Maryinsky (by Northern Dancer), won twice at up to 9f in the USA and is a half-sister to the US Grade 3 winners Bold

Place and Card Table. (Lordship Stud). *"A good mover who has done well physically since he has come into training Obviously going to be at his best as a three-year-old."*

254. UNNAMED ★★★
b.c. Oasis Dream – Modesta (Sadler's Wells).
March 4. Half-brother to the fairly useful 7f (at 2 yrs) and 1m winner Intense (by Dansili). The dam, a useful 11.5f and listed 14f winner, is closely related to the Oaks, Fillies Mile, Musidora Stakes and May Hill Stakes winner Reams of Verse and to the smart 2-y-o 1m winner and Group-placed High Walden and a half-sister to the high-class Group 1 10f Coral Eclipse Stakes and Group 1 10f Phoenix Champion Stakes winner Elmaamul. The second dam, Modena (by Roberto), is an unraced half-sister to the smart 2-y-o 7f winner and Queen Elizabeth II Stakes third Zaizafon – herself the dam of Zafonic. (Khalid Abdulla). *"A nice colt, but he's immature and not going to be early."*

255. UNNAMED ★★★
br.f. Dansili – Protectress (Hector Protector).
February 2. Closely related to the 1m and 10f winner Stand Guard (by Danehill). The dam, a 2-y-o listed 7f winner, is a half-sister several winners including the listed-placed Market Forces. The second dam, Quota (by Rainbow Quest), a useful 10f winner, is a sister to 4 winners including the top-class Group 1 1m Racing Post Trophy winner and St Leger second Armiger and the useful 2-y-o 1m and 8.5f winner and Group 1 Racing Post Trophy fourth Besiege. (Khalid Abdulla). *"She's a medium-sized, nice filly that could make a two-year-old."*

256. UNNAMED ★★★
b.f. Beat Hollow – Quandary (Blushing Groom).
May 3. Closely related to the quite useful 12f winner Clepsydra (by Sadler's Wells) and half-sister to the fairly useful 2009 2-y-o 1m winner Quiet (by Observatory), the useful listed 10.5f winner Double Crossed (by Caerleon), the quite useful dual 12f and hurdles winner Political Intrigue (by Dansili) and the fair 2m and hurdles winner Hue (by Peintre Celebre). The dam, a useful winner of 4 races from 9f to 10f including the listed James Seymour Stakes at Newmarket, is a half-sister to the high-class filly All At Sea (winner of the Group 1 Prix du Moulin and second in the Oaks and the Juddmonte International) and to the Free Handicap winner Over The Ocean. The second dam, Lost Virtue (by Cloudy Dawn), an unraced half-sister to the US Grade 2 Shuvee Handicap winner Anti-Lib, is out of a half-sister to Damascus. (Khalid Abdulla). *"Doing everything right at this early stage and could be alright later this year."*

257. UNNAMED ★★★★
b.c. Empire Maker – Reams Of Verse (Nureyev).
March 25. Brother to the US Grade 3 placed Eagle Poise and half-brother to the smart listed 10f winner of 4 races Many Volumes (by Chester House), to the useful 2-y-o 7f winner and Group 3 7f Prestige Stakes second Ithaca (by Distant View), the fairly useful 2-y-o 6f winner Western Verse (by Gone West) and the fair 1m to 10f winner General Knowledge (by Diesis). The dam, a very smart winner of the Oaks, the Fillies Mile, the Musidora Stakes and the May Hill Stakes, is a half-sister to numerous winners including the high-class Group 1 10f Coral Eclipse Stakes and Group 1 10f Phoenix Champion Stakes winner Elmaamul. The second dam, Modena (by Roberto), is an unraced half-sister to the smart 2-y-o 7f winner and Queen Elizabeth II Stakes third Zaizafon – herself the dam of Zafonic. (Khalid Abdulla). *"A good mover and likeable. He could make a two-year-old from July onwards."*

258. UNNAMED ★★★
b.c. Dansili – Shirley Valentine (Shirley Heights).
May 15. Closely related to the French 7f (at 2 yrs) and listed 1m winner Multiplex (by Danehill) and half-brother to the very useful 10f winner Valentine Band (by Dixieland Band), to the very useful 10f and Irish Group 3 14f winner Memorise (by Lyphard), the useful 7.5f winner and listed 1m placed Sparkling Water (by Woodman), the useful 2-y-o 7f winner Fully Invested (by Irish River) and the useful 12f to 2m winner of 9 races Greenwich Meantime (by Royal Academy). The dam, a useful 11.8f winner, was fourth in the Park Hill Stakes and the Lancashire Oaks. She is a sister to the high class Irish Derby second Deploy

and a half-sister to the Derby and Irish Derby winner Commander in Chief, the champion 2-y-o and miler Warning and the Grade 1 10f Flower Bowl Invitational Handicap winner Yashmak. The second dam, Slightly Dangerous (by Roberto), won the 7.3f Fred Darling Stakes, was second in the Oaks and is a half-sister to the dam of Rainbow Quest. (Khalid Abdulla). *"A good mover and very likeable, he may do something later this season but I expect him to be more of a three-year-old."*

259. UNNAMED ★★★★
b.f. Cadeaux Genereux – Violet Ballerina (Namid).
February 21. First foal. The dam, a fair 7f (at 2 yrs) and 6f winner, is a half-sister to the very useful 2-y-o Group 2 6f Richmond Stakes winner Carizzo Creek. The second dam, Violet Spring (by Exactly Sharp), a 5-y-o 2m winner in Ireland, is a half-sister to 3 other minor winners and to the placed dam of the US Grade 3 winner Doc Holiday. (Racegoers Club). *"A nice, medium-sized, good moving filly. Likeable."*

MICK CHANNON

260. ARABIAN STAR (IRE) ★★★★
b.c. Green Desert – Kassiopeia (Galileo).
January 29. First foal. The dam, a quite useful 12f winner, was fourth in a listed event and is a half-sister to several winners including the French listed-placed Craft Fair. The second dam, Brush Strokes (by Cadeaux Genereux), is an unraced half-sister to several winners including the Group 1 Racing Post Trophy second Mudeer. (George & Jackie Smith). *"A lovely horse and he'll be a two-year-old from the end of May onwards. A smashing horse, being out of a Galileo mare might make stretch him to seven furlongs but I don't think that matters too much. I like him and he's one to follow."*

261. BEACH PATROL (IRE) ★★
b.c. Antonius Pius – Slip Ashore (Slip Anchor).
May 6. Twelfth foal. £26,000Y. Doncaster St Leger. Gill Richardson. Half-sister to 5 winners including the fairly useful 2-y-o 6f winner and Group 3 Princess Margaret Stakes second Valentin (by King Of Kings) and the Irish and US winner and listed-placed Storm Ashore (by Storm Cat). The dam is an unraced half-sister to 4 winners including the listed 7f Irish 1,000 Guineas Trial winner Welsh Muffin (herself dam of the champion Japanese sprinter and Horse of the Year Taiki Shuttle). The second dam, Muffitys (by Thatch), won the listed Marble Hill Stakes in Ireland and is a half-sister to 6 winners. (Box 41). *"He disappointed me first time up because he ran badly. I know he's a May foal but he was showing plenty of dash. Maybe we got on with him too soon, but the jury's out really."*

262. BINT YAZMOUNA ★★★
ch.f. Cadeaux Genereux – Resistance Heroine (Dr Fong).
March 25. Second foal. 42,000Y. Tattersalls October Book 2. Gill Richardson. Half-sister to the fairly useful 2009 2-y-o 5f winner and listed-placed Nosedive (by Observatory). The dam is a placed half-sister to 6 winners including the Group 3 winners Violette and Silca's Gift. The second dam, Odette (by Pursuit Of Love), a fair 3-y-o 5f and 5.7f winner, is a half-sister to 4 winners. (Jaber Abdullah). *"She's lovely filly for the middle of the season. A sprinter/miler, she's a big two-year-old that just needs a bit of time."*

263. BOUNTIFUL GUEST ★★★★
ch.c. Bahamian Bounty – Perfect Partner (Be My Chief).
January 26. Sixth foal. 32,000Y. Tattersalls October Book 2. R Frisby. Half-brother to the fair 2009 2-y-o 5f winner Hot Pursuits (by Pastoral Pursuits), to the modest 2-y-o 6f winner Molly Dancer (by Emarati) and a winner in Saudi Arabia by Medicean. The dam is an unraced half-sister to 6 winners including the 6f Ayr Gold Cup and Washington Singer Stakes winner Funfair Wane and the Italian listed 7.5f winner Cabcharge Striker. The second dam, Ivory Bride (by Domynsky), won the listed 6f Rose Bowl Stakes and is a half-sister to 7 winners including the useful listed 8.5f and listed 10f winner Putuna and the useful sprinter Lochonica. (J D Guest). *"A nice big horse, he's been wrong for a while with different issues it's held him up but I have a sneaking fancy for him. He's a fine colt and we won't hang around when he's ready. Look out for him."*

264. CHILWORTH LAD ★★★★
b.c. Diktat – Dowhatjen (Desert Style).
February 23. The dam, a fair winner of 4 races over 6f and 7f (including at 2 yrs), is a half-sister to numerous winners including the useful 5f ad 6f winner Cupids Ray. The second dam, Cupid Miss (by Anita's Prince), won over 6f at 2 yrs in Ireland and is a half-sister to numerous winners. *"He looks a two-year-old type, he's sharp and he's got plenty of speed, so he'll be out early doors."*

265. BINT NAS (IRE) ★★★
b.f. Clodovil – Molomo (Barathea).
January 26. Sixth foal. €90,000Y. **Arqana Deauville August. Gill Richardson.** Half-sister to the quite useful 2-y-o 7f winner Onida (by Noverre). The dam, an Irish 12f winner and second in both the Group 2 10f Pretty Polly Stakes and the Group 2 10f Royal Whip Stakes, is a sister to the Irish 1m and 9f winner and listed-placed Pepperwood and a half-sister to 2 winners. The second dam, Nishan (by Nashwan), is a placed half-sister to 3 winners including the Group 3 Prix de Sandringham winner and good broodmare Orford Ness. (Jaber Abdullah). *"A lovely big filly with bags of size and scope, she's one for the middle of the season onwards."*

266. BLUE DEER (IRE) ★★★
b.c. Bahamian Bounty – Jaywick (Jade Robbery).
January 29. First foal. 34,000Y. **Tattersalls December. Gill Richardson.** The dam is an unplaced half-sister to 5 winners including the listed winner Icklingham. The second dam, Braiswick (by King Of Spain), winner of the Group 1 E P Taylor Stakes and the Group 2 Sun Chariot Stakes, is a half-sister to 6 winners including the Group 3 11f September Stakes winner Percy's Lass (dam of the Derby winner Sir Percy). (Jaber Abdullah). *"A nice, big horse for later in the year. He does everything right but I don't think you'll see him until the second half of the season."*

267. DREAMS OF DAWN ★★★
b.c. Invincible Spirit – Castilian Queen (Diesis).
March 2. Tenth foal. 72,000Y. **Tattersalls October Book 1. Gill Richardson.** Half-brother to the high-class Group 1 5f Prix de l'Abbaye winner Carmine Lake (by Royal Academy), the useful 2-y-o 5f and 6f winner Major Eazy (by Fasliyev), the fairly useful 3-y-o 7f winner and listed-placed Three Secrets (by Danehill), the fairly useful Irish 2-y-o 6f winner Progreso (by Danehill Dancer) and the fair 2-y-o 7f winner Star Of Grosvenor (by Last Tycoon). The dam, a fair 2-y-o 6f winner, is a half-sister to 4 winners including the useful 6f and 7f winner and Diomed Stakes third Regal Sabre. The second dam, Royal Heroine (by Lypheor), won 10 races including the 6f Princess Margaret Stakes (at 2 yrs) and the 9f Hollywood Derby, the 9f Matriarch Stakes and the Breeders Cup Mile (all Grade 1 events). (Jaber Abdullah). *"A nice colt, he's not quite ready yet but he has a bit of size and scope. I like him."*

268. ESCAPE THE HEAT ★★
b.c. Singspiel – Takarna (Mark Of Esteem).
February 4. Fifth foal. 22,000Y. **Tattersalls October 2. Gill Richardson.** Half-brother to the quite useful 2009 2-y-o 1m winner Jibrrya (by Motivator). The dam is a placed half-sister to 5 winners including the Group 2 Royal Whip Stakes winner Takali and the Group 3 12f Meld Stakes winner Takarian, subsequently winner of the Bay Meadows Derby in the USA. The second dam, Takarouna (by Green Dancer), a very useful winner of the Group 2 12f Pretty Polly Stakes at the Curragh, is a sister to the smart Group 2 Dante Stakes winner Torjoun. (Jaber Abdullah). *"A nice colt but he's more of a back-end type two-year-old and he'll be better next year."*

269. EXTRA POWER (IRE) ★★★★♣
b.c. Acclamation – Vintage Escape (Cyrano de Bergerac).
May 15. Ninth foal. 37,000Y. **Tattersalls October Book 2. Gill Richardson.** Half-brother to the useful 1m (at 2 yrs) and listed 8.5f winner Vinthea (by Barathea) and to the fair Irish 10f winner High Vintage (by High Chaparral). The dam was placed 6 times in Ireland at up to 9f and is a half-sister to one winner. The second dam, Overstay (by Be My Guest), is an unraced half-sister to 10 winners including the Melbourne Cup and Irish St Leger winner Vintage Crop. (Jaber Abdullah). *"A nice colt, he'll make a two-year-old alright,*

he goes well and he'll definitely be winning come May/June time."

270. FALKLAND FLYER (IRE) ★★
b.c. Johannesburg – Tree Chopper (Woodman).
March 23. First foal. £30,000Y. Doncaster St Leger. Gill Richardson. The dam, a modest 1m winner at 2 yrs, is a half-sister to 5 winners including Mubtaker, winner of the Group 2 Geoffrey Freer Stakes and second in the Prix de l'Arc de Triomphe. The second dam, Gazayil (by Irish River), a winner over 7f at 2 yrs here, later won in Australia and is a half-sister to 4 winners including the Group 3 Brigadier Gerard Stakes winner Husyan. (Box 41). *"I've just have a few niggling problems with him so although I liked him and was getting on with him, I've had to back off for a bit."*

271. FOG CUTTER (IRE) ★★★
b.c. Mujadil – Park Approach (Indian Ridge).
April 29. Second foal. 55,000Y. Tattersalls October 2. Gill Richardson. Half-brother to the quite useful 2009 2-y-o 6f winner Tasmeem (by Acclamation). The dam, a fair 5f to 7f placed maiden (including at 2 yrs), is a half-sister to 4 winners. The second dam, Abyat (by Shadeed), is an unraced half-sister to 9 winners including the Group 1 Middle Park Stakes winner Hayil. (Jaber Abdullah). *"A lovely colt but he's just going to need a bit of sun on his back. He's not quite ready and is more of a June type two-year-old."*

272. GALLOPING QUEEN (IRE) ★★★★
b.f. Refuse To Bend – Rouge Noir (Saint Ballado).
May 11. Fourth foal. €32,000Y. Goffs Orby. Gill Richardson. Half-sister to the useful 2009 2-y-o 7f winner and listed placed Cadley Road (by Elusive City), to the useful 2-y-o listed 5f winner Light The Fire (by Invincible Spirit) and the minor French 3-y-o winner Blanc Sur Blanc (by Hold That Tiger). The dam, a minor winner at 3 yrs in the USA, is a half-sister to 2 winners in Japan. The second dam, Ardana (by Danehill), won the Group 3 Premio Bagutta and is a half-sister to 5 winners. (Jaber Abdullah). *"No one likes the sire anymore but this is a nice filly, she's got a bit of speed, she'll want six or seven furlongs to be at her best and I like her. She does everything right and she's nice."*

273. GALTYMORE LAD ★★★★
b.c. Indesatchel – Right Answer (Lujain).
February 14. First foal. £28,000Y. Doncaster St Leger. Gill Richardson. The dam, a fairly useful 2-y-o 5f winner, was third in the listed St Hugh's Stakes and is a half-sister to 3 winners. The second dam, Quiz Show (by Primo Dominie), a quite useful 7f winner, is a half-sister to 4 winners including the high-class sprinter Mind Games, winner of the Group 2 Temple Stakes (twice), the Norfolk Stakes and the Palace House Stakes. (Mrs M Findlay). *"A lovely colt. He'll be a two-year-old, he'll be running sometime in May and if he doesn't win we're in trouble! A proper horse."*

274. GOLDEN SHINE ★★★★★♣♣
b.f. Royal Applause – Branston Jewel (Prince Sabo).
March 2. Ninth foal. £28,000Y. Doncaster St Leger. Gill Richardson. Half-sister to the fairly useful 2009 2-y-o 5f and 1m winner and listed-placed Raine's Cross (by Cape Cross) and to the useful dual listed 6f winner of 5 races Falcon Hill (by Polar Falcon). The dam, a fairly useful 2-y-o dual 5f winner, was second in the Group 3 5.5f Prix d'Arenburg and is a half-sister to 11 winners including the Group Sandown Mile winner Desert Deer and the very useful and tough mare Branston Abby, a winner of 24 races at up to 7f including numerous listed events. The second dam, Tuxford Hideaway (by Cawston's Clown), a useful sprint winner of two races at 2 yrs, is a half-sister to 4 winners. (Jaber Abdullah). *"Queen Mary!...and I won't say another word...but if you push me I'd just say that she's a natural and although she's not very big if you want a star this is her."* This filly ran third on her debut at Newmarket.

275. HOLY MACKEREL (IRE) ★★★★
b.c. Cape Cross – Sparky's Song (Electric).
May 10. Tenth foal. €35,000Y. Goffs Orby. Gill Richardson. Half-brother to the fair 2-y-o 5f winner White Daffodil (by Footstepsinthesand), to the dual listed 6f winner (including at 2 yrs) Lady Links (by Bahamian Bounty), the fairly useful Irish 2-y-o 7f winner Braydeen (by Barathea), the quite useful 2-y-o 6f winner and Group 1 Moyglare Stud Stakes fourth Umniya (by Bluebird), the quite useful 2-y-o 6f and subsequent Hong Kong winner King

Malachi (by King Charlemagne) and the fair 12f and hurdles winner Stolen Song (by Sheikh Albadou). The dam, a moderate 10.2f and 12f winner, is a half-sister to the very smart Group 1 6.5f winner Bold Edge and to the listed winner and Group 3 5f Temple Stakes second Brave Edge. The second dam, Daring Ditty (by Daring March), ran unplaced twice and is a half-sister to 5 minor winners. (Box 41). *"He's done very well. He was very small as a yearling and we took a chance on him at the sales, but he's thrived since he came here. One for later in the year, but he's a nice horse."*

276. HORTENSIA (IRE) ★★★★
b.f. *Holy Roman Emperor – Snippets (Be My Guest).*
March 9. Third foal. €32,000Y. Goffs Orby. Gill Richardson. The dam was an Irish 7f, 1m (both at 2 yrs) and listed 12f winner and is a half-sister to 2 winners. The second dam, Sniffle (by Shernazar), is an unplaced half-sister to 4 winners including the Grade 1 12f Hollywood Turf Cup and Group 3 1m Beresford Stakes winner Frenchpark and the Group 1 Prix Vermeille winner Pearly Shells. (Box 41). *"She'll be one of the early ones and she'll win. An April/May type two-year-old and she's a real nice filly that could be anything."*

277. INDIAN NARJES ★★★
b.f. *Sleeping Indian – Flora Burn (Jade Robbery).*
March 10. First foal. 13,000foal. Tattersalls December. Rabbah Bloodstock. The dam is an unraced half-sister to 5 winners including Campsie Fells (Group 3 Prix Vanteaux). The second dam, Queen's View (by Lomond), won twice and was second in the Group 3 Rockfel Stakes and is a half-sister to 6 winners. (Jaber Abdullah). *"She's very nice, goes well and she's a two-year-old, so don't leave her out."*

278. JASMINE FLOWER ★★★
ch.f. *Kyllachy – Triple Sharp (Selkirk).*
March 1. Fifth foal. 55,000Y. Tattersalls October Book 1. Gill Richardson. Sister to the useful 2-y-o dual 6f winner and listed-placed Nasri and half-sister to the useful 2-y-o 6f all-weather winner and Group 2 7f Superlative Stakes third Ellmau (by Dr Fong), to the listed-placed Laureldean Express (by Inchinor) and a winner in Spain by Vettori. The dam, a quite useful 10f and hurdles winner, is a half-sister to 4 winners including the US stakes winner and Grade 2 placed Pina Colada. The second dam, Drei (by Lyphard), placed fourth over 1m at 3 yrs on her only outing, is a half-sister to 3 winners. (Jaber Abdullah). *"A nice filly that's grown quite a bit. She's outgrown her strength a touch and is one for a bit later in the year."*

279. KADOODD (IRE) ★★
b.c. *Motivator – Briery (Salse).*
March 9. Fifth foal. 120,000Y. Tattersalls October 2. Shadwell Estate Co. Half-brother to the 2009 Swiss 2-y-o winner Story Of Dubai (by Dubai Destination), to the quite useful 6f and 7f winner of 5 races Great Charm (by Orpen), the quite useful 7f to 15f winner of 5 races Fregate Island and the fair 10f, 11f and hurdles winner Pearl (both by Daylami). The dam, a modest 3-y-o 7f winner, is out of the unraced Wedgewood (by Woodman), herself a half-sister to 10 minor winners. (Sheikh Ahmed Al Maktoum). *"A lovely big horse with plenty of size and scope, but he's one for the back-end of the season and next year."*

280. KALLEIDOSCOPE ★★★
ch.f. *Pivotal – Brush Strokes (Cadeaux Genereux).*
April 22. Half-sister to the quite useful 12f winner Kassiopeia (by Galileo), to the French 10.5f winner and listed-placed Craft Fair (by Danehill), the modest 10f winner My Girl Jode (by Haafhd) and the moderate 5f and 6f winner Tenancy (by Rock Of Gibraltar). The dam is an unraced sister to the Japanese 2-y-o winner Christian Name and a half-sister to 4 winners including the very useful 2-y-o dual 7f winner and Group 1 Racing Post Trophy second Mudeer. The second dam, Colorvista (by Shirley Heights), is an unraced half-sister to 9 winners including Colorspin (winner of the Irish Oaks and dam of the Group 1 winners Zee Zee Top, Opera House and Kayf Tara), Bella Colora (winner of the Prix de l'Opera and dam of the very smart colt Stagecraft) and the Irish Champion Stakes winner Cezanne. (George & Jackie Smith). *"She's big and she's got her faults, but she'll make a two-year-old and she ought to be in the book."*

281. LOCAL SINGER (IRE) ★★★
b.c. *Elusive City – Alinga (King's Theatre).*
February 22. Fourth foal. €35,000Y. Goffs Orby. Gill Richardson. The dam, a useful 2-y-o dual 6f and subsequent US stakes winner, is a half-sister to one winner. The second dam, Cheyenne Spirit (by Indian Ridge), a useful winner of 7 races including a listed event over 6f, was third in the Group 3 Phoenix Sprint and is a half-sister to 5 winners including the dam of the Group winners Ashdown Express and Hoh Buzzard. (Jaber Abdullah). *"A nice colt but he's just thrown a splint so he's been held up and is behind everything else. Once we get him going he'll be a nice horse later on."*

282. MAJESTIC DUBAWI ★★★★
b.f. *Dubawi – Tidal Chorus (Singspiel).*
January 31. First foal. 22,000Y. Tattersalls October Book 3. Gill Richardson. The dam ran twice unplaced and is a half-sister to 6 winners including the French listed winner South Rock. The second dam, South Shore (by Caerleon), a useful winner of 4 races at up to 12f, is a half-sister 4 winners including to the Lockinge Stakes winner Soviet Line. (Jaber Abdullah). *"A very nice filly. She'll probably need six furlongs but she's doing everything really well, she has a bit of quality about her and I like her."*

283. MIDNIGHT MIRAGE (FR) ★★★
b.f. *Kheleyf – Lily Valley (Poliglote).*
March 29. First foal. €65,000Y. Arqana Deauville August. Gill Richardson. The dam was placed twice at 3 yrs in France and is a half-sister to 2 minor winners. The second dam, Shining Candle (by Bering), was a minor 3-y-o winner and a half-sister to 2 winners. (Jaber Abdullah). *"A nice, big filly, she's just had little setbacks that have held us up and she's one that needs time and six furlongs plus."*

284. PLAY MUSIC ★★★★
ch.f. *Proclamation – Zacchera (Zamindar).*
April 9. Fourth foal. 27,000Y. Tattersalls October Book 2. Gill Richardson. Half-sister to the modest dual 1m winner Oriental Girl (by Dr Fong). The dam, a quite useful 6f winner, is a half-sister to 9 winners including the high-class Group 1 July Cup winner Sakhee's Secret and the smart listed winner of 6 races from 5f to 7f Palace Affair. The second dam, Palace Street (by Secreto), a useful winner over 6f and 7f including the listed Cammidge Trophy, is a half-sister to 7 winners including the Extel Handicap winner Indian Trail and the Italian Group 3 winner Sfriss. (Jaber Abdullah). *"A very nice filly, I think she'll be a six/seven furlong type and she does everything real nice. A big filly with some size and scope."*

285. PLENTY POWER ★★★★ ♣
b.c. *Acclamation – Maugwenna (Danehill).*
April 24. Fourth foal. 60,000Y. Tattersalls October Book 2. Gill Richardson. Half-brother to the useful 2009 2-y-o dual 5f winner and Group 2 5f Flying Childers second Bould Mover (by Kyllachy) and to the modest 5f and 6f winner of 5 races including sellers at 2 yrs Mac Dalia (by Namid). The dam, a fair 2-y-o 5f winner, is a half-sister to 3 winners. The second dam, River Abouali (by Bluebird), is an unraced half-sister to 3 winners including the Irish Group 3 winner Psalm. (Jaber Abdullah). *"He needs a bit of time to get his act together because he's had little niggling two-year-old problems. He wouldn't be a early type but he'll be a nice colt to look for in the middle of the season."*

286. RED MERCURY ★★★
ch.c. *Majestic Missile – Fey Rouge (Fayruz).*
February 28. Seventh foal. £22,000Y. Doncaster St Leger. Gill Richardson. Half-brother to the Irish 7f and 1m winners and Group placed Crystal View (by Imperial Ballet) and Miss Trish (by Danetime), the Irish 5f winner Bye Bye Ben (by Beckett) and the minor Italian winner of 8 races Schumichel (by Imperial Ballet). The dam is an unplaced full or half-sister to 9 winners. The second dam, Isa (by Dance In Time), is an unraced half-sister to 4 winners. (Ridgeway Downs Racing). *"This is a nice horse and he goes well although he just gave a few coughs after working yesterday. He'll be ready to go soon and the owners are lucky."*

287. ROSAMUNDE FFRENCH ★★
b.f. *Piccolo – Wansdyke Lass (Josr Algharoud).*
March 3. Second foal. 3,000Y. Ascot Sales. M Channon Bloodstock. Half-sister to the quite useful 2009 2-y-o 7f winner Universal Circus (by

Imperial Dancer). The dam, a modest 10f seller winner, is a half-sister to 2 minor winners (both by Piccolo). The second dam, Silannka (by Slip Anchor), a moderate 12f and 13f winner, is a half-sister to numerous winners. (Mr S Fisher). *"She's a very nice filly. She's grown though, so she's one for a bit later on in the season. The mare needed ten furlongs but she's OK."*

288. SACRED SOUND (IRE) ★★
b.c. Oratorio – Affaire Royale (Royal Academy).
February 16. Fourth foal. 34,000foal. Tattersalls December. Gill Richardson. Half-brother to the modest 7f winner Dancing Duo (by Groom Dancer). The dam, a fairly useful 3-y-o 7f winner, was listed-placed and is a half-sister to 3 winners. The second dam, Fleet Amour (by Afleet), is an unplaced three-parts sister to the US Grade 1 winner Quiet American. (Jon & Julia Aisbitt). *"A big horse, he's done everything right and he's got bags of scope so he needs time. A nice horse for July/August I would have thought."*

289. SAUCY BUCK (IRE) ★★★★
b.c. Mujadil – Phantom Ring (Magic Ring).
March 18. Eighth foal. £24,000Y. Doncaster St Leger. Gill Richardson. Half-brother to the fair 7f winner of 7 races Inaminute (by Spectrum) and to the modest 1m to 12f winner Double Spectre (by Spectrum). The dam, a modest 5f winner at 3 yrs, is a half-sister to 9 other minor winners. The second dam, Follow The Stars (by Sparkler), a quite useful 8.5f and 10f winner, is a half-sister to 9 winners. (Mrs M Findlay). *"He ran in the Brocklesbury, he's ready to go and he should win at some stage. Obviously an early type, you must put him in the book. He's a good sized colt that'll get six furlongs."* TRAINERS' BARGAIN BUY

290. SHADOW OF THE SUN ★★★
b.f. Red Ransom – Hill Welcome (Most Welcome).
April 2. Seventh foal. £45,000Y. Doncaster St Leger. Gill Richardson. Half-sister to the useful 2-y-o dual 5f winner and Group 3 Molecomb Stakes second Mary Read (by Bahamian Bounty), to the quite useful 2-y-o 6f winner Dubai Hills (by Dubai Destination), the useful 2-y-o 6f winner and listed-placed Tiana (by Diktat) and the quite useful dual 5f winner Jack Rackham (by Kyllachy). The dam was placed twice at 2 yrs and stayed 7f and is a half-sister to 5 winners including the Group 1 6f Middle Park Stakes winner Stalker and the 2-y-o listed 5f winner and Group 3 third Regal Peace. The second dam, Tarvie (by Swing Easy), won 3 races and was a useful sprinter. (Jaber Abdullah). *"One for a bit later on, but she's a nice filly that's done well. She's grown a bit so she needs that bit more time."*

291. SILCA CONEGLIANO (IRE) ★★★★♠
b.f. Alhaarth – Sarah Stokes (Brief Truce).
February 15. Fifth foal. £55,000Y. Doncaster St Leger. Gill Richardson. Half-sister to the fairly useful Irish 2-y-o dual 5f winner and listed-placed Nubar Lady (by Danetime). The dam, a fair 3-y-o 6f winner, is a half-sister to 5 winners including the very useful Group 3 5f Curragh Stakes and Group 3 5f Molecomb Stakes winner Almaty. The second dam, Almaaseh (by Dancing Brave), placed once over 6f at 3 yrs, is a half-sister to 7 winners including the 2,000 Guineas and Champion Stakes winner Haafhd and the Group 2 Challenge Stakes winner Munir. (Aldridge Racing Partnership). *"What's the race at Ascot we normally win? Oh yes...the Albany Stakes! She's very nice and a two-year-old that's very correct and has a good attitude. I think she's one of the better ones."*

292. SILVER SHOW (IRE) ★★★★
b.f. Noverre – Incense (Unfuwain).
April 1. Second foal. 65,000Y. Tattersalls October Book 2. Gill Richardson. Half-sister to the unplaced 2009 Irish 2-y-o Petit Chou (by Captain Rio). The dam, a modest dual 1m placed maiden, is a half-sister to 6 winners including the useful Group 3 7f Prestige Stakes winner Icicle. The second dam, Blessed Honour (by Ahonoora), a quite useful 2-y-o 7f winner, is a half-sister to 6 winners including the smart Group 2 11.9f Great Voltigeur Stakes winner Sacrament and the unraced dam of the Group 1 winner Chorist. (Jaber Abdullah). *"She's a lovely filly but she's been coughing and what have you, so she's not quite there yet. But she's pretty decent and six/seven furlongs should suit her I would have thought. She'll be sharp but she's just been held up with typical two-year-old problems."*

293. SMART RED ★★★★
b.f. Bachelor Duke – Zarannda
(Last Tycoon).
April 25. Ninth living foal. €44,000Y. Goffs Orby. Gill Richardson. Half-sister to 6 winners including the useful Irish 1m winner and dual Group 3 placed Zarad (by Selkirk), the fairly useful Irish 12f to 2m winner Zaralabad (by Fantastic Light) and the fair dual 7f winner Zarabad (by King's Best). The dam, a dual French listed winner over 7f and 1m, is a half-sister to 2 winners including the dam of the Group 3 Prix de Sandringham winner Zarkiya. The second dam, Zarna (by Shernazar), won once at 3 yrs and is a half-sister to 4 winners including the dam of the French Oaks and Prix Saint-Alary winner Zainta. (Jaber Abdullah). *"She'll win – so put her in your horses to follow list! A nice filly, she's not the biggest but she's pretty correct and she knows her job well."*

294. STAR NOW ★★★
b.f. Librettist – Affair Of State
(Tate Gallery).
February 8. Fourteenth foal. 7,000Y. Tattersalls October. Gill Richardson. Half-sister to the useful 2-y-o listed 6f and 7f winner Bibury Flyer, to the useful 10f and 11.8f winner Mojalid (both by Zafonic), the fairly useful 6f winner Diplomat (by Deploy), the quite useful 7f (at 2 yrs) and 9f winner Nordic Affair (by Halling), the quite useful 2005 2-y-o 7f winner Celestial Princess (by Observatory), the fair 2-y-o 5f winner Ice Maiden (by Polar Falcon), the fair 5f (at 2 yrs) and 6f winner Stately Princess (by Robellino), the modest 6f all-weather winner Gun Salute (by Mark Of Esteem) and the German and Swedish 5f to 1m winner Statesman (by Doyoun). The dam, a very useful Irish 2-y-o 6f winner, is a half-sister to 7 minor winners. The second dam, All Hat (by Double Form), won over 5f at 3 yrs and is a half-sister to 5 winners including the Cherry Hinton and Musidora Stakes winner Everything Nice – herself dam of the Irish 1,000 Guineas winner Nicer. (Jaber Abdullah). *"Not very big, I trained the mother and a lot of the others in the family. She's had a few two-year-old problems that have held her up, but if she comes clean she could easily be out in May. These horses need some decent weather now."*

295. STELLA POINT (IRE) ★★
b.f. Pivotal – Venturi (Danehill Dancer).
March 23. Third foal. €150,000Y. Arqana Deauville August. Gill Richardson. Half-sister to the fair Irish 1m winner Cilium (by War Chant). The dam, winner of the Group 3 7f C L Weld Park Stakes, was subsequently second in two US Grade 3 events and is a sister to the French listed winner and Group 1 Criterium de Saint-Cloud third Feels All Right. The second dam, Zagreb Flyer (by Old Vic), is an unraced half-sister to 8 winners including the listed winner and Group 1 Italian Oaks second Flying Girl. (Jon & Julia Aisbitt). *"A lovely, big filly but she's growing and needs time. One for next year really."*

296. YOJIMBO (IRE) ★★★
gr.c. Aussie Rules – Mythie
(Octagonal).
April 12. Third living foal. £65,000Y. Doncaster St Leger. Gill Richardson. Half-brother to Rahaala (by Indian Ridge), unplaced in one start at 2 yrs in 2009 and to the fairly useful 2-y-o 6f winner Versaki (by Verglas). The dam, a minor French 3-y-o 1m winner, is a half-sister to 4 winners including the French listed winner Mytographie. The second dam, Mythologie (by Bering), won two races at 2 and 3 yrs in France and is a half-sister to 7 winners. (Jon & Julia Aisbitt). *"He's gone the right way but he grew very quickly and just went a bit weak on us, but he's coming good now and I think he'll definitely be a two-year-old. He'll be a nice horse and you'll have to put him in the book."*

297. UNNAMED ★★★
b.f Imperial Dancer – Aileen's Gift (Rainbow Quest).
February 3. Fourth foal. Half-sister to the 2-y-o Group 3 Albany Stakes winner Nijoom Dubai (by Noverre) and to the fair 7f winner of 6 races La Gifted (by Fraam). The dam is an unraced half-sister to several winners including the fairly useful listed-placed Roker Park. The second dam, Joyful (by Green Desert), a fair 7f all-weather winner at 3 yrs, is a half-sister to 7 winners including the Golden Opinion, winner of the Group 1 1m Coronation Stakes and placed in the French 1,000 Guineas and the

July Cup. (Norman Court Stud). *"She's a nice filly that just needs a bit of time. A half-sister to two nice winners of ours, she's had a few minor problems and is a bit behind the others, but she'll be alright."*

298. UNNAMED ★★★
b.f. Beat Hollow – Catch (Blushing Groom).
March 21. Twelfth living foal. 22,000Y. Tattersalls October Book 3. David McGreavy. Half-sister to the quite useful Irish dual 10f winner Eldorado, to the fair 7f (including at 2 yrs) and 10f winner Hidden Chance, the moderate 1m and 14f winner Captivate (all by Hernando) and three minor winners in the USA by Boundary (2) and Conquistador Cielo. The dam, a minor 3-y-o winner in the USA, is a half-sister to 5 winners including the US Grade 3 winner Swear. The second dam, Suave (by Majestic Prince), was a stakes-placed winner of 5 races in the USA and a half-sister to 8 winners. *"I have two Beat Hollow's and they both go well and yet being by him you'd think they'd need a bit more time. She's a bit behind some of the others but she'll make a two-year-old later on."*

299. UNNAMED ★★★★
b.f. Exceed And Excel – Guana Bay (Cadeaux Genereux).
March 2. Seventh foal. €60,000Y. Goffs Orby. Gill Richardson. Half-sister to the quite useful 2-y-o 5f winner Pelican Key (by Mujadil) and to the Italian 2-y-o winner and listed-placed Enrika's Gift (by Orpen). The dam is an unraced sister to one winner and a half-sister to 5 winners including the Group 2 winners Prince Sabo and Millyant and the listed winner Bold Jessie (herself dam of the Group 2 Gimcrack Stakes winner Abou Zouz). The second dam, Jubilee Song (by Song), won once at 3 yrs and is a sister to the dual winner and Nell Gwyn Stakes second Shark Song and to the winner of 10 races and listed-placed Band On The Run. (Jaber Abdullah). *"A lovely filly, she's in the early group and she goes well. I think she could start at five furlongs but she'll be better at six and she's got to go in the book – she's lovely."*

300. UNNAMED ★★
b.c. Singspiel – Moonmaiden (Selkirk).
April 30. Second foal. 25,000Y. Tattersalls December. G Howson. The dam, a modest 7f winner, is a half-sister to 6 winners including the useful listed winners Zato and Krispy Knight. The second dam, Top Table (by Shirley Heights), a modest 12f placed maiden, is a half-sister to 5 winners including the very smart 1m listed winner and Group 1 Juddmonte Lockinge Stakes third Centre Stalls. (Derek & Jean Clee). *"A nice filly and she hasn't missed a day, but being by Singspiel she'll need time. One for the back-end of the season really."*

301. UNNAMED ★★
ch.c. Byron – Shbakni (Mr Prospector).
February 3. Seventh foal. Closely related to the UAE 10f winner Pentland Firth (by Green Desert). The dam was placed in France and the UAE at up to 9f and is a daughter of the Kentucky Derby winner Winning Colors (by Caro). (A Ali). *"A nice big horse that was late coming in and it'll take me a month to find out which group to put him in. He goes alright though."*

302. UNNAMED ★★★
br.c. Imperial Dancer – Wrong Bride (Reprimand).
February 22. Half-brother to the quite useful 2-y-o 5f winner Opal Noir (by Lujain) and to the quite useful 11f and 12f winner Lucky Leo (by Muhtarram). The dam ran once unplaced and is a half-sister to 6 winners including the dual Ayr Gold Cup winner Funfair Wane. The second dam, the fairly useful listed 2-y-o 6f winner Ivory Bride (by Domynsky), is a half-sister to 7 winners including the listed 8.5f and listed 10f winner Putuna. (Capital). *"A lovely horse, he'll need six or seven furlongs but he's nice and he'll make a two-year-old alright."*

PETER CHAPPLE-HYAM
303. CADORE (IRE) ★★★★
b.c. Hurricane Run – Mansiya (Vettori).
February 11. First foal. €62,000foal. Goffs. Scuderia Amalita. The dam, a modest 7f (at 2 yrs) to 9f placed maiden, is a half-sister to 5 winners including the useful listed 11.4f Cheshire Oaks winner Abury. The second dam, Bay Shade (by Sharpen Up), a fairly useful 2-y-o 7f and Italian 1m listed winner, is a half-sister to 10 winners including the Group/Grade 3 winners Bex and Daarik. (P W Chapple-Hyam).

"A big colt that's going to take quite a bit of time, but he moves well and goes along really nicely. He'd probably be the pick of my two-year-olds but I don't see him being out until August time over seven furlongs or a mile. A horse I like a lot."

304. DIVINITE GREEN ★★★
b.c. Diamond Green – Divinite (Alleged).
€15,000Y. SGA, Italy. Scuderia Eledy. Half-brother to the French listed 12f winner Mondovino (by Black Minnaloushe), to the fairly useful French 2-y-o 1m winner War Academy (by Royal Academy) and the French 1m (at 2 yrs) to 11f winner Divin Tremp (by Trempolino). The dam won 2 minor races at 3 yrs and is a half-sister to 3 winners including the smart 7f performer Dreams To Reality. The second dam, D'Arqueangel (by Raise A Native), won over 6f in the USA and is closely related to the Kentucky Oaks winner Native Street (herself dam of the good US colts Regal And Royal and Royal And Regal). "He does everything right but he's a big horse and won't run until the second half of the season over seven furlongs, but he's alright and certainly no slouch."

305. FOGHORN LEGHORN ★★★★♠
ch.c. Medicean – Dance Away (Pivotal).
March 22. Third foal. £26,000Y. Doncaster St Leger. Blandford Bloodstock. Half-brother to the modest 5f winner Azif (by Where Or When). The dam, a fairly useful 2-y-o 5f winner, is a half-sister to one winner. The second dam, Dance On (by Caerleon), a fairly useful 2-y-o dual 5f winner, is a half-sister to 4 winners. (The Comic Strip Heroes). "He'll be my sharpest two-year-old and he goes really well. He'll go to Newbury to start with and he's more than useful. I can see him winning his maiden without a problem, but what level he can get to I don't know yet." This colt refused to enter the stalls on his intended debut.

306. HERE TO ETERNITY (USA) ★★★
b.br.f. Stormy Atlantic – Heat Of The Night (Lear Fan).
January 8. The dam, a dual 9f winner here, subsequently won a listed 1m event in Germany and is a half-sister to the Irish 7f and Grade 2 hurdles winner Convincing. The second dam, Hot Thong (by Jarraar), was a Brazilian Grade 3

7f winner. (Miss K Rausing). "She's quite sharp and has done a couple of nice canters up the grass. More a six furlong type in May time I'd say. She goes well and there's nothing bad to say about her at all."

307. MALAKEH (IRE) ★★★
b.f. Green Desert – Bakhoor
(by Royal Applause).
March 10. First foal. The dam, the fair dual 6f and 7f winner, is a half-sister to numerous winners including the UAE 6f winner Desert Whisper (by Green Desert) and the very useful triple 1m and hurdles winner Atlantic Rhapsody. The second dam, First Waltz (by Green Dancer), a winner of the Group 1 6f Prix Morny and second in the Cheveley Park Stakes, is a half-sister to the dam of the Prix Lupin second Angel Falls. (Z A Galadari). "Not the biggest filly in the world, but she looks very sharp and she'll be suited by five furlongs in May. She shows ability and I like her."

308. MARKED CARD (IRE) ★★★
b.c. Kheleyf – Kelsey Rose
(Most Welcome).
April 25. Fifth foal. 50,000Y. Tattersalls October 2. J Fretwell. Half-sister to the very useful 2009 2-y-o 6f and 2010 Group 3 7f Fred Darling Stakes winner Puff (by Camacho) and to the fair 2-y-o 6f winner Golden Rosie (by Exceed And Excel). The dam, a fairly useful 2-y-o 5f winner of 3 races, was listed-placed three times and is a half-sister to 3 winners. The second dam, Duxyana (by Cyrano de Bergerac), is an unraced half-sister to 8 winners including the dam of the Group 2 Mill Reef Stakes winner Indian Rocket. (J C Fretwell). "He's just started doing canters up the grass and he's a late April foal so he needs a bit of time still. But I can see him being out over six furlongs in May or June. I like him quite a bit."

309. MISS EXHIBITIONIST ★★★
b.f. Trade Fair – Miss McGuire (Averti).
February 11. First foal. 3,700Y. Tattersalls October 3. Steve Troy. The dam, a fair 3-y-o 1m winner, is a half-sister to 2 minor winners. The second dam, Friend For Life (by Lahib), is a placed half-sister to 2 winners and to the placed dam of the Australian Group 1 winner Markham. (Mandy Whitlock). "She's done little

bits up the grass and although she was cheap at the Sales she's really impressed me. She'll be running in May or maybe slightly later and she does everything really good." TRAINERS' BARGAIN BUY

310. PIAVE (IRE) ★★★★
b.c. Oratorio – Peace In The Park (Ahonoora).
February 18. €32,000foal. Goffs. Scuderia Amalita. Half-brother to the Italian 2-y-o listed 7f winner and Group 2 placed Morena Park (by Pivotal) and to the modest Irish 1m winner Jinx Johnson (by Desert King). The dam was unplaced twice and is a half-sister to 6 winners including the 1999 Irish 2-y-o listed winner and Group 1 Phoenix Stakes third Buffalo Berry (by Sri Pekan). The second dam, Palm Dove (by Storm Bird), is a twice-raced close relative of the very smart sprinter Nabeel Dancer. "He'll want a bit of time but he's very good-looking and I see him being an August type two-year-old over seven furlongs. Looking at his action he'd want pretty quick ground, he's going the right way and is probably the best looking two-year-old I have – he's beautiful. One to follow."

311. RED SPADES ★★★
b.c. Kyllachy – Quevada (Mark Of Esteem).
April 29. Third foal. 52,000Y. Tattersalls October 2. Allan Bloodlines. The dam, a minor French 2-y-o winner, is a half-sister to 6 winners including the French listed winners Play Around and Playact (subsequently Grade 2 placed in the USA). The second dam, Play Or Pay (by Play Fellow), won twice in France and was listed-placed and is a half-sister to 9 winners. "He shows plenty and does everything right, he just had a touch of a sore shin but that's fine again now. I see him being a six furlong horse in May. The trouble is everyone will be bringing their nice ones out then to see if they're good enough for Ascot! He goes along real good and could be alright."

312. SNOW CANNON ★★★
gr.f. Verglas – Kanun (Dancing Brave).
February 17. Seventh foal. €19,000Y. SGA, Italy. Half-sister to 2 minor winners by Wixim and Celtic Swing. The dam is an unraced half-sister to 6 winners including Oratorio (Eclipse Stakes, Irish Champion Stakes etc). The second dam, Mahrah (by Vaguely Noble), a fairly useful 3-y-o 1m winner, is a half-sister to 6 winners including the Group 2 12f Blandford Stakes winner Andros Bay. "She'll need a bit of time and will probably want six furlongs in July. But she does everything right and I'm very pleased with her."

313. STAR FERRY ★★★
b.f. Fasliyev – Donna Giovanna (Mozart).
February 21. First foal. 4,500Y. Tattersalls October 3. S Ballinger. The dam, a fair 7f winner, is a half-sister to 2 winners here and abroad. The second dam, Chelsea (by Miswaki), a French 9f winner, is a half-sister to the US Grade 1 10f winner Super Staff and to the French and US Grade 2 winner Public Purse. "Named after the cheap and cheerful way of getting across to Hong Kong! She goes really well and hopefully she'll be out by June over six/seven furlongs."

314. ZAFARAAN ★★★
b.f. Royal Applause – Sakhya (Barathea).
February 21. Second foal. Half-sister to Falakee (by Sakhee), unplaced in one start at 2 yrs in 2009. The dam was unplaced on her only start and is a half-sister to 4 winners including the useful 2-y-o 6f winner Mr Sandancer and the useful 2-y-o 7f winner Fantasy Island. The second dam, Um Lardaff (by Mill Reef), a winner over 11f and 12f at 3 yrs in France, is a sister to the Derby winner and high-class sire Shirley Heights and a half-sister to the good mare Bempton – dam of the Group 3 winners Mr Pintips and Banket and of the Group 2 winner Gull Nook (herself dam of the smart filly Spring). (Z A Galadari). "This filly isn't the biggest in the world, but although she looks like she should be sharp and early, she isn't. I can see her being out in July or August and she does everything right."

315. UNNAMED ★★★♠
b.f. Holy Roman Emperor – Dabiliya (Vayrann).
April 11. Thirteenth foal. €150,000Y. Arqana Deauville August. Blandford Bloodstock. Half-sister to the listed 10f Ballyroan Stakes winner Dabtiya (by Shirley Heights), to the 10f winner and listed placed Dabaya (by In The Wings), the French flat and jumps winner Dabistan (by Kahyasi) and the minor 3-y-o winner 1m Dabali (by Doyoun).

The dam is an unraced half-sister to 12 winners including the French Derby winner and high-class sire Darshaan, the Prix Vermeille winner Darara and the Prix de Royallieu winner Dalara (herself dam of the Coronation Cup winner Daliapour). The second dam, Delsy (by Abdos), won over 12f and was third in the Group 3 Prix de Pomone. (Mr L J Inman). *"She's done a couple of canters up the grass but I just found her out, weakness-wise, so I'm leaving her alone for a bit. She'll be one for the end of May or early June over six furlongs and she'd want quick ground. Another one that's done nothing wrong so far."*

316. UNNAMED ★★★
b.c. *Araafa – Frond (Alzao).*
April 2. Ninth foal. 70,000foal. Tattersalls December. Mr A Nerses. Half-brother to the smart triple listed winner (from 7f to 10f) Nashmiah (by Elusive City), to the useful 2-y-o 7f and listed 1m winner Streets Ahead (by Beat Hollow), the fairly useful 2-y-o 6f winner and listed-placed Ridder (by Dr Fong), the fair dual 10f winner Addikt (by Diktat), the German 10f winner Portcullis (by Pivotal) and the Scandinavian 1m and 9f winner Azolla (by Cadeaux Genereux). The dam, a quite useful 2-y-o 7f winner, is a half-sister to 6 winners. The second dam, Fern (by Shirley Heights), a useful 12f winner and third in the listed 10f Lupe Stakes, is a half-sister to the Group 1 Fillies Mile winner and Oaks second Shamshir. *"He goes along really well and is in the same situation as the Kheleyf two-year-old Marked Card in that he's just doing his first bits of work. He does everything right and will hopefully start at Newmarket over six furlongs in May."*

317. UNNAMED ★★★
b.c. *Mujadil – Walk On Quest (Rainbow Quest).*
March 20. Sixth foal. 37,000Y. Tattersalls October Book 2. Blandford Bloodstock. Half-brother to the smart Group 3 12f John Porter Stakes winner Enroller (by Marju) and to the Irish 1m winner Polish Odyssey (by Polish Precedent). The dam, a minor French 3-y-o winner, is a half-sister to 10 winners including the Group 2 11f Prix Noailles winner Walk On Mix. The second dam, Walk On Air (by Cure The Blues), is a placed half-sister to 7 winners including the Group 1 Prix Vermeille winner Walensee. (Daffey, Markwick, Black). *"He goes well and I see him as a six furlong horse. Hopefully he'll be Royal Ascot class although we don't know that yet. He start off in May I should think and he's done enough to suggest he can definitely go."*

ROGER CHARLTON

318. EMBEZZLE ★★
b.c. *Sadler's Wells – Trick (Shirley Heights).*
April 30. Tenth foal. 110,000Y. Tattersalls October Book 1. Charlie Gordon-Watson. Half-brother to the fairly useful 2-y-o 6f winner and listed-placed White Rabbit (by Zilzal), to the fairly useful 6f (at 2 yrs) to 12f winner Cap Ferrat (by Robellino), the fair 14f winner Onyergo (by Polish Precedent) and the modest 2-y-o 6f winner Shinner (by Charnwood Forest). The dam, a fair 10f winner, is a half-sister to 6 winners. The second dam, Hocus (by High Top), a fair 10f winner, is a half-sister to 10 winners including the Group 1 6f Middle Park Stakes winner Hittite Glory. (Mr B E Nielsen).

319. LUCY LIMELITES ★★
b.f. *Medicean – In The Limelight (Sadler's Wells).*
April 8. Fourth foal. 60,000Y. Tattersalls October 1. Not sold. The dam, an Irish listed 1m winner, is a sister to the Irish listed winner On The Nile, closely related to the Singapore Gold Cup, Group 1 Gran Premio del Jockey Club and dual German Group 1 winner Kutub and a half-sister to 3 winners. The second dam, Minnie Habit (by Habitat), an Irish 4-y-o 9f winner, is closely related to the dual sprint Group 3 winner Bermuda Classic (herself dam of the Coronation Stakes winner Shake The Yoke) and a half-sister to 6 winners. (Marston Stud).

320. MARLINKA ★★★
b.f. *Marju – Baralinka (Barathea).*
March 2. Sister to the quite useful 2009 5f to 7f placed maiden State Fair. The dam, a useful 5f (at 2 yrs) and triple 6f winner, is a half-sister to the Group 1 Fillies Mile, Falmouth Stakes, Sussex Stakes and Matron Stakes winner Soviet Song (by Marju). The second dam, Kalinka (by Soviet Star), a quite useful 2-y-o 7f winner, is a half-sister to 2 winners. (Elite Racing Club).

321. PROUDIE ★★★
b.c. King's Best – Strut (Danehill Dancer).
February 6. First foal. The dam, a 2-y-o listed 5.2f winner, was Group 3 placed twice and is a half-sister to the quite useful 2-y-o 5f winner Brag (by Mujadil). The second dam, Boast (by Most Welcome), a useful 5f and 6f winner, is a half-sister to 6 winners including the fairly useful 2-y-o 5f and 4-y-o 1m winner Great Bear. (Lady Rothschild).

322. SAILING NORTH (USA) ★★★
b.c. Mizzen Mast – Silver Star (Zafonic).
May 2. Half-brother to the fairly useful 2-y-o 6f winner Faraway Flower (by Distant View). The dam won over 1m at 2 yrs in France, was listed placed over 1m at 3 yrs and is a sister to the champion European 2-y-o Xaar (winner of the Group 1 Dewhurst Stakes and the Group 1 Prix de la Salamandre) and a half-sister to the Group 3 10.5f Prix Corrida winner Diese and the Group 3 1m Prix Quincey winner Masterclass. The second dam, Monroe (by Sir Ivor), a useful Irish 5f and 6f winner, is a sister to the good 2-y-o Gielgud and to the very smart Malinowski and a half-sister to the dual Grade 1 winner Blush With Pride and to Sex Appeal – the dam of El Gran Senor and Try My Best. (Khalid Abdulla).

323. SEATTLE DAWN ★★★
b.c. Avonbridge – Silky Dawn
(Night Shift).
April 23. Fifth foal. Half-brother to the fairly useful 2-y-o 5f winner Sun Ship (by Xaar) and to the fair 7f all-weather winner Catbang (by Zafonic). The dam, a fairly useful 1m winner, is a half-sister to 3 winners. The second dam, Bluffing (by Darshaan), a 2-y-o 1m winner at the Curragh, was listed-placed over 9f (at 2 yrs) and 12f and is a half-sister to 6 winners. (Mr D J Deer).

324. SERGEANT TROY (IRE) ★★♣
br.c. Aussie Rules – Et Dona Ferentes
(Green Desert).
March 22. First foal. 67,000Y. Tattersalls December. Amanda Skiffington. The dam, a moderate 1m seller winner, is a half-sister to 5 winners including the Canadian Grade 3 winner Alexis and the Irish listed winner Freshwater Pearl. The second dam, Sister Golden Hair (by Glint Of Gold), a listed-placed winner at 2 yrs in Germany, is a half-sister to 2 winners. (Mr M Pescod).

325. ST OSWALD ★★
b.c. Royal Applause – Susun Kelapa
(St Jovite).
March 5. Half-brother to the fairly useful 9f and 10f winner Military Power (by Dubai Destination), to the fair Irish 7f winner Monsusu (by Montjeu), the modest 5f winner Royal Composer (by Mozart) and the 1m seller winner Non Ultra (by Peintre Celebre). The dam won 2 races, over 7.8f (at 2 yrs) and 9f and is a half-sister to the US stakes winner Lac Dessert. The second dam, Tiramisu (by Roberto), a minor French 3-y-o winner, is a half-sister to the dam of the French 2,000 Guineas winner Green Tune and the Cheveley Park Stakes winner Pas de Reponse. (Mr P Hearson).

326. SUGAR BEET ★★
b.f. Beat Hollow – Satin Bell (Midyan).
May 5. Eighth foal. Half-sister to the very useful 6f (at 2 yrs) and 9f winner Zabaglione (by Zilzal), to the quite useful 1m and 9f winner Strawberry Leaf (by Unfuwain) and the fair 12f winner Snake's Head (by Golden Snake). The dam, a useful 7f winner, is a half-sister to several winners including the useful listed 6f winner Star Tulip. The second dam, Silk Petal (by Petorius), a useful German listed 1m winner and third in the Group 3 10.5f Prix de Flore, is a half-sister to numerous winners including the dam of the Group 2 12f Ribblesdale Stakes winner Fairy Queen. (Mr Nicholas Jones).

327. TREASURED (IRE) ★★
b.f. Red Ransom – Takarouna
(Green Dancer).
April 5. Half-sister to the Group 3 12f Meld Stakes winner Takarian (by Doyoun), subsequently winner of the Bay Meadows Derby in the USA, the very useful 7f (at 2 yrs) and listed 12f Galtres Stakes winner and dual Group 2 third Tanoura (by Dalakhani), the smart Irish 10f and 12f winner Takali (by Kris), the Irish 2-y-o 6f winner Takariya (by Arazi) and the fair French 10.5f winner Takaniya (by Rainbow Quest). The dam, a very useful winner of the Group 2 12f Pretty Polly Stakes at the Curragh, is a sister to the smart Group 2 Dante

Stakes winner Torjoun and a half-sister to the quite useful 2m Northumberland Plate winner Tamarpour (by Sir Ivor). The second dam, Tarsila (by High Top), won over 1m and 9f and is a sister to Top Ville. (The Queen).

328. WATERBORNE ★★★
b.c. Diktat – Waterfall One (Nashwan).
January 26. Third foal. Half-sister to the fair 2009 2-y-o 7f winner Water Biscuit (by Bertolini). The dam is an unplaced half-sister to 3 winners. The second dam, Spout (by Salse), was a very smart winner of the Group 3 12f John Porter Stakes and the Group 3 Lancashire Oaks and is a half-sister to numerous winners including the French listed winner Mon Domino. (Lady Rothschild).

329. UNNAMED ★★★
gr.c. Maria's Mon – Danzante (Danzig).
April 19. Eleventh foal. Brother to the US Grade 1 9.5f Eddie Read Handicap winner Monzante and half-brother to the useful French 2-y-o 7f winner Alpha Plus (by Mr Prospector), the fairly useful 2-y-o triple 5f winner and listed-placed Tentative (by Distant View), the 10f winner Roman Villa (by Chester House), the 7f winner Dance West (by Gone West) and the 2-y-o 5f winner Forante (by Forty Niner) – all quite useful. The dam, a sprint winner in France and in the USA, is a half-sister to the Breeders Cup Classic winner Skywalker and to the French Group 3 7f winner Nidd. The second dam, Bold Captive (by Boldnesian), was a sprinter. (Khalid Abdulla).

330. UNNAMED ★★
gr.c. Invincible Spirit – Diamond Line (Linamix).
April 11. Third foal. 82,000Y. Tattersalls October Book 2. Charlie Gordon-Watson. The dam ran once unplaced and is a sister to the Group 3 Prix de Royaumont winner Diasilixa and the Group 2 10.5f Prix Greffulhe winner Diamond Mix and a half-sister to 7 winners including the Group 3 10.5f Prix Penelope winner Diamond Dance and the Group 2 placed Diamonaka (the dam of 3 French Group winners). The second dam, Diamond Seal (by Persian Bold), won 3 races including the listed 10f Woodpark Stud Stakes. (HRH Sultan Ahmad Shah).

331. UNNAMED ★★★
b.f. Oasis Dream – Zante (Zafonic).
February 2. Half-sister to the modest 10f winner Kefalonia (by Mizzen Mast). The dam, a very useful 1m and listed 10f winner, is a half-sister to the 11f winner and dual US Grade 1 second Requete. The second dam, Danthonia (by Northern Dancer), a quite useful 2-y-o 5f winner, is closely related to the Group 3 1m Prix Quincey winner Masterclass and a half-sister to the Group 3 10.5f Prix Corrida winner Diese. (Khalid Abdulla).

PAUL COLE

332. ALREADY BASKING (CAN) ★★★
ch.c. More Than Ready – Basking (Alydar).
April 12. Tenth foal. $95,000Y. Keeneland September. Paul Cole. Half-brother to 5 winners including the US Grade 3 winners Ballymore Lady (by War Chant) and Sunray Spirit (by Hennessey) and the US stakes-placed winner Dehere Of The Dog (by Dehere). The dam is an unplaced half-sister to 2 winners. The second dam, Slewbasque (by Seattle Slew), a stakes-placed US winner, is a half-sister to the US Grade 1 winner Bounding Basque. (Mrs F H Hay).

333. END OR BEGINNING ★★
b.c. Sadler's Wells – Smart 'n Noble (Smarten).
April 1. Eighth foal. 330,000Y. Tattersalls October Book 1. Paul Cole. Half-brother to the 1m (at 2 yrs), listed 10f and Group 3 2m Jockey Club Cup winner Royal And Regal (by Sadler's Wells), to the listed 2-y-o 7f Chesham Stakes winner and Group 2 Dante Stakes second Celtic Silence and the dual listed-placed Celtic Sapphire (both by Celtic Swing). The dam won 12 races in the USA including the Grade 2 7f Barbara Fritchie Handicap and is a half-sister to 7 winners. The second dam, Noble Station (by Executioner), won 3 races in the USA and is a half-sister to the Grade 3 winner Dihela. (Mrs F H Hay).

334. EZZLES (USA) ★★★
b.br.c. Speightstown – Paris Glory (Honour And Glory).
February 24. Second foal. 35,000Y. Tattersalls October Book 1. Not sold. The dam is an unraced half-sister to 3 winners including the

Group 1 Prix Morny winner and sire Elusive City. The second dam, Star Of Paris (by Dayjur), is an unraced half-sister to 8 winners including Millions, winner of the Grade 3 Laurel Futurity.

335. FLODDEN (USA) ★★
ch.c. Henny Hughes – Dundrummin'
(Gone West).
March 14. Second foal. $170,000Y. Keeneland September. P Cole. The dam is an unraced sister to the US Grade 2 Lexington Stakes winner and Kentucky Derby second Proud Citizen. The second dam, Drums Of Freedom (by Green Forest), was placed in France and is a half-sister to 6 winners including the US Grade 2 winner Drapeau Tricolore and the French Group 3 winner Dampierre. (Mrs F H Hay).

336. FRANKISH DYNASTY (GER) ★★★
br.c. Holy Roman Emperor – Fantastic Belle
(Night Shift).
April 24. Seventh foal. €80,000Y. Goffs Orby. Not sold. Half-brother to the fairly useful triple 6f winner (including at 2 yrs) Fantaisiste (by Nashwan), to the fair 2-y-o 9f winner Fandangerina (by Hernando) and the modest 6f winner Fairnilee (by Selkirk). The dam, a quite useful 6f winner, is a half-sister to 10 winners including the smart Group 3 10f Gordon Richards Stakes winner Germano, the listed 1m Prix de Saint-Cyr winner Fantastic Bid, the Canadian Grade 2 winner Moon Solitaire and the US stakes winner Fantastic Don. The second dam, Gay Fantastic (by Ela-Mana-Mou), is an unraced sister to the Group 3 Prix de Flore winner Gay Hellene. (Mr P Fahey).

337. MEMEN (IRE) ★★★
gr.c. Verglas – Pride Of My Heart
(Lion Cavern).
March 16. Fifth foal. 65,000Y. Tattersalls October Book 2. Paul Cole. Half-brother to the Group 2 5f Temple Stakes winner of 8 races Night Prospector (by Night Shift), to the fair 2-y-o 6f winner Soliniki (by Danzero), the minor Italian 2-y-o winner Pazzo Pazzini (by Tiger Hill) and a winner in Russia by Spectrum. The dam, a fair 3-y-o 7f winner, is a half-sister to 7 winners including the Group 3 Phoenix Sprint Stakes winner Northern Goddess. The second dam, Hearten (by Hittite Glory), is an unraced half-sister to 7 winners. (Mr J J O'Sullivan).

338. NO HERETIC ★★★
b.c. Galileo – Intrigued (Darshaan).
February 29. First foal. 260,000Y. Tattersalls October Book 1. P Cole. The dam, a very useful 2-y-o 8.5f winner, was listed-placed and fourth in the Group 1 Prix Marcel Boussac and is a sister to the 7.5f (at 2 yrs) and listed 10f winner and US Grade 2 second Approach and a half-sister to the French 2,000 Guineas and US Grade 1 winner Aussie Rules. The second dam, Last Second (by Alzao), winner of the 10f Nassau Stakes and the 10f Sun Chariot Stakes, is a half-sister to 7 winners including the Moyglare Stud Stakes third Alouette (herself dam of the Group 1 winners Albanova and Alborada), the Group 2 Doncaster Cup winner Alleluia (dam of the Group 1 Prix Royal-Oak winner Allegretto) and to the placed dam of the Group 1 winners Yesterday and Quarter Moon. (Mrs F H Hay).

339. PARADISE WAY ★★★
b.f. Elusive Quality – Fin
(Groom Dancer).
February 27. First foal. 115,000Y. Tattersalls October Book 1. Paul Webber. The dam won 4 races in France and the USA including a US stakes event and is a half-sister to 5 winners including the listed winner Bonne Etoile. The second dam, Bonne Ile (by Ile de Bourbon), won 7 races here and in the USA including the Grade 1 Yellow Ribbon Invitational Handicap and is a sister to the Group 3 winner Ile de Nisky and a half-sister to the Group 3 winner Hi Lass. (Denford Stud).

340. RIMTH ★★★
b.f. Oasis Dream – Dorelia (Efisio).
February 26. First foal. The dam, a fair 1m winner, is a half-sister to 3 winners including the smart Group 2 5f Kings Stand Stakes and Group 3 5f Cornwallis Stakes winner Dominica. The second dam, Dominio (by Dominion), a useful 5f winner and second in the Group 2 5f Temple Stakes, is a half-sister to the very smart Group 1 5f Nunthorpe Stakes winner Ya Malak. (Denford Stud).

341. STRATEGIC BID ★★♠
b.c. Selkirk – Eminencia
(Sadler's Wells).
January 10. First foal. 260,000Y. Tattersalls October Book 2. Paul Cole. The dam is an unraced half-sister to 3 winners including the smart 12f and listed 14f winner Moments Of Joy. The second dam, My Emma (by Marju), a smart winner of the Group 1 12f Prix Vermeille, is a half-sister to 5 winners including the Group 1 St Leger and Group 1 Ascot Gold Cup winner Classic Cliché. (Mrs F H Hay).

342. TINKERTOWN (IRE) ★★
gr.c. Verglas – Kelly Nicole
(Rainbow Quest).
March 3. Second foal. €55,000Y. Goffs Orby. P Cole. Half-brother to the unplaced 2009 Irish 2-y-o Super Hoofer (by Shamardal). The dam, a fair 1m to 10f winner of 3 races, is a half-sister to 3 winners including the Irish dual 9f and subsequent US stakes winner Cold Cold Woman. The second dam, Banquise (by Last Tycoon), won over 2m in France and is a half-sister to 8 winners including the French dual Group 2 winner Modhish, the French Group 2 12.5f Prix de Royallieu winner Russian Snows and the Group 3 winner and good broodmare Truly Special. (Mrs F H Hay).

343. UNNAMED ★★★
b.f. Sadler's Wells – Wosaita (Generous).
January 19. Ninth foal. 115,000Y. Tattersalls October Book 1. Not sold. Closely related to the quite useful 2-y-o 7f and 1m winner Special Envoy (by Barathea), to the quite useful 2-y-o all-weather 8.6f winner Whatizzit (by Galileo) and half-sister to the useful 7f (at 2 yrs), listed 1m and Italian Group 3 1m winner Whazzis (by Desert Prince), to the useful 2-y-o listed 7f Chesham Stakes winner Whazzat (by Daylami) and a hurdles winner by Selkirk. The dam, a fair 12.3f placed maiden, is a half-sister to 9 winners including the very smart Group 1 10.5f Prix de Diane winner Rafha (herself the dam of 4 stakes winners including the Haydock Sprint Cup winner Invincible Spirit) and the Group 3 12f Blandford Stakes winner Chiang Mai. The second dam, Eljazzi (by Artaius), a fairly useful 2-y-o 7f winner, is a half-sister to 8 winners including the high-class miler Pitcairn (the sire of Ela-Mana-Mou). (Mr J J Sullivan).

JO CROWLEY

344. DESTINY OF DREAMS ★★
b.f. Dubai Destination – Valjarv (Bluebird).
March 6. Second foal. 28,000Y. Tattersalls October Book 2. Kilstone. Half-sister to the modest 2009 5f placed 2-y-o Val C (by Dubawi). The dam, a fairly useful 2-y-o 6f winner, was listed-placed and is a half-sister to 5 winners including the listed-placed Qadar and Ikan. The second dam, Iktidar (by Green Desert), a quite useful Irish 1m placed maiden, is a half-sister to 6 winners. (Kilstone Ltd).
"She's a lovely, big filly but a late season two-year-old I think will be suited by seven furlongs to start with. I haven't rousted her along yet but she moves like a dream."

345. DUBARSHI ★★★
b.c. Dubawi – Asheyana (Soviet Star).
March 24. Second foal. 26,000Y. Tattersalls October Book 2. Kilstone. Half-brother to the modest 2009 7f placed 2-y-o Ashkalara (by Footstepsinthesand). The dam is an unraced sister to the high-class miler Ashkalani, winner of the Group 1 Prix du Moulin and the Group 1 French 2,000 Guineas. The second dam, Ashtarka (by Dalsaan), won over 1m in France and is a half-sister to 4 winners including Shafaraz (Group 1 Prix du Cadran) and Ajarann (Group 1 Premio Roma second). (Kilstone Ltd).
"He's a nice colt and quite precocious. Six furlongs in May will be his starting point but he's certainly a colt! So he might need his first run to help make him grow up. A good-sized, chunky two-year-old type."

346. PRINCESS ICICLE ★★★
b.f. Iceman – Sarabah (Ela-Mana-Mou).
January 31. Ninth foal. 15,000Y. Tattersalls October Book 2. Kilstone. Closely related to the useful 5f to 6f winner Cryhavoc, the useful 7f to 9f winner Ice, the quite useful dual 1m winner Miss Polaris and the German 7f winner Euro Falcon (all by Polar Falcon) and half-sister to the useful 7f (at 2 yrs) and 10.4f winner Saratov (by Rudimentary), the quite useful 2-y-o 5f winner Basbusate Nadia (by Wolfhound) and the German 1m and 9f winner Manguista (by Shareef Dancer). The dam, a quite useful 10f winner, is a half-sister to 5 winners including the very smart triple Group 2 1m winner Gothenburg. The second

dam, Be Discreet (by Junius), won 5 races in France at up to 7f and is a half-sister to 9 winners including 3 stakes winners. (Kilstone Ltd). *"She won't be an early type because she's a big, scopey filly. One for the autumn over a mile."* TRAINERS' BARGAIN BUY

347. UNNAMED ★★
b.f. Diktat – Hoh Dancer (Indian Ridge).
March 2. Seventh foal. 20,000Y. Tattersalls October Book 2. Kilstone. Sister to the fairly useful dual 7f winner (including at 2 yrs) Dixey and to the fair 7f to 9f winner of 9 races Dichoh and half-sister to the quite useful 2-y-o 5f and 6f winner Harry Patch (by Lujain). The dam was placed over 5f and is a half-sister to 3 winners including the listed Doncaster Stakes winner Infanta Real. The second dam, Alteza Real (by Mansingh), won 3 sprint races at 2 and 3 yrs and is a full or half-sister to 10 winners including the US Grade 1 winner and useful sire Forzando. (Kilstone Ltd). *"She isn't likely to make a two-year-old but she's nice and will hopefully be out in the autumn. A lovely filly and I probably like her the most, but she's very tall and much more of a three-year-old type."*

348. UNNAMED ★★
ch.c. Footstepsinthesand – Sunset (Polish Precedent).
May 20. Fourth foal. 15,000Y. Tattersalls October Book 3. Not Sold. The dam ran once unplaced and is a half-sister to 4 winners including Red Sea (Coventry Stakes) and the useful 7f (at 2 yrs) and Italian Group 3 12f winner Sailing. The second dam, Up Anchor (by Slip Anchor), won four races including the Group 3 12f St Simon Stakes, was third in the Italian Oaks and is a half-sister to 5 winners including the triple US Grade 3 winner at around 8.5f Just Class. (Kilstone Ltd). *"A nice sort of colt, he's nearly there and he'll be suited by six furlongs. He looks a two-year-old type, quite compact and the perfect size. I really like him and he takes everything you can throw at him. He's available for purchase if anyone wants him."*

LUCA CUMANI
349. ALKIMOS (IRE) ★★★
b.c. High Chaparral – Bali Breeze (Common Grounds).
March 4. Second foal. 50,000Y. Tattersalls October Book 2. Charlie Gordon-Watson. The dam, a quite useful 10f, 12f and hurdles winner, is a sister to the fairly useful listed-placed winner Amicable and a half-sister to 3 minor winners. The second dam, Bahia Laura (by Bellypha), a minor winner over 10.5f at 4 yrs in France, is a sister to the Group 3 10.5f Prix de Flore winner Benicia and a half-sister to 6 winners. (L Marinopoulos). *"I like him a lot. He was weak as a yearling but he's done very well and is getting stronger all the time. I don't expect him to be at his best as a two-year-old, but the sire has picked up after a slow start and I think this colt will show some promise at two."*

350. AKRIAS (USA) ★★
b.c. Lemon Drop Kid – Prevail (Danzig).
May 5. Seventh foal. 40,000Y. Tattersalls October 2. Charlie Gordon-Watson. Half-brother to the minor French 11f and 12f winner Persistent Memory (by Red Ransom) and a winner in Russia by Chester House. The dam, a winner in France and third in the Group 3 Prix des Reservoirs, is a half-sister to 4 winners including the triple Group 1 winner Priolo. The second dam, Primevere (by Irish River), a listed-placed winner of 3 races in France, is a half-sister to 4 winners. (L Marinopoulos). *"He seems like a nice horse. He's a good mover and a good-looking colt that does everything right. Being by Lemon Drop Kid he'll be a middle distance three-year-old but hopefully he'll be able to run sometime this year."*

351. BARY ★★★
b.c. Noverre – Saada One (Polish Precedent)).
February 20. Brother to the quite useful 2-y-o 5f winner Mahusay. The dam is closely related to the fairly useful 1m and 8.5f winner Invader and a half-sister to the fairly useful 8.3f (at 2 yrs) and 10.3f winner Jumaireyah and the useful 10.5f and 12f winner Altaweelah. The second dam, Donya (by Mill Reef), was placed once over 10f from 2 outings and is a half-sister to the useful Irish winner at up to 12f Golden Isle. (Sheikh Mohammed Obaid Al Maktoum). *"A neat, compact, smallish colt and a two-year-old type. There's a bit of speed in the family and he should be running in June or July over six furlongs."*

352. BRICK DUST (IRE) ★★★
ch.c. Noverre – Reddening (Blushing Flame).
February 15. Fifth foal. 46,000Y. Tattersalls October 2. Charlie Gordon-Watson. Half-brother to the very useful 2-y-o 6f and 7f winner and Group 1 Nunthorpe Stakes third Pivotal Flame (by Pivotal) and to the fairly useful 5f and 6f winner Olynard (by Exceed And Excel). The dam, a fairly useful 2m winner, is a sister to the Italian winner and Group 3 placed Musical Score and a half-sister to 5 winners. The second dam, Music In My Life (by Law Society), a modest 7.5f and 1m placed 3-y-o, is a half-sister to 4 winners. (L Marinopoulos). *"Another nice looking horse by Noverre, he's a different type to another Noverre two-year-old of mine, Bary, in that he's got a lot more scope and will be more of a seven furlong two-year-old."*

353. CARSULAE (IRE) ★★★
b.f. Marju – Trois Heures Apres (Soviet Star).
April 9. Ninth foal. 92,000Y. Tattersalls October Book 2. Rachel Boffey. Half-sister to the quite useful 2-y-o 6f and 7f winner and 1m listed placed Laurentina (by Cadeaux Genereux), to the French 9m to 10f winner of 9 races and listed placed Rising Talent (by Bering), the fairly useful 10f winner Feaat (by Unfuwain), the fair 1m to 2m and hurdles winner Groomsman (by Groom Dancer) and a minor winner in Italy by King's Theatre. The dam is an unraced half-sister to 4 winners including the very useful 7f (at 2 yrs) and 10f listed winner and Oaks third Mezzogiorno (herself dam of the Group 2 Blandford Stakes winner Monturani). The second dam, Aigue (by High Top), a fairly useful 4-y-o dual 1m winner, is a sister to the listed middle-distance winner Torchon. (Mr S A Stuckey). *"She's a nice filly, a bit unfurnished, weak and backward at the moment but she goes well and is a very good mover. More likely to be a July/August type over six or seven furlongs."*

354. DANADANA (IRE) ★★
b.c. Dubawi – Zeeba (Barathea).
April 11. First foal. The dam, a fair 12f winner, is a sister to the useful listed 14f winner Lost Soldier Three and a half-sister to 5 winners including the useful 10.5f and 12f winner Altaweelah. The second dam, Donya (Mill Reef), was placed once over 10f from 2 outings and is a half-sister to the Rothmans International winner French Glory and the useful Irish winner at up to 12f Golden Isle. (Sheikh Mohammed Obaid Al Maktoum). *"A biggish sort of horse, he's a bit backward and plain at the moment. It's a family I know quite well and although he's by Dubawi he's much more likely to be a middle distance horse next year, but as a two-year-old he'll be suited by seven furlongs to a mile."*

355. DRESDEN (IRE) ★★★
b.c. Diamond Green – So Precious (Batshoof).
March 30. Third living foal. £48,000Y. Doncaster St Leger. G Howson. Half-brother to the 2-y-o 7f and subsequent US Grade 3 winner Oil Man (by Pyrus). The dam, a quite useful 7f (at 2 yrs), 11f and hurdles winner, is a half-sister to 4 winners. The second dam, Golden Form (by Formidable), an Irish listed 9f winner, was Group 3 placed and is a half-sister to 6 winners. (L Marinopoulos). *"A nice big horse. It's difficult to know what trip he'll want being by a first-season sire, but he should run as a two-year-old."*

356. DUBAI QUEEN (USA) ★★★★
b.f. Kingmambo – Zomaradah (Deploy).
February 9. Half-sister to the high-class miler Dubawi (by Dubai Millennium), to the listed 10f winner Princess Nada (by Barathea) and the quite useful 8.5f winner Suba (by Seeking The Gold). The dam, a winner of 6 races including the Group 1 Italian Oaks, the Group 2 Royal Whip Stakes and the Group 2 Premio Lydia Tesio, is a half-sister to several winners. The second dam, Jawaher (by Dancing Brave), was placed over 1m and 9f and is a half-sister to the Derby winner High Rise. *"A bit on the small side, but she's neat and she goes well. Most of the dam's foals haven't stayed further than ten furlongs and I see this filly as a six/seven furlong type."*

357. DYSIOS (IRE) ★★★★
b.c. Invincible Spirit – Hataana (Robellino).
April 29. Fourth foal. 72,000Y. Tattersalls October 2. Charlie Gordon-Watson. Closely related to the Italian 2-y-o listed 1m winner Desert Cry (by Desert Prince). The dam ran once unplaced and is a half-sister to one winner. The second dam, Katakana (by Diesis),

a useful 2-y-o 6f winner, was third in the Group 1 Coronation Stakes and is a half-sister to 2 winners. (L Marinopoulos). *"A really nice horse, very good-looking and moves well. He'll be a July type two-year-old starting at six furlongs and he should get seven."*

358. FAIRY FAMILIAR (USA) ★★★
b.f. Smart Strike – Arabian Spell
(Desert Prince).
March 11. Half-sister to Blissful Moment (by Dynaformer), placed fourth over 1m on his only start at 2 yrs in 2009. The dam, a 1m winner and third in the Group 3 Prix Miesque, is a half-sister to 2 winners including the useful 7f and 1m winner Truly Enchanting. The second dam, Truly Bewitched (by Affirmed), a quite useful 2-y-o 6f winner, is a half-sister to 4 winners including the US Grade 2 winner Chinese Dragon. (W McAlpin). *"A home-bred from an American owner, she's a bit small but strong and she'll make a two-year-old over five or six furlongs."*

359. FIMIAS ★★★
b.br.c. Aussie Rules – Miss Lacey (Diktat).
February 14. First foal. £33,000Y. Doncaster St Leger. G Howson. The dam is an unraced half-sister to 5 winners including the Group 2 Superlative Stakes and Group 3 Rose Of Lancaster Stakes winner Halicarnassus. The second dam, Launch Time (by Relaunch), is a US placed half-sister to 4 winners including the US Grade 2 winner Palace March and the Group/Grade 1 placed Executive Pride. (Mr L Marinopoulos & Partners). *"He's worth putting in the book. He's a medium-sized colt and he looks like he should make a two-year-old and do something this year."*

360. FRANCISCAN ★★
b.c. Medicean – Frangy (Sadler's Wells).
April 19. Seventh foal. Half-brother to the very useful 12f and listed 14f winner Savarain (by Rainbow Quest) and to the quite useful 9f winner Forte Dei Marmi (by Selkirk). The dam, a fair dual 12f winner, is a full or half-sister to 8 winners including the German 1m to 9.5f winner of 7 races and listed-placed Flying Heights. The second dam, Fern (by Shirley Heights), a useful 12f winner and third in the listed 10f Lupe Stakes, is a half-sister to 6 winners including the Group 1 Fillies Mile winner and Oaks second Shamshir. (Fittocks Stud). *"It's a slow-developing family so I don't expect him to do much as a two-year-old, but he's very good-looking – probably the best looking colt the mare has produced so far."*

361. GUARDS CHAPEL ★★★★★
b.c. Motivator – Intaaj (Machiavellian).
March 20. First foal. 150,000Y. Tattersalls October 2. John Warren. The dam was placed at 3 yrs in France on her only start and is a half-sister to 4 winners including the Group 3 6f Prix de Meautry winner of 15 races Indian Maiden. The second dam, Jinsiyah (by Housebuster), a useful 2-y-o 7f winner, is a half-sister to 5 winners including the fairly useful dual 1m winner Bintalshaati. (Highclere Thoroughbred Racing, Matilda). *"A very nice colt and he was our most expensive yearling. Being by Motivator you wouldn't expect him to be a speedster but he should run this year and do well from August onwards."*

362. GULBARG ★★★
b.f. Dubawi – Jade Chequer (Green Desert).
March 7. Seventh foal. 55,000Y. Tattersalls October Book 1. L Cumani. Half-sister to the German winner and listed-placed Jurako (by Surako), to the 6f seller winner Jazenio (by Auenadler) and the German 2-y-o winner Jade Rheinberg (by Platini). The dam is a placed half-sister to 2 winners. The second dam, Draft Board (by Rainbow Quest), a fair 3-y-o 6f winner, is a sister to 2 winners including the very useful 1m winner and 10f listed placed Star Selection and a half-sister to 4 winners including the multiple Group 1 winner Ouija Board. (Sheikh Mohammed Obaid Al Maktoum). *"A nice, good-looking filly that goes well and there's nothing negative to say about her. She should be a mid-season filly and I wouldn't really have an idea about her distance but I would say a mile maximum and she'll probably start off at six furlongs."*

363. IPPIOS ★★★
b.c. Cadeaux Genereux – Siena Gold
(Key Of Luck).
February 28. First foal. 27,000Y. Tattersalls October 2. Charlie Gordon-Watson. The dam, a useful winner of the 2-y-o 5f Weatherbys

Supersprint, is a half-sister to 6 winners including the very useful 2-y-o Crazee Mental (a winner over 6f and placed in the Cheveley Park Stakes, the Queen Mary Stakes and the Cherry Hinton Stakes). The second dam, Corn Futures (by Nomination), a fair 2-y-o 6f winner, is a half-sister to 7 winners including the dam of the March Stakes and Glorious Stakes winner Midnight Legend. (L Marinopoulos). *"He's a son of Cadeaux Genereux who doesn't normally get precocious types, but the dam line does produce two-year-olds which means there's a chance that this colt will do something this year. However quickly he appears on the track, he'll be a sprinter."*

364. KHOR SHEED ★★★★
ch.f. *Dubawi – Princess Manila (Manila)*.
April 23. Twelfth foal. 42,000Y. Tattersalls October Book 1. L Cumani. Half-sister to the Group 1 Prix d'Ispahan winner Prince Kirk (by Selkirk), to the Italian winners Prince Esteem (by Mark Of Esteem), Prince Honor (by Highest Honor) and Princer (by Irish River) and the French winner Platel (by Alysheba). The dam is an unplaced half-sister to 3 winners including the Group 1 Italian Derby winner Hailsham. The second dam, Halo's Princess (by Halo), won the Grade 1 Princess Elizabeth Stakes in Canada and is a half-sister to 6 winners and to the unraced dam of the Australian Grade 1 winners Curata Storm and Voile d'Or. (Sheikh Mohammed Obaid Al Maktoum). *"A nice, well put-together filly. The sire has started his stud career very well and I like this filly. She'll make a two-year-old and eventually she'll stay a mile or more but she should do something this year. I'd say she'll be one to follow."*

365. KIRTHILL (IRE) ★★★
b.c. *Danehill Dancer – Kirtle (Hector Protector)*.
March 12. Third foal. 90,000Y. Tattersalls October Book 1. Charlie Gordon-Watson. The dam, a fairly useful 8.2f winner here and subsequently a listed-placed winner in the USA, is a half-sister to one winner. The second dam, Kyle Rhea (by In The Wings), winner of the listed Cheshire Oaks, is a half-sister to 6 winners including the Park Hill Stakes winner Coigach and the Park Hill Stakes second Applecross (herself the dam of 3 Group winners). (L Marinopoulos). *"A nice, good-looking horse, he's quite big but he should run this year from July or August onwards."*

366. KYZYL KUM ★★★
b.c. *Green Desert – Rise (Polar Falcon)*.
April 28. Third foal. £48,000Y. Doncaster St Leger. G Howson. Brother to the moderate 1m winner Join Up (by Green Desert). The dam won 3 races from 6f to 7f at 2 and 3 yrs and is a half-sister to 4 winners including the smart 6f winner Feet So Fast and the Group 2 Lowther Stakes winner Soar. The second dam, Splice (by Sharpo), a smart winner of 7 races including the listed 6f Abernant Stakes, is a full or half-sister to 7 winners. (L Marinopoulos). *"He's quite a compact, forward two-year-old. A fairly strong colt, he should eventually be a seven furlong/mile horse but he'll start off at six furlongs in June or July."*

367. LADY FASHION ★★★
b.f. *Oasis Dream – Carinae (Nureyev)*.
April 23. Fifth foal. 60,000Y. Tattersalls December. Gill Richardson. Half-sister to the fair 2-y-o 6f winner Carina Nebula (by Grand Slam) and to the minor US 2-y-o winner Sweet And Sassy (by Lear Fan). The dam, a useful 2-y-o 6f winner, was listed placed here and in the USA and is a half-sister to 4 winners including the smart 2-y-o 7f and 1m winner and Group 3 1m UAE 2,000 Guineas third Rallying Cry (by War Chant). The second dam, Turning Wheel (by Seeking The Wheel), winner of the Group 3 10f La Coupe de Maisons-Laffitte, is a half-sister to 7 winners including the 1,000 Guineas third Ajfan and the St Leger second Minds Music. (Jaber Abdullah). *"A little Oasis Dream filly, she's nice and well put-together. Likely to be one of our earlier types, I'd hope to have her out in June or July."*

368. MASTER PERFECT ★★
ch.c. *Dubai Destination – My Mariam (Salse)*.
March 31. Tenth foal. 30,000Y. Tattersalls October 2. Charlie Gordon-Watson. Half-brother to the fairly useful Irish 10f winner Crookhaven (by Dansili), to the Irish 12f winner and listed-placed In the Ribbons (by In The Wings), the quite useful 1m, 10f and hurdles winner Sam Lord (by Observatory), the fair 10f seller winner Yashin (by Soviet Star) and a minor

winner of 10 races in the USA by Revoque. The dam, a quite useful 2-y-o 6f winner, is a sister to the Group 1 7f Moyglare Stud Stakes and Group 2 6f Lowther Stakes winner Bianca Nera and a half-sister to 3 winners including the Group 1 Moyglare Stud Stakes second Hotelgenie Dot Com (herself dam of the Group 1 Fillies' Mile winner Simply Perfect). The second dam, Birch Creek (by Carwhite), was placed five times including when third in the Group 3 1m Premio Royal Mares and is a half-sister to 7 winners including the useful Group 3 winning sprinter Great Deeds. (Samanda Racing). *"The sire has been a bit disappointing but this is a nice, good-looking horse – albeit on the small side."*

369. MUNDANA (IRE) ★★★★
b.f. *King's Best – Mail Express (Cape Cross).*
March 23. First foal. €65,000Y. Goffs Orby. L Cumani. The dam, a fair 6f winner at 3 yrs, is a half-sister to 5 winners including the Group 1 1m Premio Vittorio di Capua, Group 2 Challenge Stakes and Group 2 Italian 2,000 Guineas winner Le Vie dei Colori. The second dam, Mystic Tempo (by El Gran Senor), won over 6f at 2 yrs and two 6f sellers on the all-weather at 3 yrs and is a half-sister to 3 winners including the useful dual 3-y-o 1m winner and Group 1 Moyglare Stud Stakes third Timely. (Sheikh Mohammed Obaid Al Maktoum). *"She's a very good-looking filly, there's speed in the family and the dam's half-brother Le Vie Dei Colori was not only a good two-year-old but he has produced plenty of precocious types too. This filly will be a six/seven furlong two-year-old from June or July onwards."*

370. NAQSHABBAN (USA) ★★★
b.c. *Street Cry – Ream Three (Mark Of Esteem).*
The dam, a useful 8.6f to 10.4f winner, was listed placed and is a half-sister to one winner. The second dam, Jumaireyah (by Fairy King), a fairly useful 8.3f (at 2 yrs) and 10.3f winner, is a half-sister to numerous winners including the useful 10f to 14f winner Lost Soldier Three and the useful 10.5f and 12f winner Altaweelah. (Sheikh Mohammed Obaid Al Maktoum). *"He's a good-looking horse that goes well and he should run as a two-year-old for sure."*

371. OMID ★★★
b.c. *Dubawi – Mille Couleurs (Spectrum).*
April 24. Fifth foal. 55,000Y. Tattersalls October Book 2. Shadwell Estate Co. Half-brother to the minor French winner of 7 races (including over 5f at 2 yrs) Mindbend (by Verglas) and to a bumper winner by Limnos. The dam is an unraced half-sister to 5 winners including the French listed winner and Group 2 placed Misbegotten. The second dam, Mistreat (by Gay Mecene), a minor French 3-y-o winner, is half-sister to 6 winners. (Sheikh Mohammed Obaid Al Maktoum). *"A big son of Dubawi, he's nice enough and he goes well enough. One for the second half of the season."*

372. PICENO (IRE) ★★★
b.c. *Camacho – Ascoli (Skyliner).*
April 29. 13,000Y. Tattersalls Book 2. Charlie Gordon-Watson. Half-brother to the useful Irish listed 6f winner Spencers Wood (by Pips Pride), to the fair Irish 1m and 10f winner Liscoa (by Foxhound), the modest 12f, 15f and hurdles winner Precious Mystery (by Titus Livius) and a winner in Turkey by Prince Rupert. The dam, an Irish, 10f, 12f and hurdles winner, is a half-sister to 3 winners. The second dam, Yamadori (by Charlottesville), won and was listed-placed and is a half-sister to the Derby winner Parthia. (Team Spirit 2). *"He'll be one of our first to run. Well put-together and strong, he was cheaply bought but should win races."*
TRAINERS' BARGAIN BUY

373. POPLIN ★★
ch.f. *Medicean – Pongee (Barathea).*
March 8. Second foal. Half-sister to the fair 10f winner Paisley (by Pivotal). The dam, a very useful Group 2 12f Lancashire Oaks winner, is closely related to the smart listed 12f and listed 14f winner Lion Sands and a half-sister to the very useful 10f (at 2 yrs) and 11f winner and listed-placed Pukka. The second dam, Puce (by Darshaan), a very useful listed 12f winner, is a half-sister to 7 winners. (Fittocks Stud). *"A nice, well put-together filly. The family takes time and wants distance so she's much more likely to come into her own next year, but hopefully she should be able to do something at two."*

374. SAMANDA (IRE) ★★★
b.c. Ad Valorem – Presently Blessed (Inchinor).
March 6. First foal. 50,000Y. Tattersalls October 2. Charlie Gordon-Watson. The dam is an unplaced half-sister to the 2-y-o winner and Group 3 7f Nell Gwyn Stakes third Hector's Girl. The second dam, Present Imperfect (by Cadeaux Genereux), a modest 5f placed 3-y-o, is a half-sister to 5 winners including the high-class sprinter College Chapel and the dams of the Group winners Leap For Joy, Barrow Creek and Last Resort. (Samanda Racing). *"He's by a first season sire so it's difficult to know where we are with him, but he's a good-looking horse that seems to be going well and he looks a two-year-old type that's likely to want six or seven furlongs."*

375. SET ME FREE (IRE) ★★★★
b.c. Noverre – Lonesome Me (Zafonic).
February 1. Second foal. 62,000Y. Tattersalls October Book 2. Charlie Gordon-Watson. The dam, a French 2-y-o 7f winner, was listed placed over 9f at 3 yrs and is a half-sister to one winner. The second dam, Lone Spirit (by El Gran Senor), is an unraced sister to the US Grade 2 and Group 3 Chester Vase winner Panama City and to the useful 8.5f to 10.8f winner Morgana (subsequently a Grade 2 8.5f winner in the USA). (L Marinopoulos). *"A nice, good-looking son of Noverre, he cost quite a bit of money and I like him. He should be a two-year-old and he's strong and well put-together."*

376. UNNAMED ★★
gr.f. Medicean – Dali's Grey (Linamix).
April 21. Sixth foal. Half-sister to the useful 10f to 14f winner Bauer (by Halling), to the fairly useful 10.2f to 12f winner Batik (by Peintre Celebre), the fair 10f winner Surrealism (by Pivotal) and the fair 10f to 14f winner Boz (by Grand Lodge). The dam, a French 11f winner, is a sister to the French Group winners Diamilina and Diamonixa and a half-sister to the Group winner Diamond Green. The second dam, Diamonaka (by Akarad), a French 10.5f winner, was Group 2 placed and is a half-sister to the French Group winners Diamond Mix, Diasilixa and Diamond Dance. (Aston House Stud). *"She's a bit small and weak at the moment and the family take a bit of time to get going, so I don't expect her to do much this year. It's a family that produces lots of multiple winners though, so hopefully she'll carry on the family trait."*

377. UNNAMED ★★
b.c. Cadeaux Genereux – Hawait Al Barr (Green Desert).
April 27. Eleventh foal. 52,000Y. Tattersalls October Book 2. Charlie Gordon-Watson. Brother to the 1m winner and listed-placed Blue Dream and half-brother to 5 winners including the 1m (at 2 yrs) and 9f winner and German Group 3 second Equity Princess (by Warning), the quite useful dual 12f winner Blaze Of Colour, the fair 10f winner Questive (both by Rainbow Quest) and the quite useful 2-y-o dual 6f winner Feisty Royale (by Royal Applause). The dam, a useful 12f and listed 2m winner, is out of the winner and Group 2 Park Hill Stakes third Allegedly Blue (by Alleged), herself a half-sister to 4 winners including the dam of the Kentucky Derby and Preakness Stakes winner Real Quiet. (B Corman). *"He's a bit backward and he was a fairly late foal, so he'll take his time and although he's a good-looking horse, time will tell with him."*

378. UNNAMED ★★★
b.c. Le Vie Dei Colori – So Glam So Hip (Spectrum).
March 10. Second foal. £24,000Y. Doncaster St Leger. G Howson. Brother to the fair 2009 6f and 7f placed 2-y-o Pictures. The dam is an unplaced daughter of the minor 3-y-o winner With A Prayer (by Caerleon), herself a half-sister to 4 winners. (Mrs A S Silver). *"A strong sort of colt, he seems alright and although I don't think he's a world beater he's going to be one of the first ones to run, in June or July over six or seven furlongs."*

379. UNNAMED ★★★
gr.c. Motivator – Zarawa (Kahyasi).
February 18. Sixth living foal. 45,000Y. Tattersalls October Book 2. Charlie Gordon-Watson. Half-brother to the quite useful 10f winner Plymouth Rock (by Sadler's Wells), to the fair 12f all-weather winner Dawaarr (by Indian Ridge) and a winner over hurdles by Danehill. The dam ran once unplaced in France and is a half-sister to 3 winners including the French listed winner Zarannda and the dam of the

Group 3 Prix de Sandringham winner Zarkiya. The second dam, Zarna (by Shernazar), won once at 3 yrs and is a half-sister to 4 winners including the dam of the French Oaks and Prix Saint-Alary winner Zainta. (Scuderia Rencati Srl). "Very nice. He was cheaply bought, but he goes very well. The way he's bred I don't expect him to be a speedster, but seven furlongs to a mile in the autumn should suit him."

TOM DASCOMBE

Having been very successful in Lambourn, Tom is now set up at footballer Michael Owen's yard near Malpas in Cheshire. It's a beautiful location with great facilities and plenty of money has been spent at the Sales to try and get the yard into the Premier League of Racing Stables. Tom and his team must be looking forward to sending out plenty of winners and it was a pleasure to chat to him about his two-year-olds. As well as the ones below, Tom reminded me he has a couple of fillies by Deep Impact that were bought as foals in Japan. It will be fascinating to see how they get on this year too.

380. ADDOCK AND EGG ★★★
b.c. Danbird – Luanshya (First Trump).
April 14. Fifth foal. £16,000Y. Doncaster St Leger. Kern/Lillingston. Half-brother to the useful 2-y-o listed 5f Roses Stakes and 3-y-o 6f winner Tabaret (by Bertolini), to the modest 5f (at 2 yrs) and 6f winner African Breeze (by Atraf) and the modest dual 1m winner Aussie Blue (by Bahamian Bounty). The dam, a fair 3-y-o 6f winner, is a half-sister to 4 winners. The second dam, Blues Indigo (by Music Boy), won over 6f and was second in the Group 3 Palace House Stakes and is a half-sister to 5 winners. (Addock and Egg Partnership). "He's a bit weak and plain at the moment but he's a nice little colt that should be out soon. He's not a superstar but he should win."

381. ADORABLE CHOICE (IRE) ★★★
b.br.f. Choisir – Burnin' Memories (Lit de Justice).
April 12. Third foal. €45,000Y. Tattersalls Ireland. Kern/Lillingston. Half-sister to the useful Irish 2-y-o 6f winner and Group 2 Railway Stakes second In Some Respect (by Indian Haven) and to the quite useful 1m winner Glebe Queen (by Hawkeye). The dam won 5 races at 2 to 5 yrs in the USA including a minor stakes event and is a half-sister to 6 winners. The second dam, Adorable Vice (by Vice Regent), a US stakes-placed winner of 3 races, is a half-sister to 4 winners including the Italian Group 1 winner Looking For and the Italian Group 2 winner Life On Mars. (John and Diane Brown). "She's not going to be an early type as she's a big filly that's taking a bit of time. She'll want six furlongs to begin with and she should go on any ground. We've put her in the Tattersalls Ireland Sales race."

382. ANGEL FISA (IRE) ★★
b.f. High Chaparral – Angel Isa (Fayruz).
March 1. First foal. 14,000Y. Tattersalls October Book 2. Winston Wing Kin Chow. The dam, a moderate 7f winner, is a half-sister to 8 winners including the German listed winner and Group placed Time To Go Home. The second dam, Isa (by Dance In Time), is an unraced half-sister to 4 winners. (Mr W Chow). "She's going to want a lot of time, there's no rush with her and she's one for the back-end. More of a three-year-old type."

383. ANKH (IRE) ★★★★
b.f. Cape Cross – Everlasting Love (Pursuit Of Love).
February 22. Fourth living foal. €64,000Y. Arqana Deauville October. Kern/Lillingston. The dam, a useful 2-y-o 7f winner and third in the Group 3 May Hill Stakes, is a half-sister to 3 winners. The second dam, Now And Forever (by Kris), is an unraced half-sister to 8 winners including the Group 3 Curragh Cup winner Witness Box. (Andrew Black & Partners). "She's one of the best-bred fillies we've got and I thought she was ever so cheap – a bargain in fact. She's beautiful, moves really nicely but won't be early. There's no reason why she shouldn't start off at six furlongs though, because she's not slow."

384. BACK FOR TEA (IRE) ★★★
b.c. Redback – Jasmine Pearl (King Of Kings).
March 21. €12,500Y. Tattersalls Ireland. Kern/Lillingston. The dam, a modest 4-y-o 6f winner, is a half-sister to the 2-y-o Group 2 5f Queen Mary Stakes winner Gilded. The second dam, Tumbleweed Pearl (by Aragon),

a fairly useful 5.7f (at 2 yrs) and 6f winner, is a half-sister to 5 winners including the Group 3 Horris Hill Stakes, Ballycorus Stakes and Prix de la Porte Maillot winner Tumbledown Ridge. (The China Plates). *"A sharp, early two-year-old. He had a little setback but nothing that's going to hold him up for long. He'll be aimed at one of the sales bonus races and he's up to winning two-year-old races."*

385. BALLISTA (IRE) ★★★★
b.c. Majestic Missile – Ancient Secret (Warrshan).
February 28. Ninth foal. €11,000Y. Goffs Orby. Kern/Lillingston. Half-brother to the quite useful 2-y-o 6f winner Secret Formula, to the fair 6f to 8.5f winner Artifact (both by So Factual), the fair 2-y-o 8.5f winner Old Opium, the fair 6f 2-y-o and subsequent US winner Secret Spice (both by Dilum) and the minor 3-y-o winner of 6 races in Italy Aztec Robber (by Robellino). The dam is an unraced half-sister to 9 winners including the smart stayer Primitive Rising and the dam of the Group 2 Flying Childers Stakes winner Poker Chip. The second dam, Periquito (by Olden Times), is an unplaced half-sister to 4 winners. (Well Done Top Man Partnership). *"He's a lovely, lovely colt. He looked like a two-year-old when he was a yearling and he looks like he's three now. One of our nicest, he won't be rushed and we're hoping he'll be a Royal Ascot type. His sire was fast and I think five or six furlongs will suit him too. I think he's nice."* TRAINERS' BARGAIN BUY

386. BLACKLEYF (IRE) ★★★
br.g. Kheleyf – Cuca Vela (Devil's Bag).
March 28. Third foal. £17,000Y. Doncaster St Leger. Kern/Lillingston. The dam is an unraced half-sister to 5 winners including the US Grade 2 placed Halo's Stride. The second dam, Moscow Tap (by Moscow Ballet), is an unplaced half-sister to 3 winners including the US stakes winner Perceived Value. (The Folly Racers). *"He's already been gelded because he was a bit naughty, but he has a ability and he's as good as gold now. As soon as my horses start firing he'll be winning. Six furlongs will suit him I would say."*

387. BROWN PANTHER ★★
b.c. Shirocco – Treble Heights (Unfuwain).
March 3. Half-brother to the modest 15f and hurdles winner Holoko Heights (by Pivotal). The dam, a listed 12f winner, was Group 2 placed over 14f in France and is a half-sister to numerous winners including the very useful winner of 5 races and Group 1 Ascot Gold Cup third Warm Feeling and the useful 7.6f (at 2 yrs) and 10f (all-weather) winner Rainbow Heights. The second dam, Height Of Passion (by Shirley Heights), is an unplaced half-sister to 8 winners. (Owen Promotions Ltd). *"A big, strong colt and a really nice horse. He's not going to be running until the second half of the season and hopefully he can win a maiden this year or next."*

388. CHOSEN CHARACTER (IRE) ★★★★
b.c. Choisir – Out Of Thanks (Sadler's Wells).
May 9. Third foal. €55,000Y. Goffs Orby. Kern/Lillingston. Half-brother to the 2009 2-y-o Group 3 6f Sirenia Stakes and listed 6f winner Love Lockdown (by Verglas). The dam, a fairly useful dual 10f winner in Ireland, is a half-sister to 3 winners. The second dam, Trust In Luck (by Nashwan), an Irish 7f winner, is a half-sister to 9 winners including the Grade 1 winner Dress To Thrill. (Aykroyd & Sons Ltd). *"Over the last month he's improved tremendously both physically and mentally. He's a very nice two-year-old. A fairly late foal, we won't rush him but he might be out at the end of May. Possibly more the type for Newmarket's July meeting than Ascot."*

389. CLASSIC GEM (IRE) ★★★★
br.f. Diamond Green – Undercover (Grand Lodge).
February 22. Second foal. €40,000Y. Tattersalls Ireland. Kern/Lillingston. Half-sister to Muleta (by Daggers Drawn), winner of 2 minor races in France at 3 and 4 yrs and listed-placed in Italy and to the minor Italian winner San Ana (by Iron Mask). The dam was placed four times at 3 yrs in France and is a half-sister to 5 winners including the Group 1 Italian Oaks winner and Group 2 Premio Lydia Tesio second Nydrion. The second dam, Nabila (by Foolish Pleasure), won once at 3 yrs and is a half-sister to 6 winners including the

US stakes winner and Grade 3 placed Forty Weight. (Not Another Horse Partnership). *"A beauty. She's the nicest walker we've got and she'll have had a race by the time the book is published. She'll be better over six furlongs and maybe even seven, but she's a really kind filly that will get better as the year goes on. Possibly one to get a bit of black type before the end of the year."*

390. COCONUT ICE ★★★★
ch.f. Bahamian Bounty – Winter Ice (Wolfhound).
March 9. Eighth foal. £20,000Y. Doncaster St Leger. Kern/Lillingston. Half-sister to 6 winners including the minor French winners Emperor Jones, Numerous, Gold Away and Bering. The dam is an unraced half-sister to 3 winners abroad. The second dam, Ice Pool (by Diesis), won once at 3 yrs and is a half-sister to 3 winners including the US Grade 1 third Fadeyev. (Timeform Betfair Racing Club Ltd). *"The owners wanted horses that would run often and you'd be thoroughly disappointed if this filly didn't win a couple and run a lot. There's not a lot of her, she's tall and light framed, but the dam has bred loads of winners and this will be another one."*

391. COUNTESS ELLEN (IRE) ★★★★
b.f. Fasliyev – Princess Ellen (Tirol).
March 15. 55,000Y. Tattersalls October Book 1. Kern/Lillingston). Half-sister to the useful listed 1m winner Prince Of Dance (by Danehill Dancer), to the French 2-y-o listed 5f placed Candelabro (by Elusive Quality), the quite useful 9f to 14f and hurdles winner La Estrella (by Theatrical) and the fair 1m winner Stravella (by Stravinsky). The dam, a smart listed 7f Sweet Solera Stakes winner at 2 yrs, was second in the 1,000 Guineas and the Coronation Stakes and third in the Nassau Stakes (all Group 1 events). She is a half-sister to one winner out of the unraced Celt Song (by Unfuwain), herself a half-sister to 3 minor winners. (Five Horses Ltd). *"A really beautiful filly, she could be one of the nicest of those likely to be at their best as two-year-olds. If you had to push me now, I would say she'd be our Queen Mary type two-year-old. She'll probably start off at Salisbury in a Conditions race and I like her a lot."*

392. CUBAN PIECE (IRE) ★★★★
b.c. Azamour – Naazeq (Nashwan).
February 23. Tenth foal. €90,000Y. Goffs Orby. Kern/Lillingston. Half-brother to the 7f, 1m and subsequent US Grade 1 placed stakes winner Tamweel, to the fair 9.5f all-weather winner Thunder Canyon (both by Gulch), the fairly useful 10f to 2m 1f winner of 12 races Mostarsil (by Kingmambo) and to the quite useful 7f winner Sharapova (by Elusive Quality). The dam, a quite useful 10.5f winner, is a full or half-sister to 9 winners including the very useful 10f winner Shaya. The second dam, Gharam (by Green Dancer), a very useful 2-y-o 6f winner, was third in the French 1,000 Guineas and is a half-sister to 7 winners including the US Grade 1 9f winner Talinum. (The Cuban Partnership). *"A beautiful looking horse and to look at he's probably the nicest colt we've got. Despite his pedigree, he's quite forward mentally and he might just be earlier than you'd think. I'd be surprised if he wasn't out in June."*

393. CUBAN QUALITY (USA) ★★★
b.br.c. Elusive Quality – Russian Lullaby (Galileo).
March 1. First foal. €50,000Y. Goffs Orby. Kern/Lillingston. The dam is an unraced half-sister to 8 winners including the dual listed winner and Irish Derby second Dr Johnson. The second dam, Russian Ballet (by Nijinsky), a minor 6f and 7f placed 2-y-o, is closely related to El Gran Senor and Try My Best. (The Cuban Partnership). *"He's a lovely two-year-old and if he had a bit more quality he would have made a lot of money. It's difficult to tell what trip he'll want and because he's showing a bit of speed I'll start him off at five furlongs, but I'd say he'll want further as the year progresses. He's on the small side and he looks like a staying type, but he's not the slowest."*

394. CUBAN SPIRIT (IRE) ★★★★
b.c. Invincible Spirit – Shesasmartlady (Dolphin Street).
April 29. Sixth foal. 150,000Y. Tattersalls October Book 1. Not sold. Brother to the smart Group 2 6f Criterium de Maisons-Laffitte winner and Group 1 Middle Park Stakes third Captain Marvelous and half-brother to the fairly useful 10f and 12f winner Hero Worship

(by Kalanisi), the fair Irish 6f winner Smartest (by Exceed And Excel) and the minor US 4-y-o winner French Fern (by Royal Applause). The dam is an unplaced half-sister to 7 winners including the listed winners Dashing Colours and Dash Of Red. The second dam, Near The End (by Shirley Heights), is an unraced half-sister to 2 minor winners. (The Cuban Partnership). *"A beautiful looking horse, he's just a bit backward mentally at present but he's doing nice bits of work and when the penny drops he'll improve by a stone. If you were to draw a picture of a nice racehorse, then this is what you'd have. A strong, stocky, close-coupled type that looks an out-and-out sprinter."*

395. FIRSTKNIGHT ★★★★
b.c. Kyllachy – Wedding Party (Groom Dancer).
March 6. Second foal. 80,000Y. Tattersalls October Book 1. Dwayne Woods. Half-brother to the 2009 2-y-o dual 7f listed-placed Party Doctor (by Dr Fong). The dam, a quite useful 6f and 7f winner, was listed-placed and is a half-brother to 2 winners. The second dam, Ceanothus (by Bluebird), was placed over 7f and 12f and is a half-sister to 4 winners including the US Grade 2 12f Orchid Handicap and Grade 3 8.5f Suwannee River Handicap winner Golden Pond. (Mr W A Tinkler). *"He couldn't be more different to look at than his half-brother Party Doctor. I would hope that he'd be just as good and be a winning two-year-old as well. He's dropped more riders than all the other horses put together, and he's a bit like the Azamour colt we have in that if I got stuck into him I bet he'd cope with it well. A nice type of colt and I won't be too hard on him, but he's one to watch out for."*

396. FULL PELT (USA) ★★★★
b.br.c. Orientate – Class (Thunder Gulch).
April 5. Sixth foal. £44,000Y. Doncaster St Leger. Kern/Lillingston. Half-brother to 4 minor winners in North America by Running Stag, Golden Missile, El Prado and Touch Gold). The dam, a stakes winner in the USA and Grade 3 placed, is a half-sister to 3 winners. The second dam, Happenchance (by Alydar), a US stakes-placed winner of 4 races, is a half-sister to 2 winners. (Gary & Linnet Woodward). *"He's got an American pedigree and you'd think that ideally he'd probably start over six furlongs at either Lingfield or even Wolverhampton. If he were to win first time out I should think we'd get a good few quid for him from America. A beautiful horse who was quite small and fine in the winter when he was working, and yet he was coping with it all. But we decided to leave him alone to let him develop and as a result he's grown and he's a proper horse to look at."*

397. GENTLE LORD ★★★
b.c. Ishiguru – Soft Touch (Petorius).
March 23. Fourth living foal. £32,000Y. Doncaster St Leger. David Redvers. Brother to the fair 6f (including at 2 yrs) and 5f winner Gentle Guru and half-brother to the minor Italian winner of 5 races Beecroft (by Fraam). The dam, a fair 1m and hurdles winner, is a full or half-sister to 9 winners including the dual French listed winner and Group 3 Horris Hill Stakes second Hollow Hand. The second dam, Fingers (by Lord Gayle), won over 12f in Ireland, is a full or half-sister to 6 winners. (K P Trowbridge). *"Unfortunately he's had a bit of a setback and it'll be a few months before he's back but he showed us plenty of ability and he's entered for a few of the Sales races."*

398. HIGHLAND COLORI ★★★★
b.c. Le Vie Dei Colori – Emma's Star (Darshaan).
February 1. Seventh foal. €13,000Y. Tattersalls Ireland. David Redvers. Brother to the useful 2009 2-y-o 6f winner and listed 7f second Za Za Zoom and half-brother to the useful 6f winner of 5 races and listed-placed Genki (by Shinko Forest), the fair 6f winner Hazelrigg (by Namid) and the modest 1m winner The Happy Hammer (by Acclamation). The dam, a winner over 8.5f in Italy at 3 yrs, is a half-sister to 4 other winners in Italy. The second dam, Notte Chiara (by Artaius), won the listed Premio Minerva and is a half-sister to 8 winners. (Mr E M Sutherland). *"He was a huge yearling but he's always grown in proportion. I thought his sales price was unbelievably cheap, because I paid 13 Grand and I would have paid 50. I hope at the end of the year I still feel clever! He's got everything you'd want in a horse. A little bit backward thinking at the moment, but when the penny does drop he looks like he'll be able to go a bit.*

We had two by the same sire last year and they both did well. I don't see why this colt should be any different."

399. HIGH TABLE (IRE) ★★★
b.c. High Chaparral – Inner Strength
(Take Risks).
March 3. First foal. €45,000Y. Arqana Deauville August. Kern/Lillingston. The dam, a minor winner at 3 yrs in France, is a half-sister to the US Grade 3 Laurel Dash winner and Group 3 Prix Thomas Bryon second Mayoumbe and to the useful Irish 10f and 12f listed winner Tipperary All Star. The second dam, Moucha (by Fabulous Dancer), a winner of 3 races in France and listed-placed, is a half-sister to 7 winners including the US Grade 3 winner Daloma. (De La Warr Racing). "He's really turned into a nice horse and if all went well with him in the next two months I can't see why he wouldn't be the type to go for the Chesham Stakes at Royal Ascot. A medium-sized, close-coupled and strong looking colt."

400. HOPPY'S FLYER (FR) ★★★★
b.f. Country Reel – Madeleine's Blush (Rahy).
April 14. Sixth foal. €20,000Y. Arqana October. Kern/Lillingston. Half-sister to the minor French winner Agua de Mayo (by Mr Greeley), to the minor US winner Legacy Hunter (by Jade Hunter) and the Swiss winner of 7 races Maintop (by Royal Academy). The dam is an unraced half-sister to 3 minor winners. The second dam, Madeleine's Dream (by Theatrical), won the French 1,000 Guineas and is a half-sister to 4 winners. "A French-bred that will run in England in April before campaigning for a while in France to try and win their owner's premiums. A really, really sweet horse, she's quite strange in a way because she cut her leg in early January and probably didn't even canter until early February, but was ready to run a month later. It's incredible how sharp she proved herself to be, nothing phases her, she knows her job and she's a proper two-year-old."

401. IN BABYLON (GER) ★★★
b.c. Oasis Dream – Ice Dream (Mondrian).
April 4. Seventh foal. 60,000Y. Tattersalls October Book 2. Kern/Lillingston. Half-brother to the winner of 4 races and German listed-placed Ianina (by Monsun) and to 3 minor winners in Germany and Italy by Big Shuffle, Dashing Blade and Grand Lodge. The dam won twice in Germany (including at 2 yrs) and is a half-sister to 3 winners. The second dam, Iriyana (by Nishapour), is an unraced half-sister to 8 winners. (Sir Robert Ogden). "A lovely, big, strong colt, he's still growing a bit and although I'd love to rush him we certainly won't do that. A July type two-year-old, maybe for around Goodwood time, everything about him is lovely. He's not been pushed yet because he's not mentally forward."

402. JULIUS GEEZER (IRE) ★★★
b.c. Antonius Pius – Victoria's Secret
(Law Society).
April 5. Ninth foal. £22,000Y. Doncaster St Leger. Kern/Lillingston. Half-brother to the useful 6f (at 2 yrs) and 7f winner of 12 races Master Robbie, to the fairly useful 7f, 1m and hurdles winner Grand Opera (by City On A Hill), the Italian 7f (at 2 yrs) and 1m winner of 7 races Small Secret (both by Piccolo), the modest 1m winner of 6 races Legal Lover (by Woodborough) and the moderate 6f winner Private Passion (by Captain Rio). The dam, a fair 12f winner, is a half-sister to 5 winners. The second dam, Organdy (by Blakeney), a quite useful 3-y-o 1m winner, is a full or half-sister to 9 winners. (Basing, Bellman, Newman, Stroud). "We took him for his first race in Ireland and the whole thing was a disaster – everything went wrong for him. He should win in April, he looks amazing and he goes like a rocket. The only thing with him is that he doesn't like to stand still – he's a born runner and a 'buzzy' horse."

403. LENJAWI PRIDE ★★★
b.f. Elusive City – Clarice Orsini
(Common Grounds)
April 9. Seventh foal. 16,000Y. Doncaster St Leger. Kern/Lillingston. Half-sister to Johnny Jumpup (by Pivotal), a winner of 3 races at 2 yrs from 5f to 7.6f and second in a German Group 2 1m event, the Group 3 Horris Hill Stakes and the Group 3 Greenham Stakes, to the 6f (at 2 yrs) and 7f winner Tiber Tilly (by King Charlemagne), the fair 6f winner Here Comes Danny (by Kyllachy), the modest 6f winner Klarity (by Acclamation) and the modest all-weather 6f (at 2 yrs) and 8.3f winner Ally Makbul (by Makbul). The dam was placed over

1m in France and is a half-sister to 2 minor winners. The second dam, Be My Everything (by Be My Guest), won once at 3 yrs and is a half-sister to 9 winners including the Irish 1,000 Guineas winner Nicer. (Abdul Aziz Lenjawi). "She's grown a lot recently and she looks a bit like a dragster – she's well up-behind, but that'll change. She was just struggling with a couple of bits of work, so we've backed off her and she'll be out in May all being well. She's up to winning races and I would have thought six furlongs would be her trip."

404. MALPAS MISSILE ★★★
b.f. Elusive City – Second Prayer (Singspiel).
January 27. Fourth foal. £30,000Y. Doncaster St Leger. Kern/Lillington. Half-sister to the fair Irish 7f (at 2 yrs) and UAE 1m winner First Empire (by Desert Prince). The dam is an unraced half-sister to 5 winners including the listed Galtres Stakes winner Firecrest. The second dam, Trefoil (by Blakeney), won 3 races in France and is a half-sister to 6 winners including the French Group 2 winner First Prayer, the US Grade 3 winner Water Lily (herself dam of the Grade 1 winner Talinum) and the dam of the Melbourne Cup winner Jeune. (Andrew Black & Michael Owen). "A lovely filly, she's small, sharp and racy although she might be a little bit green when she makes her debut this month. Looking at her, you'd say she wouldn't get much further than five furlongs."

405. MILLENNIUM STAR ★★★★
b.f. High Chaparral – Diamonaka (Akarad).
April 20. Twelfth foal. 210,000Y. Tattersalls December. Dwayne Woods. Half-sister to 8 winners including the 2-y-o Group 3 7f Prix la Rochette winner Diamond Green (by Green Desert), the Group 2 12f Prix de Malleret winner Diamilina, the Group 3 Prix Cleopatre winner Diamonixa, the minor 12f winner Dianimix and the minor French winner Dali's Grey (dam of the Melbourne Cup winner Bauer) – (all by Linamix). The dam, a French 10.5f winner, was Group 2 placed and is a half-sister to the very smart Group 2 10.5f Prix Greffulhe winner Diamond Mix (by Linamix) and the Group 3 winners Diamond Dance and Diasilixa. The second dam, Diamond Seal (by Persian Bold), won 3 races including the listed 10f Woodpark Stud Stakes. (Mr W A Tinkler). "She's a beautiful filly, by far and away the best bred two-year-old we've got and obviously I'm not going to rush her, but hopefully she won't just have the odd race at the back-end. She'll get better but there's nothing that says she won't make a two-year-old. She's sharp, she wants to do it and I like her a lot. Her pedigree says she'll want seven furlongs to start with, but looking at her you don't get that opinion."

406. MIRROR LAD ★★★
gr.c. Proclamation – Shaieef (Shareef Dancer).
March 13. Eleventh living foal. £9,000Y. Doncaster St Leger. Not sold. Half-brother to 7 winners including the fair 2-y-o 5f winner Capture The Moment (by Keen), the fair 9f to 12f winner of 5 races Kyle Of Lochalsh (by Vettori) and the moderate 1m winner Bounty Reef (by Bahamian Bounty). The dam, a modest triple 1m winner, is a half-sister to 2 winners. The second dam, Shaiyneen (by Kalamoun), won twice at 3 yrs and is a half-sister to Shergar. "He was hugely disappointing in the Brocklesbury but maybe the ground was too soft and in any case our horses weren't firing at the time. He'll be out again in April and he's a little rocket, even though on pedigree you'd think he'd want a lot further. I'd almost eat your book if he didn't win over five furlongs and he's got bags of toe."

407. MY MATE AL ★★★
b.f. Deportivo – Yes Dear (Fantastic Light).
February 18. First foal. 1,000Y. Ascot December. T Dascombe. The dam is an unplaced half-sister to numerous winners including the useful 2-y-o 7.2f winner and listed-placed Makfool and the useful triple 7f winner Raheibb. The second dam, Abeyr (by Unfuwain), a useful 3-y-o 7f and 8.2f winner, was listed-placed over 1m and is a half-sister to the useful 2-y-o 7.3f Radley Stakes winner Boojum. (S E Roberts). "She came in looking little and hairy, but she's improved tremendously. God knows what trip she'll need because she's working with fillies I would consider good enough for five furlongs, but her pedigree says otherwise. She's working well and if she comes soon enough I don't see why I shouldn't start her at five."

408. OLLIANNA ★★★★
b.f. Majestic Missile – Aspired (Mark Of Esteem).
April 19. Second foal. €7,000Y. Tattersalls Ireland. Kern/Lillingston. Half-sister to the quite useful 2009 2-y-o 7f winner Janeiro (by Captain Rio). The dam ran twice unplaced and is a half-sister to 4 winners including the fairly useful listed winner of 6 races at around 10f First Fantasy. The second dam, Dreams (by Rainbow Quest), a quite useful 3-y-o 10.3f winner, is a half-sister to 4 winners including the Melbourne Cup winner Jeune and the very useful Group 2 12f King Edward VII Stakes winner Beneficial. (Basing, Bellman, Newton, Stroud). *"Named after my two children, she's a half-sister to a filly we sold to Hong Kong and I think she's a lovely filly. She's so well she kicked the stable door off last night and was loose, chasing round the colts. I thought she was going to be really early but she had a setback and I guess she'll be a five/six furlong horse but to look at her you'd say she'd want further. I like her a lot."*

409. PRESS RELEASE ★★★
b.c. Elnadim – Last Impression (Imp Society).
March 9. £18,000Y. Doncaster St Leger. McKeever St Lawrence. Half-brother to the fair 2-y-o 5f winner Davaye (by Bold Edge) and to the modest dual 6f winner Fulford (by Elmaamul). The dam, a fair 2-y-o 5f winner, is a half-sister to one winner. The second dam, Figment (by Posse), a fair 5f and 6f winner, is a half-sister to 3 winners. (Timeform Betfair Racing Club Ltd). *"He looks speedy, he's a small, strong, racy two-year-old and once we get him fit we probably wouldn't need to work him, we'd just run him weekly instead. He's probably not got the quality of some, but he'd be capable of winning and I think he's as tough as old boots."*

410. RED PRESENCE (IRE) ★★★★
ch.c. Redback – Birthday Present (Cadeaux Genereux).
March 7. Fourth foal. €52,000Y. Goffs Orby. Kern/Lillingston. Half-brother to the quite useful 2-y-o 6f winner and Group 3 6f third May Day Queen (by Danetime) and to the quite useful 2-y-o 7f and 1m winner Call It On (by Raise A Grand). The dam is an unraced half-sister to 3 winners including the Group 1 Moyglare Stud Stakes third Supposition. The second dam, Topicality (by Topsider), won once at 3 yrs and is a sister to the Cherry Hinton and Fred Darling Stakes winner Top Socialite and a half-sister to the US Grade 1 winners Expelled and Exbourne. (The Folly Racers). *"A beautiful moving horse with a lot of quality, he was bought for the owners as a replacement for Orpen Grey. Redback's tend to want cut in the ground and the way this colt moves you would say he'd want a bit of ease too. Both the way he moves and his attitude to his work suggests he'll be an above average two-year-old."*

411. RHYTHM OF LIGHT ★★
b.f. Beat Hollow – Luminda (Danehill).
February 16. Third foal. 500Y. Ascot December. Tom Dascombe. Half-sister to the French 1m listed-placed Lazy Afternoon (by Hawk Wing) and to the quite useful triple 7f winner She's In The Money (by High Chaparral). The dam won 2 races in France at 2 and 4 yrs and is a half-sister to 3 winners including the US Grade 2 winner Little Treasure. The second dam, Luminosity (by Sillery), won once at 2 yrs in France and is a half-sister to 4 minor winners. (Mr G Lowe, Mr P Deal & Mr M Silver). *"Not an obvious two-year-old but the dam's done well with her first two foals and I don't see any reason why this one shouldn't continue the trend. She's a nice enough two-year-old, tall, scopey and reasonably plain, so she's not going to be an early type."*

412. ROWAN SPIRIT (IRE) ★★★
gr.c. Captain Rio – Secret Justice (Lit De Justice).
April 6. Fourth foal. €10,000Y. Tattersalls Ireland. Kern/Lillingston. Half-brother to the fairly useful 2-y-o 6f winner and Group 3 6f Albany Stakes fourth Aide Memoir (by Lend A Hand). The dam is an unplaced half-sister to 3 winners. The second dam, Secret Form (by Formidable), won the Group 2 Prix de l'Opera. (Deva Racing). *"He's done nothing but improve. The first time he worked he looked hopeless but now I'd be surprised if he didn't win as a two-year-old."*

413. SALMON ROSE (IRE) ★★★

b.f. *Iffraaj – North East Bay (Prospect Bay)*.
February 6. Fourth foal. €87,000Y. Arqana Deauville August. Paul Nataf. Half-sister to the fairly useful 1m (at 2 yrs) and 10f winner Strategic Mission (by Red Ransom) and to the quite useful 2-y-o 6f winner Acquiesced (by Refuse To Bend). The dam was unplaced on her only start and is a half-sister to 5 winners including the listed winner Hold To Ransom. The second dam, Wassifa (by Sure Blade), a fairly useful 11f winner here, subsequently won 3 minor races in the USA and was stakes-placed. (Mrs Sandra Bell & Tony Bloom). *"A gorgeous looking filly, she looked like being early but then grew. She's really filling out and I would say she'll be a six/seven furlong horse. When I bought her I had the Albany Stakes at Royal Ascot in mind for her. She won't be ready in time for that, but I liked her when I bought her and I'm not going to stop liking her now."*

414. SIZZLE (FR) ★★★
b.f. *Muhtathir – Lizzysue (Prospect Bay)*.
March 5. Sixth foal. €13,000Y. Arqana October. Kern/Lillingston. Half-sister to 2 minor winners in France by Sir Cat and Enrique. The dam is an unraced half-sister to 5 winners. The second dam, All For Hope (by Sensitive Prince), is an unraced half-sister to 4 winners including the Prix de Diane and Prix Saint-Alary winner Lacovia (herself the dam of Tobougg). (Chris McHale, Lawrence Bellman, Graham Newton & Partners). *"She's French bred, she's going to want a trip and she's one for the mid-summer. She's a gorgeous looking filly and I'd be surprised if she's not a seven furlong/mile winning two-year-old."*

415. SNOW LEGEND (IRE) ★★★
gr.f. *Proclamation – Royal Consort (Green Desert)*.
March 3. Second foal. 5,500Y. Tattersalls October Book 3. Not sold. The dam is an unraced half-sister to 4 winners including the Group 2 Gimcrack Stakes winner and Group 1 Middle Park Stakes second Carrowkeel. The second dam, Par Un Nez (by Cyrano de Bergerac), is an unraced half-sister to 2 winners and the Group 3 Nell Gwyn Stakes second Tetradonna. (Living Legend Racing Partnership IV). *"Her dam is by Green Desert so there's a bit of speed there, but she'll want at least six furlongs. She's had a few niggles through sore shins and growing, and my horses haven't been right, so at the moment she's just cantering. I could see her being out in late May, she has a good attitude and she does everything right. She's a bit angular and has gone a bit tall, but she's improving all the time."*

416. WATER ICE ★★★
b.f. *Shamardal – Cumulate (Gone West)*.
May 3. Seventh foal. 21,000Y. Tattersalls October 2. Kern/Lillingston. Half-sister to the useful 2-y-o 7f and Group 3 Sweet Solera Stakes second Princess Taise (by Cozzene), to the French winner of 21 races Graphic Design (by Swain) and 2 minor winners in the USA by Broad Brush and Theatrical. The dam, a fair 7f placed 2-y-o, is a half-sister to 6 winners including the US Grade 2 9f Jim Dandy Stakes winner Composer. The second dam, Honoria (by Danzig), won the Group 3 Railway Stakes, was second in the Group 1 Moyglare Stud Stakes and is a sister to two listed winners and a half-sister to 8 winners including the Irish St Leger second Father Rooney and the dam of the Group/Graded stakes winners King Ivor, Linney Head and Snake Eyes. (De La Warr Racing). *"She was a small, May foal but she's now a strong May foal and she'll win in May. Possibly not a star but she's a nice, good two-year-old filly. I'd say she's the type you could work three times a week."*

417. WOLF SLAYER ★★★♣
b.f. *Diktat – Bolsena (Red Ransom)*.
May 9. Fifth foal. 20,000Y. Tattersalls October Book 2. Blandford Bloodstock. Half-sister to the quite useful dual 1m winner Cactus Rose (by Zamindar). The dam is an unraced half-sister to 8 winners including the US Grade 3 winner De Niro and the Italian Group 3 winner Vidalia. The second dam, Waya (by Faraway Son), won four Grade 1 events in the USA and the Group 2 Prix de l'Opera and is a half-sister to the US Grade 1 winner Warfever. (Michael Owen & Andrew Black). *"A really nice little horse, she was a May foal and she's not a superstar but is capable of winning races. She'll probably be alright over five furlongs but six will more than likely suit her better."*

418. UNNAMED ★★
b.f. Striking Ambition – Angel's Camp
(Honour And Glory).
January 30. First foal. £24,000Y. Doncaster St Leger Festival. Kern/Lillingston. The dam, a moderate Irish 3-y-o 1m winner, is a half-sister to 4 winners including the US stakes winner Sirmione. The second dam, Desert Digger (by Mining), won the Grade 2 Sorrento Stakes in the USA and is a half-sister to 2 winners. (Manor House Stables LLP). *"She's not been sold and she's a difficult horse to assess. A January foal and yet not very big, but she is now starting to grow at last. We were hoping she'd be early but she's improving now and I haven't worked out what her trip will be yet. She's had a couple of niggling issues but she's back now and I think she'll be above average."*

419. UNNAMED ★★
b.c. Indesatchel – Charlie Girl
(Puissance).
January 26. Seventh foal. £30,000Y. Doncaster St Leger. Kern/Lillingston. Half-brother to the useful 2-y-o dual 6f winner and listed-placed Josh (by Josr Algharoud), the quite useful 2-y-o 6f winner Russian Reel (by Reel Buddy), the fair 5f (including at 2 yrs) and 6f winner of 7 races and listed-placed Feelin Foxy (by Foxhound) and the 2-y-o 5f seller winner Gone To Ground (both by Foxhound). The dam, a 2-y-o 5f winner, is a half-sister to 4 winners. The second dam, Charolles (by Ajdal), is a placed half-sister to 4 winners including the French dual Group 1 winner Creator. (Mrs M Findlay). *"I thought this was one of the nicest looking yearlings we bought. I haven't changed my mind except that he hasn't stopped growing and he's enormous now. He's a lovely colt and I'm assuming he'll want seven furlongs, but he could end up being faster than I'm giving him credit for because we haven't done much with him at this point. He's one to keep an eye out for."*

420. UNNAMED ★★★★
b.f. Danehill Dancer – Corrine (Spectrum).
May 9. Third foal. 48,000Y. Tattersalls October Book 2. Kern/Lillingston. Half-sister to the fairly useful Irish 1m (at 2 yrs) and 14f winner Liszt and to Marie Cuddy, placed over 7f on her only start at 2 yrs in 2009 (both by Galileo). The dam won 4 races, including a listed event, in Norway and is a half-sister to 6 winners. The second dam, La Luna (by Lyphard), a winner over 9f at 3 yrs in France, is a sister to the Group 3 Prix Daphnis and Group 3 Prix Thomas Bryon winner Bellypha and a half-sister to the Prix Eugene Adam winner Bellman and the Peruvian Grade 1 winner Run And Deliver. (Manor House Stables LLP). *"She was a May foal but I don't mind that with a filly because it enables you to give them a bit of time. She's filled out and is a different horse than two months ago so I haven't done much with her. But for a Danehill Dancer that cost 48 Grand I'd say she looks like she's worth twice that. She's really done well, she'll make a two-year-old and I would think she'd win a maiden before we try and get a bit of black type.*

421. UNNAMED ★★
b.f. Aussie Rules – Dream Genie (Puissance).
April 11. €10,000Y. Goresbridge September. G Mullins. Half-sister to the quite useful 1m and 9f winner Gaily Noble (by One Cool Cat), to the fair 7f winner Raspberry Beret (by Danehill Dancer) and the moderate 1m seller winner One Night In May (by Choisir). The dam is an unraced sister to the high-class sprinter Mind Games, winner of the Group 2 Temple Stakes (twice), the Norfolk Stakes and the Palace House Stakes and a half-sister to 4 winners. The second dam, Aryaf (by Vice Regent), is an unplaced half-sister to 6 winners including the Group 2 Tripleprint Celebration Mile third Peartree House. (Mrs M Findlay). *"We've had a few niggling issues with her, but nothing drastic. Her breeder Joe Foley recommended her and he'd be a better judge than me. I haven't been able to do much with her yet because of the issues she's had, but she's bred for speed so we'll give her the benefit of the doubt at the moment."*

422. UNNAMED ★★★
b.c. Acclamation – Eman's Joy (Lion Cavern).
April 29. Sixth foal. €27,000Y. Goffs Orby. Kern/Lillingston. Half-brother to Pleasant Way, unplaced in two starts at 2 yrs in 2009, to the 2-y-o Group 3 1m Autumn Stakes winner Blitzkrieg, the quite useful 1m and 10f winner Summer Gold (all by Barathea) and the fair 2-y-o 6f winner Toledo Gold (by Needwood

Blade).. The dam, a modest 3-y-o 6f winner, is a half-sister to 8 winners including the Group 3 Diomed Stakes winner Eton Lad. The second dam, Carolside (by Music Maestro), a very useful 2-y-o 5f winner, was second in the Cherry Hinton Stakes and is a half-sister to 6 winners. (Mrs M Findlay). *"I thought he was an absolute steal when we bought him, but when we brought him home he fell apart. It's taken about three months to build him back up, but now he's a horse and I'll start training him. One for the middle of the season."*

423. UNNAMED ★★★
b.c. One Cool Cat – Escouades (General Assembly).
April 12. Eighth foal. €30,000Y. Arqana Deauville October. Kern/Lillingston. Half-brother to the French listed-placed winner Squad (by Johann Quatz) and to 4 minor winners in France by Perugino, Orpen, Loup Solitaire and King's Theatre. The dam is a placed half-sister to 5 winners including the German Group 3 winner Saperlipoupette. The second dam, Emmanuelle (by Margouillat), won 8 minor races in France from 2 to 4 yrs and is a half-sister to 7 winners. (Manor House Stables LLP). *"All the horses by this sire have been tricky but he's not that way at all. We haven't sold him yet, but he'll probably have a run here before racing in France for the owner's premiums they have over there. He should be winning over six or seven furlongs, he'd go on soft and the all-weather at Deauville and he could pay for himself in one run."*

424. UNNAMED ★★★★
b.c. Ad Valorem – Gladstone Street (Waajib).
March 16. Ninth foal. €30,000Y. Goffs Orby. Lillingston Bloodstock. Half-brother to the 2-y-o Group 2 6f Flying Childers Stakes and listed St Hugh's Stakes winner Madame Trop Vite (by Invincible Spirit), to the quite useful Irish 7f (including at 2 yrs) and 9f winner Patrickswell (by Iron Mask), the modest 10f, 12f and hurdles winner Gardasee (by Dashing Blade) and 4 winners abroad by Nicolette, Dolphin Street, Brief Truce and Perugino. The dam, a winner over 1m at 2 yrs in Germany, is a half-sister to 7 winners. The second dam, Grafton Street (by Pentathlon), a listed-placed winner at 3 yrs in Germany, is a half-sister to 8 winners. (Gallop Bookmakers, Bellman, McCormack and Newton). *"A big, gangly two-year-old that looks like he'd need ten furlongs – but I don't think he will. He's got such a big stride on him and I think he'll be faster than he looks physically. He'll start off on a proper galloping track and I really do think he's a nice colt. I may be way off mark but I can't help but think of the Superlative Stakes for him."*

425. UNNAMED ★★★
b.c. Motivator – Holy Nola (Silver Deputy).
April 24. Seventh foal. 52,000Y. Tattersalls October Book 1. Kern/Lillingston. Half-brother to the US Group 2 and dual Group 3 winner Preachinatthebar (by Silver Charm), to the listed placed winner Nolas Lolly (by Lomitas) and the French 2-y-o 1m winner Royal Lolly (by King's Best). The dam, a stakes winner of 5 races in the USA, is a half-sister to 5 winners including the triple US Grade 3 winner Bare Necessities. The second dam, Shrewd Vixen (by Spectacular Bid), a listed-placed winner of 6 races, is a half-sister to 3 winners. (Manor House Stables LLP). *"He was a very small, weak looking horse at the Sales and I don't really know why but I just loved him. He's had plenty of time and he's not the typical horse I would buy really – but he's one of those you look at and decide to buy because there's something about him. Motivator was a Derby winner but he was a good two-year-old too and the dam won over three furlongs in America! I'm quite looking forward to him."*

426. UNNAMED ★★★
b.f. Cadeaux Genereux – Lighthouse (Warning).
March 20. Seventh foal. 200,000Y. Tattersalls October Book 1. Blandford Bloodstock. Sister to the very useful 7f and 1m winner Kehaar and to the fairly useful 2-y-o 5f winner and listed placed All For Laura (herself dam of the Group 2 Cherry Hinton Stakes winner Misheer) and half-sister to the winner Point Of Light and a minor US winner at 4 yrs by Barathea. The dam, a fairly useful 3-y-o 8.3f winner, is a half-sister to 4 winners including the Group 1 Middle Park Stakes, Group 3 July Stakes and Group 3 Richmond Stakes winner First Trump. The second dam, Valika (by Valiyar), was placed three times from 1m to 12f at 3

yrs and is a half-sister to 6 winners including the high-class sprinter Mr Brooks. (A Black & M Owen). *"She went back to the stud after the Sales and when she came here she was all gangly and hairy, so we've given her plenty of time. She's looking a different horse now and she'll definitely be aimed at the second half of the season. She'll want a trip I should imagine – probably seven furlongs, although the dam's half-sister has bred a Cherry Hinton winner. A big, scopey filly with an excellent walk to her."*

427. UNNAMED ★★★
b.f. Hurricane Run – Nasharaat
(Green Desert).
April 15. First foal. 40,000Y. Tattersalls October Book 2. Kern/Lillingston. The dam, a minor Irish 7f winner, is a half-sister to one winner. The second dam, Daqtora (by Dr Devious), a minor Irish 11f winner, is a half-sister to the 2-y-o Group 1 1m National Stakes winner Mus-If and to the very smart 1m (at 2 yrs) and 10f winner of 3 listed events Jammaal. (Manor House Stables LLP). *"She had an injury the first day we had her in the yard, but she's gorgeous and has a lovely attitude. She's only just started cantering and although there's not a lot to get excited about yet, she's one of my favourites. A seven furlong filly, there's no rush with her and if looks are anything to go by she'll be a black type filly."*

428. UNNAMED ★★★
ch.c. Compton Place – Our Sheila
(Bahamian Bounty).
February 21. First foal. £32,000Y. Doncaster St Leger. Kern/Lillingston. The dam, a fair 6f winner of 4 races at 3 yrs, is a half-sister to 4 winners including the Italian Group 3 winner Shifting Place. The second dam, Shifting Mist (by Night Shift), a modest 10f to 14f winner of 5 races, is a half-sister to 7 winners including the dam of the Group/Grade 3 winner Needwood Blade. (Manor House Stables LLP). *"A proper little racehorse, the dam won over five furlongs and he'll do the same before winning over six. He'll run regularly and he's as tough as old boots. You could say I'm not expecting him to be a Group class horse but he'll be a winner."*

429. UNNAMED ★★★
ch.c. Kyllachy – Red Ryding Hood
(Wolfhound).
March 21. Fifth foal. €20,000Y. Goffs Orby. Kern/Lillingston. Half-brother to the modest 2007 2-y-o 7f winner Belle Eponine (by Fraam) and to the fair triple 5f winner (including at 2 yrs) Baileys Outshine (by Inchinor). The dam, a quite useful 3-y-o dual 5f winner, is a half-sister to the useful 2-y-o listed 6f Sirenia Stakes winner and Group 2 6f Lowther Stakes second Arethusa. The second dam, Downeaster Alexa (by Red Ryder), won 2 races at 2 yrs over 5f, was second in the Group 3 Shernazar Curragh Stakes and is a half-sister to 3 winners. (Clive Clarke, Phil Slater and Partners). *"We thought we'd sold this colt, but the guy let us down. That's happened two or three times to me and each time the horse has turned out to be a superstar – that's just the way it works out. So were hopeful for him just on that basis! There isn't a great deal of pedigree there, but he was a nice looking Kyllachy at the Sales. A strong, good-looking horse for July onwards."*

430. UNNAMED ★★★
b.c. Numerous – Sensational Mover
(Theatrical).
April 3. Fourth foal. €48,000Y. Arqana Deauville October. Kern/Lillingston. Half-brother to the 2009 2-y-o listed 6f and 6.5f Watership Down Stud Sales Race winner Shamandar (by Exceed And Excel). The dam, a moderate 12f placed maiden, is a half-sister to 8 winners including the US listed winner Winsome. The second dam, Blushing Heiress (by Blushing John), won the Grade 2 Wilshire Handicap and the Grade 3 Palomar Handicap and is a half-sister to 4 winners including the US Grade 3 winner Really Fancy. (The Tipperary Partners). *"He's just like his dam – a Sensational Mover! The sire isn't fashionable by any stretch of the imagination but he's a really good looking horse and a half-brother to a really good filly from last year. He'll be a two-year-old alright but he'll be much better next year. I'd go as far as saying that I think we'd like to run him in a race at Deauville (not a black type race) in August before he makes up into a nice miler next year."*

431. UNNAMED ★★★
b.f. Intikhab – Tharwa (Last Tycoon).
May 14. Seventh foal. £20,000Y. Doncaster St Leger Festival. Kern/Lillingston. Half-sister to the useful 5f and 6f winner of 5 races Enchantment (by Compton Place), to the quite useful 6f and 7f winner Nisr (by Grand Lodge), the modest dual 5f winner Minnow (by Averti) and the modest 7f and 1m winner Taiyo (by Tagula). The dam, a modest 5.2f and 6f winner, is a half-sister to 8 winners including the French listed winner Blushing All Over and good broodmare Come On Rosi (the dam of 4 stakes winners). The second dam, Victory Kingdom (by Vice Regal), was a stakes-placed winner of 5 races in the USA. (Manor House Stables LLP). "An unsold filly and although Intikhab's aren't fashionable, they win races. She was a late foal, broken in, got going, cantered, given a break and she grew three inches. She's starting back now, has a great attitude and she's a nice filly with speed."

ANN DUFFIELD

432. ALASKAN SPIRIT ★★
b.c. Kodiac – Alexander Phantom (Soviet Star).
March 5. Second foal. €18,000Y. Goffs Orby. Ann Duffield. Half-brother to the quite useful 2009 6f placed 2-y-o Ghost (by Invincible Spirit). The dam is an unraced half-sister to 3 minor winners. The second dam, Phantom Waters (by Pharly), won twice at 3 yrs and is a half-sister to 9 winners including the Group 3 Solario Stakes winner Shining Water (herself dam of the Grand Criterium and Dante Stakes winner Tenby). "He goes really well and he should be out at the end of May, possibly over five furlongs because he's got pace but I think he'll stay a bit further. A great-moving horse that does everything naturally."

433. BETTER SELF ★★
b.f. With Approval – Alter Ego (Alzao).
March 20. Half-sister to Chilean Fizz (by Domedriver), placed fourth once over 5f at 2 yrs in 2009. The dam, a quite useful 2-y-o 7f winner, was listed-placed over 9f at 2 yrs in Germany and is a half-sister to several winners. The second dam, Kirsten (by Kris), won over 12f and is a half-sister to the high-class colt Petoski. (Miss K Rausing). "She's going to be a mid-season two-year-old and she gets up our stiff gallop very easily. A lovely mover with a good attitude. Seven furlongs should suit."

434. INDIESLAD ★★★
b.c. Indesatchel – Sontime (Son Pardo).
February 22. Fifth foal. £24,000Y. Doncaster St Leger. Mrs A Duffield. Half-brother to the 2-y-o 5f winner Auction Time and the 3-y-o 6f winner Somni (both by Auction House) – both moderate. The dam, a fair 5f and 6f winner at 2 yrs, is a half-sister to one winner. The second dam, Fact Of Time (by Known Fact), is an unraced half-sister to 3 minor winners. (Mr T Wilson). "A compact, racy, athletic horse with a good temperament. I think the sire is going to be successful and we're looking forward to seeing this colt. He's got pace but he's probably going to be better suited by six furlongs than five."

435. JANET'S PEARL (IRE) ★★
ch.f. Refuse To Bend – Sassari (Darshaan).
April 28. Third foal. 3,000Y. Tattersalls October Book 2. Not sold. Half-sister to the quite useful 2009 2-y-o 6f winner Chicago Cop (by Fasliyev). The dam, a fair 10f placed maiden, is a half-sister to 3 winners. The second dam, Alwiyda (by Trempolino), won once at 3 yrs in France and is a half-sister to 6 winners. (Middleham Park Racing XL). "She's strengthened up a lot over the winter because she was small as a yearling but she's done well. A good moving filly and very willing and she's got a bit of pace despite the middle-distance pedigree, but she'll probably want seven furlongs this year."

436. RIVERDALE (IRE) ★★★
ch.c. Choisir – Hollow Haze (Woodman).
March 13. Eighth foal. £8,000Y. Doncaster St Leger. Ann Duffield. Half-brother to the fair 7f to 9f winner Ella Woodcock (by Daggers Drawn), to the moderate triple 5f winner (including at 2 yrs) Handsinthemist (by Lend A Hand) and 4 winners abroad by Singspiel, Southern Halo, Dayjur and Mujadil. The dam, a fair 8.5f all-weather winner, is a half-sister to 2 minor winners. The second dam, Libeccio (by Danzatore), is an unraced daughter of the US stakes winner Windy Triple K (by Jaklin

Klugman), herself a half-sister to the top-class colt Generous. (James Warrender & Mrs Elaine Culf). *"A very tall colt, he's not going to be early but he's a big, strapping colt and a good mover with a good attitude. He'll make a two-year-old late on this season."*

437. SMART VIOLETTA (IRE) ★★
b.br.f. Smart Strike – Dubai Diamond (Octagonal).
April 4. Fourth foal. 19,000Y. Tattersalls October Book 2. Not sold. Half-sister to the fair 10f and 12f winner Bavarian Nordic (by Barathea). The dam, a French 7f placed maiden, is a half-sister to numerous winners including Riviera, a listed-placed winner of 4 races in France and the USA. The second dam, Manureva (by Nureyev), won the listed 1m Prix des Tuilleries at Longchamp and is a half-sister to numerous winners including the Prix Marcel Boussac winner Macoumba, the Prix de la Foret winner Septieme Ciel and the dual US Grade 3 winner Maxigroom. (Six Iron Partnership). *"A lovely filly, I like her a lot and she's by a very good stallion but she won't be ready to run until the second half of the season. A great mover with a good attitude, she's doing nothing wrong but she's a bit immature at the moment. One for the back-end of the season and more of a three-year-old type."*

438. SOVEREIGN STREET ★★★
ch.f. Compton Place – Mint Royale (Cadeaux Genereux).
April 28. Fourth foal. Half-sister to the useful 2-y-o 5f winner and Group 3 6f Sirenia Stakes second La Neige (by Royal Applause), to the fairly useful 2009 2-y-o dual 7f winner Spying (by Observatory) and the fair 5f to 8.5f 3-y-o winner of 3 races Ten Shun (by Pivotal). The dam is an unplaced sister to the very smart Group 1 6f Prix Morny and Group 1 6f Middle Park Stakes winner and sire Bahamian Bounty and a half-sister to 2 winners. The second dam, Clarentia (by Ballad Rock), a very useful winner of 5 races at up to 6f, was third in the Group 3 Cornwallis Stakes. (The Duchess of Sutherland). *"She's very backward and weak at present so we're not doing a lot with her yet, but she's easier to train than her half-brother Spying who won for us last year. One for the back-end of the season."*

439. TAHITIAN PRINCESS (IRE) ★★★
b.f. One Cool Cat – Akarita (Akarad).
January 29. Sixth foal. 7,000Y. Tattersalls October 2. Ann Duffield. Half-sister to the quite useful Irish 6f winner Scarsdale (by Polar Falcon) and to the moderate Irish 7f winner Soviet Trooper (by Soviet Lad). The dam won over 7.5f at 3 yrs and was listed placed twice. She is a half-sister to 9 winners including the useful 2-y-o 5f winner and Group 3 third Safka (herself dam of the listed winner Speedfit Too), the Group 2 7f Lockinge Stakes winner Safawan and the dam of the Group 2 12f Prix Hocquart winner Sayarshan. The second dam, Safita (by Habitat), won the listed 1m Prix de la Calonne and was second in the French 1,000 Guineas and the Prix Saint-Alary. (David & Carole McMahon). *"She's nice, she's going very well and isn't far off a run. She'll be better over six furlongs and might stay seven. A very nice filly and she's doing everything right."*

440. TOM BOWLER ★★★
b.c. Marju – Tembladora (Docksider).
February 3. First foal. £7,000Y. Doncaster St Leger. Ann Duffield. The dam, placed once at 3 yrs, is a sister to the UAE listed winner and US Grade 2 placed Clinet and a half-sister to 3 winners. The second dam, Oiche Mhaith (by Night Shift), won once at 3 yrs and is a half-sister to 7 winners. (The Lucky Dip Syndicate). *"He was cheap for a Marju, maybe because he looked very small at the Sales, but he's grown a lot during the winter, he's very cheeky, has a really good temperament, is strong-bodied and he goes quite well. We'll probably start him off at seven furlongs, maybe six."* TRAINERS' BARGAIN BUY

441. ZENELLA ★★★★♠
b.f. Kyllachy – West One (Gone West).
March 16. Fifth foal. €26,000Y. Goffs Orby. Ann Duffield. Half-sister to the modest all-weather 7f and 9f winner of 7 races Hoh Wotanite (by Stravinsky) and to the Italian winner of 3 races West Act (by Act One). The dam ran twice unplaced and is closely related to the US stakes-placed winner Go Baby Go. The second dam, Bequest (by Sharpen Up), a very useful 2-y-o 6f winner here, subsequently won the Grade 1 10f Santa Barbara Handicap and is a half-sister to 4 winners. (H Findlay). *"A

very nice filly, she'll make a two-year-old, she's got natural speed but needs a bit more time. One for the middle of the season."

442. UNNAMED ★★
b.f. Araafa – Puzzling (Peintre Celebre).
March 26. First foal. 4,000Y. Tattersalls December. Ann Duffield. The dam is an unraced half-sister to several winners including the useful listed 10.5f winner Double Crossed (herself dam of the high-class colt Twice Over) and the dam of the 2-y-o Group 1 winner Passage Of Time. The second dam, Quandary (by Blushing Groom), a useful winner of 4 races from 9f to 10f including the listed James Seymour Stakes at Newmarket, is a half-sister to 8 winners including the Group 1 Prix du Moulin winner All At Sea. *"We haven't done a lot with her but the way she's turned herself inside out over the last two months is extraordinary. A lovely moving filly."*

ED DUNLOP

443. ANA EMARATI (USA) ★★
b.c. Forestry – Triple Edition (Lear Fan).
February 27. First foal. $70,000Y. Keeneland September. Blandford Bloodstock. The dam, placed at 2 yrs in France, is a sister to the winner and listed-placed Starfan and a half-sister to the Group 1 Prix de la Foret winner Etoile Montante. The second dam, Willstar (by Nureyev), a minor French 3-y-o winner, is a sister to the listed winner Viviana (herself dam of the Grade 1 winners Sightseek and Tates Creek) and a half-sister to US Grade 2 winner Revasser. (Ahmad & Abdulla Al Shaikh). *"A scopey colt with a good temperament, he goes OK but is a bit lazy. One for the latter part of the season."*

444. APPAREL (IRE) ★★★
b.f. Cape Cross – Independence (Selkirk).
April 12. Sixth foal. Half-sister to the Group 1 1m Criterium International and Group 1 Eclipse Stakes winner Mount Nelson (by Rock Of Gibraltar), to the Group 2 12f Great Voltigeur Stakes winner Monitor Closely (by Oasis Dream), the quite useful 1m winner Stone Of Scone (by Pivotal) and the quite useful 9.5f winner Off Message (by In The Wings). The dam won four races at 3 yrs from 7f to 1m including the Group 2 Sun Chariot Stakes and the Group 3 Matron Stakes and is a half-sister to one winner. The second dam, Yukon Hope (by Forty Niner), a fair maiden, is out of a half-sister to Reference Point. (Cliveden Stud Ltd). *"Not here yet, but she's nice. Most of the family are later-developers and although this filly isn't huge she's grown a lot. One for the second half of the season."*

445. CANADA FLEET (CAN) ★★★
gr.c. Afleet Alex – Marieval (El Prado).
March 23. First foal. $150,000Y. Keeneland September. Bluehills Racing Ltd. The dam won minor races at 3 and 4 yrs and is a half-sister to 3 winners including the Grade 1 Preakness Stakes third Icabad Crane. The second dam, Adorahy (by Rahy), a minor US 3-y-o winner, is a half-sister to the US Grade 3 winner Adcat and two Grade 2 placed winners. (Bluehills Racing Ltd). *"A good-looking colt, he moves very well and is a racy, good-moving type. Probably a six furlong horse, he's done some work and so far he's OK."*

446. CRAFTY ROBERTO ★★★
ch.c. Intikhab – Mowazana (Galileo).
February 5. First foal. £25,000Y. Doncaster St Leger. Angie Sykes. The dam, a fair 10.2f winner, is a half-brother to 5 winners including the useful 2-y-o 6f winner Shohrah and the useful 7f winner and 1m listed second Ma-Arif. The second dam, Taqreem (by Nashwan), was second four times over middle-distances and is a half-sister to Ibn Bey (a winner of 4 Group 1 events including the Irish St Leger and second in the Breeders Cup Classic) and to the very smart Group 1 Yorkshire Oaks winner and smart broodmare Roseate Tern. (Mrs M Findley). *"He's nice, he was quite tall and leggy to start with but he's filled out and strengthened up. He has a good temperament, moves well and I should think he'll be a six/seven furlong horse in mid-season. Not a backward horse, he looks OK so far."*

447. ERAADAAT (IRE) ★★★
ch.f. Intikhab – Ta Rib (Mr Prospector).
February 19. Half-sister to the fairly useful 7f and 1m winner Fajr, to the quite useful dual 6f winner Estihlal (both by Green Desert), the fairly useful 11f winner Mawaheb (by Nashwan), the quite useful 3-y-o 7f winner and listed 1m third Khaizarana (by Alhaarth)

and the quite useful triple 1m winner Kabeer (by Unfuwain). The dam, a smart winner of the French 1,000 Guineas and second in the 1m Falmouth Stakes, is a half-sister to several winners including the useful 2-y-o listed 6f winner Tabdea. The second dam, Madame Secretary (by Secretariat), won 2 races in America at around 1m including a minor stakes and is a half-sister to 4 winners including the Stewards Cup winner Green Ruby. (Hamdan Al Maktoum). "Much more precocious and racy than anything I've had out of the mare – they've all been enormous. She was a bit scatty to start with but she's settled down well and although she hasn't done much fast work yet she has a nice shape about her. So far so good."

448. GOLD PENDANT (USA) ★★★★
b.f. Medaglia d'Oro – Forty Carats (Forty Niner).
April 24. Eighth foal. $90,000Y. Keeneland September. Bluehills Racing Ltd. Half-sister to 2 winners including the minor US winner Forestlee (by Forestry). The dam is an unraced half-sister to 2 winners including the US Grade 3 winner Minister's Melody (herself dam of the US Grade 1 winner Bob And John). The second dam, My Song For You (by Seattle Song), a US stakes-placed winner, is a half-sister to the US champion 2-y-o and dual Grade 1 winner Capote. (Bluehills Racing Ltd). "A pretty filly, she'll probably need some time but she has a very attractive head and is a good mover with a good temperament. She looks nice."

449. HAYLAMAN (IRE) ★★★
b.c. Diamond Green – Schonbein (Persian Heights).
February 1. 14,000Y. Tattersalls October Book 2. Ed Dunlop. Half-brother to the useful 7.9f (at 2 yrs) to 10f winner of 7 races and subsequent jumps winner Football Crazy (by Mujadil), to the fairly useful Irish 5f, 6f (both at 2 yrs) and 9f winner Warrimoo (by Flying Spur), the fair 6f winner Man Crazy (by Foxhound) and the modest 7f all-weather (at 2 yrs) and 10f winner Finn McCool (by Blues Traveller). The dam is a placed half-sister to 6 winners including the Group 1 Heinz 57 Phoenix Stakes winner Bradawn Breever. The second dam, Ozone by Auction Ring), won 4 races in Ireland at 2 and 3 yrs and is a half-sister to 8 winners. (Ahmad & Abdulla Al Shaikh). "A strong, powerful horse, I loved the Diamond Greens at the Sales and this is a good goer."

450. HEAVEN KNOWS WHY ★★
b.f. Pivotal – Red Heaven (Benny The Dip).
January 30. Second foal. The dam, unplaced in one start, is a half-sister to the US triple Grade 1 winner in the USA Megahertz and to the dual Group 3 9f winner Heaven Sent (both by Pivotal). The second dam, Heavenly Ray (by Rahy), a fairly useful 7f and 1m winner, is a half-sister to 3 winners. (Cheveley Park Stud Ltd). "A big, backward filly, she's turned out at the moment and won't be racing until the back-end of the season."

451. ILLANDRANE (IRE) ★★★★
b.f. Cape Cross – Lalindi (Cadeaux Genereux).
January 9. Sixth foal. 50,000Y. Tattersalls October 1. Not sold. Half-sister to the Group 3 7f Craven Stakes winner Adagio (by Grand Lodge) and to the 9.5f (at 2 yrs) and Grade 2 La Prevoyante Handicap winner and Group 1 10f Prix Saint-Alary third Arvada (by Hernando). The dam, a fair middle-distance winner of 7 races, is a half-sister to 5 winners including the useful 2-y-o winner Sumoto (herself dam of the Group 1 winners Summoner and Compton Admiral). The second dam, Soemba (by General Assembly), a quite useful 9f winner, is a half-sister to 4 minor winners here and abroad. "A very nice filly with a good temperament, she's strong, scopey, moves well and looks to have some speed. Nice."

452. INCITEMENT ★★
b.c. Motivator – Dardshi (Darshaan).
April 23. Sixth foal. 80,000Y. Tattersalls October Book 2. John Warren. Half-brother to 2 minor winners abroad by Barathea. The dam is an unraced half-sister to one winner. The second dam, Ozette (by Dancing Brave), won 4 races including the listed Mooresbridge Stakes and is a half-sister to 6 winners including Takfa Yahmed (Group 2 Prix Dollar). (Highclere Thoroughbred Racing, Bahram). "A nice colt, but he's had a problem and has gone home. Up to that point he'd done well but he was always going to be one for the latter part of the year,

given his breeding. A good mover with a good temperament, he's nice but probably won't be back in training until May."

453. MABSAM ★★★
b.f. Green Desert – Week End (Selkirk).
January 22. First foal. £50,000Y. Doncaster St Leger. Shadwell Estate Co. The dam is an unraced daughter of the Group 2 Pretty Polly Stakes winner Tarfshi (by Mtoto), herself a half-sister to 5 winners including the Group 1 Cheveley Park Stakes winner Embassy. (Hamdan Al Maktoum). *"A good-looking filly, she looks racy but she won't be that early. Probably a six/seven furlong filly, she has a good action and doesn't cause me any problems. Looks well and I'm pleased so far."*

454. MUHANDIS (IRE) ★★★
b.c. Muhtathir – Ahdaaf (by Bahri).
March 15. Second foal. Half-brother to the modest 2009 2-y-o 6f winner Athwaab (by Cadeaux Genereux). The dam, a quite useful 7f winner, is a half-sister to 2 winners. The second dam, Ashrakaat (by Danzig), a very useful 6f and 7f listed winner, is a sister to the July Cup winner Elnadim and is closely related to the Irish 1,000 Guineas winner Mehthaaf. (Hamdan Al Maktoum). *"Still in Dubai but I've seen him and he's very nice. A scopey, good-looking horse but obviously he won't be ready until later in the season as he's not here yet."*

455. MUNAASEB ★★★
ch.c. Zafeen – Miss Prim (Case Law).
March 16. Third foal. 70,000Y. Tattersalls October Book 1. Shadwell Estate Co. Half-brother to the unplaced 2009 2-y-o Sydney Bridge (by Danbird) and to the Group 3 5f Cornwallis Stakes (at 2 yrs) and Group 3 5f Palace House Stakes winner Amour Propre (by Paris House). The dam is an unplaced half-sister to 3 winners including the listed winner and Group 3 placed Corrybrough. The second dam, Calamanco (by Clantime), won 2 races at 3 and 4 yrs and is a sister to the dam of the Group 1 Golden Jubilee Stakes winner Cape Of Good Hope. (Hamdan Al Maktoum). *"He grew enormously after coming here and was sent back to the stud. He's done well for that and he'll obviously be a sprinter but I'm not convinced how precocious he'll be."*

456. MUSHARAKAAT (IRE) ★★★★♠
b.f. Iffraaj – Gift Of Spring (Gilded Time).
April 11. Third foal. 70,000Y. Tattersalls October Book 1. Shadwell Estate Co. Half-sister to the fair 2009 7f placed 2-y-o Key Art and to the quite useful 5f (at 2 yrs) and 6f winner Vegas Baby (both by Kheleyf). The dam, placed at 3 yrs in France, is a half-sister to 6 winners including the listed-placed and smart broodmare Witch Of Fife (the dam of 3 stakes winners). The second dam, Fife (by Lomond), a winner at 3 yrs and third in the listed Lupe Stakes, is a half-sister to 5 winners including the dam of the Prix Vermeille winner Pearly Shells. (Hamdan Al Maktoum). *"Nice. She's a very good-looking filly with scope, size and a good temperament. Goes nicely and we'll probably wait for the six furlong races."*

457. ONE FLAG PLEASE ★★★
b.c. Hurricane Run – Teller (Southern Halo).
April 24. Seventh foal. 35,000Y. Tattersalls October Book 1. Not sold. Closely related to a winner in Greece by Montjeu and half-brother to the quite useful 5f winner of 6 races at 2 and 5 yrs Argentine (by Fasliyev), the fair triple 5f winner Corton Charlemagne (by King Charlemagne) and 2 winners in South Africa by Spaceship and Gold Press. The dam, a dual winner in South Africa, is a full or half-sister to 4 winners including the high-class Argentinian sprinter Teologa. The second dam, Teodelina (by Logical), won 3 races in Argentina and is a half-sister to 4 winners. (Mrs M Findlay). *"A very good-looking horse, he moves very well. He'll be a seven furlong two-year-old and is a bit behind the others because obviously he's going to need a bit of time."*

458. PALM PILOT (IRE) ★★★
b.f. Oasis Dream – Off Message (In The Wings).
April 8. First foal. The dam, a quite useful 9.5f winner, is a half-sister to 3 winners including the Group 1 1m Criterium International and Group 1 Eclipse Stakes winner Mount Nelson and the Group 2 Great Voltigeur winner Monitor Closely (by Oasis Dream). The second dam, Independence (by Selkirk), won four races at 3 yrs from 7f to 1m including the Group 2 Sun Chariot Stakes and the Group 3 Matron Stakes and is a half-sister to one winner. (Cliveden

Stud Ltd). *"The dam needed some time, but this filly is a lot finer than anything that came out of the second dam, Independence. I think she'll be a mid-season two-year-old and she's a good-looking, racy filly. A bit of a mixture on pedigree, but she moves well."*

459. RED LOVER ★★★★♠
b.c. Azamour – Love Me Tender (Green Desert).
January 31. Second foal. 45,000Y. Tattersalls October Book 2. Charlie Gordon-Watson. The dam, a fair 3-y-o dual 7f placed maiden, is a half-sister to 2 winners. The second dam, Easy To Love (by Diesis), a quite useful 4-y-o 11.5f winner, is a half-sister to numerous winners including the high-class Group 1 12f Oaks and listed Lupe Stakes winner Love Divine, the listed 12f winner Floreeda and the French 12f winner and listed-placed Laurentine. (Mr R J Arculli). *"Bred by Willie Carson, this is a very nice horse, he's strong, looks to have a good attitude, moves well and has quite a lot of speed. I like this colt – he's nice."*

460. SADAFIYA ★★★★
b.f. Oasis Dream – Nidhaal (Observatory).
February 3. First foal. The dam, a very useful 2-y-o listed 6f winner and second in the Group 3 6f Princess Margaret Stakes, is a half-sister to 2 winners. The second dam, Jeed (by Mujtahid), a quite useful 2-y-o 6f winner, is a half-sister to 2 winners. (Hamdan Al Maktoum). *"The dam was small and won a listed race for us. This filly is small, racy and neat. She'll be early and is an active, powerful two-year-old."*

461. TAMAREEN (IRE) ★★★★
b.c. Bahamian Bounty – Damjanich (Mull Of Kintyre).
February 12. First foal. £60,000Y. Doncaster St Leger. Shadwell Estate Co. The dam, a modest 2-y-o 6f winner, is a half-sister to one winner. The second dam, Lions Den (by Desert Style), a modest Irish 6.5f winner, is a half-sister to 4 other minor winners. (Hamdan Al Maktoum). *"He looks OK, goes well and is doing some faster work now. Neat, racy and sound, he does everything well so far. We might start him over five furlongs and he's a good-looking horse that looks to go quite well."*

462. TANFEETH ★★★
ch.c. Singspiel – Nasij (Elusive Quality).
April 15. Fourth foal. Half-brother to the fair 2-y-o 1m winner Rezwaan (by Alhaarth). The dam, a useful 6f (at 2 yrs) and listed 1m winner, was Group 3 placed twice and is a half-sister to 3 winners. The second dam, Hachiyah (by Generous), a fairly useful 10f winner, is closely related to the Italian Derby third Mutawwaj and a half-sister to the Peruvian champion Faaz. (Hamdan Al Maktoum). *"A very nice horse but one for the back-end of the season and next year."*

463. TIME FOR APPLAUSE ★★★
b.f. Royal Applause – Spitting Image (Spectrum).
February 10. Second foal. 13,000Y. Tattersalls October Book 2. Rabbah Bloodstock. The dam, a modest 2m winner of 6 races, is a half-sister to 4 winners. The second dam, Decrescendo (by Polish Precedent), is a half-sister to 3 winners including Calando (Group 3 May Hill Stakes). *"A small, racy, strong filly. I like her, she goes OK and is certainly worth including in your list."*

464. VOODOO PRINCE ★★★★
b.c. Kingmambo – Ouija Board (Cape Cross).
February 9. First foal. The dam was a top-class winner of 10 races from 7f (at 2 yrs) to 12f including seven Group/Grade 1 races and is a half-sister to 6 winners. The second dam, Selection Board (by Welsh Pageant), was placed over 7f at 2 yrs and is a sister to the top-class Queen Elizabeth II Stakes and Budweiser Arlington Million winner Teleprompter. (The Earl of Derby). *"He's done very well physically and although he's not going to be early he's a lot more like Kingmambo than Ouija Board. He finds life easy so far and although we haven't pushed any buttons so far he's likely to start off at seven furlongs in mid-season."*

465. WIQAAYA (IRE) ★★★
gr.f. Red Ransom – Masaader (Wild Again).
March 21. Third foal. Half-sister to the fair 2009 6f placed 2-y-o Almadaa (by Exceed And Excel). The dam, a fairly useful dual 6f winner (including at 2 yrs), is a half-sister to the smart 2-y-o Group 1 6f Middle Park Stakes winner Hayil and the useful 2-y-o winners Mizhar, Farqad and Elnahaar. The second dam, Futuh

(by Diesis), a fairly useful 2-y-o 6f winner, is a half-sister to the Canadian Selene Stakes winner Rose Park (herself the dam of the smart US Grade 2 winner Wild Rush). (Hamdan Al Maktoum). *"She's in Dubai and I liked her particularly when I saw her over there. She looks racy, the mother was fast and although I don't know much about her she's definitely well-thought of."*

466. YA HAFED ★★★
ch.c. Haafhd – Rule Britannia (Night Shift).
February 18. 3,000Y. Tattersalls October Book 2. Ed Dunlop. Half-brother to a bumper winner by Indian Danehill. The dam, a quite useful 10f and 12f winner, is a half-sister to 5 winners here and abroad. The second dam, Broken Wave (by Bustino), won 5 races including two listed events in France and is a half-sister to 6 winners. (Ahmad & Abdulla Al Shaikh). *"A strong, powerful horse and it wouldn't surprise me if he was relatively early. Goes OK."* TRAINERS' BARGAIN BUY

467. ZAFARANA ★★
b.f. Tiger Hill – Miss Meltemi (Miswaki Tern).
April 3. Sixth foal. 45,000Y. Tattersalls October Book 1. Rabbah Bloodstock. Sister to the very useful 7f (at 2 yrs) and listed 1m winner and Group 3 Dahlia Stakes third Don't Dili Dali, to the fairly useful 1m winner Ada River (both by Dansili), the quite useful 2-y-o 5f winner Haigh Hall (by Kyllachy) and the fair 7f to 8.7f winner Willie Ever (by Agnes World). The dam, a 7f and 1m 2-y-o winner in Italy, was third in the Group 1 Italian Oaks and is a half-sister to 2 winners. The second dam, Blu Meltemi (by Star Shareef), won 5 races at 2 and 3 yrs and was second in the Italian Oaks. (Mr M Al Suboosi). *"A nice filly but she's backward at the stage, as you'd expect from a Tiger Hill."*

468. ZARAFSHAN (IRE) ★★
b.c. Halling – Gipsy Moth (Efisio).
March 16. Seventh foal. 50,000Y. Tattersalls October 1. Rabbah Bloodstock. Brother to the quite useful 7f winner Fly Free and to the minor winner abroad Gipsy Hall and half-brother to the quite useful 2009 2-y-o 6f and 7f winner Leviathan (by Dubawi), the smart Group 3 12f Glorious Stakes winner of 8 races Illustrious Blue (by Dansili), the useful listed 6f winner of 5 races Mullein (by Oasis Dream) and the quite useful 5f (including at 2 yrs) and 6f winner of 8 races Romany Nights (by Night Shift). The dam, a quite useful dual 5f winner at 2 yrs, subsequently won a listed event in Germany and is a half-sister to 4 winners including the useful listed 1m winner and Group 2 Falmouth Stakes second Heavenly Whisper. The second dam, Rock The Boat (by Slip Anchor), a modest 6f (at 2 yrs) and 1m placed maiden, is a half-sister to 9 winners including the 1,000 Guineas second Kerrera and the high-class multiple Group winner Rock City. (Mr Mohammed Sultan). *"A nice horse, but he's immature and will need time."*

469. UNNAMED ★★★★
ch.c. Dubawi – Clear Impression (Danehill).
April 30. Second foal. 57,000Y. Tattersalls October Book 1. Rabbah Bloodstock. The dam, a fairly useful 3-y-o 6f winner, was listed-placed 3 times and is a half-sister to one winner. The second dam, Shining Hour (by Red Ransom), won the Group 3 5f Queen Mary Stakes and is a full or half-sister to 6 winners. (Mrs S Ali). *"A strong, powerful, racy colt and a six furlong type, he'll certainly do a job. He's out of a Danehill mare so there's a lot of strength about him. He has a very good attitude and is workmanlike in what he does but is one of those that will probably keep improving. So far so good."*

470. UNNAMED ★★★
ch.f. Shamardal – Ekleel (Danehill).
April 3. First foal. The dam is an unraced half-sister to the high-class Group 1 7f Prix de la Salamandre and Group 1 1m Sussex Stakes winner Aljabr, to the useful 10f winner Jabaarto and the useful French 2-y-o winner Makaarem. The second dam, Sierra Madre (by Baillamont), a very smart winner of the Group 1 1m Prix Marcel Boussac and the Group 1 12f Prix Vermeille, is a half-sister to several minor winners. (Hamdan Al Maktoum). *"In Dubai until mid-April, but I've seen her and she's a nice, racy filly. Strong and powerful – she could be nice."*

471. UNNAMED ★★
b.f. Alhaarth – Hachiyah (Generous).
March 29. Half-sister to the quite useful 10f

winner Adraaj (by Sahm), to the useful 6f (at 2 yrs) and listed 1m winner and dual Group 3 third Nasij (by Elusive Quality), the quite useful 10f and 14f winner Madaarek (by Kingmambo), the UAE 10f and 11f winner Musaayer (by Erhaab) and the fair 12f winner Turjuman (by Swain). The dam, a fairly useful 10f winner, is closely related to the Italian Derby third Mutawwaj and a half-sister to the Peruvian champion Faaz. The second dam, Charmie Carmie (by Lyphard), is a placed half-sister to numerous winners including the triple Grade 1 winner Chris Evert (the grandam of Chief's Crown) and All Rainbows (dam of the Kentucky Derby winner Winning Colors). (Hamdan Al Maktoum). *"In Dubai, she'll need more time, which is typical of the mare."*

472. UNNAMED ★★★
b.f. Encosta De Lago – Model Queen (Kingmambo).
March 18. Sixth foal. 280,000Y. Tattersalls October Book 1. Hugo Lascelles. Half-sister to the fairly useful 2009 2-y-o 1m winner Hot Prospect (by Motivator), to the Group 1 6f Haydock Sprint Cup and listed 7f winner Regal Parade (by Pivotal), the useful French 11f and 12f winner and Group 2 Prix Noailles fourth Mount Helicon (by Montjeu) and the minor French 10f winner Sister Sylvia (by Fantastic Light). The dam, a fair 3-y-o 7f winner, is a half-sister to 5 winners including the French listed 1m winner Arabride. The second dam, Model Bride (by Blushing Groom), is an unraced half-sister to 6 winners including the smart Queen Elizabeth II Stakes third Zaizafon (herself the dam of Zafonic and Zamindar) and to the unraced Modena (the dam of Elmaamul and Reams Of Verse). (St Albans Bloodstock LLP). *"A beautiful, beautiful filly. We paid a lot for her and she's backward – as you'd expect from the pedigree. She's only just being broken-in, so clearly she'll be a back-end of the season type."*

473. UNNAMED ★★★
b.c. Cape Cross – Polly Perkins (Pivotal).
March 15. Second foal. 40,000Y. Tattersalls October Book 1. Rabbah Bloodstock. The dam, a useful 2-y-o dual listed 5f winner, is a half-sister to 2 winners. The second dam, Prospering (by Prince Sabo), a moderate 7f winner at 3 yrs, is a half-sister to 6 winners. (Mr M Al Suboosi). *"He's small like his mother and he's tough. I love him – not for any reason other than he's a real tough little horse. I think he'll be a six furlong colt to start with and then we'll step him up in trip. He has a good temperament and there's speed in the pedigree."*

474. UNNAMED ★★
b.br.f. Kingmambo – Saree (Barathea).
February 2. Second foal. Half-sister to the quite useful 2-y-o 7f winner North East Corner (by Giant's Causeway). The dam, a fairly useful 2-y-o 7f winner, subsequently won once at 3 yrs in the USA and was Grade 3 placed in Canada and is a sister to the 2-y-o Group 1 6f Cheveley Park Stakes winner Magical Romance and a half-sister to the high-class 1m (at 2 yrs), Oaks, Irish Oaks And Yorkshire Oaks winner Alexandrova). The second dam, Shouk (by Shirley Heights), a quite useful 10.5f winner, is closely related to the listed winner and Group 3 Park Hill Stakes third Puce and a half-sister to 7 winners. (Ballygallon Stud Ltd). *"Not here yet, she's backward and still at stud in Ireland."*

475. UNNAMED ★★★
b.f. Dubawi – Sea Angel (Nashwan).
February 12. Second foal. 10,000Y. Tattersalls October Book 1. Not sold. Half-sister to the fair 2009 1m placed 2-y-o Inner Angel (by Motivator). The dam won 2 minor races at 3 yrs in France including over 12f and is a full or half-sister to 5 winners. The second dam, Nadma (by Northern Dancer), a fair 10f winner, is closely related to the dual US Grade 1 winning filly Sabin and a half-sister to the Musidora Stakes winner Fatah Flare. *"Tall and scopey, she's not going to be early but she's a nice filly and a very good mover. She wasn't expensive for a Book 1 filly with a pedigree."*

476. UNNAMED ★★★
b.f. Bertolini – Seed Al Maha (Seeking The Gold).
April 4. Third foal. The dam is an unraced half-sister to one winner. The second dam, Fairy Queen (by Fairy King), won 5 races including the Group 2 12f Ribblesdale Stakes and the Group 2 12.5f Prix de la Royallieu and is a half-sister to the smart Group 2 1m Falmouth

Stakes winner Tashawak. (M Jaber). *"She looks quite racy and she's done a bit of faster work. She may have just grown slightly but she looks to have some speed and we'll probably start her over six furlongs. So far, no problem."*

477. UNNAMED ★★★
b.f. Cape Cross – Sister Sylvia (Fantastic Light).
February 5. First foal. 50,000Y. Tattersalls December. Berri Schroder. The dam, a minor French 10f winner, is a half-sister to 3 winners including the Group 1 6f Haydock Park Sprint Cup winner Regal Parade. The second dam, Model Queen (by Kingmambo), a fair 3-y-o 7f winner, is a half-sister to 5 winners including the French listed 1m winner Arabride. (Mr Berri Schroder & Partners). *"A neat, racy filly but the pedigree doesn't shout speed. She had a few little niggles to start with but she's come on and I like her so far. Small and strong, I think she'll probably be a six/seven furlong filly."*

478. UNNAMED ★★★♣
ch.c. Ivan Denisovitch – Top Of The Form (Masterclass).
April 27. 10,000Y. Tattersalls October Book 3. Blandford Bloodstock. Closely related to the quite useful 7f winner Flying Goose (by Danehill Dancer) and half-brother to the fair 6f to 1m winner of 8 races Glencalvie (by Grand Lodge) and the fair 2-y-o 6f winner Top Form (by Almutawakel). The dam, a fair 5f (at 2 yrs) and 6f winner of 4 races, is a half-sister to 3 winners including the useful sprinter and listed winner of 6 races Double Quick. The second dam, Haraabah (by Topsider), a useful 5f to 7f winner, is a half-sister to 3 winners. (Byculla Thoroughbreds). *"Small and racy, she hasn't been in long but she looks OK for a cheap filly and she'll fit in auction races."*

479. UNNAMED ★★★★
b.f. Shamardal – Wimple (Kingmambo).
February 3. Fourth foal. 120,000Y. Tattersalls October Book 1. Hugo Lascelles. Half-sister to the quite useful 2-y-o 6f winner Master Rooney (by Cape Cross) and a winner in Russia by Daylami. The dam, a useful 5f and 6f winner at 2 yrs, was listed-placed and is a half-sister to 2 winners. The second dam, Tunicle (by Dixieland Band), won 4 minor races in the USA and is a half-sister to 5 winners.

(St Albans Bloodstock LLP). *"Very nice – a strong, powerful and racy two-year-old. She's definitely going to be fairly early, looks to have a good temperament and she might be a decent two-year-old."*

HARRY DUNLOP

480. CAPE GOOSEBERRY ★★
b.f. Cape Cross – Macadamia (Classic Cliché).
January 26. Half-sister to the fairly useful 2009 2-y-o 7f winner Kona Coast (by Oasis Dream). The dam, a smart winner of 5 races including the Group 2 1m Falmouth Stakes, is a half-sister to 6 winners including the very useful winner and listed-placed Azarole and the useful 2-y-o 5f and 6f winner Pistachio – subsequently a Group 3 winner in Scandinavia. The second dam, Cashew (by Sharrood), a quite useful 1m winner, is a half-sister to 6 winners here and abroad. (The Gauchos). *"A filly that's going to need some time, she's obviously very well-bred but she's very much a three-year-old type. A big, good-looking filly that has a look of her sire Cape Cross, but it'll be the autumn before we see her on the track."*

481. CAPTAIN SHARPE ★★★
ch.c. Tobougg – Helen Sharp (Pivotal).
March 26. Third foal. £10,000Y. Doncaster St Leger. H Dunlop. Half-brother to the modest 2009 5f placed 2-y-o Sharp Eclipse (by Exceed And Excel) and to the fair dual 5f winner Angelo Poliziano (by Medicean). The dam ran once unplaced and is a half-sister to 7 winners including the useful 6f (at 2 yrs) to 1m (in Sweden) winner Warming Trends. The second dam, Sunny Davis (by Alydar), was a fair 2-y-o 7f winner. (Here Come The Boys). *"He's done some faster work already and I like this colt a lot. I would envisage he'd be running in mid-May once the six furlong races start and I'm very pleased with his progress. A bonny little horse that looks very racy."*

482. ELFINE (IRE) ★★★♣
b.f. Invincible Spirit – Donnelly's Hollow (Docksider).
January 18. First foal. 82,000foal. Tattersalls December. Lawn Stud. The dam, a modest 1m placed Irish maiden, is a half-sister to 5 winners including the Group 1 12f Italian Derby winner and King George VI and Queen Elizabeth Stakes

second White Muzzle and the Group 2 German St Leger winner Fair Question and the listed 10f winner Elfaslah (dam of the Dubai World Cup winner Almutawakel). The second dam, Fair of the Furze (by Ela-Mana-Mou), won the Group 2 10f Tattersalls Rogers Gold Cup and is a half-sister to the listed winners Majestic Role, Norman Style and Proconsular. (Mr J H Richmond-Watson). *"An interesting filly that hasn't stopped improving. By a good sire and from a good family, she's taken time to come to hand but I would say she's really going the right way now. I would say she'll make a two-year-old by June or July. Hopefully the sire will inject some speed into what is predominantly a middle-distance pedigree."*

483. INVIGILATOR ★★★★
b.c. *Motivator – Midpoint (Point Given).*
March 18. First foal. The dam is an unraced half-sister to several winners including the US Grade 2 Buena Vista Handicap, Group 3 Queen Mary Stakes and Group 3 Fred Darling Stakes winner Dance Parade, the Grade 3 9f Bay Meadows Derby winner Ocean Queen ad the US stakes winner Jig. The second dam, River Jig (by Irish River), a useful 2-y-o 9f winner here, later won over 12f in Italy and is a half-sister to 6 winners. (David and Paul Hearson). *"He's done some fast work despite the fact that being by Motivator you think he'd need some time. He shows speed and I'd recommend him as a two-year-old to follow."*

484. NUTSHELL ★★★
b.f. *Dubai Destination – Cashew (Sharrood).*
April 25. Half-sister to the smart Group 2 1m Falmouth Stakes and Royal Hunt Cup winner Macadamia (by Classic Cliché), to the very useful 6f (at 2 yrs) to 1m winner and Group 3 placed Azarole (by Alzao), the useful 2-y-o 5f and 6f winner Pistachio (by Unblest) – subsequently a Group 3 winner in Scandinavia, the useful triple 1m winner Cashier (by Alhaarth), the fairly useful 2-y-o 6f winner Prime Version (by Primo Dominie), the quite useful 1m and 10f winner Nutkin (by Act One) and the modest dual 10f winner Hazelnut (by Selkirk). The dam, a quite useful 1m winner, is a half-sister to 6 winners here and abroad. The second dam, Kashmiri Snow (by Shirley Heights), was a quite useful 1m winner at 3 yrs.

(The Gauchos). *"She's a big filly that will take a bit of time but she's a lovely mover and a filly I like very much. She's obviously well-bred too and is from the same family as another of our two-year-olds, Cape Gooseberry. She has a bit of class about her and could be quite an interesting filly. One for August time I would think."*

485. SUMMER JASMINE ★★★
b.f. *Kyllachy – Blodwen (Mister Baileys).*
April 13. Sixth foal. 7,800Y. Tattersalls October 3. Highflyer Bloodstock/H Dunlop. Half-sister to the quite useful 11f winner Ostaadi (by Nayef) and to the German 3-y-o winner and 2-y-o Group 3 1m Premio Dormello third Carolines Secret (by Inchinor). The dam is an unplaced full or half-sister to 6 winners including the UAE listed winner Kassbaan. The second dam, Ma Biche (by Key To The Kingdom), was a top-class filly and winner of the 1,000 Guineas, the Prix de la Foret, the Cheveley Park Stakes and the Prix Robert Papin. (Here Come The Girls). *"She's not the biggest and I would hope she'd be relatively sharp and appear in May or June over six furlongs before progressing to seven. She's racy and I like her a lot."*

486. VIKING STORM ★★★★
b.c. *Hurricane Run – Danehill's Dream (Danehill).*
February 18. Second foal. 24,000Y. Tattersalls October 2. Not sold. The dam is an unraced sister to the 2-y-o winner and Group 1 Criterium de Saint-Cloud second Summerland and a half-sister to 2 minor winners. The second dam, Summerosa (by Woodman), a fair 3-y-o 8.5f winner, is a half-sister to 4 winners including the Group 1 Racing Post Trophy second Zind and to the unraced dam of the Derby winner Dr Devious. (Be Hopeful Partnership). *"We bought him privately for 20k after he failed to sell. He's a big horse that will take a bit of time but he's going nicely and I like him a lot. He's very good-looking, a very good mover and he'll want seven furlongs to start with."* TRAINERS' BARGAIN BUY

487. WAR IN BABYLON (IRE) ★★
b.c. *Montjeu – Three Owls (Warning).*
March 11. Sixth foal. Brother to the useful

10f winner and listed-placed Three Moons and half-brother to the useful 2-y-o 5f winner and listed-placed Black Velvet (by Inchinor). The dam, a fair 1m winner, is a half-sister to 6 winners including the listed winners Thames and Three Wrens. The second dam, Three Terns (by Arctic Tern), won over 9f in France and is a half-sister to 3 winners including the Group 3 1m Prix des Reservoirs winner Three Angels. (Mrs Ben Goldsmith). *"A horse that's going to take some time, but he's very straightforward for a Montjeu and he's a brother to Three Moons, a nice filly we had last year. I suspect he's going to want seven furlongs to a mile and we're in no hurry with him."*

488. UNNAMED ★★★
b.c. Chineur – Finty (Entrepreneur).
March 11. Fourth foal. 9,500Y. Tattersalls October Book 2. Highflyer/H Dunlop. Half-brother to the unplaced 2009 2-y-o Hathaway and to the fair 2-y-o 5f winner Ocean Glory (both by Redback). The dam is an unraced half-sister to one winner in Japan. The second dam, Touch Of Magic (by Brief Truce), placed once over 7f in 2 starts in Ireland, is a half-sister to 10 winners including the German Group 3 winner Premier Amour and the dam of the US Grade 1 winner Running Flame. (Mrs M Findlay). *"He's definitely going the right way, we very much bought him to make a two-year-old and he's a big powerful colt. If he takes after his sire he should be a mid-season two-year-old. Six furlongs to begin with before progressing to seven I would think."*

489. UNNAMED ★★★
b.f. Holy Roman Emperor – Tafseer (Grand Lodge).
May 21. Second foal. 9,500Y. Tattersalls December. Harry Dunlop. Closely related to Plus Ultra (by Rock Of Gibraltar), unplaced in one start at 2 yrs in 2009. The dam is an unraced half-sister to 8 winners including the Group 2 1m Royal Lodge Stakes second Tholjanah and the Group 2 Jockey Club Stakes third Ta-Lim. The second dam, Alkaffeyah (by Sadler's Wells), is an unraced sister to the listed 12f Galtres Stakes winner and Group 1 12f Prix Vermeille third Larrocha and a half-sister to 8 winners including the outstanding middle-distance stayer Ardross and the Group 3 Prix de Flore winner Gesedeh. *"She's going very much the right way. A little bit temperamental you might say, but I like her a lot. She could start off in May over six furlongs and I like her."*

490. UNNAMED ★★★
b.c. King's Best – Thermopylae (Tenby).
March 28. Seventh foal. 25,000Y. Tattersalls October Book 1. Not sold. Half-brother to the Group 3 Give Thanks Stakes winner and Group 1 St Leger second Unsung Heroine (by High Chaparral) and to the quite useful triple 7f winner Ghostmilk (by Golan). The dam is a placed full or half-sister to 9 winners including the Group 1 Gran Premio d'Italia winner Posidonas and to the dam of the Group 2 Italian 2,000 Guineas winner Spirit of Desert. The second dam, Tamassos (by Dance In Time), won at 3 yrs and is a half-sister to the Group 1 Juddmonte International winner Ile de Chypre. *"He's a very nice horse and I like him a lot. He's going to take some time and his sister Unsung Heroine was obviously better as a three-year-old. He's gone a bit gangly and obviously needs some time, so perhaps seven furlongs in late summer would be his starting point."*

JOHN DUNLOP

491. ABBAKHAM (IRE) ★★★
gr.c. Dalakhani – Agnetha (Big Shuffle).
April 3. Fifth foal. 25,000Y. Tattersalls October Book 2. Charlie Gordon-Watson. Half-brother to the quite useful 2009 7f placed 2-y-o Averna (by Galileo), to the quite useful Irish 7f winner Scarlet O'Hara (by Sadler's Wells), the fair Irish 5f winner April (by Rock Of Gibraltar) and the fair UAE 7f winner Pure Bluff (by Indian Ridge). The dam was a smart winner of the listed Silver Flash Stakes (at 2 yrs) and the Group 3 5f King George Stakes at 3 yrs. She is a sister to the smart German Group 2 sprint winner Areion and to the Irish listed winner Anna Frid and a half-sister to 5 winners. The second dam, Aerleona (by Caerleon), a German 2-y-o 6f winner, is a half-sister to 5 winners including the Fillies' Mile winner Nepula. (M.C.C Armitage). *"A nice and compact individual from a rather speedy and precocious dam line. He should show some talent this year even if his sire is not known to produce 2-y-o's."*

492. ANTON DOLIN (IRE) ★★
ch.c. Danehill Dancer – Ski For Gold (Shirley Heights).
February 16. Eighth foal. Brother to the quite useful 2-y-o 10f winner Eglevski and half-brother to the fairly useful 10f to 2m winner Downhiller (by Alhaarth), the quite useful 2-y-o 1m winner Alpine Gold (by Montjeu) and the quite useful 2-y-o 1m winner Ski For Me (by Barathea). The dam, a fair 2-y-o 7f winner, stayed 2m and is a half-sister to the very useful 6f (at 2 yrs) and subsequent Grade 1 10f Santa Barbara Handicap winner Bequest and the useful 2-y-o 7f winner Fitzcarraldo. The second dam, Quest (by The Minstrel), won 3 races from 9f to 10f at 3 yrs, was third in the Group 3 Queen Mary Stakes, is a sister to the Group 1 Grand Criterium winner Treizieme and a half-sister to the Group 2 Yorkshire Cup winner Eastern Mystic. (Windflower Overseas Holdings Inc). *"A well-made colt, he's a half-brother to the smart stayer Downhiller and will need time."*

493. BAKOURA ★★★★
b.f. Green Desert – Bunood (Sadler's Wells).
January 22. First foal. The dam, a fairly useful 2-y-o 1m winner, was third in the Group 3 12f Princess Royal Stakes, is a half-sister to 4 winners. The second dam, Azdihaar (by Mr Prospector), a quite useful dual 7f at 3 yrs is a half-sister to the high-class and genuine filly Shadayid, winner of the 1,000 Guineas and the Prix Marcel Boussac and to the very useful listed 7f winner and Jersey Stakes third Dumaani. (Hamdan Al Maktoum). *"First foal out of a useful stakes placed filly. Well put together and really attractive."*

494. CHEWDEH (USA) ★★
b.br.f. Cape Cross – Jaish (Seeking The Gold).
April 12. The dam, a useful 2-y-o 6f winner, was listed-placed over 1m and 10f and is a half-sister to 2 winners. The second dam, Khazayin (by Bahri), was placed over 10f and is a sister to the high-class Prix de l'Arc de Triomphe and Juddmonte International winner Sakhee and closely related to the useful 7f (at 2 yrs) and 10f winner Nasheed. (Hamdan Al-Maktoum). *"Still in Dubai."*

495. CLASSICAL AIR ★★★
b.f. Dubai Destination – Claxon (Caerleon).
April 12. Sixth foal. Half-sister to the fairly useful 2009 2-y-o triple 7f winner and listed-placed Clarietta (by Shamardal), to the useful 7f (at 2 yrs) and listed Lingfield Oaks Trial and subsequent US Grade 3 winner and Group 1 Nassau Stakes second Cassydora (by Darshaan), the listed 10f winner Classic Remark (by Dr Fong) and the quite useful 10f winner Circle Of Love (by Sakhee). The dam, a very useful 1m (at 2 yrs) and Group 2 10f Premio Lydia Tesio winner, is a half-sister to 3 winners including the Group 2 placed Bulwark. The second dam, Bulaxie (Bustino), a very useful winner of the Group 3 7.3f Fred Darling Stakes, was second in the Group 2 Premio Lydia Tesio and is a half-sister to 6 winners including the Group 3 10f Prix de la Nonette winner and smart broodmare Dust Dancer. (Bluehills Racing Ltd). *"A big, scopey filly. Will need some time to come into her own."*

496. COACHLIGHT ★★★
b.c. Cape Cross – Spotlight (Dr Fong).
March 4. Second foal. Half-brother to the unplaced 2009 2-y-o Spring Heather (by Montjeu). The dam, a listed 1m and subsequent US Grade 2 Lake Placid Handicap winner, is a full or half-sister to 3 winners including the listed-placed Dusty Answer. The second dam, Dust Dancer (by Suave Dancer), won 4 races including the Group 3 10f Prix de la Nonette and is a half-sister to 6 winners including the Group 3 7.3f Fred Darling Stakes winner Bulaxie (herself dam of the Group 2 winner Claxon). (Bluehills Racing Ltd). *"A smart, bulky colt by Cape Cross, he has plenty of quality and is a nice goer."*

497. CUPANI ★★★
b.c. Dansili – Sweet Pea (Persian Bold).
March 10. Seventh foal. Half-brother to the 2009 2-y-o 7f winner (on his only start) Bronze Prince (by Oasis Dream), to the Group 3 Princess Margaret Stakes and Group 3 Nell Gwyn Stakes winner Scarlet Runner (by Night Shift) and the minor Irish 12f winner Scent (by Groom Dancer). The dam, a fairly useful winner of 4 races at around 1m, is a half-sister to 4 winners including the useful listed 6f winner Star Tulip. The second dam, Silk Petal (by

Petorius), a useful German listed 1m winner and third in the Group 3 10.5f Prix de Flore, is a half-sister to 5 winners including the good broodmare Dedicated Lady (dam of the Group 2 winners Fairy Queen and Tashawak). (N M H Jones). *"A nice son of Dansili from a good family. One for the second part of the season."*

498. ELRASHEED ★★
b.c. Red Ransom – Ayun (Swain).
February 24. Third foal. Half-brother to the very useful Group 3 2m winner of 7 races Akmal (by Selkirk). The dam, a useful 1m and 10f winner, is a half-sister to the smart 7f (at 2 yrs) and Group 3 1m Desmond Stakes winner Haami. The second dam, Oumaldaaya (by Swain), a very useful filly, won over 7f at 2yrs and the Group 2 10f Premio Lydia Tesio and listed 10f Lupe Stakes at 3 yrs. She is a half-sister to 6 winners including the Derby winner Erhaab. (Hamdan Al Maktoum). *"A big scopey horse that will need some time."*

499. FLEETING TIGER ★★
b.c. Tiger Hill – Fleeting Rainbow (Rainbow Quest).
May 4. Twelfth foal. 29,000Y. Tattersalls October Book 2. Angie Sykes. Half-brother to the high-class Group 1 10.5f Tattersalls Gold Cup and Group 2 10f Pretty Polly Stakes winner Rebelline, to the Group 2 Blandford Stakes and Group 3 Gallinule Stakes winner Quws (both by Robellino), the useful 2-y-o 6f and 7f winner Moonlight Man (by Night Shift), the fair Irish 1m and 10f winner Danzelline (by Danzero) and the French 1m winner Partly Sunny (by Alhaarth). The dam, a modest 10f placed 3-y-o, is a half-sister to 3 winners. The second dam, Taplow (by Tap On Wood), is an unraced half-sister to 7 winners including the dams of the Group winners Adam Smith, Braashee, Ghariba, Careafolie, Gouriev and Run And Gun. (Gail Brown Racing). *"A nice sort for the second part of the season."*

500. GAMESMANSHIP ★★
b.c. Beat Hollow – Artful (Green Desert).
January 12. Second foal. 80,000Y. Tattersalls October Book 2. Shadwell Estate Co. Half-brother to the 2009 2-y-o listed 6f winner Duplicity (by Cadeaux Genereux). The dam, a minor 3-y-o winner in France, is a half-sister to 3 winners including the Irish Group 3 winner Chintz. The second dam, Gold Dodger (by Slew O'Gold), a listed 10f winner of 2 races in France, is a half-sister to 9 winners including the French Group winners Prospect Wells and Prospect Park. (Hamdan Al Maktoum). *"A backward looking colt for the second part of the season."*

501. HIGH ON THE HOG (IRE) ★★★
b.c. Clodovil – Maraami (Selkirk).
March 22. Fourth foal. £10,500 2-y-o. Goffs Kempton Breeze Up. J Dunlop. Half-brother to the quite useful 2-y-o 1m winner Calaloo (by Dansili). The dam, placed 5 times from 6f (at 2 yrs) to 2m, is a half-sister to 4 winners including the Group 3 Meld Stakes winner Latino Magic. The second dam, Tansy (by Shareef Dancer), won once at 2 yrs and is a half-sister to 7 winners including the Lockinge Stakes winner Most Welcome. *"A bonny and athletic colt by a sire who can produce 2-y-o's."*

502. ISABA ★★★
b.f. Shamardal – White Queen (Spectrum).
March 15. Third foal. 65,000Y. Tattersalls October Book 2. J Dunlop. Half-sister to the quite useful 11f, 12f and hurdles winner Hibiki (by Montjeu). The dam, an Irish 12f winner, is a half-sister to 3 winners including the 2-y-o Group 2 1m Royal Lodge Stakes winner and 2,000 Guineas second Snow Ridge. The second dam, Snow Princess (by Ela-Mana-Mou), a smart winner of 6 races at up to 2m including the November Handicap and an Italian listed event, was second in the Group 1 Prix Royal-Oak and is a half-sister to 7 winners. (F Hernandez-Font). *"Quite a tall individual but he's pleasant and by a really hot sire. He will need time though."*

503. ISTISHAARA (USA) ★★★
b.c. Kingmambo – Itnab (Green Desert).
March 2. Fourth foal. Half-brother to the useful 7f (at 2 yrs), 10f and UAE 6f winner Alazeyab (by El Prado). The dam won the Group 3 12f Princess Royal Stakes and is a sister to the very useful 6f winner of 4 races Haafiz and the useful 7f and 1m winner and Irish 1,000 Guineas third Umniyatee and a half-sister to numerous winners including the Group 1 Epsom Oaks winner Eswarah. The second dam,

Midway Lady (by Alleged), won the Prix Marcel Boussac, the 1,000 Guineas and the Oaks and is a half-sister to 5 winners including the very useful 11.8f listed winner Capias. (Hamdan Al Maktoum). *"Still in Dubai."*

504. KORNGOLD ★★★♠
b.c. Dansili – Eve (Rainbow Quest).
February 23. Fifth living foal. 170,000Y. Tattersalls October 1. Peter Doyle. Half-brother to the fairly useful 1m and 10f winner Dubai Twilight (by Alhaarth) and to the fairly useful 7f winner Charm School (by Dubai Destination). The dam, a quite useful winner of 3 races over 1m, is a half-sister to 7 winners including the listed 11.5f winner Birdie and the French middle-distance winner of 10 races (including 4 listed events) Faru. The second dam, Fade (by Persepolis), is an unraced half-sister to Tom Seymour, a winner of five Group 3 events in Italy. (B Andersson). *"A nice, scopey colt and a good mover."*

505. LEJAAM ★★★★
b.c. Dansili – Acts Of Grace (Bahri).
March 9. First foal. 160,000Y. Tattersalls October Book 1. Shadwell Estate Co. The dam won 3 races including the Group 3 12f Princess Royal Stakes and is a half-sister to 10 winners including the Group 1 6f Haydock Park Sprint Cup winner and good sire Invincible Spirit and the dual Group 3 winner Sadian. The second dam, Rafha (by Kris), a very smart winner over 6f (at 2 yrs) and the Group 1 10.5f Prix de Diane, the Group 3 Lingfield Oaks Trial and the Group 3 May Hill Stakes, is a half-sister to 9 winners. (Hamdan Al Maktoum). *"An attractive first foal from the really good family of Invincible Spirit. A colt with plenty of scope, he's a really good mover but he should require a bit of time."*

506. LOVE NEST ★★★★
b.c. Compton Place – Encore My Love (Royal Applause).
March 6. Fifth foal. Half-brother to the fair 2009 dual 6f placed 2-y-o Gundaroo (by Oasis Dream) and to the quite useful 2-y-o 5f and 6f winner Prospect Place (by Compton Place). The dam, a modest 6f placed 2-y-o, is a half-sister to 6 winners including the Group 1 Racing Post Trophy winner Be My Chief. The second dam,

Lady Be Mine (by Sir Ivor), a minor 3-y-o 1m winner at Yarmouth, is a half-sister to 6 winners including Mixed Applause (dam of both the high-class miler Shavian and the Ascot Gold Cup winner Paean). (Mrs M Burrell). *"A smart looking colt that's bred for speed."*

507. MAFROODH ★★★★
ch.c. Pivotal – Khulood (Storm Cat).
January 22. Fourth foal. Brother to the quite useful dual 7f winner Imaam (by Pivotal) and half-brother to the quite useful 2-y-o 5f winner Kashoof (by Green Desert). The dam, a useful listed 7f (at 2 yrs) and Group 3 7f Nell Gwyn Stakes winner, is a half-sister to numerous winners including the Irish 1,000 Guineas winner Mehthaaf and the July Cup winner Elnadim. The second dam, Elle Seule (by Exclusive Native), a very smart winner of the Group 3 1m Prix d'Astarte, also won over 10.5f and is a half-sister to the Group/Grade 1 winners Fort Wood, Hamas and Timber Country and to the Group winners Northern Aspen, Colorado Dancer and Mazzacano. (Hamdan Al Maktoum). *"A strong looking son of Pivotal with plenty of scope from a very good family."*

508. MAKYAAL (IRE) ★★★★
b.c. Nayef – Ros The Boss (Danehill).
February 7. Fourth foal. 250,000Y. Tattersalls October Book 1. Shadwell Estate Co. Brother to the 2009 Irish 1m placed 2-y-o Alsalwa and half-brother to the quite useful 2-y-o 5f winner Kate The Great (by Xaar). The dam, a quite useful 7f and 1m winner, is a half-sister to 5 winners including the Irish 2-y-o 1m and listed 9f winner Yehudi. The second dam, Bella Vitessa (by Thatching), is an unplaced half-sister to 6 winners including the German Group 1 12f Aral-Pokal winner Wind In Her Hair (herself dam of the Japan Cup winner Deep Impact). (Hamdan Al Maktoum). *"A bulky colt, he's a really good mover with a lot of quality."*

509. MARAHEB ★★★★
b.c. Redoute's Choice – Hureya (Woodman).
February 1. Fifth foal. Half-brother to the 2-y-o listed 7f Star Stakes and 3-y-o Group 3 7f Fred Darling Stakes winner Muthabara (by Red Ransom), to the fairly useful 7f (including at 2

yrs) and 1m winner Aqmaar (by Green Desert) and the quite useful 9f winner Estiqraar (by Alhaarth). The dam, a quite useful 3-y-o 1m winner, is a half-sister to the very smart listed 7f (at 2 yrs) and listed 10f winner Muqbil. The second dam, Istiqlal (by Diesis), is an unraced half-sister to the Group 1 1m St James's Palace Stakes and Group 1 1m Queen Elizabeth II Stakes winner Bahri and to the high-class 2-y-o Group 2 7f Laurent Perrier Champagne Stakes winner Bahhare. (Hamdan Al Maktoum). *"An attractive and powerful son of the outstanding top Australian sire. He has plenty of scope and a lot to like about him. One for the second part of the season."*

510. MISKKHITAAM (USA) ★★★
b.c. *Distorted Humor – Tashawak (Night Shift).*
January 10. Half-brother to the quite useful 7f and 1m winner Nadawat (by Kingmambo). The dam, a smart 6f (at 2 yrs) and Group 2 1m Falmouth Stakes winner, is a sister to the fair 6f (at 2 yrs) and 1m winner of 8 races Speedfit Free and a half-sister to the Irish 8.5f (at 2 yrs) and 10f winner and Group 1 1m Criterium International third Acropolis and the smart Group 2 12f Ribblesdale Stakes and Group 2 12.5f Prix de la Royallieu winner Fairy Queen. The second dam, Dedicated Lady (by Pennine Walk), a useful Irish 2-y-o 5f and 6f winner, is a half-sister to 5 winners including the German listed winner and Group 3 10.5f Prix de Flore third Silk Petal (herself dam of the listed Sandy Lane Stakes winner Star Tulip). (Hamdan Al-Maktoum). *"Still in Dubai."*

511. MISS TOPSY TURVY (IRE) ★★★★★
br.f. *Mr Greeley – Cara Fantasy (Sadler's Wells).*
March 22. Third foal. Closely related to the very smart 2009 2-y-o Group 3 7f Acomb Stakes winner and Group 1 Racing Post Trophy second and subsequent Craven Stakes winner Elusive Pimpernel (by Elusive Quality) and half-sister to the smart 1m (at 2 yrs), Group 3 10f Strensall Stakes and listed 9f winner Palavicini (by Giant's Causeway). The dam, a quite useful dual 12f winner, is closely related to the Group 2 winner Lucky Guest and a half-sister to numerous winners. (Windflower Overseas Holdings Inc). *"A three-parts sister to the classic hope Elusive Pimpernel. She's a big, scopey filly with a lot of quality and a fine action. Really attractive."*

512. MUJARAH (IRE) ★★★
b.f. *Marju – Tanaghum (Darshaan).*
May 21. Fourth foal. Half-sister to the fair 2009 2-y-o 1m winner Zahoo (by Nayef), to the useful 12f winner and Group 3 placed Tactic (by Sadler's Wells) and the quite useful 1m winner Taaresh (by Sakhee). The dam, a useful listed-placed 10f winner, is a half-sister to 5 winners including the smart Group 2 10f Premio Lydia Tesio winner Najah. The second dam, Mehthaaf (by Nureyev), won the Irish 1,000 Guineas, the Tripleprint Celebration Mile and the Nell Gwyn Stakes and is closely related to the Diadem Stakes winner Elnadim and to the French 2-y-o 7.5f winner Only Seule (herself dam of the Group 1 7f Prix de la Foret and Group 1 6.5f Prix Maurice de Gheest winner Occupandiste). (Hamdan Al Maktoum). *"A witty little filly, she was a late foal but she's a nice mover."*

513. MUZDAHI (USA) ★★★
b.c. *Smarty Jones – Reem Al Barari (Storm Cat).*
January 1. Half-brother to the quite useful 2009 2-y-o 7f winner Saafia (by Swain) and to the quite useful 10f winner Rafaan (by Gulch). The dam, placed fourth over 6f on her only start, is a half-sister to the 1994 Derby winner Erhaab and the very useful Group 2 10f Premio Lydia Tesio and Lupe Stakes winner Oumaldaaya. The second dam, Histoire (by Riverman), won once in France over 10.5f and is a half-sister to the Group 3 7f Prix de la Porte Maillot winner Hamanda. (Hamdan Al Maktoum). *"Still in Dubai."*

514. NUZOOL (IRE) ★★
b.c. *Red Ransom – Eternity Ring (Alzao).*
February 18. Third foal. £65,000Y. Doncaster St Leger. Shadwell Estate Co. The dam is an unraced half-sister to 7 winners including the Group 3 winners Baron Ferdinand and Love Everlasting. The second dam, In Perpetuity (by Great Nephew), a fairly useful 10f winner, is a half-sister to 6 winners including the Derby winner and high-class sire Shirley Heights and to the placed Bempton (herself dam of

the Group winners Gull Nook, Mr Pintips and Banket). (Hamdan Al Maktoum). *"Hasn't arrived from the stud yet."*

515. SALVATIONIST ★★★★
b.c. Invincible Spirit – Salvia (Pivotal).
January 23. The dam, unplaced in one start, is a half-sister to 3 winners including the very useful 6f (at 2 yrs) and 9f winner Zabaglione. The second dam, Satin Bell (by Midyan), a useful 7f winner, is a half-sister to several winners including the useful listed 6f winner Star Tulip. (N M H Jones). *"A smart and precocious looking colt with a really nice swinging action."*

516. SPANISH PRIDE (IRE) ★★★★
b.f. Night Shift – Spanish Lady (Bering).
March 17. Sister to the fairly useful 1m (at 2 yrs) and listed Italian St Leger winner Spanish Hidalgo and half-sister to the quite useful 2009 2-y-o 7f and 1m winner Spanish Duke (by Big Bad Bob) and the fair 12f winner Spanish Ridge (by Indian Ridge). The dam is an unplaced half-sister to several winners. The second dam, Belle Arrivee (by Bustino), a quite useful 3-y-o 10f winner, is closely related to the top-class King George and Eclipse Stakes winner Mtoto and a half-sister to 13 other winners including Savoureuse Lady (Group 3 Prix Fille de l'Air) and the dam of the smart sprinter Lugana Beach. (Windflower Overseas Holdings Ltd). *"A quality filly and a really good mover."*

517. TAMEEN ★★★
b.f. Shirocco – Najah (Nashwan).
March 15. The dam, a smart Group 2 10f Premio Lydia Tesio winner, is a sister to 3 winners and a half-sister to the useful 10f winner and listed-placed Tanaghum. The second dam, Mehthaaf (by Nureyev), won the Irish 1,000 Guineas, the Tripleprint Celebration Mile and the Nell Gwyn Stakes and is closely related to the Diadem Stakes winner Elnadim and to the French 2-y-o 7.5f winner Only Seule (herself dam of the Group 1 7f Prix de la Foret and Group 1 6.5f Prix Maurice de Gheest winner Occupandiste). (Hamdan Al Maktoum). *"A good-looking filly by the freshman sire Shirocco. Not an early type."*

518. TANASSUQ (USA) ★★★
b.c. Rahy – Wasnah (Nijinsky).
February 13. Tenth foal. Half-sister to the top-class colt Bahri, a winner over 6f (at 2 yrs) and the Group 1 1m St James's Palace Stakes and Group 1 1m Queen Elizabeth II Stakes, to the fair 12f winner Winsa (both by Riverman), the very smart Bahhare (by Dayjur), winner of the Group 2 7f Laurent Perrier Champagne Stakes and third in the Champion Stakes and the fair 1m winners Amwaal (by Seeking The Gold) and Ashwaaq (by Gone West). The dam, a fairly useful maiden, was placed five times from 7f (at 2 yrs) to 10.5f. She is closely related to the Group 3 Tetrarch Stakes winners Dance Bid and Northern Plain and a half-sister to the US Grade 2 winner Winglet. The second dam, Highest Trump (by Bold Bidder), won the Group 2 5f Queen Mary Stakes at Royal Ascot. (Hamdan Al Maktoum). *"Still in Dubai."*

519. THEKRAYAAT (IRE) ★★★
b.f. Red Ransom – Mokaraba (Unfuwain).
March 12. Second foal. Half-sister to the quite useful 2009 2-y-o 7f winner Qaraaba (by Shamardal). The dam, a quite useful 12f winner, is a half-sister to the fairly useful triple 10f winner Kaateb. The second dam, Muhaba (Mr Prospector), a fairly useful 2-y-o 1m winner, is a sister to the very useful 2-y-o 6f and 7f winner Sahm and a half-sister to the very useful 6f to 10f winner Bint Salsabil. (Hamdan Al Maktoum). *"Still in Dubai."*

520. VELOCE (IRE) ★★★★
b.c. Hurricane Run – Kiftsgate Rose (Nashwan).
April 27. Fourth foal. 40,000Y. Tattersalls October Book 2. J Dunlop. The dam is an unraced half-sister to 3 winners including the French listed 13f winner and Group 3 10.5f Prix de Flore second Kentucky Rose. The second dam, Kapuchka (by Soviet Star), is an unplaced half-sister to 7 winners including the Canadian Grade 2 and dual French listed winner Calista. (Mrs H I Slade). *"An attractive colt with a lot of quality, he's an extravagant mover and is one for the second part of the season."*

521. YAIR HILL (IRE) ★★★
b.c. Selkirk – Conspiracy (Rudimentary).
March 12. Brother the useful 2-y-o triple 7f and 3-y-o Group 3 7f Minstrel Stakes winner Jedburgh and half-brother to the useful 10f

to 11.6f winner In Disguise (by Nashwan), the fairly useful 2-y-o 7f winner and 3-y-o listed-placed Presbyterian Nun (by Daylami) and the fairly useful 2-y-o 7f winner Impersonator (by Zafonic). The dam, a useful 2-y-o listed 5f winner, is a half-sister to 7 winners including the Group 2 10f Sun Chariot Stakes winner Ristna and the dual listed winner Gayane. The second dam, Roussalka (by Habitat), won 7 races at up to 10f including the Coronation Stakes and the Nassau Stakes (twice) and is a half-sister to the Fillies Triple Crown winner Oh So Sharp (herself dam of the Prix Saint Alary winner Rosefinch). (The Earl Cadogan). *"A nice, strong looking colt with plenty of scope. A full brother to our Group 3 winner Jedburgh."*

522. UNNAMED ★★★
ch.c. Dalakhani – Kalagold (Magical Strike).
April 30. Sixth living foal. 38,000Y. Tattersalls October 1. Not sold. Half-brother to the smart dual Group 3 7f winner Wake Up Maggie (by Xaar). The dam, a quite useful 2-y-o 1m winner, is a half-sister to 6 winners. The second dam, Showing Style (by Pas de Seul), is an unraced half-sister to 5 winners. *"A smart colt with a really nice action. He's very attractive."*

PAT EDDERY

523. CHEF ★★
b.c. Selkirk – Ego (Green Desert).
April 7. Third foal. Brother to the fair 7f winner I'm Sensational and half-brother to the fair dual 7f winner (including at 2 yrs) Cut And Thrust (by Haafhd). The dam, a very useful 2-y-o dual 6f winner, was listed-placed twice and is a half-sister to 2 winners including the useful 2-y-o 6f winner and Group 2 7f Champagne Stakes third Ghayth. The second dam, Myself (by Nashwan), a smart winner of the Group 3 7f Nell Gwyn Stakes, is a half-sister to 12 winners including the Group 3 Princess Margaret Stakes winner Bluebook. (Brook Farm Bloodstock). *"Definitely a later type, he's done everything we want for now so he's been turned out to let him mature a bit more. A very nice type, he's one for seven furlongs or a mile later on, he's a nice size but he does have to fill his frame a bit more. More of a three-year-old type."* Pat's Assistant Derek Shockledge was kind enough to discuss their horses with me.

524. DA PONTE ★★★
b.c. Librettist – Naharnook (Fantastic Light).
February 29. First foal. £15,000Y. Doncaster St Leger Festival. P Eddery. The dam is an unraced sister to a winner in Japan and a half-sister to 7 winners including the Group 2 Mill Reef Stakes and Group 2 Godolphin Mile winner Firebreak. The second dam, Breakaway (by Song), a useful 5f winner, was listed-placed and is a full or half-sister to 5 winners. (Mrs B V Evans). *"Quite a nice type for early on in the season, he'd start off at six furlong but he'll probably get a mile next year. Not very big but nice and strong, he's a typical two-year-old."*

525. UNNAMED ★★★
b.c. Avonbridge – Feeling Blue (Missed Flight).
April 25. Third foal. £11,000Y. Doncaster St Leger. Pat Eddery. The dam, a moderate winner over 5f at 3 yrs, is a half-sister to 3 winners. The second dam, Blues Indigo (by Music Boy), won over 6f and was second in the Group 3 Palace House Stakes and is a half-sister to 5 winners. (Pat Eddery Racing, Reference Point). *"He looks real sprinter, a lovely size, well developed and mature enough. We're hopefully going to start him off at the end of April or early May. From what he's showing he'll be a five/six furlong type. There are shares available on two year deal basis."* TRAINERS' BARGAIN BUY

526. UNNAMED ★★
gr.c. Proclamation – Persian Fortune (Forzando).
April 19. Eighth foal. 7,500Y. Tattersalls December. Pat Eddery Racing. Half-brother to the fair 6f (at 2 yrs) and 5f winner Demolition Molly (by Rudimentary). The dam, a modest 2-y-o 5f winner, is a full or half-sister to 6 winners including the useful 5f (at 2 yrs) and 6f winner and listed-placed Turnkey. The second dam, Persian Air (by Persian Bold), is an unplaced half-sister to 3 minor winners. (Pat Eddery Racing, Colorspin). *"Quite a nice size of horse, he's just done a bit of growing and has weakened a little bit. One for the back-end of June most probably and although we're likely to start him off at six furlongs he'll be better over further. He moves very well and there are*

two shares still available as a one year deal if anyone is interested."

527. UNNAMED ★★
b.c. Sadler's Wells – Red Bloom (Selkirk).
February 20. First foal. 73,000Y. Tattersalls December. Owen O'Brien. The dam, winner of the Group 1 Fillies' Mile and Group 2 10f Blandford Stakes, is a half-sister to the listed winner Red Gala. The second dam, Red Camellia (by Polar Falcon), won of the Group 3 7f Prestige Stakes, was third in the French 1,000 Guineas and is a half-sister to 4 winners. "Beautifully bred, he was relatively cheap and I believe he was the last Sadler's Wells to enter the ring. When you look at him he's got a lot of white about him and he needs time obviously, so he's turned out at the moment. A real nice type and we're quite excited about him."

528. UNNAMED ★★★
b.f. Noverre – Summerhill Parkes (Zafonic).
February 20. Third foal. 28,000Y. Tattersalls December. Pat Eddery. Half-sister to the fair 8.5f and subsequent minor Italian winner Seleet (by Sakhee). The dam, a useful 3-y-o listed 6f winner, is a half-sister to 7 winners including the useful 2-y-o 5f and 6f winner Ace Of Parkes, the useful dual 5f winner and Moyglare, Lowther and Queen Mary Stakes placed My Melody Parkes and the useful winner of 13 races over 5f Lucky Parkes. The second dam, Summerhill Spruce (by Windjammer), a fair 3-y-o 6f seller winner, is a half-sister to 6 winners including the German Group 2 winner Jimmy Barnie. (Mr Heffer & Mick Hawkett). "She's a nice sized filly, very nicely put-together and one for the middle of the season. What he's done so far is very encouraging. We stayed behind until quite late in the Sale just to get her, Pat was pleased with her there and she looks quite nicely bought."

DAVID ELSWORTH

529. COLD SECRET ★★★
ch.c. Iceman – Dance Sequence (Mr Prospector).
May 10. Tenth foal. 60,000Y. Tattersalls October 2. Suzanne Roberts. Half-brother to Theymistim (by Kyllachy), a 5f winner on his only start at 2 yrs in 2009, to the fairly useful 10f and 12.3f winner Sequential (by Rainbow Quest), the fairly useful 2-y-o dual 5f winner Dance On (by Caerleon), the quite useful 2-y-o 6f winner Hornpipe (by Danehill) and the fair 2-y-o 6f winner Albaher (by Oasis Dream). The dam, a very useful winner of the Group 2 6f Lowther Stakes, is a sister to the US dual Grade 2 winner Souvenir Copy and to the Japanese Grade 2 1m winner Shake Hand. The second dam, Dancing Tribute (by Nureyev), a very useful 6f and 1m winner and second in the Cheveley Park Stakes, is a full or half-sister to 4 winners including the dam of the Cherry Hinton Stakes winner Dazzle. (Mr Leung Kai Fai & Mr Vincent Leung). "He looks like a two-year-old type. He's a baby but he's coming on nicely. A nice, quality horse and expensive for an Iceman, he was a late foal, but it's a good family and I wouldn't be surprised if he made a mid-season two-year-old."

530. FREEDOM TRAIL ★★★
b.f. Bertolini – Film Buff (Midyan).
February 4. Sixth foal. 37,000Y. Tattersalls October Book 1. R Frisby. Sister to the 2-y-o 5f winner and Group 2 Queen Mary Stakes third Nina Blini and half-sister to the minor US 3-y-o winner Red Film (by Robellino). The dam is a placed half-sister to 4 winners including the Irish listed 1m winner and Irish 1,000 Guineas third Starbourne. The second dam, Upper Circle (by Shirley Heights), ran twice unplaced and is a sister to the dam of the Oaks winner Lady Carla. (G B Partnership). "She's a precocious filly and she shows a fair bit. An early runner and one I like."

531. HURSLEY HOPE (IRE) ★★★
b.f. Barathea – Hendrina (Daylami).
February 9. First foal. 20,000Y. Tattersalls October Book 2. Not sold. The dam, unplaced in 2 starts, is a half-sister to numerous winners including the Irish Group 3 7.5f Concorde Stakes winner Hamairi and the Irish 5f (at 2 yrs) and 3-y-o listed 6f winner Hanabad. The second dam, Handaza (by Be My Guest), a 1m winner at 3 yrs in Ireland, is out of Hazaradjat (by Darshaan), herself a half-sister to the Middle Park Stakes winner Hittite Glory. (J C Smith). "A very nice filly, but one for much later in the year and as a three-year-old. With luck she'll turn into a May Hill type in the autumn."

532. MALANOS (IRE) ★★★

b.c. Lord Of England – Majorata (Acatenango). **February 5.** Half-brother to 4 winners including the Group 1 German Oaks winner Mystic Lips (by Generous). The dam, unlaced in one start, is a half-sister to 8 winners including the Group 1 German Derby winner Malinas and the German Derby third Masterplayer. The second dam, Majoritat (b Konigsstuhl), won the German Oaks. *"A lovely, strong colt – I think he's a star. He's by a sire you won't have heard of because he stands in Germany, but this a powerful beast that throws us off like a rag doll when he has a go! His size and his pedigree both show he'll be a better three-year-old."*

533. ODIN (IRE) ★★★
b.c. Norse Dancer – Dimelight (Fantastic Light). **February 13. First foal.** The dam, a fair 9f and 10f placed maiden, is a half-sister to numerous winners including the smart Group 3 Prix La Rochette winner Guys And Dolls, the smart 1m (including at 2 yrs) to 11f listed winner Pawn Broker and the useful dual 7f 2-y-o winner and Group 3 placed Blushing Bride. The second dam, Dime Bag (by High Line), a quite useful winner of 4 races at up to 2m (including on the all-weather), is a half-sister to 7 minor winners. (J C Smith). *"The owner has supported his own stallion, Norse Dancer, by sending him some very nice mares. This is a very nice, strong colt that's more of a three-year-old in type but he should be able to show us something this year in the second half of the season."*

534. SAMMY ANY TWO (IRE) ★★★
b.c. Royal Applause – Mandolin (Sabrehill). **March 16. Fifth foal. 51,000Y. Tattersalls October Book 2. Suzanne Roberts.** Half-brother to the unplaced 2009 2-y-o Althabea (by Avonbridge) and to the modest 1m winner The Mumbo (by Bahamian Bounty). The dam ran once unplaced and is a half-sister to the listed winner and Group 1 placed Alboostan and a half-sister to 8 winners. The second dam, Russian Countess (by Nureyev), a listed-placed winner at 2 yrs in France, is a half-sister to 5 winners. (Mr J Dwyer). *"I keep trying to buy the odd early two-year-old and I thought this colt would be one of them, but at this point in time I don't see him being early at all, although he looks the part. He's named after a poker player."*

535. SEATTLE DRIVE (IRE) ★★★
b.c. Motivator – Seattle Ribbon (Seattle Dancer). **March 29.** Closely related to the very useful listed 1m (at 2 yrs) and listed 10f winner Snoqualmie Girl and to the smart listed 10f winner and Group 2 Dante Stakes third Snoqualmie Boy (both by Montjeu) and half-brother to the quite useful 2-y-o 6f winner Robocop, the modest 9f and 10f winner Seattle Robber, the fair 10f winner Seattle Storm (all by Robellino) and the fair 7f and 10f winner Seattle Express (by Salse). The dam, placed over 9f and 10f at 3 yrs, is a sister to the 2-y-o Group 1 1m winner Seattle Dancer. The second dam, Golden Rhyme (by Dom Racine), was a quite useful 3-y-o 7f winner. (J C Smith). *"A colt out of a good mare, he ought to be a nice two-year-old later on. He's well-grown and impressive."*

536. SOLE BAY ★★
ch.f. Compton Place – Barboukh (Night Shift). **April 2. Tenth foal. £24,000Y. Doncaster St Leger. Suzanne Roberts.** Half-sister to the Group 3 10f Prix Exbury winner and Group 1 Premio Presidente della Repubblica third Barbola (by Diesis), to the fairly useful 10f winner Tarboush (by Polish Precedent) and a hurdles winner by Fantastic Light. The dam, a fairly useful winner of the 1m listed Fern Hill Stakes, is a half-sister to 6 winners. The second dam, Turban (by Glint Of Gold), a fair 10f and 11.7f winner at 3 yrs, is a half-sister to 6 winners including the top-class French and Irish Derby winner Old Vic. (G B Partnership). *"The Compton Place – Night Shift cross is very good I always think and I know this family well. An autumn type two-year-old."*

537. SWISS DREAM ★★★★♠
b.f. Oasis Dream – Swiss Lake (Indian Ridge). **February 2. Fourth foal.** Half-sister to the quite useful 2009 2-y-o 7f winner Swiss Cross (by Cape Cross), to the smart 2-y-o 5f winner and triple Group 2 placed Swiss Franc (by Mr Greeley) and the 6f winner (including at 2 yrs) and listed-placed Swiss Diva (by Pivotal). The dam, a dual listed 5f winner (including at 2 yrs), is a half-sister to the useful 2-y-o dual 5f winner and listed placed Dubai Princess. The second dam, Blue Iris (by Petong), a useful winner of 5

races over 5f and 6f including the Weatherbys Super Sprint and the Redcar Two-Year-Old Trophy, is a half-sister to 9 winners. (Lordship Stud). *"This could be a Royal Ascot filly if all goes right for her. She does everything nicely, the other foals out of the dam have been fast and I'd be disappointed if she didn't deliver at a fairly high standard as a two-year-old."*

538. WESTHAVEN (IRE) ★★★
b.c. Alhaarth – Dashiba (Dashing Blade).
February 20. Half-brother to the fair 2009 2-y-o 1m winner Dashing Doc, to the useful 2-y-o listed 1m winner Doctor Dash (both by Dr Fong) and the smart 7f (at 2 yrs) and Group 2 Lancashire Oaks winner of 5 races Barshiba (by Barathea). The dam, a useful 9f and 10f winner, is a half-sister to several winners including the fairly useful 10f and 12f winner Smart Blade. The second dam, Alsiba (by Northfields), a modest winner of one race at 4 yrs, was a staying half-sister to several winners and to the dam of the Irish St Leger winner Oscar Schindler. (J C Smith). *"A strong, well-made colt from a family that's been very good to me – they all seem to win. He's going to go middle-distances next year but he's very nicely made, pretty correct and certainly something to go to work with."*

539. UNNAMED ★★
bl.f. Halling – Digger Girl (Black Minnaloushe).
January 30. First foal. 32,000Y. Tattersalls October Book 2. Suzanne Roberts. The dam ran once unplaced and is a half-sister to the listed 14f winner and Group 3 second Art Eyes (by Halling). The second dam, Careyes (by Sadler's Wells), is an unraced half-sister to 2 minor winners. *"An attractive filly with the same mannerisms as her dam's half-sister Art Eyes. You won't see her until later on this season and I'd like to think she'll make up into a decent three-year-old."*

JAMES EUSTACE

540. CIRCUS MASTER ★★★
b.c. Kyllachy – Alegria (Night Shift).
April 22. Fifth foal. Half-brother to the quite useful dual 6f winner (including at 2 yrs) Fast Bowler and to the fair 1m winner Integria (both by Intikhab). The dam, a fairly useful dual 6f winner (including at 2 yrs), is out of the fair middle-distance placed maiden High Habit (by Slip Anchor), herself a half-sister to the smart sprinter Blue Siren. (J C Smith). *"He's quite mature and he will be a two-ear-old although he didn't come in very early and we then had a delay when we were breaking him in. So in terms of education he's a bit behind the rest, but I do love the look of him. I'm slightly wary of the fact that both Fast Bowler and Integria looked more forward than they really were, but nonetheless he's a well-grown, strong horse now. He's the best-looking that the mare has had and he's bred for speed so although he's only cantering still, I'd be quite hopeful for him. He'll have the speed for six furlongs, maybe even five, because he has the physique of a sprinter."*

541. NOVERTON ★★★
b.f. Noverre – Quintrell (Royal Applause).
February 15. First foal. The dam, a fair dual 7f winner at 3 yrs, is a half-sister to 6 winners. The second dam, Peryllis (by Warning), a modest 6f (at 2 yrs) to 10.2f placed maiden, is a half-sister to 6 winners including the French listed 11.5f winner Honest Word and the very useful sprinter Cragside. (Major M G Wyatt). *"She's been very straightforward, a little bit backward in her coat, but I can see her being a two-year-old. I won't be in any rush with her and she's one of those fillies that's been problem free in every way – she just gets on with it and is a TRAINERS' dream in that regard. I think she'd be quick enough for six furlongs to start off with and then we'll take it from there. An average-sized filly that's perfectly 'together enough' to be a two-year-old."*

542. PAID UP FRONT ★★
b.c. Dr Fong – Duty Paid (Barathea).
March 12. Fourth foal. Brother to the modest 7f and 1m winner Duty Doctor. The dam, a useful 2-y-o listed 6f winner, is a sister to the useful 1m winner and listed-placed Lady Miletrian and a half-sister to 3 winners. The second dam, Local Custom (by Be My Native), was placed at up to 7f at 2 yrs and is a sister to the listed winner Tribal Rite and a half-sister to the Middle Park Stakes winner Balla Cove. (J C Smith). *"Interestingly enough I think he's going to need quite a lot of time despite the fact the dam won a listed six furlong race as

a two-year-old. I like him but physically he's very immature. He has a great attitude and I have to admit that now he's on the heath cantering he doesn't look as backward as I first thought. But he won't be doing anything in the first half of the season. A seven furlong type for later on."

543. SCOTTISH STAR ★★★★
gr.c. Kirkwall – Child Star (Bellypha).
April 29. Ninth foal. 35,000Y. Tattersalls October Book 3. James Eustace. Half-brother to the modest 5f (at 2 yrs) to 10f winner of 7 races King After (by Bahamian Bounty), to the modest 2-y-o 5f winner Animal Cracker (by Primo Dominie), the modest 2-y-o 7f winner Colmar Supreme (by Woodborough) – all 3 only modest, the moderate 9f to 2m winner of 4 races Vandenberghe (by Millkom) and the moderate 5f to 1m winner of 3 races Lucky Star (by Emarati). The dam, a moderate 2m and hurdles winner, is a half-sister to 12 winners, mostly in Japan. The second dam, Miss Shirley (by Shirley Heights), won once at 3 yrs and is a half-sister to 9 winners including Mendez (Prix du Moulin). (J C Smith). *"I like him, he's going well, he's quite forward in his coat and he's quite a mature horse that's been going for quite some time, so in terms of education he's quite forward too. I'm just increasing his work a little bit all the time and he's coping well. A six furlong type and I think he'll be early enough for Royal Ascot if he's good enough – and I do underline the 'if'! You could see him running a couple of times before the middle of June and he does give the impression of being a nice horse."*

544. SPEED DANCER ★★★
b.c. Norse Dancer – Speed Of Sound (Zafonic).
January 25. First foal. The dam, a fair dual 5f placed 2-y-o, is a half-sister to several winners including the useful 2-y-o listed 5.2f winner and Group 2 Flying Childers Stakes third Speed Cop and the fairly useful dual 5f winner (including at 2 yrs) Siren's Gift. The second dam, Blue Siren (by Bluebird), a very useful winner of three races from 5f to 7f, was disqualified from first place in two more, notably the Group 1 5f Nunthorpe Stakes (the winner on merit) and is a half-sister to several winners including the quite useful 9f winner Northern Habit. (Mr J C Smith). *"A lovely, well-grown colt and very straightforward, he could just be alright as a two-year-old later on. Not the type you'd rush, but he could be OK in the second half of the season."*

545. TENBA (IRE) ★★★
b.g. Kheleyf – Kathy Jet (Singspiel).
April 3. Fourth foal. 16,000Y. Tattersalls October Book 2. James Eustace. Half-brother to the fair Irish 5f winner He's Got Rhythm (by Invincible Spirit) and to a minor winner in Italy by Desert Prince. The dam, an Italian 3-y-o winner, is a half-sister to 5 other minor winners. The second dam, Hollow Haze (by Woodman), a fair 8.5f winner, is a half-sister to 4 minor winners. (The Macdougall Partnership). *"An enormous horse, he was a great, big, stroppy colt at the Sales and I suspect that's why I got him so cheaply. I had to geld him straightaway, he's cantering on the heath now but he has gone 'up behind' and he'll be massive when he's levelled up. I do like him though, the sire has done well and I think he'll be worth waiting for. He's not slow, so he'll make a two-year-old in the second half of the season."* TRAINERS' BARGAIN BUY

546. VIKING ROSE (IRE) ★★★
ch.f. Norse Dancer – Rosy Outlook (Trempolino).
March 12. Half-sister to the fair 2009 1m placed 2-y-o Tiger Star (by Tiger Hill), to the very useful 2-y-o 6f and Group 3 7f Horris Hill Stakes winner Rapscallion (by Robellino) and very useful the 6f (at 2 yrs) and Group 3 12f St Simon Stakes winner Orcadian (by Kirkwall). The dam, a quite useful 6f winner, is out of Rosyphard (by Lyphard), herself a sister to the dual French Group 3 winner Tenue de Soiree and a half-sister to the European champion 2-y-o filly Baiser Vole. (Mr J C Smith). *"A very straightforward filly, which is a bit of a surprise given the fact that the family tend to be quirky, so it could be the sire's influence. She's a bit backward in her coat, but apart from that she gives the impression of being pretty early and I'm sure she'll make a two-year-old."*

RICHARD FAHEY
547. ABOVE THE STARS ★★★
b.f. Piccolo – Swindling (Bahaman Bounty).

February 5. First foal. £11,000Y. Doncaster St Leger. R O'Ryan. The dam is an unraced half-sister to one winner. The second dam, Fiddling (by Music Boy), won once at 3 yrs and is a half-sister to 4 winners including the dual Group 3 winning sprinter Clantime. *"She's not very big, but she's quite quick, very sharp and genuine."* TRAINERS' BARGAIN BUY

548. ADLINGTON ★★★
b.c. Dansili – Kiralik (Efisio).
March 27. Third foal. Half-sister to Green Secret (by Green Desert), unplaced in one start at 2 yrs in 2009. The dam, an Italian listed winner and third in the Group 2 Italian 1,000 Guineas, is a full or half-sister to 5 winners including the 2-y-o Group 3 6f Princess Margaret Stakes and subsequent US 3-y-o Grade 2 8.5f winner and Grade 1 9f third River Belle. The second dam, Dixie Favor (by Dixieland Band), was a quite useful Irish 6f (at 2 yrs) to 1m winner. *"Quite a backward colt at the moment, but he'll make a two-year-old in the second half of the season. He moves well and he's quite a nice horse but I haven't done much with him yet. Possibly a seven furlong type."*

549. BAHAMIAN SUNSET ★★★
b.f. Bahamian Bounty – Jalissa (Mister Baileys).
February 26. Second foal. Half-sister to the quite useful 2009 2-y-o 6f winner Folly Bridge (by Avonbridge). The dam, a quite useful 6f winner, is a half-sister to 3 winners including the smart 7f (at 2 yrs) to 10f winner of 7 races Vintage Premium. The second dam, Julia Domna (by Dominion), is an unplaced half-sister to the Hungerford Stakes winner Norwich. *"We'll be stepping her up shortly, we're still learning about her but she could be sharp and I'd expect her out in late May."*

550. BRIDAL BELLE ★★★
b.f. Dansili – River Belle (Lahib).
March 11. Second foal. £80,000Y. Doncaster St Leger. Gill Richardson. Half-sister to the quite useful 2009 2-y-o 7f and subsequent UAE 1,000 Guineas winner Siyaadah (by Shamardal). The dam, winner of the Group 3 6f Princess Margaret Stakes and subsequently the US Grade 2 8.5f Mrs Revere Stakes, was Grade 1 placed and is a half-sister to the Italian listed winner and Group 2 Italian 1,000 Guineas third

Kiralik and the useful 7.5f and 1m winner of 5 races Rio Riva. The second dam, Dixie Favor (by Dixieland Band), was a quite useful Irish 6f (at 2 yrs) to 1m winner of 3 races. *"She hasn't grown a lot so we'll just give a bit of time but she's a good-moving filly and seven furlongs should suit."*

551. CHISWICK BEY (IRE) ★★★★♣
b.c. Elusive City – Victoria Lodge (Grand Lodge).
February 10. Second foal. £90,000Y. Doncaster St Leger. Gill Richardson. The dam is an unraced half-sister to one winner. The second dam, Lake Victoria (by Lake Coniston), was listed-placed in Ireland and is a half-sister to 5 winners including the US Grade 1 winner Delighter and the Oaks third Oakmead. *"He did well to win the Brocklesby because he wasn't really wound-up. I thought he'd get the trip in the soft ground so I ran him. We'll give him a chance now because he'll improve a lot and he'll get six furlongs I should think but we may go for the National Stakes at Sandown first. He's big enough and he's doing well and getting stronger all time."*

552. CORSICAN RUN (IRE) ★★★
ch.c. Medicean – Castara Beach (Danehill).
April 8. Sixth foal. 175,000Y. Tattersalls October Book 1. R O'Ryan. Half-brother to the very smart 2009 2-y-o 6f winner and Group 1 Dewhurst Stakes fourth Steinbeck (by Danehill Dancer) and to the fairly useful 2-y-o 7.5f winner and Italian listed-placed Varenka (by Fasliyev). The dam, placed fourth once over 7f at 2 yrs, is a sister to the useful Group 3 7f Criterion Stakes winner Hill Hopper and a half-sister to 5 winners including the Australian Grade 1 winner Water Boatman. The second dam, Sea Harrier (by Grundy), ran twice unplaced and is a half-sister to 5 winners including the Group 2 12f King Edward VII Stakes winner Sea Anchor. *"He's quite a nice horse but I'm in no hurry with him at all. He's quite immature, a very good mover and I like him but it'll be the back-end of the season before we go with him."*

553. DUNMORE BOY (IRE) ★★★
ch.c. Iffraaj – Night Club (Mozart).
March 4. Second foal. €28,000Y. Goffs

Orby. R O'Ryan. The dam is an unplaced half-sister to 12 winners including the French 1,000 Guineas and Group 1 7f Prix de la Foret winner Danseuse du Soir (herself dam of the Group 1 Gran Criterium winner Scintillo), the smart 7f (at 2 yrs) to 12f winner Don Corleone and the very useful 1m to 12f winner Dana Springs. The second dam, Dance By Night (by Northfields), a quite useful 2-y-o dual 7f winner, is a half-sister to 3 winners. *"He's quite sharp and might run in April. He's got plenty of speed but he was getting a bit 'buzzy' and we laid off him a bit. He's back in work again, he's big enough and he's quite quick."*

554. EAVES LANE (IRE) ★★★
b.f. Whipper – Cape Columbine (Diktat).
February 27. First foal. 30,000foal. Tattersalls December. Highfield Farm. The dam, a useful 2-y-o 6f winner, was fourth in the Group 1 Coronation Stakes and is a half-sister to several winners including the Group 1 Golden Jubilee Stakes and Australian Group 1 winner Cape Of Good Hope. The second dam, Cape Merino (by Clantime), a useful winner of 4 races over 5f and 6f, is a sister to the fair dual 5f winner Calamanco and a half-sister to one winner. *"A big, backward filly, she's very tall just like the dam, so she'll be one for the second half of the season. A very good-moving filly, it's a good family but she is very tall."*

555. EL VIENTO (FR) ★★★★
ch.c. Compton Place – Blue Sirocco (Bluebird).
February 23. £20,000Y. Doncaster St Leger. Robin O'Ryan. Closely related to the fairly useful 5f and 6f winner of 5 races Bluebok (by Indian Ridge) and half-brother to the useful 6f winner of 5 races (including at 2 yrs) and listed-placed Johannes (by Mozart), the fair 11f winner Zamboozle (by Halling) and the modest 1m and 10f winner Blue Mistral (by Spinning World). The dam ran once unplaced and is a half-sister to 8 winners including the listed 7f winner and Group 1 7f Moyglare Stud Stakes second Tamnia, the Group 2 13.3f Geoffrey Freer Stakes winner Azzilfi and the Group 3 15f Coppa d'Oro di Milano winner Khamaseen. The second dam, Tanouma (by Miswaki), a very useful 6f (at 2 yrs) and 7f winner, was third in the Group 3 7.3f Fred Darling Stakes and is a half-sister to 7 winners. *"He's quite quick and looked being one of my sharper ones but he just started with a few niggling things like a dirty nose. We'll get him round to our way of thinking soon and he's got loads of speed."*

556. GOLDENVEIL (IRE) ★★★
b.f. Iffraaj – Line Ahead (Sadler's Wells).
January 27. Third foal. €19,000foal. Goffs. Gill Richardson. Half-sister to Silkenveil (by Indian Ridge), unplaced in one start at 2 yrs in 2009. The dam was unplaced on her only start and is a half-sister to 2 winners. The dam was placed 3 times including when second in the Group 3 Prestige Stakes and is a half-sister to 4 winners including the Group 2 Great Voltigeur winner Bonny Scot and the dam of the King George and 2,000 Guineas winner Golan. The second dam, Scots Lass (by Shirley Heights), won over 13f. *"She's out of a Sadler's Wells mare but she still shows some toe – just as all our Iffraaj two-year-olds do. Quite a nice filly that'll want six or seven furlongs."*

557. HEARTBREAK ★★★
b.c. Iffraaj – Romantic Myth (Mind Games).
March 23. Sixth foal. 9,000Y. Ascot December. Not sold. Half-sister to the fair 2-y-o 6f winner Mythicism (by Medicean), to the modest triple 7f winner Headache (by Cape Cross) and the moderate dual 7f winner Stargazy (by Observatory). The dam won 3 races at 2 yrs including the Group 3 5the one Queen Mary Stakes and is a half-sister to 5 sprint winners including Romantic Liason – also winner of the Queen Mary. The second dam, My First Romance (by Danehill), ran twice unplaced and is a full or half-sister to 6 minor winners here and abroad. *"I don't understand why he didn't sell at the Sales because I saw him and couldn't see anything wrong with him. He's only just come to us, but the pedigree would suggest he'd have the speed for six furlongs. We have five Iffraaj two-year-olds and we like them all."*

558. HONEYMEAD (IRE) ★★★★
b.f. Pivotal – Camaret (Danehill).
March 7. Fourth foal. 120,000foal. Tattersalls December. Gill Richardson. Sister to the useful dual 1m winner (including at 2 yrs) and listed placed La Conquistadora (by Pivotal) and half-sister to the quite useful 2009

Irish 2-y-o 7f winner Ejteyaaz (by Red Ransom). The dam, a fairly useful 7f winner, is a sister to the useful Irish 6f (at 2 yrs) and 7f winner Darwin and a half-sister to the modest 2-y-o 7f all-weather winner Tiger Dawn (by Anabaa) and the modest 10.2f winner Crozon (by Peintre Celebre). The second dam, Armorique (by Top Ville), a minor winner and listed placed at 3 yrs in France, is a half-sister to 8 winners including the French Group winners Modhish, Russian Snows and Truly Special. *"A lovely filly, I like her and she's one of my nicest. She's got natural ability, she's breezed well and worked a couple of times, so despite being by Pivotal she could be out sooner than you'd think. She's very nice and if I have a really good two-year-old this could be the one."*

559. INTRUSION ★★
b.f. Indesatchel – Waterfowl Creek (Be My Guest).
February 6. Eighth living foal. 16,000Y. Tattersalls October Book 2. McKeever St Lawrence. Half-sister to the useful 10f listed winner Maid Of Camelot (by Caerleon), to the modest 10f and hurdles winner Dark Energy (by Observatory), the Italian winner of 6 races Doctor Destiny (by Vettori) and a winner in Sweden by Belmez. The dam, a quite useful 3-y-o dual 1m winner, is a sister to the very useful dual 1m winner Guest Artiste, closely related to the very useful Inchmurrin (a winner of 6 races including the Group 2 Child Stakes and herself dam of the very smart colt Inchinor) and a half-sister to numerous winners including the very useful 2-y-o Group 2 6f Mill Reef Stakes winner Welney. The second dam, On Show (by Welsh Pageant), a fairly useful 3-y-o 10f winner, is a half-sister to 5 winners. *"A very genuine and honest filly, we haven't had her long and we haven't breezed her yet, so I don't know much about her."*

560. JAMESWAY (IRE) ★★★★
b.c. Camacho – Charlene Lacy (Pips Pride).
April 4. Eighth foal. 40,000Y. Tattersalls October Book 2. Not sold. Brother to the very useful 2009 2-y-o listed 5f winner of 5 races Star Rover and half-brother to the minor Italian 2-y-o winner Bod Common Pride (by Bad As I Wanna Be) and the modest 4-y-o 8.6f winner Tetcott (Definite Article). The dam won once over 5f at 2 yrs and is a half-sister to 4 winners. The second dam, Friendly Song (by Song), is a placed sister to the sire and winner of 7 races Fayruz. *"He's not very big but he won one of the Sales Bonus race for the lads. I'll give him a bit of a break now and we'll probably go to Beverley next. He's very genuine and has a bit of speed but he's not an early foal and I want to give him a bit of a chance now."*

561. LADY INTRIGUE (IRE) ★★★★
b.f. Hurricane Run – Intriguing (Fasliyev).
March 31. Second foal. €50,000Y. Goffs Orby. Robin O'Ryan. Half-sister to the unplaced 2009 2-y-o Historic Occasion (by Royal Applause). The dam, a quite useful 2-y-o 6f winner, is a half-sister to 7 winners including the Group 3 6f Greenlands Stakes winner Nautical Pet. The second dam, Sea Mistress (by Habitat), is an unraced half-sister to 2 minor winners. *"A lovely filly, she was looking quite sharp but being by Hurricane Run I couldn't believe it so I've given her six weeks off. A filly I like a lot, she has a bit of natural ability. The dam was meant to be very smart but she got injured. She won over six and although being by Hurricane Run you'd think this filly would want seven, she does appear to have some speed."*

562. LAS VERGLAS STAR (IRE) ★★★
gr.c. Verglas – Magnificent Bell (Octagonal).
March 15. Third foal. 20,000Y. Tattersalls October Book 2. R O'Ryan. Half-brother to the fairly useful 10f to 2m and hurdles winner Inventor (by Alzao). The dam is an unraced half-sister to 6 winners including the very useful 7.5f (at 2yrs) and listed 10f winner Esyoueffcee (by Alzao). The second dam, Familiar (by Diesis), a fairly useful 3-y-o 1m winner, is a half-sister to 8 winners including the high-class Prix du Moulin winner and Epsom Oaks second All At Sea and the smart French dual Group 3 winner Over The Ocean. *"He's won over five furlongs but it was an uncompetitive race and I would imagine he'd want six or seven furlongs. A nice colt and I'm sure the owners will have some fun with him."*

563. LEXINGTON BAY (IRE) ★★★
b.c. High Chaparral – Schust Madame (Second Set).

April 1. Sixth foal. 85,000Y. Tattersalls October Book 2. R O'Ryan. Half-brother to the Group 3 Killavullan Stakes winner and dual Group 3 placed Confuchias (by Cape Cross), to the Irish 2-y-o 6f and 7f winner and listed-placed Little Whisper (by Be My Guest), the fairly useful 2-y-o dual 7f winners Secret Pact (by Lend A Hand) and Soaring Falcon (by Hawk Wing). The dam won over 11f in Ireland and is a half-sister to 4 winners including the dual US Grade 2 winner Sweet Ludy and Late Parade, a winner of 23 races in France and Italy including the Group 3 Gran Premio Citta di Napoli (3 times). The second dam, Skisette (by Malinowski), was placed in France and is a half-sister to 5 minor winners here and abroad. *"Quite a scopey horse, we're just stepping him up and the lads are very keen on him. Let's hope they're right because I haven't really found out yet but he could be a York horse."*

564. LOUIS GIRL ★★
b.f. Araafa – Crumpetsfortea (Henbit).
May 18. Eighth foal. 10,000Y. R Fahey. Half-sister to the fair 2009 2-y-o 7f winner Layla's Dancer, to the quite useful 2-y-o 8.3f winner Prohibition (both by Danehill Dancer), the French Group 3 7f Prix Miesque winner Contemporary (by Alzao), the useful 2-y-o 7f winner James Joyce (by Danehill), the French dual 1m winner Yippee (by Orpen) and the French 1m to 9.5f winner Heinstein (by Night Shift). The dam is an unraced half-sister to 4 winners. The second dam, Butter Knife (by Sure Blade), is an unraced half-sister to 10 winners including the US Grade 1 winner Danish. *"She'll take a bit of time, the fillies are a bit backward this year and they haven't done much yet."*

565. MR OPTIMISTIC ★★★
b.c. Kyllachy – Noble Desert (Green Desert).
February 4. Third foal. £38,000Y. Doncaster St Leger. Robin O'Ryan. Half-brother to the quite useful 2009 2-y-o 6f winner The Human League (by Tobougg) and to the modest 2-y-o 1m winner Noble Dictator (by Diktat). The dam is an unplaced half-sister to 6 winners. The second dam, Sporades (by Vaguely Noble), won 3 races in France including the Group 3 10.5f Prix de Flore and is a half-sister to 9 winners including the high-class colts Mill Native (Grade 1 10f Arlington Million) and French Stress (three Group 3 1m wins in France) and the 2-y-o Group 3 5f Prix du Bois winner American Stress. *"A strong colt that suffered a bit from sore shins but he's fine now and he'll win one of the Sales Bonus races."*

566. PANDORO DE LAGO (IRE) ★★★
ch.f. Encosta De Lago – Fig Tree Drive (Miswaki).
April 25. Ninth foal. 130,000Y. Tattersalls October Book 1. Sir Robert Ogden. Half-sister to the listed 1m and 10f winner Sublimity (by Selkirk) and the UAE Group 3 1m winner Marbush (by Linamix) and the fair 2m and hurdles winner Estate. The dam, a fairly useful 2-y-o 6f winner on her only start, is a half-sister to 4 winners. The second dam, Rose O'Riley (by Nijinsky), won over 1m in France at 2 yrs and is a sister to the US Grade 1 winners Upper Nile and De La Rose (herself dam of the Grade 1 winner Conquistarose). *"A big, scopey filly, she's lovely and a good mover but she's one for the second half of the season. A sweet filly."*

567. PETERS SPIRIT (IRE) ★★
b.f. Invincible Spirit – Khatela (Shernazar).
April 3. Seventh living foal. 55,000Y. Tattersalls October Book 1. R O'Ryan. Half-sister to the modest 15f winner Khayar (by Refuse To Bend), to the 2-y-o 7.2f and listed 1m Heron Stakes winner and Group 3 9f Prix de Conde second Massive (by Marju), the modest 2-y-o 9f winner Khandala (by Soviet Star), the French 11f winner Jimbeck and a winner over jumps in France (both by Night Shift). The dam won over 1m and 9f in Ireland and is a half-sister to 4 minor winners. The second dam, Khatima (by Relko), won at 3 yrs and is a half-sister to the French triple listed winner Kaldoun. *"She was at home with a dirty nose for a couple of months, so although she could have been sharp we didn't gee the chance. We're stepping her up now."*

568. PREMIER CLARETS (IRE) ★★★★
b.c. Ivan Denisovich – Blueberry Walk (Green Desert).
January 30. Eleventh foal. £25,000Y. Doncaster St Leger. Robin O'Ryan. Half-brother to the 1m winner Basserah (by Unfuwain), to the French 1m (at 2 yrs) and 10f

winner Jungle Rumbler (by Charnwood Forest), the 2-y-o 7f all-weather winner Buona Sera (by Marju), the 6f winner Spartan Duke (by Xaar), the 9.4f winner Joondey (by Pursuit Of Love) – all 5 quite useful – and the Italian winner Armenian Heritage (by Bluebird). The dam is an unraced sister to the listed 2m George Stubbs Stakes winner Hawait Al Barr and a half-sister to 3 winners. The second dam, Allegedly Blue (by Alleged), won once at 3 yrs, was placed in the Park Hill Stakes and is a full or half-sister to 4 winners including the dams of the Kentucky Derby and Preakness Stakes winner Real Quiet and the Queen Anne Stakes winner Allied Forces. *"A nice colt and a big horse that shows a lot of speed. I like him and he'll be running by the end of May I should think."*

569. SAPPHIRE GIRL ★★★
ch.f. Compton Place – Centre Court (Second Set).
March 23. Eighth foal. £6,000Y. Doncaster St Leger Festival. Robin O'Ryan. Sister to the fairly useful 2-y-o 7f winner and listed placed The Old Fella and to the modest dual 5f winner (including at 2 yrs) Blue Neptune and half-sister to the modest 2-y-o 5.2f winner Service (by College Chapel). The dam, a fair 2-y-o 5f winner, is a half-sister to 3 winners including the useful winner of 4 races at around 7f Rasan. The second dam, Raffle (by Balidar), a quite useful 3-y-o 5.8f winner, is a half-sister to the good sprinters Mummy's Pet, Parsimony and Arch Sculptor. *"A sharp filly but like all our fillies she wants some sun on her back. She's not big but she's very genuine and game. I'm sure she'll do something."*

570. SHIROCCO VICE (IRE) ★★
b.f. Shirocco – Viscaria (Barathea).
April 6. Seventh foal. 28,000Y. Tattersalls October Book 1. R O'Ryan. Half-sister to the quite useful 10f and 12f winner of 3 races Excape (by Cape Cross), to the modest 9.5f winner Pivotalia (by Pivotal) and a winner over hurdles by Desert Prince. The dam, an Irish 1m (at 2 yrs) and 10f winner, is closely related to the UAE Group 3 winner Stagelight and a half-sister to 6 winners including the 1,000 Guineas third Hathrah, the smart Group 2 12f Premio Ellington winner Ivan Luis and the French/German listed winners Amathia and Zero Problemo. The second dam, Zivania (by Shernazar), a useful Irish winner of 4 races from 1m to 9.5f, is a half-sister to 4 stakes winners. *"She's had six weeks off to grow and develop, so she'll take a bit of time. A good-moving filly but I don't know a lot about her yet."*

571. VENTURA SANDS (IRE) ★★★★
b.c. Footstepsinthesand – Beautiful Noise (Piccolo).
February 29. Second foal. 92,000Y. Tattersalls October Book 2. R O'Ryan. The dam, a moderate 1m placed maiden, is a half-sister to 3 winners including the very useful listed 1m winner Soviet Flash. The second dam, Mrs Moonlight (by Ajdal), is an unraced half-sister to 11 winners including the high-class 2-y-o Precocious, the Group 1 Japan Cup winner Jupiter Island and the Mary Stakes winner Pushy (herself dam of smart fillies Bluebook and Myself). *"A lovely, big horse that I like a lot. The lads are keen on him, he's breezed a couple of times but he's 16.1 hands – a big fine horse with a bit of quality about him."*

572. WOOTTON BASSETT ★★★★
b.c. Iffraaj – Balladonia (Primo Dominie).
February 4. Fifth foal. £46,000Y. Doncaster St Leger. Bobby O'Ryan. Half-brother to the fairly useful 5f (at 2 yrs) to 1m winner of 6 races and listed-placed Mister Hardy (by Kyllachy), to the fairly useful 2-y-o 6f to 1m and subsequent Hong Kong winner Zaal (by Alhaarth) and the quite useful triple 6f winner (including at 2 yrs) Mister Laurel (by Diktat). The dam, a useful 9f winner, was listed-placed twice over 10f and is a half-sister to 5 winners. The second dam, Susquehanna Days (by Chief's Crown), a fair 1m and 8.2f winner, is a half-sister to 6 winners including Clare Bridge (Group 3 Gilltown Stud Stakes). *"I like him a lot and I trained his two half-brothers Mister Hardy And Mister Laurel. This looks like the best of the three, he's a shade back at the knee but he's a nice type of colt and were giving him a bit of time. He's breezed lovely."*

573. UNNAMED ★★
b.c. Iffraaj – Aljafliyah (Halling).
April 3. Third foal. 50,000Y. Tattersalls October Book 2. R O'Ryan. Half-brother to

the fairly useful 2009 2-y-o 5f and 6f winner The Only Boss (by Exceed And Excel). The dam is an unplaced half-sister to 4 winners including the US Grade 3 winner Sohgol. The second dam, Arruhan (by Mujtahid), a quite useful 5f (at 2 yrs) and 7f winner, is a half-sister to 5 winners including the smart listed 7f winner Royal Storm. *"They call him Big Dave – he's about 16.2 hands! The strongest horse in the yard but for a big horse he's very active and probably won't take as much time as you'd think."*

574. UNNAMED ★★★★
b.c. Compton Place – Clincher Club (Polish Patriot).
April 17. Ninth foal. 75,000Y. Tattersalls October Book 1. R O'Ryan. Half-brother to the smart 2-y-o 6f winner and Group 1 1m Racing Post Trophy third Henrik (by Primo Dominie), to the quite useful 2-y-o 6f winners Bishop's Lake (by Lake Coniston) and Spritzeria (by Bigstone) and a minor winner abroad by Soviet Star. The dam, a fair 5f (at 2 yrs) and 7.5f winner, is a half-sister to 9 winners. The second dam, Merry Rous (by Rousillon), won once at 2 yrs and is a half-sister to 5 winners including the dual Group 3 winning sprinter Tina's Pet. (Jim McGrath). *"Probably my favourite yearling last year, he was the nicest one we bought. We're just stepping him up now, he'll probably be a six furlong type."*

575. UNNAMED ★★
ch.c. Compton Place – Flying Finish (Priolo).
March 16. Second foal. €43,000Y. Goffs Orby. Robin O'Ryan. Half-brother to the fair 2009 2-y-o 7f winner Newton Circus (by Verglas). The dam, a minor French 2-y-o winner, is a sister to the Group 2 Prix de Chaudenay winner Flyway and a half-sister to 6 winners including the US dual Grade 2 winner Falcon Flight. The second dam, Flying Circus (by Gay Mecene), won 3 minor races at 2 yrs in France and is a half-sister to 7 winners including the German Group 2 and Group 3 winner Flying Brave. *"He went a bit light on me so we gave him a break and he's just come back in. I don't really know a lot about him yet."*

576. UNNAMED ★★★
b.c. Marju – Irina (Polar Falcon).
April 12. Fifth foal. £42,000Y. Doncaster St Leger. Highflyer Bloodstock. Brother to the fairly useful 7f to 9f winner of 4 races (including at 2 yrs) and subsequent US winner Icemancometh and half-brother to the modest 7f winner of 4 races (including at 2 yrs) Imperial Lucky (by Imperial Ballet). The dam, a fairly useful Irish 7f and 1m winner at 3 and 4 yrs, is a half-sister to one winner. The second dam, Bird Of Love (by Ela-Mana-Mou), is a placed half-sister to 6 winners including the Australian Grade 1 winner Water Boatman and the Group 3 winner Hill Hopper (herself dam of the Group 1 Fillies' Mile and Coronation Stakes winner Nannina). *"Funnily enough I was under bidder to him as a yearling and the owner sent him to me six weeks later. I was mad about him as a yearling and I'm delighted to have him. I'm only just stepping him up now, so I don't know a lot about him."*

577. UNNAMED ★★
b.f. Encosta De Lago – Reematna (Sabrehill).
April 23. 20,000Y. Tattersalls December. Bobby O'Ryan. Half-sister to the fairly useful dual 6f winner (including at 2 yrs) Ebn Reem (by Mark Of Esteem), to the fairly useful 2-y-o dual 6f winner Dahteer (by Bachir), the quite useful dual 1m and subsequent UAE 6f winner My Verse (by Exceed And Excel) and the fair UAE 7f winner Fire Two (by Cape Cross). The dam, a fair 7f placed 3-y-o, is a full or half-sister to 2 winners including the Italian Derby winner and Irish Derby second Morshdi. The second dam, Reem Albaraari (by Sadler's Wells), was a fair dual 6f placed 2-y-o. *"She's not very big but she looks very genuine. We're just stepping her up now, so we're still learning about her."*

578. UNNAMED ★★★
b.f. Alhaarth – She's Classy (Boundary).
March 28. Sixth foal. £24,000Y. Doncaster St Leger. Robin O'Ryan. Sister to the fair 1m and 10f winner Miss Sophisticat (by Alhaarth) and half-sister to the modest 7f winner Royal Manor (by King's Best) and the minor US 3-y-o winner Swanky (by Saint Ballado). The dam a winner of 2 races at 2 yrs in the USA including a stakes event, was Grade 1 placed twice and is a half-sister to 3 minor winners. The second dam, Stately Dance (by Stately Don), won 2 minor races in the USA and is a half-sister to 4

winners including the Coronation Cup winner and sire Be My Native. *"Quite a nice filly and for an Alhaarth she's got plenty of speed, but she'll want six or seven furlongs in time."*

579. UNNAMED ★★
ch.c. Araafa – Truly Bewitched (Affirmed).
April 21. Seventh foal. £34,000Y. Doncaster St Leger. Highflyer Bloodstock. Half-brother to the modest 2009 2-y-o 7f winner Truly Magic (by Traditionally), to the useful 12f winner of 5 races Red Merlin, to the fair 2-y-o 5f winner Red Trance (both by Soviet Star), the fairly useful 7f and 1m winner Truly Enchanting (by Danehill Dancer) and the 1m winner and Group 3 Prix Miesque third Arabian Spell (by Desert Prince) and the fair 2-y-o 7f winner Trueblue Wizard (by Bachelor Duke). The dam, a quite useful 2-y-o 6f winner, is a half-sister to 4 winners including the US Grade 2 winner Chinese Dragon. The second dam, Fabulous Fairy (by Alydar), a fair 3-y-o 10f winner, is a half-sister to 5 winners and to the dam of the top-class miler Desert Prince. *"Early on he looked like being sharp and we gave him a chance but he's one for seven furlongs, so we've laid off him for now because he thought he was quicker than he is!"*

JEREMY GASK
Jeremy's assistant, Kevin Blake, was good enough to chat about these two-year-olds with me.

580. AMUN RA (USA) ★★★
b.br.c. E Dubai – Pocketbrook (Montbrook).
March 15. Fourth foal. $52,000Y. Keeneland September. D Farrington. Brother to the US Grade 2 Churchill Downs Stakes winner Accredit and half-brother to the minor 2009 2-y-o 4.5f winner Grand Times (by Greatness). The dam, a minor US 3-y-o winner, is a half-sister to 5 winners including the stakes winner and Grade 3 placed Sing Me Back Home. The second dam, Pocket Tunes (by Tunerup), won 13 minor races in the USA. (Horses First Racing Ltd). *"He's very well-bred, being a full brother to a Grade 2 winner in America. A big, scopey colt and a very nice mover, although he's doing well now he looks like being one for the mid- to-back end of the season, probably starting at six furlongs but he'll stay seven. He's growing into a really nice colt."*

581. CREW CUT (IRE) ★★
gr.c. Acclamation – Carabine (Dehere).
April 22. Sixth foal. £50,000Y. Doncaster St Leger. D Farrington. Brother to the fair 6f winner of 4 races Sutton Veny and half-brother to the fair 5f, 6f (both at 2 yrs) and 9.5f winner Fiore Di Bosco (by Charnwood Forest) and the Irish 7f and subsequent minor US stakes winner Glorificamus (by Shinko Forest). The dam is an unraced half-sister to 8 winners including the 2,000 Guineas winner Mystiko. The second dam, Carracciola (by Zeddaan), was placed four times in France and is a half-sister to 10 winners including the Group 2 Prix de Malleret winner Calderina. (Horses First Racing Ltd). *"He's going to be like his sister Sutton Veny and be a two-year-old for the back-end of the season. She won four races for us but didn't run at two. This is a big, scopey colt with a really nice attitude and if his body was as forward as his mind he'd be running now, but we won't be rushing him. A very nice colt that'll be much better next year."*

582. PALINDRAMIC (IRE) ★★★
ch.c. Chineur – Compton Girl (Compton Place).
February 24. Fourth foal. 11,000Y. Tattersalls October Book 3. Half-brother to the fair 2009 2-y-o 5f winner Night Trade (by Trade Fair). The dam is an unraced half-sister to 5 winners including Repertory (winner of the Group 3 Prix du Petit Couvert three times). The second dam, Susie's Baby (by Balidar), was an unplaced half-sister to 7 winners including The Go-Between (Group 3 Cornwallis Stakes). (Mr S A Herbert). *"He's quite small and strong and the type that should be going early. He's doing everything asked of him, galloping and going along fine and he should be out for late May. His pedigree is all about being fast and early, and he wouldn't be sure to stay further than six furlongs."* TRAINERS' BARGAIN BUY

583. UNNAMED ★★★
b.c. Encosta De Lago – Duchy Of Cornwall (The Minstrel).
May 23. Twelfth foal. €80,000Y. Goffs Orby. Horses First Racing/D Farrington. Half- brother to 7 winners including the Australian

Group winners Newquay and Civil List (both by Last Tycoon), the Australian listed winner Lands End (by Vettori), the Australian Group-placed winners Point Of Honour and St Pirion (both by Danehill) and the modest 6f and 7f winner of 4 races Downhill Skier (by Danehill Dancer). The dam, a fair 3-y-o 7f winner, is a half-sister to 5 winners. The second dam, Queen Of Cornwall (by Cornish Prince), a winner of 6 races here and in the USA, was third in the Group 2 Flying Childers Stakes and is a half-sister to 9 winners. (Horses First Racing Ltd). *"Despite the fact he was a May foal he'd be our most forward two-year-old. He's not over-big, which is a family trait I believe, and he's a hardy little colt. He'll be out by the end of May at the latest, probably over six furlongs."*

584. UNNAMED ★★
b.f. Iffraaj – Lucky For Me (King Of Kings).
April 14. Third foal. 32,000Y. Tattersalls October Book 2. Horses First Racing. Half-sister to the 2009 6f placed 2-y-o Serhaal (by Green Desert) and to a winner in Spain by Okawango. The dam is an unraced full or half-sister to 7 winners including the minor US stakes winner Legend Of Russia. The second dam, Vilikaia (by Nureyev), won the Group 2 Prix de la Porte Maillot and is a sister to the Group 2 Prix d'Astarte winner Navratilovna and a half-sister to the good filly Maximova (herself dam of the Group 1 winners Septieme Ciel and Macoumba). (Horses First Racing Ltd). *"A nice filly with a very likeable attitude, she was going along quite nicely but she had a little muscle problem – nothing major and she's doing light work now. She's not over-big and I should think she'll come up quite quickly and be ready for August, starting over six furlongs."*

JAMES GIVEN

585. ALHORALHORA ★★★
b.f. Rock Hard Ten – Rahcak (Generous).
March 25. Sixth foal. 52,000Y. Tattersalls October Book 2. Anthony Stroud. The dam is a placed half-sister to 3 winners including the top-class colt Mark of Esteem, winner of the 2,000 Guineas, the Queen Elizabeth II Stakes and the Tripleprint Celebration Mile. The second dam, Homage (by Ajdal), was unraced and is closely related to the very smart Group 1 9.2f Prix Jean Prat winner Local Talent and a half-sister to the Group 2 6f Mill Reef Stakes winner Local Suitor. (Danethorpe Racing).

586. JACK SMUDGE ★★★
b.br.c. One Cool Cat – Forever Fine (Sunshine Forever).
January 28. Ninth foal. 26,000Y. Tattersalls October Book 2. Anthony Stroud. Closely related to the minor US stakes winner Stormy Forever (by Storm Boot) and half-brother to the fairly useful 2-y-o 1m winner Familiar Territory (by Cape Cross), the quite useful 2-y-o 5f and 6f winner Oasis Breeze (by Oasis Dream) and the minor US and Mexican winners by Peaks And Valleys and Announce. The dam, a US stakes-placed winner at 2 yrs, is a half-sister to 7 winners. The second dam, She's Sofine (by Bold Hour), won 5 races in the USA and is a half-sister to 9 winners including the US Grade 1 winner Rest Your Case. (Danethorpe Racing).

587. NELLA SOFIA ★★
bl.f. Diktat – Night Symphonie (Cloudings).
April 12. Fourth foal. 13,000Y. Tattersalls October Book 2. James Given. Half-brother to the quite useful 1m and 10f winner Buddy Holly (by Reel Buddy) and to the Italian 2-y-o winner Bacco (by Lucky Owners). The dam, a minor 3-y-o winner in Germany, is a half-sister to 12 winners including the German Group 2 winner Network. The second dam, Note (by Reliance), a minor German winner, is a half-sister to 11 winners in Germany. (Mrs Lynne Daykin).

588. PIZZARRA ★★★★
b.f. Shamardal – Pizzicato (Statoblest).
January 25. Seventh foal. 35,000Y. Tattersalls October Book 1. Anthony Stroud. Half-sister to the 2-y-o Group 2 5f Flying Childers Stakes and Group 3 5f Molecomb Stakes winner Wunders Dream (by Averti), to the very useful Irish Group 3 Ridgewood Pearl Stakes winner Grecian Dancer (by Dansili), the fairly useful 6f (at 2 yrs) and 7f winner Go Between (by Daggers Drawn), the quite useful Irish 5f and 1m winner Astonish (by Cape Cross) and the quite useful 7f winner Plucky (by Kyllachy). The dam, a modest 5f and 5.3f winner at 3 yrs, is a half-sister to 5 winners including the high-class

Hong Kong horses Mensa and Firebolt. The second dam, Musianica (by Music Boy), was a fairly useful 2-y-o dual 6f winner. (Danethorpe Racing).

589. SILK BOUNTY ★★
b.c. Bahamian Bounty – Sahara Silk (Desert Style).
February 11. First foal. The dam, a fair winner of 10 races over 5f and 6f, is a half-sister to one winner. The second dam, Buddy And Soda (by Imperial Frontier), is a half-sister to 9 winners. (Danethorpe Racing).

590. SKY DIAMOND (IRE) ★★★
b.f. Diamond Green – Jewell In The Sky (Sinndar).
February 29. First foal. €20,000Y. Goffs Orby. Anthony Stroud. The dam is an unraced half-sister to several winners including the very useful 2-y-o 7f winner and Group 3 Horris Hill Stakes third Aahaykid. Closely related to the 2004 2-y-o Tiny Petal (by Grand Lodge) and half-sister to the Irish dual 10f winner Out Of Thanks (by Sadler's Wells), the minor Irish 3-y-o 10f winner Trusted Instinct (by Polish Precedent) and the Irish 2-y-o 6f winner Whistle Down (by Danehill). The second dam, Trust In Luck (by Nashwan), an Irish 7f winner, is a half-sister to numerous winners including the US Grade 1 winner Dress To Thrill. (Danethorpe Racing).

591. STILETTOESINTHEMUD ★★
ch.f. Footstepsinthesand – The Stick (Singspiel).
March 16. Third foal. 7,000Y. Tattersalls October. Anthony Stroud. The dam, placed fourth once over 7f from 10 starts, is a sister to one winner and a half-sister to 6 winners. The second dam, Fatah Flare (by Alydar), won over 6f (at 2 yrs) and the Group 3 10.5f Musidora Stakes at 3 yrs. She is a half-sister to 8 winners including Sabin, a dual US Grade 1 winner over 9f and 10f. (Danethorpe Racing Partnership).

592. TSARINA LOUISE ★★★
b.f. Red Ransom – Imperial Bailiwick (Imperial Frontier).
March 25. Eleventh foal. £37,000Y. Doncaster St Leger. James Given. Half-sister to the fair 2009 5f and 6f placed 2-y-o Autocracy (by Green Desert), to the high-class Haydock Park Sprint Cup and the Nunthorpe Stakes winner Reverence (by Mark Of Esteem), the very useful 2-y-o listed 6f Chesham Stakes winner and 1m Britannia Handicap second Helm Bank (by Wild Again), the quite useful 6f (at 2 yrs) and 5f winner of 5 races Impressible (by Oasis Dream), the fairly useful 5f (at 2 yrs) and 6f winner Quiet Elegance (by Fantastic Light), the modest 6f winner Fortress (by Generous), the modest 10f winner Sedgwick (by Nashwan) and a winner at up to 7.5f in Italy by Efisio. The dam, a useful winner of 3 races at around 5f including the Group 2 Flying Childers Stakes, was placed in the Molecomb Stakes and the Prix du Petit-Couvert and is a half-sister to 3 winners in France (all over 1m+). The second dam, Syndikos (by Nashua) was second 6 times in the USA and is a half-sister to 5 minor winners. (Danethorpe Racing).

593. UNNAMED ★★★
b.f. Diktat – Me (Green Desert).
January 4. First foal. The dam is an unplaced sister to the useful 2-y-o dual 6f winner Ego and a half-sister to 2 winners including the useful 2-y-o 6f winner and Group 2 7f Champagne Stakes third Ghayth. The second dam, Myself (by Nashwan), a smart winner of the Group 3 7f Nell Gwyn Stakes, is a half-sister to 12 winners including the Group 3 Princess Margaret Stakes winner Bluebook. (Brighton Farm Ltd).

594. UNNAMED ★★★
b.br.c. Sky Mesa – Melrose Morning (Shadeed).
February 11. Seventh foal. $62,000Y. Fasig-Tipton Kentucky. David Eiffe. Half-brother to 3 minor winners in the USA by Pyramid Peak. The dam is a placed half-sister to 6 winners including the dual US Grade 3 winner Jambalaya Jazz. The second dam, Glorious Morning (by Graustark), is an unraced sister to the US dual Grade 1 winner Tempest Queen and the Grade 2 winner Steal A Kiss and a half-sister to two other Graded stakes winners. (Brighton Farm Ltd).

595. UNNAMED ★★
gr.c. Tapit – Scootie Utie (Fappiano).
March 5. Eighth foal. $25,000Y. Fasig-Tipton Kentucky. David Eiffe. Half-brother to a minor US 3-y-o winner by Glitterman. The dam is a

placed half-sister to 3 winners including the Japanese $1 million earner Sugino Cutie and the dam of the Group 3 Norfolk Stakes winner Warm Heart and the Irish listed winners Miguel Cervantes and Royal Tigress. The second dam, Summer Mood (by Raja Baba), a winner of 17 races and a champion sprinter in Canada, is a half-sister to the multiple Graded stakes winner Present Value. (Brighton Farm Ltd).

596. UNNAMED ★★★
b.br.f. Medaglia d'Oro – Sheena's Gold (Fast Gold).
April 7. Thirteenth foal. $80,000Y. Fasig-Tipton Kentucky. David Eiffe. Half-sister to 3 winners including the US Grade 1 Champagne Stakes winner The Groom Is Red (by Runaway Groom) and the minor US 3-y-o winner Factual Evidence (by Known Fact). The dam, a minor winner in the USA, is a half-sister to 8 winners including the dams of the Group 1 Queen Elizabeth II Stakes winner Where Or When and the Group 1 Prix Saint-Alary winner Air de Rien. The second dam, Afasheen (by Sheshoon), is a placed sister to the Prix de Minerve winner Flaming Heart (dam of the Prix Jean-Prat winner Maroun) and a half-sister to the Group 3 winner Afayoun. (Brighton Farm Ltd).

597. UNNAMED ★★★♣
br.c. Marju – Unreal (Dansili).
April 5. Second foal. 65,000Y. Tattersalls December. Anthony Stroud. The dam, a quite useful 2-y-o 5f winner, is a half-sister to 7 winners including the 1m and 9f winner Phantom Quest, the dual 7f winner Sensory and the 10f winner and Group 1 Racing Post Trophy third Illustrator – all very useful. The second dam, Illusory (by Kings Lake), a quite useful 3-y-o 6f winner, is a sister to the Group 2 Lowther Stakes winner Kingscote (herself dam of four stakes winners) and a half-sister to 7 winners. (Mr J Williams).

598. UNNAMED ★★★
br.f. Cape Cross – Wunders Dream (Averti).
March 14. Third foal. 30,000Y. Tattersalls October Book 2. Not sold. Half-sister to the modest 5f placed 2-y-o Paradise Dream (by Kyllachy). The dam, a winner of 4 races at 2 yrs including the Group 2 5f Flying Childers Stakes and the Group 3 5f Molecomb Stakes, is a half-sister to 4 winners including the Irish Group 3 winner Grecian Dancer. The second dam, Pizzicato (by Statoblest), a modest 5f and 5.3f winner at 3 yrs, is a half-sister to 5 winners including the high-class Hong Kong horses Mensa and Firebolt. (Mr J Ellis).

GODOLPHIN (SAEED BIN SUROOR)

I owe a big thank you to Diana Cooper for helping me out once again with this information on some of the Godolphin horses. The stable had a terrific season with their two-year-olds in 2009, so look out for this lot!

599. ACHAEMENES ★★★
b.c. Singspiel – Forum Floozie (Danasinga).
March 16. First foal. The dam won 5 races and was Group 1 placed twice over 1m in Australia and is a half-sister to Starcraft, a winner of six Grade 1 events in Australasia and Europe including the Queen Elizabeth II Stakes. The second dam, Flying Floozie (by Pompeii Court), is a lightly raced half-sister to the South African Group 2 winner Happy Heiress. *"This colt is a big, rangy good-looking type who won't be early, but he has a good outlook and is one to look out for at the back-end of the season."*

600. ARTEMISIA (IRE) ★★★
b.f. Cape Cross – Cashel Queen (Kingmambo).
March 27. Third foal. 200,000Y. Tattersalls October 1. John Ferguson. Half-sister to the fair 2009 2-y-o 7f winner Cash Queen Anna (by Dr Fong). The dam was placed over 1m and 9.5f and is a half-sister to 7 winners including the French 1,000 Guineas and Irish 1,000 Guineas placed La Nuit Rose (herself dam of the US Grade 2 winner Tam Lin). The second dam, Caerlina (by Caerleon), won the Group 1 Prix de Diane and is a half-sister to 8 winners. *"An eye moving filly and although she's still a little weak, she is very pleasing. She still has some way to go but has a great attitude and is improving all the time."*

601. BATTLE ENSIGN (IRE) ★★★★
b.c. Invincible Spirit – Priere (Machiavellian).
January 21. First foal. €260,000Y. Arqana Deauville August. John Ferguson. The dam won twice and was listed-placed in France and

Germany at 3 and 4 yrs. She is a half-sister to 3 winners out of the French listed winner Play Around (by Niniski), herself a half-sister to 6 winners. *"This is a good-looking, athletic colt with a very positive attitude. He's well-grown and should be out mid-summer."*

602. BEDEVILMENT (USA) ★★★★★
b.f. *Street Cry – Bedazzle (Dixieland Band).*
April 23. Sister to the Breeders Cup Juvenile, Kentucky Derby and Travers Stakes winner Street Sense. The dam won four races at 3 and 5 yrs in the USA and is a half-sister to 6 winners including the stakes winner Binalegend. The second dam, Majestic Legend (by His Majesty), was a US stakes winner of 7 races and is a half-sister to 7 winners including the US triple Grade 3 winner and sire Mr Greeley. *"A very laid-back filly, she loves her work and is very professional, is a nice type and should be racing in early summer. Looks to have some class."*

603. BEYOND REASON (IRE) ★★★
b.c. *Cape Cross – Easy Option (Prince Sabo).*
April 14. Eighth foal. Half-brother to the Group 1 1m Sussex Stakes and Group 1 7f Prix de la Foret winner Court Masterpiece (by Polish Precedent), to the useful 6f (at 2 yrs) and 7f winner Easy Air, the French 5f winner (including at 2 yrs) Maybe Forever (both by Zafonic), the quite useful 6f (at 2 yrs) and 7f winner Generous Option (by Cadeaux Genereux) and the fair 6f winner Pride In Me (by Indian Ridge). The dam, a smart winner of the listed 5f St Hugh's Stakes and second in the Group 2 5f Prix du Gros-Chene, is a half-sister to 8 winners including the useful 2-y-o 5f winner and Group 2 Flying Childers Stakes third Wanton (herself dam of the Irish 1,000 Guineas winner Classic Park). The second dam, Brazen Faced (by Bold And Free), a quite useful 2-y-o 5f winner, is a half-sister to 8 winners including the Musidora Stakes winner Lovers Lane. *"Very easy-moving and straightforward, he has some strengthening still to do and it's a bit early to know how much speed he'll have, but we would hope to have him out in June/July."*

604. BLACK AURA (IRE) ★★★
b.c. *Dalakhani – Canouan (Sadler's Wells).*
April 23. Fourth foal. 75,000Y. Tattersalls October 1. John Ferguson. Half-brother to the unplaced 2009 2-y-o Ilston Lord (by One Cool Cat). The dam was placed 5 times in Ireland including in a listed event and is a half-sister to 5 winners including the Group 1 Irish Oaks winner Winona. The second dam, My Potters (by Irish River), an Irish 3-y-o 1m handicap winner, was listed-placed and is a half-sister to numerous winners including the champion US sprinter My Juliet (herself the dam of two Grade 1 winners) and the very smart middle-distance colt Lyphard's Special. *"This is a middle-distance type for next season so he won't be out early, but he's done nothing but please."*

605. BLUE TIGER'S EYE (IRE) ★★★
b.br.c. *Motivator – Bush Cat (Kingmambo).*
April 9. Fourth foal. 110,000Y. Tattersalls October 2. Blandford Bloodstock. Half-brother to Jack O'Lantern (by Shamardal), placed third over 7f on his only start at 2 yrs in 2009, to the quite useful 2-y-o 1m winner and subsequent US Grade 3 placed Meer Kat (by Red Ransom) and the moderate dual 1m seller winner Ask Dan (by Refuse To Bend). The dam, a quite useful 2-y-o 7f winner, is a half-sister to 6 winners. The second dam, Arbusha (by Danzig), won the listed 1m Schwarzgold Rennen, was third in the Group 3 Royal Whip Stakes and is a sister to the Group 2 6f Goldene Peitsche winner Nicholas and a half-sister to 9 winners. *"This colt grew quite a bit during the winter, but he's now settled down well to his work and is quite forward-going, enjoying himself and active."*

606. BURJ HATTA (USA) ★★★★
b.br.c. *Kingmambo – Vadahilla (Danehill).*
January 23. Third foal. $750,000Y. Saratoga August. John Gosden. The dam, a minor winner at 3 yrs in France and 4 yrs in North America, is a half-sister to 10 winners including the Grade 1 Breeders Cup Mile winner and sire Val Royal and the dam of the Group 1 Prix d'Ispahan winner Valixir. The second dam, Vadlava (by Bikala), won at 2 yrs and listed-placed in France. *"We like this horse, he's a very athletic, straightforward colt with plenty of quality and a seven furlong type for mid-summer."*

607. DRAGON STORM (USA) ★★★
b.br.c. Bernardini – Windsharp (Lear Fan).
January 26. Half-brother to the Grade 1 12f Breeders Cup Turf and Grade 1 Hollywood Derby winner Johar (by Gone West), to the Grade 1 Del Mar Oaks winner Dessert (by Storm Cat) and the quite useful 10f winner Game Stalker (by Elusive Quality). The dam won 11 races in France, Canada and the USA including the Grade 1 San Luis Rey Stakes and the Grade 1 Beverly Hills Handicap. The second dam, Yes She's Sharp (by Sharpen Up), won at 3 yrs in Ireland and is a half-sister to 4 winners. *"This colt has a lot to live up to in his pedigree, he's not the most precocious but he's really beginning to shape up and progress with fitness. He has quite a laid-back attitude and it will be very exciting to see the first Bernardini's on the track."*

608. FARHH ★★★
b.c. Pivotal – Gonbarda (Lando).
March 4. First foal. The dam, a German dual Group 1 12f winner, is a full or half-sister to numerous winners including Gonfilia, a winner of the Group 3 8.5f Princess Elizabeth Stakes and four listed events. The second dam, Gonfalon (by Slip Anchor), is a half-sister to several winners. *"He's improving all the time, he's athletic, showing promise and shaping up to be a nice prospect for mid-summer."*

609. FAVART (IRE) ★★★
b.c. Invincible Spirit – Urgele (Zafonic).
February 9. Fourth foal. €90,000Y. Goffs Orby. John Ferguson. Half-brother to the fairly useful 1m winner of 3 races (including at 2 yrs) Cordell (by Fasliyev). The dam, a listed winner of 4 races in France and third in the Group 2 Prix Miesque, is a half-sister to 7 winners. The second dam, Urmia (by Persian Bold), a listed-placed winner in France, is a half-sister to 10 winners including the Group 2 Prix Noailles winner Gunboat Diplomacy. *"This is a tough horse who is coming together nicely. He looks as though six furlongs will be his trip and he shouldn't take too long to come to hand. One of our earlier runners all being well."*

610. HFLAH (USA) ★★★★
b.c. Monsun – Maids Causeway (Giant's Causeway).
March 20. First foal. The dam won Group 1 1m Coronation Stakes and the Group 2 7f Rockfel Stakes and was second in the Group 1 Fillies' Mile. The second dam, Vallee des Reves (by Kingmambo), is an unraced half-sister to the Group 2 Prix du Muguet winner Vetheuil, the Group 3 Prix de l'Opera winner Verveine (herself dam of the Grade 1 winners Vallee Enchantee and Volga) and the dam of the Group 1 Grand Prix de Paris winner Vespone. *"A very pleasing, quality type colt, he's proving very professional and let's hope he shows some of his dam's precocity."*

611. KONSAL (USA) ★★★
ch.c. Storm Cat – Elbaaha (Arazi).
January 25. Seventh foal. €900,000Y. Arqana Deauville August. John Ferguson. Half-brother to 4 winners including the Group 1 Juddmonte International Gran Premio di Milano and Dubai World Cup winner Electrocutionist (by Red Ransom) and the listed Prix des Lilas winner Grogorieva (by Woodman). The dam was a useful 11.5f winner and a half-sister to the dams of the Group 1 winners Royal Highness and Robertico. The second dam, Gesedeh (by Ela-Mana-Mou), winner of the Group 3 10.5f Prix de Flore and the Pretty Polly Stakes, was placed in the Sun Chariot Stakes and the Prince of Wales's Stakes and is a half-sister to the top-class middle-distance stayer Ardross. *"This is a half-brother to Electrocutionist, so he's close to our hearts. He's a very good-looking horse with a lot of scope and is just beginning to shape up. He won't be early but should be a seven furlong type for the second half of the season."*

612. LASTARRIA (IRE) ★★★★
b.f. Cape Cross – Villarrica (Selkirk).
January 10. First foal. The dam, a fair 10f and 11f winner, is a half-sister to 2 winners. The second dam, Melikah (by Lammtarra), was a smart winner of the listed 10f Pretty Polly Stakes and was third in the Oaks. She is a half-sister to the outstanding colt Sea The Stars, to the top-class Galileo and the Group 1 12f Gran Premio del Jockey Club and Group 1 10.5f Tattersalls Gold Cup winner Black Sam Bellamy. *"A really nice individual who still needs to get some sun on her back and is not bred to be early. She's very attractive and will hopefully*

race in the second half of the season with a view to a middle-distance career next season."

613. NAJOUM (USA) ★★★
b.f. Giant's Causeway – Divine Dixie (Dixieland Band).
February 16. Seventh foal. Half-sister to the Grade 1 Blue Grass Stakes winner Bandini (by Fusaichi Pegasus). The dam, a stakes-placed winner of 2 races at 3 yrs in the USA, is a half-sister to 2 minor US stakes winners. The second dam, Hail Atlantis (by Seattle Slew), won the Grade 1 Santa Anita Oaks. *"There is both speed and stamina in her family and this filly shows some precocity, so she'll be a June/July type two-year-old over six/seven furlongs. She is keen to please but is not one to rush."*

614. PIERIDES (USA) ★★★
ch.f. Medicean – Musical Treat (Royal Academy).
March 5. Fifth living foal. 500,000Y. Tattersalls October 1. John Ferguson. Half-sister to the useful 2009 2-y-o French 7f winner Frozen Power (by Oasis Dream), to the Prix Marcel Boussac, 1,000 Guineas and Irish 1,000 Guineas winner Finsceal Beo (by Mr Greeley), the quite useful 7f winner and listed placed Musical Bar (by Barathea) and a 3-y-o winner abroad by Red Ransom. The dam, a useful 3-y-o 7f winner and listed-placed twice, subsequently won 4 races at 4 yrs in Canada and the USA and is a half-sister to 6 winners. The second dam, Mountain Ash (by Dominion), won 10 races here and in Italy including the Group 3 Premio Royal Mares and is a half-sister to 7 winners. *"Pierides is showing some precocity as well as the tough professionalism of her half-siblings Finsceal Beo and Frozen Power. She should be racing by early summer."*

615. QUEEN'S JOURNAL (USA) ★★★★
b.c. Kingmambo – Marienbad (Darshaan).
March 22. Half-brother to the Group 1 12f Prix de l'Arc de Triomphe and dual German Group 1 winner Marienbard (by Caerleon), to the fair 12f and 14f winner Cape Marien (by Cape Cross), the fair 12f winner Marine City (by Carnegie), the modest 12f winner Genscher (by Cadeaux Genereux) and a 3-y-o winner in Japan by Polish Precedent. The dam, a French 1m winner at both 2 and 3 yrs, is a half-sister to 6 winners including the French and Italian listed winner Kentucky Coffee. The second dam, Marie de Fontenoy (by Lightning), won once in France and is a half-sister to 7 winners including the Group 1 Prix Morny winner Sakura Reiko. *"A half-brother to our Arc winner Marienbard, he's a neat, forward going type who should debut over seven furlongs in mid-summer."*

616. RAGSAH (IRE) ★★★
ch.f. Shamardal – Colorado Dancer (Shareef Dancer).
April 19. Half-sister to the outstanding Dubai Millennium (by Seeking The Gold), winner of the Dubai World Cup, the Prix Jacques le Marois, the Prince Of Wales's Stakes and the Queen Elizabeth II Stakes (all Group 1 events), the Group 2 10.5f Prix Greffulhe second Denver County (by Mr Prospector), the useful French 12f winner Fort Morgan (by Pleasant Colony), the UAE 1m to 12f winner and listed-placed Hobb Alwahtan, the fair UAE 9f and 10f winner Dubai Vision (both by Machiavellian) and the 2-y-o 7f winner (on his only start) Dubai Excellence (by Highest Honor). The dam, a very smart winner of the Group 2 13.5f Prix de Pomone and the Group 3 12f Prix de Minerve, was placed in the Group 1 Prix Vermeille and two US Grade 1 events. She is closely related to the very useful Grade 1 Gamely Handicap winner Northern Aspen, to the Group 1 July Cup winner Hamas and the Group 1 Grand Prix de Paris winner Fort Wood and a half-sister to the Prix d'Astarte winner Elle Seule (herself dam of the Irish 1,000 Guineas winner Mehthaaf) and the champion US 2-y-o colt Timber Country. The second dam, Fall Aspen (by Pretense), won 8 races notably the Grade 1 7f Matron Stakes. *"This is a strong, mature, forward-going type who is straightforward and moves well. She's very enthusiastic and although it remains to be seen how much speed she has, she's looking like a mid-summer type at the moment."*

617. RAW SPIRIT ★★
ch.c. Shirocco – Reem Dubai (Nashwan).
May 10. Ninth foal. 160,000Y. Tattersalls October 1. John Ferguson. Closely related to the US Grade 1 Beverly D Stakes winner Royal Highness (by Monsun) and half-brother

to German Group 3 winner Royal Dubai (by Dashing Blade) and the moderate Irish 9f winner Ardwelshin (by Ajdayt). The dam was placed once over 12f and is a half-sister to 2 winners including the dam of the Group 1 Dubai World Cup winner Electrocutionist and to the placed dam of the Group 1 German Derby winner Robertico. The second dam, Gesedeh (by Ela-Mana-Mou), a smart middle-distance filly and winner of the Group 3 10.5f Prix de Flore and the Pretty Polly Stakes, was second in the Group 2 Sun Chariot Stakes and is a half-sister to the top-class middle-distance stayer Ardross. *"This colt goes well for a big horse at this time of the year. He's easy-going, with a good action and willing with it, but he is bred for next year and won't be early."*

618. ROAYH (USA) ★★★★
ch.c. Speightstown – Most Remarkable (Marquetry).
March 31. Fifth foal. $220,000Y. Keeneland September. R O'Gorman. Half-brother to the US stakes winner of 5 races Remarkable Remy (by Hennessy) and to the minor US 3-y-o winner Remarkable Storm (by Stormy Atlantic). The dam is an unplaced half-sister to the US triple Grade 2 winner and Grade 1 placed Snow Dance and to two US stakes-placed winners. The second dam, Northern Pageant (by Spectacular Bid), is an unraced half-sister to the Grade 1 placed Southern Halo and to the dam of the US Grade 1 winner General Challenge. *"An active type who is coming together nicely at the moment, he's very straightforward and he could debut in May. He looks like a six furlong type at the moment and there is a lot of speed in the family."*

619. SAHAFH (USA) ★★★★
b.br.f. Rock Hard Ten – Fireman's Ball (Hennessy).
February 2. Fifth foal. $475,000Y. Saratoga August. John McCormack. Sister to the minor US 2-y-o stakes winner Pamona Ball and half-sister to a minor US winner by Grand Slam. The dam is an unplaced half-sister to Ozone Friendly, a useful 2-y-o winner of the Group 1 5.5f Prix Robert Papin and fourth in the Group 1 6f Prix Morny. The second dam, Kristana (by Kris), a fairly useful 10f winner, was placed in the Group 3 Prix de Royaumont and is a half-sister to the dams of the good winners Ardkinglass, Reprimand, Wiorno and Fawzi. *"A very athletic filly with a good stride, she promises quality and will be out in mid-summer."*

620. SIDERA (IRE) ★★★
b.c. Medicean – Alluring Park (Green Desert).
February 5. Fourth foal. 150,000Y. Tattersalls October 1. John Ferguson. The dam, a 2-y-o 6f winner and dual listed-placed, is a sister to the Japanese stakes winner Shinko Forest and a half-sister to 6 winners including the champion 2-y-o and Epsom Derby winner New Approach and the Group 3 1m Matron Stakes winner and dual Group 1 placed Dazzling Park. The second dam, Park Express (by Ahonoora), won 5 races including the Group 1 10f Phoenix Champion Stakes and is a half-sister to 6 winners including the listed 6f Firth of Clyde Stakes winner Myra's Best. *"This is a good-looking individual who moves well. He has a very laid-back attitude and it's still early days for him but he seems to be a nice type in the waiting."*

621. SIGNS IN THE SAND ★★★★
b.c. Cape Cross – Gonfilia (Big Shuffle).
February 18. First foal. The dam won 7 races including the Group 3 8.5f Princess Elizabeth Stakes and four listed events and is a full or half-sister to 6 winners including the German dual Group 1 12f winner Gonbarda. The second dam, Gonfalon (by Slip Anchor), is a half-sister to several winners. *"This is a very bonny horse who seems to love his job. He's thriving, showing some speed and should be one of our earlier runners."*

622. STAR BLOSSOM (USA) ★★★
ch.f. Good Reward – Princess Kris (Kris).
March 20. Eighth foal. €220,000Y. Goffs Orby. John Ferguson. Half-sister to the 2009 2-y-o Group 1 7f National Stakes winner Kingsfort (by War Chant), to the US Grade 1 11f winner Prince Arch, the fair 10f to 12f winner Arty Crafty (both by Arch) and a minor winner in the USA. The dam, a quite useful 3-y-o 1m winner, is half-sister to 8 winners including the Group 3 May Hill Stakes winner Intimate Guest. The second dam, As You Desire Me (by Kalamoun), won 2 listed events in

France over 7.5f and 1m and is a half-sister to 7 winners including the Group 2 King Edward VII Stakes winner Classic Example. *"A half-sister to Kingsfort, she's going through a growing patch and has gone a little weak on us, but she's a very willing filly and will hopefully go forward again shortly."*

623. TANFEER ★★★
b.br.f. *Dansili – Mawaakeb (Diesis)*.
March 20. First foal. The dam is an unraced half-sister to one winner. The second dam, Muwakleh (by Machiavellian), winner of the UAE 1,000 Guineas and second in the Newmarket 1,000 Guineas, is a sister to the high-class Dubai World Cup and Prix Jean Prat winner Almutawakel and to the useful 10f winner Elmustanser and a half-sister to the smart 10f winner Inaaq. *"This is a lovely, tough little filly who is progressing daily and loves to please. We will see what her best trip will be in the next couple of months."*

624. TOUQUES (IRE) ★★★
b.c. *Dalakhani – Lisieux Orchid (Sadler's Wells)*.
April 27. Third foal. 135,000Y. Tattersalls October 1. John Ferguson. The dam, a quite useful Irish 12f winner, is a half-sister to 5 winners including the Group 1 National Stakes third Force Of Will. The second dam, Clear Issue (by Riverman), won once over 7f in Ireland at 3 yrs and is a half-sister to 8 winners including the US Grade 1 winner Twilight Agenda and the dam of the Group 1 winners Media Puzzle and Refuse To Bend. *"He covers the ground well and shows quality and promise, but he won't want to be rushed and is an interesting prospect for later in the season. He has the same Dalakhani-Sadler's Wells cross as another of our two-year-olds Black Aura."*

625. UNNAMED ★★★
ch.c. *Shamardal – Akrmina (Zafonic)*.
May 2. Third foal. The dam, a fair 7f winner, is a sister to the high-class triple Group 2 7f winner Iffraaj and the useful 2-y-o Group 3 7f Prix du Calvados winner Kareymah and a half-sister to the useful 7 winner of 4 races and listed-placed Taqdeyr. The second dam, Pastorale (Nureyev), a fairly useful 3-y-o 7f winner, is a half-sister to 7 winners including Cape Cross. *"He's shaping up nicely and at this stage he looks like he has the speed his breeding suggests. He could be out in a couple of months' time."*

626. UNNAMED ★★★
b.c. *Singspiel – My Dubai (Dubai Millennium)*.
March 2. Second foal. The dam, placed over 7f on her only start, is a half-sister to 7 winners including the very smart triple Group 2 7f winner Iffraaj, the useful 2-y-o Group 3 7f Prix du Calvados winner Kareymah and the useful dual 1m winner Jathaabeh. The second dam, Pastorale (by Nureyev), a fairly useful 3-y-o 7f winner, ran only twice more including in a walk-over. *"Like a few of our two-year-olds he's from the same family of Iffraaj, he's taking everything in his stride and pleasing at the moment. Probably one for the second half of the season."*

627. UNNAMED ★★★
ch.c. *Dubai Destination – Pastorale (Nureyev)*.
March 6. Brother to the useful 7 winner of 4 races and listed-placed Taqdeyr and half-brother to the high-class triple Group 2 7f winner Iffraaj, the useful 2-y-o Group 3 7f Prix du Calvados winner Kareymah, the fair 7f winner Akrmina (all by Zafonic), the useful dual 1m winner Jathaabeh (by Nashwan), the fairly useful 1m winner Mofarij (by Bering), the fair 1m and 11.5f winner Krosno (by Kris) and the French 11f winner In Arcadia (by Slip Anchor). The dam, a fairly useful 3-y-o 7f winner, is a half-sister to 7 winners including Cape Cross. The second dam, Park Appeal (by Ahonoora), won four 6f races including the Group 1 Cheveley Park Stakes and the Group 1 Moyglare Stud Stakes and is a sister to the Group 3 9f winner Nashamaa and a half-sister to the Irish Oaks and Ribblesdale Stakes winner Alydaress and the Cheveley Park Stakes winner Desirable – herself dam of the 1,000 Guineas winner Shadayid. *"Another from the same family, he is a half-brother to Iffraaj. He's straightforward, has a good attitude and although a little weak, it will be interesting to see how much speed he has mid-season."*

628. UNNAMED ★★★
b.f. *Distorted Humor – Fleet Lady (Avenue Of Flags)*.

May 3. Sister to the Grade 1 Breeders Cup Juvenile and Grade 1 Del Mar Futurity winner Midshipman and half-sister to the US Grade 2 placed winner Fast Cookie (by Deputy Minister). The second dam, Dear Mimi (by Roberto), is a half-sister to Salse. "She's going well at the moment, having taken time earlier in the year to pull herself together. She shows quality and at the moment it looks as though she could make into a six or seven furlong filly for June/July."

JOHN GOSDEN

629. AIKEN ★★
b.c. Selkirk – Las Flores (Sadler's Wells).
May 10. Brother to the useful 10f winner and Group 3 10f Prix de la Nonette third Felicity and half-brother to the very smart Group 2 7f Challenge Stakes winner Sleeping Indian (by Indian Ridge), the useful 10f winner Jalisco (by Machiavellian), the fairly useful 1m winner Spanish Spur (by Indian Ridge) and the quite useful 12f winners La Paz (by Nashwan) and Teeky (by Daylami). The dam, a useful 10f winner, was second in the Lingfield Oaks Trial and third in the Italian Oaks. She is a full or half-sister to numerous winners including the useful Irish 6f and 10f winner Dancing Goddess. The second dam, Producer (by Nashua), a top-class winner of the Group 1 7f Prix de la Foret and the Group 2 Prix de l'Opera, was second in the Irish Oaks and is a half-sister to the Grade 3 stakes winners Deb Marion and D O Lady and to the dam of the triple Grade 1 winner Yankee Affair. "He's a rangy, backward type but typical of the sire. Potentially a nice type of colt."

630. ANEEDAH ★★★
b.f. Invincible Spirit – Fairy Of The Night (Danehill).
February 12. First foal. 170,000Y. Tattersalls October Book 1. Not sold. The dam, an Irish 7f listed and 9.5f winner, is a half-sister to the US Grade 3 winner Dress Rehearsal. The second dam, Sassenach (by Night Shift), a winner over 13f at 4 yrs in Ireland, is a half-sister to 3 winners including the Group 3 2m 2f Doncaster Cup winner Far Cry. "She's shot up behind, so she's going through a growing stage at the moment. She canters away, has a grand attitude and was bred by the late Liam Cashman – what a great loss to our business he is. A nice type of filly, but not a precocious one."

631. APEZINE (USA) ★★★★
b.br.f. Storm Cat – Fanzine (Cozzene).
February 12. Second foal. $190,000Y. Keeneland September. Blandford Bloodstock. The dam is an unraced sister to the Group 3 Prix de Guiche and subsequent US Grade 1 Malibu Stakes winner Mizzen Mast and a half-sister to 6 winners including the Group 3 placed Red Earth and Kinema Red. The second dam, Kinema (by Graustark), a minor US 3-y-o winner, is a half-sister to the US Grade 2 winners Sweet Alliance (the dam of Shareef Dancer) and Dancing Champ. "A strong filly that goes nicely, she was bought for very little money out of the W T Young dispersal with no reserve on the stock. I like her and see her as an August two-year-old."

632. BIOGRAPHICAL (USA) ★★★
b.br.c. Dynaformer – Tell It (Storm Cat).
March 12. Fourth foal. $270,000Y. Keeneland September. Blandford Bloodstock. Half-brother to the minor US 2-y-o 6f winner Spoken (by Unbridled's Song). The dam, a stakes-placed winner of 4 races in the USA at 2 to 4 yrs, is a half-sister to 6 winners including the dual US Grade 2 winner Pulpit. The second dam, Preach (by Mr Prospector), won the 2-y-o Grade 1 1m Frizette Stakes and was Grade 1 placed twice and is a half-sister to 3 stakes-placed winners and to the dam of the Middle Park Stakes winner Minardi. "A strong colt, he's done well and his half-brother had speed. A nice type for seven furlongs on the July course, so he looks like making a two-year-old – and not many Dynaformers do."

633. BRAVESTOFTHEBRAVE (USA) ★★★
b.c. Elusive Quality – Victoria Cross (Mark Of Esteem).
April 21. Fifth foal. 100,000Y. Tattersalls October Book 1. Not sold. Brother to the fair 2009 Irish dual 7f winner Elusive Award and half-brother to the very smart Group 2 12f Hardwicke Stakes and Group 2 12f Jockey Club Stakes winner Bronze Cannon, the quite useful 12f winner Crimson Ribbon (both by Lemon Drop Kid) and the fairly useful 2-y-o 7f winner

and listed placed Valiance (by Horse Chestnut). The dam, a useful 7f winner here and listed-placed in France, is a half-sister to 6 winners including the Grade 2 San Marcos Handicap winner Prize Giving and to the placed dam of the dual US Grade 1 winner Alpride. The second dam, Glowing With Pride (by Ile de Bourbon), a smart 7f and 10.5f winner, was second in the Park Hill Stakes and is a half-sister to 7 winners. *"A nice of horse, he's gone through a growing spell recently and he's the type of horse we'll hopefully see out in August or September. He has potential and is out of a mare we know quite a lot about. A very likeable horse."*

634. BUTHELEZI (USA) ★★★
b.br.c. Dynaformer – Ntombi (Quiet American). **March 26. Fourth foal. $300,000Y. Keeneland September. Blandford Bloodstock.** The dam, a US stakes winner of 3 races at 2 and 3 yrs, is a half-sister to 9 winners including the US Grade 1 winners Cetewayo and Dynaforce and the US Grade 2 winner Bowman Mill. The second dam, Aletta Maria (by Diesis), won 3 races in the USA at 3 and 4 yrs and is a sister to the Group 3 winner Pharian and a half-sister to the Group 2 winner Raah Algharb. *"A big, strong horse with a good action, he looks like starting off in a seven furlong maiden before graduating to a mile. A nice horse."*

635. CATOPUMA (USA) ★★★
b.br.f. Elusive Quality – Golden Cat (Storm Cat). **April 14.** Half-sister to the 2009 US Grade 2 1m Breeders Cup Juvenile (Turf) winner and Group 1 Prix Jean-Luc Lagardere second Pounced (by Rahy), to the useful dual 10f winner and Group 3 placed Big Bound (by Grand Slam), the useful dual 10f winner and Group 3 placed Pampas Cat (by Seeking The Gold), the useful Irish 5f winner and listed 7f Acomb Stakes second Celtic Cat (by Danehill) and the modest 8.7f winner Mozie Cat (by Mozart). The dam won over 1m at 3 yrs in Ireland and was listed-placed and is a half-sister to 7 winners including the very useful Irish listed 1m and 10f winner and subsequent US winner Eurostorm, the useful 10.3f winner Tamiami Trail and the useful 12f winner Garden Society. The second dam, Eurobird (by Ela-Mana-Mou), a smart winner of 4 races including the Irish St Leger and the Blandford Stakes, is a half-sister to the French Derby winner Bikala and to the Irish Derby and French Derby winner Assert. *"A rangy type, she needs to furnish but is a promising filly for the latter part of the season."*

636. COBBS QUAY ★★★
b.c. Danehill Dancer – Rave Reviews (Sadler's Wells). **January 15. First foal. 270,000Y. Tattersalls October Book 1. M H Goodbody.** The dam, a very useful listed 10f winner and second in the Group 1 Premio Lydia Tesio, is closely related to the listed winners Fermion and Sail and a half-sister to the Group 3 winner Hearthstead Maison. The second dam, Pieds De Plume (by Seattle Slew), placed second once over 1m at 3 yrs in France, is closely related to the French listed and US stakes winner Slew The Slewor and a half-sister to 7 winners including the Group 1 Prix Lupin winner and sire Groom Dancer and the French Group 3 winner Tagel. *"A big, strong, long-striding son of Danehill Dancer, he's a nice type of horse with a good way of going. He'll be suited by seven furlongs and a mile this year."*

637. COURT DRESS (USA) ★★★★
b.f. Speightstown – Well Dressed (Notebook). **March 25. Seventh foal. $350,000Y. Keeneland September. Blandford Bloodstock.** Half-sister to the Group 1 Dubai World Cup and US Grade 1 Goodwood Stakes winner Well Armed (by Tiznow), to the US Grade 3 winner Witty, the US winner and Grade 1 Travers Stakes third Helsinki (both by Distorted Humor) and the minor US 2-y-o winner Formalities Aside (by Awesome Again). The dam won 3 races in the USA at 3 and 4 yrs, including a minor stakes event, and is out of the placed Trithenia (by Gold Meridian), herself a half-sister to the US Grade 3 winner and smart broodmare Tee Kay. *"A half-sister to Well Armed, she's active, quick and light on her feet. The type that could be racing over six furlongs in June or July."*

638. DEVASTATION ★★★
b.f. Montjeu – Attraction (Efisio). **March 26. Second foal.** Half-sister to the promising 2009 2-y-o winner Elation (by Cape Cross). The dam, a high-class 1,000 Guineas, Irish 1,000 Guineas, Coronation Stakes, Matron Stakes and Sun Chariot Stakes winner, is a half-

sister to 2 winners including the 2-y-o 1m winner Racketeer. The second dam, Flirtation (by Pursuit Of Love), ran unplaced once over 7f at 3 yrs and is a half-sister to 4 winners including the French listed 12f winner and Group 2 placed Carmita. *"A good-looking filly, she's at the owner's stud at the moment but she's due in any time. A good-bodied filly with a nice outlook."*

639. FALLEN FROM GRACE ★★★
b.f. Singspiel – Fallen Star (Brief Truce).
April 1. Half-sister to the 2009 2-y-o 7f debut winner Fallen Idol (by Pivotal), to the useful 2-y-o 1m winner and Group 2 12f Lancashire Oaks second Fallen In Love (by Galileo) and the quite useful 12f winner Star Of Gibraltar (by Rock Of Gibraltar). The dam, a listed 7f winner and Group 3 placed twice, is a half-sister to 6 winners including the Group 1 7f Lockinge Stakes winner Fly To The Stars. The second dam, Rise And Fall (by Mill Reef), is an unplaced full or half-sister to 7 winners including the listed winners Special Leave, Spring To Action and Laughter. (Normandie Stud). *"She's typical of the sire in that she'll improve with age, so I can see her coming out in the autumn and she's likeable."*

640. FIELD OF MIRACLES (IRE) ★★★
b.f. Galileo – Landmark (Arch).
May 5. Second foal. 155,000Y. Tattersalls October Book 1. Cheveley Park Stud. Half-sister to Sourmash (by Danehill Dancer), unplaced in one start at 2 yrs in 2009. The dam, a minor 2-y-o winner in the USA, is a sister to the Grade 1 E P Taylor Stakes and Grade 1 Del Mar Oaks winner Arravale. The second dam, Kalosca (by Kaldoun), won 3 races in France and the USA, was Grade 2 placed and is a half-sister to the listed winners Mykonos and Crillon. *"A nice type of filly, light-framed with a good stride to her. The kind of filly you'd point towards August and September."*

641. FOLLOW MY DREAM ★★★★
ch.f. Kyllachy – Follow A Dream (Gone West).
March 3. Fourth living foal. Half-sister to the very smart Group 2 10.5f York Stakes and Group 2 10f Prix Dollar winner Pipedreamer (by Selkirk). The dam, a fairly useful maiden, was placed 5 times at up to 8.3f at 2 and 3 yrs and is a half-sister to the useful middle-distance winner of 4 races Elusive Dream. The second dam, Dance a Dream (by Sadler's Wells), a smart winner of the Cheshire Oaks and second in the Epsom Oaks, is a sister to the 2,000 Guineas winner and Derby fourth Entrepreneur and to the very useful middle-distance listed winner Sadler's Image and a half-sister to numerous winners including the Coronation Stakes winner Exclusive. (Cheveley Park Stud). *"A sharp type, she has a lot of the sire about her and she has a good action. A filly that gets on with the job, she should be a mid-season two-year-old starting off at six furlongs and I should think she'll get seven. Kyllachy was a sprinter but this filly is a nice type and her half-brother Pipedreamer was a tough horse."*

642. GATEWOOD ★★
b.c. Galileo – Felicity (Selkirk).
February 27. Third foal. The dam, a useful winner of the Group 3 10f Golden Daffodil Stakes, is a half-sister to the Group 2 7f Challenge Stakes winner Sleeping Indian and to the useful 10f winner Jalisco. The second dam, Las Flores (by Sadler's Wells), a useful 10f winner and second in the Lingfield Oaks Trial and third in the Italian Oaks, is a full or half-sister to numerous winners including the useful Irish 6f and 10f winner Dancing Goddess. *"A nice type of horse but very much one for the one mile maidens in the autumn. The mother was a big, rangy Selkirk we won a Group 3 with."*

643. GAWAARIB (USA) ★★★
b.c. Anabaa – Beautifulballerina (Nureyev).
February 4. Second foal. €190,000Y. Arqana Deauville August. Shadwell Estate Co. Brother to the French 10f winner Arbat Bello. The dam, a quite useful 3-y-o 1m winner in Ireland, is a half-sister to the 2-y-o winner and Group 3 Horris Hill second Josephus. The second dam, Khulasah (by Affirmed), a minor US 3-y-o winner, is a half-sister to 7 winners. (Hamdan Al Maktoum). *"A nice, athletic horse, he's light on his feet and he should make a nice two-year-old come June or July. We'll probably start him over six furlongs and then pick up in trip."*

644. GAY GALLIVANTER ★★★
b.f. Iceman – Gallivant (Danehill).
March 1. Fourth foal. Closely related to the quite useful dual 6f winner Pumpkin (by Pivotal). The dam, a quite useful 2-y-o 6f winner, is a closely related to the smart 2-y-o Group 2 6f Mill Reef Stakes winner Byron and a half-sister to 3 winners including the useful 1m and 10.3f winner Gallant Hero. The second dam, Gay Gallanta (by Woodman), a very smart winner of the Group 1 6f Cheveley Park Stakes and the Group 3 5f Queen Mary Stakes, was second in the 1m Falmouth Stakes and is a half-sister to 10 winners including the Group 2 10f Gallinule Stakes winner Sportsworld. (Cheveley Park Stud). *"A solid type. He has a good attitude and a good way of going. Some of the Iceman two-year-olds do look like being racehorses."*

645. HAMASAT ★★★★
b.br.f. Pivotal – Moon's Whisper (Storm Cat).
February 10. Fourth foal. Half-sister to the useful dual 1m winner Yazamaan (by Galileo) and to the fair 2m winner Hamsat Elqamar (by Nayef). The dam is an unraced half-sister to 3 winners including the 2-y-o Group 3 5.5f Prix d'Arenburg winner Moon Driver and the US winner and Grade 2 Californian Stakes second Mojave Moon. The second dam, East Of The Moon (by Private Account), was a high-class winner of the French 1,000 Guineas, the Prix de Diane and the Prix Jacques le Marois and is a half-sister to the top class miler and sire Kingmambo and to the smart Miesque's Son. *"A nice filly, she has a bit of quality and looks the nicest one yet out of the mare. She's a very likeable type and I'd like to get her on the track in July or August."*

646. HIGHEST ★★★★
b.f. Dynaformer – Solaia (Miswaki).
April 15. Third foal. Half-sister to the French listed 12f and US Grade 2 12f Long Island Handicap winner Olaya (by Theatrical), to the very useful 7f (at 2 yrs) to 10f winner and listed-placed Wasan (by Pivotal) and the quite useful 1m winner Fifty Cents (by Diesis). The dam won the listed Cheshire Oaks and was second in the Group 3 12f Lancashire Oaks and is a half-sister to 3 winners. The second dam, Indian Fashion (by General Holme), a stakes winner of 8 races in the USA, was Grade 2 and Grade 3 placed and is a half-sister to 5 winners. *"An attractive filly, she's grown a lot through the spring and she needs to furnish. Very much one that's likely to start around September time and she has a lot of quality about her. I like her."*

647. INTERCEPT (IRE) ★★★
b.c. Iffraaj – Sharp Catch (Common Grounds).
April 24. Sixth foal. 62,000Y. Tattersalls October Book 2. Blandford Bloodstock. Half-brother to the fairly useful triple 7f winner (including at 2 yrs) Slate (by Rock Of Gibraltar), to the fairly useful dual 5f winner (including at 2 yrs) Littlemisssunshine (by Oasis Dream), the quite useful 3-y-o 6f winner of 3 races Bohola Flyer (by Barathea) and the fair Irish 7f winner Cappa Blanca (by Giant's Causeway). The dam won over 5f (at 2 yrs) and 1m in Ireland and was third in the Group 3 5f Ballyogan Stakes. She is a half-sister to 6 winners including the smart Ballyogan Stakes winner and Group 1 Haydock Park Sprint Cup third Catch The Blues. The second dam, Dear Lorraine (by Nonoalco), won over 10f in France and is a half-sister to 4 winners. *"He's a nice-looking horse and the Iffraaj two-year-olds seem to have good tops to them. I don't think he's one to rush in any way and you'd want to be looking for a nice bit of juice in the ground in the autumn. But he's a very likeable colt at this stage."*

648. JOHNNY CASTLE ★★★
b.c. Shamardal – Photogenic (Midyan).
March 26. Half-brother to the fairly useful 7f winner Baby Houseman (by Oasis Dream) and to the quite useful 12f winner Gifted Musician (by Sadler's Wells). The dam, a fairly useful 6f and listed 7f winner at 2 yrs, is a half-sister to numerous winners including the listed winner and Group 1 placed Mona Lisa and the very useful 2-y-o 5f and 7f Italian listed winner and Group 2 1m Falmouth Stakes second Croeso Cariad. The second dam, Colorsnap (by Shirley Heights), is an unraced half-sister to 8 winners including the Irish Oaks winner Colorspin (dam of the Group 1 winners Opera House, Zee Zee Top and Kayf Tara), the Prix de l'Opera winner Bella Colora (dam of the very smart colt Stagecraft) and the Irish Champion Stakes winner Cezanne. *"A tough little character, he's*

a 'street fighter' of a colt like these Shamardals often are. Not particularly big, but he'll punch his weight."

649. JOVIALITY ★★★
b.f. Cape Cross – Night Frolic (Night Shift).
February 19. Third foal. 200,000Y. Tattersalls October Book 1. Blandford Bloodstock. Half-sister to the fair 2009 2-y-o 5f winner Chicita Banana (by Danehill Dancer) and to the fair 1m winner Burns Night (by Selkirk). The dam, a modest 1m winner, is a half-sister to 5 winners including the US Grade 3 Cardinal Handicap winner Miss Caerleona (by Caerleon and herself dam of the Group winners Karen's Caper and Miss Coronado) and the French listed-placed winners Mr Academy (by Royal Academy) and Mister Shoot (by Shining Steel). The second dam, Miss d'Ouilly (by Bikala), won a listed event over 9f in France and is a half-sister to the Prix Jacques le Marois winner Miss Satamixa and the dam of the Group/Graded stakes winners Mister Riv, Mister Sicy and Manninamix. *"She's a nice filly and I like her, but her joints are immature at this stage and I won't be rushing her."*

650. JUSTINIAN ★★★
ch.c. Muhtathir – Jeritza (Rainbow Quest).
January 28. First foal. 32,000Y. Tattersalls October 2. Blandford Bloodstock. The dam won over 12f in France and is a half-sister to 7 winners including the US stakes winner and Grade 2 placed Green Light. The second dam, Jade Jewel (by Mr Prospector), is an unplaced sister to the US dual Grade 1 winner Jade Hunter. *"He's a tough, solid colt, a nice sort of a horse and I like his attitude."*

651. KEY WEST ★★★★
ch.c. Kheleyf – Quinzey (Carnegie).
April 20. Fifth foal. £65,000Y. Doncaster St Leger. R O'Gorman. Half-brother to the useful 2-y-o 5f and subsequent US Grade 3 1m Senorita Stakes winner Mrs Kipling (by Exceed And Excel) and to the fair 2-y-o 1m all-weather winner Stanley George (by Noverre). The dam is an unraced half-sister to 2 winners. The second dam, Quinpool (by Alydar), won 3 races in the USA and was third in the Grade 1 Kentucky Oaks and is a half-sister to 7 winners.

"A neat, sharp type. He's an active two-year-old I'd like to have out in April."

652. LIBERTY CAP (USA) ★★★★
b.br.c. Street Cry – Binavicar (Vicar).
February 28. First foal. $150,000Y. Saratoga August. John Gosden. The dam, a minor US 2-y-o winner, is a half-sister to one winner. The second dam, Binalegend (by Binalong), a minor stakes winner of 8 races in the USA, is a half-sister to 9 winners including the dam of the champion 2-y-o colt and triple Grade 1 winner Street Sense. *"A sweet little horse, he was on the Al Bahathri gallop this morning and he has a good attitude. Not very big, but a real nice two-year-old type. He cost a lot of money, but actually for a Street Cry from the Saratoga sale not as much as it might have been. I hope to have him out in May over six furlongs."*

653. LIGHT WELL (IRE) ★★★★
b.c. Sadler's Wells – L'Ancresse (Darshaan).
March 7. Fourth foal. 160,000Y. Tattersalls December. Blandford Bloodstock. The dam, a 7f (at 2 yrs) and listed 12f winner, was second in the Group 1 Breeders Cup Filly Mare & Turf and is a sister to 2 winners including the Group 1 10f Prix Saint-Alary winner Cerulean Sky and a half-sister to 6 winners including the Group 1 Irish Oaks winner Moonstone. The second dam, Solo de Lune (by Law Society), a French 11f winner, is a half-sister to 7 winners including the Grade 2 E P Taylor Stakes winner Truly A Dream and the French Group 2 winner Wareed. *"A big, good-looking horse with a fine action. He's going to be a nice horse in the second half of the year and a staying three-year-old. He has a lot to like about him – a lot of quality."*

654. MAQAASID ★★★★
b.f. Green Desert – Eshaadeh (Storm Cat).
January 21. Third foal. The dam, unplaced in 2 starts, is a half-sister to 6 winners including the useful dual 1m winner Mawatheeq. The second dam, Sarayir (by Mr Prospector), winner of a 1m listed event, is closely related to the top-class Champion Stakes winner Nayef and a half-sister to numerous winners including the 2,000 Guineas, Eclipse, Derby and King George winner Nashwan and the high-class

middle distance colt Unfuwain. (Hamdan Al Maktoum). *"I like her, she's strong and did some upsides work on the Al Bahathri gallop this morning. She did it well, looks like a six furlong two-year-old and is a good filly. One to watch out for."*

655. MARIE JEANNE ★★
b.f. Montjeu – Carafe (Selkirk).
February 7. Second living foal. 120,000Y. Tattersalls October Book 1. Cheveley Park Stud. The dam, a quite useful 7f winner, is a half-sister to the fairly useful 1m winner and listed-placed Coyote (herself the dam of two stakes winners). The second dam, Caramba (by Belmez), a smart winner of the Group 2 1m Falmouth Stakes and the Group 2 10f Nassau Stakes, is a half-sister to 7 winners including the Moyglare Stud Stakes and Falmouth Stakes winner Lemon Souffle. *"A backward type who's done a lot of growing, she's quite long in herself at the moment and seems to have a good mind on her. Very much an autumn filly."*

656. MIDNIGHT CALLER ★★★
br.f. Dansili – Midnight Air
(Green Dancer).
April 27. Half-sister to the Grade 2 Long Island Handicap, Group 3 May Hill Stakes and Group 3 Prestige Stakes winner Midnight Line (by Kris S), to the quite useful 1m winner L'Amour, the fair 9.3f all-weather winner Westerly Air (both by Gone West), the fair 11.6f winner Thinking Positive (by Rainbow Quest) and the modest 8.5f all-weather winner Midnight Watch (by Capote). The dam won the Group 3 1m May Hill Stakes at 2 yrs and is a half-sister to 5 minor winners and to the dam of the Group 1 5f Prix de l'Abbaye winner Imperial Beauty. (Mr. G Strawbridge). *"She's done well. She recently had a growing spurt and went a little weak with it and with her pedigree I'm very much looking towards September. That's when these type of horses come out."*

657. MONTEFINO (IRE) ★★★★
b.f. Shamardal – Monturani (Indian Ridge).
May 14. Third foal. 62,000Y. Tattersalls October Book 1. Blandford Bloodstock. Half-sister to the quite useful 1m and 9f winner Ithinkbest (by King's Best). The dam, winner of the Group 2 Blandford Stakes, is a half-sister to 4 winners including the smart 6f and 7f listed winner Monnavanna and to the very useful 2-y-o 7f winner Mezuzah. The second dam, Mezzogiorno (by Unfuwain), a very useful 7f (at 2 yrs) and 10f listed winner and third in the Oaks, is a half-sister to 3 winners. *"A nice filly that goes well. She's one of the more forward fillies and I'd hope to see her running in late May or early June. A filly with a good attitude."*

658. MUSAWAMA (IRE) ★★★★
b.c. Azamour – Chater (Alhaarth).
April 6. Fourth foal. The dam is an unraced half-sister to 3 winners including the 1,000 Guineas and Group 2 7f Rockfel Stakes winner Lahan. The second dam, Amanah (by Mr Prospector), a useful 1m winner, is a half-sister to 2 winners including the fairly useful 2-y-o winners Alhufoof and Habub. (Hamdan Al Maktoum). *"A big, strong horse with a good action. I like him and I could see him starting on the July course in a seven furlong maiden."*

659. NAQASH (IRE) ★★★
b.c. Medicean – Varenka (Fasliyev).
April 18. Second foal. €240,000Y. Goffs Orby. Shadwell Estate Co. Brother to the fair 2009 2-y-o 7f winner Meezaan. The dam, a fairly useful 2-y-o 7.5f winner, was listed-placed in Italy and a half-sister to one winner. The second dam, Castara Beach (by Danehill), placed fourth once over 7f at 2 yrs, is a sister to the useful Group 3 7f Criterion Stakes winner Hill Hopper (herself dam of the dual Group 1 winner Nannina) and a half-sister to 5 winners including the Australian Grade 1 winner Water Boatman. (Hamdan Al Maktoum). *"A very active, very athletic colt for the mid-season. He's a nice horse with a good way of going."*

660. NASHAAT ★★★
b.br.f. Redoute's Choice – Sulaalah (Darshaan).
February 14. Third foal. Half-sister to the fairly useful 2-y-o 1m winner and 3-y-o 10f and 12f listed-placed Mooakada (by Montjeu). The dam is an unraced half-sister to 2 winners. The second dam, Bint Shadayid (by Nashwan), a very useful winner of the Group 3 7f Prestige Stakes, was placed in the 1,000 Guineas and the Fillies Mile. (Hamdan Al Maktoum). *"A perfectly acceptable filly. At this stage I'd say

nothing more than she looks the type to be starting off in August over six furlongs, then we'll step her up in trip."

661. NATHANIEL (IRE) ★★★
b.c. Galileo – Magnificent Style (Silver Hawk).
April 24. Closely related to the Group 1 Fillies' Mile winner Playful Act, to the Group 3 11.5f Lingfield Derby Trial winner Percussionist and the 10f winner and Group 3 10f Prix de Psyche second Changing Skies (all by Sadler's Wells) and half-brother to the Group 2 1m Sun Chariot Stakes and Group 2 14.6f Park Hill Stakes winner Echoes In Eternity (by Spinning World), the US stakes winner and Grade 3 placed Stylelistick (by Storm Cat), the 1m (at 2 yrs) and listed 9f winner and Group 2 placed Petara Bay (by Peintre Celebre) and the quite useful 9f winner Distinctive Look (by Danehill). The dam won the Group 3 10.5f Musidora Stakes and is a half-sister to the Grade 1 10f Charles H Strub Stakes winner Siberian Summer. The second dam, Mia Karina (by Icecapade), a minor 3-y-o winner in France, is a half-sister to the dam of the US Grade 1 Pegasus Handicap winner Silver Ending. *"Obviously this is a family we know well, having had Playful Act and Percussionist out of the mare. He's a nice, big, rangy colt and a lovely middle-distance/ staying horse in the making."*

662. NESSINA (USA) ★★★★
ch.f. Hennessy – Didina (Nashwan).
January 31. Sixth foal. Half-sister to the smart dual listed 7f winner Tantina (by Distant View), to the quite useful 10f winner Trekking (by Gone West) and the quite useful 2-y-o 1m winner Auction Room (by Auction House). The dam, a winner over 6f at 2 yrs here, subsequently won the Grade 2 8.5f Dahlia Handicap in the USA and is a sister to one winner and a half-sister to 4 winners including the French listed 10f winner Espionage. The second dam, Didicoy (by Danzig), a useful winner of 3 races over 6f, is closely related to the Group 3 1m Prix Quincey winner Masterclass and a half-sister to the champion 2-y-o Xaar. (Khalid Abdulla). *"She's a long-backed, strong filly and I like the way she goes. A six furlong filly for the middle of the summer, she has a quick, top of the ground action."*

663. NEW HAMPSHIRE (IRE) ★★
b.c. Elusive Quality – Downtown Blues (Seattle Song).
March 7. Tenth foal. $175,000Y. Keeneland September. Blandford Bloodstock. Half-brother to 6 winners including the US Grade 2 and Grade 3 winner Night Patrol , the minor US stakes-placed winner Gumshoe (both by Storm Boot) and the US stakes winner and Grade 2 placed Harbor Blues (by Petionville). The dam, a minor US 3-y-o winner, is a half-sister to 4 winners out of the minor US 2-y-o winner Sultry Sally (by Raja Baba). *"I'm just going along quietly with him at the moment, but he's a strong colt and I'd hope to get him out in August."*

664. OLD NAVY ★★
b.c. Shirocco – So Admirable (Suave Dancer).
March 23. Fifth foal. 125,000Y. Tattersalls October Book 2. Blandford Bloodstock. Half-brother to La Di Da (by Oratorio), placed fourth over 1m on her only start at 2 yrs in 2009, to the fair 10f winner on her only start Come April (by Singspiel) and a winner in Japan by Fantastic Light. The dam is an unraced sister to the Group 1 10f Coral Eclipse Stakes, Group 3 1m Craven Stakes and Group 3 7f Solario Stakes winner Compton Admiral and a half-sister to 6 winners including the Group 1 1m Queen Elizabeth II Stakes winner Summoner. The second dam, Sumoto (by Mtoto), a useful 6f (at 2 yrs) and 7f winner, is a half-sister to 5 winners. *"The Shirocco's looked quite nice individuals at the Sales. This horse is immature of his knees, he's a staying type but I'd be very hopeful of him running a couple of times in the autumn."*

665. PALITANA (USA) ★★★★
b.br.f. Giant's Causeway – Glatisant (Rainbow Quest).
March 10. Sister to the 2,000 Guineas winner Footstepsinthesand and half-sister to the fairly useful 2-y-o 6f winner Frappe (by Inchinor and herself dam of the Ribblesdale Stakes winner Thakafaat) and the Irish 12f to 2m and bumper winner Theme Song (by Singspiel). The dam, a very useful winner of the Group 3 7f Prestige Stakes at 2 yrs, is a half-sister to 8 winners including the very useful triple 10f winner Gai Bulga and to the placed dam of the very smart

2-y-o Superstar Leo. The second dam, Dancing Rocks (by Green Dancer), won over 5f and 6f at 2 yrs and the Group 2 10f Nassau Stakes at 3 yrs and is a half-sister to 4 winners. *"A good-looking filly, strong with a good action. She has the attitude of a colt – she's aggressive. Very likeable, I would have thought she'd be out in mid-season and she has the power to start at six furlongs."*

666. PLEA ★★★★♠
b.c. Motivator – Request (Rainbow Quest).
April 8. Half-brother to the Group 1 12f Coronation Cup and Group 1 2m Prix Royal-Oak winner Ask and the quite useful 10f winner Kensington Oval (both by Sadler's Wells). The dam was placed over 10f and is a half-sister to 4 winners including the Group 2 12f Jockey Club Stakes winner Blueprint and the listed 10f winner Fairy Godmother. The second dam, Highbrow (by Shirley Heights), a very useful 2-y-o 1m winner, was second in the Group 2 12f Ribblesdale Stakes, is closely related to the good middle-distance colt Milford and a half-sister to the Princess of Wales's Stakes winner Height of Fashion – herself the dam of Nashwan, Nayef and Unfuwain. *"A real character, he's very active and I have to keep his mind occupied. If he was in the classroom he'd be disruptive because he gets bored easily. I'm moving along with him, I'd like to get him out in early May and he might make up into a Chesham Stakes horse."*

667. PRINCE OF BURMA (IRE) ★★★★
b.c. Mujadil – Spinning Ruby (Pivotal).
February 28. First foal. €100,000Y. Goffs Orby. Blandford Bloodstock. The dam, a quite useful 6f (at 2 yrs) and 1m winner, is a half-sister to 4 winners. The second dam, Red Rabbit (by Suave Dancer), was placed three times over 7f including at 2 yrs and is a half-sister to 7 winners including the listed 1m winner Barboukh (herself dam of the Group 3 10f Prix Exbury winner Barbola). *"He needed to grow and he has done. I can see him being out on the July course over six furlongs. A likeable colt, he's what I call a 'proper TRAINERS' horse' in that there's nothing fussy about him, he's a good individual and a nice horse to be around."*

668. PURIFICATION (IRE) ★★★★♠
b.c. Hurricane Run – Ceanothus (Bluebird).
April 13. Sixth foal. 180,000Y. Tattersalls October Book 1. Amanda Skiffington. Closely related to the 2009 2-y-o Group 2 1m May Hill Stakes winner Pollenator (by Motivator) and half-brother to the fairly useful 7f (at 2 yrs) and 1m winner of 3 races Prince Hector (by Hector Protector), the quite useful 6f and 7f winner and listed-placed Wedding Party (by Groom Dancer) and the modest 1m (at 2 yrs) to 12f winner of 8 races Competitor (by Danzero). The dam, a maiden who stayed 12f, is a half-sister to 4 winners including the US Grade 2 12f Orchid Handicap and Grade 3 8.5f Suwannee River Handicap winner Golden Pond. The second dam, Golden Bloom (by Main Reef), is an unraced half-sister to the Group 3 Matron Stakes winner Spring Daffodil and the Grade 1 Australian Derby winner Dance The Day Away. *"A big, strong horse that almost looks like a three-year-old already. An arrogant horse – he likes getting up on his hind legs and letting you know he's around the place. He does everything very easily and he's done bits of work already because he's one of those I have to stay on top of. Obviously he's bred to start off in a seven furlong maiden and if he's in good form at the time I might start him off in the first of them, which is in the third week of June."*

669. QUESTIONING (IRE) ★★★
b.c. Elusive Quality – Am I (Thunder Gulch).
March 29. First foal. 160,000Y. Tattersalls October Book 1. Blandford Bloodstock. The dam, a minor 2-y-o winner in the USA, is a half-sister to 6 winners including the US Grade 3 winner Certainly Classic and the French Group 3 winner Mahfooth. The second dam, I Certainly Am, a minor winner in the USA, is a sister to the Group 2 Premio Lydia Tesio winner Medi Flash and a half-sister to the US Grade 1 Flower Bowl Invitational winner Laugh And Be Merry. *"He's a good, strong type of horse and looks the type for top of the ground in mid-summer. I'd say he'd be wanting seven furlongs."*

670. RASHEED ★★★
b.c. Oasis Dream – Alexandrine (Nashwan).
April 27. Sixth foal. 180,000foal. Tattersalls December. Shadwell Estate Co. Closely

related to the quite useful 1m (at 2 yrs) and 10f winner Algarade (by Green Desert) and half-brother to the fairly useful 12f to 14f winner of 6 races and listed-placed Alambic (by Cozzene), the quite useful 1m, 10f (both at 2 yrs) and 11f winner Alcalde (by Hernando) and the modest 11f and 12f winner Astrodome (by Domedriver). The dam, a fair 10f to 13f winner of 4 races, is a half-sister to 7 winners including the Nassau Stakes and Sun Chariot Stakes winner Last Second (dam of the French 2,000 Guineas winner Aussie Rules), the Doncaster Cup winner Alleluia (dam of the Prix Royal-Oak winner Allegretto) and the Moyglare Stud Stakes third Alouette (herself dam of the dual Champion Stakes winner Alborada and the triple German Group 1 winner Albanova) and to the placed dam of the Group 1 winners Yesterday and Quarter Moon. The second dam, Alruccaba (by Crystal Palace), a quite useful 2-y-o 6f winner, is out of a half-sister to the dams of Aliysa and Nishapour. *"This is a colt from a mare that was a 'Sir Mark Prescott special' as she won four in a short space of time! I wouldn't know about the correct trip for this colt yet, because Oasis Dream seems to have the knack of siring winners at all types of distances. He seems to put speed into stamina-bred horses and compliment them – which is quite a rare gift. I think I'll probably end up looking for the seven furlong maidens in mid-season. He's a nice type."*

671. ROSE WILLOW (USA) ★★★
b.f. Artie Schiller – Divi (Bustino).
March 22. Sixth foal. $170,000Y. Saratoga August. Blandford Bloodstock. Half-sister to 3 winners including the US stakes winner and Grade 2 placed Understood. The dam, a listed winner in France, is a half-sister to 6 winners. The second dam, Syzygy (by Kenmare), won 3 races at 2 and 3 yrs in France and is a half-sister to 4 winners. *"An attractive filly, the dam was listed-class in France and the sire won the Breeders Cup Mile – this is his first crop. A nice filly, she'll appreciate some cut in the ground over seven furlongs or a mile in early autumn."*

672. RYTON RUNNER (IRE) ★★★★
b.c. Sadler's Wells – Love For Ever (Darshaan).
February 16. Eighth foal. 115,000Y.
Tattersalls October Book 1. Blandford Bloodstock. Brother to the 7f (at 2 yrs) and Group 3 Dee Stakes winner Gypsy King, to the useful 12f winner Albanov, the fairly useful 12f winner King O'The Gypsies, the French 10f winner Salila and the Irish 10f winner Napoleon. The dam, a dual 3-y-o winner in France, is a half-sister to 6 winners including French listed winner and US Grade 2 placed Wedding Ring. The second dam, Fleur d'Oranger (by Northfields), won the listed 12f Prix de la Ville Trouville, was placed in three Group 3 events in France and is a half-sister to 9 winners including the German Group 3 winner and French Oaks third Premier Amour. *"A very active, athletic colt, his full brother Gypsy King was decent and won at Chester before sadly dying in the Irish Derby. I'm very happy with him and he could be out early. Another Chesham Stakes possibility."*

673. SCHOOLMASTER ★★
b.c. Motivator – Londonnetdotcom (Night Shift).
March 6. Third foal. 75,000Y. Tattersalls October Book 1. Blandford Bloodstock. Half-brother to the fair 7f winner Loveinanelevator (by Dr Fong). The dam, a useful 7f (at 2 yrs) and listed 1m winner, is a half-sister to one winner. The second dam, Hopeful Sign (by Warning), ran once unplaced and is a half-sister to 8 winners including the Group 3 winners Ecologist, Green Reef and Infrasonic and the dam of the St Leger winner Toulon. *"An attractive colt, leggy and immature at this stage and one for the autumn."*

674. SKIP ALONE ★★★
ch.f. Galileo – Peony (Lion Cavern).
March 30. Sixth foal. 200,000Y. Tattersalls October Book 1. Blandford Bloodstock. Half-sister to the smart listed 11f Predominate Stakes winner and Group 3 placed Unfurled (by Unfuwain), to the fairly useful 10.5f winner Broomielaw (by Rock Of Gibraltar) and the modest 14f to 17f and hurdles winner Synonymy (by Sinndar). The dam won 4 races in France over 7f and 1m including the listed Prix Imprudence, was second in the French 1,000 Guineas and is a half-sister to 4 winners. The second dam, Persiandale (by Persian Bold), is an unraced half-sister to 3 winners including

the Australian dual Grade 1 winner Raffindale. *"A rangy filly with a lovely action, she grew and got a bit unfurnished but she's overcoming that now and looks a nice, staying filly to run in the latter part of the season."*

675. SPANISH FLEET ★★★
b.c. Cadeaux Genereux – Santisima Trinidad (Definite Article).
February 25. Third foal. €70,000Y. Goffs Orby. Blandford Bloodstock. The dam, a fairly useful winner of 8 races at around 7f, is a half-sister to the Italian listed winner Meanya and to the dam of the Group 2 July Stakes winner Classic Blade. The second dam, Brazilia (by Forzando), a modest 6f placed 2-y-o, is a half-sister to 4 winners including the Group 2 5f Kings Stand Stakes winner Dominica. *"A big boy, he's good looking and a good topped horse. A bit open of his knees at the moment so I wouldn't be rushing him, but I like him."*

676. STARS IN YOUR EYES ★★★★
b.f. Galileo – Apache Star (Arazi).
May 4. Seventh living foal. 210,000Y. Tattersalls October Book 1. John Gosden. Closely related to the promising 2009 2-y-o 1m winner Coordinated Cut (by Montjeu) and half-sister to the useful 2-y-o 6f and listed 1m winner New Mexican (by Dr Fong), to the useful 10f winner of 4 races and listed-placed Wild Savannah (by Singspiel), the useful Irish 6f (at 2 yrs) to 2m winner Sahara Desert and the fairly useful 1m (including at 2 yrs) and 10f winner Cactus King (both by Green Desert). The dam, a fairly useful 7f (at 2 yrs) to 9f winner, was listed placed twice at up to 11.4f and is a half-sister to 6 winners including the US stakes winner and Grade 3 placed Duke Of Green. The second dam, Wild Pavane (by Dancing Brave), is an unraced half-sister to 6 winners including the listed winner Nuryana (dam of the Group 1 Coronation Stakes winner Rebecca Sharp). *"A nice type of filly, she's athletic with a good stride to her, looks very typical of the sire and well-balanced, I could see her being out in August."*

677. TRADE COMMISIONER (IRE) ★★★★★
b.c. Montjeu – Spinning Queen (Spinning World).
February 3. First foal. The dam, winner of the Group 1 1m Sun Chariot Stakes and the Group 3 7f Brownstown Stakes and third in the Group 2 Cherry Hinton Stakes, is a half-sister to 4 winners including the useful 10f and 12f winner and 2-y-o 7f listed-placed Shannon Springs. The second dam, Our Queen Of Kings (by Arazi), is an unraced half-sister to 7 winners including the Grade 1 9f Hollywood Derby winner Labeeb, the Grade 2 Arlington Handicap winner Fanmore and the Group 2 9f Budweiser International Stakes winner Alsassam. *"A nice-looking colt and the first foal of a good racemare. He looks a proper type of horse and he'll start off at seven furlongs. One to watch out for."*

678. UNEX EL GRECO ★★★
b.c. Holy Roman Emperor – Friendlier (Zafonic).
March 2. Fourth foal. Half-brother to the fair 2009 2-y-o 1m winner Comradeship (by Dubawi) and to the fairly useful 7f (at 2 yrs) and 1m winner Foolin Myself (by Montjeu). The dam is an unraced half-sister to 3 winners including the top-class filly User Friendly, winner of the Oaks, the St Leger, the Irish Oaks and the Yorkshire Oaks and second in the Prix de l'Arc de Triomphe. The second dam, Rostova (by Blakeney), a fairly useful winner of 4 races from 12f to 14f, is a half-sister to 7 winners including the very successful Italian filly Judd. (Mr Bill Gredley). *"This is an active horse, he should be out in May and he looks a tough individual."*

679. UTLEY (USA) ★★★
b.c. Smart Strike – No Matter What (Nureyev).
March 10. Half-brother to the Group 1 Fillies' Mile and Group 1 1m Matron Stakes winner Rainbow View (by Dynaformer), the Canadian Grade 1 winner Just As Well (by A P Indy) and the US Grade 3 9f and Grade 3 12f winner Winter View (by Thunder Gulch). The dam, winner of the Grade 1 Del Mar Oaks, is a half-sister to the Grade 2 Suburban Handicap and Grade 2 Dwyer Stakes winner E Dubai. The second dam, Words Of War (by Lord At War), a US stakes winner of 9 races, is a sister to the Grade 3 Miesque Stakes winner Ascutney (the dam of Raven's Pass). *"A half-brother to Mr Strawbridge's Rainbow View, we like him and we'll try to get him on the racecourse in the second half of the season."*

680. WILAYA (USA) ★★★★
b.br.f. Bernardini – Tanzania (Alzao).
April 23. Ninth foal. $100,000Y. Keeneland September. Blandford Bloodstock. Half-brother to the US Grade 1 John C Mabee Handicap and Grade 1 Del Mar Oaks winner Amorama (by Sri Pekan), to the fairly useful 9f and 10f winner Serengeti (by Singspiel), the quite useful triple 12f winner Milwaukee (by Desert King) and the minor French 3-y-o winner Shangani (by Giant's Causeway). The dam, a minor Irish 12f and 13f winner, is out of the unplaced Triple Couronne (by Riverman), herself a half-sister to the top-class filly Triptych. *"A nice type of filly at this stage. I'm going quietly with her but she's shown a great attitude and a good action. I'm looking forward to running her in mid-season. I've got three Bernardini two-year-olds and I like them all. This filly will be one to follow."*

681. ZANAZZI (USA) ★★★★
b.f. Bernardini – Silken Cat (Storm Cat).
April 27. Eighth foal. $360,000Y. Keeneland September. Blandford Bloodstock. Half-sister to the Grade 1 Breeders Cup Sprint winner Speightstown (by Gone West). The dam, a stakes winner and champion 2-y-o filly in Canada, is a half-sister to several winners including the Group 1 Racing Post Trophy third Juyush. The second dam, Silken Doll (by Chieftain), was a US stakes winner of 4 races at 3 yrs and a half-sister to the US Grade 1 winner Turk's Passer. *"She's going to take a little bit of time, she's grown but she's nice and is a good-looking filly. You get a feel of quality about her, she has a good action and will be a second half of the season two-year-old. I like her."*

682. UNNAMED ★★★
b.c. Galileo – Arabesque (Zafonic).
April 2. Seventh foal. Half-brother to the 2009 Group 2 6f Gimcrack Stakes winner Showcasing, to the fairly useful triple 6f winner (including at 2 yrs) and listed-placed Bouvardia (both by Oasis Dream) and the very smart listed 6f winner Camacho (by Danehill). The dam, a useful listed 6f winner, is a sister to 2 winners including the useful 5f and 6f winner Threat and a half-sister to 5 winners including the Group 2 1m Prix de Sandringham winner Modern Look. The second dam, Prophecy (by Warning), was a very useful winner of the Group 1 6f Cheveley Park Stakes and was second in the Group 3 7f Nell Gwyn Stakes. (Khalid Abdulla). *"He's had a hold up and is on the easy list now, but he's a nice, strong type of horse with a big, hind-end on him. He might not be guaranteed to stay because the dam was speedy and I think her influence is strong here."*

683. UNNAMED ★★★★
b.f. Galileo – Ballette (Giant's Causeway).
The dam, a fair Irish 10f and 12f winner, is a half-sister to numerous winners including the very smart 10f to 14f winner and Irish Derby second Dr Johnson. The second dam, Russian Ballet (by Nijinsky), a minor 6f and 7f placed 2-y-o, is closely related to El Gran Senor and Try My Best. *"She goes alright and she'll be out on the July course in a seven furlong maiden. She's very likeable."*

684. UNNAMED ★★★★
b.c. Bernardini – Crystal Music (Nureyev).
February 22. Fifth foal. $1,000,000Y. Saratoga August. Not sold. Half-brother to the fairly useful 2-y-o 6f winner and listed-placed Crystany (by Green Desert). The dam, a smart winner of the Group 1 Fillies' Mile at 2 yrs, is closely related to the Group 3 12f John Porter Stakes winner Dubai Success and the smart 7f (at 2 yrs) and 10f winner Tchaikovsky and a half-sister to the Group 3 1m May Hill Stakes winner Solar Crystal and the Group 3 12f Lancashire Oaks winner State Crystal. The second dam, Crystal Spray (by Beldale Flutter), a minor Irish 4-y-o 14f winner, is a half-sister to 8 winners including the Group 3 Scottish Classic winner Crystal Hearted. *"A lively, rangy horse but very much one for September time onwards, so he'll take a bit of time but he's a quality horse and I like him."*

685. UNNAMED ★★★★
b.f. Orpen – Delta (Zafonic).
March 7. Third foal. Half-sister to the fairly useful 2009 2-y-o 7f winner Hunting Tartan (by Oasis Dream) and to the quite useful 2-y-o 1m winner Sampi (by Beat Hollow). The dam was a French 3-y-o dual 1m winner. The second dam, Fleet River (by Riverman), a fairly useful 2-y-o 7f winner, is a half-sister

to the very smart Eltish, winner of the 7f Lanson Champagne Stakes and the 1m Royal Lodge Stakes and runner-up in the Grade 1 8.5f Breeders Cup Juvenile, to the useful 8.3f winner Yamuna, the useful 5f and 6f winner Forest Gazelle and the French listed 10f winner Souplesse. (Khalid Abdulla). *"She's a nice type of filly, likeable and very much a mid-season type of two-year-old."*

686. UNNAMED ★★★
b.f. *Danehill Dancer – Hawala (Warning).*
April 14. Seventh foal. €80,000Y. Goffs Orby. Blandford Bloodstock. Half-sister to the very smart 2009 2-y-o 7f winner and Group 1 6f Phoenix Stakes second Air Chief Marshal, to the listed 6f (at 2 yrs) and listed 7f winner and Group 3 placed Misu Bond, the dual sprint listed winner and Group 3 placed Slip Dance (by Celtic Swing), the fairly useful 2-y-o 7f and 1m winner Numen (by Fath), the quite useful 6f winner Winged Harriet (by Hawk Wing) and the minor French 3-y-o winner Hawazi (by Ashkalani). The dam, a useful 8.3f winner, is a half-sister to 3 winners including the French Group 3 winner Afaf. The second dam, the minor French 3-y-o winner Halawa (by Dancing Brave), is a half-sister to 7 winners. *"A nice filly that's a bit open of her knees at this stage so we'll take our time with her. But she's an athletic filly that looks as if she'll go on top of the ground and I like her."*

687. UNNAMED ★★★★
b.f. *Oasis Dream – Innocent Air (Galileo).*
March 7. First foal. The dam, a 2-y-o listed 7f winner, is a half-sister to 6 winners including the French listed and US stakes winner and US Grade 1 placed Skipping and the dual Group 3 placed Minority. The second dam, Minskip (by The Minstrel), won once at 2 yrs and is a sister to the US Grade 2 winner Savinio and a half-sister to the Italian dual Group 1 winner St Hilarion and the dam of the dual Group 1 winner Muhtarram. (Khalid Abdulla). *"A strong, very good-looking filly. Her mother was on the nevous side and this filly is the same. She's a bit keen and wants to do too much, but if we get her to settle nicely she could be a real quality filly. I see her being out in mid-season."*

688. UNNAMED ★★★★
b.c. *Sadler's Wells – Jude (Darshaan).*
May 20. Tenth foal. 290,000Y. Tattersalls October Book 1. Charlie Gordon-Watson. Brother to the unraced 2009 2-y-o Loveisallyouneed, to the Irish 1,000 Guineas winner Yesterday and to the Group 1 7f Moyglare Stud Stakes winner and Irish 1,000 Guineas, Oaks and Irish Oaks placed Quarter Moon, the Group 2 placed winners All My Loving and Hold Me Love Me and the listed-placed winner Magicalmysterytour. The dam, a moderate 10f placed maiden, is a sister to the very useful Irish listed 14f winner and Irish Oaks third Arrikala and to the useful Irish 12f listed winner Alouette (herself dam of the Group 1 winners Albanova and Alborada) and a half-sister to the very smart Group 2 10f Nassau Stakes and Sun Chariot Stakes winner Last Second (dam of the dual Group 1 winner Aussie Rules) and the Group 2 Doncaster Cup winner Alleluia (dam of the Group 1 winner Allegretto). The second dam, Alruccaba (by Crystal Palace), a quite useful 2-y-o 6f winner, is a half-sister to 3 winners. *"A strong colt, at the moment he's a bit springy of his pasterns and immature of his joints but a nice horse. Very much the type that will want a bit of cut in the ground come September. I like him."*

689. UNNAMED ★★★
ch.c. *Noverre – Landela (Alhaarth).*
March 12. Second foal. £12,000Y. Doncaster St Leger. Blandford Bloodstock. Half-brother to the quite useful 2009 2-y-o 1m winner Get A Grip (by Royal Applause). The dam, placed fourth on both her starts over 7f and 1m at 4 yrs, is a half-sister to 4 winners including the Group 1 Grand Prix de Paris and Group 2 Prix Foy winner Zambezi Sun and the Group 2 Prix Guillaume d'Ornano winner Kalabar. The second dam, Imbabala (by Zafonic), was a placed half-sister to the French Group 3 winner Short Pause, the French 1m listed winner Cheyenne Dream and the dam of the Group 1 winner Continent. *"A nice type of horse with a lovely action. He's grown and is good-bodied colt and a mid-summer, seven furlong type. I like him."*

690. UNNAMED ★★★
b.br.c. Street Cry – Lords Guest
(Lord At War).
March 27. Seventh foal. $190,000Y. Keeneland September. Blandford Bloodstock. Half-brother to the US Grade 3 winner Lisa M (by Banker's Gold) and to two minor winners by With Approval. The dam won 3 minor races in the USA at 3 and 4 yrs and is a sister to the US dual Grade 1 winner John's Call. The second dam, Calling Guest (by Be My Guest), was unplaced. *"He's going the right way at this stage, his joints are a little immature but he's a likeable, well-balanced colt for the second half of the season."*

691. UNNAMED ★★★
b.c. Dansili – Summer Shower
(by Sadler's Wells).
February 26. The dam, a French listed-placed dual 12f winner, is a sister to the very smart 1m (at 2 yrs) and Group 2 12f Princess of Wales's Stakes winner Doctor Fremantle. The second dam, Summer Breeze (Rainbow Quest), won over 1m at 2 yrs, was third in the Group 3 1m Prix des Reservoirs and is sister to the high-class Rothmans International and Prix Royal-Oak winner Raintrap and to the very smart Criterium de Saint-Cloud and Prix du Conseil de Paris winner Sunshack. (Khalid Abdulla). *"A small colt, he does lack some scope and will be out early. He's bred to stay but because he lacks scope I'll get him out earlier than his pedigree would indicate."*

692. UNNAMED ★★★
b.c. Medaglia d'Oro – Thousand Thrills
(Crafty Prospector).
April 23. First foal. $390,000Y. Keeneland September. Blandford Bloodstock. The dam is an unraced half-sister to 3 minor winners. The second dam, Vivano (by Island Whirl), won 10 races in the USA including the Grade 3 Honeybee Handicap, was Grade 1 placed five times and is a half-sister to 6 winners. *"He's a nice, rangy horse and like a lot of them by this sire he's quite European looking. He has a good shape to him and a good action but he's a little bit weak at the moment so I'd be looking towards the autumn with him – but he has quality."*

693. UNNAMED ★★★★★
b.c. Montjeu – Waldmark
(Mark Of Esteem).
March 6. Fourth foal. €260,000Y. Arqana Deauville August. J Brummitt. The dam, a smart 2-y-o 7f winner, was second in the Group 2 1m Falmouth Stakes and is a half-sister to 4 winners including the German listed winner and Group 3 placed Waldvogel. The second dam, Wurftaube (by Acatenango), won two Group 2 events over 12f and 14f in Germany and is a half-sister to 7 winners. *"A strong colt that came from the Deauville sales, he's improved in looks in every way. He's got quality, a great mind and a good stride. A very promising horse"*

MICHAEL GRASSICK

694. INVINCIBLE DON (IRE) ★★★★
b.c. Invincible Spirit – Dame Alicia
(Sadler's Wells).
May 2. Fourth foal. €52,000Y. Goffs Orby. Not sold. Half-brother to the fair 2009 2-y-o 6f winner Flip Flop (by Footstepsinthesand) and to the fair Irish 12f winner Lady Alicia (by Hawk Wing). The dam, fourth in the Group 3 7f C L Weld Park Stakes at 2 yrs, won over 9f at 3 yrs and is a half-sister to the Irish Group 2 1m and US Grade 2 9f winner Century City. The second dam, Alywow (by Alysheba), a champion filly in Canada, won 7 races including the Grade 3 8.5f Nijana Stakes, was second in the Grade 1 Rothmans International and the Grade 1 Flower Bowl Invitational and is a half-sister to 6 winners. (Miss P F O'Kelly). *"I've only had him two months, but he's a lovely big, colt with a super temperament and I love everything about him. I would say you'd be talking about July or August before he put in an appearance – probably over six furlongs. I trained the dam and she was a decent filly."*

695. MARTINE'S SPIRIT (IRE) ★★
b.f. Invincible Spirit – Mayenne (Nureyev).
May 25. Half-sister to the useful 2-y-o 6f to 7f winner of 3 races Sutter's Fort (by Seeking The Gold), to the very useful 12f listed winner My Renee (by Kris S), the quite useful 1m winner Menaggio (by Danehill), the quite useful Irish 10f winner Carnbridge (by Giant's Causeway) and the fair 12f winner Dalaval (by Dalakhani).

The dam is an unraced three-parts sister to the top-class colt Carnegie, winner of the Prix de l'Arc de Triomphe and the Grand Prix de Saint-Cloud, to the smart Group 2 10f Prix Guillaume d'Ornano winner Antisaar, the useful 10f and 12f winner Wayne County and the useful listed 13.5f winner Honfleur and a half-sister to the smart Group 3 St Simon Stakes winner Lake Erie. The second dam, Detroit (by Riverman), won the Prix de l'Arc de Triomphe and is a half-sister to 5 winners including the Cheveley Park Stakes winner Durtal (herself dam of the Ascot Gold Cup winner Gildoran). (Miss P F O'Kelly). *"An attractive filly, she's backward and is going to take a bit of time, so September or October would be her time. She's nice and it's a good family but they've all got a bit of a trip and they're not precocious."*

696. SWEET DIAMOND (IRE) ★★
b.f. Diamond Green – Love Knot (Lomitas).
January 12. First foal. €3,000Y. Tattersalls Ireland. Not sold. The dam, a minor French 2-y-o winner, is a half-sister to 3 winners including the listed winner and Group 2 Champagne Stakes second Playfellow. The second dam, Love And Adventure (by Halling), a French listed-placed winner of 3 races, is a half-sister to 7 winners. (P Croke). *"A small, sharp, racy filly. She'll be out over five furlongs in late April and she'll be my first runner."*

RAE GUEST
697. CHASING PIRATES ★★★
ch.f. Bahamian Bounty – Amorette (King's Best).
February 28. First foal. 4,000Y. Tattersalls October 3. Rae Guest. The dam, unplaced in Norway, is a half-sister to 6 winners including the French 7f listed winner Bezrin. The second dam, Darling Flame (by Capote), a useful 6f (at 2 yrs) and 7f winner, is a half-sister to 7 winners including the very smart Japanese Group 1 winning miler Heart Lake. *"She's the sharpest of our two-year-olds at the moment, she's done very well and I should think she'll start off at six furlongs."* TRAINERS' BARGAIN BUY

698. KALGOOLIE ★★
b.f. Aussie Rules – Kilbride (Selkirk).
February 15. Third foal. The dam is an unraced half-sister to several winners including the fairly useful 1m (at 2 yrs) and subsequent German listed 14f Kiswahili. The second dam, Kiliniski (by Niniski), a very smart winner of the Group 3 12f Lingfield Oaks Trial and second in the Yorkshire Oaks and fourth in the Epsom Oaks and is a half-sister to 5 winners including the dam of the US Grade 2 winner Bienamado. (Miss K Rausing). *"She's a bit backward at the moment and she's bred to stay. A nice filly for the future though, and she's out of a Selkirk mare which is always a bonus. I'd say she's been doing well since she came in and that she's coming along nicely but will want seven furlongs this year."*

699. UNNAMED ★★★
b.c. Oasis Dream – Break Point (Reference Point).
April 22. Half-brother to the quite useful 6f and 7f winner Daniella, to the moderate dual 9f winner Head First (both by Dansili) and the quite useful 10f winner Play Time (by Unfuwain). The dam, unplaced in one start, is a half-sister to numerous winners out of Cut Loose (by High Top). (Brian and Elaine Cooper). *"He came in very late but he's a very nice horse and another one for towards the end of the season. We had the half-sister Daniella and I think this colt will be very nice in the future."*

700. UNNAMED ★★★
br.f. Where Or When – Icing (Polar Falcon).
February 19. Second foal. The dam, a fair 2-y-o 7f winner, is a half-sister to numerous winners including the useful Italian 2-y-o 7f winner and subsequently US stakes winner La Martina. The second dam, Dance Steppe (by Rambo Dancer), showed no form but is a half-sister to 8 winners including the smart 12f winner Carlingford Rose. (T J Cooper). *"She's a very light filly – there's not a lot of her. But she moves beautifully and she's very elegant. One for the middle of the season."*

701. UNNAMED ★★★
ch.f. Selkirk – Perfect Solution (Entrepreneur).
January 22. First foal. 15,000Y. Tattersalls October 2. Boyce Bloodstock. The dam, a modest 6f winner at 3 yrs, is a half-sister to a bumper winner. The second dam, Pearl Barley (by Polish Precedent), won once at 4 yrs and is a half-sister to 5 winners including Nayyir

(Group 2 Lennox Stakes and Group 2 Challenge Stakes). (Perfect Partnership). *"She's well-bred, she's doing very well and we're very pleased with her. She'll be a mid-summer 2-y-o."*

702. UNNAMED ★★★
b.f. Sadler's Wells – Sweet Gypsy Rose (Darshaan).
May 1. Third foal. 65,000Y. Tattersalls October Book 1. Rae Guest. The dam, a fairly useful Irish 2-y-o 6f winner, is out of the very useful Group 3 7f Killavullan Stakes and listed Athasi Stakes winner Kincara Palace (by Fairy King), herself a half-sister to 6 winners. (E P Duggan). *"She's beautifully-bred and she was bought with that in mind but she's very much a late season type and one for next year really. A big, strong, lovely filly."*

703. UNNAMED ★★★
b.br.f. Noverre – Teide Lady (Nashwan).
January 9. The dam, a modest 9f winner, is a half-sister to the 2-y-o Group 2 7f Superlative Stakes and US Grade 3 7f winner Hatta Fort. The second dam, Oshiponga (by Barathea), a fair 9f winner, is a half-sister to the useful Tattersalls Houghton Sales Stakes winner and German Group 1 fourth Sir George Turner and the 7f (at 2 yrs) and Thirsk Classic Trial winner Tissifer. (E P Duggan). *"This filly was home-bred, she's a sharp type and will definitely make a two-year-old."*

704. UNNAMED ★★★
ch.f. Barathea – Top Row (Observatory).
February 9. First foal. 11,000Y. Tattersalls October Book 2. Rae Guest. The dam is an unplaced half-sister to 8 winners including the useful 2-y-o Group 3 7f C L Weld Park Stakes winner Rag Top and the dam of the 2-y-o Goffs Million winner Lucky General. The second dam, Petite Epaulette (by Night Shift), a fair 5f winner at 2 yrs, is a full or half-sister to 3 winners including the Group 1 1m Gran Criterium second Line Dancer. (Showhouse Furniture). *"A nice filly and one for the mid-summer onwards, she'll start off at six furlongs."*

WILLIAM HAGGAS

705. ABOVE ALL ★★
b.c. Nayef – Anyaas (Green Desert).
February 5. Third foal. Half-brother to the fair 2-y-o 7f winner Pearl Dealer (by Marju). The dam was a 1m winner at 3 yrs in the UAE. The second dam, Anwaar (by Machiavellian), was an Irish 2-y-o 1m winner. (Hadi Al Tajir). *"He's backward and still at the stud. I've only seen him once and he's quite nice but I wouldn't know enough about him to comment."*

706. ALHEERA (IRE) ★★★
b.f. Haafhd – Ghazal (Gone West).
February 5. Fourth foal. Half-sister to the quite useful 5f to 1m winner Muftarres (by Green Desert) and to the quite useful triple 1m winner at 3 to 5 yrs Hassaad (by Danehill). The dam, a useful dual 6f winner (including at 2 yrs), is a sister to the US dual Grade 3 winner and good sire Elusive Quality and closely related to 4 winners including the 2-y-o Group 2 5.5f Prix Robert Papin winner Rossini. The second dam, Touch Of Greatness (by Hero's Honor), is an unraced half-sister to the German Group 1 and Royal Lodge Stakes winner Gold And Ivory and to the dam of the Group 1 National Stakes winner Heart Of Darkness. (Hamdan Al Maktoum). *"I like this filly. I trained the half-brother Hassaad and he was handy but not very sound. She's quite nice but one for later on and over seven furlongs."*

707. ALJANA (IRE) ★★★
b.f. Exceed And Excel – Bush Baby (Zamindar).
March 26. Fourth foal. 90,000Y. Tattersalls October Book 1. Shadwell Estate Co. Sister to the quite useful 6f (at 2 yrs) and 5f winner Aakef and half-sister to the fair 2009 Irish 2-y-o 1m winner Plum Sugar (by Footstepsinthesand). The dam is an unplaced half-sister to 9 winners including the very smart Group 2 12f Ribblesdale Stakes winner Gull Nook (herself dam of the top-class colt Pentire), the equally smart Group 3 12f Princess Royal Stakes winner Banket and the useful Group 3 Ormonde Stakes winner Mr Pintips. The second dam, Bempton (by Blakeney), was placed three times at up to 11f and is a half-sister to 6 winners including Shirley Heights. (Sheikh Hamdan bin Maktoum al Maktoum). *"We've had a bit of luck with the sire and this filly is quite forward going. We're just going quietly with her at the moment so I wouldn't think we'd see her until July, but she'll be alright."*

708. AMJAAD ★★★★
br.f. Dansili – Frappe (Inchinor).
February 27. Eighth foal. 330,000Y. Tattersalls October Book 1. Shadwell Estate Co. Half-sister to the 7f (at 2 yrs) and Group 2 12f Ribblesdale Stakes winner Thakafaat (by Unfuwain), to the fairly useful 10f winner Quantum (by Alhaarth) and the quite useful 2-y-o 7f all-weather winner Applauded (by Royal Applause). The dam, a fairly useful 2-y-o 6f winner, is a half-sister to 2 winners including the 2,000 Guineas winner Footstepsinthesand. The second dam, Glatisant (by Rainbow Quest), winner of the Group 3 7f Prestige Stakes, is a half-sister to 8 winners and to the placed dam of the very smart 2-y-o Superstar Leo. (Hamdan Al Maktoum). *"There are bits and pieces of this pedigree which say she'll stay a mile and a half next year and yet she looks an absolute dead-set two-year-old. She's still got slightly open knees so she's on the back burner at the moment. I see her being out in July and she's a sweet filly. Definitely a two-year-old."*

709. ANOINT ★★
b.c. Pivotal – Pious
(Bishop Of Cashel).
February 12. Fifth foal. Brother to the fairly useful 2-y-o 7f winner Blithe and to the fair 5f winner of 5 races Solemn and closely related to the useful 7f and 2010 1m Lincoln Handicap winner Penitent (by Kyllachy). The dam, a fair dual 6f winner (including at 2 yrs), is a half-sister to 3 winners including the fair 6f, 8.5f and hurdles winner Mister RM. The second dam, La Cabrilla (by Carwhite), a fairly useful 2-y-o 5f and 6f winner, was third in the Group 3 Princess Margaret Stakes and is a half-sister to 6 winners including the Group 1 Nunthorpe Stakes winner Ya Malak. (Cheveley Park Stud). *"He's backward, just like all the family at this stage. Penitent never ran at two and I have the three-year-old, Divine Call who was just the same."*

710. APPROVE (IRE) ★★★
b.c. Oasis Dream – Wyola (Sadler's Wells).
March 13. Second foal. 65,000Y. Tattersalls October Book 1. Not sold. The dam, placed fourth once over 10f in Ireland at 3 yrs, is a half-sister to two listed-placed winners. The second dam, Rubies From Burma (by Forty Niner), won 3 races from 5f to 6f and was listed placed over 5.5f in Ireland and is a half-sister to 9 winners including the French 1,000 Guineas, Fillies Mile and Prix Marcel Boussac winner Culture Vulture. (Highclere Thoroughbred Racing, Bahram). *"Quite a sharp horse, I don't know quite what to make of him really because he looks very much like a two-year-old but the dam was slow and she's by Sadler's Wells. But he looks fast and early, so he'll probably be our first runner. I just hope it's controlled speed rather than 'cheap speed' and he's certainly showing all the indications that he wants to go."*

711. AROWANA (IRE) ★★★
b.f. Kodiac – Bali Royal
(King's Signet).
April 13. Third foal. 17,000Y. Tattersalls October 3. Gill Richardson. The dam was a very useful winner of 10 races over 5f including a listed event and is a half-sister to 2 winners. The second dam, Baligay (by Balidar), a fair winner of 7 races from 5f to 7f, is a half-sister to 3 winners. (Smith, Duke, Netherthorpe, Morecambe). *"I always like to have a relatively cheap filly or two and aim for the Weatherbys Supersprint – a race we have a good record in. This filly is quite sharp and quite long in the back but she's got a bit of speed."* TRAINERS' BARGAIN BUY

712. BARAAYA ★★★★
ch.f. Dalakhani – Sayedati Eljamilah
(Mr Prospector).
March 1. Half-sister to the quite useful 2-y-o 6f winner Motarassed, to the fair 2-y-o 6f winner Nudrah (both by Green Desert), the fair 11f winner Mujahaz (by Act One) and the modest 7f seller winner Sairaam (by Marju). The dam, unplaced in 2 starts, is a half-sister to numerous winners including the Derby winner Erhaab and the very useful Group 2 10f Premio Lydia Tesio winner Oumaldaaya. The second dam, Histoire (by Riverman), won once in France over 10.5f and is a half-sister to the Group 3 7f Prix de la Porte Maillot winner Hamanda. (Hamdan Al Maktoum). *"She's in Dubai but I like her a lot. When I saw her there she looked gorgeous and they love her. Obviously we have to see how she goes on when she arrives here, but she gets a good review."*

713. BLESSED BIATA (USA) ★★★★
b.f. *Mr Greeley – June Moon*
(Sadler's Wells).
March 31. Twelfth foal. 45,000Y. Tattersalls October Book 1. Not sold. Closely related to the smart 6f, 7f (both at 2 yrs) and Group 2 1m German and Italian 2,000 Guineas winner Dupont, to the Japanese 7f and 1m stakes winner Zachariah, the German 2,000 Guineas winner Pacino (all by Zafonic) and the French 3-y-o 1m winner Moon West (by Gone West) and half-brother to the useful 1m and UAE 9f winner Moon Dazzle (by Kingmambo), the 2-y-o 7f all-weather winner Lunar Express (by Giant's Causeway), the all-weather 1m and UAE 10f winner Dawn Piper (by Desert Prince) and the 7f (at 2 yrs) to 12f winner Winsome George (by Marju) – the last 3 all quite useful. The dam is an unraced half-sister to 7 winners including the French 1,000 Guineas second Firth Of Lorne. The second dam, Kerrera (by Diesis), a smart winner of the Group 3 Cherry Hinton Stakes and second in the 1,000 Guineas, is a half-sister to the high-class 2-y-o Rock City. (Mr B Kantor). *"The nicest we've had out of this mare for a while. She's got speed and she's useful. She had a slight setback in February but she's fine now and I think she'll be a two-year-old for sure. Six or seven furlongs will suit her this season."*

714. CAPE CLASSIC (IRE) ★★★★
b.c. *Cape Cross – Politesse (Barathea).*
March 14. Fourth foal. 320,000Y. Tattersalls October Book 1. Not sold. Half-brother to the very smart Group 1 6.5f Prix Maurice de Gheest and Group 2 6f Diadem Stakes winner of 6 races King's Apostle (by King's Best). The dam is an unraced half-sister to one winner out of the Group 1 6f Cheveley Park Stakes and Group 3 6f Princess Margaret Stakes winner Embassy (by Cadeaux Genereux), herself a half-sister to 5 winners including the Group 2 Pretty Polly Stakes winner Tarfshi. (Mr B Kantor). *"A nice-looking horse, he's well-bred and will make a two-year-old in the second half of the season. I'm glad he wasn't sold because he's a nice horse. His half-brother King's Apostle began his career in the late summer as a two-year-old and I can see this colt doing the same."*

715. DANCING RAIN (IRE) ★★★★
ch.f. *Danehill Dancer – Rain Flower*
(Indian Ridge).
April 24. Seventh foal. €200,000Y. Goffs Orby. Norris/Huntingdon. Sister to the fair 2-y-o 7f winner Captain Dancer, closely related to the 2-y-o listed 5f St Hugh's Stakes winner Sumora and the useful Irish 7f winner Fleeting Shadow (both by Danehill) and half-sister to the fairly useful 12f winner Mikhail Fokine (by Sadler's Wells). The dam is an unraced three-parts sister to the top-class Epsom Derby, Irish Champion Stakes and Dewhurst Stakes winner Dr Devious and a half-sister to 5 winners including the Japanese listed winner Shinko King and the Group 3 winners Royal Court and Archway. The second dam, Rose Of Jericho (by Alleged), is an unraced half-sister to 5 winners. *"A nice, big, backward looking filly. I can see her getting a mile this year, she's got a bit of quality about her and I can see her being put in the good races at the back-end of the season like the Fillies Mile at Ascot. A good type, she's a big, galloping filly."*

716. DUBAWI DANCER ★★★
ch.f. *Dubawi – Adees Dancer*
(Danehill Dancer).
February 15. Second foal. 39,000Y. Tattersalls October Book 1. N Callaghan. The dam is an unplaced half-sister to 13 winners including the German Group 2 winner Network and the good broodmare Nona (the dam of four German stakes winners). The second dam, Note (by Reliance II), won once in Germany and is a half-sister to 11 winners. (Callaghan, Golding, Kirtland). *"A nice, solid filly, she'll be running in the summer and she's a big, strong type."*

717. EXCHANGE ★★★
b.c. *Kheleyf – Quantum Lady (Mujadil).*
April 3. Fourth foal. 45,000Y. Tattersalls October Book 2. John Warren. Half-brother to the fair 2-y-o dual 5f winner Amber Sunset (by Monsieur Bond), to the modest 7f winner Johnny Friendly (by Auction House) and the moderate 1m winner Jemima Godfrey (by Ishiguru). The dam, a fair 5f and 6f winner at 2 yrs, is a half-sister to 4 other minor winners. The second dam, Folly Finnesse (by

Joligeneration), a 7f (at 2 yrs) to 10.8f winner, is a half-sister to 6 winners including the useful listed 5f Harry Rosebery Trophy and listed 5f Field Marshal Stakes winner Westcourt Magic. (Highclere Thoroughbred Racing Ltd). *"He's sixteen hands already but he's not slow! He looks a two-year-old, he's been doing a bit and his pedigree suggests he'll be precocious. Not quite ready yet, but he moves well and I think he'll be sprinter."*

718. EXPOSE ★★★
ch.c. Compton Place – Show Off (Efisio).
February 21. Seventh foal. 62,000Y. Tattersalls October Book 2. John Warren. Half-brother to the fairly useful 2-y-o 6f winner Bling (by Mark Of Esteem), to the fair 7f winner Bluff (by Bluebird) and the modest 6f and 7f winner Excessive (by Cadeaux Genereux). The dam, placed fourth once over 6f at 2 yrs, is a half-sister to 9 winners including the listed 5f winner and Group 2 5f second Easy Option (dam of the Group 1 Prix de la Foret winner Court Masterpiece) and the Group 2 5f third Wanton (dam of the Irish 1,000 Guineas winner Classic Park). The second dam, Brazen Faced (by Bold And Free), a quite useful 2-y-o 5f winner, is a half-sister to 8 winners. (Royal Ascot Racing Club). *"I trained Bluff who I thought was early and he proved me wrong. I think this family need time, so he'll be one for the second half of the season. He's grown a bit since we bought him, but he's strong and I think he'll be a two-year-old."*

719. FIGARO ★★★★
ch.c. Medicean – Chorist (Pivotal).
March 22. Half-brother to the moderate 10f seller winner King's Chorister (by King's Best). The dam won the Group 1 10f Curragh Pretty Polly Stakes and two Group 3 events and is a half-sister to the very useful 2-y-o 7f winner and Group 3 7f Prestige Stakes second Choirgirl. The second dam, Choir Mistress (Chief Singer), is an unraced half-sister to 6 winners including the smart Group 2 11.9f Great Voltigeur Stakes winner Sacrament. (Cheveley Park Stud). *"I'd love this to be a good horse. I've had one other out of the mare that was no good but this colt has done very well, he's a lovely mover and although he's tall, leggy and backward at the moment he's a nice horse alright."*

720. FIREBEAM ★★★
b.c. Cadeaux Genereux – Firebelly (Nicolotte).
March 10. Third foal. 100,000Y. Tattersalls October Book 1. John Warren. Half-brother to the fair dual 1m winner (including at 2 yrs) Bombina (by Lomitas). The dam, a fairly useful 2-y-o dual 6f and Italian listed 1m winner, is a half-sister to 3 winners including the South African listed winner L'Passionata. The second dam, Desert Delight (by Green Desert), is an unraced half-sister to 9 winners including the Group 3 May Hill Stakes winner Intimate Guest and the dams of the Grade 1 winners Luas Line and Prince Arch. (Highclere Thoroughbred Racing, Blue Peter). *"Firebeam reminds us very much of a horse we trained for Highclere called Bonus. This is a big, tall horse but he doesn't look that backward. I guess he'll need time being by Cadeaux Genereux but he's not bad at all. A nice horse."*

721. FLYING PHOENIX ★★★
b.f. Phoenix Reach – Rasmalai (Sadler's Wells).
February 14. 20,000foal. Tattersalls December. Lodge Farm Stud. Half-sister to the modest 12f winner Starburst (by Fantastic Light) and the modest 10f and 12f winner Urban Space (by Sulamani). The dam, a modest 9f placed maiden, is a half-sister to the winners and Group 3 placed Rayouni and Raiyoun. The second dam, Raymouna (by High Top), a minor Irish 1m winner, is a half-sister to 5 winners including the Group 3 Royal Whip Stakes winner and Irish St Leger second Rayseka. (Mr A Christou). *"A nice filly, she's definitely going to be a second half of the season two-year-old, unless she grows a lot which seems unlikely. Worth putting in the book."*

722. FURY ★★★★♠
b.c. Invincible Spirit – Courting (Pursuit Of Love).
March 28. Half-brother to the fairly useful 7f to 10f winner of 6 races Secret Liaison (by Medicean), to the fairly useful 7f winner Tryst (by Highest Honor), the modest 9f winner Speed Dating (by Pivotal) and the modest 6f winner Vibe (by Danzero). The dam was a fairly useful winner of four 2-y-o 7f events and two listed races over 1m and 10f at 3 yrs. The second dam, Doctor's Glory (by Elmaamul), a fairly useful 5.2f (at 2 yrs) and 6f winner, is a half-sister to 4

winners including the useful On Call, a winner of 7 races at up to 2m. (Cheveley Park Stud). *"Fury has always gone well, he's very good-natured, strong and a mid-season type two-year-old. He's a nice colt and I like him."*

723. GAINSBOROUGHS BEST (IRE) ★★★
b.f. *Invincible Spirit – Catherinofaragon (Chief's Crown).*
March 15. Eighth living foal. 65,000Y. Tattersalls October Book 1. Shadwell Estate Co. Half-sister to the quite useful 2-y-o dual 7f winner Lucayan Legacy (by Persian Bold), to the fair 2-y-o 1m winner Centenary (by Traditionally) and the modest all-weather 1m and 8.5f winner Catstreet (by Catrail). The dam is an unraced half-sister to 3 winners including the Canadian Grade 3 8.5f and 10f winner Gold Alert. The second dam, Croquis (by Arts And Letters), won 6 races in the USA including a stakes event, was placed in the Grade 1 CCA Oaks and the Grade 1 Delaware Handicap and is a half-sister to the Grade 1 winner Linkage. (Sheikh Hamdan bin Maktoum Al Maktoum). *"In the same ownership as the two-year-old Aljana, this filly's knees aren't the best but she should be a two-year-old because she's quite sharp. Probably a six furlong type."*

724. GOBOOLL ★★★★
gr.c. *Invincible Spirit – Exclusive Approval (With Approval).*
March 30. Fifth foal. 260,000Y. Tattersalls October Book 2. Shadwell Estate Co. Half-brother to the modest 2009 7f placed 2-y-o Turf Trivia (by Alhaarth), to the very useful 6f and 10.5f winner and listed-placed In The Light (by Inchinor), the quite useful 1m and 10f winner Thumbs Up (by Intikhab) and the French 1m to 10f winner of 4 races By Appointment (by Mojave Moon). The dam, a minor US 3-y-o winner, is a sister to the stakes winner Be Elusive and a half-sister to 8 winners. The second dam, Be Exclusive (by Be My Guest), won 5 races in France and the USA including the Group 3 Prix Chloe and is a half-sister to 2 winners. (Sheikh Ahmed Al Maktoum). *"He was a beautiful yearling and everyone loved him at the Sales. A very nice, straightforward, good moving horse. He's having a break at the moment but he will be a nice horse. Sheikh Ahmed is another new owner for me."*

725. HAAMAAT (IRE) ★★★
b.f. *Shamardal – Exultate Jubilate (With Approval).*
March 25. Fifth foal. 110,000Y. Tattersalls October Book 2. Shadwell Estate Co. Half-sister to the fair 2-y-o 7f winner One Cool Kitty (by One Cool Cat). The dam ran twice unplaced in the USA and is a half-sister to 8 winners including the Group 3 Prix Quincey winner Heraldiste and two French listed winners. The second dam, Heiress (by Habitat), is an unraced half-sister to the Group 1 Prix Saint-Alary and Prix Vermeille winner Saraca. (Hamdan Al Maktoum). *"I like her. She's very much a Shamardal in that he gets them plain and they're not great movers but they can run. I fancy Shamardal has a chance of being a good sire and we have one or two of his this year. This filly has open knees at the moment so she'll be a mid-season two-year-old, but if she stays sound she'll be alright."*

726. HAKEEKA ★★★★
b.f. *Cape Cross – Bourbonella (Rainbow Quest).*
February 22. Fifth foal. 300,000Y. Tattersalls October Book 1. Shadwell Estate Co. Half-sister to the high-class Group 1 1m Prix du Moulin, Group 2 Summer Mile and Group 3 7f Jersey Stakes winner Aqlaam (by Oasis Dream) and to the fair 12f and 14f winner Curacao (by Sakhee). The dam is an unraced half-sister to 9 winners including the high-class and multiple winning stayer Persian Punch and the Group 3 7f Solario Stakes winner Island Magic. The second dam, Rum Cay (by Our Native), a fair 14.6f winner, is a half-sister to 3 winners including the listed winner of 10 races Gymcrak Premiere. (Hamdan Al Maktoum). *"A sweet filly that cost a lot of money, she's out in a field at the moment because she went 'up behind' and just needs a bit of time. But she's a very attractive, good natured filly and a good mover, so although the dam has bred some slow ones she's also bred Aqlaam. I hope this filly is more like him!"*

727. IBSAAR ★★★
gr.c. *Red Ransom – Mosquera (Acatenango).*
February 4. Sixth foal. £80,000Y. Doncaster St Leger. Shadwell Estate Co. Half-brother to the quite useful 1m winner Mosqueras Romance (by Rock Of Gibraltar), to the French

1m winner Manita (by Peintre Celebre) and the fair Irish 6f winner Bonanza (by Danehill). The dam won 5 races including two listed events in Germany, was third in the Group 3 Prix de Psyche and is a full or half-sister to 8 winners. The second dam, Midnight Society (by Imp Society), won a stakes event in the USA and was Grade 2 placed. (Hamdan Al Maktoum). *"He'll want seven furlongs to a mile as a two-year-old, he's strong, not really backward and an August type two-year-old. Quite a nice horse."*

728. JAWHAR (IRE) ★★★★
ch.c. Halling – Kawn (Cadeaux Genereux).
February 7. Second foal. The dam, unplaced in one start, is a half-sister to the Group 2 1m Prix du Rond-Point and Group 3 8.5f Diomed Stakes winner Trans Island, to the Italian Group 3 winner Welsh Diva and the useful 2-y-o 7f winner Nothing Daunted (all by Selkirk). The second dam, Khubza (by Green Desert), a quite useful 3-y-o 7f winner, is a half-sister to 7 winners including the Group 2 winners Barrow Creek and Last Resort and the listed winners Arctic Char and Heard A Whisper. (Hamdan Al Maktoum). *"I've got the first foal out of the dam, Safwaan and he's quite a good horse. This colt is the one that got the rave reviews among the Sheikh Hamdan home-breds that were allocated to me. He's a very nice, straightforward, good-moving two-year-old for the second half of the season."*

729. LORDOFTHEHOUSE (IRE) ★★★★★
ch.c. Danehill Dancer – Bordighera (Alysheba).
May 1. Closely related to the Phoenix Stakes, National Stakes, 2,000 Guineas and Queen Elizabeth II Stakes winner George Washington (by Danehill) and half-brother to the Irish Champion Stakes, Prince Of Wales's Stakes and Singapore Airlines International Cup winner Grandera, to the UAE 1m and 10f winner Ampelio, the modest 13f, 2m and hurdles winner Wyeth (all by Grand Lodge) and the French 10f winner Fifty Five (by Lake Coniston). The dam won once over 13f in France, was second in the listed 12f Prix des Tuileries and is a half-sister to 7 winners. The second dam, Blue Tip (by Tip Moss), won 4 races including the Group 3 10.5f Prix Penelope, was Group 2 placed and is a half-sister to 7 winners. (Lael Partnership). *"He's got a bit of a temperament, but what a pedigree he has! He's very flashy, with white legs and a flaxen mane and tail – so I'm not sure about his colour but he's as hard as nails. He could be anything and should certainly be worth waiting for."*

730. LUDICROUS (IRE) ★★★
ch.f. Pivotal – Pretty As Can Be (Giant's Causeway).
February 2. Second foal. 82,000Y. Tattersalls October Book 1. William Haggas. The dam is an unraced half-sister to 6 winners including the high-class Group 1 St Leger and Group 1 Ascot Gold Cup winner Classic Cliché, the smart Group 1 12f Prix Vermeille winner My Emma (by Marju) and the smart 1m (at 2 yrs) and 14f Tote Ebor Handicap winner Mediterranean. The second dam, Pato (by High Top), a fairly useful 2-y-o 7f and triple 4-y-o 10f winner, was listed-placed and is a sister to the very smart sprinter Crews Hill and a half-sister to 3 winners. (St Albans Bloodstock LLP). *"It's a funny pedigree to suggest she might be sharp, but she's very racy. Pivotal's need time and although it's a lovely female line you can see from the pedigree that they need time as well. She's nice though and, as I say, she does look like making a two-year-old."*

731. MAP OF HEAVEN ★★★★★♣
b.f. Pivotal – Superstar Leo (College Chapel).
February 2. Sister to Enticing, a very smart Group 3 5f Molecomb Stakes and Group 3 5f King George Stakes winner and to Praesepe, placed second over 5f on her only start at 2 yrs in 2009 and half-sister to the quite useful dual 5f winner (including at 2 yrs) Speed Song (by Fasliyev). The dam, a very smart 2-y-o, won 5 races including the Group 2 5f Flying Childers Stakes and the Weatherbys Super Sprint and is a full or half-sister to numerous winners. The second dam, Council Rock (by General Assembly), a fair 9f and 10f placed 3-y-o, is a half-sister to 6 winners including the Group 3 Prestige Stakes winner Glatisant and the listed Virginia Stakes winner Gai Bulga. (Lael Stable). *"She's beautiful. A different class to the dam's three-year-old and bigger already. A charming filly, she's having a break for a month so she's one for the middle of the season. Her sister Enticing was useful but she was hot, whereas*

this filly isn't . I'd have to mark her as one of my favourites."

732. PARVANA (IRE) ★★★★
b.f. *Galileo – Lucina (Machiavellian)*.
February 5. Second foal. €140,000Y. Goffs Orby. Cheveley Park Stud. Half-sister to the fair 2009 2-y-o 6f and 7f winner My One Weakness (by Bertolini). The dam is an unraced half-sister to 7 winners including the triple Group 3 winner and Group 1 third Blue Monday and the Group 1 Italian Derby third Lundy's Lane. The second dam, Lunda (by Soviet Star), ran three times unplaced at 3 yrs and is a half-sister to the high-class middle-distance horses Luso (winner of the Aral-Pokal, the Italian Derby and the Hong Kong International Vase) and Warrsan (Coronation Cup and Grosser Preis von Baden), the smart Group 3 7f Nell Gwyn Stakes winner Cloud Castle and the smart Group 3 12f Meld Stakes winner Needle Gun. (Cheveley Park Stud.) *"This is a nice-natured filly, quite small but charming. One for the second half of the season and I think she was well-bought. One of my favourite fillies, I'd say."*

733. RED RIVERMAN ★★★
b.c. *Haafhd – Mocca (Sri Pekan)*.
March 17. Second foal. 37,000Y. Tattersalls October Book 2. W Haggas. Half-brother to the fair 2009 7f placed 2-y-o Café Greco (by Red Ransom). The dam, a quite useful 1m (at 2 yrs) and 10f winner, was listed-placed in Germany is a half-sister to one winner. The second dam, Ewan (by Indian Ridge), is an unraced half-sister to one winner. (Options O Syndicate). *"He was a real pain to break-in – very tricky, but he's had a break and has settled down well. He's back in work, doing well and he's a nice mover. A backward colt at the moment."*

734. SCENTED ★★
b.f. *Medicean – Red Garland (Selkirk)*.
April 16. Fifth foal. Sister to the quite useful dual 10f winner Aromatic and to the fair 11f winner Red Petal and half-sister to the quite useful 7f and 1m winner of 4 races King's Colour (by King's Best). The dam is an unraced sister to the smart Group 1 Fillies' Mile and Group 2 10f Blandford Stakes winner Red Bloom and to the smart listed 13f winner Red Gala. The second dam, Red Camellia (by Polar Falcon), winner of the Group 3 7f Prestige Stakes and third in the French 1,000 Guineas, is a half-sister to the German middle-distance winner Red Bouquet. (Cheveley Park Stakes). *"A backward, weak filly with a good bottom, no middle and long legs! She moves well, but I don't think there's a man alive who knows if she's any good because she's just not built right at the moment. She just needs three months to allow her to come to herself and who knows, she might turn out to be a nice back-end two-year-old."*

735. SHUHRA (IRE) ★★★
b.f. *Marju – Wijdan (Riverman)*.
April 25. Sister to the Group 2 1m Premio Ribot winner Oriental Fashion and to the quite useful dual 10f winner Tanfidh and half-sister to the very useful listed 7f and subsequent US Grade 2 10f winner Makderah (by Danehill), the useful 1m and 10f winner Ezdiyaad (by Galileo) and the modest 10f all-weather winner Mohafzaat (by Sadler's Wells). The dam, a useful 1m and 10.4f winner, is a sister to the 7f (at 2 yrs) and 1m listed winner Sarayir and a half-sister to the brilliant 2,000 Guineas, Derby, Eclipse and King George winner Nashwan and to the high-class middle distance colt Unfuwain. The second dam, Height of Fashion (by Bustino), a high-class winner of 5 races from 7f to 12f including the Group 2 Princess of Wales's Stakes, is a half-sister to the good middle-distance colt Milford. (Hamdan Al Maktoum). *"This filly is from Sheikh Hamdan's great family. She's a nice, backward filly and she could be an Oaks candidate, who knows? This is just the sort of animal that floats along and you think 'Mmm, maybe she isn't much good', then you give her a piece of work and she shows you she is!."*

736. SILVER SHINE (IRE) ★★★★
gr.c. *Verglas – Dream Time (Rainbow Quest)*.
February 14. Fifth foal. 60,000Y. Tattersalls October Book 2. Blandford Bloodstock. Half-brother to the 2-y-o Group 3 7f Silver Flash Stakes third Mark Of An Angel (by Mark Of Esteem) and to a minor winner abroad by Spinning World. The dam, placed once over 12f at 3 yrs, is a half-sister to 4 minor winners. The second dam, Grey Angel (by Kenmare), won 8 races at around 1m including two Group 3

events in South Africa and was Group 1 placed. (M Jaber). *"He'll be sharp and I think he'll be a tough, six furlong two-year-old from May onwards. If he's any good he'll go to Ascot. One of my sharper ones."*

737. SKELETON (IRE) ★★★
b.f. Tobougg – Atamana (Lahib).
February 7. Fifth foal. €25,000Y. Tattersalls Ireland. A Skiffington. Half-sister to the Group 3 10.5f winner Mulaqat and the fair 10f winner Emshabb. The dam, a quite useful 1m winner, is a half-sister to 6 winners including the Irish 2-y-o 6f winner and Group 3 7f Killavullen Stakes third Dance Clear – subsequently a winner of 4 races and Grade 3 placed in the USA. The second dam, Dance Ahead (by Shareef Dancer), a quite useful 2-y-o 7f winner, is a half-sister to 6 winners. (R Tooth). *"She was bought at Fairyhouse in the hope she might run in their Sales race. She was named Skeleton because we wanted to name her Toboggan (after the sire) and when that was turned down so we thought of the Olympic Gold Medal winner Amy Williams in the Skeleton Bob! She's a good mover and she'll be alright."*

738. SKY BOOSTER ★★★
b.c. Indesatchel – Myths And Verses (by Primo Valentino).
January 29. 13,000Y. Tattersalls October. W Haggas. The dam, a modest 5f (at 2 yrs) to 9f placed maiden, is a half-sister to 3 winners. The second dam, Romantic Myth (by Mind Games), won 3 races at 2 yrs including the Group 3 5f Queen Mary Stakes and is a half-sister to 5 sprint winners including the Queen Mary winner Romantic Liason. (Option O Syndicate). *"This colt is bred to be sharp, but we don't know about the sire yet as it's his first season. He was relatively cheap, he's tough and he'll run a lot. A proper trainer would have had him out by now!."*

739. STARBOUND (IRE) ★★★★
ch.f. Captain Rio – Glinting Desert (Desert Prince).
February 16. Second foal. 400,000Y. Tattersalls October Book 1. Cheveley Park Stud. Half-sister to the Group 1 Phoenix Stakes and Group 2 Railway Stakes winner Alfred Nobel (by Danehill Dancer). The dam, a fair 2-y-o 7f winner, is a half-sister to 2 winners. The second dam, Dazzling Park (by Warning), a very smart winner of the Group 3 1m Matron Stakes and a listed 9f event, was placed in the Group 1 Irish Champion Stakes and the Irish 1,000 Guineas. She is a half-sister to 7 winners including the Derby, Champion Stakes, Dewhurst Stakes and National Stakes winner New Approach. (Cheveley Park Stud). *"Obviously she's very well-bred being a half-sister to a Group 1 winner and she must be the most expensive Captain Rio there's ever been. She's changed a fair bit because she looked an early type at the Sales but she's got a bit longer and seems to have a bit more scope now. In a way that's good (though not in the short term) and it's hard not to like her because she's a very attractive filly."*

740. STARSTUDED (IRE) ★★★
b.f. Galileo – Miss Demure (Shy Groom).
May 23. Thirteenth foal. 75,000Y. Tattersalls December. Not sold. Half-sister to 9 winners including the useful 2009 Irish 2-y-o 6f winner and listed-placed Miracle Match (by Oratorio), the useful 6f and US stakes winner and Group 1 Cheveley Park Stakes third Royal Shyness (by Royal Academy), the fairly useful 2-y-o 6f winner and Group 3 Coventry Stakes third Missel (by Storm Bird), the fairly useful 10f to 2m winner of 9 races Steamroller Stanly (by Shirley Heights), the quite useful 7f winner Dangerous Fortune (by Barathea) and 2 minor winners in Japan and the USA by Siphon and Private Terms. The dam won the Group 2 6f Lowther Stakes and is a half-sister to one winner. The second dam, Larosterna (by Busted), ran once unplaced and is a full or half-sister to 6 winners. (Hirschfield, Scott & Piggott). *"The mare was a good two-year-old but Galileo's record with juveniles isn't that good because they need time. However, this is the sort of mare that should help him get a nice two-year-old and this filly doesn't look that backward, so hopefully we'll be able to get cracking with her from July onwards."*

741. TO THE SPRING ★★★
b.f. Medicean – Humouresque (Pivotal).
May 13. Fourth foal. 38,000Y. Tattersalls October Book 1. Not sold. Half-sister to

the fair Irish 7f and 1m winner Solid Air (by Linamix). The dam, a smart Group 3 10.5f Prix Penelope winner, is a sister to the winner and Group 2 placed Mighty and a half-sister to the very smart sprinter Danehurst, winner of the Cornwallis Stakes (at 2 yrs), the Curragh Flying Five, the Prix de Seine-et-Oise and the Premio Umbria (all Group 3 events). The second dam, Miswaki Belle (by Miswaki), second over 7f on her only start, is a half-sister to 8 winners including the smart Group 3 6f Cherry Hinton Stakes winner and 1,000 Guineas third Dazzle. (Cheveley Park Stud). *"She's just gone home for a break. She wasn't much at the sales, where she didn't sell, but she's done really well since. She goes well and her pedigree tells you she has a chance of being good."*

742. TROJAN NIGHTS (USA) ★★★★
ch.c. Street Cry – Dabaweyaa (Shareef Dancer).
April 11. Half-brother to the very useful 2-y-o 6f winner and UAE Group 2 1m second Western Diplomat, the fairly useful 1m winner Blue Snake (both by Gone West), to the fairly useful 5.7f (at 2 yrs) and 7f winner Ascot Cyclone, the quite useful 2-y-o 7f winner Dubai Magic (both by Rahy), the 2-y-o 6f winner and Group 1 7f Prix de la Salamandre second Bin Nashwan (by Nashwan), the US Grade 2 winner Magellan (by Hansel), the useful listed 6f winner and Group 2 second Damaniyat Girl (by Elusive Quality), the useful 7.6f to 1m winner Faithful Warrior, the 2-y-o 6f winner Oman Gulf (both by Diesis), the 6f winner and Group 3 7f Supreme Stakes second Alanees (by Cadeaux Genereux), the 2-y-o 6f winner Dare Hunter (by Gulch) and the 1m winner Aneesati (by Kris) – the last 4 all quite useful. The dam was a smart winner of the 1m Atalanta Stakes and was placed in the 1,000 Guineas and the Child Stakes. She is a half-sister to the Group 3 winning sprinter Bruckner and the smart Hoover Fillies Mile and Nassau Stakes winner Acclimatise. The second dam, Habituee (by Habitat), won over 1m in France and was second in the Prix d'Aumale. (Mohammed Obaida). *"We had his half-sister Damaniyat Girl who wasn't a bad filly at all, being a listed winner and second in a Group 2. This colt is a nice mover, although a bit 'springy of his pasterns' which might accentuate his movement. He's by a very good sire in Street Cry and from a hell of a family, so he could be anything."*

743. UNEX GOYA (IRE) ★★★
b.c. Medicean – Arabica (Red Ransom).
May 2. Second foal. 20,000Y. Tattersalls October 1. David Redvers. The dam is an unraced half-sister to 4 winners in France including the listed placed Red Mo. The second dam, the 2-y-o Group 2 7f Criterium de Maisons-Laffitte winner Moiava (by Bering), is a half-sister to 8 winners including the 2-y-o Group 1 10f Criterium de Saint-Cloud winner Special Quest. (Mr Bill Gredley). *"I think he'll certainly be a two-year-old and quite an early one at that. I can see him running in May, he's a real runner and a nice little horse."*

744. WATNEYA ★★★
b.f. Dubawi – Quickstyx (Night Shift).
February 27. Third foal. 70,000Y. Tattersalls October Book 2. Shadwell Estate Co. Half-sister to the fairly useful 2-y-o dual 6f winner Hairspray (by Bahamian Bounty) and to the modest 2-y-o 7.5f winner Blusher (by Fraam). The dam, a fair 1m winner, is a half-sister to 5 winners including the smart 12f listed winner and US Grade 1 second Red Fort and the useful 12f listed winner Red Carnation. The second dam, Red Bouquet (by Reference Point), won 3 minor races from 12f to 13f at 4 yrs in Germany and is a half-sister to 4 winners including the Group 3 7f Prestige Stakes winner Red Camellia (herself dam of the Group 1 Fillies' Mile winner Red Bloom). (Sheikh Ahmed Bin Rashid Al Maktoum). *"She's a fat, strong filly and she should be a two-year-old. I think Dubawi's can be a bit squat and she's that way too. Not small, I think the quicker she goes the better she moves. It's a two-year-old family and she'll be out around July time."*

745. UNNAMED ★★
ch.c. Cadeaux Genereux – Bread Of Heaven (Machiavellian).
April 28. Third foal. 55,000Y. Tattersalls October Book 1. W Haggas. Half-sister to the unplaced 2009 2-y-o Nefyn (by Tiger Hill). The dam, a quite useful 2-y-o 6f winner, is a half-sister to 5 winners including the Group 2 1m Prix du Rond-Point and Group 3 8.5f Diomed Stakes winner Trans Island and the Italian

Group 3 winner Welsh Diva. The second dam, Khubza (by Green Desert), a quite useful 3-y-o 7f winner, is a half-sister to 7 winners including the Group 2 winners Barrow Creek and Last Resort and the listed winners Arctic Char and Heard A Whisper. (Mr J Fretwell). *"He's going to need time, he will be fine but he has open knees and he's going to be a back-end two-year-old. It's a nice family, so again he's got a chance."*

746. UNNAMED ★★★
b.f. Encosta De Lago – Fille De Joie (Royal Academy).
April 6. Third foal. 120,000Y. Tattersalls October 1. A O Nerses. The dam, a modest 7f and 1m placed maiden, is a half-sister to 5 winners including the Group 3 Park Hill Stakes and Group 3 Princess Royal Stakes winner Delilah. The second dam, Courtesane (by Majestic Light), is a placed half-sister to the Group 3 5f Greenlands Stakes winner Drama (dam of the US Grade 3 winner Tycoon's Drama). (Saleh Al Homaizi). *"She's quite tall but a great mover with a wonderful presence. A charming filly, she's nice and don't leave her out."*

747. UNNAMED ★★★★
b.f. Exceed And Excel – Mellow Jazz (Lycius).
January 24. Half-sister to the fairy useful 6f winner and listed placed Improvise (by Lend A Hand). The dam, a quite useful 6f (at 2 yrs) and 1m all-weather winner, is a half-sister to the Italian listed winner Mister Cavern. The second dam, Slow Jazz (by Chief's Crown), a French listed 1m winner, is a three-parts sister to the smart Group 1 6f Middle Park Stakes and Group 2 7f Challenge Stakes winner Zieten and to the Group 1 6f Cheveley Park Stakes and Group 3 5f Queen Mary Stakes winner Blue Duster. (S Ali). *"We had a problem with her in February but she's sound now. She's a big, strong filly and will make a two-year-old alright. She's nice and should be one to watch out for."*

748. UNNAMED ★★★
b.f. Marju – Opera Comica (Dr Fong).
February 29. First foal. The dam, a fair 1m to 10f placed maiden, is a half-sister to Viva Pataca (by Marju), a winner of 15 races and nearly £5 million in prize money here and in Hong Kong from 6f (at 2 yrs) to 12f including seven Grade One events. The second dam, Comic (Be My Chief), a quite useful 10f and 11.5f winner, is a half-sister to 4 winners including the very useful 2-y-o Group 3 Solario Stakes winner Brave Act and the dual listed winner Jellaby Ashkir. (Mr H T Lok). *"This is a nice horse. He's a medium-sized colt and a nice mover that'll need a bit of time. He'll be one for the seven furlong maidens at the back-end and he could be anything."*

749. UNNAMED ★★
b.c. Tiger Hill – Vayavaig (Damister).
March 14. Twelfth foal. 32,000Y. Tattersalls October Book 1. William Haggas. Half-brother to the useful 2-y-o 1m winner and Group 3 1m Autumn Stakes second Taameer (by Beat Hollow), to the useful 6f and 6.5f (at 2 yrs) and dual listed 1m winner Expensive (by Royal Applause), the useful 6f (at 2 yrs) and 8.5f winner and US Grade 3 placed Sweet Prospect (by Shareef Dancer), the fairly useful dual 6f all-weather winner Wolfhunt (by Wolfhound) – subsequently a minor winner in the USA, the quite useful 11.6f to 14f winner Dr Cool (by Ezzoud), the fair 9f winner Ainia (by Alhaarth), the Irish 3-y-o 6f winner Green Pursuit (by Green Desert) and the Italian winner of 7 races Zaigon (by Zilzal). The dam, a fair 2-y-o 6f winner, is a half-sister to 6 winners including the Group 3 Palace House Stakes winner Vaigly Great and July Cup second Vaigly Star (herself dam of the Group 3 winners Sahara Star and Yalaietanee). The second dam, Dervaig (by Derring-Do), won over 5f at 2 yrs and is a half-sister to 6 winners including the dam of the Group 1 Premio Presidente Della Repubblica winner Hoche. (K Bailey & P Watson). *"He has a nice pedigree and we bought him because the dam has a bit of speed. I quite like the sire but they need time. He's a backward horse but he isn't bad at all."*

750. UNNAMED ★★★
b.c. Giant's Causeway – Winds Of Time (Danehill).
March 10. First foal. The dam, a fairly useful 2-y-o 6f winner, subsequently won in the USA and Canada and is a half-sister to 2 winners. The second dam, Windmill (by Ezzoud), a fair 13.8f

winner, is a half-sister to 8 winners including the very smart Group 2 12f Ribblesdale Stakes winner Gull Nook (herself dam of the top-class colt Pentire), the equally smart Group 3 12f Princess Royal Stakes winner Banket and the useful Group 3 Ormonde Stakes winner Mr Pintips. (Mr & Mrs R Scott). *"This colt is a bit small, he goes well and looks like having a bit of speed. The dam won over six furlongs but overall it's a stoutly bred family. He looks like making a two-year-old."*

MICHAEL HALFORD

751. CASAMENTO ★★★
ch.c. Shamardal – Wedding Gift (Always Fair).
March 20. €54,000foal. Goffs. Bobby O'Ryan. Half-brother to Inler (by Red Ransom), a promising 6f winner on his only start at 2 yrs in 2009, to the fair 2-y-o 7f winner Brosna Cry (by Cape Cross) and to the French 7f and 1m winner Sky Gift (by Stravinsky) and the French 2-y-o 1m winner Wana Doo (by Grand Slam). The dam, a French 2-y-o listed 1m winner, was Group 3 placed twice and is a half-sister to 7 winners. The second dam, Such Style (by Sassafras), is a placed half-sister to 5 winners including the Group 2 Prix Hocquart winner Regency. (Sheikh Mohammed). *"A big horse, he's lovely and a great mover that'll need a bit of time, so he's one for the second half of the year. A colt with plenty of size and scope, he'll be a seven furlong two-year-old and along with Mereli he'll be one of our best colts."*

752. DARIKA (IRE) ★★★
b.f. Barathea – Darariyna (Shirley Heights).
March 9. Half-sister to the quite useful 10f and 12f winner Dakiyah (by Observatory) and to the 2m and hurdles winner Darenjan (by Alhaarth). The dam, a quite useful 12f and 13.4f winner, is a half-sister to numerous winners including the smart Group 2 Goodwood Cup winner Darasim (by Kahyasi) and to the quite useful 12f and 13.4f winner Darariyna (by Shirley Heights). The second dam, Dararita (by Halo), a winner in France over 12.5f at 3 yrs, is a half-sister to the Group 2 12.5f Prix Maurice de Neiuil winner Darazari, to the listed 10.5f and 12f winner Dariyoun (by Sharastani), the smart King Edward VII Stakes second Kilimanjaro (by Shirley Heights) and the 2-y-o 8.2f winner and French Derby third Rhagaas. (H H Aga Khan). *"She's a nice filly, she'll make a 2-y-o and we like her. A good actioned filly, it'll be the second half of the season before she runs. Seven furlongs with some ease in the ground should suit her."*

753. ELIZABETH COFFEE ★★★
b.f. Byron – Queen's Wharf (Ela-Mana-Mou).
April 20. Fourth foal. The dam, a useful Irish listed 14f winner, is a half-sister to 4 winners. The second dam, Lady Bennington (by Hot Grove), is an unplaced half-sister to 6 winners including the dual Group 3 winner Ahohoney. (Ms R Hines). *"A filly with a nice shape to her, she'll probably need seven furlongs being out of Queen's Wharf – a filly we trained. She has a bit of pace, she's correct and she's a nice filly.*

754. INEXCUSED (IRE) ★★★
ch.f. Medicean – Miss Intimate (War Chant).
January 29. First foal. €50,000Y. Goffs Orby. A O'Ryan. The dam is an unraced half-sister to the Irish 2,000 Guineas winner Bachelor Duke and the German listed 12f winner Translucid. The second dam, Gossamer (by Seattle Slew), a winner of 2 races in the USA at up to 9f, is a half-sister to 5 winners including the German Group 3 winner Miss Tobacco. (Gigginstown I louse Stud). *"She's done very well physically but it'll be the second half of the season before she's ready to run, over seven furlongs. A medium-sized, good-balanced filly with a good attitude."*

755. MERELI (IRE) ★★★
b.c. Cape Cross – Mariyba (Be My Guest).
April 25. Half-brother to the quite useful 1m (at 2 yrs) and 11f winner Mariydi (by Kalanisi). The dam, a fair Irish 1m and 9f placed maiden, is a half-sister to several winners. The second dam, Mariyada (by Diesis), won once at 3 yrs and is a half-sister to 6 winners. (HH Aga Khan). *"The most forward of the Aga Khan horses we have, he's a nice horse that's certainly worth putting in the book. A strong, good-sized colt, he's correct and he goes well. He'd be one of the best of our colts."*

756. MORE THAN A LOT (IRE) ★★★★
ch.f. Mr Greeley – Jellett (Green Desert).
March 21. Second foal. €110,000Y. Goffs Orby. M Halford. Half-sister to Smart Striking

(by Smart Strike), unplaced in one start at 2 yrs in Ireland in 2009. The dam is an unraced sister to the Irish 2,000 Guineas, Prix du Moulin and Queen Elizabeth II Stakes winner Desert Prince and a half-sister to 6 winners including the 2-y-o Group 3 6.5f Anglesey Stakes winner Ontario. The second dam, Flying Fairy (by Bustino). placed twice at up to 12f, is a half-sister to 6 winners including the Group 3 Prix Penelope third Fleet Fairy. (Gigginstown House Stud). *"She should be running by the end of May and she's a good, strong filly, well-balanced with a good attitude."*

757. MULLINGAR ★★★
b.c. *Dubawi – Crystal Gazing*
(El Gran Senor).
May 13. Eleventh foal. €24,000Y. Tattersalls Ireland. Not sold. Half-brother to the fair 2009 2-y-o 10f winner Futurist (by Halling), to the UAE dual Group 3 6f winner of 7 races Conroy (by Gone West), the fairly useful 2-y-o 7f winner Fen Shui (by Timber Country), the minor Irish 10f winner Dark Veil (by Gulch) and the minor French 9f winner Key Circle (by Jade Robbery). The dam won the Group 3 7f Nell Gwyn Stakes, was third in the 1,000 Guineas and is a half-sister to numerous winners. The second dam, Crystal Bright (by Bold Lad, Ire), won once in the USA and is a half-sister to 4 minor winners. (Sheikh Mohammed). *"A lovely, well-balanced colt and a good actioned horse, he's medium-sized and because he's a May foal he'll just take a bit of time, but he'll make a two-year-old in the second half of the year."*

758. UNNAMED ★★★★
b.f. *Mujadil – Perle d'Irlande (Top Ville).*
March 12. Twelfth foal. €31,000Y. Goffs Orby. John Wholey. Half-sister to the French 11f and 12f listed winner Paraiyor (by Lomitas), to the useful Irish triple 7f winner and Group 3 placed Excelerate (by Mujadil), the quite useful 14f winner Irish Blade (by Kris) and 2 minor winners in France by Sillery and Bigstone. The dam, a listed-placed winner of 3 races in France, is a half-sister to 4 winners including the Prix Marcel Boussac winner Sierra Madre (herself dam of the Sussex Stakes winner Aljabr). The second dam, Marie d'Irlande (by Kalamoun), won once at 3 yrs in France and is a sister to the Prix Jean Prat winner Dom Racine. (Mr J Wholey). *"She'll be running in late May and she's a fine, big filly that goes well. She'll be suited by six furlongs and the way she's going at the moment she wouldn't need to go further!"*

RICHARD HANNON

759. ALDWICK BAY (IRE) ★★★
b.c. *Danehill Dancer – Josie Doocey (Sadler's Wells).*
April 12. First foal. €50,000Y. Goffs Orby. Peter Doyle. The dam is an unraced sister to the Group 3 Gallinule Stakes winner Puerto Rico, closely related to the Group 1 Fillies' Mile winner Fairy Heights and the stakes-placed winner Peace Offering and half-sister to the Group 3 St Simon Stakes winner Persian Brave. The second dam, Commanche Belle (by Shirley Heights), was placed four times from 10f to 2m and is a half-sister to 11 winners including the Yorkshire Cup winner Band and the Ormonde Stakes winner Zimbalon. (Mrs A Williams). *"A nice, big colt. We won't be racing him until the six or seven furlong races but he's a bonny horse."*

760. ATTRACTED TO YOU (IRE) ★★★
b.f. *Hurricane Run – Haute Volta (Grape Tree Road).*
February 27. Second foal. €110,000Y. Goffs Orby. Peter Doyle. The dam is an unraced half-sister to 7 winners including the 2-y-o Group 1 National Stakes winner Heart Of Darkness. The second dam, Land Of Ivory (by The Minstrel), a very useful winner over 7f (at 2 yrs) and 1m, was placed in the Prix Cleopatre and Lupe Stakes and is a half-sister to the high-class middle-distance colt Gold and Ivory and to the unraced dams of the Grade 1 winner Anees and the Graded stakes winners and sires Elusive Quality and Rossini. (Mr W P Drew). *"A nice looking colt and a lovely mover, we won't be looking at him until mid-season but he's in good form."*

761. AULD BURNS ★★★★★
gr.c. *Pastoral Pursuits – Crackle (Anshan).*
March 28. Fifth foal. 160,000Y. Tattersalls October Book 1. Peter Doyle. Half-brother to the US dual Grade 3 winner, over 1m and 9f, Pickle (by Piccolo), to the fair French 6f and 7f winner Pivock (by Pivotal) and a winner in

Spain by Mujahid. The dam, a quite useful 5.7f (at 2 yrs) to 10f winner of 3 races, is a half-sister to 5 winners including the listed winner of 4 races Ronaldsay. The second dam, Crackling (by Electric), a modest 9f and 12f winner, is a half-sister to 4 winners including the Group 1 7f Moyglare Stud Stakes winner Bianca Nera. (P A Byrne). *"One of my favourites. A gorgeous horse, he could be a Coventry Stakes horse – there's no reason why not."*

762. AVONMORE STAR ★★★★
b.c. *Avonbridge – Pooka's Daughter (Eagle Eyed).*
March 5. Third foal. £14,000Y. Doncaster St Leger. Peter Doyle. The dam, a modest 1m (including at 2 yrs) and 7f winner is a half-sister to 3 winners. The second dam, Gaelic's Fantasy (by Statoblest), won once at 3 yrs in Italy and is a half-sister to 7 winners including the French and Irish 2,000 Guineas and Richmond Stakes winner Bachir. (Mr K Gearing). *"A nice, early type of two-year-old, he wasn't expensive but I think he'll do well this year."*

763. BAHCELI (IRE) ★★★★
gr.c. *Mujadil – Miss Shaan (Darshaan).*
March 12. Eighth foal. £48,000Y. Doncaster St Leger. Ross Doyle. Half-brother to the very useful 2-y-o 6f winner and listed-placed Damien (by Namid) and to two minor 2-y-o winners in France by Welkin and Homme de Roi. The dam is an unplaced half-sister to 8 winners abroad. The second dam, Miss Mendez (by Bellypha), won twice at 3 yrs in France and is a sister to the Prix du Moulin winner Mendez. *"He'll be an early two-year-old. A lovely colt and a sharp one too."*

764. BARKING (IRE) ★★★
b.c. *Bahri – Pivot d'Amour (Pivotal).*
March 27. Third foal. £21,000Y. Doncaster St Leger. Ross Doyle. The dam, a moderate 5f placed 2-y-o, is a half-sister to 9 winners. The second dam, Miss Loving (by Northfields), a fairly useful 2-y-o 5f and 7f winner, is a half-sister to 6 winners including the useful 5f to 1m winner Cremation. (R Tooth). *"A nice, good-moving horse, but you won't be seeing him out until mid-season."*

765. BILKO PAK (IRE) ★★★
b.c. *Barathea – Vale View (Anabaa).*
March 26. First foal. €25,000Y. Goffs Orby. Peter Doyle. The dam, placed fourth twice in France over 7f and 1m, is a half-sister to the Irish 2,000 Guineas winner Saffron Walden, the Grade 1 E P Taylor Stakes winner Insight and the Group 1 Prix de la Foret winner Dolphin Street. The second dam, Or Vision (by Irish River), won over 5.5f and 7f at 2 yrs and the listed 7f Prix de l'Obelisque at 3 yrs and is a half-sister to the dams of Listen (Fillies Mile), Sequoyah (Moyglare Stud Stakes) and the US Grade 2 winner Dance Master. (Middleham Park Racing II). *"He'll be early, I'll be making an entry for him soon and he goes very well. A nice horse."* This colt made a fair start to his career in mid-April, finishing fifth at Newmarket.

766. BRANDY SNAP (IRE) ★★★
b.f. *Hennessy – Natural Skill (Aptitude).*
March 28. First foal. €64,000Y. Goffs Orby. Peter Doyle. The dam is an unraced half-sister to 7 winners including the Grade 1 Eddie Read Handicap winner Monzante and the useful French 2-y-o listed 7f winner Alpha Plus. The second dam, Danzante (by Danzig), a sprint winner in France and in the USA, is a half-sister to the Breeders Cup Classic winner Skywalker, the US Grade 2 winner Pac Mania and the French Group 3 7f winner Nidd. (Thurloe Thoroughbreds XXVIII). *"A sharp filly, she moves well and she'll be an early type."*

767. BUNCE (IRE) ★★★
b.c. *Good Reward – Bold Desire (Cadeaux Genereux).*
February 9. Second foal. 65,000Y. Tattersalls October Book 2. Peter Doyle. Half-brother to Freedom Pass (by Gulch), placed fourth over 7f on her only start at 2 yrs in 2009. The dam, placed once over 6f, is a sister to the fairly useful 5f (at 2 yrs) and listed 6f winner Irresistible (herself dam of the Group 3 Nell Gwyn Stakes winner Infallible) and a half-sister to one winner. The second dam, Polish Romance (by Danzig), a minor 7f winner in the USA, is a full or half-sister to 6 winners. (R C Tooth). *"A nice horse, he's a bit 'on the leg' at the moment so he won't be early – he's more of a mid-season type."*

768. BYRONY (IRE) ★★★★
ch.f. Byron – Saphire
(College Chapel).
February 29. Fifth foal. 24,000Y. Tattersalls October Book 2. Axom. Closely related to the fairly useful 2-y-o 5f winner and Group 3 5f Cornwallis Stakes second Waffle (by Kheleyf) and half-sister to the modest Irish 1m winner King's Road (by King's Best). The dam, a fairly useful 2-y-o 5f and 6f winner, was listed-placed twice and is a half-sister to 4 minor winners. The second dam, Emerald Eagle (by Sandy Creek), a fair 6f to 1m winner of 5 races, is a half-sister to 4 winners. (Axom XIII). *"She'd be one of my picks – a very nice filly and she's going to be sharp. A strong, good-moving sort with a big backside on her."*

769. CAE SHEN (IRE) ★★★
ch.c. Iffraaj – Collada
(Desert Prince).
February 27. Third foal. €22,000foal. Goffs. Bath Bloodstock. Half-brother to the quite useful 2009 Irish 7f and 1m placed 2-y-o Crying Time (by Chevalier). The dam is an unplaced half-sister to the smart 2-y-o Group 3 7f Horris Hill Stakes winner Clearing and to the useful dual 7f winner (including at 2 yrs) Blazing Thunder. The second dam, Bright Spells (by Alleged), a French 12f winner, is a half-sister to the Group 2 German winner Non Partisan, the Grade 3 Canadian stakes winner Jalaajel and the useful dual 2-y-o 7f winner and Group 3 Prix d'Aumale third Suntrap (herself dam of the Grade/Group 1 winners Raintrap and Sunshack). (Mrs Julie Wood). *"Another nice horse, but we haven't 'opened the box' yet. He goes very well but he's hanging on to his coat at present. With every bit of work he's moving on – so I'm happy with him."*

770. CAPE TO RIO (IRE) ★★★
b.c. Captain Rio – Misaayef (Swain).
March 6. Third foal. £26,000Y. Doncaster St Leger. Peter Doyle. Half-brother to the quite useful 6f winner Solar Spirit (by Invincible Spirit). The dam, a quite useful 10.5f winner, is a half-sister to 3 winners including the dam of the US Grade 1 winner Alwajeeha. The second dam, Zakiyya (by Dayjur), a minor US 3-y-o winner, is a half-sister to 11 winners including the dam of the US Grade 1 winner Scorpion. (Kennet Valley Thoroughbreds I). *"He'll probably run before your book is out but he's not just an early sort, he's a nice type of horse that goes well and he has enough scope to continue throughout the season."* Cape To Rio won on his debut in mid-April.

771. CASUAL GLIMPSE ★★★★
b.c. Compton Place – Glimpse
(Night Shift).
February 17. Ninth foal. 40,000Y. Tattersalls October Book 2. Peter Doyle. Half-brother to the 2-y-o dual 1m winner Shenley Charm (by First Trump), to the 2-y-o 6f winner Focus (by First Trump), the 10f winner Raakaan (by Halling) – all quite useful, the Italian 7.5f and 1m winner of 8 races Masazza (by Elmaamul) and a winner in Macau by Primo Dominie. The dam, a fair 2-y-o 6f winner, is a half-sister to 5 minor winners here and abroad. The second dam, Lovers Light (by Grundy), is an unplaced half-sister to 4 winners including the good broodmare Lady Moon (dam of the Group winners Moon Cactus and Shining Steel). (N A Woodcock & John Manley). *"He worked the other morning and showed us he's a very nice horse. He goes well but he's got plenty of size about him so I won't go too early with him. A really nice type, I might wait for six furlongs with him."*

772. CENSUS (IRE) ★★★★★♠
b.c. Cacique – Slieve (Selkirk).
February 1. First foal. 50,000Y. Tattersalls October Book 2. John Warren. The dam is an unraced sister to the Group 1 Gran Premio di Milano winner Leadership and a half-sister to two minor winners abroad. The second dam, Louella (by El Gran Senor), is a placed half-sister to 7 minor winners in Europe and the USA. (Highclere Thoroughbred Racing, Beeswing). *"A very nice colt. He's a bit 'on the leg' at the moment but he looks like making up into a really nice horse one day. He won't be early – he's more of a seven furlong type."* Stable jockey Richard Hughes was quick to point out that this was one of the real quality two-year-olds in the yard, saying *"He was the first of the two-year-olds I sat on and I said to the Head Lad 'you'll go a long way before you get me a better two-year-old to sit on than this' – I think he's a nice horse."*

773. CHAIN LIGHTNING ★★★
ch.c. Hurricane Run – Sachet (Royal Academy).
March 29. Fourth foal. €55,000Y. Arqana Deauville August. Peter Doyle. The dam ran once unplaced and is a sister to the US listed winner and the Group 1 6f Cheveley Park Stakes third Royal Shyness. The second dam, Miss Demure (by Shy Groom), won the Group 2 6f Lowther Stakes. (M Pescod). *"A beautiful horse, he's well-grown but he's one for the second half of the season onwards."*

774. CLASSIC VOICE (IRE) ★★★
b.c. Oratorio – Pearly Brooks (Efisio).
March 14. Fifth foal. €32,000Y. Tattersalls Ireland. Peter Doyle. The dam, a fair 3-y-o 6f winner, is a sister to 4 winners including the Group 1 Phoenix Stakes winner Pips Pride and a half-sister to 4 winners. The second dam, Elkie Brooks (by Relkino), is a placed half-sister to one winner. (Byerley Racing Ltd). *"He's going to take time, but he'll be alright in the second half of the season."*

775. CULT CLASSIC (IRE) ★★★★♣
ch.c. Choisir – Fashion Guide (Bluebird).
March 8. Third foal. £42,000Y. Doncaster St Leger. Amanda Skiffington. Half-brother to the fair 1m winner Spotty Muldoon (by Mull Of Kintyre). The dam, a 2-y-o 6f winner in Ireland, is a half-sister to 7 winners including the Group 3 1m Premio Dormello winner Foolish Heart. The second dam, Honorine (by Blushing Groom), placed once in France over 1m, is a half-sister to 6 winners including the Group 3 10.5f Prix Corrida winner Echoes. (Cariolan Links Partnership III). *"A lovely, big horse. A really nice mover, he's strong and we like him that much that Amanda Skiffington bought the dam's foal. With a bit of luck he'll be a nice horse but we won't be starting him until the six furlong races."*

776. CUSTOM HOUSE (IRE) ★★★
b.c. Tale Of The Cat – L'Acajou (Gulch).
March 4. First foal. 50,000Y. Tattersalls October Book 2. Peter Doyle. The dam is an unraced half-sister to 8 winners including the Canadian listed stakes winner Noble Strike. The second dam, Green Noble (by Green Dancer), a stakes winner of 8 races in Canada, is a half-sister to 10 winners including the US Grade 2 winner Abigailthewife. (Mr H R Heffer). *"A big, backward, leggy horse, but he moves well and he's a nice horse for the future."*

777. DANCEYOURSELFDIZZY (IRE) ★★
b.c. Danehill Dancer – Gamra (Green Desert).
May 11. Third foal. 65,000Y. Tattersalls October Book 2. Peter Doyle. Closely related to the 2-y-o listed 5f winner and Group 3 Firth Of Clyde Stakes second Roxan (by Rock Of Gibraltar) and half-brother to the quite useful Irish 12f winner Boulay (by Montjeu). The dam, a fair 3-y-o 1m winner, is a full or half-sister to 6 winners including the very smart Group 2 9.7f Prix Dollar winner Wiorno and the very smart Trusthouse Forte Mile, Gimcrack Stakes and Earl of Sefton Stakes winner Reprimand. The second dam, Just You Wait (by Nonoalco), is an unraced half-sister to 7 winners. (Mrs Julie Wood). *"He's one we haven't really got into yet, so we don't know much about him. A nice horse, but he needs plenty of time."*

778. DATE WITH DESTINY (IRE) ★★★★♣
b.f. George Washington – Flawlessly (Rainbow Quest).
February 4. Twelfth foal. 320,000Y. Tattersalls October Book 1. Peter Doyle. Half-sister to 6 winners including the Group 3 10.5f Prix Penelope winner Ombre Legere (by Double Bed and herself dam of the Japanese Group 3 winner Germinal), the French winner and US Grade 1 placed Flawly (by Old Vic and herself dam of the US Grade 3 winner Best Name) and two minor French winners by Halling and Epervier Blue. The dam is a placed sister to the winner and listed-placed Profusion and a half-sister to 8 winners including the French listed winners and Group-placed Video Rock and Lady Day. The second dam, Pauvresse (by Home Guard), is an unraced half-sister to 6 winners. (Mrs Julie Wood). *"What more can you say that's not already been said. A beautiful filly, she's a lovely mover and there's absolutely nothing wrong with her. Most likely a seven furlong two-year-old, but she might have the speed for six."* This filly is the only horse George Washington ever managed to sire of course and she was certainly the centre of attention when she was in the sales ring.

779. DR DARCEY ★★★★

b.c. Dr Fong – Ballet (Sharrood).
February 9. Twelfth foal. 25,000Y. Tattersalls October Book 2. Peter Doyle. Half-brother to Fair Trade (by Trade Fair), second over 1m on his only start at 2 yrs in 2009, to the smart 1m (at 2 yrs) and listed 10f winner Island Sound (by Turtle Island), the useful 10f and 11.6f winner Serge Lifar (by Shirley Heights), the fairly useful Irish 10f winner Ballyhaunis (by Daylami), the quite useful 10f winner Quintoto (by Mtoto), the German 7f winner Batanga (by Primo Dominie) and the modest 14.8f all-weather winner Charlie's Gold (by Shalford). The dam, a moderate 5f and 6f placed maiden, is a half-sister to 10 winners including the May Hill Stakes winner Satinette. The second dam, Silk Stocking (by Pardao), won 3 races including the listed 9f Strensall Stakes and is a half-sister to 5 winners including the smart sprinter Shiny Tenth. (Aristotle's Elements). *"A lovely horse, he has a plain head but I suppose that's the sire's influence. A good goer and a nice mover, but he won't be a five furlong horse – he's more a seven furlongs plus horse."* Richard Hughes likes him too, saying *"A smashing horse, he'll not be too late, probably a mid-season type and he's a nice colt."*

780. DR GREEN (IRE) ★★★

b.c. Diamond Green – Tikitano (Dr Fong).
February 14. Second foal. £24,000Y. Doncaster St Leger. Peter Doyle. The dam is an unplaced half-sister to 3 winners including the US listed winner and Grade 2 placed Californian. The second dam, Asterita (by Rainbow Quest), won the listed Oaks Trial and is a half-sister to 7 winners including the top-class broodmare Loxandra (dam of four Group winners). (K T Ivory). *"We're happy with him. He goes very well and he looks pretty sharp too, but having said that I think the further he goes this year the better he'll be."*

781. DUKE OF FLORENCE (IRE) ★★★

b.c. Medicean – Bonheur (Royal Academy).
April 24. Sixth foal. 26,000Y. Tattersalls October Book 1. Peter Doyle. Half-brother to Othello (by Azamour), unplaced in 3 starts at 2 yrs in 2009, to the Group 3 Irish 1,000 Guineas Trial winner Carribean Sunset (by Danehill Dancer), the minor French 2-y-o winner Happy Lodge (by Grand Lodge) and the fair 12f winner Ommadawn (by Montjeu). The dam won over 6f at 3 yrs in Ireland and is a half-sister to 7 winners including the German 1,000 Guineas winner Quebrada. The second dam, Queen To Conquer (by King's Bishop), won the Grade 1 Yellow Ribbon Handicap and is a half-sister to 5 winners. (The Actual Partnership). *"A lovely, big horse, he's a little bit on the backward side as you might expect from his foaling date and pedigree. One for the mid-season onwards."*

782. EMPEROR'S PRINCESS (FR) ★★★

b.f. Holy Roman Emperor – Elanaaka (Lion Cavern).
March 13. Sixth foal. €125,000Y. Arqana Deauville August. Peter Doyle. Half-sister to the minor French winner of 3 races Kibaar (by Red Ransom). The dam won twice in France and was third in the Group 3 Prix de la Nonette and is a half-sister to 3 winners. The second dam, Mousaiha (by Shadeed), is an unraced half-sister to 6 winners including the Grade 1 Top Flight Handicap winner Chain Bracelet. (Mr W P Drew). *"She's a very nice filly, but we haven't done a lot with her yet, she's just cantering away until I feel she's ready."*

783. ENABLING (IRE) ★★★★

b.c. High Chaparral – Joyful (Green Desert).
January 20. Tenth foal. €80,000Y. Goffs Orby. Peter Doyle. Closely related to the minor French 4-y-o winner Dorset (by Sadler's Wells) and half-brother to the fairly useful 5f and 6f winner and listed-placed Roker Park (by Choisir) and the moderate 1m winner Cooden Beach (by Peintre Celebre and herself dam of the Group 2 Gimcrack Stakes winner Shaweel) and the unraced dam of the Group 3 Albany Stakes winner Nijoom Dubai. The dam, a fair 7f all-weather winner at 3 yrs, is a half-sister to 7 winners including the Golden Opinion, winner of the Group 1 1m Coronation Stakes and placed in the French 1,000 Guineas and the July Cup. The second dam, Optimistic Lass (by Mr Prospector), won the Group 2 10f Nassau Stakes and the Group 3 10.5f Musidora Stakes and is a half-sister to 9 winners. (Mr B C M Wong). *"I like him, but he's not going to be very early. One for the middle of the season I'd say."*

784. ENERGIZING ★★★
b.c. Zamindar – Maria Bonita (Octagonal).
May 9. First foal. 24,000Y. Tattersalls October Book 2. Peter Doyle. The dam, a moderate 4-y-o 10f winner, is a half-sister to 3 winners including the Italian listed winner of 7 races at around 1m Golden Cavern. The second dam, Nightitude (by Night Shift), a fairly useful 2-y-o 5f winner and listed-placed over 6f, is a half-sister to 9 winners including the useful 2-y-o 7f winner Normanby Lass. (Mr B C M Wong). *"A nice colt, he won't be long considering he was a May foal. The two-year-olds belonging to this owner might end up in Hong Kong."*

785. ENLIGHTENING (IRE) ★★★
b.c. Elusive City – Mono Star (Soviet Star).
April 24. Third foal. 32,000Y. Tattersalls October Book 2. Peter Doyle. Half-brother to the unplaced 2009 2-y-o Sacred Star (by Xaar). The dam is an unraced half-sister to the listed 6f winner and Group 3 placed Topkamp and to the listed 5f winner Morinqua. The second dam, Victoria Regia (by Lomond), a stakes winner of 3 races from 6f to 1m here and in the USA, is a half-sister to 9 winners. (Mr B C M Wong). *"We're working him now and he should be out in April. He wasn't an early foal and yet he's doing alright."*

786. EUCHARIST (IRE) ★★★
b.f. Acclamation – Satin Rose (Lujain).
February 17. First foal. £18,000Y. Doncaster St Leger. Peter Doyle. The dam, a moderate 12f winner, is a half-sister to 4 other minor winners. The second dam, Shamwari (by Shahrastani), is a placed half-sister to the Derby winner Golden Fleece. (Mrs Julie Wood). *"She's nice and sharp and she'll be fairly early. A five furlong type two-year-old."*

787. GENERAL SYNOD ★★★
b.c. Invincible Spirit – New Assembly (Machiavellian).
March 21. Sixth foal. Closely related to the useful dual 6f winner (including at 2 yrs) Instalment (by Cape Cross) and to the quite useful 10f winner Regent's Park (by Green Desert) and half-brother to the quite useful 7f winner Victoria Reel (by Danehill Dancer) and the fair 1m winner Small Fortune (by Anabaa).

The dam, a useful 9f and 10f winner, is a sister to the 7f (at 2 yrs) and Group 1 9f Dubai Duty Free Stakes winner Right Approach and a half-sister to 6 winners. The second dam, Abbey Strand (by Shadeed), a fair Irish 10f winner, is a half-sister to numerous winners including the 2-y-o Group 3 winners Grand Chelem and Splendid Moment. (The Queen). *"A fine, big two-year-old, one of the best lookers in the yard."*

788. HIGHCLIFFE ★★★
ch.f. Bertolini – Galapagar (Miswaki).
March 3. Third foal. 16,000Y. Tattersalls October Book 2. Peter Doyle. The dam, a French 1m and 9f winner, is a half-sister to 3 other minor winners in the USA. The second dam, Runaway Fair Lady (by Runaway Groom), was a stakes winner of 5 races in the USA. (A J Ilsley & G Battocchi). *"A little bit on the weak side at present, but she's getting better and she'll make a two-year-old alright."*

789. HUMDRUM ★★★
b.f. Dr Fong – Spinning Top (Alzao).
February 24. Half-sister to the fairly useful 7f (at 2 yrs) to 11f winner Full Toss (by Life's A Whirl) and to the moderate triple 1m winner Life's A Whirl (by Machiavellian). The dam, a useful 10f winner, is a half-sister to 4 winners including the fairly useful 3-y-o 7f and subsequent US dual 9f winner Daytime. The second dam, Zenith (by Shirley Heights), was a fairly useful 2-y-o 8.5f winner. (The Queen). *"A lovely filly. There's definitely nothing wrong with her but she's hanging on to her coat, so I think she's one for later on."*

790. INAGH RIVER ★★★
b.f. Fasliyev – Bolshaya (Cadeaux Genereux).
February 16. Seventh foal. £20,000Y. Doncaster St Leger. Peter Doyle. Half-sister to the Irish 2-y-o 7f and subsequent Hong Kong winner Carnegie Hall (by Danehill). The dam, a fair triple 6f winner, is a half-sister to 8 winners including the very smart King's Stand Stakes and Temple Stakes winner Bolshoi and the useful sprinters Mariinsky, Great Chaddington and Tod. The second dam, Mainly Dry (by The Brianstan), is an unraced half-sister to 4 winners. (D J Barry). *"A fast, early sort, he's a typical two-year-old type and he'll be out early."*

791. JAMBO BIBI (IRE) ★★★
b.f. Iffraaj – Nouveau Riche (Entrepreneur).
February 10. Second foal. 40,000Y. Tattersalls October Book 2. Peter Doyle. Half-sister to the fair 2009 7f placed 2-y-o Old Money (by Medicean). The dam, a fair 3-y-o 1m winner, is a half-sister to the smart Group 3 Prix La Rochette winner Guys And Dolls, to the smart 1m (at 2 yrs) to 11f listed winner Pawn Broker and the useful dual 7f 2-y-o winner and Group 3 placed Blushing Bride. The second dam, Dime Bag (by High Line), a quite useful winner of 4 races at up to 2m (including on the all-weather), is a half-sister to 7 minor winners. (J Palmer-Brown). "A sharp, early two-year-old, she's fine and won't take long to get ready."

792. JOLLYWOOD (IRE) ★★★
b.br.f. Holy Roman Emperor – Save The Table (Tale Of The Cat).
March 24. First foal. €24,000foal. Goffs. Not sold. The dam was unplaced at 2 yrs in the USA and is a half-sister to 5 winners including the listed Thirsk Classic Trial winner Royal Dignitary. The second dam, Star Actress (by Star de Naskra), is an unplaced half-sister to 5 winners including the US Grade 1 winner Dreamy Mimi. (Mrs Julie Wood). "She's just hanging on to her coat but I don't think she'll be long. Not very big, but a lovely filly."

793. KALAHAAG ★★★
ch.f. Iffraaj – Verbania (In The Wings).
March 26. Fourth foal. 50,000Y. Tattersalls October Book 1. Peter Doyle. Half-sister to the fair 12f winner Summerlea (by Alhaarth). The dam, an Irish 10f winner, is a half-sister to the useful 2-y-o 5.5f winner Pescara and to the useful French listed 10.8f winner Mistra (herself dam of the Group 1 Prix Saint-Alary winner Marotta). The second dam, Mackla (by Caerleon), won the Group 3 1m Prix d'Aumale and is a half-sister to 6 winners. (B Andersson). "A lovely filly for the six and seven furlong races. Her owner prefers us to hang on with them for a bit."

794. KING OF JAZZ (IRE) ★★★
b.c. Acclamation – Grand Slam Maria (Anabaa).
March 3. First foal. £48,000Y. Doncaster St Leger. Peter Doyle. The dam, a moderate 9f placed Irish maiden, is a half-sister to 7 winners. The second dam, Kate Marie (by Bering), a listed-placed winner of 3 races in France, is a half-sister to 6 winners. (Justin Dowley & Michael Pescod). "A six furlong type two-year-old, he's picking up and improving every day this horse."

795. KING TORUS (IRE) ★★★
b.c. Oratorio – Dipterous (Mujadil).
April 12. Second foal. €30,000Y. Goffs Orby. Peter Doyle. The dam, a quite useful Irish 2-y-o 6f winner, is a half-sister to 2 winners. The second dam, Dajarra (by Blushing Groom), is an unraced half-sister to 7 winners. (Dick Hitchcock & Alan King). "He goes well, he'll be fairly early and he'll probably want six furlongs."

796. KOJAK (IRE) ★★★
b.c. Kodiac – Face The Storm (Barathea).
April 30. Fifth foal. 26,000Y. Tattersalls October Book 1. Peter Doyle. Half-brother to the useful 2009 2-y-o 5f and 6f winner and Group 2 7f Superlative Stakes second Roi de Vitesse (by Chineur) and to the quite useful 6f (at 2 yrs) and 9f winner Cavort (by Vettori). The dam, a fair 2-y-o 1m winner, is a half-sister to 3 winners including the listed winner Santa Isobel. The second dam, Atlantic Record (by Slip Anchor), is an unraced half-sister to 4 winners. (Mrs Julie Wood). "A fairly early two-year-old, he goes quite well and has plenty of speed. We might start him over five furlongs and the sire has already had a winner from his first crop. A good-looking horse, and a good mover."

797. LATER (IRE) ★★★
b.f. Marju – Liege (Night Shift).
May 7. Eighth foal. €25,000Y. Tattersalls Ireland. Peter Doyle. Sister to the useful Irish 2-y-o 6f and listed 7f winner Bruges, to the minor French dual 1m winner Moore's Melody and the minor Hong Kong 3-y-o winner Sounds Better. The dam is an unraced half-sister to 2 winners. The second dam, Wedding Bouquet (by King's Lake), a useful winner of 6 races from 5f to 7f including the Group 3 C L Park Stakes and the US Grade 3 Monrovia Handicap, is closely related to the outstanding Derby, Irish Derby and King George winner

Generous and to the Oaks and Irish 1,000 Guineas winner Imagine. (Mr J N Reus). *"A lovely filly. She's strong, a nice sort and from a good family too."*

798. LIBRANNO ★★★★
b.c. Librettist – Annabelle Ja (Singspiel).
February 13. First foal. 26,000Y. Tattersalls October Book 3. Not sold. The dam, a quite useful 2-y-o 7f winner, is a half-sister to 11 winners in Europe (mainly Germany). The second dam, Alamea (by Ela-Mana-Mou), won 2 minor races at 2 and 3 yrs in Germany and is a half-sister to 8 winners. (McDowell Racing Ltd). *"A really good-looking horse. We don't know much about the sire yet but this colt goes well."*

799. MAJOR DUDE ★★★★♣
ch.c. Sakhee – Diliza (Dilum).
February 11. Third foal. 34,000Y. Tattersalls October Book 2. Peter Doyle. The dam, a moderate 1m winner, is a half-sister to one winner. The second dam, Little White Lies (by Runnett), is a placed half-sister to 5 winners. (Green Pastures Farm). *"A proper horse. He's going to make a real nice two-year-old, he's strong and he goes well."*

800. MEASURING TIME ★★★
b.c. Dubai Destination – Inchberry (Barathea).
April 2. Fourth foal. Tattersalls October Book 1. 28,000Y. Not sold. Half-brother to the modest 14f winner Berry Baby (by Rainbow Quest). The dam, placed 7 times including when second in a listed event over 1m at 2 yrs and fourth in the Oaks, is a half-sister to the very useful listed 12f winner Inchiri. The second dam, Inchyre (by Shirley Heights), a useful 1m winner, is a half-sister to 7 winners including the very smart and tough triple Group 3 7f winner and sire Inchinor. (Woodcote Stud). *"A nice horse, he goes very well and despite his pedigree he's quite sharp. He moves well and I'm delighted with him."*

801. MEMORY (IRE) ★★★★
b.f. Danehill Dancer – Nausicaa (Diesis).
March 28. Fifth foal. 72,000Y. Tattersalls October Book 1. John Warren. Sister to the quite useful 6f (at 2 yrs) and 7f winner Kafuu and half-sister to the quite useful Irish 2009 7f placed 2-y-o Hedaaya (by Indian Ridge) and the quite useful 6f (at 2 yrs) and 1m winner Naughty Frida (by Royal Applause). The dam won 3 races at 2 and 3 yrs in France and the USA over 7f and 1m, was third in the Grade 3 Miesque Stakes and is a half-sister to 3 winners. The second dam, Blushing All Over (by Blushing Groom), won 6 races in France and the USA including a listed event and is a half-sister to 8 winners including the good broodmare Come On Rosi. (Highclere Thoroughbred Racing, Masquerade). *"She's just starting to pick up now. A bit of a Madam early on, she's knuckling down now, seems to go very well and we're all pleased with her."*

802. MISS DUTEE ★★★
b.f. Dubawi – Tee Cee (Lion Cavern).
April 3. Seventh foal. Half-sister to the useful 2-y-o triple 6f winner and listed placed Yajbill (by Royal Applause), the quite useful 2-y-o 7f winner Bold Crusader (by Cape Cross) and the fair 7f all-weather winner Fantastic Cee (by Noverre). The dam, a fair 3-y-o 7f winner, is a half-sister to 5 winners including the useful 7f and 1m winner Bishr. The second dam, Hawayah (by Shareef Dancer), a modest 2-y-o 7f winner, is a half-sister to 6 winners. (Alan, Franklin, Neville, Poole, Stuart, Laws). *"A backward filly, but she's nice and she should make a two-year-old later on."*

803. MIXED EMOTIONS (IRE) ★★★
b.f. Exceed And Excel – L-Way First (Vision).
April 20. Eleventh foal. 30,000Y. Tattersalls October Book 2. Peter Doyle. Half-sister to the useful 2-y-o 7f winner, Group 3 Solario Stakes second and subsequent dual US Grade 3 winner Embossed (by Mark Of Esteem), to the quite useful 2-y-o 7f winner Gypsy Baby (by Modigliani), the quite useful 2-y-o 5f winner First Village (by Danehill) and the fair 2-y-o 1m winner Shooting Party (by Noverre). The dam, placed at up to 2m in Ireland, is a half-sister to 5 winners. The second dam, Lacey Brief (by Roi Dagobert), won once at 3 yrs and is a half-sister to 2 winners. (Mr P D Merritt). *"She goes particularly well, in fact she's trying to do too much, but she can certainly run."*

804. MORIARTY (IRE) ★★★
b.c. Clodovil – Justice System (Criminal Type).
March 28. Ninth foal. 52,000Y. Tattersalls October Book 2. Peter Doyle. Half-brother to the modest 2-y-o 5f and 6f winner Just A Carat (by Distinctly North), to the quite useful 1m winner Leave To Appeal (by Victory Note) and a winner in Greece by Mujadil. The dam is an unplaced half-sister to 9 winners including the Group 2 10f Prince Of Wales's Stakes winner Lear Spear. The second dam, Golden Gorse (by His Majesty), won 5 minor races in the USA and is a half-sister to 9 winners including the listed Irish 2,000 Trial and subsequent US dual Grade 3 winner Lotus Pool. (Justin Dowley & Michael Pescod). *"A big, strong, fine colt and a seven furlong type two-year-old. He's just cantering away nicely at the moment."*

805. MY SON MAX ★★★★
b.c. Avonbridge – Pendulum (Pursuit Of Love).
March 27. Sixth foal. £31,000Y. Doncaster St Leger. Peter Doyle. Half-brother to the quite useful 2-y-o 5f winner Every Second (by Kyllachy), to the fair 1m winner Pendulum Star (by Observatory) and the fair 5f and 6f winner Medici Time (by Medicean). The dam, a quite useful 3-y-o 7f winner, is a half-sister to 6 winners. The second dam, Brilliant Timing (by The Minstrel), is a placed half-sister to the US Grade 1 winners Timely Writer and Timely Assertion. (Mr D C McKay). *"He goes very well and will be racing before the book is published."* This is another one that jockey Richard Hughes told me he thinks a fair bit of. Ten days later he won first time out at Nottingham.

806. NOVEL DANCER ★★★
b.c. Dansili – Fictitious (Machiavellian).
February 28. Closely related to the useful 2009 2-y-o 6f and 7f winner Quadrille (by Danehill Dancer) and half-brother to the quite useful dual 1m winner Hunting Tower (by Sadler's Wells). The dam, a useful 10f listed winner, is a sister to the smart Group 2 12f Ribblesdale Stakes and Group 2 13.3f Geoffrey Freer Stakes winner Phantom Gold (herself dam of the Oaks second Flight Of Fancy). The second dam, Trying For Gold (by Northern Baby), was a useful 12f and 12.5f winner at 3 yrs. (The Queen). *"A nice filly, she's just cantering away at the moment and she'll continue doing that for a couple of months."*

807. NUMERAL (IRE) ★★★♠
b.c. Holy Roman Emperor – Savieres (Sadler's Wells).
March 28. Fourth foal. 85,000Y. Tattersalls October Book 2. John Warren. Half-brother to Bitter Man (by Azamour), placed third over 7f on his only start at 2 yrs in 2009. The dam, a minor Irish 11f winner, is a full or half-sister to 7 winners including the Irish 9f winner and Group 1 National Stakes second Coliseum. The second dam, Gravieres (by Saint Estephe), won the Grade 1 Santa Ana Handicap and the Grade 3 California Jockey Club Handicap and is a half-sister to 9 winners. (Highclere Thoroughbred Racing, Flying Fox). *"He goes very well, he's a nice horse and will be on his way when the six furlong races start."*

808. OMNIPOTENT (IRE) ★★★♠
b.c. Tagula – Bobbydazzle (Rock Hopper).
February 7. Sixth foal. £52,000Y. Doncaster St Leger. Peter Doyle. Half-brother to the fair Irish dual 5f winner Shinko Dancer (by Shinko Forest), to the fair dual 9f winner Distiller (by Invincible Spirit) and the moderate 2-y-o 5f winner Areweplayingout (by Namid). The dam, a quite useful dual 1m winner (including at 2 yrs), is a half-sister to 6 winners including the Group 3 Horris Hill Stakes, Ballycorus Stakes and Prix de la Porte Maillot winner Tumbledown Ridge. The second dam, Billie Blue (by Ballad Rock), is a placed half-sister to 4 minor winners. (Mrs Julie Wood). *"A nice type, we might wait for the six furlong races with him, but he's not far away from a run."*

809. PACO BELLE (IRE) ★★★
b.f. Whipper – Raindancing (Tirol).
April 2. Ninth foal. €26,000Y. Goffs Orby. Peter Doyle. Half-sister to the fairly useful triple 5f winner and listed-placed Jack Spratt (by So Factual), the fair 3-y-o 7f winner Dash For Cover (by Sesaro), the fair 12f winner Yossi (by Montjeu) and the modest dual 1m winner Ballare (by Barathea). The dam, a fairly useful 2-y-o 6f winner, was third in the Group 3 6f Princess Margaret Stakes and is a sister to the smart 7f (at 2 yrs) to 10f winner and Group 1 National Stakes third Mountain Song and a

half-sister to 6 winners including the Group 2 Cherry Hinton Stakes winner Please Sing. The second dam, Persian Song (by Persian Bold), is an unplaced sister to the Kentucky Derby second Bold Arrangement. (The Calvera Partnership No.2). *"A nice filly, she'll be sharp and she goes well."*

810. PAUSANIAS ★★★★
b.c. Kyllachy – The Strand (Gone West).
March 5. Fifth foal. 29,000Y. Tattersalls December. Peter Doyle. The dam is an unraced sister to the US triple Grade 3 winner Gold Land and a half-sister to 6 winners. The second dam, Lajna (by Be My Guest), is an unplaced half-sister to 5 winners including the dual Group 1 1m Lockinge Stakes winner Soviet Line. (Ferguson, Hassiakos, Morrin). *"A big, strong, fine horse. I'm very happy with him but he's one for a bit later on. A very good-looking colt."* Jockey Richard Hughes likes him too – *"A nice, big horse part owned by Sir Alex Ferguson, he'll need a bit of time but he's not bad at all."*

811. QUEEN MYRINE (IRE) ★★
b.f. Oratorio – Slewvera (Seattle Slew).
April 29. Seventh foal. £58,000Y. Doncaster St Leger. Peter Doyle. Half-sister to the Grade 1 Hollywood Turf Handicap winner Boboman (by Kingmambo) and to 2 minor winners in the USA by Atticus and Dare And Go. The dam won 3 races in France and the USA, was second in the Grade 2 Palomar Handicap and the Group 3 Prix d'Aumale and is a full or half-sister to 4 winners. The second dam, Hedgeabout (by Riva Ridge), a listed stakes winner in the USA and Grade 2 placed, is a half-sister to 6 winners. (A M Doyle, David & Dermot Cox). *"A nicely-bred filly, she'll want seven furlongs so I'm in no rush with her."*

812. RECKLESS REWARD (IRE) ★★★★♠
ch.c. Choisir – Champagne Toni (Second Empire).
March 13. Second foal. £38,000Y. Doncaster St Leger. Peter Doyle. The dam ran unplaced twice and is a half-sister to 9 winners including the smart Group 3 6f Prix de Meautry winner Andreyev. The second dam, Missish (by Mummy's Pet), is an unraced full or half-sister to 4 minor winners here and abroad. (Mr W P Drew). *"A lovely horse, there's absolutely nothing wrong with him but we're hanging on to him for a few weeks yet."*

813. REFLECT (IRE) ★★★
b.c. Hurricane Run – Raphimix (Linamix).
February 19. First foal. 40,000Y. Tattersalls October Book 2. Peter Doyle. The dam is an unraced half-sister to 2 minor winners in France. The second dam, Restifia (by Night Shift), a listed-placed French 2-y-o winner, is a half-sister to 3 winners. (Mrs Julie Wood). *"We've got him cantering away and he'll be a very nice horse once we get him over a mile or ten furlongs, but he just needs time."*

814. REGAL ROCKET (IRE) ★★★★
b.f. Majestic Missile – Frenzy (Zafonic).
March 29. Fourth foal. 32,000Y. Tattersalls October Book 3. Peter Doyle. Half-sister to the fair Irish 11f and hurdles winner Spanish Parade (by Mujadil). The dam is an unraced half-sister to 7 winners including the very useful filly Shamshir, winner of the Group 1 Brent Walker Fillies Mile and placed in the Oaks, Yorkshire Oaks, Nassau Stakes and Musidora Stakes and the useful 12f winner and Lupe Stakes third Fern. The second dam, Free Guest (by Be My Guest), was a high-class winner of nine races from 2 to 4 yrs and from 7f to 12f, notably the Sun Chariot Stakes (twice) and the Nassau Stakes and is a half-sister to 7 winners including the Group 2 Blandford Stakes winner Royal Ballerina. (J D Manley). *"She goes well, she's sharp and good-looking. A fine, strong filly that won't take long."*

815. RETAINER (IRE) ★★★★
br.c. Acclamation – Felicita (Catrail).
April 15. Eighth foal. £26,000Y. Doncaster St Leger. Peter Doyle. Half-brother to the fairly useful 2-y-o 5f winner and Group 3 5f Queen Mary Stakes fourth Bunditten (by Soviet Star), to the French 6f winner Facilita (by Fasliyev) and the modest 5f and hurdles winner Midnite Blews (by Trans Island). The dam won 3 races in France at 2 yrs including two 5f listed events and is a half-sister to 5 winners. The second dam, Abergwrle (by Absalom), ran unplaced twice at 2 yrs and is a half-sister to 4 winners. (B Bull). *"He goes very well and wherever he goes early on this season he won't be far*

away." Retainer won nicely on his debut at Newmarket's Craven meeting.

816. ROCHE DES VENTS ★★★★
b.c. Bahamian Bounty – Tokyo Rose
(Agnes World).
March 31. First foal. £15,000Y. Doncaster St Leger. Peter Doyle. The dam, a fair 5f and 6f placed 2-y-o, is a half-sister to 6 winners. The second dam, Wildwood Flower (by Distant Relative), a very useful winner of 6 races including the Ayr Gold Cup, is a half-sister to 8 winners including the minor US stakes winner His Tern To Win. (Mr R J Blunt). *"A really nice colt, he'll be early and he goes very well."*

817. ROI DU BOEUF (IRE) ★★★
b.c. Hurricane Run – Princess Killeen (Sinndar).
March 16. Second foal. 37,000Y. Tattersalls October Book 2. Fanny Kirk. Half-brother to Lady Of Namid (by Namid), unplaced in one start at 2 yrs in 2009. The dam ran once unplaced and is a half-sister to the Group 1 6f Cheveley Park Stakes winner Indian Ink and the fairly useful 2-y-o 6f and 1m winner Unavailable. The second dam, Maid Of Killeen (by Darshaan), a fairly useful 2-y-o 9f winner, was listed-placed and is a half-sister to 2 winners. (The Heffer Syndicate). *"A lovely horse, he's on the small side but I won't hang around with him. He'll be earlyish and I might go six furlongs with him."*

818. ROYAL EXCHANGE ★★★★
b.c. Royal Applause – Diamond Lodge
(Grand Lodge).
February 21. Second foal. Brother to Royal Box, a fair 6f winner at 2 yrs in 2009. The dam, a fairly useful 1m and 9f winner of 4 races at 3 yrs, is a half-sister to numerous minor winners. The second dam, Movielea (by Nureyev), won the Group 3 1m Prix des Reservoirs and is a half-sister to the Group 3 Prix de Sandringham winner Only Star. (The Queen). Looked a sure-fire future winner when just getting caught on the line at Newbury on his debut.

819. SHEER COURAGE (IRE) ★★★★
b.c. Invincible Spirit – Mood Swings
(Shirley Heights).
March 25. Tenth foal. 120,000Y. Tattersalls October Book 1. Shadwell Estate Co. Half-brother to the fairly useful 2009 2-y-o 6f winner Lowdown (by Shamardal), to the 7f (at 2 yrs) and Group 3 10f Gallinule Stakes winner Grand Ducal (by Danehill Dancer), the useful 6f (at 2 yrs) to 1m winner Al Khaleej (by Sakhee), the useful 2-y-o 6f winner and listed placed Hurricane Floyd (by Pennekamp), the Irish 7f (at 2 yrs) and 1m winner and listed-placed Best Side (by King's Best), the fairly useful 1m and 10f winner Tears Of A Clown (by Galileo) and the fair 3-y-o 5f winner Psychic (by Alhaarth). The dam, a fair 2-y-o 6f winner, is a sister to the listed 2-y-o Sweet Solera Stakes winner Catwalk and a half-sister to 5 winners. The second dam, Moogie (by Young Generation), a useful 2-y-o 6f winner, was fourth in the Coronation Stakes and is a half-sister to 6 winners. (The Socrates Partnership). *"He's lovely and he'll make a nice six furlong colt."*

820. SHEWALKSINBEAUTY (IRE) ★★★★
b.f. Byron – Election Special
(Chief Singer).
April 15. Ninth living foal. £8,000Y. Doncaster St Leger. Mrs J Wood. Half-sister to the smart 12f to 2m and jumps winner First Ballot, to the fairly useful dual 7f winner La Speziana (both by Perugino), the quite useful 1m and 10f winner Devolution (by Distinctly North), the moderate 6f winner Stoneacre Donny and the moderate 7f winner Stoneacre Fred (both by Lend A Hand). The dam won over 6f at 2 yrs and is a half-sister to 2 winners including the dam of the Goodwood Cup winner Grey Shot. The second dam, Electo (by Julio Mariner), is an unplaced half-sister to 5 winners. (Mrs Julie Wood). *"A nice, strong filly and a good mover, she'll be fine. She knows her job and she won't take long to get ready."* This filly won first time out at Lingfield in April.

821. SILENZIO ★★★
b.c. Cadeaux Genereux – All Quiet
(Piccolo).
January 21. First foal. 34,000Y. Tattersalls October Book 2. Peter Doyle. The dam, a fair 7f and 1m winner of 3 races, is a half-sister to 4 winners. The second dam, War Shanty (by Warrshan), is an unplaced half-sister to 4 winners including the Group 1 Prix Maurice de Gheest winner Bold Edge and the listed winner Brave Edge. (White Beech Farm). *"A nice horse,*

he's backward and hanging on to his coat but he'll make a two-year-old."

822. SILVERWARE (USA) ★★
b.br.c. Eurosilver – Playing Footsie (Valiant Nature).
April 22. Third foal. Half-brother to the very useful 9f and 10f winner (including at 2 yrs) and listed-placed Heliodor (by Scrimshaw). The dam, a winner of 5 races in the USA from 2 to 4 yrs, is a half-sister to 3 other minor winners. The second dam, Put Your L'il Foot (by Explodent), won 4 minor races in the USA and is a half-sister to 7 winners. (Mrs Julie Wood). *"One for a bit later in the season, he's a nice colt from America that moves well but we're not doing anything with him yet."*

823. SIR ROCKY (IRE) ★★★★
b.c. Shirocco – Bolero Again (Sadler's Wells).
March 18. Second foal. 28,000Y. Tattersalls October Book 1. Peter Doyle. Half-brother to Duchess Ravel (by Bachelor Duke), placed third over 5f on her only start. The dam, a fair 10f winner, is a sister to 5 winners including the Irish 9f winner and Group 1 National Stakes second Coliseum and a half-sister to 2 winners. The second dam, Gravieres (by Saint Estephe), won the Grade 1 Santa Ana Handicap and the Grade 3 California Jockey Club Handicap and is a half-sister to 9 winners. (The Moonrakers II). *"He'll be an early two-year-old, he looks well and although he's not over-big he has a great physique and he's a strong horse. I like him."*

824. SISTER RED (IRE) ★★
b.f. Diamond Green – Red Fuschia (Polish Precedent).
March 10. Third foal. £22,000Y. Doncaster St Leger. Peter Doyle. Half-sister to the fairly useful 2009 2-y-o 7f winner Red Badge (by Captain Rio). The dam is an unraced half-sister to 3 winners including the Group 3 placed Red Peony. The second dam, Red Azalea (by Shirley Heights), a fairly useful 7f (at 2 yrs) and 10f winner, is a half-sister to 4 winners including the smart Group 3 Prestige Stakes winner and French 1,000 Guineas third Red Camellia (herself dam of the Fillies Mile winner Red Bloom). (M Pescod). *"She's a biggish, backward filly, not a five furlong type and more one for later on."*

825. SLEEPING WOLF ★★★★★♣♣
ch.c. Sleeping Indian – Sound Of Sleat (Primo Dominie).
February 15. Sixth foal. £24,000Y. Doncaster St Leger. Will Edmeades. Half-brother to the fair 2009 2-y-o dual 5f winner Mahiki (by Compton Place) and to a minor winner in Italy by Dr Fong. The dam is an unraced half-sister to 7 winners including the Group 3 Prix de la Jonchere winner Soft Currency, the listed winner Fawzi and the 2-y-o winner of three races over 6f Choire Mhor – all useful. The second dam, Little Loch Broom (by Reform), is a placed half-sister to the dams of the Group winners Ozone Friendly, Ardkinglass, Wiorno and Reprimand. (Thurloe Thoroughbreds XXVII). *"This is a nice colt and I like him a lot. He'll be early and could go five or six furlongs. A nice, strong type of horse, he goes well and it won't be long before he's running."*

826. SO CHOOSY ★★★
b.f. Choisir – Roxy (Rock City).
March 11. Seventh living foal. 15,000Y. Tattersalls October Book 3. Peter Doyle. Half-sister to the modest 2009 7f placed 2-y-o Golden Tiger (by Kyllachy) and to the fair dual 7f winner (including at 2 yrs) Night Kiss. The dam is an unraced half-sister to 3 winners including the Irish 1,000 Guineas second Goodnight Kiss. The second dam, Hyatti (by Habitat), is a placed half-sister to 3 minor winners abroad. (Mrs B G Horne). *"A nice, big, good-moving filly, she just needs a lot of time and she'll make a two-year-old later on."*

827. STRICTLY RHYTHM ★★★
b.f. Hawk Wing – Esteemed Lady (Mark Of Esteem).
March 21. Third foal. 27,000Y. Tattersalls October Book 3. Peter Doyle. Half-sister to the quite useful 2009 2-y-o dual 6f winner Edgewater (by Bahamian Bounty) and to the modest 6f winner Sleepy Blue Ocean (by Oasis Dream). The dam, placed once over 6f at 2 yrs, is a half-sister to 4 winners including the 2-y-o Group 2 6f Richmond Stakes winner Revenue. The second dam, Bareilly (by Lyphard), is an unraced three-parts sister to the Group 3 1m Prix de la Grotte winner Baya and the Italian Group 2 winner Narrative. (Mr P D Merritt). *"This filly goes very well, she's by the same sire*

as our Goffs Million winner, Lucky General. An early two-year-old type."

828. STRONG SUIT (USA) ★★★★
ch.c. Rahy – Helwa (Silver Hawk).
February 9. Fifth foal. £40,000Y. Doncaster St Leger. Peter Doyle. Half-brother to the US winner of 3 races at 3 and 4 yrs Whimsical Day (by Spinning World). The dam is an unraced sister to the 2-y-o listed 1m winner Silver Colours and a half-sister to 4 winners including the Japanese Grade 2 winner God Of Chance. The second dam, Team Colors (by Mr Prospector), is an unraced half-sister to 4 winners. (Mrs Julie Wood). *"A fine horse, he's strong and a lovely mover that won't take long. Should be one to look out for over six furlongs."*

829. SUPER (IRE) ★★★
b.f. Royal Academy – Super Supreme (Zafonic).
May 24. Sixth foal. €60,000Y. Goffs Orby. Peter Doyle. Sister to the quite useful 7f winner Super Academy and half-sister to the fairly useful Irish 2-y-o 6f winner and Group 2 6f Coventry Stakes fourth Moran Gra (by Rahy) and the Irish 2-y-o 7.5f and subsequent minor US winner Vorteeva (by Bahri). The dam is an unraced sister to the listed winners White Gulch and Bodyguard. The second dam, White Wisteria (by Ahonoora), is an unraced half-sister to 6 winners including the dam of the Irish 2,000 Guineas winner Bachelor Duke. (Mrs Julie Wood). *"Despite her foaling date she'll be fairly sharp. A nice filly, she'll make a 2-y-o alright."*

830. SWEET CECILY (IRE) ★★★
b.f. Kodiac – Yaqootah (Gone West).
March 15. Second foal. €3,000foal. Goffs. Bath Bloodstock. The dam, a fair 5f winner at 3 yrs, is a half-sister to 6 winners including the useful 2-y-o 6f winner and listed-placed Elsahiba and the minor US stakes winner Jah. The second dam, Sweet Roberta (by Roberto), won the Grade 2 Selima Stakes and was second in the Grade 1 Breeders Cup Juvenile Fillies. (Mrs Julie Wood). *"A fairly sharp filly, we'll see her racing soon and she'll go either five or six furlongs."*

831. TAKEAWAY ★★★
b.c. Sleeping Indian – Bon Vivant (Salt Lake).
April 12. Second foal. £5,000Y. Doncaster St Leger. Peter Doyle. The dam, a minor US 3-y-o winner, is a half-sister to 5 winners including a US stakes winner. The second dam, Shes A Calling (by Clever Trick), won 2 minor races in the USA and is a half-sister to 7 winners. (Mahal, Morecombe, Anderson). *"A winner already and he had to give a lot of weight away on soft ground next time up. He'll win again."*

832. TALE UNTOLD (USA) ★★★♠
ch.f. Tale Of The Cat – Bank On Her (Rahy).
May 7. Eighth foal. 26,000Y. Tattersalls October Book 1. Peter Doyle. Half-sister to the quite useful 1m (at 2 yrs), 7f and subsequent US winner and Grade 3 second I'm In Love (by Zafonic) and to a 5f to 7f winner in Hong Kong by Marju. The dam, a 7f winner at 3yrs, is a half-sister to 7 winners including the listed winner and Group 2 placed Weldnaas. The second dam, Bank On Love (by Gallant Romeo), is an unraced sister to the Group 2 Richmond Stakes winner Gallant Special. (Trevor Stewart & Anna Doyle). *"A lovely filly that's grown a bit lately, but she won't take long and we're very happy with her."*

833. TEES AND CEES (IRE) ★★★★
ch.c. Bahamian Bounty – Berkeley Lodge (Grand Lodge).
April 11. Second foal. €52,000Y. Goffs Orby. Peter Doyle. The dam is an unraced half-sister to 7 winners including the smart 1m winner and Irish 2,000 Guineas second Fa-Eq and the listed 7.3f and 1m winner Corinium. The second dam, Searching Star (by Rainbow Quest), a modest 6f (at 2 yrs) to 11.3f placed maiden, is a half-sister to 8 winners including the smart listed Blue Riband Trial winner Beldale Star and the listed winner and useful broodmare Moon Drop. (S Dartnell). *"A strong two-year-old type, he'll go five furlongs but may be better over six. A lovely colt."*

834. THE SYDNEY ARMS (IRE) ★★★
b.f. Elusive City – Daftara (Caerleon).
March 25. Seventh foal. €18,000Y. Goffs Orby. Peter Doyle. Half-sister to the fairly

useful 2-y-o 5f winner Dahindar (by Invincible Spirit) and to the quite useful 10f to 2m 1f winner Dafarabad (by Cape Cross). The dam is an unraced half-sister to 4 winners including the Irish 3-y-o 7f and 1m winner Darayna. The second dam, Dafayna (by Habitat), was a smart winner of the Group 3 Cork and Orrery Stakes and the Salisbury 1,000 Guineas Trial and was placed in the July Cup, the Vernons Sprint Cup and the Diadem Stakes. She is a sister to the high-class 7f colt Dalsaan and a half-sister to the 2,000 Guineas winner Doyoun and the high-class Champion Stakes second Dolpour. (Morecombe, Reus, Anderson). "She goes very well, she'll be early and we've just waiting for the owners to give her a name, then we can look towards entering her."

835. TOUCH OF RED (USA) ★★★
b.c. Touch Gold – Cleveland Browni
(Allen's Prospect).
February 25. Seventh foal. 43,000Y. Tattersalls December. Peter Doyle. Half-brother to the US stakes winner Cross Creek Rosie (by Castine) and 3 minor winners in the USA by Meadow Monster, Sultry Song and Yarrow Brae. The dam won 2 minor races in the USA at 2 and 3 yrs and is a half-sister to 4 winners including 2 minor US stakes winners. The second dam, Danielle's Darling (by State Dinner), won 5 minor races in the USA and is a half-sister to the US Grade 2 winner Meadow Monster. (Terry Neill). "I won't be in that much of a rush with him although he's a lovely colt. He's doing well and showing up a bit, but he's not entered for the EBF races which might make him a bit difficult to place."

836. TUSCAN BLUE ★★★
ch.c. Medicean – Belle Et Deluree
(The Minstrel).
May 10. Sixteenth foal. €50,000Y. Goffs Orby. Peter Doyle. Closely related to the useful 2-y-o dual 7f winner Hypnotize (by Machiavellian) and half-brother to 8 winners including the Group 3 6f Cherry Hinton Stakes winner and 1,000 Guineas third Dazzle (by Gone West), the useful 7f (at 2 yrs) and 1m listed winner Fantasize (by Groom Dancer) and the fairly useful 7f winner Enchant, the dual Italian winner Jinx Joke (by Miswaki) and the placed dam of the Group winners Danehurst and Humouresque. The dam won over 1m (at 2 yrs) and 10f in France and is a half-sister to 5 winners including the US Grade 2 winner Doneraile Court and the very useful Cheveley Park Stakes second Dancing Tribute (herself dam of the Group/Grade 2 winners Dance Sequence and Souvenir Copy). The second dam, Sophisticated Girl (by Stop The Music), a very smart American 2-y-o, was second in the Grade 1 8.5f Oak Leaf Stakes. (M Pescod). "A fine, big, strong colt, he's a great mover and a good goer but we haven't opened the box with him yet."

837. TWEENIE (IRE) ★★★
b.f. Kheleyf – Housekeeper
(Common Grounds).
January 25. Fifth foal. £32,000Y. Doncaster St Leger. Ms F Carmichael. Half-sister to the fair 2009 2-y-o dual 6f winner Jeannie Galloway (by Bahamian Bounty) and to the modest 9f and 10f placed and subsequent Belgian winner Postprofit (by Marju). The dam, a fairly useful 7f (at 2 yrs), 1m and subsequent US winner, is a half-sister to 4 winners including the very smart Group 1 10f Premio Presidente della Repubblica winner Polar Prince. The second dam, Staff Approved (by Teenoso), a fairly useful 2-y-o 1m winner, is a full or half-sister to 11 winners. (Coriolan Links Partnership). "A sharp filly, she's quick and will be an early two-year-old."

838. VALERA (IRE) ★★
gr.f. Ad Valorem – Tipperary Honor
(Highest Honor).
February 6. Second foal. £15,000Y. Doncaster St Leger. Peter Doyle. The dam, placed once at 3 yrs, is a sister to the useful Irish 10f and 12f listed winner Tipperary All Star and half-sister to 5 winners including the US Grade 3 Laurel Dash winner and Group 3 Prix Thomas Bryon second Mayoumbe. The second dam, Moucha (by Fabulous Dancer), a winner of 3 races in France and listed-placed, is a half-sister to 7 winners including the US Grade 3 winner Daloma. (Valerie Shears & Peter Marshall). "She went back on us a bit as if something was amiss with her, but she's fine now and she'll be OK in mid-summer."

839. WELSH DANCER ★★★
b.c. Dubawi – Rosie's Posy (Suave Dancer).
March 10. Fourth foal. £42,000Y. Doncaster St Leger. Peter Doyle. Brother to the useful 2009 2-y-o Group 2 6f Lowther Stakes third Dubawi Heights and half-brother to the useful 6f (at 2 yrs) and 1m winner Generous Thought (by Cadeaux Genereux). The dam, a quite useful 2-y-o 5.7f winner, is a half-sister to 4 winners including the Group 1 6f Haydock Sprint Cup winner Tante Rose and the useful 2-y-o listed 7f winner Bay Tree. The second dam, My Branch (by Distant Relative), a very useful winner of the listed 6f Firth Of Clyde Stakes (at 2 yrs) and the listed 7f Sceptre Stakes, was second in the Group 1 Cheveley Park Stakes and third in the Irish 1,000 Guineas and is a half-sister to 5 winners. (David & Gwyn Joseph). *"A nicely-bred colt, we're doing a bit with him now and he'll be a two-year-old alright. He'll be quick too, so five or six furlongs will be fine for him."*

840. YASHILA (IRE) ★★★
b.f. Indian Haven – Tara's Girl (Fayruz).
March 15. Seventh foal. 110,000Y. Tattersalls October Book 1. Peter Doyle. Sister to the 2-y-o Group 3 7f Somerville Tattersall Stakes winner and Group 3 Jersey Stakes third Ashram and half-sister to the very useful 7f and 1m winner (including in the UAE) Blackat Blackitten (by Inchinor) and the quite useful 6f and 7f winner (including at 2 yrs) Triple Two (by Pivotal). The dam, a fairly useful 2-y-o dual 5f winner, was listed placed twice and fourth in the Queen Mary Stakes and is a full or half-sister to 5 winners. The second dam, Florissa (by Persepolis), a Belgian 2-y-o 7f winner, is a half-sister to a winner over jumps in France. (Mrs Julie Wood). *"She's a nice filly, but still a bit backward in her coat at the moment so we're not doing too much with her at present."*

841. ZEBEDEE ★★★★
gr.c. Invincible Spirit – Cozy Maria (Cozzene).
February 24. Fourth foal. 70,000Y. Tattersalls October Book 1. Peter Doyle. Half-brother to Satwa Son (by Oasis Dream), unplaced in two start at 2 yrs in 2009. The dam, a useful 10f winner, was listed-placed twice and is a half-sister to 6 winners in the USA. The second dam, Mariamme (by Verbatim), won twice at 3 yrs in the USA and is a half-sister to 7 winners including the Grade 1 Breeders Cup Turf winner Miss Alleged. (Mrs Julie Wood). *"One of our earliest colts, he works well and should win races this year, maybe before your book is out."* Jockey Richard Hughes likes the colt too and commented that he's a nice, sharp sort that should be out in April. He was a winner on his debut in mid-April at Windsor."

842. UNNAMED ★★★
b.f. Antonius Pius – Affirmed Crown (Affirmed).
February 2. Second foal. €12,000Y. Tattersalls Ireland. Peter Doyle. The dam, a moderate 2m placed maiden, is a half-sister to 7 winners here and abroad including the £1m Hong Kong earner Floral Pegasus. The second dam, Crown Crest (by Mill Reef), won once at 3 yrs and is a sister to the high-class middle-distance horses Glint Of Gold and Diamond Shoal. (Mr R Morecombe). *"There's nothing wrong with her, she'll be fairly sharp and she wasn't expensive either."*

843. UNNAMED ★★★
b.f. Pivotal – Dance Solo (Sadler's Wells).
April 18. Second foal. 30,000Y. Tattersalls October Book 1. Not sold. Half-sister to the quite useful 2009 2-y-o 7f and 1m winner Diam Queen (by Lando). The dam, placed 4 times from 7f to 11f here and in Germany, is a full or half-sister to 5 winners including the Group 1 St James's Palace Stakes winner Excellent Art. The second dam, Obsessive (by Seeking The Gold), a useful 2-y-o 6f winner and third in the Group 3 10.4f Musidora Stakes, is a half-sister to 7 winners. (Kingwood Stud Racing). *"A beautiful filly, she's doing all the right things and is a lovely mover. Not a five furlong two-year-old by any means, but she could make a nice one alright."*

844. UNNAMED ★★★
b.c. Chevalier – Meranie Girl (Mujadil).
January 30. Seventh foal. 52,000Y. Tattersalls October Book 2. Peter Doyle. Half-brother to the quite useful 2-y-o dual 6f winner Transaction, to the quite useful 6f (at 2 yrs) and 5f winner Meridian Line, the fair 2-y-o 6f winner Transit (all by Trans Island) and the modest 2-y-o triple 6f winner Cheverak

Forest (by Shinko Forest). The dam is an unplaced half-sister to 7 winners. The second dam, Christoph's Girl (by Efisio), won 3 races including a listed event in Belgium and is a sister to the Group 1 Prix de l'Abbaye winner Hever Golf Rose and a half-sister to 7 winners. (Mrs M Findlay). *"A nice, big horse but he's a lazy beggar and we're working him hard now to get some weight off."*

845. UNNAMED ★★★♠
b.f. *Montjeu – Quiet Waters (Quiet American).*
March 28. First foal. 50,000Y. Tattersalls October Book 1. Peter Doyle. The dam ran once unplaced and is a half-sister to 5 winners including French Group 3 winner Summertime Legacy. The second dam, Zawaahy (by El Gran Senor), a quite useful 1m winner, is a half-sister to 4 winners including the Derby winner Golden Fleece. (Mrs S M Roy). *"A good-moving filly, everything's fine with her but she's one for a bit later on this season."*

BEN HASLAM

846. DANCE FOR LIVVY (IRE) ★★★
br.f. *Kodiac – Dancing Steps (Zafonic).*
February 18. Fourth foal. £13,000Y. Doncaster St Leger. B Haslam. Half-sister to the fair 2009 2-y-o 6f winner Dance For Julie (by Redback). The dam is an unraced sister to the winner and UAE Group 3 placed Seeking The Prize and a half-sister to 7 winners including the smart Group 3 placed Firebet. The second dam, Dancing Prize (by Sadler's Wells), a useful maiden and third in the listed Lingfield Oaks Trial, is a sister to 3 winners including the Group 1 Fillies Mile second Dance To The Top and a half-sister to 5 winners. (Mark James). *"Her half-sister won for us last season and this filly is a similar stamp. She's a strong, compact filly and she's definitely going to be a two-year-old. Her sire Kodiac has already had a winner and I should imagine that she'd be winning, or at least running well, in May or June over six furlongs."*

847. BLAKE DEAN ★★
b.c. *Halling – Antediluvian (Air Express).*
February 25. Second foal. 15,000Y. Tattersalls October Book 1. Not sold. Half-brother to the modest 2009 6f placed 2-y-o Picnic Party (by Indian Ridge). The dam, a very useful 7f (at 2 yrs) and 1m listed winner, is a half-sister to numerous winners including the fairly useful dual 7f winner Ekhtiaar. The second dam, Divina Mia (Dowsing) a modest 2-y-o 6f winner, stayed 11f and is a half-sister to the dam of the Australian Grade 1 winner Markham. (Widdop Wanderers). *"We probably won't see him until September over seven furlongs. He's a typical Halling in that he's quite rangy and will probably be better as a three-year-old but he'll definitely run as a two-year-old."*

848. KINLOCHRANNOCH ★★★
b.f. *Kyllachy – Guermantes (Distant Relative).*
April 17. Fifth foal. 6,500Y. Doncaster October. Ben Haslam. Half-sister to a 1m winner in France by Marju. The dam, a listed-placed French winner, is a half-sister to the smart 7.2f (at 2 yrs) and Group 3 1m Leopardstown 2,000 Guineas Trial winner Yasoodd and to the French listed 1m Prix Montenica winner Gript. The second dam, Needwood Epic (Midyan), a modest all-weather 14f winner, is a half-sister to 7 winners. (Mr S A Dinsmore). *"She's not ready yet, but on her pedigree and on the way she looks I'd say she'd be quite quick, although her time probably won't come until later in the year."* TRAINERS' BARGAIN BUY

849. MAUNBY RUMBA ★★★
b.f. *Kheleyf – Chantilly (Sanglamore).*
March 19. Eighth foal. 8,000Y. Tattersalls October Book 2. Ben Haslam. Half-sister to the quite useful 6f (at 2 yrs) and 1m winner Jebel Tara (by Diktat). The dam is an unraced half-sister to the listed 1m winner Penang Pearl (herself dam of the Group 2 winner Harbinger). The second dam, Guapa (by Shareef Dancer), won twice over 1m and is a half-sister to 7 winners including the Group 2 winners Dusty Dollar and Kind Of Hush. (Andrew Sparks). *"She's been going quite nicely and she's a small two-year-old type. I can see her running over six furlongs in May."*

850. VIENNA WOODS (IRE) ★★★
ch.f. *Redback – Naraina (Desert Story).*
March 19. Fourth foal. 5,000Y. Tattersalls October 2. Ben Haslam. Half-sister to the fair 6f (at 2 yrs) and 1m winner Outside Edge (by Danetime). The dam is an unraced half-sister

to 4 winners including the Group 3 Princess Royal Stakes winner Narwala. The second dam, Noufiyla (by Top Ville), is a placed half-sister to the Group 3 Cherry Hinton Stakes winner Nasseem. (Mr S A Dinsmore). *"She'll make her debut in April, I think she'll run well and she's sharp and early."*

851. UNNAMED ★★★
br.f. *Statue Of Liberty – Miss Megs (Croco Rouge).*
April 10. Third foal. £7,000Y. Doncaster St Leger. Not sold. Half-brother to the quite useful 2-y-o 6f winner Chips O'Toole (by Fasliyev). The dam, a fair 9f and 11f winner in Ireland, is a half-sister to 3 winners including the listed winner Santa Isobel. The second dam, Atlantic Record (by Slip Anchor), is an unraced full or half-sister to 4 winners. (Ian Lindsay). *"She'll be running in late April/early May, she looks sharp and I imagine she's one that could win."*

852. UNNAMED ★★
b.g. *Kodiac – Counting Blessings (Compton Place).*
March 28. Second foal. £12,000Y. Doncaster St Leger. B Haslam. The dam was a moderate 1m placed maiden. The second dam, Banco Suivi (by Nashwan), a fairly useful 12f winner, is a half-sister to 5 winners including the very useful listed 6f and 7f winner and dual Group 1 placed My Branch (herself the dam of the Group 1 Sprint Cup winner Tante Rose). (Mr T Hussein). *"A big gelding, we probably won't see him until the second half of the season. He's a good stamp of a horse, but I couldn't tell you anything else because I haven't done a lot with him yet."*

853. UNNAMED ★★★
b.g. *Choisir – Guignol (Anita's Prince).*
March 23. Fifth foal. £13,000Y. Doncaster St Leger. T Hussain. Half-sister to Texan Star (by Galileo), placed second over 7f from 2 starts at 2 yrs in 2009. The dam, a minor Irish 3-y-o 5f winner, is a half-sister to 8 winners including the US Grade 3 winner Down Again and to the dam of the Irish and French 2,000 Guineas winner Bachir. The second dam, Dawn Is Breaking (by Import), won twice over 5f at 2 yrs in Ireland at 2 yrs and is a half-sister to 6 winners. (Mr T Hussain). *"I like him, he's very strong and he's one for the middle of the season over six or seven furlongs. A typical Choisir, he's definitely going to be alright."*

854. UNNAMED ★★★
b.g. *Avonbridge – Runs In The Family (Distant Relative).*
April 30. Ninth foal. £8,000Y. Doncaster St Leger. T Hussain. Half-brother to the quite useful 6f (including at 2 yrs) and 5f winner of 5 races Angel Sprints (by Piccolo), to the Italian winner of 6 races, including at 2 yrs, Red Bamboo (by Daggers Drawn) and the Italian 2-y-o winner of 3 races Jolly God (by Compton Place). The dam, a fair 5f and 6f winner of 4 races, is a half-sister to 4 other minor winners. The second dam, Stoneydale (by Tickled Pink), won 5 races at 2 and 4 yrs and is a half-sister to 6 winners. (Mr T Hussain). *"He's nice and he'll be the earliest of this owner's two-year-old to run because he's the racier of the three. He'll be a six furlong type in June, he definitely looks quite smart."*

BARRY HILLS

Thank you to Kevin Mooney for helping me out again with these comments about the two-year-olds.

855. ABOVE STANDARD (IRE) ★★
ch.c. *Shamardal – Prealpina (Indian Ridge).*
May 14. Fourth foal. €80,000Y. Goffs Orby. BBA (Ire). The dam won 3 minor races at 2 and 3 yrs in Italy and is a half-sister to 7 winners. The second dam, Karvis (by Be My Guest), a listed-placed winner of 4 races in Italy, is a half-sister to 7 winners including the Group 2 Italian 1,000 Guineas winner Shenck. *"A great big horse with scope, he's nice but he'll want a bit of time and seven furlongs I'd say."*

856. ANOTHER WHISPER (IRE) ★★★♣
b.c. *Montjeu – Heavenly Whisper (Halling).*
March 20. Sixth foal. 100,000Y. Tattersalls October Book 1. Will Edmeades. Half-brother to the useful triple 1m winner River Tiber (by Danehill), to the quite useful 2-y-o 1m and 9f winner Premier Banker (by Cape Cross) and the quite useful triple 1m winner Twilight Star (by Green Desert). The dam, a useful listed 1m winner and second in the Group 2 Falmouth

Stakes, is a half-sister to 4 winners including the German listed winner Gipsy Moth (herself dam of the Group 3 winner Illustrious Blue). The second dam, Rock The Boat (by Slip Anchor), a modest 6f (at 2 yrs) and 1m placed maiden, is a half-sister to 9 winners including the smart Cherry Hinton Stakes winner Kerrera and the high-class colt Rock City. *"He's got scope but he looks very hairy at the minute so he'll want plenty of time. One for the back-end of the season."*

857. APTICANTI ★★★★
b.f. Aptitude – Musicanti (Nijinsky).
February 28. Half-sister to the champion 1999 2-y-o Distant Music, winner of the Group 1 7f Dewhurst Stakes, the Group 2 7f Champagne Stakes and the Group 2 9f Goffs International Stakes, to the useful 10.3f winner Fragrant View (both by Distant View), the useful 10f winner and Group 3 Lancashire Oaks third New Orchid (by Quest For Fame) and the quite useful dual 12f winner Mirthful (by Miswaki). The dam, a French 14.5f winner, is a half-sister to the top-class American middle-distance colt Vanlandingham, winner of the Washington D.C. International, the Jockey Club Gold Cup and the Suburban Handicap. The second dam, Populi (by Star Envoy), a winner of 2 minor races at 2 yrs, is a half-sister to the Grade 1 Belmont Stakes winner Temperance Hill. (Khalid Abdulla). *"A lovely filly, she moves like a dream but she's altering a lot at the moment because she's going through a stage where she's growing and has probably gone a bit weak. But she gives you the impression she'll be a good filly."*

858. ARAMID (IRE) ★★★
b.c. Aussie Rules – Bollicina (Woodman).
April 25. Tenth foal. 40,000Y. Tattersalls October Book 2. BBA (Ire). Half-brother to 7 minor winners including three in Italy by Alzao, Bigstone and Indian Danehill. The dam, a minor winner in Italy, is a half-sister to 6 other minor winners. The second dam, Secret Amie (by Caro), a US stakes winner of 5 races, is a half-sister to the US Grade 2 winner Secret Prince. *"He'll be racing in April although it might just come too some for him. He wasn't really doing anything out of the ordinary but than all of a sudden he's come right. He'll improve for the run but he's tough and he'll be alright."*

859. BARNEY REBEL (IRE) ★★
b.c. Holy Roman Emperor – Opera Ridge (Indian Ridge).
May 7. Second foal. 40,000Y. Tattersalls October Book 1. BBA (Ire). Closely related to the fair 2009 1m placed 2-y-o Street Entertainer (by Danehill Dancer). The dam was placed over 10f in France and is a half-sister to 7 winners including the French Group winners Stretarez and Street Shaana. The second dam, Street Opera (by Sadler's Wells), a minor Irish 14f winner, is a half-sister to 10 winners including the Group 1 Grand Prix de Paris winner Grape Tree Road, the Group 2 Geoffrey Freer Stakes winner Red Route and the Group 3 Queens Vase winner Windsor Castle. *"A late foal, he's just hacking around at the minute and he's been growing like mad. One for the second half of the season."*

860. CANNA (IRE) ★★★
b.c. High Chaparral – Brave Madam (Invincible Spirit).
January 23. First foal. €42,000Y. Tattersalls Ireland. BBA (Ire). The dam is an unraced half-sister to 4 winners including the US listed stakes winner Insan Mala. The second dam, Madame Claude (by Paris House), a fair 2-y-o 6f winner, is a half-sister to 4 winners. *"He got sore shins quite early but he's a chunky horse and a nice one actually. He's not showing signs of being too excitable like a lot by this sire and I think he'll be relatively early."*

861. CAPAL LIATH (IRE) ★★★
br.c. Iffraaj – Bethesda (Distant Relative).
April 8. Sixth foal. £7,000Y. Doncaster St Leger. D Hanaein. Half-brother to the fair 2009 2-y-o 5f winner Gwynedd (by Bertolini), to the fairly useful 2-y-o dual 5f winner Masamah (by Exceed And Excel) and to the fair 2-y-o 5f all-weather winner Fluttering Rose (by Compton Place). The dam, a fairly useful 5.7f and 6f winner at 4 yrs, is a half-sister to 4 winners including the Group 1 6f Middle Park Stakes winner Fard. The second dam, Anneli Rose (by Superlative), a plating-class winner of one race over 6f on the all-weather at 3 yrs, is a half-sister to the Middle Park Stakes and Flying Childers Stakes winner Gallic League. *"The owner sent him to us from the Sales and he looked weedy and he then got sore shins*

because he was quite excitable. He's grown and he's just hacking around now because he needs a bit of time but he'll be a two-year-old. I'd say six furlongs would be his starting point because he shows a bit of speed." TRAINERS' BARGAIN BUY

862. CAPTAIN BERTIE (IRE) ★★★
ch.c. Captain Rio – Sadika (Bahhare).
April 29. Fourth foal. 34,000Y. Tattersalls October Book 2. BBA (Ire). Half-brother to the fairly useful 2-y-o 7f winner Amazing Star (by Soviet Star). The dam is an unplaced half-sister to 9 winners including the Group 3 Fred Darling Stakes winner Sueboog (herself dam of the Prix d'Ispahan winner Best Of The Bests). The second dam, Nordica (by Northfields), was a useful 6f (a listed event in Ireland) and 1m winner. *"He's got a bit of size about him and he's a well-balanced horse that's done nothing wrong. He's straightforward but I don't think he'll be rushed because he's quite big. He could be alright in the second half of the year."*

863. CHINOOK WIND (IRE) ★★★
b,br.f. Encosta De Lago – Dedicated Lady (Pennine Walk).
March 14. Twelfth living foal. 125,000Y. Tattersalls October Book 1. BBA (Ire). Closely related to the smart Group 2 12f Ribblesdale Stakes and Group 2 12.5f Prix de la Royallieu winner Fairy Queen (by Fairy King) and half-sister to the Irish 8.5f (at 2 yrs) and listed 10f winner and Prix de l'Arc de Triomphe fourth Acropolis, the fair Irish 12f winner De Laurentiis (both by Sadler's Wells), the smart Group 2 1m Falmouth Stakes winner Tashawak and the fair 6f (at 2 yrs) and 1m winner of 8 races Speedfit Free (both by Night Shift). The dam, a useful Irish 2-y-o 5f and 6f winner, was listed-placed and is a half-sister to 5 winners including the German listed winner and Group 3 third Silk Petal (herself dam of the listed winner Star Tulip). The second dam, Salabella (by Sallust), is a placed half-sister to 7 winners including the Irish St Leger and the Grosser Preis von Baden winner M-Lolshan. *"She looked a million dollars when she first came in and we all thought that when she grew and matured she'd be fine, but that hasn't happened yet. She's just stayed the same and she's on the back burner, ticking over. A lovely looking filly but we're waiting for he to tell us she's ready."*

864. COMMENDED ★★
b.c. Royal Applause – Granted (Cadeaux Genereux).
February 29. Sixth foal. Half-brother to the useful 7f (including at 2 yrs) and listed 1m winner Perfect Star (by Act One), to the quite useful 9f and 11f winner Barodine (by Barathea) and the modest 1m and 9f winner Bestowed (by Kyllachy). The dam, a useful 1m and 8.3f winner, was listed placed at up to 9f and is a half-sister to 2 winners. The second dam, Germane (by Distant Relative), a useful winner of the Group 3 7f Rockfel Stakes and placed in 2 listed events, is a half-sister to 9 winners including the very useful German 10f winner Fabriano. *"Didn't come in until late February or early March because he had bad colic. So he's an unknown quantity for now until we see how he gets on, but I think he'll be alright."*

865. DIAMOND GEEZAH (IRE) ★★★★
b.c. Diamond Green – Lanark Belle (Selkirk).
February 4. Second foal. £28,000Y. Doncaster St Leger. BBA (Ire). The dam is an unplaced half-sister to 6 winners including the listed Winter Derby winner Adiemus. The second dam, Anodyne (by Dominion), a useful 6f winner, is a sister to the very useful US Grade 3 winner Domynsky and a half-sister to 9 winners. *"He ran a nice race in the Brocklesbury at Doncaster and he'll come on a lot for that. Wherever he runs next he should go close. Robert Winston rode him, liked him and said there's a lot more to come. He's laid back so he should get further than five furlongs."* On his second start, this colt was just touched off by the Hannon two-year-old My Son Max.

866. EARLY APPLAUSE ★★★★
b.c. Royal Applause – Early Evening (Daylami).
February 4. First foal. 50,000Y. Tattersalls October Book 2. BBA (Ire). The dam was a quite useful dual 10f winner. The second dam, a fair 1m winner, is a sister to the Irish 5f winner, Group 3 Curragh Stakes third and subsequent Hong Kong winner Nevada and a half-sister to 4 winners. *"He stands over a lot of ground, he's good-actioned and a good-bodied horse. He'll*

be running in April at the Craven meeting, he's a bit long, but he goes well and he's kept his condition. Considering the dam's stamina it's a bit unusual to see him out so early."

867. EDMAAJ (IRE) ★★★★
ch.c. Intikhab – Lady Angola (Lord At War).
March 14. Fourth foal. 70,000Y. Tattersalls October Book 2. Shadwell Estate Co. Half-brother to the fair 2009 6f placed 2-y-o Tislaam (by With Approval) and to the fair 2-y-o dual 6f and subsequent US winner Raiding Party (by Orpen). The dam, a quite useful 12f winner, is a half-sister to 6 winners including the dam of the US Grade 1 winner Honor In War. The second dam, Benguela (by Little Current), won twice at 4 yrs in the USA and is a half-sister to the US Grade 1 winners La Gueriere and Al Mamoon. (Hamdan Al Maktoum). "A lovely, big horse for the second half of the season. He's a good mover, his temperament's OK and there's a lot to like about him. I think he's going to be a nice horse."

868. EKTIBAAS ★★
ch.c. Haafhd – Aspen Leaves (Woodman).
May 6. Sixth foal. Brother to the fair 2-y-o 7f winner Awfeyaa and half-brother to the useful Irish 10f winner Agenda (by Sadler's Wells) and the fair 3-y-o 7f winner Deira Dubai (by Green Desert). The dam, a minor Irish 7f winner, is a sister to the champion American 2-y-o colt Timber Country and a half-sister to the very smart Group 2 13.5f Prix de Pomone winner Colorado Dancer (herself the dam of Dubai Millennium), the Grade 1 Gamely Handicap winner Northern Aspen, the Group 1 July Cup winner Hamas, the Group 1 Grand Prix de Paris winner Fort Wood and the Prix d'Astarte winner Elle Seule (herself dam of the Group 1 winners Elnadim and Mehthaaf). The second dam, Fall Aspen (by Pretense), one of the finest broodmares of recent times, won 8 races notably the Grade 1 7f Matron Stakes. (Hamdan Al Maktoum). "Still in Dubai, they don't come in until the 18th April."

869. ENCORE UN FOIS ★★★
br.c. Val Royal – Factice (Known Fact).
March 22. Eleventh foal. 37,000foal. Tattersalls December. Bobby O'Ryan. Brother to the 2,000 Guineas and Irish 2,000 Guineas winner Cockney Rebel and half-brother to the modest 2009 2-y-o 5f winner Billie Jean (by Bertolini), the Irish 2-y-o 7f and subsequent Spanish 1m and 12f winner Mejhar (by Desert Prince), the Italian winner of 8 races Cap d'Ail (by Common Grounds), the minor Irish 2-y-o 7f winner Factice Royal (by Royal Academy) and the Irish 3-y-o 7f winner Festina Famosa (by Priolo). The dam, an Irish 2-y-o 5f winner, is a half-sister to 5 winners including the US stakes winner Play Waki For Me. The second dam, Wacky Princess (by Miswaki), was a stakes winner in the USA and a half-sister to 4 winners. "He was in Ireland and he must have been in a bad hotel because he was clipped from top to toe! He's only just got his coat coming through now, but he's done fantastically well and he looks like he can go a bit. He's always going forward, he wants to please and I think he'll be alright."

870. FACE THE PROBLEM (IRE) ★★★★
b.c. Johannesburg – Foofaraw (Cherokee Run).
March 20. Second foal. €75,000Y. Goffs Orby. BBA (Ire). Brother to the fair 2009 2-y-o 7f winner Thomas Baines. The dam won 2 races at 2 and 3 yrs in North America and is a half-sister to 4 winners. The second dam, All The Rage (by Lyphard), is a placed daughter of the US Grade 1 winner Laugh And Be Merry. "He's just arrived on the radar – and all the boys who ride him say he goes well. He's ready to run now and he may have won before your book comes out. One to follow."

871. FAILASOOF (USA) ★★★
b.br.c. Dynaformer – Curriculum (Danzig).
March 18. Fifth foal. $650,000Y. Keeneland September. Shadwell Estate Co. Brother to Temple City, a minor winner in the USA at 3 and 4 yrs. The dam is an unraced half-sister to 4 minor winners out of the Group 1 Prix Marcel Boussac winner Macoumba (by Mr Prospector), herself a half-sister to 4 stakes winners including the Group 1 Prix de la Foret winner Septieme Ciel. (Hamdan Al Maktoum). "Still in Dubai."

872. FITYAAN ★★★
b.c. Haafhd – Welsh Diva (Selkirk).
January 31. Fourth foal. 100,000Y. Tattersalls October Book 1. Shadwell Estate Co. Half-

brother to the unplaced 2009 2-y-o Swansea Jack (by Singspiel) and to the modest 5f and 6f winner Welsh Opera (by Noverre). The dam, an Italian Group 3 1m and Ascot listed 1m winner, is a sister to the Group 2 1m Prix du Rond-Point and Group 3 8.5f Diomed Stakes winner Trans Island and the useful 2-y-o 7f winner Nothing Daunted and a half-sister to 2 winners. The second dam, Khubza (by Green Desert), a quite useful 3-y-o 7f winner, is a half-sister to 7 winners including the Group 2 winners Barrow Creek and Last Resort and the listed winners Arctic Char and Heard A Whisper. (Hamdan Al Maktoum). *"We had a couple of these Haafhd's last year and the Boss thought they were lacking in concentration, so he told us not to hang around with them this time. We had three working and this was the one that fell by the wayside with sore shins. But he has done alright. So I think as soon as possible we'll be back on the trail again and he's shown enough to suggest he'll be OK."*

873. JANICELLAINE (IRE) ★★★
b.f. Beat Hollow – Danielli (Danehill).
March 16. Second foal. 28,000Y. Tattersalls October Book 2. Not sold. Half-sister to the fair 2009 7f placed 2-y-o Akula (by Soviet Star). The dam, placed four times at up to 13f in Ireland, is a sister to the Group 3 C L Weld Park Stakes winner Eva's Request and a half-sister to 7 winners including the Group 1 7f Moyglare Stud Stakes winner Priory Belle and the Group 3 7f Concorde Stakes winner Wild Bluebell. The second dam, Ingabelle (by Taufan), won the Group 3 Phoenix Sprint Stakes and is a half-sister to 4 winners. *"A nice filly, she was prepped by Malcolm Bastard so she knew her job when she came in. But the Boss thought we needed to take a pull on her, so that's what we've done. All the boys like her and she goes up there like a three-year-old. She's a nice filly with a good temperament and she's a nice mover. She rides as if she's got speed."*

874. LAMASAAS (IRE) ★★
b.c. Henny Hughes – Quick Feet (Dynaformer).
March 29. First foal. $230,000Y. Keeneland September. Shadwell Estate Co. The dam is an unraced sister to a US stakes winner and to the Group 1 Prix Marcel Boussac second New Story (herself dam of the Group 2 Prix Robert Papin winner New Girlfriend). The second dam, Dancey Kate (by Danzig), is an unraced half-sister to 8 winners. (Hamdan Al Maktoum). *"Still in Dubai."*

875. MADANY (IRE) ★★★★
b.f. Acclamation – Belle de Cadix (Law Society).
April 29. Ninth foal. 130,000Y. Tattersalls October Book 1. Shadwell Estate Co. Half-sister to the 2009 2-y-o Group 3 Prix du Bois winner and Group 2 Prix Robert Papin second Dolled Up (by Whipper), to the 2-y-o listed Prix Zeddaan and subsequent US stakes winner Zeiting (by Zieten), the fairly useful 2-y-o 7f winner Barrissimo (by Night Shift), the fair 2-y-o 7f winner In A Flash (by Night Shift), the Swedish winner of 5 races from 2 to 5 yrs Ardbeg (by Lake Coniston) and the Italian winner of 5 races (including at 2 yrs) Permise Men (by Catrail). The dam, a minor 13f winner at 3 yrs in Ireland, is a half-sister to 5 winners including 3 in India. The second dam, Gourgandine (by Auction Ring), ran once unplaced and is a half-sister to the Group winners Harmless Albatross, Fortune's Wheel and Libertine. (Hamdan Al Maktoum). *"She's had a couple of niggling problems but she's a nice, quality filly that the Boss likes. He thinks the Acclamation fillies are better than the colts. She'll be alright and she'll be a two-year-old in May or June."*

876. MAKE A DANCE (USA) ★★
b.f. Empire Maker – Clog Dance
(Pursuit Of Love).
April 25. Fourth foal. Half-sister to the very useful 2-y-o 7f winner, Group 3 7f Somerville Tattersall Stakes third and Group 1 Criterium International fourth Yankadi (by Johannesburg) and to the very useful 6f, listed 7f (both at 2 yrs) and listed 1m winner Short Dance (by Hennessy). The dam, a useful maiden, was second in the Group 3 7f Rockfel Stakes and the listed 10f Pretty Polly Stakes and is a half-sister to the smart 14f Ebor Handicap winner Tuning. The second dam, Discomatic (by Roberto), won over 9f in France and is a half-sister to the Phoenix Stakes winner Digamist. (Khalid Abdulla). *"This filly is going to need a lot of time but she's nice and I'm glad to say her temperament is fine, because the mother's wasn't. She's growing like mad at the moment*

so we've dropped her back to fourth lot and she's be a back-end filly."

877. MANAABER (IRE) ★★★★
ch.f. Medicean – Needlecraft
(Mark Of Esteem).
February 7. Second foal. €130,000Y. Goffs Orby. Shadwell Estate Co. The dam won 4 races including the Group 3 Prix Chloe and the Group 3 Premio Sergio Cumani and is a half-sister to 3 winners. The second dam, Sharp Point (by Royal Academy), a useful Irish listed 5f winner at 3 yrs, was fourth in the Group 1 5f Nunthorpe Stakes and is a half-sister to the listed winner High Target. (Hamdan Al Maktoum). *"This filly is one for later on but she's lovely. She does everything right, she's grown and developed and we'll just take our time with her because she's probably one for seven furlongs."*

878. MAQARAAT (IRE) ★★★
ch.c. Dalakhani – Raghida (Nordico).
February 4. Tenth foal. €150,000Y. Arqana Deauville August. Shadwell Estate Co. Half-brother to the smart Irish 5f (at 2 yrs) and dual Group 3 (7.5f and 1m) winner Marionnaud (by Spectrum), to the useful Irish dual 6f winner (including at 2 yrs) and Group 3 placed Rock Moss and the fair 5f and 7f winner Bravely (both by Rock Of Gibraltar). The dam, a fairly useful Irish 2-y-o dual 5f winner, was second in the Group 3 5f Curragh Stakes and the Group 3 Molecomb Stakes and is a sister to the useful 6f to 7f winner and Group 3 placed Nordic Fox and a half-sister to 7 winners including the Group 1 Gran Criterium winner Sholokhov and the listed winner Affianced (dam of the Group 1 Irish Derby winner Soldier Of Fortune). The second dam, La Meilleure (by Lord Gayle), a quite useful listed 1m winner in Ireland at 3 yrs, is a half-sister to 6 winners. (Hamdan Al Maktoum). *"A big, powerful horse, Dalakhani's usually take a bit of time so I'd say he's one for the back-end of the season. He's got a good temperament considering his sire, he's a nice, big horse to sit on and a good mover, so he just needs some time."*

879. MOONLIGHT RHAPSODY (IRE) ★★
b.f. Danehill Dancer – Moon Flower
(Sadler's Wells).
March 5. Ninth foal. 50,000Y. Tattersalls October Book 1. BBA (Ire). Half-sister to the 2009 French 2-y-o listed 5f placed Around Me (by Johannesburg), to the Australian Grade 2 winner Fantastic Love (by Peintre Celebre), the French 2-y-o 5.5f winner Enchanting Muse (by Fusaichi Pegasus) and a winner of 3 races in Japan by Spectrum. The dam, a winner over 1m (at 2yrs) and 10f in Ireland, is a sister to the listed winners Side Of Paradise and Flowerdrum and a half-sister to the triple Grade 1 winner Last Tycoon, the Group 2 6f Premio Melton winner Astronef and the dam of the Group 1 winners Valentine Waltz and Sense Of Style. The second dam, Mill Princess (by Mill Reef), won over 10f at 2 yrs in France and is a half-sister to the Irish Sweeps Derby winner Irish Ball and the top-class broodmare Irish Bird, dam of the classic winners Assert, Bikala and Eurobird. *"There's not a lot of her, she's very light framed, has had a touch of sore shins and she's a bit buzzy even before she's done anything, so the jury's out on her."*

880. MOUNT CRYSTAL ★★
b.f. Montjeu – State Crystal
(High Estate).
May 14. Twelfth foal. €165,000Y. Goffs Orby. BBA (Ire). Closely related to the 10f winner True Crystal, to the 12f winner Time Crystal (both fairly useful) and the 17f and hurdles winner Malakiya (all by Sadler's Wells), the fairly useful 2-y-o 7f winner Crystal Curling (by Peintre Celebre) and the fair 8.5f and hurdles winner Jack The Giant (by Giant's Causeway). The dam was a very useful winner of the Group 3 12f Lancashire Oaks and was placed in the Yorkshire Oaks and the Prix Vermeille. She is a half-sister to 6 winners including the Group 1 Fillies' Mile winner Crystal Music, the Group 3 winners Dubai Success and Solar Crystal and the Irish Derby third Tchaikovsky. The second dam, Crystal Spray (by Beldale Flutter), a minor Irish 4-y-o 14f winner, is a half-sister to 8 winners. *"She's a late foal and she's still growing. One for next year really."*

881. MRS DEE BEE (IRE) ★★★★
b.f. Barathea – Daqtora (Dr Devious).
April 22. Fifth foal. €32,000Y. Goffs Orby. BBA (Ire). Half-brother to the fairly useful 2-y-o 6f winner Qalahari (by Bahri), to the fair Irish

7f winner Nasharaat (by Green Desert) and the fair Irish 2m and hurdles winner Almolahek (by Red Ransom). The dam, a minor Irish 11f winner, is a half-sister to the 2-y-o Group 1 1m National Stakes winner Mus-If and to the very smart 1m (at 2 yrs) and 10f listed winner Jammaal. The second dam, Navajo Love Song (by Dancing Brave), placed once at 4 yrs, is a half-sister to 5 minor winners in France and Italy. *"She's going to take a bit of time because she's growing like hell at the minute, but the Boss really likes her. Baratheas need a bit of cut in the ground normally and I don't think she'll be rushed. One for a bit later on, but she might be worth watching out for."*

882. OUR PLAY (IRE) ★★★
b.c. Oratorio – Red Shoe (Selkirk).
January 27. Third foal. €58,000Y. Goffs Orby. BBA (Ire). The dam is an unraced half-sister to 5 winners including the French listed winner and Group 1 Prix Morny third Barricade. The second dam, Balleta (by Lyphard), a quite useful 10f winner and also a winner of 3 races in the USA, is a sister to the great 'Arc', 'King George' and 2,000 Guineas winner Dancing Brave and to Jolypha (winner of the Group 1 12f Prix Vermeille and Group 1 10.5f Prix de Diane). *"The sire hasn't done too bad and this is a nicely balanced horse and a good mover. He's still growing, so we'll take our time with him and we might see him out in mid-season."*

883. PIVOT BRIDGE ★★
ch.c. Pivotal – Specifically (Sky Classic).
April 30. Tenth foal. 185,000Y. Tattersalls October Book 1. M H Goodbody. Half-brother to the 1,000 Guineas and Group 2 Rockfel Stakes winner Speciosa (by Danehill Dancer), to the US Grade 3 stakes winner of 13 races and Grade 1 placed Major Rhythm (by Rhythm), the minor US winner of 6 races Bold Classic (by Pembroke), the fair 1m and 10f winner Liberally (by Statue Of Liberty), the fair 9.7f and 10f winner Thundermill (by Thunder Gulch) and the modest all-weather 5f and 6f winner Shadow Jumper (by Dayjur). The dam won once at 2 yrs in the USA and is a half-sister to 7 winners including the Group 1 Champion Stakes, Grand Prix de Saint-Cloud and Hong Kong Cup winner Pride. The second dam, Specificity (by Alleged), a useful winner of the listed 12.2f George Stubbs Stakes, is a half-sister to the 10 winners including the St Leger and Irish St Leger winner Touching Wood. *"A good-bodied colt, but he's a chestnut with four white feet and a white face! Having said that, he's done nothing wrong, he was easy to break, he's grown and he goes alright. It's just that I've never seen a horse with so much white on him!"*

884. POWER PUNCH (IRE) ★★★
b.c. Medicean – Peneia (Nureyev).
January 30. Sixth foal. €52,000Y. Goffs Orby. BBA (Ire). Half-brother to the fair Irish 1m winner Addicted (by Machiavellian), to the fair Irish 9f and 10f winner Nurenberg (by Giant's Causeway) and the modest 5f winner La Quinta (by Indian Ridge). The dam was placed 5 times in France and is a half-sister to the Group 3 5f King George Stakes and Group 3 5f Ballyogan Stakes winner Dietrich. The second dam, Piquetnol (by Private Account), a French 3-y-o winner and second in the Group 1 Prix Marcel Boussac, is a sister to the Moyglare Stud Stakes and Coronation Stakes winner Chimes of Freedom (the dam of two Grade 1 winners) and a half-sister to the multiple US Grade 1 winner Denon and the 2-y-o listed 6f winner Imperfect Circle – herself the dam of Spinning World. *"He's a nice little horse, quite a forward going and cocky colt and he's definitely got a bit about him. He hasn't done any fast work but he's a nice horse for later on."*

885. PURE SCIENCE (IRE) ★★
ch.c. Galileo – Rebelline (Robellino).
February 7. Fourth foal. 160,000Y. Tattersalls October Book 1. M H Goodbody. Half-brother to the Group 3 Irish 2,000 Guineas Trial winner Recharge (by Cape Cross) and to the fair Irish 1m winner Regalline (by Green Desert). The dam won 6 races from 7f to 10.5f including the Group 1 10.5f Tattersalls Gold Cup and the Group 2 10f Pretty Polly Stakes and is a half-sister to 4 winners including the Group 2 Blandford Stakes winner Quws. The second dam, Fleeting Rainbow (by Rainbow Quest), a modest 10f placed 3-y-o, is a half-sister to 3 winners. *"A great big horse, he won't make a two-year-old until much later in the year."*

886. RAASEKHA ★★★★♣
b.f. Pivotal – Tahrir (Linamix).
February 15. Second foal. Half-sister to the quite useful 2009 2-y-o 7f winner Tamaathul (by Tiger Hill). The dam, a useful dual 7f winner, is a sister to the listed 7f Prix Djebel winner and dual Group 3 placed Mister Charm and to the French listed 7f winner Green Channel and a half-sister to the Group 3 Prix de Guiche winner Mister Sacha. The second dam, Miss Sacha (by Last Tycoon), won the listed Topaz Sprint Stakes in Ireland at 3 yrs and is a half-sister to 6 winners including the Italian listed 7.5f winner Pinta. (Hamdan Al Maktoum). *"A lovely filly, she'll be one to look out for. She's growing at the minute so she's changing and lengthening, but she looks like being a very nice two-year-old."*

887. RED LARGO (IRE) ★★★
b.c. Encosta De Lago – Speciale (War Chant).
April 2. Second foal. 90,000Y. Tattersalls October Book 1. BBA (Ire). Half-brother to Love Action (by Motivator), placed fourth over 7f from three starts at 2 yrs in 2009. The dam won 2 races including the 2-y-o listed 6f Prix Yacowlef and is a half-sister to the Group 3 Gladness Stakes and German Group 3 winner Common World. The second dam, Spenderella (by Common Grounds), won once at 3 yrs in France and is a full or half-sister to 7 winners including the US Grade 1 Yellow Ribbon Invitational winner Aube Indienne. *"He's just lost his shape a bit at the moment so he's definitely going to need time, but he's a nice mover with a good temperament."*

888. RED MARLING (IRE) ★★★★
b.c. Danehill Dancer – Marling (Lomond).
April 10. Seventh living foal. €100,000Y. Goffs Orby. BBA (Ire). Half-brother to the smart listed 6f winner and Group 3 second Mugharreb, to the 7f and 1m winner Pilgrim's Way (both by Gone West), the 2-y-o 6f winner Half-Hitch (by Diesis), the 6f winner Chatline (by One Cool Cat) and the 7f winner Moonshiner (by Irish River) – al quite useful. The dam, a high-class winner of the Cheveley Park Stakes, the Irish 1,000 Guineas, the Coronation Stakes and the Sussex Stakes is a half-sister to 7 winners including the Irish 2,000 Guineas and Prix de l'Abbaye second Caerwent. The second dam, Marwell (by Habitat), a sister to the Mill Reef Stakes winner Lord Seymour, won the July Cup, the Prix de l'Abbaye, the Kings Stand Stakes and the Cheveley Park Stakes. *"This is another horse the Guvnor has just got on with. He's got a good temperament, he's done nothing wrong, been through the stalls and everything, so he'll be out early although you'd think he'll be better over six furlongs than five."*

889. RED REMANSO ★★★
ch.f. Redback – Esterlina (Highest Honor).
February 25. Fifth foal. 35,000Y. Tattersalls October Book 1. BBA (Ire). Sister to the smart 7f (at 2yrs) and listed 1m Heron Stakes winner and Group 1 1m Criterium International third Redolent and half-sister to the fair 6f winner Hightime Heroine (by Danetime). The dam won over 1m at 3 yrs in Ireland and is a half-sister to 3 minor winners in France. The second dam, Shaquick (by Shadeed), won in France and is a half-sister to 8 winners including the dual Group 3 winner Leap Lively (dam of the Irish 1,000 Guineas winner Forest Flower). *"She's turned herself inside out because she was a scrawny little thing when she came in. Very straight in front, she's going to need time but she's going upsides now just to make her use herself a bit. She looks quite nice and she isn't a late foal, so there's very chance she'll make a two-year-old."*

890. REROUTED (USA) ★★★
ch.c. Stormy Atlantic – Rouwaki (Miswaki).
February 28. Fourth foal. Half-brother to the useful 2009 2-y-o 7f winner Critical Moment (by Aptitude) and to the quite useful 1m winner Rattan (by Royal Anthem). The dam is an unplaced half-sister to the Grade 1 Kentucky Oaks winner Flute. The second dam, Rougeur (by Blushing Groom), won over 10f and 12f in the USA. (K Abdulla). *"Growing a lot at the moment, he's a big, plain horse with a lot of bone. I can't knock him and I think he'll be alright in time."*

891. ROUGETTE ★★
b.f. Red Ransom – Never A Doubt (Night Shift).
February 7. Fourth foal. Half-sister to the useful 5f (at 2 yrs) and listed 7f winner and Group 2 7f Rockfel Stakes third Royal

Confidence (by Royal Applause). The dam, a very useful 2-y-o Group 2 5.5f Prix Robert Papin winner, is a half-sister to 3 winners. The second dam, Waypoint (by Cadeaux Genereux), a fairly useful 6f and 7f winner (including on the all-weather), is a half-sister to 5 winners including the Group 2 6f Diadem Stakes winner Acclamation. *"She's had a few problems, so although it's a successful family we might have to wait quite a while for her."*

892. SHROPSHIRE (IRE) ★★★
gr.c. Shamardal – Shawanni (Shareef Dancer).
April 21. Eleventh foal. €70,000Y. Goffs Orby. BBA (Ire). Brother to the smart 2009 2-y-o Group 3 6f Round Tower Stakes winner Arctic and half-brother to the very useful 10f (including at 2 yrs) and Group 3 2m Queens Vase winner Shanty Star (by Hector Protector), the listed 6f and listed 7f winner Hinton Admiral (by Spectrum), the quite useful 7f to 1m winner of 14 races Mystic Man, the fair dual 7f winner Sharaby (both by Cadeaux Genereux), the quite useful 2-y-o dual 5f winner Twilight Sonnet (by Exit To Nowhere) and the fair 9f winner Lucky Token (by Key Of Luck). The dam, a useful 2-y-o 7f winner, is a half-sister to 5 winners including the Group 3 winners Blatant and Songlark. The second dam, Negligent (by Ahonoora), a champion 2-y-o filly and winner the 7f Rockfel Stakes at 2 yrs, was third in the 1,000 Guineas and is a sister to the dual 2-y-o 6f winner and 1,000 Guineas fourth Ala Mahlik. *"He's just taking plenty of time, mainly because he's been growing and changing all the time. He was hard to break because he's quite spunky. We're just ticking away with him at present."*

893. SOLE DANSER (IRE) ★★★
b.c. Dansili – Plymsole (Diesis).
April 17. Fifth foal. €60,000Y. Goffs Orby. BBA (Ire). Half-brother to the modest 11f and 12f winner She's So Pretty (by Grand Lodge). The dam, a quite useful 2-y-o 7.5f winner, is a full sister to 2 winners including the very smart Group 2 1m Berlin Brandenburg Trophy and Hong Kong Group 2 International Mile winner Docksider and a half-sister to 6 winners. The second dam, Pump (by Forli), is an unraced daughter of a half-sister to Thatch. *"A very heavy-topped horse, he got sore shins early on so we've had to keep him going as best we can to stop him getting too heavy. He's a nice horse and a nice size, he's got a good temperament but hopefully we'll have no more hold-ups."*

894. SQUIRES GATE (IRE) ★★★★
b.c. Namid – Roselyn (Efisio).
March 10. Fifth foal. £50,000Y. Doncaster St Leger. BBA (Ire). Half-brother to the fair 1m to 10f winner of 5 races Kimono My House (by Dr Fong) and to a minor Italian 4-y-o winner by Mark Of Esteem. The dam, a modest maiden, was placed fourth 3 times at 2 yrs over 6f and 7f. She is a half-sister to 3 winners including Riberac, a winner of 3 listed events and third in the Group 2 Sun Chariot Stakes. The second dam, Ciboure (by Norwick), a fair 6f (at 2 yrs) and 1m winner of 3 races, is a half-sister to 4 winners. *"He ran at Doncaster where he finished third and he just needed the run. There's a lot of improvement in him, he'll be better with a bit of give in the ground and he'll be out soon. A good stamp of a horse, he's a good two-year-old type and I'm sure he'll do well this season."*

895. SULTAH (USA) ★★★
b.f. Redoute's Choice – Judhoor (by Alhaarth).
January 21. Third foal. The dam, a useful listed 6f winner, is a half-sister to 2 winners including the fairly useful 7f and 1m winner Muzher. The second dam, Almurooj (by Zafonic), a moderate 5f and 6f placed maiden, is a half-sister to 7 winners including the smart 6f (at 2 yrs), Group 2 7f Challenge Stakes and Group 3 7f Greenham Stakes winner Munir and the very useful Irish 1m listed stakes winner and Group 1 Coronation Stakes second Hasbah. *"Still in Dubai."*

896. SUPREME SEDUCTRESS (IRE) ★★★
b.f. Montjeu – Private Seductress (Private Account).
May 14. Seventh foal. €80,000Y. Goffs Orby. BBA (Ire). Half-sister to the Group 1 Italian Oaks winner and Group 1 Moyglare Stud Stakes third Menhoubah (by Dixieland Band) and to the modest 14f and 2m winner Russian Music (by Stravinsky). The dam, a US stakes-placed winner of 3 races at 3 and 4 yrs, is a half-sister to 3 minor winners. The second dam, In Full Cry (by Seattle Slew), a winner at 2 and 3 yrs in the USA, was second in the Grade

2 6f Adirondack Stakes and is a half-sister to 6 winners including the top-class miler Posse. *"A big filly that's grown like hell, she's straightforward (considering that Montjeu's can be difficult) and she's a big, scopey filly and a good mover."*

897. TALBYAH (USA) ★★★
b.f. *Forestry – Sarayir (Mr Prospector).*
April 5. Half-sister to the 1,000 Guineas and Coronation Stakes winner Ghanaati (by Giant's Causeway), to the Group 3 12f Cumberland Lodge Stakes winner and Group 1 Champion Stakes second Mawatheeq, the quite useful 1m winner Itqaan (both by Danzig), the quite useful 10f winner Sundus (by Fairy King), the 2009 2-y-o 1m debut winner Rumoush and the fair 12f winner Atayeb (both by Rahy). The dam, winner of a 1m listed event, is closely related to the Champion Stakes winner Nayef and a half-sister to Nashwan and Unfuwain. The second dam, Height Of Fashion (by Bustino), a high-class winner of 5 races from 7f to 12f including the Group 2 Princess of Wales's Stakes, is a half-sister to the good middle-distance colt Milford. (Hamdan Al Maktoum). *"Still in Dubai."*

898. TASHEYAAT ★★★
b.f. *Sakhee – Almurooj (Zafonic).*
April 3. Ninth foal. Half-sister to the useful listed 6f winner Judhoor (by Alhaarth), to the fairly useful 7f and 1m winner Muzher (by Indian Ridge) and the quite useful 2-y-o 6f winner Al Sifaat (by Unfuwain). The dam, a moderate 5f and 6f placed maiden, is a half-sister to 7 winners including the smart 6f (at 2 yrs), Group 2 7f Challenge Stakes and Group 3 7f Greenham Stakes winner Munir and the very useful Irish 1m listed stakes winner and Group 1 Coronation Stakes second Hasbah. The second dam, Al Bahathri (by Blushing Groom), was a high-class winner of 6 races from 6f to 1m, notably the Irish 1,000 Guineas and the Coronation Stakes. (Hamdan Al Maktoum). *"Still in Dubai."*

899. TOMS RIVER TESS (IRE) ★★★
b.f. *Kodiac – Sonorous (Ashkalani).*
March 28. Fourth foal. 20,000Y. Tattersalls October Book 2. BBA (Ire). Closely related to the fairly useful 6f (at 2 yrs) and 7f winner Glen Molly (by Danetime). The dam, an Irish 1m and 10f winner, was listed-placed and is a half-sister to 4 winners. The second dam, Nymphs Echo (by Mujtahid), is an unraced sister to the 2-y-o winner and Group 3 Fred Darling Stakes second Glen Rosie and a half-sister to 5 winners including the Group 3 10f Derrinstown Stud Derby Trial and triple US stakes winner Artema. *"Not over-big but an athletic filly, she's quite narrow and she'll need a bit of time. She's quite willing though and she always does her work."*

900. WEST LEAKE BRIDGE (IRE) ★★★
b.c. *Avonbridge – Miss Amadeus (Mozart).*
February 25. Second foal. £28,000Y. Doncaster St Leger. BBA (Ire). The dam is an unplaced half-sister to one winner. The second dam, Markova's Dance (by Mark Of Esteem), is a placed half-sister to 8 winners including the Group 2 Geoffrey Freer Stakes winner Azzilfi. *"A nice, two-year-old type, he just had a bit of a setback with a nasty cut on the eye but it won't take him long to get back together again. He'll make an early two-year-old."*

901. WEST LEAKE MELODY ★★★
b.c. *Royal Applause – Rada's Daughter (Robellino).*
May 12. Sixth foal. 22,000Y. Tattersalls October Book 2. BBA (Ire). Brother to the moderate 10f winner Theatre Royal. The dam, a useful winner of 5 races at up to 12f, was second in the Group 3 Park Hill Stakes and is a half-sister to 8 winners. The second dam, Drama School (by Young Generation), is an unplaced half-sister to 3 winners. *"A late foal but all the boys who ride him like him. They say he goes better than the ones that are working, but the Boss says he's heard all that before! We're hanging fire with him at the moment, but he might just be alright and he won't be too late."*

902. WHISTLE ON BY ★★★
b.c. *Piccolo – Glory Oatway (Desert Prince).*
January 23. First foal. 6,000Y. Doncaster October. Not sold. The dam, unplaced in 2 starts, is a half-sister to 3 winners. The second dam, Seasonal Blossom (by Fairy King), is an unplaced half-sister to 6 winners including the smart Group 3 7f C L Weld Park Stakes winner

Token Gesture and the US Grade 2 9f winner Wait Till Monday. (Mr R Morecombe & Mr J Netherthorpe). *"When he came in he looked a million dollars and he was a good goer too. But he got sore shins, otherwise he'd have been in the Brocklesbury. He's on the back burner but he's a bonny horse and for six grand he's a nice little horse."*

903. YASMEENA (USA) ★★★
ch.f. *Mr Greeley – La Cucaracha (Piccolo).*
January 28. First foal. $330,000Y. Keeneland September. Shadwell Estate Co. The dam, a high-class sprinter, won the Group 1 Nunthorpe Stakes, the Group 3 King George Stakes and the Group 3 Ballyogan Stakes and is a half-sister to 3 winners. The second dam, Peggy Spencer (by Formidable), a fair 6f and 7f all-weather winner, is a half-sister to the very smart sprinter Gift Horse. (Hamdan Al Maktoum). *"Still In Dubai. It'll be nice to have this mare's first foal, as she was trained here."*

904. UNNAMED ★★★★
b.c. *Oasis Dream – Achieve (Rainbow Quest).*
April 23. Fourth foal. Half-brother to the fair 6f winner High Achieved (by Dansili). The dam is an unraced sister to the Derby and Hollywood Turf Handicap winner Quest For Fame and to the Group 3 Queens Vase second Silver Rainbow and a half-sister to the Grade 2 Long Island Handicap winner and Prix Vermeille second Yenda. The second dam, Aryenne (by Green Dancer), was a high-class winner of the French 1,000 Guineas and the Criterium des Pouliches and is a half-sister to 3 winners. (Khalid Abdulla). *"A quality colt, he's lovely and he could be anything. A seven furlong type two-year-old and he'll definitely be alright."*

905. UNNAMED ★★
ch.c. *Haafhd – Balmy (Zafonic).*
May 1. Third living foal. The dam, a fairly useful 1m winner, is a sister to winner in Greece and a half-sister to the very useful French 6f (at 2 yrs) and 1m listed winner Barricade and the useful 14f winner War Cabinet. The second dam, Balleta (by Lyphard), a quite useful 3-y-o 10f winner, also won 3 races in the USA and is a sister to the great 'Arc', 'King George' and 2,000 Guineas winner Dancing Brave and to Jolypha (winner of the Group 1 12f Prix Vermeille and Group 1 10.5f Prix de Diane). (Khalid Abdulla). *"A big, chunk of a horse, he's had a few issues so he's one for the back-end of the season."*

906. UNNAMED ★★★
b.f. *Oasis Dream – Far Shores (Distant View).*
February 28. The dam is an unplaced half sister to numerous winners including the top-class sprinter and sire Danehill, the US Grade 2 9f winner Eagle Eyed, the very smart Group 3 Criterion Stakes winner Shibboleth and the listed 7f winner Euphonic. The second dam, Razyana (by His Majesty), was placed over 7f at 2 yrs and 10f at 3 yrs. (Khalid Abdulla). *"A nice filly, she's not very big and she has a good temperament but she's had a number of niggling issues to contend with. She's just ticking along at present."*

907. UNNAMED ★★
b.c. *Oasis Dream – Five Fields (Chester House).*
January 21. The dam, a fair 10f winner, is a half-sister to numerous winners including the US Grade 1 11f United Nations Handicap winner Senure, the useful French 6f (at 2 yrs) and 1m winner Speak In Passing and the French listed 1m winner Dexterity. The second dam, Diese (by Diesis), winner of the Group 3 10.5f Prix Corrida and a listed event over 10f in France, is a half-sister to numerous good winners including the champion European 2-y-o Xaar, winner of the Group 1 Dewhurst Stakes and the Group 1 Prix de la Salamandre and the Group 3 1m Prix Quincey winner Masterclass. (Khalid Abdulla). *"Not arrived here yet."*

908. UNNAMED ★★★
b.c. *Noverre – Midnight Partner (Marju).*
January 22. Fourth foal. 50,000Y. Tattersalls October Book 2. BBA (Ire). Half-brother to the unplaced 2009 2-y-o Buona Sarah (by Bertolini), to the German 3-y-o winner and listed-placed Terre Neuve (by Verglas) and the minor French winner of 4 races at 2 to 4 yrs Desert Nights (by Desert Style). The dam is an unraced half-sister to the winner of 5 races and Group 1 Criterium International second Top Seed. The second dam, Midnight Heights (by Persian Heights), won 5 races including 2 listed events in Italy, was second in the Group 2 10f Premio Lydia Tesio and is a half-sister to the Group 3 Sandown Classic Trial winner Galitzin.

"He's on the back burner at the minute, he's grown a lot and he's a nice, big, good-moving horse with a good temperament."

909. UNNAMED ★★★
b.f. *Danehill Dancer – Singing Diva (Royal Academy).*
April 16. Fourth foal. 68,000Y. Tattersalls October Book 1. Brian Grassick Bloodstock. Half-sister to the modest 10f, 11f and hurdles winner Rising Force (by Selkirk). The dam is an unraced half-sister to 8 winners including the Group 2 12f King Edward VII Stakes winner Amfortas and the Group 3 10.5f Prix de Royaumont winner Legend Maker (herself dam of the 1,000 Guineas winner Virginia Water). The second dam, High Spirited (by Shirley Heights), was quite useful and won two of her seven races over 14f and 2m at 3 yrs. She is a sister to the Premio Roma, Ribblesdale Stakes and Park Hill Stakes winner High Hawk (herself dam of the Breeders Cup Turf winner In the Wings) and a half-sister to the dams of the Derby winner High Rise and the Rothmans International winner Infamy. *"A filly that's growing a lot now, she's nice though and everyone that rides her says she's real nice. A good mover, but she might want a bit of time."*

910. UNNAMED ★★★
b.c. *Cacique – Sound Asleep (Woodman).*
May 7. Fourth foal. Closely related to the promising 2009 2-y-o 7f winner (on his only start) Sierra Alpha (by Dansili) and half-brother to the modest 12f winner Warming Up (by Kalanisi). The dam is an unraced half-sister to a minor winner in the USA. The second dam, Sleep Easy (by Seattle Slew), won the Grade 1 Hollywood Oaks and the Grade 2 Railbird Stakes and is a half-sister to 5 winners including the US dual Grade 1 winner Aptitude. (Khalid Abdulla). *"A nice big horse, he's done nothing wrong but he'll be a seven furlong two-year-old."*

911. UNNAMED ★★★★
b.f. *Cacique – Stormy Channel (Storm Cat).*
May 6. Half-sister to the quite useful 2-y-o 6f winner Senatorial (by Oasis Dream). The dam, a fairly useful 1m winner, is a half-sister to numerous winners including the very useful 7f winner Akimbo, the useful listed 1m winner Insinuate and the useful 6f and 7f winner and listed-placed Imroz. The second dam, All At Sea (by Riverman), a high-class winner of 5 races from 1m to 10.4f including the Group 1 Prix du Moulin, the Musidora Stakes and the Pretty Polly Stakes, was second in the Oaks, the Juddmonte International and the Nassau Stakes and is a half-sister to the Free Handicap winner Over the Ocean, the listed 10f winner Quandary and the US stakes winner Full Virtue. (Khalid Abdulla). *"A nice, quality filly and the Guvnor likes her a lot – he says she's got natural ability. I can see her making a two-year-old from the mid-summer onwards."*

912. UNNAMED ★★
b.f. *Araafa – Black Belt Shopper (Desert Prince).*
March 15. Fifth foal. 11,000Y. Tattersalls October Book 2. BBA (Ire). Half-sister to the modest dual 6f winner Exit Strategy (by Cadeaux Generereux). The dam, a quite useful 2-y-o 6f winner, was listed-placed and is a half-sister to the quite useful 2-y-o 1m winner Lucayan Beauty. The second dam, Koumiss (by Unfuwain), a French maiden, stayed 10f and is a half-sister to 8 winners including the useful 7f (at 2 yrs) and 11.5f winner Mystery Play, the Queen's Vase winner Arden, the French listed winner Kerulen and the dam of the US Grade 1 winner Kiri's Clown. *"We're still waiting for an owner, or maybe someone wanting to lease her. There's nothing wrong with her at all and she'll give the owner a lot of fun."*

JOHN HILLS

913. BROKEN BELLE (IRE) ★★★
gr.f. *Clodovil – Lady Express (Soviet Star).*
May 5. Tenth foal. €36,000Y. Goffs Orby. Not sold. Half-brother to the modest all-weather dual 6f winner Rahlex (by Rahy) and to a winner in Norway and Sweden by Desert King. The dam, a 7f winner in France, is a half-sister to the Derby winner New Approach, to the Japanese Group 1 winner Shinko Forest and the Group 3 Matron Stakes winner and Irish 1,000 Guineas third Dazzling Park. The second dam, Park Express (by Ahonoora), won the Group 1 10f Phoenix Champion Stakes and the Group 2 10f Nassau Stakes and is a half-sister to 6 winners. (Mrs C Corbett & Mr C

Wright). *"She looks quite sharp, even though on the dam's side it could go either way. The mare has been a bit disappointing but this filly is well-developed, she's done a few bits of work already and she's lovely. Her debut should come in early May and I think she'll be able to go five furlongs but will be better over six."*

914. DEVEZE (IRE) ★★★
b.f. Kyllachy – La Caprice (Housebuster).
April 10. Sixth foal. 26,000Y. Tattersalls October Book 2. Anthony Stroud. Sister to the modest 5f and 6f winner of 5 races La Capriosa and half-sister to the quite useful 2-y-o 5f winner and listed-placed Empire's Ghodha (by Mujadil) and the fair 5f and 6f winner of 4 races Milton Of Campsie (by Medicean). The dam, a quite useful 5f winner at 2 and 3 yrs, is a half-sister to 8 winners including the Group 2 6f Richmond Stakes winner Muqtarib and the listed winners Ra'A and Janib. The second dam, Shicklah (by The Minstrel), a useful 2-y-o 5f and 6f winner here, subsequently won a Group 2 event in Germany and is a half-sister to 3 winners. (Wood Hall Stud) *"Only recently arrived, she's very well-developed but we haven't been able to get stuck into her yet. She looks quite powerful, so you'd expect her to have some speed. She might just need to get her toe in the ground because she's quite a heavy filly."*

915. DIAMOND RUN ★★★
b.f. Hurricane Run – Rubies From Burma (Forty Niner).
March 25. Seventh foal. Half-sister to the useful 11.8f winner and listed 12f second Ivory Gala (by Galileo) and the quite useful 2-y-o 1m and subsequent UAE winner Alo Pura (by Anabaa). The dam, a winner of 3 races from 5f to 6f and listed placed over 5.5f in Ireland, is a half-sister to 9 winners including the French 1,000 Guineas, Fillies Mile and Prix Marcel Boussac winner Culture Vulture. The second dam, Perfect Example (by Far North), is an unraced half-sister to the dams of the Grade/Group 1 winners Awe Inspiring, Polish Precedent and Zilzal. (Mrs Fiona Hills & Partners). *"She's interesting. Physically she's still a baby but ability-wise she's definitely got speed. She carries herself perfectly and I should imagine the way she's bred she'll be one for the mid-season onwards. I think she'll make a two-year-old once she strengthened."*

916. FLO MOTION (IRE) ★★
b.f. Sadler's Wells – Darling (Darshaan).
March 25. Fifth foal. 42,000Y. Tattersalls October Book 1. A Skiffington. Half-brother to the fair Irish 11f winner Tony's Treasure (by Sakhee). The dam is an unraced half-sister to 3 winners including the Group 3 winner Shemozzle. The second dam, Reactress (by Sharpen Up), a US 2-y-o stakes winner, is a half-sister to 6 winners. (Mr P A Abberley). *"A very sweet filly and a nice mover but very much one for the autumn onwards. A filly more for next year really."*

917. GALIVANT (IRE) ★★★
b.br.f. Galileo – Valdara (Darshaan).
April 8. Ninth foal. 52,000Y. Tattersalls October Book 1. Not sold. Half-sister to the dual listed 10f winner Musha Merr (by Sadler's Wells), to the useful German listed 10f winner Cymbal (by Singspiel), the useful Irish 10f and 11f winner Queen's Colours (by Rainbow Quest) and the quite useful UAE 7f to 9f winner Valdancer (by Groom Dancer). The dam, a French 2-y-o 1m winner, was third in the Group 3 1m Prix des Reservoirs at 2 yrs and is a half-sister to 8 winners including the listed winner Valley Quest. The second dam, Valverda (by Irish River), a minor 3-y-o winner in France, is a half-sister to the Group 3 winners Verria and Voreas. (Wauchope, Cottam, Mason, Baxter, Caroe). *"A beautiful filly, she's big and scopey and she goes well. Not the most backward in the yard despite her pedigree, but she's still one for the second half of the season. Potentially the nicest I've got."*

918. GOLDEN TAURUS (IRE) ★★★
b.c. Danehill Dancer – Nadwah (Shadeed).
April 26. Seventh foal. €40,000Y. Goffs Orby. J Hills/A Skiffington. The dam, winner of the Group 3 5f Queen Mary Stakes and third in the Group 2 Lowther Stakes and is a half-sister to 7 winners. The second dam, Tadwin (by Never So Bold), was a very useful sprint winner of 3 races including the listed Hopeful Stakes and is a half-sister to 4 winners including the very smart sprinter Reesh and the dam of the smart sprinter Averti. (N Hubbard & Partners). *"He's*

an interesting horse. Peter Walwyn trained the mare to win the Queen Mary and the offspring of the sire Danehill Dancer can do anything. He looks racy, I've started to do a bit more with him and he looks quite fast. He'll definitely make a two-year-old, I like him a lot and although he's not over-big he's got al the bits in the right places. The mare has been disappointing but the sire can overcome lots of things and it wouldn't be the biggest feat of his career to overcome a Queen Mary winner that's been disappointing. A colt for the middle of May onwards."

919. MAJOR CONQUEST (IRE) ★★★★
b.c. Librettist – Arabis (Arazi).
March 27. 14,000Y. Tattersalls October Book 2. J R Best. Half-brother to the fairly useful 2-y-o dual 5f winner Great Scott (by Fasliyev), to the modest 12f and jumps winner Petrosian (by Sakhee) and the moderate 15f and jumps winner Spring Charm (by Inchinor). The dam, a quite useful 10f winner, is closely related to the useful 7f (at 2 yrs) and 10.3f winner Yeltsin and a half-sister to 8 winners including the listed 15f winner Bosham Mill. The second dam, Mill On The Floss (by Mill Reef), a winner over 7f at 2 yrs and the Group 3 12f Lingfield Oaks Trial at 3 yrs, is a half-sister to 8 winners including the Lancashire Oaks second Shadywood (dam of the Park Hill Stakes winner and good broodmare Madame Dubois). *"By a first season sire in Librettist, this colt weighs over 500kgs and he's strong – much more mature than some. He's done a couple of bits of work and he could be our first two-year-old runner. I like him and he's done everything I've asked so far."*

920. RAVE (IRE) ★★★
b.c. Oratorio – Almaaseh (Dancing Brave).
March 4. Eleventh foal. €40,000Y. Goffs Orby. A Skiffington/J Hills. Half-brother to the very useful Group 3 5f Curragh Stakes and Group 3 5f Molecomb Stakes winner Almaty (by Dancing Dissident), to the useful 10f winner and listed-placed Salee (by Caerleon), the fairly useful 7f (at 2 yrs) to 10f winner of 9 races Impeller (by Polish Precedent), the fair 1m winner Miss Brown To You (by Fasliyev), the fair 6f winner Sarah Stokes (by Brief Truce) and the modest Irish 7f and hurdles winner Collingwood

(by Machiavellian). The dam, placed once over 6f at 3 yrs, is a half-sister to 8 winners including the 2,000 Guineas and Champion Stakes winner Haafhd and the Group 2 Challenge Stakes winner Munir and to the unraced dam of the Group 1 Dubai Duty Free Stakes winner Gladiatorus. The second dam, Al Bahathri (by Blushing Groom), won the Irish 1,000 Guineas and is a half-sister to the US Grade 2 winner Geraldine's Store and to the dam of the US Grade 1 winner Spanish Fern. (Gary & Linnet Woodward). *"A lovely, scopey horse, he's very attractive and is going to take some time – I would say from July onwards. At the moment I'm not sure how much speed he has and currently I would say he's more a seven furlong type than six. A very likeable horse that stands over a lot of ground, but he's been growing a lot and we haven't much with him yet."*

921. REMOTELINX (IRE) ★★★
ch.c. Choisir – La Tintoretta (Desert Prince).
February 28. Second foal. £28,000Y. Doncaster St Leger. A Skiffington/J Hills. Half-brother to the modest Irish 7f placed Vera Lilley (by Verglas). The dam, an Irish 5f winner, is a half-sister to the useful 2-y-o 6f winner Oreana. The second dam, Lavinia Fontana (by Sharpo), a very smart sprinter and winner of the Group 1 6f Haydock Sprint Cup, the Group 2 6f Premio Umbria, the Group 3 5f Prix du Petit-Couvert and the Group 3 7f Premio Chiusura, is a half-sister to 3 winners. (Prolinx Ltd). *"He's pretty forward, he's got natural speed, has done a couple of bits of work and finds everything easy. He should be able to run at the end of April or the beginning of May. He's a nicely balanced horse that does everything in a straightforward manner."*

922. WHAT ABOUT NOW ★★★★
b.f. Encosta De Lago – Mini Driver (Danehill).
March 9. First foal. £20,000Y. Doncaster St Leger. A Skiffington/J Hills. The dam is an unraced daughter of the listed Oaks Trial winner Birdie (by Alhaarth), herself a half-sister to 7 winners. (Gary & Linnet Woodward). *"She's a lovely, deep-bodied filly, very attractive and hardy, and I love everything about her. I don't think she'll be early and it's more than likely*

she'll be one for June onwards. As an individual I like her as much as anything in the yard." TRAINERS' BARGAIN BUY

923. WONG AGAIN ★★★
b.f. Araafa – Susi Wong (Selkirk).
April 17. 10,000Y. Tattersalls October Book 2. Not sold. Half-sister to the smart 7f (at 2 yrs) to 12f winner of 8 races (including the Group 3 St Simon Stakes and the Group 3 13f Ormonde Stakes) Buccellati (by Soviet Star), to the Italian listed 2-y-o winner and Group 3 6f Premio Primi Passi second Golden Stud (by In The Wings), the Scandinavian listed winner La Petite Chinoise (by Dr Fong) and the quite useful 10.2f winner Hope An Glory (by Nashwan). The dam won once at 3 yrs in Germany, was listed-placed and is a half-sister to 4 winners. The second dam, Stay That Way (by Be My Guest), is an unraced half-sister to the Coronation Stakes winner Chalon (dam of the Prix Ganay and Prix d'Ispahan winner Creator) and to the Irish listed winner Elegance In Design (dam of the Irish Oaks winner Dance Design). (Burton Agnes Stud). *"She looks pretty tough and has a lovely way of going."*

924. UNNAMED ★★
b.f. Motivator – Orange Sunset (Roanoke).
March 10. Fifth foal. 26,000Y. Tattersalls October Book 2. J Hills/A Skiffington. Half-sister to the quite useful dual 1m winner French Art (by Peintre Celebre). The dam won 5 races including listed events in Ireland (over 12f) and the USA and was third in the Grade 2 La Prevoyante Handicap. She is a half-sister to 3 winners out of the unplaced Classical Flair (by Riverman), herself a half-sister to 6 winners. *"A lovely, scopey, quite classy-looking filly. One for the second half of the year, she's very smooth in everything she does but we're not pushing her yet."*

925. UNNAMED ★★★
ch.f. Speightstown – Terri's Charmer (Silver Charm).
February 26. First foal. €20,000Y. Goffs Orby. J Hills/A Skiffington. The dam, a minor US 3-y-o winner, is a half-sister to 7 winners including US Grade 3 winner Gone For Real and the dam of the US Grade 2 winner Josh's Madelyn. The second dam, Intently (by Drone), a US stakes winner of 8 races and Grade 3 placed, is a half-sister to 7 winners including the US Grade 3 winner and Grade 1 placed Percipient. (Gary & Linnet Woodward). *"She's pretty sharp and she'll be racing in late April or early May. A real two-year-old type, I like her and she looks quite speedy."*

MICHAEL JARVIS
926. AGBALAT ★★
b.f. Cape Cross – Tarfshi (Mtoto).
March 22. The dam, a winner of 5 races from 7f (at 2 yrs) to 10f including the Group 2 Pretty Polly Stakes, is a full or half-sister to 4 winners including the champion 2-y-o filly and Cheveley Park Stakes winner Embassy. The second dam, Pass The Peace (by Alzao), won the Cheveley Park Stakes, was second in the French 1,000 Guineas and is a half-sister to 3 winners. (Sheikh Ahmed Al Maktoum). *"The dam has been disappointing and although this filly is by a good stallion, she's on the backward side and we won't see her until the autumn."*

927. AMALLNA ★★
b.f. Green Desert – Walesiana (Star Appeal).
April 27. Half-sister to the Group 1 10f Nassau Stakes and Group 10.4f Musidora Stakes winner Zahrat Dubai, to the quite useful 9f winner Yaahomm (both by Unfuwain), the fairly useful 2-y-o 7f all-weather winner Waiting Game (by Reprimand), the fair 2-y-o 6f winner Samorra (by In The Wings) and the fair 12f all-weather winner Warluskee (by Dancing Brave). The dam won the German 1,000 Guineas and is a half-sister to 6 winners. The second dam, Wondrous Pearl (by Prince Ippi) won a listed event over 9f. (Sheikh Ahmed Al Maktoum). *"She's not a typical Green Desert and is a lengthy filly with plenty of improving to do."*

928. BOOGIE SHOES ★★★♣
b.c. Bertolini – Space Time (Bering).
April 12. Eighth foal. 20,000Y. Tattersalls October Book 2. M Jarvis. Half-brother to the 7f (at 2 yrs) and listed 10f winner Splashdown (by Falbrav), to the listed 10f winner Cosmodrome (by Bahri), the fairly useful 2-y-o 8.2f winner Muscida (by Woodman) and the US triple turf winner at around 1m and 9f and Grade 3 placed Tadreeb (by Theatrical). The dam was placed over 7f at 2 yrs in France and

THE SUMMER FESTIVALS BETTING GUIDE 2010

Last year's Summer Festivals Betting Guide highlighted several big priced winners including:

Genki	: won 12/1
Fleeting Spirit	: won 12/1
Red Merlin	: won 15/2

TRENDS SUCCESS CONTINUED ON THE FLAT

- In-Depth Analysis of over 30 races
- Individual Horse Appraisals for the Derby and Oaks
- Previews of some of the major two-year-old races

PUBLISHED MAY 2010

ORDER NOW **ONLY £10.95** (+ £2.00 post & packing)

Online and Text updates also available for every race

WEATHERBYS
COMMERCIAL SERVICES

Order Now at
www.weatherbysshop.co.uk
or call **01933 304776**

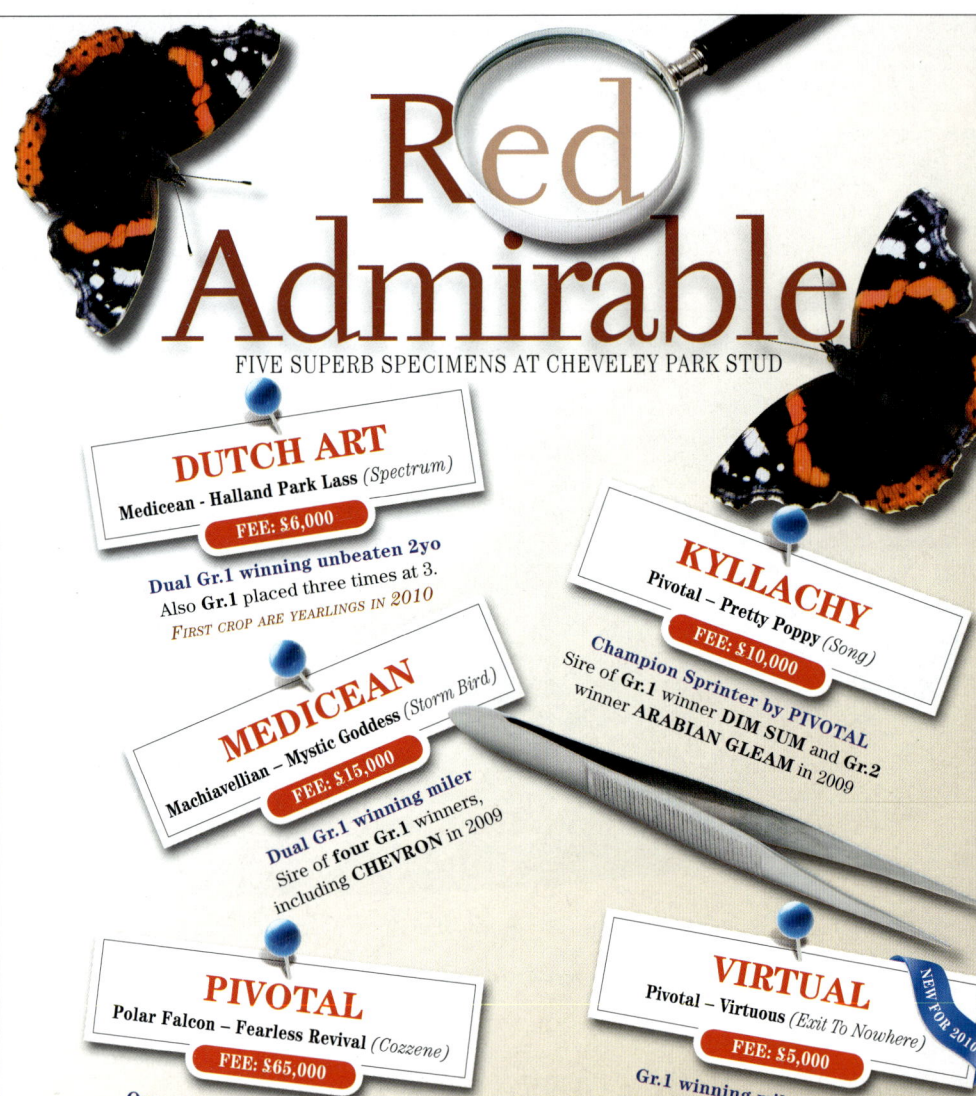

AQLAAM
FULLY BOOKED FOR 2010

Bay, 2005, by OASIS DREAM - BOURBONELLA, by RAINBOW QUEST

NEW FOR 2010
Good looking, Group 1 winning son of Oasis Dream.

Winner of Prix du Moulin de Longchamp (**Gr.1**), Summer Mile Stakes (**Gr.2**), Jersey Stakes (**Gr.3**), 2nd Prix Jacques Le Marois (**Gr.1**).

Stud fee for 2010: £7,000/€7,500 (1st Jan SLF)

NAYEF
FULLY BOOKED FOR 2010

Bay, 1998, by GULCH - HEIGHT OF FASHION, by BUSTINO

The Ultimate Racehorse.
Sire of **Gr.1** winners **TAMAYUZ** and **LADY MARIAN**, Group winning 2-y-o **TABASSUM** (**Gr.3**), **SPACIOUS** (**Gr.2**) and **CONFRONT** (**Gr.3**).

Stud fee for 2010: £15,000/€16,000 (1st Jan SLF)

SAKHEE

Bay, 1997, by BAHRI - THAWAKIB, by SADLER'S WELLS

Best Middle Distance Horse 2001.

Sire of Top Rated sprinter **SAKHEE'S SECRET**, **PRESVIS** (**Gr.1**), **ROYAL ROCK** (**Gr.3**) and Group 1 placed **PERMESSO** and **REGAL FLUSH**.

Stud fee for 2010: £6,000/€6,400 (1st Jan SLF)

HAAFHD

Chestnut, 2001, by ALHAARTH - AL BAHATHRI, by BLUSHING GROOM

2000 Guineas and Champion Stakes winner.

62.5% winners/runners in his first crop, including 14 2-y-o winners. His second crop, 2-y-os of 2009, includes Superlative Stakes **Gr.2** winner **SILVER GRECIAN**, **AZIZI** (4th Autumn Stakes **Gr.3**), **SUNNANDAEG**, etc.

Stud fee for 2010: £6,000/€6,400 (1st Jan SLF)

Contact: **RICHARD LANCASTER**, **JOHNNY PETER-HOBLYN** or **AUDREY LEYVAL**
on +44 (0)1842 755913
e-mail: nominations@shadwellstud.co.uk
www.shadwellstud.co.uk

SHADWELL
STANDING FOR SUCCESS

is a half-sister to 4 minor winners in France and Australia. The second dam, Space Ritual (by Top Ville), won at 2 yrs in France and is a half-sister to the Canadian Grade 2 winner Calista. (A D Spence). *"He's a nice, workmanlike horse that grew a lot since we bought him. He looked like being a sharp type but now he's looking more of a mid-summer two-year-old. He's quite nice and bigger than most Bertolini two-year-olds so he has a bit more scope. Seven furlongs should be his starting point."* TRAINERS' BARGAIN BUY

929. CLARKE LANE (USA) ★★★
b.c. Giant's Causeway – Wonder Lady Anne L (Real Quiet).
March 18. First foal. $190,000Y. Keeneland September. Gulf Coast Farm. The dam won 3 races including the Grade 1 CCA Oaks and the Grade 2 Bonnie Miss Stakes. The second dam, Ancho (by Wild Zone), is an unraced half-sister to 6 winners. (S Dartnell). *"He looks quite forward and although he's not a big horse he's quite a tough character, so we might just get on with him. Probably a six furlong colt to start with, but he looks a speedy type."*

930. DOMINANT (IRE) ★★★
bl.c. Cacique – Es Que (Inchinor).
February 22. First foal. 95,000Y. Tattersalls October Book 1. John Warren. The dam won once at 3 yrs in France and is a half-sister to a winner in Greece. The second dam, Bellona (by Bering), won a listed race in France and was Group 3 placed and is a half-sister to 6 winners. (Highclere Thoroughbred Racing, Isinglass). *"This horse looks like being a middle-distance horse next year. A good-looking colt, he'll make a two-year-old in the second half of the season."*

931. DUBAI METRO ★★★
b.c. Oasis Dream – Merle (Selkirk).
February 28. Third foal. 200,000foal. Tattersalls December. Shadwell Estate Co. The dam is an unraced half-sister to 11 winners including the multiple Group 3 winner Solo Mio. The second dam, Marie de Flandre (by Crystal Palace), a French listed 10f winner, is a full or half-sister to 7 winners including the high-class Prix Morny winner Sakura Reiko. (Hamdan Al Maktoum). *"Very typical of the sire in appearance, he's strong with good quarters and is a nice horse but had a cough during the winter and I haven't done much with him so far. I think he'll be alright by the mid-season and he'll be a sprinter."*

932. EKHRAAJ (USA) ★★★
b.f. El Prado – Mostaqeleh (Rahy).
April 1. First foal. The dam, a very useful 2-y-o 6f and 7f winner, was second in the Group 2 1m Prix de Sandringham and is a half-sister to the very smart listed 7f (at 2 yrs) and listed 10f winner Muqbil. The second dam, Istiqlal (by Diesis), is an unraced half-sister to the Group 1 1m St James's Palace Stakes and Group 1 1m Queen Elizabeth II Stakes winner Bahri and to the high-class 2-y-o Group 2 7f Laurent Perrier Champagne Stakes winner Bahhare. (Hamdan Al Maktoum). *"Still in Dubai until mid-April."*

933. ELZAAM (AUS) ★★★★♠
b.c. Redoute's Choice – Mambo In Freeport (Kingmambo).
January 24. Fourth foal. €280,000Y. Arqana Deauville August. Shadwell Estate Co. Half-brother to a minor winner in Australia by Anabaa. The dam, a minor US 3-y-o winner, is a half-sister to 7 winners including Point Ashley (Grade 1 Del Mar Debutante Stakes) and Raw Gold (Grade 2 Landaluce Stakes). The second dam, Golden Thatch (by Slew O'Gold), is an unraced half-sister to 5 winners. (Hamdan Al Maktoum). *"He's Australian-bred and they tell me he's typical of the sire. A very nice colt, he's a precocious two-year-old and he's one we could start off at five furlongs, so we'll be getting on with him now."*

934. EMKANAAT ★★★
b.c. Green Desert – Miss Anabaa (Anabaa).
March 3. Fourth foal. 160,000foal. Tattersalls December. Shadwell Estate Co. The dam, a winner of 3 races including the Group 3 5f Ballyogan Stakes, is a half-sister to 5 winners including Out After Dark, a smart 5f and 6f winner of 6 races, including the Portland Handicap. The second dam, Midnight Shift (by Night Shift), a fair dual 6f winner at 3 yrs, is a half-sister to 8 winners including the high-class Group 1 6f July Cup winner Owington. (Hamdan Al Maktoum). *"He's a typical Green Desert and*

is nicely put-together. A nice mover and a mid-season type two-year-old."

935. FORJATT (IRE) ★★★
b.c. Iffraaj – Graceful Air (Danzero).
March 17. Third foal. 60,000Y. Tattersalls October Book 2. Shadwell Estate Co. Half-brother to the fair 2009 2-y-o 6f winner Amenable (by Bertolini). The dam, a fair 8.3f and 10f winner, is a half-sister to the very useful 2-y-o 5f winner and Group 2 6f Mill Reef Stakes second Mystical Land. The second dam, Samsung Spirit (by Statoblest), a fair dual 6f winner (including at 2 yrs), is a half-sister to 7 winners and to the placed dam of the Group 2 6f Mill Reef Stakes winner Indian Rocket. (Sheikh Ahmed Al Maktoum). *"We trained Iffraaj and he was a big horse, but this looks a sharp two-year-old. He's big enough though and we'll be getting on with him because he was bought as a potential two-year-old type."*

936. GARMOOSHA (USA) ★★
b.f. Kingmambo – Eswarah (Unfuwain).
The dam won the Group 1 Epsom Oaks and is a half-sister to numerous winners including the Group 3 12f Princess Royal Stakes winner Itnab and the Irish 1,000 Guineas third Umniyatee. The second dam, Midway Lady (by Alleged), won the Prix Marcel Boussac, the 1,000 Guineas and the Oaks and is a half-sister to 5 winners including the very useful 11.8f listed winner Capias. (Hamdan Al Maktoum). *"Still in Dubai until mid-April."*

937. INDIAN MIST (IRE) ★★★
gr.f. Cape Cross – Indian Belle (Indian Ridge).
April 6. Third foal. 75,000Y. Tattersalls October Book 1. Will Edmeades. Half-sister to the fairly useful Irish 5f winner Sioduil (by Oasis Dream). The dam, a fairly useful Irish 10f winner, is a half-sister to 3 winners. The second dam, Abyat (by Shadeed), is an unraced half-sister to 9 winners including the Group 1 Middle Park Stakes winner Hayil. (Thurloe Thoroughbred XXVII). *"She's done well since she's been in, having originally looked a bit weak after being broken in. Having said that she's going to be an autumn two-year-old."*

938. JAARYAH (IRE) ★★
ch.f. Halling – Albahja (Sinndar).

March 1. Second foal. Half-sister to the 2009 7f placed 2-y-o (on her only start) Kronful (by Singspiel). The dam, a useful 12f winner, was second in the Group 3 10f Golden Daffodil Stakes and in the listed 12f Galtres Stakes and is a half-sister to one winner. The second dam, Eshq Albahr (by Riverman), is an unraced half-sister to the useful 1m to 10f winner Dayflower. (Sheikh Ahmed Al Maktoum). *"Quite typical of Halling, she's a nice mover and has good conformation, but very much from a staying family and is one for the second half of the year."*

939. JIWEN (USA) ★★★★
b.br.f. Singspiel – Love Medicine (Mining).
March 25. Sixth foal. $300,000Y. Saratoga August. Shadwell Estate Co. Half-sister to 4 winners including the US Grade 1 winner I'm The Tiger (by Siphon). The dam, a minor stakes winner in the USA, is a half-sister to 8 winners including the stakes winners Intern and Hot Lear. The second dam, Medicine Woman (by Dr Blum), was a Grade 3 stakes winner in the USA. *"Still in Dubai until mid-April, but I've heard that they like her over there."*

940. KAWSSAJ ★★
b.c. Dubawi – Ameerat (Mark Of Esteem).
March 11. Half-brother to Sowaylm (by Tobougg), a winner over 1m at 2 yrs in 2009 and to the quite useful 7f winner Own Boss (by Seeking The Gold). The dam won the 1,000 Guineas and is a full or half-sister to 3 winners including the smart UAE 1m winner of 11 races Walmooh. The second dam, Walimu (by Top Ville), a quite useful winner of 3 races from 1m to 12f, is a half-sister to 6 winners. (Sheikh Ahmed Al Maktoum). *"He's on the small side and he needs to grow and improve, so I'll hold judgement on him for now."*

941. LAAJOOJ (IRE) ★★★★
b.c. Azamour – Flanders (Common Grounds).
May 12. Seventh foal. 150,000Y. Tattersalls October Book 2. Shadwell Estate Co. Half-brother to the fair 2009 2-y-o 5f winner Desert Poppy (by Oasis Dream), to the US Grade 3 Miesque Stakes winner Louvain (by Sinndar), the fairly useful Irish 10f Lagoon (by Montjeu), the fair 2-y-o 6f all-weather winner My Love Thomas (by Cadeaux Genereux), the modest 7f

winner Wallonia (by Barathea) and the minor German 3-y-o winner Farbenspiel (by Desert Prince). The dam, a very useful sprint winner of 6 races including the listed Scarborough Stakes, was second in the Group 2 Kings Stand Stakes and is a half-sister to 7 winners. The second dam, Family at War (by Explodent), a fair 2-y-o 5f winner, is a half-sister to 4 minor winners in the USA. (Sheikh Ahmed Al Maktoum). *"He was a May foal and looks a little bit immature at the moment, but he's a scopey horse with a good action and is a horse we like. He goes well, needs a bit more confidence, but could be one of our nicer types."*

942. MARHABA ★★★
b.f. Nayef – Sil Sila (Marju).
January 23. Seventh foal. 160,000foal. Tattersalls December. Shadwell Estate Co. Half-sister to the US listed stakes winner Sol Mi Fa (by Distant Music). The dam, winner of the Group 1 10.5f Prix de Diane and placed in the Fred Darling Stakes and the Musidora Stakes, is a half-sister to the useful 2-y-o 5f and 6f winner and Group 1 placed Frequent Flyer. The second dam, Porto Allegre (by Habitat), won once in Germany at 3 yrs and is a half-sister to 4 winners. (Hamdan Al Maktoum). *"Quite a rangy filly, but an exceptionally good mover. One for seven furlongs plus and from July onwards, she's a nice filly."*

943. MASHAAREF ★★★
b.c. Cape Cross – Etizaaz (Diesis).
May 6. Seventh foal. Half-brother to the fair 2009 7f and 1m placed 2-y-o Munsarim (by Shamardal), to the fairly useful 1m (at 2 yrs) and 10f winner Almiqdaad (by Haafhd) and the smart 6f (including at 2 yrs) and listed 7f winner of 6 races Munaddam (by Aljabr). The dam, a listed 1m winner and second in the Group 1 12f Prix Vermeille, is a half-sister to the listed 6f Sirenia Stakes winner Santolina and the US Grade 3 7f Lafayette Stakes winner Trafalger. The second dam, Alamosa (by Alydar), is an unraced half-sister to the King George VI and Queen Elizabeth Diamond Stakes winner Swain out of the US Grade 1 winner Love Smitten. (Hamdan Al Maktoum). *"He's in Dubai and they tell me he's a scopey colt but until he arrives I can't tell you much about him."*

944. MIJHAAR ★★
b.c. Shirocco – Jathaabeh (Nashwan).
March 29. Sixth foal. Half-brother to the very useful 1m (including at 2 yrs) and 9f winner Yaddree (by Singspiel) and to the quite useful dual 1m winner Sky More (by Xaar). The dam, a useful dual 1m winner, is a half-sister to several winners including the useful 2-y-o Group 3 7f Prix du Calvados winner Kareymah. The second dam, Pastorale (by Nureyev), a fairly useful 3-y-o 7f winner, is a half-sister to the Group 1 Lockinge Stakes winner and high-class sire Cape Cross out of the dual Group 1 winning 2-y-o Park Appeal. (Sheikh Ahmed Al Maktoum). *"I like some of the Shirocco two-year-olds and the dam was a useful filly for us, but this colt is plain and distinctly an autumn type."*

945. MOON OVER WATER (IRE) ★★
b.f. Galileo – Velvet Moon (Shaadi).
February 11. Tenth living foal. 100,000Y. Tattersalls October Book 1. Badgers Bloodstock. Closely related to the minor French 15f winner Sirham (by Sadler's Wells) and half-sister to the Group 1 Dubai World Cup, Group 2 10.5f Dante Stakes and Group 3 10f Select Stakes winner Moon Ballad, the minor French 3-y-o winner Velvet Queen (both by Singspiel), the useful 1m winner Velvet Lady (by Nashwan) and the quite useful 11f winner Eta Draconis (by Daylami). The dam, a very useful Group 2 6f Lowther Stakes and listed 10f winner, is a half-sister to 6 winners including the Group 1 12f Italian Derby, Group 2 7f Lanson Champagne Stakes and German Group 2 12f winner Central Park and the Group 3 Lancashire Oaks winner Mellow Park. The second dam, Park Special (by Relkino), won over 10f at 3 yrs in Ireland and is a half-sister to the Group 3 winners Careafolie and Gouriev. (Moyns Park Estate & Stud Ltd). *"A good model, but on the small side and you'd be looking for seven furlongs plus in the autumn for her."*

946. MUJRAYAAT (IRE) ★★★★
b.c. Invincible Spirit – Ellen (Machiavellian).
February 24. Third foal. 280,000Y. Tattersalls October Book 1. Shadwell Estate Co. Half-brother to the French 4.5f and 5.5f 2-y-o winner and Group 3 Prix du Bois third Faslen

(by Fasliyev). The dam is an unraced half-sister to 2 winners including the Group 3 Winter Derby winner Gentleman's Deal. The second dam, Sleepytime (by Royal Academy), won the 1,000 Guineas and is a sister to the Group 1 winner Ali Royal and a half-sister to the Group 1 winner Taipan. (Hamdan Al Maktoum). *"He's well-grown and a good mover with good conformation. We're thinking of him being one of our two-year-old types. He's a good actioned horse, so we'll get on with him and he should be out in late May over six furlongs."*

947. NAHRAIN ★★★
ch.f. Selkirk – Bahr (Generous).
January 29. Sixth foal. Half-sister to the very useful dual listed 1m winner Baharah (by Elusive Quality), to the fairly useful 7.5f (at 2 yrs) and UAE 7f winner Naaddey (by Seeking The Gold), the fairly useful 2-y-o 1m winner In Dubai (by Giant's Causeway) and the quite useful 2-y-o 7f winner Raaeidd (by King's Best). The dam, winner of the listed 7f Washington Singer Stakes (at 2 yrs), the Group 3 12f Ribblesdale Stakes and the Group 3 10.4f Musidora Stakes, is a half-sister to numerous winners. (Sheikh Ahmed Al Maktoum). *"Although she's an early foal she's big and quite backward, so she'll be aimed at seven furlongs in the second half of the year."*

948. ROMAN EAGLE (IRE) ★★★★
b.c. Holy Roman Emperor – Qhazeenah (Marju).
March 3. Sixth foal. 90,000Y. Tattersalls October Book 1. M Jarvis. Closely related to the modest 2009 5f placed 2-y-o Robens Rock, to the French winner and listed 10.5f placed Londonintherain and the quite useful 10.5f and 11f winner Soul Mountain (both by Rock Of Gibraltar) and half-brother to the US Grade 2 winner Girl Warrior (by Elusive Quality). The dam, a useful 6.5f (at 2 yrs) to 7f winner, is a half-sister to 9 winners including the smart Group 2 14.6f Park Hill Stakes winner Ranin, the very useful 7f and 1m winner Ghalib and the useful 2-y-o 1m and listed 9f placed Wahchi. The second dam, Nafhaat (by Roberto), a fairly useful 12f winner, stayed 15f. (A D Spence). *"He looks like a two-year-old type, he's sharp and will be one of our early runners. He might have the speed for five furlongs and is a compact colt."*

949. ROMANY STONE (IRE) ★★★★
ch.f. Pivotal – Celtic Heroine (Hernando).
April 3. Second foal. 120,000Y. Tattersalls October Book 1. Not sold. The dam, a smart 7f (at 2 yrs) and 1m listed winner, is a half-sister to 3 winners. The second dam, Celtic Fling (Lion Cavern), a fair 3-y-o 8.3f winner, is a half-sister to the outstanding champion 2-y-o Celtic Swing, winner of the French Derby and the Racing Post Trophy. (P D Savill). *"A nice filly and she's a little bit more athletic than most Pivotal's because a lot of them come a bit later, but this looks like a mid-summer two-year-old. She's done well since being broken and looks quite nice. She should be a seven furlong filly and she has good prospects."*

950. RUN RABBIT RUN ★★★
b.c. Hurricane Run – Triple Gold (Goldmark).
March 10. Third foal. 110,000Y. Tattersalls October Book 2. M Jarvis. Half-brother to the minor US winner of 3 races Goin For The Gold (by Pulpit). The dam, a quite useful 7f (including at 2 yrs) and 1m winner, is a half-sister to 3 winners including Melina Mou (listed Prix de la Seine and herself dam of the US Grade 2 winner Leprechaun Kid). The second dam, Gold Necklace (both by Golden Fleece), a quite useful Irish 2-y-o 7f winner, is a half-sister to 3 winners. (A D Spence). *"He's a big, immature horse at present and one for the back-end of the season and next year. He's nice though and we'll be looking at the mile maidens at the back-end."*

951. SUHAILI ★★★★★★♠
b.c. Shirocco – Mezzogiorno (Unfuwain).
February 29. Ninth foal. 165,000Y. Tattersalls October Book 1. Charlie Gordon-Watson. Half-brother to the Group 2 Blandford Stakes winner Monturani (by Indian Ridge), to the smart 6f and 7f listed winner Monnavanna, the hurdles winner Menelaus (both by Machiavellian), the very useful 2-y-o 7f winner Mezuzah (by Barathea) and the fair 10f and hurdles winner Monterrico (by Dubai Destination). The dam, a very useful 7f (at 2 yrs) and 10f listed winner, was third in the Oaks is a half-sister to 3 winners. The second dam, Aigue (by High Top), a fairly useful 4-y-o dual 1m winner, is a sister to the listed middle-distance winner Torchon and a half-sister to 2

winners. (B E Nielsen). *"He's a good-looking colt, well-grown and a very good mover. Hard to fault, he's a nice horse and in the second half of the year he'll be really nice if he's as good as he looks."*

952. SWIMSUIT ★★
b.f. Sleeping Indian – Love Quest (Pursuit Of Love).
April 12. Fourth foal. 23,000Y. Tattersalls October Book 2. R Varian. Half-brother to the fair dual 5f winner La Zamora (by Lujain). The dam is an unraced half-sister to 4 winners. The second dam, Sky Red (by Night Shift), a fair 5f winner of 3 races, is a sister to the French listed winner Shoalhaven. (S Dartnell). *"She wasn't very healthy over the winter so she's only just come into training. She's got good conformation and I'd like to think she'll make a two-year-old, but we don't know much about her yet."*

953. TAFANEEN (USA) ★★★
b.br.f. Dynaformer – Cozzy Corner (Cozzene).
May 6. Third foal. $700,000Y. Keeneland September. Shadwell Estate Co. The dam, a US Grade 3 winner, is a half-sister to the US triple Grade 1 winner Riskaverse. The second dam, The Bink (by Seeking The Gold), won 3 races and was Grade 3 in the USA. *"Still in Dubai until mid-April."*

954. TARKEEBA (USA) ★★★
ch.f. Halling – Zarara (Manila).
April 29. Seventh foal. 150,000Y. Tattersalls October Book 1. Shadwell Estate Co. Sister to Hudoo, a fair 7f winner on his only start at 2 yrs in 2009 and half-sister to the very useful 10f (at 2yrs) to 14f and subsequent Australian Group 1 12f Caulfield Cup winner All The Good (by Diesis) and to the minor Italian winner of 3 races Grey Latino (by Daylami). The dam is an unraced half-sister to 10 winners including the Oaks, Irish Oaks and Yorkshire Oaks winner Ramruma and the Lingfield Oaks Trial winner Ausherra (herself dam of the Group 2 winner Strategic Prince). The second dam, Princess Of Man (by Green God), won three races including the Group 3 Musidora Stakes and is a half-sister to 6 winners. (Hamdan Al Maktoum). *"A medium-sized filly with good conformation, she looks one for the second half of the season. Very typical of her sire, I quite like her."*

955. TOOLAIN (IRE) ★★★
br.c. Diktat – Qasirah (Machiavellian).
March 10. Second foal. Brother to the fair 7f winner Kammaan. The dam, a useful 2-y-o 6f winner, was third in the Group 3 8.5f Princess Margaret Stakes is out of the this useful 10.5f and 12f winner Altaweelah (by Fairy King), herself a half-sister to numerous winners including the useful 10f to 14f winner Lost Soldier Three. (Sheikh Ahmed Al Maktoum). *"We had the dam and also this colt's full sister Kammaan who wanted mud up to her hocks like a lot of Diktats. He takes after her in that regard, the mare gets good-looking stock and he looks like a two-year-old type, so we'll kick on with him in late spring."*

956. ZOOWRAA ★★★
b.f. Azamour – Beraysim (Lion Cavern).
March 17. Half-sister to the useful 6f to 1m UAE winner of 5 races Almaram (by A P Indy), to the quite useful 2-y-o 7f winner Jadaara (by Red Ransom) and the fair 9.5f winner Noubian (by Diesis). The dam, a very useful winner of the listed 7f Oak Tree Stakes, is a half-sister to the useful 2-y-o 7f winner Velour. The second dam, Silk Braid (by Danzig), was a useful winner of a 3-y-o 9f York maiden and a 12f Italian listed event and is a half-sister to the Belmont and Preakness Stakes winner and champion 3-y-o colt Risen Star. (Sheikh Ahmed Al Maktoum). *"We've had a couple of disappointments out of this mare, but this is a better model. She's a little bit on the nervous side but quite athletic so we hope we'll get more success out of her than most of her siblings."*

957. UNNAMED ★★★★
b.f. Street Cry – Always Awesome (Awesome Again).
May 25. Third foal. $100,000Y. Saratoga August. Blandford Bloodstock. The dam, a stakes-placed winner in Canada, is a half-sister to 7 winners including the Group 1 Deuschland Preis winner Anzillero. The second dam, Anzille (by Plugged Nickle), is a placed half-sister to the Prix de l'Arc de Triomphe winner and outstanding broodmare Urban Sea and the 2,000 Guineas winner King's Best. (S Ali). *"A tall,*

athletic filly from a lovely family, she goes nicely and for a Street Cry she could be well-bought at that price, but because of her late foaling date we won't be in a hurry with her."

958. UNNAMED ★★★★
ch.f. Medicean – Fur Will Fly (Petong).
April 28. Eighth living foal. 75,000Y. Tattersalls October Book 2. Rabbah Bloodstock. Half-sister to the 2009 2-y-o Group 2 5f Flying Childers Stakes and listed St Hugh's Stakes winner Sand Vixen (by Dubawi), to the smart listed 6f winner and Group 3 Greenham Stakes third So Will I, the fair 6f winner Rubies (both by Inchinor) and the fair 2-y-o 6f winner Lille Ida (by Hawk Wing). The dam was placed once over 6f at 3 yrs and is a half-sister to 4 winners. The second dam, Bumpkin (by Free State), was a useful sprint winner of 4 races and a half-sister to 7 winners including the prolific 7f to 9f winner On Edge. (Saif Ali & Saeed H Altayer). *"She could be a nice, sharp filly. She'll be a two-year-old and is reasonably well-grown but quite athletic. In May or June time we'll be getting on with her and I think she'll go six furlongs."*

959. UNNAMED ★★★
ch.f. Monsun – Geminiani (King Of Kings).
April 15. Fourth foal. 170,000Y. Tattersalls October Book 1. Anthony Stroud. Half-sister to Gay Mirage (by Highest Honor), unplaced in one start at 2 yrs in 2009 and to the fairly useful 11f and 14f winner and Group 3 2m second Amerigo (by Daylami). The dam, winner of the Group 3 7f Prestige Stakes and second in the Group 3 Musidora Stakes, is a half-sister to 4 winners including the 2-y-o Group 1 6f Phoenix Stakes and Group 2 5f Queen Mary Stakes winner Damson. The second dam, Tadkiyra (by Darshaan), won over 10f at 3 yrs in France and is a half-sister to 8 winners including the Group 3 winners Tashtiya, Tassmoun and Tashkourgan. (B E Nielsen). *"It's very much a staying family and being by Monsun she'll need time, but she's a better type than both Gay Mirage and Amerigo so she'll be out from August onwards over seven furlongs and a mile."*

960. UNNAMED ★★★★♠
b.c. Cape Cross – Harda Arda (Nureyev).
February 16. Sixth foal. 150,000Y. Tattersalls

October Book 1. Charlie Gordon-Watson. Half-brother to the minor US stakes winner Strike Rate (by Smart Strike), to the fair 6f and 7f winner My Sweet Georgia (by Royal Applause) and the modest 10.5f winner Deccan Express (by Grand Lodge) and a minor US winner by A P Indy. The dam, a minor Irish 3-y-o 9f winner, is a half-sister to 8 winners including the Group 2 10f Derrinstown Stud Derby Trial and dual US Grade 2 winner Phantom Breeze. The second dam, Ask The Wind (by Run The Gantlet), was a useful winner of 3 races from 7f to 10f including the listed Hard Fought Stakes, was fourth in the Ribblesdale Stakes and is a half-sister to 4 minor winners. (H R H Sultan Ahmad Shah). *"A very good-looking horse. He and Suhaili are probably our two best looking colts. He's strong with good conformation and a good attitude, he goes nicely and could be a mid-summer two-year-old over seven furlongs, then we'll see where we go from there."*

961. UNNAMED ★★
b.c. Montjeu – Najmati (Green Desert).
March 18. Second foal. 250,000Y. Tattersalls October Book 1. Charlie Gordon-Watson. The dam was placed in the UAE and is a sister to the high-class Group 2 6f Lowther Stakes and Group 3 5f Queen Mary Stakes winner Bint Allayl and to the smart 2-y-o 5f and 6f and 3-y-o Group 3 7f Jersey Stakes winner Kheleyf and a half-sister to the French Group 3 winner Laa Rayb. The second dam, Society Lady (by Mr Prospector), a fair 6f and 7f placed 2-y-o, is a full or half-sister to 9 winners including the US Grade 3 winner Time Bandit. (H R H Sultan Ahmed Shah). *"He's quite a lengthy colt and stands over a fair bit of ground. A rangy type of horse that moves quite nicely, but he's one for the back-end of the season."*

962. UNNAMED ★★
b.c. Dubai Destination – Noushkey (Polish Precedent).
January 21. Half-brother to the quite useful 11f winner Anaamil (by Darshaan), to the quite useful 9f and hurdles winner January (by Daylami), the fair 10f winner Zemario (by Dalakhani) and a winner in Greece by Fantastic Light. The dam, a winner over 7f (at 2 yrs) and the Group 3 12f Lancashire Oaks, is a half-sister to 9 winners including the Group 1 2m 2f Prix du

Cadran winner San Sebastian and the German listed winner and Group 1 placed Chesa Plana (herself dam of the Japan Cup and Grand Prix de Saint-Cloud winner Alkaased). The second dam, Top Of The League (by High Top), a quite useful 2-y-o 7f winner, is a half-sister to 3 winners. (Sheikh Ahmed Al Maktoum). *"He's done well since he was broken in but he won't be out until the back-end."*

963. UNNAMED ★★★
b.f. Oasis Dream – Persian Jasmine (Dynaformer).
February 12. First foal. 80,000Y. Tattersalls October Book 1. Rabbah Bloodstock. The dam, a quite useful 2-y-o 7f winner, is a half-sister to 3 winners. The second dam, Rumpipumpy (by Shirley Heights), won 6 races in the USA including the Grade 2 Diana Handicap and is a half-sister to 10 winners including the Irish 1,000 Guineas winner Classic Park. (Saif Ali & Saeed H Altayer). *"Quite a nice filly, she's medium-sized, goes quite nicely and could be a mid-summer two-year-old."*

964. UNNAMED ★★★
b.f. Cape Cross – Pickle (Piccolo).
March 3. First foal. 40,000Y. Tattersalls October Book 1. Rabbah Bloodstock. The dam won 7 races here and in the USA including the Grade 2 Wilshire Handicap and the Grade 3 Yerba Buena Breeders Cup Handicap and is a half-sister to 2 winners abroad. The second dam, Crackle (by Anshan), a quite useful 5.7f (at 2 yrs) to 10f winner, is a half-sister to 5 winners. (Saif Ali and Saeed H Altayer). *"After being quite small as a yearling she's grown and has done well and is certainly big enough now. She goes quite nicely and is one for the second half of the year."*

965. UNNAMED ★★
b.c. Tiger Hill – Zayn Zen (Singspiel).
February 19. First foal. The dam, a useful 1m listed winner of 3 races, is a sister to the fairly useful 1m, 10f and UAE winner Zaafran. The second dam, Roshani (by Kris), a fair 1m and 10f winner at 3 yrs, is a half-sister to 8 minor winners here and in the USA. (Sheikh Ahmed Al Maktoum). *"He's quite a nice horse but being by Tiger Hill out a mare that got ten furlongs I'm expecting him to be much more of a three-year-old type. There's nothing wrong with him, he's quite nicely made and we'll be looking at the seven furlong and mile races in the autumn for him."*

WILLIAM JARVIS

966. INSIDIOUS ★★
b.c. Sakhee – Inseparable (Insan).
February 29. Sixth foal. 8,500Y. Tattersalls October 3. Blandford Bloodstock. Half-brother to the French dual 1m winner Saint Saens (by Pennekamp). The dam won over 11f in France and is a half-sister to 3 winners including the French Group 3 placed Maidment. The second dam, Lady Gerardina (by Levmoss), won 2 races at 2 and 3 yrs and is a half-sister to 8 winners including the Champagne Stakes winner Saintly Song. (Mr J Bowditch). *"I loved him at the Sales and I thought he was a cheap purchase. Sakhee is obviously capable breeding good horses and this colt is a good size and he has the right attitude. I like him."*

967. LADY WOODCOTE ★★★★
b.f. Pivotal – Ruby Rocket (Indian Rocket).
February 11. Second foal. 115,000Y. Tattersalls October Book 1. Ric Wylie. The dam, a listed 5f and 6f winner, was Group 3 placed twice and is a half-sister to 8 winners including the Irish 2-y-o 6f listed winner Alexander Alliance and the German listed winner and Group 3 6.5f Prix Eclipse second Inzar's Best. The second dam, Geht Schnell (by Fairy King), is a placed half-sister to one winner abroad. (Mr K J Hickman). *"Quite a smart little filly. Everything's OK with her, Pivotal is obviously a great stallion and the dam was pretty fast herself. Being critical she just possibly lacks an inch, but I expect her to be a summer two-year-old and she'll have the speed for six furlongs."*

968. QUSHCHI ★★★
b.f. Encosta De Lago – La Persiana (Daylami).
April 15. Second foal. Half-sister to Perse (by Rock Of Gibraltar), unplaced in one start at 2 yrs in 2009. The dam, a very useful dual listed 10f winner, is a half-sister to the champion 2-y-o Grand Lodge (Group 1 7f Dewhurst Stakes and Group 1 1m St James's Palace Stakes winner), to the useful 1m listed winner Papabile and the useful 10f winner Savannah.

The second dam, La Papagena (by Habitat), is an unraced half-sister to 7 winners including the very useful 7f and 1m winner Pamina and the very useful 11f and 12.5f winner Lost Chord. (Gillian, Lady Howard de Walden). *"This filly is from a family we know very well and it's apparent that they aren't really two-year-olds. This filly is typical of the family, she's very likeable, I should imagine she'll be an autumn two-year-old and the way she moves is very reminiscent of the family."*

969. UNNAMED ★★★★
b.f. Shamardal – Bronwen (King's Best).
March 23. Second foal. 30,000Y. Tattersalls October Book 2. W Jarvis. The dam, a fairly useful 9f to 15f winner, is a half-sister to numerous winners including the Group 1 Fillies Mile and Group 3 May Hill Stakes winner Teggiano. The second dam, Tegwen (by Nijinsky), a quite useful 10f winner, is a half-sister to 4 winners. (A S Belhab). *"I like this filly, she's big and scopey with a good action and a good nature. She's lovely, she's going nicely and will be a summer two-year-old."*

970. UNNAMED ★★★
b.c. Holy Roman Emperor – Sassy Bird (Storm Bird).
May 2. Eleventh foal. 78,000Y. Tattersalls October Book 1. W Jarvis. Half-brother to 5 winners including the very useful listed 10f winner and Group 2 Ribblesdale Stakes third Asawer (by Darshaan), the French listed 6f and 7f winner Chercheuse, the minor US winner Osprey (both by Seeking The Gold), the smart French 11f and 12f winner Sasanuma (by Kingmambo) and a minor French 15f winner by Benny The Dip. The dam is a placed sister to the Group 2 1m John Roarty Memorial and Group 3 7f Lanson Champagne Vintage Stakes winner Mukaddamah and the US listed winner Contempt and a three-parts sister to the Group 3 7.3f Horris Hill Stakes winner Tatami. The second dam, Tash (by Never Bend), won twice over 6f at 2 yrs in the USA and is a half-sister to the high-class winners Arkadina, Truly Bound, Gregorian and Blood Royal. (J Kelsey-Fry). *"A late foal and he's still got some growing to do but he's not a bad sort and he's growing nicely. He has a good attitude and he points his toe when he's going up the hill nicely, so* we're hopeful. He'll make a six furlong two-year-old."

971. UNNAMED ★★★
b.c. Tobougg – Western Sal (Salse).
February 16. 10,000Y. Tattersalls October Book 3. Blandford Bloodstock. Half-brother to the fair 2-y-o 6f winner Just One Look (by Barathea), to the Italian 2-y-o 7f winner Pemba (by First Trump) and the German winner and Group 2 German St Leger second Western Devil (by Dr Devious). The dam, a fair 10f and 12f winner, is a half-sister to 7 winners including the dual Group 3 winner and 2,000 Guineas third Redback. The second dam, Patsy Western (by Precocious), a quite useful 3-y-o 6f winner, is a half-sister to 7 winners including the Queen Anne Stakes winner Mr Fluorocarbon and the Cornwallis Stakes winner Western Jewel. *"I like him and I've had a bit of luck with Tobouggs although he's not everyone's cup of tea. This colt has a good attitude and he's been going up Warren Hill well. We like what we've seen so far."*

EVE JOHNSON HOUGHTON

972. ALLTHERIGHTMOVES (IRE) ★★★
b.f. Namid – Russian Countess (Nureyev).
March 29. Sixteenth foal. £32,000Y. Doncaster St Leger. Emerald Bloodstock. Half-sister to 9 winners including the quite useful 2009 2-y-o 5f winner and listed-placed The Hermitage, to the quite useful dual 5f winner Crimea (both by Kheleyf), the smart 7f (at 2 yrs) and 11.5f winner and Epsom Oaks third Crown Of Light (by Mtoto), the very useful 2-y-o listed 1m Stardom Stakes winner and Group 1 Grand Criterium third Alboostan (by Sabrehill), the useful 7.5f and 8.5f winner Romanzof (by Kris), the Irish 6f winners Russian Empress (by Trans Island), Russian Waltz (by Spectrum) and Cossack Count (by Nashwan) and a winner in Belgium by Reference Point. The dam, a useful French 2-y-o 1m winner and listed-placed, is a half-sister to 5 winners. The second dam, Countess Tully (by Hotfoot), won 4 races here and in the USA and was placed in the Brownstown Stakes and the Princess Royal Stakes and is a half-sister to 6 winners. (Mrs R Burns). *"At first I thought she was going to be early, but she'll be ready in late April or early May. A compact filly, she's very light on her*

feet and I like her. She's been doing all the right things at home and she'll stay further than five furlongs. I'm really pleased with the quality of my two-year-olds. Last year they were better than the previous year and once again I think we've moved up a level."

973. KINGARRICK ★★★
ch.c. Selkirk – Rosacara (Green Desert).
March 12. Half-brother to the fair 2-y-o 7f winner Papa Meilland (by Dr Fong). The dam, a modest 7f and 1m placed maiden, is a half-sister to the high-class triple Group 1 winner Notnowcato. The second dam, Rambling Rose (by Cadeaux Genereux), won over 8.2f (at 2 yrs) and the listed 12f Galtres Stakes. (Miss Y Jacques). "A nice sort, I had his half-brother who won as two-year-old and this looks much more of a two-year-old type. He's not overly big, but he's just starting to grow on me now. I think he'll be out by the beginning of June and he goes very nicely. For a Selkirk he's quite a compact horse, but hopefully he's not deceiving me because Selkirk's aren't usually as early as he seems likely to be. He'll start at six but I suspect he'll progress to seven furlongs and a mile later in the year."

974. KYNCRAIGHE (IRE) ★★★
b.c. Kyllachy – Brighella (Sadler's Wells).
March 24. Third foal. 20,000Y. Tattersalls October Book 2. Eve Johnson Houghton. The dam, placed once at 3 yrs in France, is a half-sister to 3 winners including the French listed winner Nid d'Abeilles. The second dam, Massarossa (by Mr Prospector), is an unplaced full or half-sister to 4 winners. (Deal, Brown & Wallis). "He's a really nice horse, he doesn't show up well in the box but as soon as you get the tack and a rider on him, he really pulls himself together and carries himself well. It shouldn't be long before he's out and he has plenty of toe."

975. LOVAT LANE ★★★★
b.f. Avonbridge – Pudding Lane (College Chapel).
May 19. Brother to Hounds Ditch, unplaced in two starts at 2 yrs in 2009 and half-brother to the very useful listed 5f and 6f winner of 10 races Judd Street (by Compton Place). The dam, a modest maiden, ran only at 2 yrs and stayed 7f and is a half-sister to 2 winners. The second dam, Fire Of London (by Shirley Heights), was placed over 10f and is a full or half-sister to 9 winners. (R F Johnson-Houghton). "The mare hasn't done anything apart from breed Judd Street, but this one looks the fastest since him. Even though the whole family have taken time to mature, she looks quite sharp and she'll be a sprinter. I'd like to win a race with her early doors before giving her a break because all the family grow, then I could bring her back at the end of the season."

976. MRS GREELEY ★★
b.f. Mr Greeley – Swain's Gold (Swain).
March 23. Third foal. 34,000Y. Tattersalls October Book 2. Not sold. The dam won 3 minor races at 3 yrs in the USA and is a half-sister to the US stakes winner Brazilian. The second dam, Golden Pond (by Don't Forget Me), won 7 races including the Grade 2 12f Orchid Handicap, the Grade 3 8.5f Suwannee River Handicap and the listed Prix de la Cochere a maiden who stayed 12f, is a half-sister to 3 winners. (Mrs R Arber). "She's a very nice filly with a beautiful top to her but she isn't very correct in front, so I've just got to be a bit careful with her. She's not going to be early because she's a big filly. I don't know too much about the sire, but seven furlongs around September time should be alright for her."

977. ORIENTALIST ★★★★
ch.c. Haafhd – Oriental Queen (Big Shuffle).
February 7. Third foal. 14,000Y. Tattersalls October Book 2. Eve Johnson Houghton. Half-brother to the fair 1m winner Hucking Heist (by Desert Style). The dam won once at 3 yrs in Germany and is a full or half-sister to 10 winners including 3 German listed winners. The second dam, Orange Bowl (by General Assembly), is an unraced half-sister to 4 winners. (Eden Racing IV). "He's a lovely horse. If ever I've seen a two-year-old, this is it! Really strong and compact, everything is in the right place and he looks a million dollars. He had just a touch of a sore shin otherwise I'd have run him by now, but as it is he'll be out by the first week in May because he's done two bits of work and when he's done two more I think he'll be ready to run. I really like this horse and I've never sold shares in one like it – people were queuing up! He has bags of

scope and he'll be coming out at the sort of time when we can pick either five furlongs or six, but I wouldn't mind starting him in either." TRAINERS' BARGAIN BUY

978. STRENGTH AND STAY (IRE) ★★★
b.c. Motivator – Queen's Cape (King's Best).
April 11. First foal. 10,000foal. Tattersalls December. Not sold. The dam ran once unplaced in France and is a half-sister to one winner. The second dam, Cape Grace (by Priolo), won the listed Dahlia Stakes and is a half-sister to 2 winners. (Mrs V D Neale). *"He's my 'dark horse' and he won't be out until the back-end. He's a big colt and the most beautiful mover that looks like being alright. He'll want at least seven furlongs and although he hasn't got speed he's got a lovely, long, flowing action and when the longer races come out he should come into his own."*

979. THUNDA ★★
b.f. Stormy Atlantic – Lobby Card (Saint Ballado).
February 23. Third living foal. 6,000Y. Tattersalls December. Eve Johnson Houghton. Half-sister to the minor US 3-y-o winner One Sheet (by Flying Chevron). The dam, placed once at 3 yrs in the USA, is a half-sister to 6 winners including the Japanese £2 million earner Biko Pegasus and the unraced dam of the New Zealand Grade 1 winner Redoute's Dancer. The second dam, Condessa (by Condorcet), won the Group 1 Yorkshire Oaks and the Group 3 Musidora Stakes and is a half-sister to 3 winners. (Mrs C J Hue Williams). *"She's going to take time as she's quite big and rangy and she's hanging onto her coat like no other horse in the yard. So I haven't pressed any buttons with her yet, but I like her very much. The sire has done very well in the States, he's a proper turf stallion, so there's no reason why this filly shouldn't be alright."*

980. UNNAMED ★★★
b.f. Sleeping Indian – Crofters Ceilidh (Scottish Reel).
March 29. Tenth foal. 20,000Y. Tattersalls October Book 2. Threeways Bloodstock. Half-sister to the useful 2-y-o 5f and 6f winner Cop Hill Lad (by Atraf), to the fairly useful listed 7f winner Clifton Dancer (by Fraam), the fair 2-y-o 5f winner Bahamian Ceilidh (by Bahamian Bounty), the fair 2-y-o 6f winner Okikoki (by Ishiguru) and the modest 5f winner of 4 races (including at 2 yrs) Making Music (by Makbul). The dam won 3 races over 5f including at 2 yrs and was listed placed. She is a half-sister to 4 winners including the useful 5f and 6f winner and Group 2 placed Lord Kintyre. The second dam, Highland Rowena (by Royben), a modest sprint winner of 4 races, is a half-sister to 2 minor winners. (Mr D Redvers).

981. UNNAMED ★★
b.c. Aussie Rules – Shariyfa (Zayyani).
May 3. Seventh foal. 10,000Y. Tattersalls October Book 2. Eve Johnson Houghton. Half-brother to the Italian listed winner of 4 races at 2 and 3 yrs Breaking Out (by Eagle Eyed), to a minor winner in USA by Dixieland Band and a winner in Spain by Real Quiet. The dam is an unraced half-sister to 2 winners and to the unraced dam of the multiple Group 1 winner Sendawar. The second dam, Sherniya (by Empery), ran twice unplaced. (Mrs M Findlay). *"He went backward on me a month ago after showing quite a bit early on, so he's not as early as I expected him to be. He's just waiting for some nice weather."*

MARK JOHNSTON

982. BIRDWATCHER (IRE) ★★★
ch.c. Cadeaux Genereux – Dancing Feather (Suave Dancer).
February 19. Eighth foal. 60,000Y. Tattersalls October Book 1. Mark Johnston. Half-brother to the fairly useful 1m (listed) and 9f winner of 4 races at 4 yrs Wagtail (by Cape Cross), to the fairly useful 2-y-o 7f winner and listed placed Feathers Flying, the fairly useful dual 7f winner Carniolan (both by Royal Applause), the quite useful dual 10f winner Featherweight (by Fantastic Light), the quite useful all-weather 1m (at 2 yrs) and 8.5f winner King's Empire (by Second Empire) and the quite useful 2-y-o dual 6f winner Feather Boa (by Sri Pekan). The dam, a fair 4-y-o 1m winner, stayed 12f and is a half-sister to 8 winners including the Group 3 Prix Cleopatre winner Spring Oak and the 10f Lupe Stakes winner Fragrant Hill (herself dam of the French Group 1 winner Fragrant Mix). The second dam, English Spring (by Grey Dawn II), won 7 races from 1m to 10f including

the Group 2 Prince of Wales's Stakes and is a half-sister to the US Grade 1 winner Dance of Life. (Sheikh Hamdan Bin Mohammed Al Maktoum).

983. COLEBROOKE ★★★
b.c. Shamardal – Shimna (Mr Prospector).
April 25. Seventh foal. 90,000Y. Tattersalls October Book 1. Mark Johnston. Half-brother to the 2009 1m placed 2-y-o Bab Al Shams, to the quite useful dual 10f winner Black Eagle (both by Cape Cross), the useful 2-y-o 7f winner Santa Fe (by Green Desert), the useful 1m (at 2 yrs) and 10f winner and Group 3 Derby Trial second Hazeymm (by Marju) and the fairly useful 1m (at 2 yrs) and dual 10f winner Sahrati (by In The Wings). The dam, placed fourth over 10f in Ireland on her only outing, is a half-sister to the St Leger and Gran Premio del Jockey Club winner Shantou. The second dam, Shaima (by Shareef Dancer), a very useful 7.3f (at 2 yrs) and 9f listed winner here, later won the Grade 2 12f Long Island Handicap and is a half-sister to 6 winners including the Prix Saint Alary winner Rosefinch. (Sheikh Hamdan Bin Mohammed Al Maktoum).

984. COLONEL PERCY (IRE) ★★★
ch.c. Danehill Dancer – Elite Guest (Be My Guest).
May 5. Eleventh foal. €50,000Y. Goffs Orby. Mark Johnston. Brother to the modest 2009 1m placed 2-y-o Banana Republic and to the fair 7f winner Coat Of Arms, closely related to the Group 3 6.3f Anglesey Stakes winner Amigoni and to the Irish 2-y-o 5f listed and 3-y-o 7f listed winner Newton (both by Danehill) and half-brother to the French 9f (at 2 yrs) to 10.5f winner of 5 races and Group 2 placed Hesiode and the minor French winner of 5 races Bazbine (both by Highest Honor). The dam, a French 3-y-o winner and third in the Group 3 10.5f Prix de Royaumont, is a sister to Admire Lapis (a winner of 6 races in Japan) and a half-sister to 8 winners including the smart Group 3 2m Jockey Club Cup winner Capal Garmon. The second dam, Elevate (by Ela-Mana-Mou), a fairly useful dual 3-y-o 12f winner, was listed placed and is a half-sister to the top-class winners Sun Princess and Saddlers Hall. (Mr J A Barson).

985. DORDOGNE (IRE) ★★
b.br.c. Singspiel – Riberac (Efisio).
May 9. Sixth foal. 27,000Y. Tattersalls October Book 2. Mark Johnston. Brother to the quite useful 1m winner of 3 races Montrachet and half-brother to the modest 12f all-weather winner Emilion. The dam, a smart winner of 10 races from 5f to 1m including three listed events, was third in the Group 2 Sun Chariot Stakes and is a full or half-sister to 4 winners. The second dam, Ciboure (by Norwick), was a fair 6f (at 2 yrs) and 1m winner and is a half-sister to 4 winners. (Sheikh Hamdan Bin Mohammed Al Maktoum).

986. DRESSING ROOM (USA) ★★★
b.br.c. Dixie Union – Green Room (Theatrical).
April 29. Third foal. 140,000Y. Tattersalls October Book 1. Mark Johnston. Half-brother to the 2009 6f and 7f placed 2-y-o Brannagh (by Hennessy) and to the very smart Group 1 Prix Jean Prat and Group 2 7f Mill Reef Stakes winner and Group 1 7f Dewhurst Stakes second Lord Shanakill (by Speightstown). The dam is an unraced half-sister to 5 winners including the Group 1 Yellow Ribbon Handicap winner Spanish Fern. The second dam, Chain Fern (by Blushing Groom), is an unraced sister to the Irish 1,000 Guineas and Coronation Stakes winner Al Bahathri (dam of the 2,000 Guineas and Champion Stakes winner Haafhd). (Sheikh Hamdan Bin Mohammed Al Maktoum).

987. EVENING DRESS ★★★
ch.f. Medicean – Miss Hawai (Peintre Celebre).
January 27. Fourth foal. 190,000Y. Tattersalls October Book 1. Mark Johnston. Half-sister to the quite useful 2009 6f and 7f placed 2-y-o Robinson Cruso (by Footstepsinthesand) and to the to the Irish listed 9f winner and Group 1 Pretty Polly Stakes second Beach Bunny (by High Chaparral). The dam is an unraced half-sister to 4 winners including the French listed winner Mer de Corail. The second dam, Miss Tahiti (by Tirol), won the Group 1 Prix Marcel Boussac and is a half-sister to 3 winners. (Sheikh Hamdan Bin Mohammed Al Maktoum).

988. GLITTER BUG (IRE) ★★★
b.c. Oasis Dream – Aethra (Trempolino).
March 11. Eighth foal. €85,000Y. Arqana Deauville August. M Johnston. Closely

related to the French listed 1m winner Kane Ore (by Green Desert) and half-brother to the useful 8.5f (at 2 yrs) and 10f winner Alphaeus (by Sillery), the fairly useful 12f and 14f winner Ogee (by Generous), the quite useful dual 1m winner Dalradian (by Dansili), the fair 5f and 7f winner Bob's Buzz (by Zilzal), the fair 9.5f winner View From The Top (by Mujahid) and the moderate 7f winner Barataria (by Barathea). The dam, a fairly useful 1m placed maiden, is a sister to the German listed winner Tamanna and a half-sister to 3 winners. The second dam, All For Hope (by Sensitive Prince), is an unraced half-sister to the 10.5f Prix de Diane winner Lacovia (herself the dam of the champion 2-y-o Tobougg). (A D Spence).

989. GOLDEN HINDE ★★★
b.c. Red Ransom – Treacle
(Seeking The Gold).
April 11. Fourth foal. 95,000Y. Tattersalls October Book 2. Mark Johnston. Half-brother to the Irish 2-y-o 7f winner Malacara and to a minor winner in Italy by Green Desert. The dam is an unplaced half-sister to 4 winners including the useful 1m (in France) and US Grade 2 9f All Along Stakes winner Beyrouth and the smart British/US performer at up to 10f Flame Valley. The second dam, Lightning Fire (by Kris), won the listed 7f Prix Imprudence and is a sister to the Group 1 7f Prix de la Salamandre winner and good sire Common Grounds and a half-sister to 8 winners including the Group 3 10f Prix de Psyche winner Angel In My Heart (herself dam of the Derby winner Kris Kin). (Sheikh Hamdan Bin Mohammed Al Maktoum).

990. HALIFAX (IRE) ★★★
ch.c. Halling – Lady Zonda (Lion Cavern).
April 11. Fifth foal. 80,000Y. Tattersalls October Book 2. Mark Johnston. Half-brother to the 2009 2-y-o Group 1 Fillies' Mile winner Hibaayeb (by Singspiel) and to the Irish 2-y-o 6f winner and listed 6f second (from 2 starts) May Meeting (by Diktat). The dam, a quite useful 7f and 1m winner, is a half-sister to 7 winners. The second dam, Zonda (by Fabulous Dancer), a useful listed-placed 5f to 8.5f winner here, subsequently won twice in the USA. (Sheikh Hamdan Bin Mohammed Al Maktoum).

991. HANDICRAFT (IRE) ★★
ch.f. Halling – Luana (Shaadi).
February 12. Tenth foal. 120,000Y. Tattersalls October Book 1. Mark Johnston. Sister to the Chester Vase, September Stakes and Winter Derby winner (all Group 3 events) Hattan (by Halling), to the listed Aston Park Stakes winner and Group 2 placed Tastahil (by Singspiel), the fair 14f winner General Ting (by Daylami) and a winner in the UAE by Selkirk. The dam, a useful triple 6f winner (including at 2 yrs), was listed-placed and is a half-sister to the high-class middle-distance horses and Group 1 winners Warrsan and Luso and to the Group winners Cloud Castle and Needle Gun. The second dam, Lucayan Princess (by High Line), a very useful winner of the listed 6f Sweet Solera Stakes at 2 yrs, was third in the 12.3f Cheshire Oaks and is a half-sister to 7 winners. (Sheikh Hamdan Bin Mohammed Al Maktoum).

992. ITHOUGHTITWASOVER (IRE) ★★★
b.c. Hurricane Run – Green Castle
(Indian Ridge).
January 30. Third foal. 38,000Y. Tattersalls October Book 2. Mark Johnston. Half-brother to the fairly useful 1m (at 2 yrs) and 7f winner and listed-placed Greenisland (by Fasliyev). The dam, placed once over 1m at 4 yrs in Ireland from only 2 starts, is a half-sister to 12 winners including the Group 2 placed Luchiroverte. The second dam, Green Lucia (by Green Dancer), won over 6f and 10f, was second in the Group 1 Yorkshire Oaks and third in the Irish Oaks and is a half-sister to 6 winners including the top-class middle-distance colt Old Vic and the Group 3 winner Splash of Colour. (Crone Stud Farms Ltd).

993. MUNGO PARK ★★★
b.c. Selkirk – Key Academy (Royal Academy).
March 28. Seventh foal. 150,000Y. Tattersalls October Book 1. Mark Johnston. Brother to the 2009 7f placed 2-y-o Moobeyn and half-brother to the quite useful 8.5f (at 2 yrs) to 17f winner of 4 races Keenes Day (by Daylami), to the quite useful 2-y-o dual 6f winner Adaptation (by Spectrum) and the fair 2-y-o 1m winner Razed (by King's Best). The dam, a quite useful 12f winner, subsequently won at 5 yrs in the USA and was stakes placed.

She is a half-sister to 7 winners including the Grade 1 Beverly Hills Handicap and Grade 1 Matriarch Stakes winner Squeak. The second dam, Santa Linda (by Sir Ivor), is an unraced half-sister to 5 winners including the Group 1 Premio Roma winner Noble Saint. (Sheikh Hamdan Bin Mohammed Al Maktoum).

994. LOUISE MARY (IRE) ★★★★
b.f. *Red Ransom – Iris May (Brief Truce)*.
April 24. Ninth foal. Half-sister to the useful dual 5f (at 2 yrs) and 1m winner and listed placed Joseph Henry (by Mujadil), to the quite useful 2-y-o 5f winner Royal Engineer (by Royal Applause), the fair 2-y-o 6f winner Special Cuvee (by Reset) and the fair 2-y-o 7f all-weather winner Leonard Charles (by Best Of The Bests). The dam, a dual 5f winner, including at 2 yrs, is a half-sister to 4 winners including the very useful listed sprint winner Cathedral. The second dam, Choire Mhor (by Dominion), a useful winner of three races over 6f at 2 yrs, is a half-sister to 6 winners including the Group 3 Prix de la Jonchere winner Soft Currency and the listed winner Fawzi – both useful. (J M Brown).

995. LUCKBEALADYTONIGHT (IRE) ★★★
b.f. *Mr Greeley – Sumora (Danehill)*.
February 3. Second foal. €100,000Y. Arqana Deauville August. M Johnston. The dam, a 2-y-o listed 5f St Hugh's Stakes winner, is a sister to the useful Irish 7f winner Fleeting Shadow and a half-sister to 2 winners. The second dam, Rain Flower (by Indian Ridge), is an unraced three-parts sister to the Epsom Derby, Irish Champion Stakes and Dewhurst Stakes winner Dr Devious and a half-sister to 5 winners including the Japanese listed winner Shinko King and the Group 3 winners Royal Court and Archway. (A D Spence).

996. MALTHOUSE (GER) ★★★
b.c. *Green Desert – Maltage (Affirmed)*.
April 2. Sixth living foal. 100,000Y. Tattersalls October Book 1. Mark Johnston. Closely related to the multiple German and French Group 2 winner Martillo and to the minor German 3-y-o winner Mangala (by Anabaa) and half-brother to 3 other minor winners in Germany by Monsun, Orpen and Owington. The dam was placed in Germany and is a half-sister to 7 winners including the US Grade 2 winner Terra Incognita. The second dam, Analisa (by High Echelon), won 3 minor races in the USA and is a half-sister to one winner. (Sheikh Hamdan Bin Mohammed Al Maktoum).

997. MARIE DU PLESSIS ★★★
b.f. *Invincible Spirit – Scandalette (Niniski)*.
April 14. Closely related to the very smart Group 3 7f and 9f winner and Group 1 placed Gateman (by Owington), to the useful 7f (at 2 yrs) and 10f winner Lady Jane Rigby (by Oasis Dream), the fair 2-y-o dual 6f winner Diablerette and the fair 8.6f winner Devil's Island (both by Green Desert) and half-sister to the smart 1m Royal Hunt Cup winner Surprise Encounter (by Cadeaux Genereux) and the fairly useful 7f (at 2 yrs) and dual 12f winner Night Flyer (by Midyan). The dam is an unraced half-sister to 9 winners including the Group 1 July Cup winner Polish Patriot and the Italian listed winner Grand Cayman. The second dam, Maria Waleska (by Filiberto), won 6 races including the Group 1 Gran Premio d'Italia and the Group 1 Oaks d'Italia. (Miss K Rausing).

998. MEMORABILIA ★★★
b.c. *Dansili – Sentimental Value (Diesis)*.
January 15. Third foal. 65,000Y. Tattersalls October Book 1. Mark Johnston. Half-brother to the quite useful dual 10f winner Barwell Bridge (by Red Ransom). The dam, a winner of 2 stakes events in the USA and Grade 3 placed, is a half-sister to 4 winners in Japan. The second dam, Stately Star (by Deputy Minister), a stakes winner of 6 races in the USA, is a half-sister to 7 winners. (Sheikh Hamdan Bin Mohammed Al Maktoum).

999. NAMIBIAN (IRE) ★★
b.c. *Cape Cross – Disco Volante (Sadler's Wells)*.
February 18. Fourth foal. 60,000Y. Tattersalls October Book 1. Mark Johnston. Half-brother to the quite useful 10f winner Mary Goodnight (by King's Best) and to the modest 1m winner Cinerama (by Machiavellian). The dam, a useful 1m winner, was listed-placed and is a half-sister to 3 winners including the Group 1 placed Valentino. The second dam, Divine Danse (by Kris), a smart sprinter and winner of 5 races including the Group 2 Prix

du Gros Chene and the Group 3 Prix du Ris-Orangis, is a half-sister to 5 winners including the high-class colt Pursuit of Love, winner of the Group 2 Prix Maurice de Gheest and second in the July Cup. (Sheikh Hamdan Bin Mohammed Al Maktoum).

1000. QENAA ★★★
b.f. Royal Applause – In The Woods (You And I).
April 7. Fourth foal. 80,000Y. Tattersalls October Book 1. Shadwell Estate Co. Half-sister to the fairly useful 6f (including at 2 yrs) and 7f winner El Bosque (by Elnadim) and to a winner over hurdles by Vettori. The dam, a quite useful 2-y-o listed 6f Empress Stakes winner, subsequently won and was Group placed in Scandinavia. She is a half-sister to 3 winners out of the placed Silent Indulgence (by Woodman), herself a half-sister to 6 winners. (Hamdan Al Maktoum).

1001. SERGEANT ABLETT (IRE) ★★★
b.c. Danehill Dancer – Dolydille (Dolphin Street).
February 18. Fourth foal. 120,000Y. Tattersalls October Book 1. Mark Johnston. Closely related to the very useful 10f and 12f winner and Group 2 Jockey Club Stakes third Drill Sergeant (by Rock Of Gibraltar) and half-brother to the fair 7f winner Elizabethan Age (by King's Best). The dam won 7 races including 2 listed events, from 9f to 12f and is a half-sister to 9 winners including the Irish listed 1m winner and high-class broodmare La Meilleure. The second dam, Gradille (by Home Guard), a fair 6f and 7f winner, is a half-sister to 3 winners. (Mr J A Barson).

1002. SHIRATAKI (IRE) ★★
b.c. Cape Cross – Noodle Soup (Alphabet Soup).
March 1. Third foal. 52,000Y. Tattersalls October Book 1. Mark Johnston. The dam, a minor French winner of 3 races at 3 yrs, is a half-sister to 9 winners including the US stakes winners Vignette and Be Elusive and the French listed winner On A Cloud. The second dam, Be Exclusive (by Be My Guest), won 5 races in France and the USA including the Group 3 Prix Chloe and is a half-sister to 2 winners. (Sheikh Hamdan Bin Mohammed Al Maktoum).

1003. SPASHA ★★★
b.f. Shamardal – Spa (Sadler's Wells).
March 27. Ninth foal. 25,000Y. Tattersalls October Book 1. Mark Johnston. Half-sister to the smart 1m (at 2 yrs) and listed 10f winner and Group 2 Hardwicke Stakes third Persian Majesty and to the quite useful Irish 7f and 9f winner Fitzroy (both by Grand Lodge) and 2 minor winners in Italy by Rock Of Gibraltar and Sinndar. The dam is an unraced half-sister to the Group 2 Hardwicke Stakes winner Sandmason, the smart triple 12f winner Sebastian and the listed 10f Newmarket Pretty Polly Stakes winner Sardegna. The second dam, Sandy Island (by Mill Reef), was a very useful winner of the Group 3 12f Lancashire Oaks and the 10f Pretty Polly Stakes and is closely related to Slip Anchor.

1004. STATE OPERA ★★★
b.c. Shamardal – Strings (Unfuwain).
April 16. Third foal. 75,000Y. Tattersalls October Book 1. Mark Johnston. Half-brother to the quite useful 2009 2-y-o dual 7f winner Bahamian Flight (by Bahamian Bounty) and to a winner abroad by Exceed And Excel. The dam is an unraced half-sister to 5 winners including the French 2,000 Guineas winner Victory Note. The second dam, Three Piece (by Jaazeiro), an Irish placed 2-y-o, is a half-sister to 8 winners including Orchestration (Group 2 Coronation Stakes) and Welsh Term (Group 2 Prix d'Harcourt). (Sheikh Hamdan Bin Mohammed Al Maktoum).

1005. STENTORIAN (IRE) ★★★
ch.c. Street Cry – Nomistakeaboutit (Affirmed).
March 5. First foal. 110,000Y. Tattersalls October Book 1. John Ferguson. The dam, a listed-placed winner of 2 races in Canada, is a half-sister to 3 winners including the Canadian listed stakes winner Sans Souci Island. The second dam, Faux Pas (by Sadler's Wells), is a placed half-sister to 6 winners including the Rockfel Stakes winner and smart broodmare Negligent. (Sheikh Hamdan Bin Mohammed Al Maktoum).

1006. TARTAN JURA ★★★
b.c. Green Desert – On A Soapbox (Mi Cielo).
April 30. Third foal. 65,000Y. Tattersalls October Book 1. Mark Johnston. Closely

related to the Group 2 12f Princess Of Wales's Stakes and Group 3 Queen's Vase winner Soapy Danger (by Danzig). The dam won 6 races including the Grade 1 12f CCA Oaks and is a half-sister to 4 winners. The second dam, Makin A Statement (by Stage Door Johnny), won once at 3 yrs in the USA and is a half-sister to 5 winners. (Mrs N I Bird).

1007. TASFEYA ★★★★♣
b.c. Haafhd – Nufoos (Zafonic).
April 11. Second foal. Half-brother to the 2009 2-y-o Group 1 6f and Group 2 6f Mill Reef Stakes winner Awzaan (by Alhaarth). The dam, a useful 5f, 6f (both at 2 yrs) and listed 7f winner, is a half-sister to the 5 winners including the fairly useful 2-y-o sprint winner of 3 races Valiant Romeo. The second dam, Desert Lynx (by Green Desert), a fair dual 6f winner, is a half-sister to the very smart dual listed 5f winner Watching. (Hamdan Al Maktoum).

1008. UNNAMED ★★
b.c. Selkirk – Bay Tree (Daylami).
February 24. Second foal. 85,000Y. Tattersalls October Book 1. Mark Johnston. Half-brother to the 2009 7f placed 2-y-o King's Parade (by Dynaformer). The dam, useful 2-y-o listed 7f winner, was third in the Group 3 Musidora Stakes and is a half-sister to 4 winners including the Group 1 6f Haydock Sprint Cup winner Tante Rose. The second dam, My Branch (by Distant Relative), a very useful winner of the listed 6f Firth Of Clyde Stakes (at 2 yrs) and the listed 7f Sceptre Stakes, was second in the Group 1 Cheveley Park Stakes and third in the Irish 1,000 Guineas and is a half-sister to 5 winners.

1009. UNNAMED ★★★
ch.f. Hurricane Run – Cheal Rose (Dr Devious).
April 23. Sixth foal. €40,000Y. Goffs Orby. Mark Johnston. Half-sister to the Irish listed 6f (at 2 yrs) and 1m winner and Group 1 7f National Stakes second Golden Arrow (by Danehill) and to the quite useful Irish 1m winner Perpetual Motion (by Spinning World). The dam was placed 8 times at up to 1m in Ireland and is a half-sister to 6 winners including the US Grade 3 winner Buffalo Berry (herself dam of the US Grade 3 winner and Grade 1 placed Chattahoochee War). The second dam, Palm Dove (by Storm Bird), is an unplaced half-sister to 6 winners including the very smart sprinter Nabeel Dancer. (M W Graff).

1010. UNNAMED ★★
b.f. Montjeu – In My Life (Rainbow Quest).
February 20. €90,000Y. Arqana Deauville August. Horse France. Half-sister to the fair 2010 6f placed 3-y-o Fighter Boy (by Rock Of Gibraltar). The dam is a sister to the 2-y-o Group 1 10f Criterium de Saint-Cloud winner Special Quest and a half-sister to the 2-y-o Group 2 7f Criterium de Maisons-Laffitte winner Moiava. The second dam, Mona Stella (by Nureyev), a smart winner of the Group 2 9.2f Prix de l'Opera, is closely related to the French 1,000 Guineas and Prix Vermeille winner Dancing Maid.

1011. UNNAMED ★★★
b.c. Hurricane Run – Mare Aux Fees (Kenmare).
May 8. Fifteenth foal. €100,000Y. Arqana Deauville August. Mark Johnston. Closely related to the Group 2 Royal Lodge (at 2 yrs) and Group 1 Preis von Europa winner Jukebox Jury (by Montjeu) and half-brother to 7 winners including the French listed winner The Mask (by Saint Estephe), the Group 3 Prix Vanteaux winner Belle Allure, the Italian listed winner Pierrot Solaire (by Dancing Spree) and the French 2-y-o winner Albula (by Anabaa). The dam won once at 3 yrs in France and is a half-sister to 8 winners. The second dam, Feerie Boreale (by Irish River), won once in France and was fourth in the Group 1 Prix Marcel Boussac and is a half-sister to 6 winners including the Grand Prix de Paris winner Soleil Noir. (A D Spence).

SYLVESTER KIRK

1012. AD VITAM (IRE) ★★
ch.c. Ad Valorem – Love Sonnet (Singspiel).
April 12. Third foal. £3,000Y. Doncaster St Leger Festival. Peter Doyle. The dam is an unraced sister to one winner and a half-sister to 5 winners including Isle Of Glass (Group 3 C L Weld Park Stakes). The second dam, Liffey Lass (by Irish River), won once at 2 yrs and is a half-sister to 11 winners including Trapp Mountain (US Grade 1 Futurity Stakes). *"He'll be out pretty early because he's forward*

enough and he's going well, but being out of a Singspiel mare he might be a bit better over six furlongs than five."

1013. AMORE ET LABORE ★★
br.c. Ivan Denisovich – In The Highlands (Petong).
March 30. Ninth foal. £16,000Y. Doncaster St Leger. S Kirk. Half-brother to the fair Irish 9f winner Trust In Me (by Spartacus), to the quite useful 2-y-o 5f and 6f winner Glenmorangie (by Danzig Connection), the modest dual 6f winner Strathmore (by Fath) and a winner in Jersey by Missed Flight. The dam is an unplaced full or half-sister to 5 winners. The second dam, Thevetia (by Mummy's Pet), is a placed half-sister to 7 winners. *"He's going well, he's sharp and early and has a good attitude. The owner bought him because his father owned the colt's half-brother Glenmorangie. He's nice and he'd have been racing now if he hadn't got a cough, he'll be racing soon though."*

1014. BENDIGEDIG ★★
b.f. Indesatchel – Four Legs Good (Be My Guest).
January 17. Fifth foal. 6,000Y. Tattersalls October 3. S Kirk. Half-sister to the fairly useful 6f and 7f winner of 9 races Bennlech (by Lujain) and to the fair 5f (at 2 yrs) and 7f winner Perfect Friend (by Reel Buddy). The dam is an unplaced half-sister to several minor winners here and abroad. The second dam, Karine (by Habitat), ran twice unplaced and is a half-sister to the Group 3 Oaks Trial winner Heaven Knows and to the Irish listed winner Kizzy. *"A nice filly that should be suited by six furlongs but we might even start her earlier. Her name is Welsh for 'wonderful' apparently."*

1015. DRESS UP ★★★
b.f. Noverre – Lisfannon (Bahamian Bounty).
March 6. First foal. €1,000Y. Tattersalls Ireland. Not sold. The dam is a placed half-sister to the listed 5f winner of 5 races Dazed And Amazed. The second dam, Amazed (by Clantime), a modest 5f placed 3-y-o, is a sister to the Group 3 Prix du Petit Couvert winner Bishops Court and a half-sister to 5 winners including the listed winning sprinter Astonished. *"A sharp, early filly, I had her entered up in the first Sales Bonus race at* Lingfield. *She's had a small setback though and I've just started her back. A smashing little filly with lots of speed and she's definitely one for your book."* TRAINERS' BARGAIN BUY

1016. GYPSY LEGEND ★★★
b.f. Dr Fong – Generous Gesture (Fasliyev).
April 16. Second foal. €4,000foal. Goffs. Not sold. Half-sister to the quite useful 2009 2-y-o 7f winner Gallant Eagle (by Hawk Wing). The dam, a fair dual 6f winner, is a half-sister to the smart dual listed 1m winner Harvest Queen. The second dam, Royal Bounty (by Generous), a quite useful 2-y-o 7.5f winner, is a half-sister to 3 minor winners here and abroad. (J C Smith). *"A sharp, early filly, she's forward enough, active and well-balanced. One for the first half of the season."*

1017. HEAVENLY SONG ★★
b.f. Oratorio – Lochangel (Night Shift).
March 13. Seventh foal. Half-sister to the quite useful 7f winner Star Pupil (by Selkirk) and the fair 5f winner Celestial Dream (by Oasis Dream). The dam, a very smart winner of the Group 1 5f Nunthorpe Stakes, is a half-sister to the champion sprinter Lochsong. The second dam, Peckitts Well (by Lochnager), was a fairly useful winner of five races at 2 and 3 yrs from 5f to 6f. (Mr J C Smith). *"A well-balanced filly that looks as if she'll be a two-year-old. She's shaping well and I've done enough with her but I've eased off because of sore shins. Mid-season over six furlongs should be OK for her."*

1018. IRIE UTE ★★
b.c. Sleeping Indian – Prends Ca (Reprimand).
April 24. Eighth foal. 16,000Y. Tattersalls October Book 3. S Kirk. Half-brother to the fair 7f winner Le Singe Noir (by Averti) and to the minor US 4-y-o winner Nan Scurry (by Danehill). The dam, a fairly useful 6f (at 2 yrs) to 7.5f winner of 5 races, is a half-sister to 4 winners including the listed Trigo Stakes winner Friendly Persuasion. The second dam, Cri de Coeur (by Lyphard), a quite useful 2-y-o 9f winner, is a half-sister to 3 minor winners. *"A nice horse, the family might suggest he'll need a bit more time than some of my other two-year-olds, but he'll still be racing in the first half of the season."*

1019. KING BLING (IRE) ★★★
b.c. Camacho – No Hard Feelings (Alzao).
April 12. Eleventh foal. 15,000Y. Tattersalls October Book 2. R Hannon. Half-brother to the fairly useful 2-y-o 7f winner Si Si Amiga, to the fair 1m winner Touch Of Style (both by Desert Style), the fairly useful 2-y-o dual 5f winner and subsequent US stakes-placed winner Inca Tern (by Polar Falcon), fairly useful the 12f all-weather winner Athletic Sam (by Definite Article), the modest 1m winner Distant Drums (by Distant Music) and 2 minor winners in Italy and France by Rock City and Common Grounds. The dam, a quite useful 5f (at 2 yrs) and 12f winner of 7 races, is a half-sister to 4 winners. The second dam, Coshlea (by Red Alert), is a placed half-sister to 7 winners including the Group 3 Musidora Stakes winner Princess Of Man (herself dam of the Oaks and Irish Oaks winner Ramruma). (J A Challen, I Higginson, R Hannon). *"A sharp and early two-year-old with a great attitude. He's a lovely mover, he's very strong, pretty forward and he'll be out in late April or early May. It's interesting that my father-in-law Richard Hannon is down on the owner's list – and I'm pleased to say he's a good payer!"*

1020. LADYANNE ★★
ch.f. Redback – Gillipops (Xaar).
January 14. First foal. 7,000Y. Tattersalls October 3. S Kirk. The dam, a fair 2-y-o 7f winner, is a half-sister to 4 winners. The second dam, Snoozeandyoulose (by Scenic), a fair Irish 4-y-o 7f winner, is a half-sister to 6 winners. *"A sharp, early filly, she'll be one of our first runners and five furlongs will be right up her street."*

1021. MRS NEAT ★★★
b.f. Refuse To Bend – Cambara (Dancing Brave).
May 27. Closely related to the useful 7f (at 2 yrs) and 1m winner and Group 3 7f Horris Hill Stakes second Samhari (by Indian Ridge) and half-sister to the fairly useful 2-y-o 7f and 10f winner Dubai On (by Daylami), the quite useful 4-y-o 1m winner Habshan (by Swain) and the UAE 6f winner Afreet (by Kris). The dam was a useful winner of three 1m events at 3 yrs and is a half-sister to the good French 6f to 1m winner Pluralisme, the very useful 10f Virginia Stakes winner Singletta, the very useful 11f Grand Prix Prince Rose winner Classic Tale, the useful 1m winners Only and Cambrian and to the 10f winner Ghislaine – herself dam of the high-class miler Markofdistinction. The second dam, Cambretta (by Roberto), won over 9f in Ireland and is a sister to the high-class middle-distance colt Critique. *"This filly could run over six furlongs, despite being a late foal. Mentally and physically she's forward but clearly I'll give her a bit of time. She's got the speed to do well when her time comes."*

1022. NORSE BLUES ★★★
ch.c. Norse Dancer – Indiana Blues (Indian Ridge).
April 27. Half-brother to the unplaced 2009 2-y-o Temple Queen (by Sulamani). The dam, a fair 6f winner, is a half-sister to several winners including the useful 2-y-o listed 5.2f winner and Group 2 Flying Childers Stakes third Speed Cop and the fairly useful dual 5f winner (including at 2 yrs) Siren's Gift. The second dam, Blue Siren (by Bluebird), a very useful winner of three races from 5f to 7f, was disqualified from first place in two more, notably the Group 1 5f Nunthorpe Stakes (the winner on merit) and is a half-sister to several winners including the quite useful 9f winner Northern Habit. (Mr J C Smith). *"A lovely horse by Norse Dancer and although you might expect them take a bit longer he won over six furlongs himself as a two-year-old. This is a big, well-balanced horse with a lot of presence about him and I like him a lot. He'll be a six/seven furlong two-year-old."*

1023. OPERA DANCE ★★★★
ch.f. Norse Dancer – Optaria (Song).
March 6. Half-sister to the very smart 2-y-o Group 3 7f Solario Stakes winner and Group 1 Dewhurst Stakes third Opera Cape (by Barathea), to the high-class stayer Grey Shot (by Sharrood), the smart sprint winner of 4 races Night Shot (by Night Shift), the fairly useful 7f to 9f winner Highland Shot (by Selkirk), the quite useful 3-y-o 8.5f winner Opera Glass and the 1m 5f winner Sight'n Sound (by Chief Singer). The dam, a quite useful 2-y-o 5f winner, is out of the unplaced Electo (by Julio Mariner). (J C Smith). *"One of my favourites, she's a half-sister to a few nice*

winners especially Opera Cape who did so well for us. She seems precocious enough but because she has such a nice pedigree I'll take a bit longer with her and give her a chance to mature a bit more."

1024. SHOSTAKOVIC (IRE) ★★★
b.c. Fasliyev – Hi Katriona
(Second Empire).
January 14. Second foal. 10,000Y. Tattersalls October Book 2. S Kirk. The dam is a placed half-sister to 11 winners including the Group 2 Premio Melton winner Fred Bongusto. The second dam, Hi Bettina (by Henbit), a fairly useful Irish sprinter, won twice, was second in the Group 3 Debutante Stakes in Ireland and is a half-sister to the Group 3 Norfolk Stakes winner Marouble and the Irish Oaks and Irish 1,000 Guineas second Kitza. "The oldest two-year-old I've got, he's big, strong and imposing. He has a great attitude and if I can keep him sound and injury free he could be really nice. Because of his size I'm not sure if he'll be a five furlong sprinter this year or next, but he was an early foal and he goes well."

1025. SILLY BILLY ★★
b.c. Noverre – Rock Dove (Danehill).
February 4. Second foal. €1,000Y. Tattersalls Ireland. S Kirk. Second foal. The dam, a fair 2-y-o 5f winner, is a half-sister to the useful 6f winner of 4 races and listed-placed Bee Eater. The second dam, Littlefeather (by Indian Ridge), a very useful 5f (at 2 yrs) and 6f winner, was third in the Group 1 7f Moyglare Stakes and is a half-sister to 7 winners including the high class Cheveley Park Stakes, Irish 1,000 Guineas, Coronation Stakes and Sussex Stakes winner Marling and the good 5f to 1m colt Caerwent. "He's a little bit highly strung but he's been going from the start and I'll be running him in April. He's fit and straightforward and might be one of those that runs well at a big price." TRAINERS' BARGAIN BUY

1026. TOTHEENDOFTHEEARTH ★★★★
b.f. Hurricane Run – Lightwood Lady
(Anabaa).
February 16. Second foal. 20,000Y. Tattersalls October Book 1. Not sold. Half-sister to Its Alright (by King's Best), a promising 5f debut winner on her only start at 2 yrs in 2009. The dam, a fair Irish 6f winner, is a half-sister to 3 winners including the fairly useful 7f and 1m winner Furnace. The second dam, Lyrical Dance (by Lear Fan), a minor winner at 4 yrs in the USA, is a sister to the French listed 10.5f winner Shaal and a half-sister to the Group/Grade 1 winners Black Minnaloushe, Pennekamp and Nasr El Arab and the placed dam of the US dual Grade 1 winner Round Pond. (Barouche Stud). "A lovely, good-sized filly, she'll be early enough despite being by Hurricane Run and she's well-balanced. She has enough speed but I'll hang on to her a bit longer. One to watch out for."

1027. UNNAMED ★★
b.c. Orpen – Velvet Slipper (Muhtafal).
May 3. £13,500Y. Doncaster October. Not sold. Half-brother to the fair 1m winner of 3 races Statute Book (by Statue Of Liberty). The dam, a modest 7f placed maiden, is a half-sister to 6 winners including the useful 2-y-o 6f and 7f winner Muhab. The second dam, Magic Slipper (by Habitat), a useful 10f and 11.5f winner, is a half-sister to 6 winners including the 1,000 Guineas winner Fairy Footsteps and the St Leger winner Light Cavalry. "A big colt and a bit backward, but he's one of the best balanced two-year-olds I have. He has a great attitude and is one for the second half of the season."

WILLIAM KNIGHT

1028. ALL HONESTY ★★
b.f. Medicean – Al Joudha (Green Desert).
January 25. Second foal. 45,000Y. Tattersalls October Book 2. Portanova Bloodstock. Half-sister to the fair 6f winner Premier Lad (by Tobougg). The dam ran twice unplaced and is a half-sister to the champion Swedish 2-y-o 5f to 1m winner King Quantas and to the placed dam of the dual Group 1 winner Dutch Art. The second dam, Palacegate Episode (by Drumalis), a useful sprinter and winner of 11 races here and abroad including a Group 3 race in Italy and numerous listed events, is a full or half-sister to 5 winners including the triple listed winning sprinter Palacegate Jack. (Bluehills Racing Ltd). "She's a nice type but probably won't be out until July/August time but she has a bit of size and scope about her. She's just cantering at present and seems to

take after her sire rather than the dam. I like her and she's one for seven furlongs."

1029. BLOODSWEATANDTEARS ★★★★
b.c. Barathea – Celestial Princess (Observatory).
February 29. Second foal. £16,000Y. Doncaster St Leger. Portanova Bloodstock. The dam, a quite useful 2-y-o 7f winner, is a half-sister to numerous winners including the useful 2-y-o listed 6f and 7f winner Bibury Flyer and the useful 10f and 12f winner Mojalid. The second dam, Affair Of State (by Tate Gallery), a very useful Irish 2-y-o 6f winner, is a half-sister to 7 minor winners. (Five Men & A Dream Partnership). "He's a really nice colt, a lovely mover and a big, scopey horse. Potentially he'd have the speed to start over six furlongs and then he'll make up into a nice seven furlong/mile type. He should start in May and he was good value." TRAINERS' BARGAIN BUY

1030. BRINMORE ★★★
ch.f. Kyllachy – Ringarooma (Erhaab).
January 27. First foal. £10,000Y. Doncaster St Leger. Portanova Bloodstock. The dam, a moderate 4-y-o 10f winner, is a half-sister to 2 winners and to the dams of the Group 2 winners Wi Dud and Tariq. The second dam, Tatouma (by The Minstrel), a quite useful 2-y-o 5f and 6f winner, is a half-sister to 4 winners including the dams of 2 listed winners. "I quite like her, she's quite speedy and could be our earliest two-year-old. There's a lot of the grandsire Pivotal in her I think and also a lot of speed in her family, so I think she could be quite precocious."

1031. FORTY PROOF (IRE) ★★★
b.c. Invincible Spirit – Cefira (Distant View).
February 21. Third foal. 70,000Y. Tattersalls October Book 1. Elmhurst Bloodstock. Half-brother to the quite useful 2-y-o 5f winner Sirenuse (by Exceed And Excel). The dam, a modest 3-y-o 6f winner, is a half-sister to 4 winners including Abou Zouz (Group 2 Gimcrack Stakes). The second dam, Bold Jessie (by Never So Bold), an Irish 2-y-o listed winner, is a half-sister to 5 winners including the Group 2 winners Prince Sabo and Millyant. (Mr T G Roddick). "A small, 'butty' colt and he'll be racing in late May/early June. He looks a two-year-old, shows a bit of speed five furlongs will do for him to start with."

1032. NOONENOSE ★★★★
ch.c. Compton Place – Noble View (Distant View).
April 11. Fifth foal. 52,000Y. Tattersalls October Book 2. Portanova Bloodstock. Half-brother to the useful 2009 2-y-o 6f listed winner of 3 races and Group 2 7f Vintage Stakes third Corporal Maddox, to the quite useful 6f to 1m winner of 8 races Silver Hotspur (both by Royal Applause) and the modest 6f winner Aegean Shadow (by Sakhee). The dam, placed fourth over 5f and 6f at 2 yrs, is a half-sister to 5 winners including the French 1,000 Guineas winner Houseproud. The second dam, Proud Lou (by Proud Clarion), won 4 races over 6f and 1m in the USA at 2 yrs including the Grade 1 Frizette Stakes and is a half-sister to 7 winners. (Five Men & A Dream Partnership). "A nice colt and a nice mover, he looks precocious enough and he should be out in late May or early June. He looks a nice type and he'll be a six furlong type." By the way – it's pronounced No One Knows!

1033. PROPER CHARLIE ★★★
b.c. Cadeaux Genereux – Ring Of Love (Magic Ring).
April 4. Seventh foal. 58,000Y. Tattersalls October Book 2. Portanova Bloodstock. Half-brother to the 2009 1m placed 2-y-o Claddagh (by Dubai Destination) and to the very useful 6f (at 2 yrs) and 1m dual listed winner and Group 2 placed Bahia Breeze (by Mister Baileys). The dam, a fair 5f winner of 4 races (including at 2 yrs), is a half-sister to 7 winners. The second dam, Fine Honey (by Drone), a fairly useful 2-y-o 5f winner, is a half-sister to 7 winners. (Mr P L C Oakley). "A very strong, 'butty' type of horse that's very well put together. I'm sure how early he'll be because he will be a sprinter but the sire doesn't usually get them early. A very powerful colt, he'll definitely make a two-year-old and I think he'll make up into a nice older sprinter."

1034. ROYALORIEN ★★★
b.f. Royal Applause – Lorien Hill (Danehill).
April 25. Third foal. 18,000Y. Tattersalls October Book 2. Not sold. Half-sister to the

unplaced 2009 2-y-o Fancy Star (by Starcraft). The dam, a fair 7.5f winner, is a half-sister to 2 winners. The second dam, Lothlorien (by Woodman), a quite useful 1m winner, is a sister to the useful 1m (at 2 yrs) to 10f winner Monsajem and to the US 2-y-o winner Mellifont and a half-sister to 6 winners. (D M James). *"She looks a two-year-old type, she should hopefully be out in June and she goes OK. A nice type of filly and I think she'll be a six/seven furlong horse."*

1035. UNBEATABLE ★★
b.f. Beat Hollow – Koniya (Doyoun).
March 2. Sixth foal. 30,000Y. Tattersalls October Book 3. Elmhurst Bloodstock. Closely related to the winner King Of Dreams (by Sadler's Wells) and to the minor French 14f winner Kekova (by Montjeu) and half-sister to the fairly useful 9f and 10f winner and Group 3 9f Dahlia Stakes second Casilda (by Cape Cross). The dam, a minor winner over 15f at 3 yrs in France, is a half-sister to 7 winners including the listed 7f Irish 1,000 Guineas Trial winners Khanata and Kotama, and to the unraced dam of the dual Derby winner High Chaparral. The second dam, Kozana (by Kris), was a top-class filly and won 4 races at 3 yrs over 1m (3 times) and 10f including the Prix de Malleret and the Prix de Sandringham and was third in the Prix de l'Arc de Triomphe. (Mr T G Roddick). *"She's a nicely-bred filly and I trained her half-sister Casilda. She's a bit light framed but an attractive filly that looks a bit more precocious than Casilda was, but she'll still be a late summer two-year-old over seven furlongs and is more one for next year."*

1036. UP IN TIME ★★★★♣
ch.f. Noverre – Up At Dawn (Inchinor).
February 5. First foal. 24,000Y. Tattersalls October Book 3. Portanova Bloodstock. The dam is a unplaced half-sister to 4 winners including the dam of the Group 3 winner Summer Fete. The second dam, Up And About (by Barathea), a fair all-weather 14.8f winner, is a half-sister to 5 winners including the listed Atalanta Stakes winner and Group 1 placed Musicanna. (Mrs N J Welby). *"A racy, quick-actioned filly that was bought to be a two-year-old. I should think she'll be out around* June time, she hasn't done any fast work yet but she goes quite nicely."

1037. UNNAMED ★★★
b.f. Oasis Dream – Fancy Rose (Joyeux Danseur).
May 4. First foal. 40,000Y. Tattersalls October Book 1. Rabbah Bloodstock. The dam, a minor winner at 5 yrs in the USA, is a half-sister to 4 winners including the Group 3 7f Horris Hill Stakes and dual 3-y-o 1m winner Dijeer and the US stakes-placed winner Sharp Writer. The second dam, Sharp Minister (by Deputy Minister), is an unplaced sister to the multiple Grade 2 winner Flag Down. (Saif Ali & Saeed H Altayer). *"She's got a bit of class, I don't think she'll be early because she was a May foal and she's still quite leggy. A lovely mover with a lovely temperament, I think she'll be suited by seven furlongs this year."*

1038. UNNAMED ★★★
ch.c. Exceed And Excel – Gold Strike (Rainbow Quest).
April 3. Second foal. €26,000Y. Goffs Orby. Charlie Gordon-Watson. The dam ran once unplaced and is a half-sister to 7 winners including the listed 1m winner Barboukh (herself dam of the Group 3 10f Prix Exbury winner Barbola). The second dam, Turban (by Glint Of Gold), a fair 10f and 11.7f winner, is a half-sister to 6 winners, notably the top-class middle-distance colt Old Vic. (Saif Ali & Saeed H Altayer). *"A good-looking horse, a good mover and he has a fair bit of scope and size about him. I can see him being out around June or July and he's a nice type of horse."*

1039. UNNAMED ★★
b.f. Medicean – Milly Of The Vally (Caerleon).
January 30. Eighth foal. 25,000Y. Tattersalls October Book 1. Portanova Bloodstock. Sister to the fairly useful 8.3f (at 2 yrs) and 14f winner Doctor Scott and half-sister to the very smart dual listed middle-distance winner of 12 races and dual Group 1 placed Scott's View (by Selkirk), to the Italian 2-y-o listed 7.5f winner Mac Melody (by Entrepreneur) and the modest 12f winner Antillia (by Red Ransom). The dam, a fairly useful 12f winner, is a half-sister to 9 winners including the listed winner and Group 3 third Bosham Mill. The second dam, Mill

On The Floss (by Mill Reef), a winner over 7f (at 2 yrs) and the Group 3 12f Lingfield Oaks Trial, was second in the Ribblesdale Stakes and is a half-sister to 8 winners. (D G Hardisty Bloodstock). *"Quite small but a nicely bred filly that's having a break at the moment. One for a mile towards the back-end of the season and she's a nice mover."*

DAVID LANIGAN

1040. ROYAL CITY ★★
b.c. Val Royal – City Gambler (Rock City).
February 24. Half-brother to the modest 2-y-o 6f winner Ditto Ditto (by Mark Of Esteem) and the dual middle-distance seller winner River Of Diamonds (by Muhtarram). The dam, a modest 1m and 10f winner of 4 races, is a half-sister to several winners. The second dam, Sun Street (by Ile de Bourbon), won over 2m and is a half-sister to numerous winners. (Julian May). *"We had the half-brother, Ditto Ditto, but this colt is totally different. He's very big but won't grow much more and I see him as a seven furlong/mile colt at the back-end of the season."*

1041. VIVA DIVA ★★★
ch.f. Hurricane Run – Vas Y Carla (Gone West).
January 29. Third foal. 50,000Y. Tattersalls October Book 1. Not sold. Half-sister to the fair 2009 2-y-o 7f winner Alice Alleyne (by Oasis Dream). The dam, a quite useful 7f placed 2-y-o, is a half-sister to 2 winners including the Group 2 Great Voltigeur Stakes third Avalon. The second dam, Lady Carla (by Caerleon), a high-class winner over 1m (at 2 yrs) and the Group 1 12f Oaks, is a half-sister to a minor winner. (Plantation Stud & Mrs Yvonne Jacks). *"A nice filly that needs time but she should be out in mid-to-late summer over six/seven furlongs."*

1042. UNNAMED ★★
b.c. Motivator – Abide (Pivotal).
January 21. Second foal. 85,000Y. Tattersalls October Book 2. Rabbah Bloodstock. The dam, a fair 3-y-o 7f winner, is a half-sister to 3 winners. The second dam, Ariadne (by King's Lake), won twice at 3 yrs in Germany and is a half-sister to 8 winners. (Rabbah Bloodstock). *"A nice colt but very big, he needs time and will be a nice 3-y-o but hopefully he'll be able to get out from August onwards this year over seven furlongs or a mile."*

1043. UNNAMED ★★★★
b.c. Oasis Dream – Crossmolina (Halling).
March 29. First foal. 75,000Y. Tattersalls October Book 1. Rabbah Bloodstock. The dam, a minor winner at 3 yrs in France, is a sister to the smart dual listed 10f winner Foodbroker Fancy (herself the dam of two stakes winners) and a half-sister to the listed winner Femme Fatale. The second dam, Red Rita (by Kefaah), a fairly useful 4-y-o 6f winner, was second in the Group 3 6f Cherry Hinton Stakes and the Group 3 6f Princess Margaret Stakes at 2 yrs and is a half-sister to 3 minor winners. (Saif Ali & Saeed H Altayer). *"This is a nice horse that goes well. Hopefully he'll be fairly early and will be best suited by six and seven furlongs this season."*

1044. UNNAMED ★★★★
b.f. Oasis Dream – Elegant Times (Dansili).
January 22. First foal. 52,000Y. Tattersalls October Book 1. Rabbah Bloodstock. The dam, a modest 6f all-weather winner, is a half-sister to 5 winners including the Group 2 7f Hungerford Stakes and Group 3 6f Bentinck Stakes winner Welsh Emperor, the very useful listed 5f winner Majestic Times and the useful 6f and 7f winner and Group 3 6f third Brave Prospector. The second dam, Simply Times (by Dodge), ran twice unplaced at 2 yrs and is a half-sister to 5 winners including the US 2-y-o stakes winner Bucky's Baby. *"A colt that goes well and is strengthening all the time. He should be alright around June time over six and seven furlongs."*

1045. UNNAMED ★★★
b.f. Bachelor Duke – Keepers Dawn (Alzao).
April 19. Seventh foal. Half-sister to the modest 2009 6f fourth placed 2-y-o Candleshoe (by Danehill Dancer) and to the modest 10f winner Keepers Knight (by Sri Pekan). The dam, a useful 2-y-o 6f winner and second in the Group 3 7.3f Fred Darling Stakes, is a half-sister to 2 winners. The second dam, Keepers Lock (by Sunny's Halo), is an unraced half-sister to 4 minor winners. (Tullamaine Castle Stud). *"This colt should be OK in mid-summer, he goes nicely and will be suited by six and seven furlongs."*

1046. UNNAMED ★★★
ch.f. Kingmambo – Kushnarenkovo (Sadler's Wells).
February 14. First foal. $100,000Y. Keeneland September. Rabbah Bloodstock. The dam, a fairly useful 12f winner, was second in the Group 3 12f Noblesse Stakes and is a sister to the Group 1 Racing Post Trophy and St Leger winner Brian Boru and the listed Park Express Stakes winner Kitty O'Shea and a half-sister to the Group 2 Prix de Royallieu winner Moon Search. The second dam, Eva Luna (by Alleged), won the Group 3 14.6f Park Hill Stakes and is a half-sister to 5 winners. (Rabbah Bloodstock). *"Not much to look at, but she goes well enough and should be out in June over six furlongs."*

1047. UNNAMED ★★★
b.c. Smarty Jones – Madame Anne Peters (Selkirk).
January 19. Second foal. 20,000Y. Tattersalls October Book 1. Rabbah Bloodstock. The dam is an unraced half-sister to 7 winners including the US triple Grade 3 winner Gold Land. The second dam, Lajna (by Be My Guest), is an unplaced half-sister to 5 winners including the dual Group 1 1m Lockinge Stakes winner Soviet Line. *"This filly is improving and strengthening all the time. A seven furlong type 2-y-o."*

1048. UNNAMED ★★★
br.f. Forest Wildcat – Never Gone (Gone West).
March 29. Third foal. €55,000Y. Goffs Orby. Charlie Gordon-Watson. Half-sister to a minor winner abroad by Alphabet Soup. The dam is an unplaced sister to the US Grade 3 winner Scoop and a half-sister to 5 winners. The second dam, Til Forbid (by Temperence Hill), a US Grade 3 winner, was Grade 1 placed and is a full or half-sister to 12 winners including four at stakes level. (Rabbah Bloodstock). *"She's done very well since she arrived, so we'll wait and see how she goes during the summer."*

1049. UNNAMED ★★★★
b.c. El Prado – No Frills (Darshaan).
February 9. Fifth foal. 35,000Y. Tattersalls October Book 1. Rabbah Bloodstock. Half-brother to the US stakes winner and dual Grade 2 placed Singalong, to the quite useful 9f to 11f winner of 4 races Potentiale (both by Singspiel) and the quite useful 10f winner Ephorus (by Galileo). The dam, a modest 9f placed maiden, is a half-sister to 5 winners including the dams of the North American Grade 3 winners Millennium Dragon and J'Ray. The second dam, Bubbling Danseuse (by Arctic Tern), won once over 10f and was second in the Group 3 1m Prix de Sandringham and is a half-sister to 6 winners. (Rabbah Bloodstock). *"This colt goes well and he could start off at six furlongs in June."*

1050. UNNAMED ★★★
b.c. Dubai Destination – Rah Wa (Rahy).
April 6. First foal. 1,200Y. Tattersalls October Book 3. The dam is an unraced sister to the winner and US Grade 3 placed Artic Sky and a half-sister to the US Grade 2 winner Navesink. The second dam, Sailing Minstrel (by The Minstrel), a US stakes-placed winner of 3 races, is a half-sister to 11 winners including the Group 2 winner Nemain. (Rabbah Bloodstock). *"A nice horse that should be out early. He's done nothing wrong, seems a solid horse and goes well."* TRAINERS' BARGAIN BUY

1051. UNNAMED ★★★
ch.c. Shirocco – Wivenhoe (Timber Country).
January 26. Second foal. €35,000Y. Arqana Deauville August. Charlie Gordon-Watson. The dam, a minor winner in France at 3 yrs, is a half-sister to 4 winners including the Irish listed winner Icklingham. The second dam, Braiswick (by King Of Spain), a very smart winner of the Group 1 E P Taylor Stakes and the Group 2 Sun Chariot Stakes, is a half-sister to 6 winners including the Group 3 11f September Stakes winner Percy's Lass (dam of the Derby winner Sir Percy). *"He goes well enough and he should be ready to come out in May/June over six furlongs."*

GER LYONS

1052. CELESTIAL FLYER (IRE) ★★
b.c. Balmont – Pearly Gates (Night Shift).
February 24. First foal. €32,000Y. Tattersalls Ireland. David Redvers. The dam was a useful 3-y-o 7f winner. The second dam, Pearl Shell (by Bering), won once over 12f at 3 yrs in France and is a half-sister to 3 winners including the Group 2 10.5f Prix Greffulhe winner Persifleur.

"I was disappointed with him initially but he's transformed so much in the last few months that he could be alright after all. If I have a five furlong horse it could be him, but winning with him was so far out of reach two months ago I'd be happy now if he just won his maiden."

1053. CLONDINERRY (IRE) ★★★★
b.c. Choisir – Grand Lili (Linamix).
February 20. First foal. The dam, a fair Irish 12f and hurdles winner, is a half-sister to numerous winners including the French middle-distance winner of 5 races Far From Old. The second dam, Jabali (by Shirley Heights), is an unplaced half-sister to 4 winners including the French Group winners Dadarissime and Floripedes (the dam of Montjeu). (Mr Pat Gilsenan). "A nice colt that ran really well from a bad draw and in bad ground at the Curragh. He'll improve a tremendous amount for that, he'll definitely win his maiden and hopefully he'll be a good bit better than that. A gorgeous looking horse – he's very eye-catching and I think he's smart."

1054. COSMIC LOVE (IRE) ★★★
b.br.f. Noverre – Cappa Blanca (Giant's Causeway).
February 15. Second foal. €18,000Y. Tattersalls Ireland. Ger Lyons. The dam, a fair Irish 7f winner, is a half-sister to 3 winners. The dam won over 5f (at 2 yrs) and 1m in Ireland and was third in the Group 3 5f Ballyogan Stakes. She is a half-sister to 6 winners including the smart Ballyogan Stakes winner and Group 1 Haydock Park Sprint Cup third Catch The Blues. (S Jones). "A big, strapping filly, I'd expect her to win her maiden but I although thought she's be early she's done some growing. A typical Noverre, there's plenty of strength about her but I don't think she's more than a maiden winner. She's not a rocket and so if she doesn't come out early I can't see her winning over five furlongs, she's more likely to go six."

1055. DUSTLAND FAIRYTALE (IRE) ★★★
b.f. Noverre – Subtle Affair (Barathea).
February 15. Second foal. €9,000Y. Tattersalls Ireland. Ger Lyons. Sister to the moderate 2009 5f placed 2-y-o Diamond Affair. The dam, a quite useful dual 11f winner, is a half-sister to 8 winners including the useful 12.3f and 14f winner and Group 2 Henry II Stakes second Lochbuie, the Irish 7f (at 2 yrs) and 9f winner and Group 2 placed Prize Time and the useful 12f and 14f winner Direct Bearing. The second dam, Uncertain Affair (by Darshaan), dam, a quite useful Irish 14f winner, is a half-sister to 3 winners. (S Jones). "A typical Noverre, I bought her off Liam Cashman who was lucky for me and it was totally on his recommendation that I got her so I hope she'll do the job for me. She's what Noverre's are – she'd die for you. I've had loads of success with the sire and I think there's a good day in this filly. I'll probably start her at five furlongs and she has a lovely, big stride to her for her size."

1056. JOE EILE (IRE) ★★★
b.c. Iffraaj – Encouragement (Royal Applause).
March 27. First foal. €12,500Y. Tattersalls Ireland. Ger Lyons. The dam, a fair dual 6f placed 2-y-o here, was later placed in the USA. She is a sister to the winner and listed-placed Approval and a half-sister to 4 winners including the very useful Group 2 6f Moet and Chandon Rennen winner Sharp Prod and to the unraced dam of the Group 2 German 2,000 Guineas winner Royal Power. The second dam, Gentle Persuasion (by Bustino), a fairly useful 2-y-o 6f winner, was placed in the Princess Margaret Stakes and the Rockfel Stakes and is a half-sister to 11 winners. (Mr Joe Bracken). "A lovely horse, he could run from six furlongs to a mile this year and I think he'll make a nice two-year-old."

1057. MERLIN'S OAK (IRE) ★★
b.c. Shamardal – Woodland Orchid (Woodman).
March 23. Ninth foal. €65,000Y. Goffs Orby. John Ferguson. Half-brother to the 2009 7f placed 2-y-o Lady Slippers, to the 2-y-o Group 3 6f Coventry Stakes winner CD Europe (both by Royal Academy), the French 1m winner and listed Prix Yacowlef second Cedar Sea (by Persian Bold), the quite useful UAE 7f winner Cover Drive (by Giant's Causeway) and the modest 10f winner African Pursuits (by Johannesburg). The dam is an unplaced half-sister to the Group 3 Derrinstown Stud Derby Trial winner Truth Or Dare, the UAE Group 3 winner D'Anjou and the listed winner

Sandstone. The second dam, Rose de Thai (by Lear Fan), won twice in France, was third in the Group 3 Prix Thomas Bryon and is a half-sister to 8 winners. (Darley Racing). *"He's nice, the Shamardal's all seem to have great temperaments, he's doing his job nicely and he'll be a seven furlong horse later on."*

1058. MIDNIGHT SHOW (IRE) ★★
b.c. Refuse To Bend – Sheboygan (Grand Lodge).
February 3. Second foal. €22,000Y. Tattersalls Ireland. Ger Lyons. The dam, a fairly useful 7f (at 2 yrs) and 7.5f winner, was listed placed and is a half-sister to one winner. The second dam, White Satin (by Fairy King), a 2-y-o 7f winner and third in the listed 7f Tyros Stakes in Ireland, is a half-sister to 8 winners including the US stakes winner and Grade 2 placed Chenille. *"He's a gorgeous looking horse. When we bought him we were very dubious because I'm a two-year-old trainer and Refuse To Bend's are not the type I buy. He started to show us something smart a month ago but he then started to grow, so he'll be one for the middle-to-back-end over seven furlongs. To look at he's imposing and we like what we see at the minute."*

1059. PASSION PLANET ★★
b.f. Medicean – Katch Me Katie (Danehill).
February 10. Fourth foal. €22,000Y. Goffs Orby. Ger Lyons. Half-sister to the fairly useful 12f and 2m winner Suailce (by Singspiel). The dam, a fair 9f winner, is a half-sister to 4 winners including the Grade 2 E P Taylor Stakes winner and Grade 1 Gamely Handicap and Group 2 Sun Chariot Stakes second Kool Kat Katie and to the smart 8.3f (at 2yrs) and Group 3 10.4f Musidora Stakes winner, Epsom Oaks second and Grade 1 Beverley Hills Handicap third Kalypso Katie. The second dam, Miss Toot (by Ardross), a fair 10f and 15f winner on her only starts, is a half-sister to one winner. (Mr Declan Landy). *"I'm a bit disappointed with her because I didn't see one bad Medicean at the Sales last year and yet this filly is very backward at the moment. She's looking like a filly we'll run towards the back end of the season, maybe at Dundalk."*

1060. PEAHEN ★★♣
b.f. Ishiguru – Ulysses Daughter
(College Chapel).

March 7. Fifth foal. £11,000Y. Doncaster St Leger. Not sold. Half-brother to the fairly useful 2-y-o dual 5f winner Come Out Fighting, to the fair 2-y-o 9f winner Alfredian Park and the fair 5f winner Towy Valley (all by Bertolini). The dam, a quite useful 3-y-o 5.7f winner, is a half-sister to one winner. The second dam, Trysinger (by Try My Best), is an unraced half-sister to 8 winners. (Mr D Redvers). *"A very big filly, I'll have to be careful with her for now because she's one for later on, but although I've hardly done anything with her, I like what I see. I just hope that everything falls into place because she's an imposing filly to look at but she's too big to be pushing buttons at the moment."*

1061. POSH CRACKER (USA) ★★★★
b.br.f. Johannesburg – Holly's Kid (Pulpit).
January 15. First foal. €34,000Y. Goffs Orby. Not sold. The dam won 2 minor races in the USA at 2 and 3 yrs and is a sister to the US Grade 1 Del Mar Oaks winner Rutherienne. The second dam, Ruthian (by Rahy), a listed winner of 4 races in the USA, is a half-sister to 2 minor winners. *"If I have a black type filly, it's her. Johannesburg's can be difficult temperamentally but once she got settled in here she's been fine. She's doing her job splendidly, very light on her feet and she's a real athlete. I think she's smart and, she's ready to go now."*

1062. REASONS UNKNOWN (IRE) ★★★
ch.c. Camacho – Locorotondo
(Broken Hearted).
April 2. Seventh foal. €12,000Y. Goffs Orby. Ger Lyons. Closely related to the very useful Irish 7f winner, 10f listed-placed and subsequent US Grade 2 8.5f Arlington Classic third Good Day Too (by Danetime) and half-brother to the fair Irish 12f and hurdles winner Loco Grande and the modest dual 1m (including at 2 yrs) and 6f winner Triple Zero (both by Raise A Grand). The dam, a fair 10f to 11f winner of 5 races, is a half-sister to 6 winners. The second dam, Rahwah (by Northern Baby), a fair 12f winner, is closely related to the Group 1 Moyglare Stud Stakes winner Flutter Away and a half-sister to 7 winners. (S Jones). *"A lovely horse, he has ability and will definitely win his maiden. So he's value for money. I could start him over six*

furlongs but he'd be better over seven and a mile later on."

1063. SIXTY EIGHT GUNS (IRE) ★★★★
b.g. Noverre – Misskinta (Desert Sun).
February 27. First foal. €35,000Y. Goffs Orby. Ger Lyons. The dam, a minor Irish 12f winner at 4 yrs, is a half-sister to 4 winners including the Group 3 2m 2f Doncaster Cup winner Far Cry and the dam of the US Grade 3 winner Dress Rehearsal. The second dam, Darabaka (by Doyoun), is an unraced half-sister to 6 winners including the Group 3 Prix Minerve winner Daralinsha (herself the dam of numerous winners) and the listed winner Darata (dam of the French Oaks winner Daryaba). "A big, strapping horse, we have a cracking looking bunch of two-year-olds this year – in the same league as the ones we had last year. He'll definitely win his maiden and he looks like a good Noverre I had called Summit Surge. Most of the two-year-olds this year are named after song titles – just like last year!"

1064. THE REAPER (IRE) ★★★
b.c. Footstepsinthesand – Lady Gregory (In The Wings).
February 12. First foal. €40,000Y. Tattersalls Ireland. Ger Lyons. The dam, a modest all-weather 12f winner, is a half-sister to 3 winners including the Group 3 6f Firth Of Clyde Stakes winner Princess Iris. The second dam, Athlumney Lady (by Lycius), won 3 races at 2 yrs in Ireland including the Group 3 7f Killavullan Stakes and is a half-sister to 4 winners. (S Jones). "He's very smart and I had him entered for a five furlong race – he was ready to go but that's just pure ability. He'll be better suited by six furlongs and he should be one of my horses that'll be aimed for the ten grand sales bonus – my personal ambition this year is to win ten of those races for the yard. This colt is a big, strapping sort – not an early type at all. I used to be associated with sharp, early sorts but nowadays I go for mid-to-late-season types that might be Group horses at two and the real deal at three."

1065. THE RESISTANCE (IRE) ★★★
b.c. Encosta De Lago – Cordelia (Green Desert).
March 11. First foal. £36,000Y. Doncaster St Leger. David Redvers. The dam was placed four times from 5f to 7f at 3 yrs and half-sister to 4 winners. The second dam, Bint Zamayem (by Rainbow Quest), a fairly useful 3-y-o 10f winner, was listed-placed over 10f and is a half-sister to the Group 3 Prix Chloe winner Rouquette. "He's some horse and he's well named because no matter what we throw at him he comes back with a buck and a kick. He's the toughest, hardiest horse I've dealt with. I'll probably run him over six at Leopardstown, purely in the hope that the race will make him think of something else and I won't have to geld him. We're in the business of selling our horses and as this guy is by Encosta De Lago if he wins a maiden as a colt rather than a gelding it would make the difference of a couple of zeros. I'll start him off at six and then I'll step him up later on."

1066. TRANS CITY (IRE) ★★★★
ch.c. Trans Island – Where's Charlotte (Sure Blade).
April 26. Seventh foal. €32,000Y. Tattersalls Ireland. Ger Lyons. Brother to the 5f winner of 7 races (including at 2 yrs) and dual Group 3 placed Bond City and half-brother to the quite useful 7f (at 2 yrs) to 12f winner of 6 races Quince (by Fruits Of Love), the modest 5f winner Admiral Bond (by Titus Livius) and the moderate 8.6f winner Eight Ellington (by Ali-Royal). The dam, a modest sprint maiden, is a half-sister to the listed winner Pea Green. The second dam, One Degree (by Crooner), won at 2 and 4 yrs and is a full or half-sister to 3 winners including the US stakes winner and Group 3 Lowther Stakes second Vocalist. (Vincent Gaul). "He'll be every bit as good as his brother Bond City. He's a lovely horse that covers some ground and I did everything I could not to buy him because he's a Trans Island. But he is a cracker, he's probably got the biggest stride in the yard and he's 'on the leg' at the moment and will probably be a six/seven furlong horse later on."

1067. UNION CITY BLUES (IRE) ★★★
ch.f. Encosta De Lago – Child Prodigy (Ballad Rock).
March 11. Eighth foal. €40,000Y. Goffs Orby. Ger Lyons. Half-sister to Toy Razor (by Refuse To Bend), unplaced in one start at 2 yrs in

2009, to the fairly useful Irish 13f winner Road To Mandalay (by Galileo), the quite useful 2-y-o 8.5f all-weather and subsequent US winner Menuhin (by Royal Academy), the fair 8.3f winner Du Pre (by Singspiel) and the modest 5f winner Heidi's Dash (by Green Desert). The dam, a quite useful 2-y-o 6f winner here, later won a minor race at 3 yrs in the USA and is a half-sister to 5 winners including the German and Italian Group 1 winner Kutub. The second dam, Minnie Habit (by Habitat), an Irish 4-y-o 9f winner, is closely related to the dual Group 3 sprint winner Bermuda Classic (herself dam of the Coronation Stakes winner Shake The Yoke). (S Jones). *"When we were breaking her she was a proper chestnut filly in that she was all sweaty and she wasn't nice at all, but now she's the complete opposite. She's settled into her job and she's smart and honest. She'll win her maiden over six or seven furlongs."*

1068. UNIQUE STYLE (IRE) ★★★
b.c. Desert Style – Shining Creek (Bering).
April 13. Eighth foal. €50,000Y. Goffs Orby. Ger Lyons. Brother to the 2-y-o Group 2 6f Mill Reef Stakes winner Cool Creek. The dam won twice at around 7f at 2 and 3 yrs in Italy and is a half-sister to 6 winners and to the dam of the Group 2 winners Russian Hope, Archange d'Or and Russian Cross. The second dam, High And Dry (by High Line), won once at 2 yrs, was third in the Group 3 Waterford Candelabra Stakes and is a half-sister to 8 winners. *"I'd say this was the prettiest one in the yard – not handsome, but pretty. He's just eye-catching, he's a full-brother to a Group winner and I think he could be smart. Without getting hot and bothered about him he's coming now, slowly but surely."*

GEORGE MARGARSON
1069. DOUBLE DICE ★★
gr.f. Verglas – Fiddle-Dee-Dee (Mujtahid).
January 30. Eighth foal. 7,000Y. Tattersalls October Book 2. G Margarson. Half-sister to the quite useful 6f (at 2 yrs), 5f and subsequent US winner Fiddle Me Blue (by Bluebird), to the modest all-weather 8.5f winner Panic Stations (by Singspiel) and a 4-y-o winner in Belgium. The dam is an unraced half-sister to 5 winners including the listed Ulster Harp Derby winner Sir Simon and the Sun Chariot Stakes second Dartrey. The second dam, Secala (by Secretariat), a stakes-placed winner in the USA, is a half-sister to 5 winners including the South African Group 1 winner Vigliotto and the dams of the US Grade 1 winner Latin American and the Group 2 Sandown Mile winner Wixim. (Mr M B Jenner). *"She was showing me plenty of speed early on but she just got a touch of sore shin so I put her back and I don't expect her out until May. She'll be OK and quite precocious but nothing out of the ordinary."*

1070. GREY SPEEDFIT (IRE) ★★★
gr.c. Verglas – Ladylishandra (Mujadil).
February 3. Fourth foal. £12,000Y. Doncaster St Leger. G Margarson. Brother to the useful dual 6f (at 2 yrs) and 7f winner Tropical Paradise and half-brother to the fair all-weather 9f and 10f winner Nicomedia (by Key Of Luck). The dam, an Irish 2-y-o 6f winner, is a half-sister to 6 winners including the fairly useful 2-y-o 6f winner Pigeon Point. The second dam, Mevlana (by Red Sunset), a French 11f and 12f winner, is a sister to the Group 3 10f Royal Whip Stakes winner Dancing Sunset. (J D Guest). *"This fellow has done nothing but improve. At the sales he was a bit 'squatty' at the Sales but looking at him now he looks like being a bargain. I've given him a bit more time than the year-older Tropical Paradise was given, but he worked four furlongs the other morning and he showed plenty of pace. On pedigree he should get six, maybe seven furlongs."*

1071. HURRICANE GUEST ★★★
ch.c. Hurricane Run – Figlette (Darshaan).
February 25. Fourth foal. 32,000Y. Tattersalls October Book 2. G Margarson. Closely related to the modest dual 11f winner Eightdaysaweek (by Montjeu) and half-brother to Sweet Caroline (by Motivator), unplaced in one start at 2 yrs in 2009 and the quite useful 9f (at 2 yrs) and 11f winner Moment's Notice (by Beat Hollow). The dam is an unraced half-sister to 3 winners including the listed 1m and 10f winner Sublimity and the UAE Group 3 1m winner Marbush. The second dam, Fig Tree Drive (by Miswaki), a fairly useful 2-y-o 6f winner on her only start, is a half-sister to 4 winners. (J D Guest). *"A colt from a good family, he's a proper two-year-old, there's no doubt. After he showed me plenty in his bits of work I*

stopped him because I want to bring him back in May and June for the seven furlong races. I wanted to test him out to see if he could be a Chesham Stakes horse, but I'll be training him with a longer term future in mind."

1072. NO PEACE ★★
b.f. Noverre – Gentle Peace (Orpen).
April 30. 800Y. Tattersalls October 3. Not sold. The dam, a moderate 12f winner, is a half-sister to 2 winners. The second dam, Habaza (by Shernazar), is an unplaced half-sister to 7 winners including the Group 3 winners Hazariya and Hazarista. (Graham Lodge Partnership). *"A late foal, but already showing me more than the others, she's as hard as nails, she's done stalls work and plenty of work with older horses. I'll get her out in April and she's a proper early season two-year-old."*

1073. STORM RUNNER (IRE) ★★
b.c. Rakti – Saibhreas (Last Tycoon).
April 25. Ninth foal. 20,000Y. Tattersalls October Book 2. George Margarson. Brother to the unplaced 2009 2-y-o Helaku and half-brother to the French 1m, 10f (both at 2 yrs) and listed 12f winner Hopes And Fears, to the moderate 1m winner Reigning In Rio (both by Captain Rio), the fairly useful dual 7f winner (including at 2 yrs) Dancing Guest (by Danehill Dancer), the fair 7f all-weather winner Desert Lightning (by Desert Prince) and a winner over hurdles by King's Theatre. The dam, an Irish 10f winner, is a half-sister to 7 winners including the Irish listed winner and Group 3 placed Nordic Soprano. The second dam Angor (by Lorenzaccio), won at 3 yrs and is a half-sister to 6 winners including the dual Group 1 winning sprinter Double Form. (Pitfield Partnership). *"I've had two from the family and they've both been very good. I was worried about the sire's bad temperament, but the mare and the two I trained were so well behaved. I must admit that when I broke this colt in he was really difficult, but since then I've worked him and he's improved no end. He's now got a lovely temperament. All the family are seven furlong/mile horses so I'm bringing him along with a June/July campaign in mind. He has galloped and he works like a two-year-old."*

1074. TALKATIVE GUEST ★★★
b.f. Oratorio – Pedicure (Atticus).
February 16. Fourth foal. £20,000Y. Doncaster St Leger. G Margarson. Half-sister to the French 10f winner High Perfection (by High Chaparral). The dam, placed once at 3 yrs in France, is a full or half-sister to 5 winners including the French listed 5.5f winner and Group 2 Criterium de Maisons-Laffitte second Diableneyev. The second dam, La Pitie (by Devil's Bag), won once at 2 yrs in France and is a half-sister to 4 winners. (J D Guest). *"She's not over-big but I still think she'll need a bit of time. She's done bits of work and although she's shown enough to suggest she'll be alright over five furlongs we're going to wait for six and seven. I would expect her to win at two, albeit much later on and she looks the type that'll be OK."*

1075. TIBERIUS CLAUDIUS (IRE) ★★★★
b.c. Clodovil – Final Favour (Unblest).
March 22. Fourth foal. 21,000Y. Tattersalls October 2. G Margarson. Half-brother to the fair triple 5f winner (including at 2 yrs) Sister Etienne (by Lend A Hand) and to the fair 2-y-o 5f winner Sinead Of Aglish (by Captain Rio). The dam is an unraced half-sister to 9 winners including the Irish Group 3 winner Shindella. The second dam, Antipol (by Polyfoto), is an unraced half-sister to 6 minor winners. (The Hook/Morrison Partnership). *"The apple of my eye at the moment – he's the one that you wait for. But when I bought him people wondered how much I'd had to drink – he was such a squatty looking yearling! Even when I was breaking him in I was wondering if I'd got in wrong, but since I've cantered him he's grown and filled out. No matter what I've worked him with he's never been off the bridle and all I'm training now is the brain because he's such a laid-back character. He's done everything I've asked of him, but I won't run him until the middle of May because if he's as good as I think he is he could be a Royal Ascot horse. Although that route isn't imperative with the guys who own him."* TRAINERS' BARGAIN BUY

1076. UNNAMED ★★★
b.f. Bertolini – Crinkle (Distant Relative).
March 13. 8,000Y. Doncaster St Leger. Not sold. Half-sister to the useful 2-y-o 1m winner

and listed-placed Wave Aside (by Reset), to the fairly useful dual 6f winner Mr Sandicliffe (by Mujahid) and the quite useful 7f and 1m winner Froissee (by Polish Precedent). The dam is an unraced half-sister to the useful 2-y-o 6f winner and Group 2 6f Richmond Stakes third Cedarberg. The second dam, Crinolette (by Sadler's Wells), unplaced on her only start at 2 yrs, is a half-sister to the very smart Group 3 7f Tetrarch Stakes and Group 3 7f Ballycorus Stakes winner Desert Style. (Mrs T A Foreman). *"This filly came in quite late but when I started working her she came to hand really quick. She's done upsides work but I won't push her because I think she's a filly that'll do better from June onwards. But it's a cracking family and they're all sprint types. A big, strong, powerful filly and I think she'll do well."*

1077. UNNAMED ★★
b.c. Storming Home – Sweet Angeline
(Deploy).
February 12. 5,500foal. Tattersalls December. Not sold. Half-sister to the fair 2-y-o 7f winner Rosy Alexander (by Spartacus). The dam, a fair 12f winner, is a half-sister to Medici Code, a quite useful 1m and 9f winner here and subsequently a Grade 2 winner in the USA and to the quite useful 2-y-o 5f and 6f winner and listed-placed Polly Alexander. The second dam, Fiveofive (by Fairy King), a modest 5f (at 2 yrs) and 1m winner, is a half-sister to 4 winners including the Group 3 6f July Stakes third The Old Firm. (Mrs T A Foreman). *"I haven't worked him yet, but he looks a two-year-old and he'll be trained with that in mind. I had the mare, she won over twelve furlongs but it's a good family."*

ALAN McCABE
1078. GEORGE WOOLF ★★★★
ch.f. Iceman – Beading
(Polish Precedent).
April 30. Half-brother to the quite useful 7f (at 2 yrs) and 1m winner Glowing Praise (by Fantastic Light), to the quite useful dual 7f winner Cindertrack (by Singspiel) and the modest 1m winner Satin Braid (by Diktat). The dam, a quite useful 3-y-o 1m winner, is a half-sister to 3 winners including the listed Atalanta Stakes winner Intrepidous. The second dam, Silver Braid (by Miswaki), a useful 2-y-o 7f winner, was second in the Group 3 7.3f Fred Darling Stakes and is a half-sister to 5 winners here and abroad. *"A very nice horse, he's named after the jockey who rode Seabiscuit – they called him 'The Iceman'. A big, strong, quality horse, although he shows speed I don't want to give him any hustle and bustle early on, so he'll start over six furlongs before moving up to seven. If he's good enough I'm hoping he'll shape up into a Champagne Stakes type. He's a nice individual and the pick of my two-year-olds."*

1079. GEORGINA BAILEY ★★★
ch.f. Iffraaj – Baileys First (Alzao).
February 26. Tenth foal. £3,000Y. Doncaster St Leger Festival. Not sold. Half-sister to the quite useful 7f and 1m winner Young Jemmy (by Tagula), to the 2-y-o 7f seller winner Uredale (by Bahhare) and to 2 minor winners in Germany (by Spectrum) and Italy (by Salse). The dam is a placed half-sister to 7 winners including the Group 1 Gran Criterium winner Candy Glen and the Group 3 Derrinstown Stud Derby Trial winner Ashley Park. The second dam, Maiden Concert (by Condorcet), ran once unplaced and is a half-sister to 2 winners. (Sale Of The Century). *"She was cheap, but she's showing all the right signs and the reports on the Iffraaj two-year-olds are good. She's a big, strong filly and we'd be looking to start her off over six furlongs."* TRAINERS' BARGAIN BUY

1080. IL BATTISTA ★★★
b.c. Medicean – Peace
(Sadler's Wells).
March 15. Fourth foal. 6,000Y. Tattersalls October Book 1. Alan McCabe. Half-brother to the unplaced 2009 2-y-o Cordiality (by Kingsalsa). The dam, a quite useful 10f winner, is a half-sister to the Group 1 Lockinge Stakes winner Virtual and to the 2-y-o Group 2 6f Coventry Stakes winner and Group 1 6f Middle Park Stakes third Iceman. The second dam, Virtuous (by Exit To Nowhere), a fairly useful 2-y-o 1m winner, was third in the listed 11.5f Oaks Trial and is a half-sister to 3 winners. (Alotincommon Partnership). *"I have high hopes for him. He goes very well and he was entered to run in mid-April but he got a bit of a setback. Fingers crossed, he's a very nice horse, not that big but a handy-sized horse with a nice temperament. He'd probably want six furlongs to start with, moving up to seven."*

1081. SCOT LANE ★★★
b.f. Diktat – Cape Trafalgar
(Cape Cross).
April 4. Third foal. Half-sister to the fair 2009 7f placed 2-y-o Gritstone (by Dansili). The dam, a fair 5f and 6f 2-y-o winner of 4 races, was subsequently stakes-placed in the USA and is a half-sister to 3 winners. The second dam, West Escape (by Gone West), a fairly useful 1m winner at 3 yrs, is a half-sister to 6 winners. (D W Armstrong). *"Doing all the right things, she was late in but she's looking like a nice filly that'll go six furlongs. A handy-sized, compact filly and I can see her being out in June."*

1082. UNNAMED ★★
b.c. Whipper – Caribbean Escape (Pivotal).
February 17. Fifth foal. £40,000Y. Doncaster St Leger. Not sold. Half-brother to the fairly useful 2-y-o listed 5f winner Knavesmire (by One Cool Cat), to the quite useful triple 6f winner Honey Monster (by Choisir) and the quite useful dual 6f winner (including at 2 yrs) Sleeping Storm (by Danehill Dancer). The dam is an unraced half-sister to 8 winners including the smart listed 6f Abernant Stakes winner and good broodmare Splice. The second dam, Soluce (by Junius), won the Group 3 Irish 1,000 Guineas Trial and is a half-sister to 3 winners. *"He's been showing the right signals, but although people might have expected Whipper to sire really precocious types they seem take a bit more time. He's a nice little horse that's growing at the moment – we're not in any hurry with him."*

1083. UNNAMED ★★★
b.c. Bahamian Bounty – Famcred (Inchinor).
February 6. First foal. 10,000Y. Tattersalls October Book 3. Alan McCabe. The dam, a quite useful 2-y-o dual 7f winner, is a half-sister to a winner in Italy. The second dam, Sumingasefa (by Danehill), a listed-placed winner of 5 races in Italy, is a half-sister to 7 winners. (S O'Sullivan). *"He goes well, he's showing all the right signals and he'll be out over six furlongs in May."*

ED McMAHON

1084. DIAMOND NOIR (IRE) ★★★★
br.c. Diamond Green – Danish Gem (Danehill).
April 10. Fifth foal. €24,000Y. Goffs Open. Damien Shine. Half-brother to the modest 2009 7f placed 2-y-o Jimmy The Poacher (by Verglas) and to the fairly useful 5f and 6f (at 2 yrs) and listed 1m winner Ponty Rossa (by Distant Music). The dam, a 1m winner at 3 yrs in France, is a half-sister to 6 winners. The second dam, Gemaasheh (by Habitat), is an unraced half-sister to 5 winners. *"I'm hoping he's going to turn into a nice horse. He's got a bit of growing to do and he's 'a bit on the leg'. He's a big colt with a lovely action and at the end of May/early June we might see him out. I would think six furlongs would suit to start with and he might get a mile at the end of the year."*

1085. FIGHTER JET ★★
b.c. Oasis Dream – Totality (Dancing Brave).
March 6. Eighth foal. 65,000Y. Tattersalls October Book 1. E McMahon.. Half-brother to the 10f winner Total Devotion (by Desert Prince) and to the 12f winner Total Care (by Caerleon) – both quite useful. The dam, a quite useful 14f winner from just two outings, is a sister to the Epsom and Irish Derby winner Commander in Chief and a half-sister to numerous winners including the champion 2-y-o and miler Warning, the Irish Derby second Deploy, the Great Voltigeur Stakes winner Dushyantor and the Flower Bowl Handicap and Ribblesdale Stakes winner Yashmak. The second dam, Slightly Dangerous (by Roberto), winner of the 7.3f Fred Darling Stakes, was second in the Oaks and is a half-sister to the dams of the Arc winner and top class sire Rainbow Quest and the Dewhurst Stakes dead-heater Scenic. (Ladas). *"He's a bit babyish at the moment and he'll be a back-end type anyway. A lovely, big colt, he's extremely well-bred and still growing, so he's not your normal sharp two-year-old or anything like that. One for the end of the season."*

1086. INDIAN BALLARD (IRE) ★★★
b.c. Oratorio – Cherokee Stream (Indian Ridge).
April 10. First foal. 25,000Y. Tattersalls October Book 2. Ed McMahon. The dam, a fair Irish 7f to 9f placed maiden, is a half-sister to 4 winners. The second dam, Moy Water (by Tirol), an Irish 1m (at 2 yrs) and 9f winner, is a half-sister to 8 winners including

the very useful listed sprint winners Bufalino and Maledetto. *"He's not very big but I think he's sharp enough and I'm not sure whether he'd want five or six furlongs. Sharp enough mentally, it won't be long before he's out."*

1087. LOOK WHO'S KOOL ★★★
b.br.c. Compton Place – Where's Carol (Anfield).
April 12. Half-brother to several winners including the smart listed 6f winner Now Look Here (by Reprimand) and the fairly useful 6f and 7f winner of 3 races and listed-placed Look Here's Carol (by Safawan). The dam, a fair 2-y-o 6f winner of 4 races on the all-weather, is a half-sister to several winners including the useful 7.5f to 1m winner Weet-A-Minute. The second dam, Ludovica (by Bustino), is an unraced half-sister to 6 winners out of Lorelene (by Lorenzaccio), a winner of 4 races and second in the Ebor Handicap. (S L Edwards). *"He's a nice sort with a good action and he'll make a two-year-old alright. Probably a little bit temperamental, but I find Compton Place horses are like that. I should think he'll want top of the ground and I think he'll turn out to be half decent."*

1088. OVEREASY (IRE) ★★★
ch.c. Dr Fong – Desert Alchemy (Green Desert).
April 10. Fourth foal. 15,000Y. Tattersalls October Book 2. Ed McMahon. Half-brother to the quite useful 5f winner Present Alchemy (by Cadeaux Genereux) and to a bumper winner by Selkirk. The dam, a useful listed 7f winner, is a half-sister to 5 winners including the Group 3 winner Express Wish and the listed 7f winner Madid. The second dam, Waffle On (by Chief Singer), a quite useful 3-y-o 6f winner here, subsequently won in France and is a half-sister to 5 winners including the Group 3 Premio Omenoni winner Leap For Joy. (D J Allen, S E Allen & G A Weetman). *"A well-made colt, on breeding he wants six or seven furlongs really but I've not been chasing him along. He's been growing and I'm stepping him up now so he'll be a June type two-year-old I think."*

1089. TEMPLE MEADS ★★★★
ch.c. Avonbridge – Harryana (Efisio).
April 7. Sixth foal. £16,000Y. Doncaster St Leger. J Fretwell. Half-brother to the fair 2009 5f and 6f placed Yeadon (by Fraam), to the useful 2-y-o 6f winner and Group 3 Firth of Clyde Stakes second Sneak Preview (by Monsieur Bond) and the moderate French 10f winner Flaxby (by Mister Baileys). The dam, a fair 2-y-o dual 5f winner, is out of the quite useful 3-y-o 5f winner Allyanna (by Thatching), herself a half-sister to 8 winners. (J C Fretwell). *"He's a proper two-year-old type, very well-made with plenty of size and scope. He'll be going places this year."* TRAINERS' BARGAIN BUY

1090. VENUS EMPRESS ★★★
b.f. Holy Roman Emperor – Pilgrim Spirit (Saint Ballado).
April 27. Fourth foal. 10,000Y. Tattersalls October Book 2. J Fretwell. Closely related to the fair 2009 2-y-o dual 6f winner Soul Heaven (by Oratorio). The dam, a modest 14f placed maiden, is a half-sister to a minor winner in the USA. The second dam, Oshima (by Mr Prospector), a minor dual winner in the USA, is a sister to the US Grade 2 winner and French 1,000 Guineas second Sha Tha and a half-sister to 3 winners. (J C Fretwell). *"I've not rushed her yet because she's a bit on her toes and I like them to settle a bit before I move them along. She looks very well at the moment and there's plenty to work with, but although she looks a June type I think she'll want a bit of cut in the ground. She's not over-big but she's all in proportion."*

1091. UNNAMED ★★
b.c. Royal Applause – Look Here's Carol (Safawan).
February 26. Second foal. Half-brother to the fair 2-y-o 5f winner Look Whos Next (by Compton Place). The dam, a fairly useful 6f and 7f winner of 3 races, was listed-placed and is a half-sister to several winners including the smart listed 6f winner Now Look Here. The second dam, Where's Carol (by Anfield), was a fair 2-y-o 6f winner of 4 races on the all-weather. (S L Edwards). *"He's not over-big and I'd like to have got going with him earlier but he wasn't sharp enough mentally. He's just starting to come now, so really it's just onwards and upwards."*

1092. UNNAMED ★★
b.f. Refuse To Bend – Source Of Life (Fasliyev).

March 5. Second foal. Half-sister to the quite useful 2009 2-y-o 6f debut winner Decorative (by Danehill Dancer). The dam is an unraced half-sister to 6 winners including the Group 3 Prix de Flore winner Australie. The second dam, Asnieres (by Spend A Buck), a minor winner in France at 4 yrs, is a half-sister to 9 winners including the Breeders Cup Classic and Prix d'Ispahan winner Arcangues, the Prix de Psyche winner and French 1,000 Guineas second Agathe (dam of the Group 1 winners Aquarelliste and Artiste Royal) and the dams of the 1,000 Guineas winner Cape Verdi and the dual Grade 1 winner Angara. (Barouche Stud). *"She's had a bit of a setback so she's on box rest for a bit now. Time will tell, but I think she's got a bit of depth on the dam's side, so this little problem hasn't worried me because she won't be out until later on this season."*

BRIAN MEEHAN
1093. ACIANO (IRE) ★★★★
b.c. Kheleyf – Blue Crystal (Lure).
February 24. Sixth foal. 70,000Y. Tattersalls October Book 1. Hugo Merry. Half-brother to the Italian 2-y-o winner and listed placed Golden Liberty (by Statue Of Liberty) and to a minor winner in Italy by Grand Lodge. The dam, a fair 10.5f winner in Ireland, is a half-sister to 3 minor winners. The second dam, Crystal Cross (by Roberto), a quite useful winner of 4 races at up to 14f, is a half-sister to the Group 1 Haydock Park Sprint Cup winner Iktamal, the French Group 2 winner First Magnitude and the Grade 2 Arkansas Derby winner Rockamundo. (S P Tucker). *"He's a very nice, strong horse that's in work at the moment. I'd say he's a real quality horse that would be suited by six furlongs."*

1094. ALL THE EVIL (IRE) ★★★
ch.c. Exceed And Excel – Mezzanine (Sadler's Wells).
March 30. Seventh foal. 52,000Y. Tattersalls October Book 1. Angie Sykes. Closely related to the Group 2 6f Duke Of York Stakes and Group 3 6f Greenlands Stakes winner The Kiddykid (by Danetime) and to the modest all-weather 13f and 16.5 winner Annus Iucundus (by Desert King) and half-brother to the quite useful 0f and 12f winner Mezzanisi (by Kalanisi), the fair 7f winner World Series (by Almutawakel) and the modest 1m and 10f winner Dancing Jest (by Averti). The dam is an unraced half-sister to 3 winners here and abroad. The second dam, Nazeera (by Lashkari), won in France and is a half-sister to 8 winners including the French Derby winner Natroun. (Findlay & Sangster). *"He's got a bit of size to him but he's fairly sharp. I would imagine he'd be a June type and he has a nice bit of speed about him."*

1095. ANGLE KNIGHT (USA) ★★★★
b.c. Arch – Safeen (Storm Cat).
April 23. Fifth foal. Half-brother to the fairly useful 2009 2-y-o 1m winner Manhattan Fox (by Elusive Quality). The dam is an unraced half-sister to the listed winner and Italian Group 3 winner Revere. The second dam, Bint Pasha (by Affirmed), won the Prix Vermeille, the Yorkshire Oaks and the Group 2 Pretty Polly Stakes. (Mr Catesby W Clay). *"He looks very sharp and the way he's working at the moment I'd say he'd be out in May and that he'd be happy with either five or six furlongs. A quality colt."*

1096. BLACK MOTH (IRE) ★★★★
b.c. Invincible Spirit – Tshusick (Dancing Brave).
April 26. Eleventh foal. 55,000Y. Tattersalls October Book 1. McKeever St Lawrence. Half-brother to the very smart Group 3 Prix du Petit Couvert, Cornwallis Stakes and Molecomb Stakes winner Majestic Missile (by Royal Applause), the fairly useful 2-y-o dual 5f winner and Group 3 Princess Margaret Stakes third Parisian Elegance (by Zilzal), the quite useful all-weather 5f winner of 3 races Liberty Bound (by Primo Dominie), the quite useful 7f winner of 4 races Tribal Prince (by Prince Sabo) and a winner in Italy by Elnadim. The dam, a quite useful 7f winner at 3 yrs, is a half-sister to 3 winners here and abroad. The second dam, Infanta Real (by Formidable), won the listed 5f Doncaster Stakes at 2 yrs and is a half-sister to 2 winners. (Findlay & Sangster). *"He's very sharp, he's working very well and he looks the part. A sprinting type, he might make his debut at the Guineas meeting."*

1097. BRAZZA DI MARE (IRE) ★★
b.c. Rainbow Quest – Sea Picture (Royal Academy).

April 19. Closely related to the fair 1m winner Sea Nymph (by Spectrum) and half-brother to the quite useful 7f winner Tableau Vivant (by Pivotal). The dam, placed once over 7f at 2 yrs, is a half-sister to 9 winners including the Group 1 Yorkshire Oaks winner Hellenic – herself dam of the high-class filly Islington. The second dam, Grecian Sea (by Homeric), won once in France, was fourth in the Group 3 7f Prix du Calvados and is a half-sister to 8 winners including Sailor's Mate (Group 3 Meld Stakes). (Ballymacoll Stud Farm Ltd). *"He's not been long broken and he's a nice, big horse that won't be ready until September."*

1098. BREVITY (USA) ★★★
b.f. *Street Cry – Cut Short (Diesis).*
April 9. The dam, a quite useful 1m winner, is a sister to the smart Daggers Drawn (winner of the Group 2 6f Richmond Stakes and the Group 2 7f Laurent Perrier Rose Champagne Stakes) and a half-sister to the very useful 2-y-o dual 6f winner Enemy Action. The second dam, Sun And Shade (by Ajdal), a useful 2-y-o 6f winner, is a half-sister to the very smart Group 2 Park Hill Stakes and Group 2 Prix de Royallieu winner Madame Dubois (herself dam the Irish 2,000 Guineas winner Indian Haven and the Group 1 Gran Criterium winner Count Dubois). (Mrs L Freedman). *"A filly that wants plenty of time, she's by a great stallion and it's a lovely family. She's one for around August/ September time."*

1099. BUCKLAND (IRE) ★★
b.c. *Oratorio – Dollar Bird (Kris).*
May 15. Fifth foal. €85,000Y. Goffs Orby. McKeever St Lawrence. Closely related to the winner Dollar Chick (by Dansili) and half-brother to the useful 9.7f winner and listed-placed Higher Love and to the modest 12f winner Kentucky Warbler (both by Sadler's Wells). The dam, a useful 2-y-o 8.2f winner and second in the listed 11.5f Oaks Trial, is a half-sister to 7 winners including the very useful Group 2 12f King Edward VII Stakes winner Amfortas and the Group 3 10.5f Prix de Royaumont winner Legend Maker (herself dam of the 1,000 Guineas winner Virginia Waters). The second dam, High Spirited (by Shirley Heights), a quite useful winner of two races over 14f and 2m, is a sister to the Premio

Roma winner High Hawk (dam of the Breeders Cup Turf winner In the Wings) and a half-sister to the dams of the Derby winner High-Rise and the Rothmans International winner Infamy. (Brimacombe, McNally, Vinciguerra, Sangster). *"A good-looking colt, he looks an early sort but he's had a sore shin so I'd say it'll be late May before he's ready to start."*

1100. CANAVERAL ★★★
b.br.c. *Cape Cross – Tarneem (Zilzal).*
February 10. Ninth foal. £60,000Y. Doncaster St Leger. McKeever St Lawrence. Half-brother to the smart 7f (at 2 yrs) and Group 3 9f Darley Stakes winner and Group 1 Coronation Cup third Enforcer, to the quite useful 2-y-o dual 5f winner Lord Of The Inn, the modest 1m winner Uncle Brit (all by Efisio), the fair 5.7f winner Innstyle (by Daggers Drawn) and Kris's Bank (by Inchinor), a winner of 9 races at up to 13.5f in Italy. The dam, a quite useful 3-y-o 1m winner, is a half-sister to 4 minor winners abroad. The second dam, Willowy Mood (by Will Win), won 14 races including two Grade 3 events in the USA and is a half-sister to 9 winners. (Manton Racing Partnership). *"He's going to want plenty of time but he's got speed and he's one for six or seven furlongs around August time."*

1101. DEAN SWIFT ★★★★
b.c. *Dansili – Magical Romance (Barathea).*
January 21. First foal. The dam, a 2-y-o Group 1 6f Cheveley Park Stakes winner, is a sister to the fairly useful 2-y-o 7f winner and subsequent Canadian Grade 3 placed Saree and closely related to the Oaks, Irish Oaks and Yorkshire Oaks winner Alexandrova and the smart listed 2-y-o 1m winner and Group 2 1m Beresford Stakes third Masterofthehorse. The second dam, Shouk (by Shirley Heights), a quite useful 10.5f winner, is closely related to the listed winner and Group 3 Park Hill Stakes third Puce and a half-sister to 6 winners. (Manton Racing Partnership). *"A high quality colt, he looks very nice and I can see him doing well over seven furlongs in July."*

1102. DOLCEZZA (IRE) ★★
ch.f. *Dr Fong – Wedding Cake (Groom Dancer).*
April 21. Half-sister to the modest 11f winner Mehendi (by Indian Danehill). The dam, a fair

12f winner, is a sister to the useful 7f (at 2 yrs) and listed 10f winner Athens Belle and a half-sister to the Group 2 Geoffrey Freer Stakes winner Multicolored and the Group 1 12f Grand Prix de Saint-Cloud winner Gamut. The second dam, Greektown (by Ela-Mana-Mou), a French 10f and 12f winner, is a half-sister to the high-class stayer Sought Out (dam of the Derby winner North Light) and to Scots Lass (dam of the Group 2 Great Voltigeur Stakes winner Bonny Scot). (Ballymacoll Stud Farm Ltd). *"A typical Dr Fong, she's a scopey filly and won't be seen out much later on this season."*

1103. EL MUQBIL (IRE) ★★★♠
b.c. Medicean – Tariysha (Daylami).
February 23. Second foal. 450,000Y. Tattersalls October Book 1. Shadwell Estate Co. Half-brother to the 2009 2-y-o Group 1 6f Prix Morny and Group 2 6f July Stakes winner Arcano (by Oasis Dream). The dam is an unraced half-sister to 2 winners and to the dam of the Group 2 Flying Childers Stakes winner Godfrey Street. The second dam, Tarwiya (by Dominion), won the Group 3 7f C L Weld Park Stakes, was third in the Irish 1,000 Guineas and is a half-sister to 5 winners including the Group 3 Norfolk Stakes winner Blue Dakota. (Hamdan Al Maktoum). *"A very similar horse to his half-brother Arcano. He's strong, moves well and has a very good temperament, but he'll take plenty of time."*

1104. ENJOY TODAY (USA) ★★★★
ch.c. Kingmambo – Queen's Logic (Grand Lodge).
March 14. Half-brother to the 2009 2-y-o Group 2 Lowther Stakes and Group 3 Princess Margaret Stakes winner and Group 1 Cheveley Park Stakes third Lady Of The Desert (by Rahy), to the quite useful 2-y-o 1m and subsequent UAE 6f winner Go On Be A Tiger (by Machiavellian) and the fair 9f winner Dunes Queen (by Elusive Quality). The dam, a champion 2-y-o filly and winner of the Group 1 6f Cheveley Park Stakes and the Group 2 6f Lowther Stakes, is a half-sister to the top-class multiple Group 1 winner Dylan Thomas. The second dam, Lagrion (by Diesis), was placed 5 times in Ireland and stayed 12f and is a full or half-sister to 3 winners. (Jaber Abdullah). *"He looks very nice. A quality colt for around July over seven furlongs."*

1105. GOOD MORNING DUBAI (IRE) ★★★
b.f. Dubawi – Min Asl Wafi (Octagonal).
May 5. Half-sister to the fair 2009 2-y-o 5f winner Texas Queen (by Shamardal). The dam, a fair 7f placed 3-y-o, is a half-sister to the high-class Group 1 1m St James's Palace Stakes and Group 2 6f Mill Reef Stakes winner Zafeen to the very useful listed 7f winner Atlantic Sport and the useful 2-y-o Group 3 7f Prix du Calvados winner Ya Hajar. The second dam, Shy Lady (by Kaldoun), winner of a listed event over 6f in Germany, was fourth in the Group 2 6f Moet and Chandon Rennen and is a half-sister to 4 winners. (Jaber Abdullah). *"She's sharp, she goes well and won't be too long before she's ready. I'd expect her out in May."*

1106. GUISHO (IRE) ★★★
b.c. Iffraaj – Jorghinia (Seattle Slew).
March 4. Fifth foal. €30,000Y. Goffs Orby. Not sold. Half-brother to the useful 2009 2-y-o Group 3 7f Somerville Tattersall Stakes winner Sir Parky (by Choisir) and to the minor US winner of 3 races Elements (by Charismatic). The dam is a placed half-sister to 7 winners including the US stakes winner and Grade 2 placed Green Light. The second dam, Jade Jewel (by Mr Prospector), is an unplaced sister to the US dual Grade 1 winner Jade Hunter. (Findlay & Sangster). *"He shows lots of speed but he's a big horse so he'll need a bit more time. He's nice and should be a six/seven furlong two-year-old."*

1107. HAPPY TODAY (USA) ★★★★★
b.c. Gone West – Shy Lady (Kaldoun).
April 16. Seventh foal. Closely related to the high-class Group 1 1m St James's Palace Stakes and Group 2 6f Mill Reef Stakes winner Zafeen (by Zafonic) and to the very useful listed 7f winner Atlantic Sport (by Machiavellian) and half-brother to the useful 2-y-o Group 3 7f Prix du Calvados winner Ya Hajar (by Lycius). The dam, winner of a listed event over 6f in Germany, was fourth in the Group 2 6f Moet and Chandon Rennen and is a half-sister to 4 winners. The second dam, the minor French 3-y-o winner Shy Danceuse (by Groom Dancer), is a half-sister to the dual Group 3 winner Diffident. (Jaber Abdullah). *"A quality colt with a good pedigree, he looks very nice.*

The type to be seen out from July over seven furlongs before we step him up to a mile. He's one I particularly like."

1108. INDIGO WAY ★★★
b.g. Encosta De Lago – Artistic Blue (Diesis).
March 25. Sixth foal. 20,000Y. Tattersalls October Book 2. McKeever St Lawrence. Half-brother to the fairly useful 12f winner Wandle (by Galileo) and to a 3-y-o winner in Japan by Machiavellian. The dam won the listed 7f Tyros Stakes, was second in the Group 3 7f Boland Stakes and is a half-sister to 6 winners including the Irish listed winners Queen Of Palms and Cool Clarity. The second dam, Tapolite (by Tap On Wood), won the listed 7f Tyros Stakes, is a sister to the 2-y-o Group 3 1m Killavullen Stakes winner Sedulous and a half-sister to 3 winners. (N B Attenborough, Mrs L Mann, Mrs L Way). *"We thought that these Encosta De Lago's might need a bit of time but this horse looks early. He's working very well and he'll be out in early May."* TRAINERS' BARGAIN BUY

1109. JAN SMUTS (IRE) ★★★★
b.c. Johannesburg – Choice House (Chester House).
January 12. Fourth foal. 67,000Y. Tattersalls October Book 2. McKeever St Lawrence. The dam is an unraced half-sister to one winner. The second dam, Choice Spirit (by Danzig), won the listed 1m Prix de la Calonne and is a half-sister to 8 winners including Zafonic and Zamindar. (R C Tooth). *"A sharp, good-sort of horse and a typical Johannesburg. I like him a lot, he's straightforward and I'll start him off at six furlongs before stepping him up seven. He should be racing by early June."*

1110. LITTLE HOT SHOT (IRE) ★★★★
b.f. Bertolini – Gold Queen (Grand Lodge).
January 26. Second foal. Half-sister to the quite useful 2009 2-y-o 6f winner Secret Queen (by Zafeen). The dam, a quite useful 2-y-o 7.5f winner, is a half-sister to 2 winners including the listed 1m winner Silver Pivotal. The second dam, Silver Colours (by Silver Hawk), a useful 2-y-o listed 1m winner, is a half-sister to 3 winners including the Japanese Grade 2 winner God Of Chance and the Royal Lodge Stakes third Desaru. (Jaber Abdullah). *"A nice, sharp filly as you'd expect from the pedigree. I had her half-sister who won over six furlongs last year and this filly would be a similar. A typical Bertolini, she has a good temperament and she's a nice filly that won't be long before she's out – probably early May."*

1111. MANTOBA ★★★
b.c. Noverre – Coming Home (Vettori).
February 16. Third foal. 52,000Y. Tattersalls October Book 1. McKeever St Lawrence. The dam, a minor French middle-distance winner, is a half-sister to 2 winners. The second dam, Bonne Etoile (by Diesis), a fairly useful winner of 3 races at 3 yrs including a listed event over 10f, is a half-sister to 5 winners. (Manton Racing Partnership). *"A quality colt, he's strong but needs a bit more time. He's going to go seven furlongs and he's a typical Noverre – good value for money."*

1112. MISS ELEGANCE ★★
b.f. Mind Games – Mania (Danehill).
January 13. Fifth foal. 20,000Y. Tattersalls October Book 2. Not sold. Sister to the fairly useful 2-y-o 6f winner Fanatical and half-sister to the fair 2009 2-y-o 6f winner (on her only start) Marrayah (by Fraam) and the quite useful 2-y-o 6f winner Gower Valentine (by Primo Valentino). The dam is an unraced half-sister to 4 winners including the dam of the Group 1 winners Youmzain and Creachadoir. The second dam, Anima (by Ajdal), is a placed half-sister to 8 winners including the multiple Group 1 winner Pilsudski. (Mr T & Mrs M E Holdcroft). *"A nice, big filly that wants a bit of time still. I haven't done a lot with her but the way she's bred you'd imagine she'd be a sprinter."*

1113. MORTITIA ★★★★
b.f. Dansili – Simianna (Bluegrass Prince).
March 22. Third foal. 35,000Y. Tattersalls October Book 2. Not sold. Half-sister to the moderate 2009 6f placed 2-y-o Anna's Boy (by Reel Buddy). The dam, a useful and tough listed sprint winner of 5 races, was second in the Group 3 Ballyogan Stakes and is a half-sister to 2 winners. The second dam, Lowrianna (by Cyrano de Bergerac), a moderate 2-y-o 5f winner, is a half-sister to 2 winners. (Mr T & Mrs

M E Holdcroft). *"A lovely filly, I imagine she'll make a two-year-old in mid-season, she's very classy and goes really well."*

1114. MORERMALOKE ★★★
ch.c. Bahamian Bounty – Rainbow End (Botanic).
March 18. Third foal. £60,000Y. Doncaster St Leger. McKeever St Lawrence. Half-brother to a minor winner abroad by Dr Fong. The dam, a fairly useful 10f winner, is a half-sister to 2 winners. The second dam, High Finish (by High Line), is an unplaced full or half-sister to 11 winners including Munwar (Group 3 Lingfield Derby Trial). (Findlay & Sangster). *"He looks sharp but he's not going to be that early because he's just needing a bit of time off at the moment. But he's a very nice colt and when he's ready I'd say he'd be no exception to most Bahamian Bounty's in that he'll show speed."*

1115. MUQTARRIB (IRE) ★★★
b.c. Medicean – Anna Karenina (Atticus).
March 10. Fourth foal. €140,000Y. Arqana Deauville August. Shadwell Estate Co. Half-brother to the useful Irish 7f (at 2 yrs) and listed 7.5f winner Anna's Rock (by Rock Of Gibraltar) and to the useful 1m winner and listed-placed Sugar Mint (by High Chaparral). The dam is an unraced half-sister to the Group 3 Prix de Psyche winner and French 1,000 Guineas and French Oaks placed Agathe (herself dam of the Grade/Group 1 winners Artiste Royale and Aquarelliste), to the Breeders Cup Classic winner Arcangues and the dams of the Group/Grade 1 winners Cape Verdi and Angara. The second dam, Albertine (by Irish River), a smart winner of 2 races at up to 10f, was placed in the Group 2 Prix de l'Opera and is a half-sister to 8 winners including the high-class middle-distance stayer Ashmore and the smart middle-distance filly Acoma. (Hamdan Al Maktoum). *"He still wants plenty of time but for a big horse he goes well."*

1116. MURBEH (IRE) ★★★
b.g. Elusive City – My Funny Valentine (Mukaddamah).
February 2. Seventh foal. £77,000Y. Doncaster St Leger. Shadwell Estate Co. Half-brother to the fair 2009 Irish 2-y-o 1m winner Lyle Lady (by Traditionally) and to 3 minor winners in Italy by Nashwan, Mark Of Esteem and Singspiel. The dam, a winner of 7 races at 2 to 4 yrs in Italy, was listed placed 10 times and is a half-sister to 3 minor winners. The second dam, Imperfect Timing (by Coquelin), is an unraced half-sister to 6 winners. (Hamdan Al Maktoum). *"He's quite quick and if he hadn't had a small mishap he'd have been running any time now. He should be out in May, over six or seven furlongs."*

1117. NAFEDAH (USA) ★★
b.f. Henny Hughes – Khasayl (Lycius).
March 17. The dam was a very useful listed 5f winner at both 2 and 3 yrs. The second dam, Muwajaha (by Night Shift), a fairly useful 6f winner, is a half-sister to numerous winners including the useful listed 2-y-o 7f winner Muklah. (Hamdan Al Maktoum). *"She's not arrived here yet, so I know nothing about her."*

1118. NINTH PARALLEL (USA) ★★★★
b.br.c. Mr Greeley – Nemea (The Minstrel).
January 30. Tenth foal. 210,000Y. Tattersalls October Book 1. Sir Robert Ogden. Half-brother to the very smart filly Lovers Knot, winner of the Group 2 1m Falmouth Stakes and the US Grade 3 De La Rose Handicap and to the very useful 1m (at 2 yrs) and 9f winner and listed-placed Foodbroker Founder (both by Groom Dancer) and the Irish 2-y-o 6f winner El Fuego (by Fusaichi Pegasus). The dam, a fairly useful 10f winner, stayed 2m and is a half-sister to 9 winners including the useful 12f winners Topsider Man and Bryan Station and the useful stayer Muir Station. The second dam, Donna Inez (by Herbager), a stakes winner of 4 races in the USA, is a half-sister to 6 winners including the Kentucky Derby and Breeders Cup Classic winner Ferdinand. (Sir Robert Ogden). *"A lovely big horse, he'll want plenty of time but he goes very well. I'm very pleased with him."*

1119. PAPAS FRITAS ★★
ch.c. Dr Fong – Locharia (Wolfhound).
March 6. Fifth foal. 52,000Y. Tattersalls October Book 2. BBA (Ire). Half-brother to the fair 5f winner Yanza (by Bahamian Bounty), to the quite useful 6f and 1m winner Credit Swap (by Diktat) and the modest 6f winner

Vivi Belle (by Cadeaux Genereux). The dam was a fairly useful 2-y-o 5f winner. The second dam, Lochbelle (by Robellino), a fair 10.2f winner, is a half-sister to 3 winners including the champion sprinter Lochsong (winner of the Prix de l'Abbaye (twice), the Kings Stand Stakes, the Nunthorpe Stakes, etc) and the Nunthorpe Stakes winner Lochangel. (Findlay & Sangster). *"He got a little sick otherwise he'd have been ready soon, but as he's by Dr Fong he'll want seven furlongs anyway."*

1120. QUADRANT (IRE) ★★★★
br.c. Shamardal – Quite Elusive (Elusive Quality).
February 9. Second foal. 57,000Y. Tattersalls October Book 2. Blandford Bloodstock. Half-brother to Quite Something (by Footstepsinthesand), placed fourth over 7f on her only start at 2 yrs in 2009. The dam is an unraced half-sister to 7 winners including a French listed winner. The second dam, Quarrel Over Halo (by Halo), is a half-sister to 9 winners including the US Grade 2 winner Suivi. (Highclere Thoroughbred Racing – Masquerade). *"He'll be ready for June or July, he goes well, has a nice attitude and I like him a lot."*

1121. RED EYES ★★
b.c. Beat Hollow – Kardelle (Kalaglow).
February 21. Seventh living foal. 48,000Y. Tattersalls October Book 2. Hugo Merry. Half-brother to the 6f (at 2 yrs) to 1m and subsequent US winner and Group 1 National Stakes second King's County (by Fairy King), to the quite useful 1m and 8.5f winner Airbuss (by Mozart), the modest 6f all-weather winner Deuxieme (by Second Empire), a winner in Italy by Grand Lodge and a multiple winner in Hong Kong by Salse. The dam, a quite-useful middle-distance placed maiden, is a half-sister to 6 winners including the John Porter Stakes and Lancashire Oaks winner Spout and the French listed winner Mon Domino. The second dam, Arderelle (by Pharly), a quite useful 3-y-o 10f winner, is a half-sister to 8 winners including the Group 2 Prix Greffulhe winner Arokar. (Jaber Abdullah). *"He'll be ready around mid-summer, he goes well and will want seven furlongs and a mile."*

1122. RED LITE (IRE) ★★
b.f. Red Ransom – Cloudy Bay (Zilzal).
May 15. Second foal. 28,000Y. Tattersalls October Book 2. McKeever St Lawrence. The dam won twice at 3 yrs in Germany and is a half-sister to 4 winners including Swedish Group 3 winner Calrissian. The second dam, Centaine (by Royal Academy), a winner of 3 races in Germany including the Group 2 11f Preis der Diana, is a half-sister to 6 winners. (R C Tooth). *"She should be racing by late May/early June but Red Ransom's normally want seven furlongs."*

1123. SANAABEK (IRE) ★★★
b.f. Chineur – Lulu Island (Zafonic).
April 12. Fifth foal. £38,000Y. Doncaster St Leger. Shadwell Estate Co. Half-sister to the Swedish 2-y-o winner Rock Of Lambada (by Indian Rocket). The dam is an unraced half-sister to 2 winners. The second dam, Twafeaj (by Topsider), won 3 races including the Group 1 Moyglare Stud Stakes and the Group 3 Prix de Meautry and is a half-sister to 3 winners. (Hamdan Al Maktoum). *"She goes well and I'd say she'd be racing by late May. A nice filly, we'll start her at six furlongs I should imagine."*

1124. SECRET GOLD (IRE) ★★★
b.f. Exceed And Excel – Janayen (by Zafonic)
April 19. Half-sister to the quite useful 2009 2-y-o 5f winner Nadeen (by Bahamian Bounty). The dam, a fairly useful dual 1m winner, is a half-sister to the useful 2-y-o 7f winner Manntab. The second dam, Saafeya (by Sadler's Wells), a very useful listed 10f winner of 6 races, is a half-sister to one winner. (Jaber Abdullah). *"She goes well, she'll be out in late May and she's a good-looking filly but she'll probably want a bit of a trip – seven furlongs."*

1125. SHIM SHAM (IRE) ★★★
ch.f. Danehill Dancer – Pirie (Green Dancer).
May 17. Seventh foal. 180,000Y. Tattersalls October Book 1. Blandford Bloodstock. Sister to the Group 3 7f Tetrarch Stakes and US Grade 3 stakes winner and Irish 2,000 Guineas third Decado and half-sister to the fair 2009 2-y-o 7f winner Smoky Cloud (by Refuse To Bend) and the quite useful 7f and 10f winner Another Faux Pas (by Slip Anchor).

The dam is an unraced half-sister to 8 winners including the Group 2 Derrinstown Stud Derby Trial Stakes winner Fracas. The second dam, Klarifi (by Habitat), won the listed 7f Ballycorus Stakes and is a full or half-sister to 7 winners including the smart Irish miler Captivator and to the dam of the Irish Oaks winner Wemyss Bight. (B E Nielsen). *"A smart looking filly, I'm holding her back a bit because she was a late foal, although she could be ready anytime."*

1126. SISINDU (IRE) ★★★★
b.c. *Kheleyf – Nandy's Cavern (Lion Cavern).*
April 12. Third foal. 110,000Y. Tattersalls October Book 2. Hugo Merry. The dam, placed once at 2 yrs in Italy, is a half-sister to 5 winners including the dual Italian listed winner Mister Cavern. The second dam, Slow Jazz (by Chief's Crown), a French 6f, 6.7f and listed 1m winner, is a three-parts sister to the smart Group 1 6f Middle Park Stakes winner Zieten and to the Group 1 6f Cheveley Park Stakes winner Blue Duster. (Brimacombe, McNally, Vinciguerra, Sangster). *"A big, strong horse, he goes well and I like him a lot. One for June time and he looks a quality two-year-old."*

1127. SLEEK GOLD ★★★★
b.f. *Dansili – Ya Hajar (Lycius).*
March 13. Half-sister to the quite useful 3-y-o 6f winner Muhajaar (by Cape Cross) and to the fair 10f and 11f winner Laish Al Hajar (by Grand Lodge). The dam, a useful 2-y-o Group 3 7f Prix du Calvados winner, is a half-sister to the high-class Group 1 1m St James's Palace Stakes and Group 2 6f Mill Reef Stakes winner Zafeen. The second dam, Shy Lady (by Kaldoun), winner of a listed event over 6f in Germany, was fourth in the Group 2 6f Moet and Chandon Rennen. (Jaber Abdullah). *"She's going to want plenty of time but she goes very well and I like her a lot. She'll want seven furlongs or a mile."*

1128. STAR TODAY ★★★★
b.f. *Invincible Spirit – Bint Zamayem (Rainbow Quest).*
February 25. Eleventh foal. €80,000Y. Goffs Orby. Gill Richardson. Closely related to the useful Irish 6f (at 2 yrs) and 7f winner and Group 3 Debutante Stakes third Sweet Deimos (by Green Desert) and half-sister to the listed 1m winner Mia's Boy (by Pivotal), to the quite useful 7.6f winner Queenie (by Indian Ridge) and the fair 2-y-o 1m winner Rumbalara (by Intikhab). The dam, a fairly useful 3-y-o 10f winner, was listed-placed over 10f and is a half-sister to the Group 3 Prix Chloe winner Rouquette and the US stakes winner Moody's Cat. The second dam, Zamayem (by Sadler's Wells), is an unraced half-sister to 4 winners. (Jaber Abdullah). *"She should be racing in May, probably starting over six furlongs and she looks a smart filly. In fact I'd say she looks very nice and is one to follow."*

1129. STYLE SQUAD (USA) ★★
b.br.f. *Dynaformer – Stylish (Thunder Gulch).*
February 2. Third foal. $310,000Y. Keeneland September. Hugo Merry. The dam won 8 races including two Grade 3 events in the USA and is a half-sister to 5 winners including the dual US Grade 2 placed Tangazi. The second dam, Miss Lenora (by Theatrical), a US Grade 3 9f Bewitch Stakes winner, is a half-sister to the French 1,000 Guineas winner Madeleine's Dream out of the French and Irish 1,000 Guineas winner L'Attrayante (by Tyrant). (Mr A Rosen). *"She still wants plenty of time which is typical of the sire. She goes well for a big filly but she wouldn't be ready until the back end of the season."*

1130. TALKHEES (IRE) ★★★
b.f. *Invincible Spirit – Asaafeer (Dayjur).*
February 22. Half-sister to the modest dual 6f winner Athaakeel (by Almutawakel). The dam is an unraced sister to the very useful 2-y-o Group 3 6f Cherry Hinton Stakes and listed 5f Windsor Castle Stakes winner Asfurah and a half-sister to several winners. The second dam, Mathkurh (by Riverman), a useful 5f (at 2 yrs) and 6f winner, is a half-sister to the Group 3 6f Princess Margaret Stakes winner Muhbubh. (Hamdan Al Maktoum). *"She's sharp, she missed a bit of time in march but it looks like she's catching back up now and I can her being ready in May. Either five or six furlongs would suit and I think she's quite nice."*

1131. TALK TALK (IRE) ★★★♠
b.c. *Oratorio – Sybella (In The Wings).*
March 29. First foal. £37,000Y. Doncaster St Leger. Not sold. The dam, a fair 12f placed maiden, is a half-sister to 3 winners including

the listed Oaks Trial winner Sister Sophia. The second dam, Samara (by Polish Patriot), won 2 listed events over 1m and 8.5f and is a half-sister to 8 winners including the German Group 2 winner Soto-Grande. (Mrs Carmen Burrell & Jonathan Harvey). *"Very sharp, he goes really well and it shouldn't be any later than May before he's out."*

1132. THE LONG GAME ★★★
b.c. Kyllachy – Something Blue (Petong).
February 27. Eighth foal. 90,000Y. Tattersalls October Book 2. Angie Sykes. Brother to the useful Group 3 5f Prix de Saint-Georges and triple sprint listed winner Mood Music and half-brother to the fairly useful 5f (at 2 yrs) and 6f winner of 8 races Steel Blue, the fair 6f and 7f winner of 12 races Yorkshire Blue (both by Atraf), the quite useful 5f and 6f winner of 9 races (including at 2 yrs) Memphis Man (by Bertolini) and the fair 6f winner Angel Song (by Dansili). The dam is an unplaced sister to one winner and a half-sister to 5 winners including the Group 3 5f Palace House Stakes second Blues Indigo and the 2-y-o winner Indigo (herself dam of the smart sprinters Astonished and Bishops Court). The second dam, Blueit (by Bold Lad, Ire), was a useful 2-y-o 5f winner and a full or half-sister to 3 winners. (Findlay & Sangster). *"He's just taking his time to get it all together, but he looks a smart colt and I look forward to running him in May."*

1133. VELVET UNDERGROUND (IRE) ★★★
ch.c. Exceed And Excel – Taalluf (Hansel).
March 23. Seventh foal. £35,000Y. Doncaster St Leger. McKeever St Lawrence. Half-brother to the fair 2009 2-y-o 6f winner Bathwick Gold (by Noverre), to the fairly useful 2-y-o 6f winner and dual listed placed Middleham (by Best Of The Bests), the fair 6f (including at 2 yrs) to 1m winner of 4 races Sun Catcher (by Cape Cross) and the Italian winner of 7 races at around 1m at 2 to 5 yrs Gallaccio (by Desert Style). The dam was placed 3 times over 5f and 6f at 2 yrs and is a half-sister to 2 minor winners. The second dam, Tatwij (by Topsider), won twice over 5f at 2 yrs and is a half-sister to 5 winners including the US triple Grade 1 winner Tejano. (Mrs Carmen Burrell & Jonathan Harvey). *"He wants plenty of time really, he should be out over seven furlongs in mid-summer but I do like him."*

1134. VITA LIKA ★★★
b.f. Dansili – Bayalika (Selkirk).
May 8. Fifth foal. 50,000Y. Tattersalls October Book 1. McKeever St Lawrence. Half-sister to the 2009 7f placed 2-y-o Poltergeist (by Invincible Spirit), to the Group 2 7f Champagne Stakes winner and 2,000 Guineas second Vital Equine (by Danetime) and the quite useful 1m winner Bramaputra (by Choisir). The dam is an unraced half-sister to 4 winners including an Italian listed winner. The second dam, Bayrika (by Selkirk), won the Group 3 Prix Berteux and is a half-sister to 7 winners out of the Prix Saint-Alary winner Behera. *"She's a big girl and one for the back-end of the season. She shows a nice bit of pace but I wouldn't expect to see her before August or September."*

1135. WAITER'S DREAM ★★★★
b.c. Oasis Dream – Sarah Georgina (Persian Bold).
March 16. Thirteenth foal. 85,000Y. Tattersalls October Book 2. McKeever St Lawrence. Half-brother to the Group 3 10.5f Prix de Flore winner Audacieuse (by Rainbow Quest), to the Irish listed 14f winner Lord Jim (by Kahyasi), the fairly useful 12f winner Gironde (by Sadler's Wells), the modest 10f winner Signella (by Selkirk) and the minor French 2-y-o winner Intellectuelle (by Caerleon). The dam, a quite useful 2-y-o 6f winner, is a half-sister to 11 winners including the French 1,000 Guineas winner Danseuse du Soir. The second dam, Dance By Night (by Northfields), a quite useful 2-y-o dual 7f winner, is a half-sister to 3 winners. *"A nice colt, I like him a lot, he should be racing in late May/early June and he looks sharp enough."*

1136. WARNEFORD ★★★★
b.c. Dansili – Maramba (Rainbow Quest).
May 8. Fifth foal. 115,000Y. Tattersalls October Book 1. McKeever St Lawrence. Half-brother to the very useful 2-y-o 5f, 6f listed and 6.5f Watership Down Stud Sales Race winner and Group 3 placed Nyramba (by Night Shift) and to the listed 10f winner Cape Amber (by Cape Cross). The dam, a fairly useful 3-y-o 1m winner, is a half-sister to 7 winners. The second dam, Gayane (by Nureyev), a very smart winner of the 6f Sandy

Lane Stakes and the 7f Oak Tree Stakes, was second in the Group 1 July Cup and is a half-sister to 7 winners including the Group 2 10f Sun Chariot Stakes winner Ristna and the Group 3 Beeswing Stakes winner Shahid. (Brimacombe, McNally, Vinciguerra, Sangster). *"A lovely horse but a backward type and he'll need plenty of time – September probably, but he'd be worth looking out for."*

1137. WEB OF DREAMS (IRE) ★★★♣
b.c. Oasis Dream – Web Of Intrigue (Machiavellian).
April 28. Seventh living foal. 65,000Y. Tattersalls October Book 1. McKeever St Lawrence. Half-brother to the fair 6f winner Francis Walsingham (by Invincible Spirit), to the modest 1m and 10f winner Chapter (by Sinndar), the 4-y-o winner Dubonai (by Peintre Celebre) and a bumper winner by In The Wings. The dam is a placed half-sister to 9 winners including the high-class Group 1 12f Yorkshire Oaks and Group 3 12f Lancashire Oaks winner Catchascatchcan (herself dam of the Group 2 winner and triple Group 1 placed Antonius Pius). The second dam, Catawba (by Mill Reef), a useful 3-y-o 10.5f winner, is a half-sister to 7 winners including Strigida, winner of the Ribblesdale Stakes. (Manton Racing Partnership). *"A nice colt, he's pretty sharp and should be racing sometime in mid-May."*

1138. YOUNG SAHIB (USA) ★★★
ch.g. Mr Greeley – Carefree Cheetah (Trempolino).
March 4. Sixth foal. 21,000Y. Tattersalls October Book 1. BBA (Ire). Sister to the unplaced 2009 2-y-o Balsha and half-sister to the US winner of 3 races, Grade 3 placed and smart miler Warrior Girl (by War Chant). The dam, placed over 10f at 3 yrs, is a half-sister to 6 winners including the Group 2 Mill Reef Stakes, Group 3 Hungerford Stakes and Group 3 Criterion Stakes winner Arkadian Hero. The second dam, Careless Kitten (by Caro), won once at 3 yrs in the USA and is a half-sister to 7 winners including the US Grade 1 winner Field Cat and the dams of the Group/Grade 1 winners Hold That Tiger, Editor's Note, Hennessy, Pearl City, Family Style and Lost Kitty. (Manton Racing Partnership). *"He'll be racing in late May, he's a very typical Mr Greeley and he just wants a bit of time because he's just been gelded, but he goes well."*

1139. UNNAMED ★★★★
b.c. Encosta De Lago – Autumnal (Indian Ridge).
April 28. Fourth foal. Half-brother to Harvest Dancer (by Danehill Dancer), placed fourth over 7f on his only start at 2 yrs in 2009. The dam was a useful winner of the 2-y-o 5f Windsor Castle Stakes and over 6f at 2 yrs and is a sister to the useful sprint winners Mazepa and Lord Pacal and a half-sister to the quite useful sprint winner of 12 races Storyteller. The second dam, Please Believe Me (by Try My Best), a fairly useful 2-y-o 5f winner, is out of the Group 3 12f Princess Royal Stakes winner Believer. (Paul & Jenny Green). *"A very smart colt I'd say. I trained the mare and he probably won't be as fast as her, he's more of a six/seven furlong type. A nice horse."*

1140. UNNAMED ★★★
b.f. Bernardini – Heat Lightning (Summer Squall).
May 6. Tenth foal. $250,000Y. Saratoga August. Stephen W Young. Half-sister to 7 winners including the US Grade 1 8.5f Breeders Cup Juvenile winner Stevie Wonderboy (by Stephen Got Even), the US stakes-placed winner Queen Joanne (by Mr Greeley), the fair 11f and 12f winner Imperial Bay (by Smart Strike) and the minor US winner of 12 races Game Called (by Miswaki). The dam was placed in the USA and is a half-sister to 9 winners including the Group 2 Pacemaker International Stakes winner and Group 1 Sussex Stakes fourth Fair Judgement. The second dam, Mystical Mood (by Roberto), won the Group 3 Schuylerville Stakes, was second in the Grade 1 Frizette Stakes and is a half-sister to 7 winners. (Mr A Rosen). *"I like her a lot but she wants a good bit more time. A nice filly."*

1141. UNNAMED ★★★★♣
b.c. Arch – La Reine Mambo (High Yield).
February 22. First foal. €72,000Y. Goffs Orby. McKeever St Lawrence. The dam, a listed-placed winner of 2 races over 1m at 2 and 3 yrs in France, is a half-sister to the Group 3 9f Prix Vanteaux and US Grade 1 third Danzon. The second dam, Zappeuse (by Kingmambo),

won once over 12f in France. *"He looks very sharp, five or six furlongs will suit, he should be ready in late May and he goes very well. A possible stakes horse."*

1142. UNNAMED ★★★
ch.c. Pivotal – Magicalmysterykate
(Woodman).
April 17. Fourth foal. £80,000Y. Doncaster St Leger. Favourites Racing. Half-brother to the useful dual 7f winner Mutheeb (by Danzig). The dam, a minor winner at 3 yrs in the USA, is a sister to the champion Japanese sprinter/miler Hishi Akebono and a half-sister to Agnes World and the dam of the Group 1 winners Librettist and Dubai Destination. The second dam, Mysteries (by Seattle Slew), was third in the Group 3 Musidora Stakes and is a half-sister to 5 winners. (Favourites Racing). *"A nice horse, he hasn't been in that long but he's very typical of the sire. He goes well and he's one for a bit later on."*

1143. UNNAMED ★★★
ch.c. Medicean – Pretty Sharp (Interrex).
April 10. Ninth foal. 38,000Y. Tattersalls October Book 1. Not sold. Half-brother to the Group 3 5f Duke Of York Stakes winner Twilight Blues (by Bluebird), to the quite useful 2-y-o 7f winner Sharp As A Tack (by Zafonic), the quite useful 2-y-o 5f winner and listed 5f placed Incise (by Dr Fong), the quite useful 2-y-o 7f winner Mobsir (by Mozart), the modest Irish 8.5f winner Sagittate (by Grand Lodge) and a winner abroad by Pivotal. The dam, a modest 7f placed 2-y-o, is a half-sister to 6 winners. The second dam, To The Point (by Sharpen Up), a fairly useful 2-y-o 5f winner, is a half-sister to 5 winners. *"We won't be too long with him, he goes well and he'll be a seven furlong type horse. He's going well."*

1144. UNNAMED ★★★
b.f. Oasis Dream – Silent Heir
(Sunday Silence).
April 20. Fourth foal. Sister to the very useful 2-y-o Group 3 7f Prix La Rochette winner Young Pretender and half-sister to the quite useful 2009 2-y-o 7f winner Rumool (by Exceed And Excel). The dam, a quite useful 4-y-o 10f winner, is a half-sister to 4 winners. The second dam, Park Heiress (by Sunday Silence), is an unraced half-sister to 7 winners including the champion 2-y-o and Derby winner New Approach. (Sangster Family). *"A nice, big filly, she wants a good bit more time but I like her."*

1145. UNNAMED ★★★
b.c. Oasis Dream – Thorntoun Piccolo
(Groom Dancer).
April 22. Second foal. 42,000Y. Tattersalls October Book 1. McKeever St Lawrence. Half-brother to the unplaced 2009 2-y-o Baoli (by Dansili). The dam is a placed half-sister to 10 winners including the listed Doncaster Mile, listed City Of York Handicap and subsequent Canadian Grade 2 winner Vanderlin. The second dam, Massorah (by Habitat), won the Group 3 5f Premio Omenoni and was second in the Group 3 Prix du Gros Chene and is a half-sister to 4 winners. *"He goes well and he won't be long, so I could see him racing in early May. A typical Oasis Dream, he looks a nice horse."*

1146. UNNAMED ★★★★
b.c. Invincible Spirit – Truly Generous
(Generous).
April 22. Eleventh foal. €40,000Y. Goffs Orby. McKeever St Lawrence. Half-sister to the unplaced 2009 2-y-o Thoughtful (by Acclamation), to the French listed 1m winner and Group 3 Prix de Psyche third Antique (by Dubai Millennium), the fair 10f, 12f and hurdles winner Nawamees (by Darshaan) and the minor French dual 11f winner Trouble Fete (by Fantastic Light). The dam won the listed Prix Petite Etoile, is closely related to the very smart Truly Special (winner of the Group 3 10.5f Prix de Royaumont and herself dam of the E.P. Taylor Stakes winner Truly A Dream) and a half-sister to 7 winners including the Group 2 13.5f Grand Prix de Deauville winner Modhish and the Group 2 12.5f Prix de Royallieu winner Russian Snows. The second dam, Arctique Royale (by Royal and Regal), won the Irish 1,000 Guineas and the Moyglare Stud Stakes and is a half-sister to the dam of Ardross. *"He worked very well this week and it shouldn't be long before he runs. I think he'd be sharp enough for five furlongs but he'd be better over six."*

ROD MILLMAN

1147. ALSHAZAH ★★★
b.c. Haafhd – Mountain Law (Mountain Cat).
February 10. Fourth foal. 26,000Y. Tattersalls October Book 2. Not sold. Half-brother to the fairly useful Irish 7f and 1m winner and subsequent US Grade 3 placed High Court Drama (by Theatrical) and to the fair 6f winner Pearl Of Manacor (by Danehill Dancer). The dam is an unraced half-sister to 7 winners including the smart Group 3 7f Hungerford Stakes winner With Reason and the useful Group 3 1m Curragh Futurity Stakes and 7f Sweet Solera Stakes winner Jural. The second dam, Just Cause (by Law Society), is an unraced half-sister to 5 winners out of the Group 1 Prix Saint-Alary winner Tootens. (The Links Partnership). *"He has some nice relatives, he's an athletic-looking colt and he looks like a decent horse we had called Prince Nureyev. He'll be out in late May/early June over six and then seven furlongs. A medium-sized colt and a good-moving horse that will probably want top of the ground."*

1148. BASILICA ★★★
ch.c. Zafeen – Thicket (Wolfhound).
February 17. Eighth foal. £7,000Y. Doncaster St Leger. R Millman. Half-brother to the fair 5f (including at 2 yrs) and 6f winner Diminuto (by Iron Mask), to the modest 5f winner Baileys Applause (by Royal Applause) and the moderate dual 6f winner Seductive Witch (by Zamindar). The dam, a fairly useful 2-y-o 5f winner, is a half-sister to 5 winners. The second dam, Sharpthorne (by Sharpen Up), a fairly useful dual 6f winner (including at 2 yrs), was listed-placed and is a half-sister to 9 winners. (B R Millman). *"He's a large horse, very strong and although he's had a touch of sore shins he's OK again now. I'm hoping he'll make up into a decent two-year-old, he's entered in the Supersprint and although the both the dam and the half-sister were Diminuto were small, this colt is 500kg plus. A strong, tough colt for mid-season over five and six furlongs and he's as good-looking a horse as we have in the yard."* TRAINERS' BARGAIN BUY

1149. EIGHT KEYS ★★★
b.c. Sakhee – Summertime Parkes (Silver Patriarch).
March 21. First foal. 16,000Y. Tattersalls October Book 2. Rod Millman. The dam, placed once over 7f from 2 starts at 2 yrs, is a half-sister to 6 winners including the listed Cecil Frail Stakes winner Summerhill Parkes and the useful dual 5f winner and Moyglare, Lowther and Queen Mary Stakes placed My Melody Parkes. The second dam, Summerhill Spruce (by Windjammer), a fair winner of a 6f seller at 3 yrs, is a half-sister to 6 winners. (Seasons Holidays). *"A very athletic horse out of one of Jack Berry's sprinting families, the sire seems to be able to get winners at all sorts of trips. He'll be ready by mid-season, he's a strong, good-moving sort. He looks quick enough to start at five furlongs but I can see him staying a mile in time."*

1150. ICEBUSTER ★★
ch.c. Iceman – Radiate (Sadler's Wells).
January 18. First foal. 12,000Y. Tattersalls October Book 3. Rod Millman. The dam is an unraced half-sister to 4 winners including the Group 1 Phoenix Stakes third Polar Force. The second dam, Irish Light (by Irish River), a fairly useful dual 1m winner at 3 yrs, is a half-sister to 5 winners including the US stakes winner and Grade 3 placed Solar Bound. *"A big, muscular horse, he possibly needs a bit more time despite being an early foal."*

1151. MILLDOWN MAGIC ★★★
ch.c. Lucky Story – Barnacla (Bluebird).
February 19. Seventh foal. 22,000Y. Tattersalls October Book 3. Rod Millman. Brother to the modest 3-y-o 6f winner Milldown Story and half-brother to the fair 2-y-o 6f winner Suesam (by Piccolo) and the modest 1m winner Princess Zada (by Best Of The Bests). The dam, a fairly useful 6f winner, is a half-sister to 4 winners including the fairly useful 12f winner Palua. The second dam, Reticent Bride (by Shy Groom), a fair 6f winner in Ireland, is a sister to the Group 2 Lowther Stakes winner Miss Demure. *"I've had his three sisters and he would be the best specimen. They were all small fillies whereas this is quite a strong colt. He'll be racing by the end of May over five furlongs but he'll get six and maybe more."*

1152. ROSINA GREY ★★★
gr.f. Proclamation – Rosina Mae (Danehill Dancer).

February 1. 900Y. Ascot Autumn. Not sold. Half-sister to a hurdles winner by Zaha. The dam, a fair 2m and hurdles winner, is a half-sister to numerous winners including the 2-y-o 1m Autumn Stakes and Group 2 Henry II Stakes winner Fight Your Corner. *"Quite a nice filly, she's already had a run, she works well and we'd expect her to be a nice filly this year. A very strong filly, she's stay six furlongs already."*

1153. ROYAL OPERA ★★★
b.c. Acclamation – Desert Gold (Desert Prince).
March 14. First foal. £23,000Y. Doncaster St Leger. Rod Millman. The dam, a fairly useful Irish dual 7f winner, is a half-sister to one winner. The second dam, Brief Sentiment (by Brief Truce), an Irish 2-y-o winner and second in the listed Irish 1,000 Guineas Trial, is a half-sister to 2 winners. (The Links Partnership). *"Quite a sharp type, he's on the small side so I'm hoping he'll turn into a decent two-year-old. He's athletic and he'll running by the beginning of May."*

1154. UNNAMED ★★
ch.c. Singspiel – Clear Vision (Observatory).
February 13. First foal. 31,000Y. Tattersalls October Book 2. D F Powell. The dam, a moderate 12f and 13f placed maiden, is a half-sister to 4 winners including the useful 2-y-o 7f winner, Group 1 Nassau Stakes second and subsequent US Grade 3 winner Cassydora. The second dam, Claxon (by Caerleon), a very useful 1m (at 2 yrs) and Group 2 10f Premio Lydia Tesio winner, is a half-sister to 3 winners. (E J S Gadsden). *"A medium-sized colt for seven furlongs plus in mid-to-late summer."*

1155. UNNAMED ★★
ch.c. Peintre Celebre – Desiraka (Kris).
April 22. Fifth living foal. 34,000Y. Tattersalls October Book 2. D F Powell. Half-brother to a minor 4-y-o winner in Germany by Sternkoenig. The dam won twice in Germany at 3 yrs and is a half-sister to 6 winners including two German listed winners. The second dam, Desidera (by Shaadi), a German Group 3 winner, is a half-sister to 10 winners including the Group 2 German 1,000 Guineas winner Diacada. (E J S Gadsden). *"He's* stockier than the Singspiel and I can see him starting at six furlongs but nevertheless he's not going to be out until mid-summer."

STAN MOORE

1156. ANYA AMASOVA ★★★
b.f. Red Ransom – Zabadani (Zafonic).
February 10. Second foal. €8,000Y. Goffs Orby. Not sold. The dam ran unplaced twice and is a half-sister to 6 winners including the Group 2 Prix Eugene Adam and Group 3 Prix La Force winner Radevore. The second dam, Bloudan (by Damascus), is an unraced half-sister to the Irish 1,000 Guineas and Coronation Stakes winner Al Bahathri (dam of the 2,000 Guineas and Champion Stakes winner Haafhd). *"She's named after one of James Bond's girlfriends and like the girl in the movie she seems to have a bit of class about her! The sire is very good and she's related to a couple of high-class horses, she'll be a six/seven furlong type two-year-old and I'm hoping she'll be good enough for something like the Empress Stakes at Newmarket in July."*

1157. BOOGIE STAR ★★
b.c. Tobougg – Donyana (Mark Of Esteem).
February 8. First foal. €4,000Y. Tattersalls Ireland. Stan Moore. The dam was a fairly useful 2-y-o 7f winner. The second dam, Albarsha (by Mtoto), a fair 12f placed 3-y-o, is a half-sister to 4 winners including the 1,000 Guineas winner Ameerat and the very useful multiple UAE 1m winner Walmooh. (J S Moore). *"He was cheap but I think he could be the surprise package. A mid-season type two-year-old, he's a good sized horse, strong and does everything very easily. He'll be trained for the Sales race."*

1158. DANZIG'S GRANDCHILD (USA)★★
b.f. Anabaa – Millie's Choice (Taufan).
March 23. Eleventh foal. 22,000Y. Tattersalls October Book 1. Not sold. Half-sister to the US Grade 3 winner and Grade 1 placed Millie's Quest (by Quest For Fame), to the fairly useful 2-y-o 6f winner Eat Pie (by Thunder Gulch), the US stakes-placed winners Honeypenny (by Royal Academy) and Millie's Trick (by Phone Trick), the French 7f winner Double Brandy (by Hennessy) and 2 minor winners in the USA by Hennessy and Stravinsky. The dam, an Irish 7f

winner of 7 races, is a half-sister to 2 winners including the dam of the dual Grade 1 winner Doctor Dino. The second dam, Salagangai (by Sallust), is an unraced half-sister to 6 winners. (Coleman Bloodstock Ltd). *"She's taking her time but she's just started working and she's doing nicely. She was cheap for an Anabaa and she'll be a mid-season two-year-old."*

1159. GUNMAKER'S CHOICE (USA) ★★★
b.c. More Than Ready – Trillion Wing
(In The Wings).
April 14. Fourth foal. €32,000Y. Goffs Orby. Stan Moore. The dam was placed at 3 yrs in the USA. The second dam, Diamond On The Run (by Kris S), won the US Grade 2 Davona Dale Handicap, was dual Grade 1 placed and is a half-sister to 6 winners. (Mrs F H Hay). *"A real nice horse that was bought in America as a foal. We bought him at Goffs, he'll be a seven furlong horse in mid-season and he has a lot of quality about him. A big colt, he looks like a three-year-old now and he could be very nice."*

1160. KISSING CLARA (IRE) ★★
ch.f. Elusive City – Purepleasureseeker
(Grand Lodge)
February 21. 4,500Y. Tattersalls December. Not sold. Third foal. Half-sister to the unplaced 2009 2-y-o Red Barcelona (by Indian Haven). The dam is an unplaced half-sister to the useful 2-y-o Group 3 6.5f Prix Eclipse winner Potaro. The second dam, Bianca Cappello (by Glenstal), is an unplaced half-sister to Idris, a winner of four Group 3 events in Ireland at up to 12f and to the winner and US Grade 3 placed Sweet Mazarine. *"A big filly that shows plenty of toe and she'll win races. She had a few niggling problems otherwise she'd have been out now and even though she has plenty of scope she's sharp."*

1161. PARTOUT LE MAGASIN ★★
b.c. Xaar – Mimiteh (Maria's Mon).
March 1. First foal. 3,800foal. Tattersalls December. Not sold. The dam was a fair 5f (at 2 yrs) and 6f winner. The second dam, Green Minstrel (by Green Tune), won the Group 3 Prix d'Aumale at 2 yrs and is a half-sister to 2 winners. *"He shows real good paces and we'll kick start him when the six furlong races start."*

1162. RED ZEUS ★★★
ch.g. Titus Livius – Cheviot Indian
(Indian Ridge).
April 10. Eighth foal. €16,000Y. Tattersalls Ireland. Stan Moore. Brother to the quite useful 5f (at 2 yrs) to 7f winner of 5 races Southandwest and half-brother to the modest triple 5f winner La Motta (by Sesaro) and the modest 1m winner No Trimmings (by Medecis). The dam, a fair 5f placed maiden, is a half-sister to 2 winners including the smart 7.5f to 10f winner Amalia. The second dam, Cheviot Amble (by Pennine Walk), won 8 races in Ireland including the listed 10f Mooresbridge Stakes and is a half-sister to the listed Debutante Stakes winner Alalja. (J S Moore). *"He's really nice and a six furlong type horse that seems to have plenty of pace. We've gelded him because he had the same colty traits as his brother Southandwest who did well for us. He's as good as gold now, we'll kick start him at six furlongs and he'll get seven. One to follow and he'll win."*

1163. SHEILA'S STAR ★★★
b.f. Hurricane Run – Yaselda (Green Desert).
April 2. Fifth foal. €20,000Y. Goffs Orby. Stan Moore. Half-sister to the 2009 6f placed 2-y-o Green Utopia (by Alhaarth), to the quite useful Irish dual 7f winner Magic Mornings (by Bahri) and the dual Italian 3-y-o winner Ponte Milvio (by Hernando). The dam, a fair 2-y-o 6f winner, is a sister to the 2-y-o Group 1 5.5f Prix Robert Papin winner Greenlander. The second dam, Pripet (by Alleged), a quite useful 3-y-o 2m winner, is a sister to the 1,000 Guineas and Oaks winner Midway Lady and to the listed winners Capias and Heavenly Calm. *"She's a really nice filly that's had one run. She came to herself early and she's a bit flighty so we had to send her to the races just to settle her head. We're hoping she'll be one for the Albany Stakes and at the end of the year she'll be one of the nicer fillies. Not over-big but she's seems to have a bit about her."*

1164. SLIM SHADEY ★★★★
br.c. Val Royal – Vino Veritas (Chief's Crown).
March 6. £1,000. Ascot Sales. Not sold. Half-brother to the fair Irish 12f and 13f winner Nora Chrissie (by Bahhare). The dam is an unplaced half-sister to several winners including the

multiple Hong Kong and Japanese Group 1 winner Bullish Luck. The second dam, Wild Vintage (by Alysheba), a minor French 10f winner, is a half-sister to 7 winners including the Group 1 Prix Marcel Boussac winner Juvenia and the Group 3 Prix de Guiche winner In Extremis. (P M Cunningham). *"He's a quality colt that could make a Chesham Stakes horse. Definitely a seven furlong/miler and he could end up a black type sort of horse."* TRAINERS' BARGAIN BUY

1165. TRAFFIC'S SISTER (USA) ★★★★
b.f. More Than Ready – Street Scene (Zafonic).
January 23. $50,000Y. Keeneland September. Not sold. Sister to the very smart dual 6f (at 2 yrs) and listed 1m winner and Group 1 Irish Champion Stakes second Traffic Guard. The dam was placed at 3 yrs and is a half-sister to 7 winners including the South African Grade 1 winner Chief Advocate. The second dam, Lady Vivienne (by Golden Fleece), won 3 races in Ireland and is a half-sister to the Irish Group winners Erin's Isle and Erin's Hope. (Mrs F H Hay). *"A very big filly that should be suited by seven furlongs and seems to have a lot of class about her. She goes real good but we won't race her too often this year."*

1166. VALDAW ★★★
b.c. Val Royal – Delight Of Dawn (Never So Bold).
February 24. The dam, a fair winner of 11 races from 6f to 1m, is out of the moderate 1m winner Vogos Angel (by Song). (Mayden Stud). *"He's really sharp, he'll be a five or six furlong type and the dam was tough and consistent in her grade. A real nice two-year-old with plenty of strength about him and he'll win plenty of races. He'll be ready for when the six furlong races start and he could progress to be really good."*

HUGHIE MORRISON
1167. ASTRAGAL ★★
b.f. Shamardal – Landinium (Lando).
March 12. The dam, a useful winner of the listed 10f Premio Baggio, was Group 3 placed twice and is a half-sister to a minor winner in France. The second dam, Hollywood Girl (by Cagliostro), was a German 7f to 9.5f winner. (Lady Blyth). *"She's only just appeared, so she's* backward and will hopefully be an autumn two-year-old."

1168. CAPTAIN BELLAMY (USA) ★★★
ch.c. Bellamy Road – Thesky'sthelimit (Northern Prospect).
April 9. Ninth foal. 30,000Y. Tattersalls October Book 1. Anthony Stroud. Half-brother to the US Grade 2 7f Del Mar Futurity winner Siphonizer, the 12f seller winner Dub Dash (both by Siphon), two minor winners in the USA by Harlan's Holiday and Include and a 2-y-o winner in Russia by Friends Lake. The dam won 5 minor races in the USA at 2 to 4 yrs and is a half-sister to 8 winners. The second dam, Portio (by Riva Ridge), a minor US stakes winner of 4 races, is a half-sister to Group 3 winner Flamenco. (A C Pickford). *"A beautiful looking horse with a superb temperament but he's big and as a result he's weak. He looks like a three-year-old now and he's one for later in the season over seven furlongs or a mile."*

1169. DAFFYDOWNDILLY ★★
b.f. Oasis Dream – Art Eyes (Halling).
February 29. First foal. 72,000Y. Tattersalls October Book 1. The dam, a smart 12f and listed 14f winner, was second in the Group 3 14f Lillie Langtry Fillies' Stakes and is a half-sister to 2 winners. The second dam, Careyes (by Sadler's Wells), is an unraced half-sister to 2 minor winners. (Lady Blyth). *"She's not very big but very long and 'up behind' at the moment. She has a nice pedigree and hopefully she'll make a late season two-year-old. When you look at Oasis Dream he seems to complement the dam, in that if she's a sprinter the foal will end up a sprinter, but if the mare stays the foal will too. So I think this filly will end up staying twelve furlongs next year."*

1170. DAWN GALE (IRE) ★★
b.f. Hurricane Run – Latest Chapter (Ahonoora).
March 7. Eleventh foal. 44,000Y. Tattersalls October Book 2. Mrs Robin Birley. Half-sister to the very useful Irish Group 3 7f Boland Stakes winner Social Harmony (by Polish Precedent), to the fairly useful Irish 1m winner Artist's Tale (by Singspiel), the fair 7f winner Syrinx (by One Cool Cat) and the Irish winners Lady Luck (over 1m by Kris), God Speed (over

6f by Be My Guest), Discreet Option (over 5f by Night Shift) and Bounce Back (over 7f by Alzao). The dam is an unraced half-sister to 5 winners including the Grade 1 Belmont Stakes winner Go And Go. The second dam, Irish Edition (by Alleged), won at 3 yrs and is a half-sister to 8 winners including the US Grade 1 winner Twilight Agenda and the dam of the Group 1 winners Refuse To Bend and Media Puzzle. (Robin & Lucy Birley). *"A nice filly, she'll hopefully be racing in late summer, the owners are in no hurry with her and seven furlongs should suit to start with. At the moment she looks like being a staying filly."*

1171. DELPHI DREAM ★★★
b.f. Oasis Dream – Delphic Way (Warning).
May 14. Half-sister to the fair 1m and 10f winner of 6 races Parnassian (by Sabrehill) and the modest 11f seller winner Ask The Oracle (by Where Or When). The dam is an unplaced half-sister to 10 winners including the high-class Group 1 6f July Cup winner Sakhee's Secret, to the smart listed winner of 6 races from 5f to 7f Palace Affair, the very useful listed 6f winner Palace Moon. The second dam, Palace Street (by Secreto), a useful winner over 6f and 7f including the listed Cammidge Trophy, is a half-sister to the Extel Handicap winner Indian Trail and the Italian Group 3 winner Sfriss. (Exors of the late Miss B Swire). *"A small filly and she was a fairly late foal. The dam produces unsound horses but as this filly is small like the dam, she should be able to run during the summer. I would think five or six furlongs will be right for her and she looks sharp."*

1172. DIVINE RULE (IRE) ★★
br.c. Cacique – Island Destiny (Kris).
March 30. Fifth foal. 32,000Y. Tattersalls December. Kern/Lillingston. Half-brother to the to the Italian winner of 4 races at 2 and 3 yrs Federica Vegas (by Desert Prince) and a winner in Denmark by Red Ransom. The dam, a fair 6f placed 2-y-o, is a sister to the Group 1 Coronation Stakes winner Balisada. The second dam, Balnaha (by Lomond), a modest 3-y-o 1m winner, is a sister to Inchmurrin (winner of the Child Stakes and herself dam of the very smart and tough colt Inchinor) and a half-sister to 6 winners including the Mill Reef Stakes winner Welney. (De La Warr Racing).

"A medium-sized colt, he's gone a bit 'dumpy' looking because he was sick when he came in so I haven't been able to do anything with him. We need to progress quickly with him but I'm not sure what his trip will be."

1173. DUBAI AFFAIR ★★★★
b.f. Dubawi – Palace Affair (Pursuit Of Love).
February 6. Half-sister to the useful 2009 2-y-o listed 6f winner Queen's Grace (by Bahamian Bounty) and to the fair 7f and 1m winner of 4 races April Fool (by Pivotal). The dam, a smart listed winner of 6 races from 5f to 7f, is a half-sister to the high-class Group 1 6f July Cup winner Sakhee's Secret and to the very useful 6f to 8.3f winner Duke Of Modena. The second dam, Palace Street (by Secreto), a useful winner over 6f and 7f including the listed Cammidge Trophy, is a half-sister to the Extel Handicap winner Indian Trail and the Italian Group 3 winner Sfriss. (Exors of the late Miss B Swire). *"She'll probably take a similar sort of route as her half-sister Queen's Grace. Hopefully she'll be out in July, she's a bit long in the pasterns but she's quite sharp looking and won't take long to get ready. She's maybe a bit better looking than Queen's Grace, so I'd have to be hopeful."*

1174. EXPERIMENTALIST ★★★
b.c. Monsieur Bond – Floppie (Law Society).
March 11. Eleventh foal. 22,000Y. Tattersalls October Book 2. Hugh Morrison. Half-brother to the dual Group 3 5f winner Ringmoor Down (by Pivotal), to the Irish 7f winner Still Going On (by Prince Sabo), the fairly useful 6f (at 2 yrs) and 7f winner Lindoro (by Marju), the quite useful dual 6f winner (including at 2 yrs) Bailey Gate (by Mister Baileys), the quite useful 2-y-o 5f winner Floppie Disk (by Magic Ring), the modest 6f winner Hireath (by Petong) and the 1m seller winner On Porpoise (by Dolphin Street). The dam won over 1m in France and is a half-sister to 2 minor winners. The second dam, Enfant d'Amour (by Lyphard), was an unraced half-sister to 7 winners. (Mr Macaroon). *"He's never stopped progressing and you'd hope he would make a late summer two-year-old. The sire gets plenty of two-year-old winners and it's a fast family, so he has every chance."* TRAINERS' BARGAIN BUY

1175. FANTASY FRY ★★★
b.c. Avonbridge – Footlight Fantasy (Nureyev).
May 19. Eleventh foal. 22,000Y. Tattersalls October Book 2. Hugh Morrison. Half-brother to the smart 7f and 1m winner Unscrupulous (by Machiavellian), to the quite useful dual 7f winner Hatch, the fair 2-y-o 7f winner Leading Role (both by Cadeaux Genereux), the 2-y-o 7f winner Fantasy Ridge (by Indian Ridge), the 2-y-o 6f winner Dominant Dancer (by Primo Dominie) and the 1m winner Lindop (by Nashwan) – all 3 fairly useful. The dam, a fair 3-y-o 7f winner, is a half-sister to 4 winners including the dam of the Sun Chariot Stakes winner Kissogram. The second dam, Milligram (by Mill Reef), won the Group 1 Queen Elizabeth II Stakes and the Group 2 Coronation Stakes and is a half-sister to the Coronation Stakes second Someone Special (dam of the Group winners Alnasr Alwasheek, One So Wonderful and Relatively Special). (Margadale, Scott-Barrett, Smith, Kerr-Dineen, Tullett). *"He's quite forward going, quite sharp and you would hope he'd make a two-year-old. He's part of a four horse syndicate and he was bought as the one to keep them happy this year as the others are more three-year-old types. He's never stopped developing and I've had two from the family that have been headstrong so if he turns out the same I'll just kick on with him."*

1176. GOLDEN DELICIOUS ★★★
ch.f. Cadeaux Genereux – Playgirl (Caerleon).
January 23. Half-sister to the fair 2009 6f placed 2-y-o Imperial Delight by Royal Applause). The dam was placed over 10f and is a sister to the 10f winner and listed-placed Drama Class (herself dam of the listed 10f winner and Group 1 12f Irish Oaks second Scottish Stage) and a half-sister to 3 winners. The second dam, Stage Struck (by Sadler's Wells), a quite useful 12f winner, is a sister to the high-class Group 1 7f Dewhurst Stakes winner (in a dead-heat) Prince of Dance and to the useful middle-distance winners Ballet Prince and Golden Ball. (Nicholas Jones). *"Yes, she's a nice filly, she's one for the late summer and the autumn you would hope she'd be going for the nicer maidens in October."*

1177. ISOLATE ★★★
gr.f. Verglas – Nirvana (Marju).
March 21. Half-sister to the fair dual 1m and hurdles winner Ultimate (by Anabaa). The dam, a quite useful 11.7f winner, is a half-sister to 5 winners including the very smart Group 2 12f King Edward VII Stakes winner Kingfisher Mille and the Group 3 12f St Simon Stakes and Group 3 10f Prix Gontaut-Biron winner Wellbeing. The second dam, Charming Life (by Sir Tristram), won over 7f in Australia and is a sister to the Australian Grade 1 1m winner Zabeel and a half-sister to the Australian Grade 1 winner Baryshnikov. (Gillian, Lady Howard de Walden). *"She's quite forward going but unfurnished at the moment. She could easily be out in mid-summer and she knows her job already after being prepped by Malcolm Bastard."*

1178. LITTLE CURTSEY ★★★♣
b.f. Royal Applause – Tychy (Suave Dancer).
February 16. Second foal. 30,000Y. Tattersalls October Book 2. Anthony Stroud. The dam, a quite useful 6f and 7f winner of 7 races at 3 to 5 yrs, is a half-sister to 3 winners here and abroad. The second dam, Touch Of White (by Song), won 3 races at 3 and 4 yrs and is a half-sister to 6 winners here and abroad. (Lady Faringdon). *"I quite like the look of her and she needs to come to herself but she should make a two-year-old as there's plenty of speed in the pedigree. She's strong and looks quite 'together' so I can see her running in mid-summer."*

1179. QUEEN OF CASH (IRE) ★★
b.f. Ad Valorem – Warrior Wings (Indian Ridge).
February 5. Fifth foal. €28,000Y. Goffs Orby. Amanda Skiffington. Half-sister to the fairly useful dual 7f winner (including at 2 yrs) and Group 3 7f Killavullan Stakes fourth Warriors Key (by Key Of Luck). The dam, a quite useful Irish 2-y-o 5f winner, is a half-sister to 2 winners including the dam of the French Grade 1 winner Zafisio. The second dam, Winger (by In The Wings), a fair Irish 9f winner, is a half-sister to 6 winners including the smart 1m winner Killer Instinct. (Margadale, Scott-Barrett, Smith, Kerr-Dineen, Tullett). *"A nice filly. This family generally needs some cut in the ground, she's*

straightforward and is one for late summer. She has a bit of scope to her but we'll probably push on with her a bit because she's not bred in the purple."

1180. SAGRAMOR ★★
ch.c. Pastoral Pursuits – Jasmick (Definite Article).
January 29. 500Y. Ascot Sales. H Morrison. The dam, a quite useful 10f and 14f winner, is a half-sister to 2 winners. The second dam, Glass Minnow (by Alzao), was placed three times for 5f to 9f. (Melksham Craic & Partners). "A very nice colt, he'll take more after his mother than his father and he's just been on the grass for the first time. Hopefully he'll be going for a maiden in the autumn, but I think he will be worth watching out for."

1181. SHARP RELIEF (IRE) ★★★
b.f. Galileo – Jinskys Gift (Cadeaux Genereux).
March 2. Second foal. 95,000Y. Tattersalls October Book 1. Anthony Stroud. The dam is an unraced half-sister to 7 winners including the triple listed 7f winner Modeeroch, the 2-y-o 8.5f winner and Group 1 1m Gran Criterium third Chinese Whisper and the useful Irish 2-y-o 6f winner and Group 1 6f Cheveley Park Stakes third Danaskaya. The second dam, Majinskaya (by Marignan), winner of the listed 12f Prix des Tuileries, is a half-sister to 6 winners including the dam of the Group 1 5f Prix de l'Abbaye winner Kistena. (Margadale, Scott-Barrett, Smith, Kerr-Dineen, Tullett). "A nice filly but probably not bred to be an early two-year-old. I'd say she'll be quite progressive whether it's this autumn or next year. She's a nice mover and when you put her upsides Queen Of Cash she goes better although she shouldn't really, considering the pedigree."

1182. SILENT NINJA ★★
b.f. Montjeu – Farfala (Linamix).
January 28. Closely related to the useful dual 12f winner and Group 2 Park Hill Stakes second Starfala (by Galileo) and half-sister to the 2-y-o listed 10f Zetland Stakes winner and Group 2 12f Lancashire Oaks second Under The Rainbow (by Fantastic Light), the quite useful 2-y-o 8.3f winner Speightstown (by Grand Lodge) and the moderate 5f winner Mujma (by Indian Ridge). The dam, a French listed 12f winner, is a sister to the Group 1 Grand Prix de Saint-Cloud winner Fragrant Mix and the Group 3 Prix d'Hedouville winner Fracassant. The second dam, Fragrant Hill (by Shirley Heights), was a useful winner of the listed 10f Lupe Stakes and is a half-sister to 8 winners. (Ben & Sir Martin Arbib). "A strong looking filly from a good family, I would hope to be running her in the autumn with purpose."

1183. SPARTAN SPIRIT (IRE) ★★★
b.c. Invincible Spirit – Kylemore (Sadler's Wells).
May 8. Seventh foal. 85,000Y. Tattersalls October Book 2. Anthony Stroud. Half-brother to the unplaced 2009 2-y-o Dhan Dhana (by Dubawi), to the very useful listed 1m winner Annabelle's Charm (by Indian Ridge) and the fairly useful 2-y-o 7f winner and listed UAE 1,000 Guineas third Purple Sage (by Danehill Dancer). The dam ran twice unplaced and is a sister to the Group 1 Criterium de Saint-Cloud and Grade 1 Canadian International Stakes winner Ballingarry and to the Group 1 1m Racing Post Trophy winner Aristotle and a half-sister to the Group 1 St James's Palace Stakes and Prix Jean Prat winner Starborough. The second dam, Flamenco Wave (by Desert Wine), won the Group 1 6f Moyglare Stud Stakes and is a half-sister to 3 winners. (Thurloe Thoroughbreds XXVIII). "He looked very weak as a yearling but he's done quite well physically. The lads tell me he feels quite strong but I suspect he won't be showing up too much until the autumn."

1184. UNNAMED ★★
b.f. Medicean – Easy Sunshine (Sadler's Wells).
April 30. Fifth foal. Half-sister to the quite useful 7f and 1m winner Sunshine Always (by Verglas) and to the fair Irish 10f winner Second Glance (by Lemon Drop Kid). The dam, an Irish 7f winner and third in the 2-y-o Group 3 7f C L Weld Park Stakes, is a sister to the Irish 6f (at 2 yrs) and 10f winner and listed-placed Unique Pose and a half-sister to 3 winners. The second dam, Desert Ease (by Green Desert), an Irish 2-y-o listed 6f winner, is a half-sister to 5 winners including the Group 3 Tetrarch Stakes

and Group 3 7f Concorde Stakes winner Two-Twenty-Two. (Mr Russell Swinbourne). *"Being by Medicean and out of a Sadler's Wells mare you'd think she'd be one for next year, but she's not that backward. Even so, she may just have the one run this year."*

1185. UNNAMED ★★
b.br.c. Lemon Drop Kid – Lynnwood Chase
(Horse Chestnut).
February 22. Second foal. 100,000Y. Tattersalls October Book 1. Amanda Skiffington. Brother to Ultravox, placed third over 7f from 2 starts at 2 yrs in 2009. The dam is a placed half-sister to the UAE Group 2 and Irish Group 3 Ballycorus Stakes winner Lord Admiral. The second dam, Lady Ilsley (by Trempolino), a winner in France and listed-placed twice, is a half-sister to 6 winners including the dam of the Grade 1 Breeders Cup Juvenile winner Action This Day. (Michael Kerr-Dineen & Bob Tullett). *"Physically he's up for anything – especially the fillies! He's a nice horse and he finds everything quite easy and if he keeps going the same way he could be a late summer seven furlong two-year-old. There is some stamina in the pedigree and he's quite 'together' but a bit like a dachshund with a long back and short legs!"*

WILLIE MUIR

1186. CONJUROR'S BLUFF ★★★
b.c. Tiger Hill – Portmeirion
(Polish Precedent).
February 3. First foal. 45,000Y. Tattersalls October Book 1. Willie Muir. The dam, a quite useful triple 6f winner, was listed-placed and is a half-sister to 8 winners including the smart US Grade 2 1m Colonel F W Koester Handicap and German Group 3 1m winner Ventiquattrofogli and to the German 6f to 11f listed winner Irish Fighter. The second dam, India Atlanta (by Ahonoora), is an unraced half-sister to 6 winners including the German Group 3 1m winner Sinyar. (J P Punters Racing). *"If he wasn't by Tiger Hill you'd think he was a real two-year-old. He shows he's got speed, probably from his dam, and I really do like him. He looks as if he can produce something this year, he's sound, he isn't the biggest horse you've ever seen but he has everything in the right place."*

1187. CRUISER ★★★★
b.c. Oasis Dream – Good Girl (College Chapel).
February 13. Third foal. 70,000Y. Tattersalls October Book 1. Willie Muir. Half-brother to the fairly useful 6f (at 2 yrs) and 1m winner Hood Again (by Dubai Destination) and to the quite useful 7f winner Ink Spot (by Diktat). The dam, a useful winner of the 2-y-o listed 5f Hilary Needler Trophy and third in the Group 1 6f Cheveley Park Stakes, is a half-sister to 6 winners. The second dam, Indian Honey (by Indian King), is an unraced half-sister to 7 winners. (C L A Edginton). *"I think he's special. I was lucky to be able to buy him because he had a bit of an issue with his knees. If he hadn't, he'd have been too expensive. Since then he's been in the Spa and he's turned inside out. His knees are good, he moves really well and he could be anything. A really nice horse by the right sire and I love him. I would think he'd be suited by six furlongs."*

1188. FANCOURT ★★
b.f. Diktat – Santorini (Spinning World).
March 12. Fifth foal. 30,000Y. Tattersalls October Book 1. Not sold. Half-sister to the modest 1m and 10f winner South Wales (by Sakhee), to the quite useful 5f to 7f winner of 10 races Methaaly (by Red Ransom) and the modest 7f winner Park Valley Prince (by Noverre). The dam is an unraced half-sister to the dual US Grade 1 Flower Bowl Invitational winner Dimitrova and to the multiple Group 1 winner (including the St Leger and Coronation Cup) Mutafaweq. The second dam, The Caretaker (by Caerleon), won 4 races in Ireland over 7f and 1m including 4 listed events, was Grade 3 placed in the USA and is a half-sister to 8 winners. (K J Mercer). *"A nice filly that moves well and does everything right. The family show they have speed but they aren't usually two-year-olds. She's sweet, she's over-big, she's butty and looks like a two-year-old, but her pedigree says different."*

1189. HERMINELLA ★★★
b.f. Lucky Story – Herminoe
(Rainbow Quest).
April 10. Half-sister to the fair 2009 2-y-o 1m winner Dr Mathias (by Dubai Destination). The dam, a minor French 9.5f winner, is a half-sister to a winner out of the unraced Hamasaat (by

Sadler's Wells), herself a half-sister to the Group 2 Sun Chariot Stakes winner La Confederation. (Dulverton Equine). *"I like her, she's going well and her half-brother won as a two-year-old for me. This filly has great conformation and she has the attitude to be a nice, mid-season two-year-old."*

1190. KRISTOLLINI ★★★
b.f. Bertolini – Lady Kris (Kris).
February 16. Half-sister to the very useful 7f and 1m winner Noon Gun (by Ashkalani), to the fairly useful 2-y-o dual 6f winner Lima (by Distant Relative), the quite useful middle-distance winner of 9 races Al's Alibi (by Alzao) and the fair 2-y-o 5f winner Just Sort It (by Averti). The dam, a winner in Ireland over 10f at 3 yrs, is a half-sister to 11 winners including the Gimcrack Stakes winner Bel Bolide, the Irish listed winner Milieu and the US stakes winner Excitable. The second dam, Lady Graustark (by Graustark), won twice at up to 6f at 2 yrs in the USA. (North Farm Stud). *"She's not been in training very long, she was bred by my father and she has a nice pedigree. I like her but I don't know much more about her yet. The family aren't usually early although Bertolini might put a bit more speed into her. She's actually quite stocky for this family, so you never know she might start in mid-summer."*

1191. MELODIZE ★★★
ch.f. Iceman – Rhapsodize (Halling).
February 22. First foal. 8,000Y. Doncaster St Leger. Not sold. The dam is an unraced half-sister to several winners including the useful 2-y-o listed 8.3f winner Hypnotic. The second dam, Hypnotize (by Machiavellian), a useful 2-y-o dual 7f winner, is a closely related to 2 winners including the Group 3 6f Cherry Hinton Stakes winner Dazzle and a half-sister to 4 winners including the useful 7f (at 2 yrs) and 1m listed winner Fantasize. (Foursome Thoroughbreds). *"She'll be my first two-year-old runner and my first winner. She's a sharp type that's showing speed and that she'll win this year."*

1192. MIDAS MOMENT ★★★
b.f. Danehill Dancer – Special Moment (Sadler's Wells).
February 19. The dam is a placed sister to the Irish listed 1m winner and Irish 1,000 Guineas third Starbourne and to the Irish 12f winner and listed-placed Starrystarrynight and a half-sister to 2 winners. The second dam, Upper Circle (by Shirley Heights), ran twice unplaced and is a sister to the dam of the Oaks winner Lady Carla. (Foursome Thoroughbreds). *"She's potentially very special but we'd be looking at her running her towards the back-end of the season. She has a lovely action and a lovely way about her."*

1193. PIPPA'S GIFT ★★★
b.c. Royal Applause – Pippa's Dancer (by Desert Style).
May 7. Second foal. 12,000Y. Tattersalls October Book 2. Not sold. Half-brother to the modest 2010 5f placed 3-y-o Blue Zephyr (by Pastoral Pursuits). The dam, a fair 5f and 6f winner of 4 races, is a half-sister to several winners including the smart dual 6f winner (including at 2 yrs) Strahan. The second dam, Soreze (Gallic League), a useful Irish 2-y-o listed 5f Marble Hill Stakes winner, is a half-sister to 5 winners. (Perspicacious Punters Racing Club). *"He's quite sharp and he'll be a two-year-old. He was a May foal but I'm going to crack on with him soon to see if he can win races from mid-summer onwards."*

1194. TALBOT GREEN ★★
b.c. Green Desert – One Of the Family (Alzao).
April 23. Seventh foal. Half-brother to the fairly useful 14f to 18f winner Som Tala (by Fantastic Light) and to the quite useful 1m to 14f winner of 7 races Pass The Port (by Docksider). The dam, a fair 1m placed 4-y-o, is a sister to the Rockfel Stakes winner Relatively Special and a half-sister to 7 winners including the Juddmonte International Stakes winner One So Wonderful and the Group 2 Dante Stakes winner Alnasr Alwasheek. The second dam, Someone Special (by Habitat), won over 7f, was third in the Coronation Stakes and is a half-sister to the Queen Elizabeth II Stakes winner Milligram. (K J Mercer). *"He won't be much of a two-year-old but I'm hoping he'll be a Derby horse – it's that sort of a family. He won't run until later on this year but he's nice-looking, he moves well and everything's grand."*

1195. THE GURU OF GLOOM (IRE) ★★★★
b.c. Dubai Destination – Gabriella (Cape Cross).
March 13. First foal. 15,000Y. Tattersalls October Book 2. Willie Muir. The dam is an unraced half-sister to 4 winners including the Group 1 Golden Jubilee Stakes and Australian Group 1 winner Cape Of Good Hope and the useful 2-y-o 6f winner and Group 1 Coronation Stakes fourth Cape Columbine. The second dam, Cape Merino (by Clantime), a useful winner of 4 races over 5f and 6f, is a full or half-sister to 4 winners. (Mr R Haim). *"I like him, he's from a good family and the dam cost 400, 000 but couldn't run because of a problem with her pelvis. This lad moves beautifully and shows he's a really nice horse. He'll be a two-year-old in the second half of the season."* TRAINERS' BARGAIN BUY

1196. VALLEY TIGER ★★★
b.c. Tiger Hill – Nantyglo (Mark Of Esteem).
January 24. First foal. 30,000Y. Tattersalls October Book 1. Willie Muir. The dam, a useful 6f (at 2 yrs) and listed 1m winner, was third in the Group 2 6f Mill Reef Stakes and is a half-sister to 2 winners. The second dam, Bright Halo (by Bigstone), a minor French 3-y-o 9f winner, is a half-sister to 7 winners including the Group 1 Irish Oaks winner Moonstone, the Breeders Cup second L'Ancresse and the Group 1 10f Prix Saint-Alary winner Cerulean Sky (herself dam of the Group 2 Doncaster Cup winner Honolulu). (Clive Edginton & Martin Graham). *"I love him, but although he looks sharp and he has a pedigree that suggests he could be a two-year-old, my brain tells me he can't be if he's by Tiger Hill. His pedigree says he can be a stallion if he's good enough. He's dead straightforward and I couldn't fault him."*

1197. UNNAMED ★★
b.c. Val Royal – Brecon (Unfuwain).
February 12. Second foal. 9,000Y. Tattersalls October Book 3. Willie Muir. The dam, a fairly useful 2-y-o 7f winner and fourth in two listed events, is a half-sister to one winner. The second dam, Welsh Valley (by Irish River), a modest 6f placed maiden, is a half-sister to 8 winners including the Group 2 6f Gimcrack Stakes winner Chilly Billy. *"He's not been sold yet, he's a big horse but I do like him and I think he'll make a fantastic horse one day."*

JEREMY NOSEDA

1198. BAHIA EMERALD (IRE) ★★
b.f. Bahamian Bounty – Emerald Peace (Green Desert).
May 15. Sixth living foal. 95,000Y. Tattersalls October Book 1. Cheveley Park Stud. Half-sister to the listed 6f winner and Group 3 Princess Margaret Stakes second Vital Statistics (by Indian Ridge), to the quite useful triple 6f winner (including at 2 yrs) Emerald Lodge (by Green Desert), the quite useful 7f winner Carved Emerald (by Pivotal) and the fair dual 6f winner Spiritual Peace (by Cadeaux Genereux). The dam, a useful listed 5f winner of 4 races and second in the Group 2 5f Flying Childers Stakes, is a half-sister to 3 winners. The second dam, Puck's Castle (by Shirley Heights), a fairly useful 2-y-o 1m winner and third in the listed 10f Zetland Stakes, is a half-sister to 5 winners including the champion 2-y-o filly and Cheveley Park Stakes winner Embassy and the Group 2 Pretty Polly Stakes winner Tarfshi. *"I couldn't tell you as much about her as I'd like because she had a slight setback and she's not back cantering yet. A medium-sized, good-looking filly, what little we did with her we liked but she's on the back burner for a while."*

1199. CASSINI FLIGHT (USA) ★★★
b.c. Bernardini – Cassis (Red Ransom).
February 12. Third foal. 170,000Y. Tattersalls December. Not sold. The dam, winner of the Group 3 Musidora Stakes, was placed in the Group 2 Cherry Hinton Stakes and Mill Reef Stakes and fourth in the Coronation Cup and the Del Mar Oaks. She is a half-sister to 7 winners including the dam of the champion US 2-y-o filly Storm Song. The second dam, Minstress (by The Minstrel), was a stakes winner and Grade 3 placed in the USA. *"I'm happy with him, he's a nice, strong horse and a good mover. A little bit backward at present, he's definitely a two-year-old for later in the season but I quite like him. A nice, solid horse, I trained the mare and he has a lot of her attributes and is a lot more athletic than her. There's a little question mark over the sire as to whether his stock will handle the turf, as it's not a sire line that's been very successful on the turf over the years."*

1200. CLUB OCEANIC ★★★
b.c. Cape Cross – My Lass (Elmaamul).
February 13. Seventh foal. 210,000Y. Tattersalls October Book 1. Sir Robert Ogden. Brother to Mac Love (by Cape Cross), a winner of four Group 3 races from 7f to10f and Group 1 placed and half-sister to a winner in Scandinavia by Oasis Dream. The dam won over 12f at 3 yrs, was third in the listed 10f Trigo Stakes and is a half-sister to 4 minor winners. The second dam, Be My Lass (by Be My Guest), won once at 4 yrs in France and is a half-sister to the Grade 1 Yellow Ribbon Invitational winner Bonne Ile and the Group 3 winners Ile de Nisky and Hi Lass. *"A good-moving horse, he's cantering away at the moment and is a good, solid individual. I would say he'll be a two-year-old from July onwards and although I haven't done a lot with him yet, what I see I like."*

1201. DANISH PASTRY ★★★
b.f. Danehill Dancer – Foodbroker Fancy (Halling).
January 31. Half-sister to the smart 7f (at 2 yrs), listed 10f and subsequent US Grade 3 12f winner Dalvina (by Grand Lodge) and to the very useful 7f (at 2 yrs) and listed 10f winner Soft Centre (by Zafonic). The dam, a smart 6f (at 2 yrs) and dual listed 10f winner, is a half-sister to the useful listed 2-y-o 6f winner Femme Fatale. The second dam, Red Rita (by Kefaah), a fairly useful 4-y-o 6f winner, was second in the Group 3 6f Cherry Hinton Stakes and the Group 3 6f Princess Margaret Stakes at 2 yrs and is a half-sister to 3 minor winners. (Normandie Stud). *"A small, quite set filly but she's changing and lengthening at present. A good mover with a good temperament, I hoped to have done more with her at this stage, but I think she'll make a two-year-old. She's just not as precocious as she originally looked as an individual."*

1202. DEFER ★★
b.f. Kyllachy – Succumb (Pursuit Of Love).
April 10. Fourth foal. 25,000Y. Tattersalls October Book 2. Not sold. Sister to the fair 2-y-o 5f winner Rare Art and half-sister to a winner in Greece by Pivotal. The dam is an unraced half-sister to 7 winners including the useful On Call, a listed winner of 7 races at up to 2m and herself dam of the US Grade 2 winner One Off. The second dam, Doctor Bid (by Spectacular Bid), is an unraced half-sister to 9 winners including the smart Group 3 Prix Thomas Bryon winner Glory Forever and the dam of the Group winners Verglas and Cassandra Go. *"She's cantering away and is a solid filly that should make a two-year-old, but she's had a few niggling issues so I don't know enough about her as I would have liked. A two-year-old for the second half of the season."*

1203. DEITY ★★★★
b.f. Danehill Dancer – Golden Flyer (Machiavellian).
February 2. Third foal. 110,000Y. Tattersalls October Book 1. John Warren. Half-sister to the fair 2009 7f and 1m 2-y-o winner Al Khimiya (by Van Nistelrooy). The dam is an unraced half-sister to 5 winners including the Irish Group 3 placed Gee Kel. The second dam, Shir Dar (by Lead On Time), won the US Grade 2 Palomar Handicap and is a half-sister to 9 winners. *"I looked upon her as possibly an Albany Stakes filly but unfortunately she's had a setback and won't appear now until the autumn. A lovely moving filly and definitely one to keep an eye on. She definitely has talent and although things might be delayed they will happen, because she has size and scope."*

1204. EBONY SONG (USA) ★★★★
b.br.c. Songandaprayer – Thiscatsforcaryl (Storm Cat).
March 17. Eleventh foal. $150,000Y. Keeneland September. Bluehills Racing Ltd. Half-brother to 7 winners including the US winner and Grade 1 placed Sacred Journey and the US stakes winner Be Like Mike (both by Unbridled's Song). The dam is an unplaced sister to the US stakes winner Cat Affair. The second dam, Tesio's Love (by Tom Rolfe), is an unplaced half-sister to the US Grade 1 Santa Ana Handicap winner Annual Reunion. *"A nice, big scopey horse and a good mover, with a bit of luck he should be a June type two-year-old. Songandaprayer is a good sire of two-year-olds and this is a nice, solid horse who I think will win races at six and seven furlongs this year."*

1205. ELAS DIAMOND ★★★
gr.f. *Danehill Dancer – Ela Athena (Ezzoud).*
February 4. Fifth foal. 150,000Y. Tattersalls October Book 1. P Barbe. The dam, a winner of 3 races including the Group 3 Lancashire Oaks, was placed in seven Group/Grade 1 events and is a half-sister to 4 winners. The second dam, Crodelle (by Formidable), a French 3-y-o 9.5f winner, is a half-sister to 7 winners. *"A nice scopey filly, she's definitely one for the autumn and is a good mover. She's a filly that I like and although the dam hasn't done it yet, if you forget the pedigree and look at this filly as an individual she's got great scope and size and is very athletic."*

1206. ELVIRA DELIGHT (IRE) ★★★
b.f. *Desert Style – Entente Cordiale (Ela-Mana-Mou).*
April 29. Fifth foal. 50,000Y. Tattersalls October Book 1. Richard Venn. Half-sister to the Group 1 King's Stand Stakes and Group 2 Prix du Gros-Chene winner Equiano (by Acclamation) and a winner in Spain by Key Of Luck). The dam was placed once at 4 yrs and is a half-sister to 3 winners. The second dam, Mirmande (by Kris), is an unplaced sister to the Prix Marcel Boussac fourth Aljood and a half-sister to the listed Ulster Harp Derby winner Sir Simon and the Group 2 Sun Chariot Stakes second Dartrey. *"A fairly late foal, but she's done really well over the past two months. I wouldn't be setting my sights too high but I'd certainly expect her to win races over five and six furlongs from May onwards."*

1207. ELYSIAN HEIGHTS (IRE) ★★★
b.c. *Galileo – Ziffany (Taufan).*
April 24. Seventh foal. €110,000Y. Goffs Orby. John Magnier. Half-brother to the very smart listed 7f winner of 6 races and Group 1 Lockinge Stakes second Major's Cast (by Victory Note) and to the very smart sprinter Jessica's Dream (by Desert Style), winner of the Group 3 Ballyogan Stakes and the Group 3 Premio Omenoni. The dam, a 2-y-o 7f seller winner, is a half-sister to one winner abroad. The second dam, Bonnie Banks (by Lomond), is an unplaced half-sister to 6 winners including the Group 3 Cornwallis Stakes winner Hanu. *"A good mover, I'm happy with him although ideally I would prefer him to have a bit more* substance. A well-balanced colt, he's one that will definitely run at two, probably from July onwards. Time will tell."*

1208. EPIC STORM (IRE) ★★★
b.c. *Montjeu – Jaya (Ela-Mana-Mou).*
January 24. Sixth living foal. Closely related to the quite useful Irish 13f winner Zulu Queen (by Sadler's Wells) and half-brother to the fairly useful 2-y-o 7f winner King Of Cashel (by King Of Kings). The dam is an unplaced half-sister to 3 minor winners. The second dam, Modern Dance (by Nureyev), ran once unplaced and is a half-sister to the dual US Grade 1 winner Too Chic (herself dam of the US Grade 1 winner Queena and Chic Shirine). *"A lovely, good-sized, well-balanced horse that will take a bit of time and is definitely one for the autumn, but he's a nice type of colt that goes about things in the right manner."*

1209. FANLIGHT ★★
b.f. *Shamardal – Lightsabre (Polar Falcon).*
April 3. The dam, a modest 6f placed 3-y-o, is a placed half-sister to Megahertz, a 1m (at 2 yrs) to 10f winner of 14 races including three Grade 1 events in the USA. The second dam, Heavenly Ray (by Rahy), a fairly useful 7f and 1m winner, is a half-sister to 3 winners. *"A big, backward filly that moves well but is definitely one for the autumn."*

1210. FETTUCCINE (IRE) ★★★★
b.f. *Invincible Spirit – Capannacce (Lahib).*
March 28. First foal. £75,000Y. Doncaster St Leger. W Browne. The dam won 6 races from 7f to 9f at 2 and 3 yrs in Italy, including a listed event. The second dam, Paoenia (by Pelder), is a placed half-sister to 5 winners including The Scout (Group 3 Prix La Force). *"A sharp filly that's done her first piece of work. I'll move along with her and I envisage her running at the end of April or early May. She's a little runner and although time will tell whether she has the ability to go to a good level she'll campaign and win her races."*

1211. GALIANDO ★★
b.c. *Galileo – Nando's Dream (Hernando).*
March 9. First foal. The dam, a fair 12f and 13f winner, is a half-sister to 2 winners over jumps. The second dam, Dream Quest (by Rainbow

Quest), a useful 10f winner, was listed-placed over 10f and 11f and is a sister to the smart German Group 2 12f winner Baroon and a half-sister to the Group 2 Goldene Peitsche and Group 3 6f Prix de Meautry winner Vision Of Night and the smart Group 3 5f Prix de Saint-Georges winner Struggler. *"A horse that I quite like, he's a scopey, back-end type two-year-old over a mile. A good mover, he's nicely balanced and does everything right."*

1212. GARDE COTIERE (USA) ★★★★
b.c. Giant's Causeway – Amonita (Anabaa).
February 8. Fourth foal. €500,000Y. Arqana Deauville August. Sir Robert Ogden. Half-brother to 2 minor winners in France and the USA by Kingmambo. The dam won the 2-y-o Group 1 Prix Marcel Boussac and the Grade 3 Suwannee River Handicap and is a half-sister to 9 winners including the multiple Grade 3 winner Cox Orange (herself dam of the 1,000 Guineas third Vista Bella). The second dam, Spectacular Joke (by Spectacular Bid), won the Group 2 Prix Maurice de Gheest. *"A lovely horse, he's big, strong, scopey and has done everything right since he's been with us. A well-balanced colt that carries himself well, I would hope to see him on the racetrack by July and he's a horse that I like. Definitely a horse with a future, he'll start off at seven furlongs."*

1213. GOVENOR GENERAL (IRE) ★★
b.c. Araafa – Requested Pleasure
(Rainbow Quest).
February 13. First foal. 60,000Y. Tattersalls October Book 1. Not sold. The dam, a fairly useful 1m and 10f winner in Ireland, is a half-sister to 8 winners including the very useful Group 3 1m Desmond Stakes winner Swift Gulliver and the useful 2-y-o 6f and subsequent dual US stakes winner Abderian. The second dam, Aminata (by Glenstal), a useful winner of the Group 3 5f Curragh Stakes, is a half-sister to 3 winners. *"A strong, solid type, it's taking a bit of a time to get him into a good routine but we're getting there now. More of a horse for July time, I think he'll campaign well in seven furlong nurseries."*

1214. INSTANCE ★★★
b.f. Invincible Spirit – Hannda (Dr Devious).
February 16. Second foal. 55,000Y. Tattersalls October Book 1. Kern/Lillingston. The dam, a winner over 10f in Ireland from 2 starts, is a half-sister to the Irish Group 3 7.5f Concorde Stakes winner Hamairi and to the Irish 5f (at 2 yrs) and 3-y-o listed 6f winner Hanabad. The second dam, Handaza (by Be My Guest), won over 1m winner at 3 yrs in Ireland and is a half-sister to 6 winners including the Irish Group 3 winners Hazariya and Hazarista. *"She's done her first bit of half-speed and she's a good mover with a good temperament. A filly with a bit of scope but it looks like she has speed and I'll come to an opinion in April as to when she'll be racing. Definitely a two-year-old type."*

1215. KORABUSHKA ★★
b.f. Selkirk – Russian Dance
(Nureyev).
February 4. Third foal. Half-sister to Dance East (by Shamardal), unplaced in one start at 2 yrs in 2009. The dam, a fairly useful 2-y-o 6f winner, is a half-sister to 7 winners including the Group 1 Racing Post Trophy winner Saratoga Springs. The second dam, Population (by General Assembly), is a placed half-sister to the Group/Grade 1 winners Play It Safe and Providential. (Cheveley Park Stud). *"A big, backward filly, she's a good mover and is turned out at the moment having a little break at the stud."*

1216. LUMINANCE (IRE) ★★★★
b.f. Danehill Dancer – Bright Bank
(Sadler's Wells).
February 3. Second foal. 105,000Y. Tattersalls October Book 1. Cheveley Park Stud. The dam is an unraced half-sister to 6 winners including the very useful listed 6f and 7f winner and dual Group 1 placed My Branch (herself the dam of the Group 1 Sprint Cup winner Tante Rose). The second dam, Pay The Bank (by High Top), a quite useful 2-y-o 1m winner, stayed 10f and is a half-sister to 4 winners. (Cheveley Park Stud). *"A good-moving, active filly, she had a little hold-up in late February but she's back on the go now. She has a chance to be out there in mid-May and it looks like she's got a bit of speed. Mentally she looks like a forward going filly and she'll do a good job. I like her and it strikes me that she's got a bit of talent."*

1217. MAID OF ICE ★★
ch.f. Iceman – Revival (Sadler's Wells).
March 7. Fifth foal. Half-sister to the quite useful Irish 8.5f winner Uva Fragola (by Nashwan) and to the 10f seller winner Danalova (by Groom Dancer). The dam, a quite useful 10f winner, is a half-sister to 3 winners including the Group 1 6f Nunthorpe Stakes winner and sire Pivotal. The second dam, Fearless Revival (by Cozzene), was a useful 2-y-o 6f and 7f winner and was listed-placed over 10f at 3 yrs. (Cheveley Park Stud). *"A nice, straightforward type, I'm happy with her, she has her level and she's quite sharp. She'll run at two around June time."*

1218. MOUNTAIN GLOW ★★
b.f. Araafa – Mexican Hawk (Silver Hawk).
May 18. Fifth foal. 20,000Y. Tattersalls October Book 2. J Noseda. Half-sister to the quite useful 9f and 12f winner Elegant Hawk (by Generous). The dam, a fairly useful 10f winner, is a half-sister to 8 winners. The second dam, Viva Zapata (by Affirmed), won the Group 2 Prix du Gros Chene and is a half-sister to 7 winners. *"Quite a backward filly, she's more one for the autumn but she's straightforward and a good mover."*

1219. MUSIC IN MY HEART ★★
b.f. Galileo – Rainbow Goddess (Rainbow Quest).
May 13. Fifth living foal. 100,000Y. Tattersalls October Book 1. Demi O'Byrne. Sister to the Group 3 Queen's Vase winner, St Leger second and Melbourne Cup third Mahler. The dam is an unraced sister to the very useful 2-y-o Group 3 7f Prestige Stakes winner Glatisant (dam of the 2,000 Guineas winner Footstepsinthesand) and a half-sister to 8 winners including the very useful triple 10f winner Gai Bulga and the placed dam of the very smart 2-y-o Superstar Leo. The second dam, Dancing Rocks (by Green Dancer), won over 5f and 6f at 2 yrs and the Group 2 10f Nassau Stakes at 3 yrs and is a half-sister to 4 winners including the very useful 7f winner Cragador. *"A nice filly and a good mover with size and scope. One for the last third of the season, I like her but she needs time."*

1220. NIGHT OF FANTASY (IRE) ★★★
b.f. Galileo – Kicking Bird (Darshaan).
April 18. Sixth foal. Half-sister to the Italian 2-y-o listed 10f winner Mr Bird (by Polish Precedent) and to 3 minor winners in France by Polish Precedent, Priolo and Groom Dancer. The dam won twice at 3 yrs in France and is a half-sister to 4 winners. The second dam, Antartica (by Arctic Tern), won the Group 3 Prix des Reservoirs. *"She was late being broken in but is a filly I like. Physically she's started to do very well and she's a good mover. One for July onwards and I like her – a nice type of filly."*

1221. OBSESSION (IRE) ★★★
b.c. Marju – Athlumney Lady (Lycius).
April 9. Fifth foal. 85,000Y. Tattersalls October Book 1. John Warren. Half-brother to the Group 3 6f Firth Of Clyde Stakes winner Princess Iris (by Desert Prince), to the fair 12f winner Princess Lomi (by Lomitas), the fair 9f winner Daylumni (by Daylami) and the modest all-weather 12f winner Lady Gregory (by In The Wings). The dam won 3 races at 2 yrs in Ireland including the Group 3 7f Killavullen Stakes and is a half-sister to 4 winners. The second dam, Simouna (by Ela-Mana-Mou), is an unraced half-sister to the listed winner and Group 2 Prix de Malleret second Ancara. *"A colt that I like, he'll be a July/August two-year-old and he's going to grow into a good-looking colt. He could be a nice, seven furlong two-year-old. A bonny horse."*

1222. PARADISE PLACE ★★★
ch.f. Compton Place – Passiflora (Night Shift).
February 19. Sister to the 2-y-o 6f and subsequent dual US stakes winner Passified and half-sister to the fairly useful 6f winner of 3 races (including at 2 yrs) Zomerlust (by Josr Algarhoud), the fairly useful 2-y-o dual 6f all-weather winner Bond Royale (by Night Shift) and the modest 7f winner Solis (by Josr Algarhoud). The dam, a fair 2-y-o 6f winner, is a half-sister to the Group 2 6f Cork And Orrery Stakes winner Harmonic Way. The second dam, Pineapple (by Superlative), a fair 12f winner, is a half-sister to 6 winners including the top-class filly In The Groove. *"A good mover and a straightforward filly. She's done her first little breeze and we're going to move along with*

her now. I'm not sure at the moment whether she'll be ready for May or whether we'll hold on to her for a bit, but she will campaign as two-year-old."

1223. RAINBOW RED ★★★
b.c. Dubawi – Rainbow Queen (FR) (Spectrum).
March 15. Half-brother to the fair dual 7f winner Sir Isaac (by Key Of Luck). The dam won 4 races from 6f to 1m at 3 and 4 yrs in Belgium and France and is a half-sister to the Group 3 Prix Miesque winner Stella Blue. The second dam, Libanoor (by Highest Honor), won 4 races at 3 yrs in France and is a sister to the French triple Group 3 winner Take Risks. *"A good, solid colt that should be racing from June onwards. A nice 'set' horse and a good mover with a good temperament."*

1224. REGAL SALUTE ★★
b.f. Medicean – Regency Rose (Danehill).
March 2. First foal. Sister to the useful 2-y-o Group 3 6.3f Anglesey Stakes winner Regional Counsel. The dam is an unraced sister to the Group 1 6f Cheveley Park Stakes winner Regal Rose and to the Japanese 10f stakes winner Generalist. The second dam, Ruthless Rose (by Conquistador Cielo), ran twice unplaced and is a half-sister to 9 winners including the high-class miler Shaadi. (Cheveley Park Stud). *"A filly that's taken a bit of time to furnish, I don't know enough about her yet."*

1225. SNOWY PEAK ★★★
ch.f. Pivotal – Snow Princess (Ela-Mana-Mou).
March 11. Eighth foal. 120,000Y. Tattersalls October Book 1. Not sold. Half-sister to the 2-y-o Group 2 1m Royal Lodge Stakes winner and 2,000 Guineas second Snow Ridge (by Indian Ridge), to the German listed winner Snow Gretel (by Green Desert), the French winner of 7 races White King and the Irish 12f winner White Queen (both by Spectrum). The dam, a smart winner of 6 races at up to 2m including the November Handicap and an Italian listed event, was second in the Group 1 Prix Royal-Oak and is a half-sister to 7 winners. The second dam, Karelia (by Sir Ivor), won over 1m and was third in the Group 3 12.5f Prix de Royallieu. *"She was plagued throughout the winter with a respiratory infection but I've got her right now and I'm happy with her. She's in full cantering exercise and although the family usually take a bit of time she'll make a two-year-old from mid-season onwards. She'll win this year but I haven't done enough with her to say how good she'll be yet."*

1226. SPLICE (USA) ★★
b.c. Dixie Union – Tawaaded (Nashwan).
May 4. Half-brother to the US Grade 2 Bernard Baruch Handicap winner and Grade 1 placed Shakis and to the French listed-placed winner Sahaat (both by Machiavellian). The dam, a fairly useful 7f winner, is a half-sister to 8 winners including the very useful dual 1m winner Kismah. The second dam, Thaidah (by Vice Regent), was a useful winner from 5f (at 2yrs) to 7f, was second in the Group 3 Fred Darling Stakes and is a half-sister to 8 winners including the champion US 2-y-o Devil's Bag and to the top-class filly Glorious Song (the dam of Singspiel and Rahy). *"A big, backward horse, he's a good mover but he'll need time, especially as he was a May foal. He'll get a run or two at the back-end of the season."*

1227. SUD PACIFIQUE (IRE) ★★★
b.c. Montjeu – Anestasia (Anabaa).
February 19. First foal. €600,000Y. Arqana Deauville August. Sir Robert Ogden. The dam, a minor winner in France, is a sister to the 2-y-o Group 1 Prix Marcel Boussac and the Grade 3 Suwannee River Handicap winner Amonita and a half-sister to 8 winners including the multiple Grade 3 winner Cox Orange (herself dam of the 1,000 Guineas third Vista Bella). The second dam, Spectacular Joke (by Spectacular Bid), won the Group 2 Prix Maurice de Gheest. *"A good-moving colt, he's a backward type but I think he's together enough to campaign as a two-year-old from late summer onwards. He's a horse that I like and without question he's a horse with a future."*

1228. TOKUM (IRE) ★★★
b.c. Danehill Dancer – Ibtikar (Private Account).
April 29. Fourteenth foal. 70,000Y. Tattersalls October Book 1. J Noseda. Half-brother to 6 winners including the US stakes-placed Vegas Venture (by Gold Fever), the South African stakes-placed Brown Linnet (by King

Of Kings) and the quite useful 2-y-o 7f winner Just Name It (by Miswaki). The dam, a poor 6f (at 2 yrs) and 2m placed maiden, is closely related to the Grade 1 Hollywood Gold Cup, Charles H. Strub Stakes and Californian Stakes winner Desert Wine and a half-sister to 6 winners including the dual Grade 1 winner Menifee and to the unraced dam of the dual Group 1 winner Fasliyev. The second dam, Anne Campbell (by Never Bend), won three races in the USA including a minor stakes event and is a half-sister to 4 winners including the French Group 3 winner Repercutionist. *"A good, straightforward type that's already breezed. Quite a tough, neat little horse that will go out there and do his job. I think he'll win as a two-year-old."*

1229. TRIPLE CHARM ★★★
ch.f. Pivotal – Triple Joy (Most Welcome).
May 14. Tenth foal. Half-sister to the French 1m (at 2 yrs) and listed 10.5f winner Trinity Joy (by Vettori), to the very useful 6f (at 2 yrs) and 1m winner Triple Dash (by Nashwan), the fairly useful 2-y-o dual 6f winner and listed-placed Asaawir (by Royal Applause), the fair 7f all-weather winner Tre Colline (by Efisio) and a winner in Italy by Halling. The dam, a useful 6f and 7f winner and second in the listed Abernant Stakes, is a half-sister to 7 winners including the Sun Chariot Stakes winner Talented. The second dam, Triple Reef (by Mill Reef), is an unraced half-sister to 13 winners including the 1,000 Guineas and Oaks placed Maysoon and the Ribblesdale Stakes winner Third Watch. *"She's was a late foal but she's done really well and is about to have a break now. Definitely one for the last half of the season, she's a nice sort of filly from a good family and I like her."*

1230. TWIST OF SILVER (USA) ★★★★
b.br.f. Silver Train – Twist Of Faith (Storm Cat).
$30,000foal. Keeneland November. Emerald Bloodstock. Half-sister to a minor US 2-y-o winner by Cherokee Run. The dam is an unraced half-sister to 5 minor winners. The second dam, Via Borghese (by Seattle Dancer), winner of the Grade 2 Diana Handicap and three Group/Grade 3 events, is a half-sister to the Group winners El Angelo, Miswaki Tern and Porto Varas. *"This filly has done plenty of work, she's sharp, early and ought to be running by the end of April/early May. She was a cheapish foal purchase and just might be a bargain. A nice type that goes well, she certainly looks value for money."* TRAINERS' BARGAIN BUY

1231. WAR IS WAR (IRE) ★★
b.c. Galileo – Walkamia (Linamix).
February 6. Third foal. Half-brother to the fairly useful 2-y-o 6f and 7f winner War Native (by Cape Cross). The dam won the Group 3 10.5f Prix Fille de l'Air and is a sister to the Group 2 11f Prix Noailles winner Walk On Mix. The second dam, Walk On Air (by Cure The Blues), is a placed half-sister to 7 winners including the Group 1 Prix Vermeille winner Walensee. *"He's yet to arrive as he had a setback at the farm and was a bit late being broken in. He was a gorgeous yearling and my reports are that he's going well, so I await him eagerly."*

1232. WESTERN ARISTOCRAT (USA) ★★★
b.br.c. Mr Greeley – Aristocratic Lady (Kris S).
February 7. First foal. $37,000Y. Keeneland September. Not sold. The dam, a minor winner at 3 yrs in France and the USA, is out of the US stakes winner American Dynasty (by Quiet American), herself a half-sister to 3 stakes winners. *"He's at Vinery Stud and is coming over at Easter. A big, strong horse, I've seen him do a few half-speeds, he goes well and I like him. One for the second half of the season, he's a bonny colt that's done phenomenally well since the Sales to where we're at now."*

1233. UNNAMED ★★★
gr.c. Kyllachy – Bunditten (Soviet Star).
January 21. Second foal. 45,000Y. Tattersalls October 1. A O Nerses. Half-brother to the 2009 French 1m placed 2-y-o Bundestag (by Dansili). The dam, a fairly useful 2-y-o 5f winner, was listed-placed and fourth in the Group 3 5f Queen Mary Stakes and a half-sister to 2 winners. The second dam, Felicita (by Catrail), won 3 races in France at 2 yrs including two 5f listed events, was Group 3 placed and is a half-sister to 5 winners. *"A neat, two-year-old type, he's quite lazy and has done his first little breeze. A colt with a good mind and a good, solid citizen."*

1234. UNNAMED ★★★
b.c. *Motivator – Capriole (Noverre).*
March 9. First foal. 85,000Y. Tattersalls October Book 2. Jane Allison. The dam is an unraced half-sister to 8 winners, two of them listed-placed. The second dam, Zonda (by Fabulous Dancer), a useful listed-placed 5f to 8.5f winner here, subsequently won twice in the USA. *"A bonny, straightforward colt with a good attitude, he's not that backward and I think he'll win at two in the last half of the season over seven furlongs or a mile."*

1235. UNNAMED ★★★
b.c. *Oratorio – Castelletto (Komaite).*
March 10. Second foal. €200,000Y. Goffs Orby. Sue Roy. The dam, winner of the 2-y-o Group 3 5f Cornwallis Stakes, is a sister to 8 winners including the useful 6f winner (including at 2 yrs) Lake Garda and the useful 5f winner and listed-placed Final Dynasty. The second dam, Malcesine (by Auction Ring), a 1m seller winner at 4 yrs, is a half-sister to 5 winners including the Wokingham Handicap winner Red Rosein. *"He was coming along nicely but I just had to back off him because of sore shins. I'd like to think he'll be on the track at the back end of May or early June though and he's a two-year-old type that should win his races."*

1236. UNNAMED ★★★
ch.c. *Johannesburg – Houdini's Honey (Mr Prospector).*
Half-brother to the smart 7f (at 2 yrs) and US Grade 3 8.5f Gotham Stakes winner Awesome Act (by Awesome Again). The dam, a quite useful 10f winner, was later successful in the USA and is a sister to Machiavellian and to the high-class French 2-y-o Coup' de Genie. The second dam, Coup de Folie (by Halo), won four races from 6f to 10f including the Group 3 1m Prix d'Aumale and was stakes-placed in the USA. *"He's in America at the moment, they're delighted with him out there and he's for a new owner. I look forward to seeing the colt, he's a sprinting type two-year-old."*

1237. UNNAMED ★★★
b.c. *Aussie Rules – Nymphs Echo (Mujtahid).*
April 4. Sixth foal. €62,000Y. Goffs Orby. Jane Allison. Closely related to the Irish dual 12f and hurdles winner Kirov King (by Desert King) and half-brother to the Irish 1m and 10f winner and listed-placed Sonorous (by Ashkalani), the quite useful 7f (at 2 yrs) and subsequent UAE 6f and 1m winner Jaasoos (by Noverre), the Irish 3-y-o 6f winner Camarade (by Common Grounds) and the hurdles winner Icarus Dream (by Intikhab). The dam is an unraced sister to the 2-y-o winner and Group 3 Fred Darling Stakes second Glen Rosie and a half-sister to 5 winners including the Group 3 10f Derrinstown Stud Derby Trial and triple US stakes winner Artema. The second dam, Silver Echo (by Caerleon), is an unraced sister to the listed 6f winner Dawn Success and a half-sister to the Group 3 7f Gladness Stakes winner Prince Echo. *"This colt has changed a lot since the sales but he grown and lengthened. He's done well but he's going to take a bit of time and is one for the second half of the season. A nicely-balanced horse and a good mover. I like him."*

1238. UNNAMED ★★★★
b.c. *Danehill Dancer – Park Romance (Dr Fong).*
February 15. Second foal. 340,000Y. Tattersalls October Book 1. J Noseda. Half-brother to the fair 2009 6f and 7f placed Motivational (by Motivator). The dam, a fairly useful 2-y-o 6f winner, was third in the Group 3 Sweet Solera Stakes and is a half-sister to 6 winners including the 6f (at 2 yrs) and Group 3 7f Ballycorus Stakes winner Rum Charger. The second dam, Park Charger (by Tirol), a useful winner over 1m and 10f at 3 yrs in Ireland, was listed-placed four times and is a half-sister to 9 winners. *"He's done his first bit of breeze and he looks very much a two-year-old type. A colt with good limbs and a great attitude – I like him. In my mind he'd be one of those that could be a Royal Ascot type if he shows he has the ability."*

1239. UNNAMED ★★★★
ch.f. *Pivotal – Polish Descent (Danehill).*
February 12. Eighth foal. €210,000Y. Goffs Orby. Citywest Inc Ltd. Half-sister to the Irish 1,000 Guineas winner and Group 1 Moyglare Stud Stakes third Saoire, to the quite useful 7f winner Classic Descent (both by Auction House), the fairly useful 6f and 7f winner of

4 races and listed-placed Awinnersgame (by Kyllachy), the quite useful 6f and 7f all-weather winner (including at 2 yrs) Foronlymo (by Forzando), the fair 2-y-o 1m winner Whittle Warrior (by Averti) and the Italian dual 7f winner (including at 2 yrs) Naomi de Bergerac (by Cyrano de Bergerac). The dam is an unraced half-sister to 4 winners including the Group 3 Curragh Stakes third Wistful Tune. The second dam, Nolnocan (by Colum), won twice at 4 yrs and is a half-sister to 8 winners including the Irish listed winner Lady Eileen. *"She's in America, at Vinery Stud in Florida, where she's breezing and she arrives in England in early April. I would hope she'd be ready to race in late April or early May. Definitely a two-year-old type and she should be sharp and early."*

1240. UNNAMED ★★★
ch.c. *Johannesburg – Pretty Meadow (Meadowlake).*
February 3. Second foal. $145,000Y. Keeneland September. J Noseda. The dam, a stakes winner and Grade 3 placed in Canada, is a sister to the stakes-placed winner Que Bonita and a half-sister to 3 stakes winners and to the dam of the US Grade 3 winner Seattle Borders. The second dam, Why So Much (by Northern Baby), won at 2 yrs in the USA. *"He's at Vinery Stud as well and he's done a couple of bits of work but he's going to be a July type two-year-old. I like him, he's a lengthy, scopey horse and a solid citizen. I think he'll be OK."*

1241. UNNAMED ★★★
b.br.f. *Kingmambo – Reach For The Moon (Pulpit).*
February 17. Fifth foal. $270,000Y. Keeneland September. J Noseda. Half-sister to the minor French winner Prince de Conde (by Sadler's Wells) and to a winner in Japan by Storm Cat. The dam, an Irish 2-y-o 6f winner and third in the Group 1 Fillies Mile, is a half-sister to the high-class Japanese stakes winner of 7 races from 1m to 10f Agnes Digital. The second dam, Chancey Squaw (by Chief's Crown), a minor winner in the USA, is a half-sister to 6 winners including the Royal Lodge Stakes winner Royal Kingdom and the French listed winners Beaute Dangereuse and Matador. *"She'll travel over from Vinery Stud during the Easter weekend. She's working there and physically she's done very well over the winter. I saw her canter there in February and since then she's been breezing well. They love the way she's going out there and hopefully she'll be running in the second half of May. She's grown since the sales where she was quite a neat yearling, so I'm looking forward to her arriving."*

1242. UNNAMED ★★★★
b.c. *Footstepsinthesand – Scarlett Rose (Royal Applause).*
February 15. Second foal. 105,000Y. Tattersalls October Book 1. Kerri Radcliffe. The dam, a modest 6f and 7f placed maiden, is a half-sister to 7 winners including the multiple Group 3 winner Tumbleweed Ridge and the dam of the Group 2 Queen Mary Stakes winner Gilded. The second dam, Billie Blue (by Ballad Rock), is a placed half-sister to 4 winners. *"A nice type of colt, very strong and a two-year-old type. He's breezed, I like the way he goes about things and there's a chance, all being well, that he'll make a Royal Ascot two-year-old. I'm pleased with him."*

1243. UNNAMED ★★★★
b.f. *Sadler's Wells – Shastye (Danehill).*
February 24. First living foal. 350,000Y. Tattersalls October Book 1. J Noseda. The dam, a useful 12f and 13f winner, was listed-placed and is a half-sister to 6 winners including the Prix de l'Arc de Triomphe winner Sagamix, the Group 2 Prix de Malleret winner Sage Et Jolie and the Group 1 Criterium de Saint-Cloud winner Sagacity. The second dam, Saganeca (by Sagace), was a very smart winner of the Group 3 12.5f Prix de Royallieu. *"She was a lovely filly at the Sales and she's done really well over the winter. She has size, scope, length and is a good mover. I'm going to give her a little break because she is a three-year-old in the making but she's one of those that could be running in late July/early August. A filly with a bit of quality, I like her, I think she'll do well and there's enough about her to suggest she'll show her level as a two-year-old."*

1244. UNNAMED ★★
gr.c. *Verglas – Sigonella (Priolo).*
April 7. Seventh foal. 62,000Y. Tattersalls October Book 1. Jane Allison. Half-brother to the French and Italian listed winner Round

Heels (by Daggers Drawn), to the fair 1m and 11f winner Blakfrankisch, a minor winner in France (both by Tagula) and the minor Italian winner of 8 races Sammiyo (by Revoque). The dam is an unraced half-sister to 5 winners including the French Derby third Sestino. The second dam, Stellina (by Caerleon), won at 2 yrs in France and is a half-sister to 6 winners. *"A bonny, straightforward, tough horse. When we saw him at the Sales he reminded us of another Verglas horse we had called Leahurst. Like that colt I think he's going to take a bit of time although I think he'll run at two sometime from August onwards. He wants to do his job and is just a good, solid citizen."*

1245. UNNAMED
b.f. *Dixie Union – Square Pants (King Of Kings).*
February 2. First foal. $235,000Y. Keeneland September. Not sold. The dam, a minor US 4-y-o winner, is a half-sister to the Cherry Hinton Stakes and Albany Stakes winner Sander Camillo. The second dam, Staraway (by Star de Naskra), a US stakes winner of 20 races, is a half-sister to several winners. *"This is one of the fillies I have in America that's been working. She goes well, looks very much like a two-year-old type and she'll be arriving over Easter. I would hope she'll be racing in early May and I she'll definitely win her races."*

AIDAN O'BRIEN

1246. ALEXANDER POPE (IRE) ★★★
b.c. *Danehill Dancer – Starship (Galileo).*
January 24. First foal. 100,000foal. Tattersalls. BBA (Ire). The dam, a fair 7f (at 2 yrs) to 8.3f winner, is a half-sister to numerous winners including the very smart Group 2 5f Flying Childers Stakes and Weatherbys Super Sprint winner Superstar Leo. The second dam, Council Rock (by General Assembly), a fair 9f and 10f placed 3-y-o, is a half-sister to 6 winners including the Group 3 Prestige Stakes winner Glatisant and the listed Virginia Stakes winner Gai Bulga.

1247. AMAZING BEAUTY (IRE) ★★★
b.f. *Galileo – Doula (Gone West).*
March 7. 280,000foal. Tattersalls December. Demi O'Byrne. Half-sister to the useful dual 7f (at 2 yrs) to 10f winner of 4 races Humungous (by Giant's Causeway) and to a minor 12f winner in France by Grand Lodge. The dam, a minor US 3-y-o turf winner, is a half-sister to the US Grade 2 winner sprint Cat Chat. The second dam, Phone Chatter (by Phone Trick), won 2 Grade 1 events in the USA and is a half-sister to 4 winners.

1248. AMEN (IRE) ★★★★
b.c. *Galileo – Kitza (Danehill).*
April 14. Seventh foal. 600,000Y. Tattersalls October Book 1. Demi O'Byrne. Closely related to the fair 12f winner Passerelle (by In The Wings) and half-brother to the very useful listed 8.5f winner of 3 races Fort Dignity (by Seeking The Gold) and to the French 1m winner of 3 races Ascension Island (by Rahy). The dam won 3 races including the listed Irish 1,000 Guineas Trial and was second in the Irish Oaks and the Irish 1,000 Guineas. She is a half-sister to 5 winners including the fairly useful Irish sprinter Hi Bettina (dam of the Group 2 winner Fred Bongusto) and the Group 3 Norfolk Stakes winner Marouble. The second dam, Pitmarie (by Pitskelly), won four sprint races (including two listed events) in Ireland and is a half-sister to 4 winners. This is a nice horse for the second half of the season, according reports.

1249. BALLROOM (USA) ★★★★
b.f. *Storm Cat – Virginia Waters (Kingmambo).*
January 12. Second foal. Closely related to the useful 2-y-o 6f winner and listed-placed Emperor Claudius (by Giant's Causeway). The dam won the 1,000 Guineas and is a half-sister to the Group 3 Gallinule Stakes winner and Irish Derby second Alexander Of Hales and to the Irish 2-y-o 1m winner and Group 1 1m Criterium International second Chevalier. The second dam, Legend Maker (by Sadler's Wells), won the Group 3 10.5f Prix de Royaumont, was third in the Group 2 13.5 Prix de Pomone and is a half-sister to 7 winners including the Group 2 12f King Edward VII Stakes winner Amfortas.

1250. CARD TRICK (IRE) ★★★
b.c. *Danehill Dancer – Juno Madonna (Sadler's Wells).*
February 15. Tenth foal. 115,000Y. Tattersalls October Book 1. John Magnier. Brother to the very useful 2-y-o 5f listed winner and Group 2

Cherry Hinton second Salut d'Amour and half-brother to the smart Group 3 Sandown Classic Trial and Group 3 Mooresbridge Stakes winner Regime (by Golan), the quite useful 2-y-o 1m winner Wotchalike (by Spectrum), the quite useful Irish 12f and 17f winner Coquette Rouge (by Croco Rouge) and the minor French winner Laureldean Lady (by Statue Of Liberty). The dam is an unraced half-sister to 5 winners including the Group 3 5f King George Stakes winner Title Roll and the Irish listed sprint winner Northern Express. The second dam, Tough Lady (by Bay Express), a fairly useful 2-y-o 6f winner, is a half-sister to 5 winners.

1251. CATHERINEOFARAGON (IRE) ★★★★
b.f. *Holy Roman Emperor – Monevassia (Mr Prospector).*
March 2. €240,000Y. Arqana Deauville August. Not sold. Closely related to the 2-y-o Group 1 Moyglare Stud Stakes and Group 1 Prix Marcel Boussac winner Rumplestiltskin and the quite useful 1m winner Denbera Dancer (both by Danehill) and half-sister to the fairly useful Irish 2-y-o 6f winner Great Rumpuscat (by Storm Cat) and a hurdles winner by Sadler's Wells. The dam is a placed sister to the French 2,000 Guineas, the St James's Palace Stakes and Prix du Moulin winner Kingmambo and to the smart Group 3 6f Prix de Ris-Oranges winner Miesque's Son, closely related to the listed winner Moon Is Up and a half-sister to the high-class French 1,000 Guineas, Prix de Diane and Prix Jacques le Marois winner East of the Moon. The second dam, Miesque (by Nureyev), was a great filly and the winner of 10 Group or Grade 1 events including the Breeders Cup Mile (twice), the Prix Jacques le Marois (twice), the 1,000 Guineas, the French 1,000 Guineas and the Prix du Moulin.

1252. EMPEROR HADRIAN (IRE) ★★★★
b.c. *Holy Roman Emperor – Gilded Edge (Cadeaux Genereux).*
March 13. Third foal. €140,000Y. Goffs Orby. BBA (Ire). The dam, a fairly useful 2-y-o 6f winner, is a half-sister to 2 winners including the champion Swedish 2-y-o 5f to 1m winner King Quantas and to the unplaced dam of the high-class sprinter Dutch Art. The second dam, Palacegate Episode (by Drumalis), a useful sprint winner of 11 races here and abroad including a Group 3 race in Italy and numerous listed events, is a full or half-sister to 5 winners.

1253. ENCHANTED FOREST (IRE) ★★★
b.c. *Galileo – Halland Park Lass (Spectrum).*
April 1. Third foal. Half-brother to the 2-y-o Group 1 Middle Park Stakes and Group 1 Prix Morny winner Dutch Art (by Medicean). The dam ran 3 times unplaced and is a half-sister to 4 winners including the Scandinavian Group 3 winner King Quantas. The second dam, Palacegate Episode (by Drumalis), won 11 races including the Group 3 Premio Omenoni and the listed St Hugh's Stakes and is a half-sister to the listed winners Palacegate Jack and Another Episode.

1254. ESKIMO (IRE) ★★★
b.c. *Galileo – Dietrich (Storm Cat).*
April 25. Half-brother to the Irish 2-y-o 7f winner and Group 3 6f second Marquesa, to the fairly useful Irish 7f winner Greatwallofchina (both by Kingmambo), the Irish 5f (at 2 yrs) and Group 3 6f winner Beauty Bright and the fair 7f winner Port Of Spain (both by Danehill). The dam won the Group 3 5f King George Stakes and Group 3 5f Ballyogan Stakes. The second dam, Piquetnol (by Private Account), a French 3-y-o winner and second in the Group 1 Prix Marcel Boussac, is a sister to the dual Group 1 winner Chimes of Freedom (the dam of two Grade 1 winners) and a half-sister to the multiple US Grade 1 winner Denon and the dam of Spinning World.

1255. FACTUM (USA) ★★★★
b.br.c. *Storm Cat – Starry Dreamer (Rubiano).*
May 13. Half-brother to the US Grade 2 6f winner War Front (by Danzig), to the US Grade 2 1m and 9f winner Teammate (by A P Indy), the US Grade 3 7f winner Ecclesiastic (by Pulpit) and the US Grade 2 placed Riviera Cocktail (by Giant's Causeway). The dam, a US stakes winner, was Grade 1 placed and is a half-sister to 2 stakes winners in the USA. The second dam, Lara's Star (by Forli), a minor 3-y-o winner, is a half-sister to 6 winners.

1256. FIRST SEA LORD (IRE) ★★★
b.c. *Galileo – Quiet Mouse (Quiet American).*
April 18. Half-brother to the Group 3 7f 2-y-o

C L Weld Park Stakes and 3-y-o 6f listed winner and Group 1 7f Moyglare Stud Stakes second Ugo Fire (by Bluebird) and to the quite useful Irish 2-y-o 7f winner Houston Dynamo (by Rock Of Gibraltar). The dam is an unraced half-sister to 6 winners including the fairly useful 2-y-o 6f and 7f winner and smart broodmare Witch Of Fife. The second dam, Fife (by Lomond), a fairly useful 1m winner, is a half-sister to 5 winners including Piffle (dam of the Group 1 winners Frenchpark and Pearly Shells).

1257. FLAVIA TATIANA (IRE) ★★★
b.f. *Holy Roman Emperor – Sanctify (Sadler's Wells).*
March 23. First foal. The dam ran unplaced twice and is a sister to the listed 1m Garnet Stakes winner Queen Titi and to the Irish Group 3 winner Psalm and a half-sister to the very useful 1m winner and subsequent US stakes-placed winner The Editor. The second dam, Litani River (by Irish River), was listed placed and is a sister to the listed winner and top-class broodmare Or Vision (dam of the Group 1 winners Dolphin Street, Insight and Saffron Walden) and a half-sister to 7 winners including the dam of the Group 1 winners Sequoyah and Listen.

1258. FREEDOM ★★★★♣
b.c. *Hurricane Run – Cute Cait (Atraf).*
February 12. First foal. 180,000Y. Tattersalls October Book 1. Charlie Gordon-Watson. The dam, a moderate 2-y-o 5f seller winner, is a half-sister to 8 winners including the Group 2 Prix du Gros Chene second Touch And Love and the dam of the French Group 3 winner Pallodio. The second dam, Clunk Click (by Star Appeal), is a placed half-sister to 9 winners including the triple Group 2 winner Sure Blade. Reportedly a nice colt for the second half of the season.

1259. IMPERATOR AUGUSTUS (USA) ★★★
b.c. *Holy Roman Emperor – Coralita (Night Shift).*
April 29. Eighth foal. Closely related to the quite useful Irish 6f winner Andrea Palladio, to the fair 2009 Irish 2-y-o 7f winner Flameoftheforest (both by Danehill Dancer) and the fairly useful 5f winners Peak District and Always A Star (both by Danehill). The dam won once over 5f at 2 yrs, was second in the Group 3 Anglesey Stakes and third in the Group 3 Queen Mary Stakes and is a half-sister to 5 minor winners. The second dam, Mumble Peg (by General Assembly), is an unraced half-sister to 7 winners including the Group 2 winners Little Bonny and Noelino.

1260. JACKAROO (IRE) ★★★
b.c. *Galileo – Ardbrae Lady (Overbury).*
March 19. First foal. 230,000Y. Tattersalls October Book 1. John Magnier. The dam, a useful winner of the Group 3 1m Park Express Stakes and second in the Irish 1,000 Guineas, is a half-sister to 5 winners including the useful listed 5f (at 2 yrs) to 7f winner of 6 races Obe Gold (by Namaqualand). The second dam, Gagajulu (by Al Hareb), won 5 races over 5f at 2 yrs and is a half-sister to 3 winners.

1261. JUSTIFICATION ★★
b.c. *Montjeu – Colorspin (High Top).*
March 7. Sixteenth foal. 550,000Y. Tattersalls October Book 1. John Magnier. Closely related to the top-class King George VI and Queen Elizabeth Diamond Stakes winner Opera House and to the Ascot Gold Cup and Irish St Leger winner Kayf Tara (both by Sadler's Wells) and half-brother to the Group 1 10f Prix de l'Opera winner Zee Zee Top (by Zafonic), the very useful 10f and 11.7f winner and Brigadier Gerard Stakes and Hardwicke Stakes placed Highland Dress (by Lomond) and the quite useful 12f winner Turn Of A Century (by Halling). The dam won 3 races, notably the Irish Oaks and is a half-sister to the Irish Champion Stakes winner Cezanne and the Group 2 Prix de l'Opera winner Bella Colora (herself dam of the high class colt Stagecraft). The second dam, Reprocolor (by Jimmy Reppin), won 3 races including the Group 3 Lingfield Oaks Trial and the Group 3 Lancashire Oaks.

1262. JUST INCREDIBLE (IRE) ★★★
b.f. *Galileo – Mona Lisa (Giant's Causeway).*
January 7. First foal. The dam, an Irish listed 12f winner, was third in the Group 1 Coronation Stakes and the Group 1 Irish Oaks and is a half-sister to numerous winners including the very useful 2-y-o 5f and 7f Italian listed winner and Group 2 1m Falmouth Stakes second Croeso Cariad and the Irish 2-y-o listed 7f Debutante

Stakes winner Photogenic. The second dam, Colorsnap (by Shirley Heights), is an unraced half-sister to Colorspin (winner of the Irish Oaks and dam of the Group 1 winners Opera House, Kayf Tara and Zee Zee Top), Bella Colora (winner of the Prix de l'Opera and dam of the very smart colt Stagecraft) and the Irish Champion Stakes winner Cezanne.

1263. LONG LIVE THE KING (IRE) ★★★
ch.c. Galileo – Hideaway (Cape Cross).
March 12. Second foal. €420,000Y. Arqana Deauville August. Demi O'Byrne. The dam, a listed winner of 2 races at 3 yrs in France, is a half-sister to the French Group 3 winners Homeland and High Rock and to the dam of the French 2,000 Guineas winner Silver Frost. The second dam, Hint Of Silver (by Alysheba), won once and is a sister to one listed winner and a half-sister to another.

1264. LOOKING LOVELY (IRE) ★★★
b.f. Storm Cat – Love Me True (Kingmambo).
May 16. Half-sister to the multiple Group 1 10f – 12f winner Duke Of Marmalade (by Danehill) and to the quite useful 2-y-o 7f winner So In Love With You (by Sadler's Wells). The dam, an Irish 1m winner, was third in the Group 3 Killavullan Stakes and is a half-sister to the Grade 2 Sanford Stakes winner Bite The Bullet and the smart listed 10f winner Shuailaan. The second dam, Lassie's Lady (by Alydar), a stakes-placed winner in the USA, is a half-sister to 10 winners including the dual US Grade 3 winner Weekend Surprise, the high-class sprinter Wolfhound, the US stakes winner Spectacular Spy and the French Group 3 placed Foxhound.

1265. LOVE ME ONLY (IRE) ★★★★
b.f. Sadler's Wells – Mariah's Storm (Rahy).
April 8. Half-brother to the top-class and genuine Giant's Causeway, winner of the Group 1 7f Prix de la Salamandre (at 2 yrs), the St James's Palace Stakes, Eclipse Stakes, Irish Champion Stakes, Sussex Stakes and Juddmonte International, to the Group 2 Cherry Hinton Stakes winner You'resothrilling, the smart 1m winner Freud and the Irish 2-y-o 6f winners Roar Of The Tiger and Tumblebrutus (all by Storm Cat). The dam, a winner of 10 races in the USA including six Graded stakes events from 1m to 9f, is closely related to the Group 2 Prix d'Harcourt winner Panoramic. The second dam, Immense (by Roberto), won the Grade 3 8.5f Little Silver Handicap in the USA and was a half-sister to the smart US 2-y-o Dearly Precious.

1266. LUXURIOUS (IRE) ★★★
b.f. Galileo – Parvenue (Ezzoud).
April 17. Sixth foal. €280,000Y. Goffs Orby. C Gardiner. Closely related to the Irish 2-y-o 1m winner Vivaldi (by Montjeu) and half-sister to the quite useful 2-y-o 6f winner Three Decades (by Invincible Spirit) and a winner at 2 yrs in Italy by Fasliyev. The dam, a quite useful 2-y-o 6f winner, is a half-sister to 3 winners including the useful 8.3f winner Pedrillo. The second dam, Patria (by Mr Prospector), a fair 2-y-o 7.6f winner, is a sister to Lycius (winner of the Group 1 6f Middle Park Stakes and placed in numerous Group 1 events) and to the Group 3 6f Prix de Cabourg winner Tereshkova and a half-sister to the US dual Grade 2 winner Akabir.

1267. MAGIC WORD (USA) ★★★★
ch.f. Kingmambo – Legend Maker (Sadler's Wells).
May 10. Sister to the 7f (at 2 yrs) and 1,000 Guineas winner Virginia Waters and half-sister to the Irish 2-y-o 1m winner and Group 1 1m Criterium International second Chevalier, the Group 3 Gallinule Stakes winner Alexander Of Hales (both by Danehill) and the 2-y-o 7f winner and Group 3 placed Chief Lone Eagle (by Giant's Causeway). The dam won the Group 3 10.5f Prix de Royaumont, was third in the Group 2 13.5f Prix de Pomone and is a half-sister to the Group 2 12f King Edward VII Stakes winner Amfortas. The second dam, High Spirited (by Shirley Heights), a quite useful winner over 14f and 2m, is a sister to the Premio Roma, Ribblesdale Stakes and Park Hill Stakes winner High Hawk (herself dam of the Breeders Cup Turf winner In the Wings) and a half-sister to the dams of the Derby winner High Rise and the Rothmans International winner Infamy.

1268. MASTER OF HOUNDS (USA) ★★★★
b.c. Kingmambo – Silk And Scarlet (Sadler's Wells).

March 4. Second foal. Half-brother to the Japanese Group 1 placed Eishin Apollon (by Giant's Causeway). The dam, a 2-y-o Group 2 7f Debutante Stakes winner, is a half-sister to the smart Group 3 6f Prix de Seine-et-Oise winner Danger Over. The second dam, Danilova (by Lyphard), is an unraced half-sister to the French Derby and the 9.3f Prix d'Ispahan winner Sanglamore.

1269. MEMPHIS TENNESSEE (IRE) ★★★
b.c. Hurricane Run – Hit The Sky (Cozzene).
March 10. Third foal. 150,000Y. Tattersalls October Book 1. Blandford Bloodstock. Half-brother to the 2009 French 2-y-o 1m winner Royal Bench (by Whipper). The dam is an unraced half-sister to the very smart Group 2 2m 2f Doncaster Cup winner Honolulu. The second dam, Cerulean Sky (by Darshaan), a 1m (at 2 yrs) and Group 1 10f Prix Saint-Alary winner, is a sister to the 7f (at 2 yrs) and listed 12f winner and Breeders Cup Filly & Mare second L'Ancresse and a half-sister to the Irish Oaks winner Moonstone.

1270. MIST (IRE) ★★★
b.f. Galileo – Beauty Bright (Danehill).
January 5. First foal. The dam, an Irish 5f (at 2 yrs) and Group 3 6f winner, is a sister to one winner and a half-sister to 2 winners including the Group 3 6f second Marquesa. The second dam, Dietrich (by Storm Cat), won the Group 3 5f King George Stakes and Group 3 5f Ballyogan Stakes.

1271. MOONS OF JUPITER ★★★
b.c. Galileo – Jessica's Dream (Desert Style).
March 26. Sixth foal. €350,000Y. Arqana Deauville August. Demi O'Byrne. Half-brother to the fair 5f winner of 5 races (including at 2 yrs) Rocker (by Rock Of Gibraltar). The dam, a very smart sprinter, won the Group 3 Ballyogan Stakes and the Group 3 Premio Omenoni and is a half-sister to the listed winner and dual Group 1 placed Majors Cast. The second dam, Ziffany (by Taufan), a 2-y-o 7f seller winner, is a half-sister to one winner abroad.

1272. NANTUCKET BAY (USA) ★★★
ch.c. Giant's Causeway – Saudia (Gone West).
March 31. Fifth foal. $425,000Y. Saratoga August. M V Magnier. Half-brother to the US stakes-placed winner The West's Awake (by Theatrical) and to the fair 2-y-o 10.2f winner Blue Dynasty (by Dynaformer). The dam, a quite useful 2-y-o 6f winner, is a half-sister to 7 winners including the listed winner and Italian Group 3 winner Revere. The second dam, Bint Pasha (by Affirmed), won the Prix Vermeille, the Yorkshire Oaks and the Group 2 Pretty Polly Stakes.

1273. OCTOBER (USA) ★★★★
b.c. Kingmambo – Quarter Moon (Sadler's Wells).
March 30. Brother to the 2009 2-y-o 7f winner and Group 1 Fillies' Mile third You'll Be Mine and the fairly useful 10f winner King Of Westphalia and half-brother to the fairly useful 7f winner and Group 3 2,000 Guineas Trial third Born To Be King (by Storm Cat). The dam, winner of the Group 1 7f Moyglare Stud Stakes and the Irish 1,000 Guineas, is a half-sister to the Irish 1,000 Guineas winner Yesterday. The second dam, Jude (by Darshaan), a moderate 10f placed maiden, is a sister to the very useful Irish listed 14f winner and Irish Oaks third Arrikala and to the useful Irish 12f listed winner Alouette (herself dam of the Champion Stakes winner Alborada) and a half-sister to the very smart Group 2 10f Nassau Stakes and Sun Chariot Stakes winner Last Second (dam of the French 2,000 Guineas winner Aussie Rules).

1274. ORACLE (IRE) ★★★
b.c. Danehill Dancer – Zibilene (Rainbow Quest).
February 26. Sixth foal. 160,000Y. Tattersalls October Book 1. John Magnier. Half-brother to the French 6f (at 2 yrs) and 7.5f winner and Group 2 1m third Mathematician (by Machiavellian) and to the quite useful 10f winner Aryaamm (by Galileo). The dam, a useful 12f winner and listed-placed over 10f, is a half-sister to 7 winners including the Breeders Cup Mile, Irish 2,000 Guineas and Queen Anne Stakes winner Barathea and the Fillies Mile and Irish 1,000 Guineas winner Gossamer. The second dam, Brocade (by Habitat), won 5 races including the Group 1 7f Prix de la Foret and is a half-sister to 7 winners.

1275. OUTRIDER (IRE) ★★★
b.c. Smart Strike – Adoration (Honor Grades).

February 15. The dam, a US dual Grade 1 winner, is a half-sister to numerous other winners including the US Grade 3 placed winner Mo Mon. The second dam, Sewing Lady (Key To The Mint), is an unraced half-sister to 9 winners including the Irish listed winner Astraeus.

1276. PALE MOON RISING (IRE) ★★★
b.f. Kingmambo – Baraka (Danehill).
March 11. The dam, a listed 11f winner, is a sister to the Japanese Grade 1 winner Fine Motion and a half-sister to numerous winners including the Pilsudski (winner of the Grade 1 12f Breeders Cup Turf, Grade 1 12f Japan Cup, Group 1 10f Grosser Preis von Baden and Group 1 10f Coral-Eclipse Stakes) and the Irish 2-y-o Group 3 1m winner Glowing Ardour. The second dam, Cocotte (by Troy), a very useful 10.2f winner, was second in the Group 3 Prix de Psyche, fourth in the Group 2 10f Nassau Stakes and is a half-sister to the listed winner Gay Captain.

1277. PAWNEE ★★★★
b.c. Montjeu – Red Azalea (Shirley Heights).
May 7. Tenth foal. 120,000Y. Tattersalls October Book 1. Demi O'Byrne. Brother to the useful 7f (at 2 yrs) and 12f winner and Group 3 7f Prestige Stakes third Red Peony and half-brother to the quite useful 7f all-weather winner Grandalea (by Grand Lodge) and a winner at up to 10f in Spain by Polar Falcon. The dam, a fairly useful 7f (at 2 yrs) and 10f winner, is a half-sister to 4 winners including the Group 3 Prestige Stakes winner and French 1,000 Guineas third Red Camellia (herself dam of the Fillies Mile winner Red Bloom). The second dam, Cerise Bouquet (by Mummy's Pet), a fair 2-y-o 5f winner, is a half-sister to 6 winners including the Group 1 winners Ibn Bey and Roseate Tern. This is a lovely colt the yard are hoping will do well later this season.

1278. PETRONIUS MAXIMUS (IRE) ★★★
b.c. Holy Roman Emperor – Khamseh (Thatching).
April 8. Eighth foal. €170,000Y. Goffs Orby. Blandford Bloodstock. Closely related to the very useful Irish listed 7f winner and Group 3 placed Georgebernardshaw (by Danehill Dancer) and half-brother to the smart Group 3 6f Phoenix Sprint Stakes winner of 10 races Bonus (by Cadeaux Genereux), the useful 7f to 9f listed winner of 7 races Third Set (by Royal Applause) and the quite useful 7f and 1m winner Corky (by Intikhab). The dam, a quite useful 7f winner at 3 yrs, is a half-sister to the high-class Group 2 12f Hardwicke Stakes and Group 2 12f Blandford Stakes winner Predappio. The second dam, Khalafiya (by Darshaan), won the Group 3 12f Meld Stakes and is a half-sister to 4 winners.

1279. PIRATE CHEST (IRE) ★★★
b.c. Montjeu – Cash Run (
Seeking The Gold)
May 10. Sixth foal. Half-brother to the quite useful 2009 2-y-o 6f winner Step In Time (by Giant's Causeway), to the Irish 2-y-o listed 7f winner and Group 3 Tetrarch Stakes and Group 3 Ballycorus Stakes second Great War Eagle and the quite useful Irish 2-y-o 5f winner Gstaad (both by Storm Cat). The dam won the Grade 1 Breeders Cup Juvenile Fillies' and two Grade 2 events and is a half-sister to the US Grade 1 King's Bishop Stakes winner and sire Forestry. The second dam, Shared Interest (by Pleasant Colony), won the Grade 1 Ruffian Handicap and is a half-sister to the dual Grade 1 Vosburgh Stakes winner Sewickley.

1280. PIRATEER (IRE) ★★
b.br.c. Danehill Dancer – Wannabe (Shirley Heights).
May 13. Tenth foal. €180,000Y. Goffs Orby. John Magnier. Brother to the quite useful Irish 12f winner Wanna, closely related to the Group 1 6f Cheveley Park Stakes and Group 2 6f Cherry Hinton Stakes winner Wannabe Grand (by Danehill) and half-sister to the useful 2-y-o dual 1m winner and listed placed Assaaf (by Night Shift), the useful listed 12f Galtres Stakes winner and Group 3 second Wannabe Posh (by Grand Lodge) and the minor French 3-y-o winner Masseera (by Alzao). The dam, a quite useful 1m and 10f winner, is a half-sister to 3 winners including the very useful 5f and 6f winner and Group 1 Cheveley Park Stakes second Tanami (herself dam of the Group 2 Rockfel Stakes winner Cairns). The second dam, Propensity (by Habitat), a fairly useful 2-y-o 5f winner, was second in the Queen Mary Stakes and is a half-sister to 2 winners.

1281. POINSETTIA (IRE) ★★★
b.f. *Galileo – Mermaid Island (Mujadil)*.
April 15. Second foal. 360,000Y. Tattersalls October Book 1. Demi O'Byrne. The dam, an Irish 2-y-o 1m winner, was listed-placed and is a half-sister to the Group 1 Irish 1,000 Guineas winner Nightime. The second dam, Caumshinaun (by Indian Ridge), won 5 races from 6f to 1m in Ireland at 3 and 4 yrs including a listed event.

1282. PRESIDENT LINCOLN (USA) ★★★★
b.br.c. *First Samurai – Preach (Mr Prospector)*.
April 25. Eleventh foal. $775,000Y. Keeneland September. Demi O'Byrne. Half-brother to 7 winners including the dual US Grade 2 winner Pulpit, the minor US 2-y-o winners Orate and Convent (all by A P Indy) and the minor US stakes-placed winner Tell It (by Storm Cat). The dam won the 2-y-o Grade 1 1m Frizette Stakes and was Grade 1 placed twice and is a half-sister to 3 stakes-placed winners and to the dam of the Middle Park Stakes winner Minardi. The second dam, Narrate (by Honest Pleasure), won 8 races including the Grade 3 8.5f Falls City Handicap and is a half-sister to the US Graded stakes winners Announce, Double Feint and Region.

1283. QUEEN OF SPAIN (IRE) ★★★★
b.f. *Holy Roman Emperor – Starlight Dreams (Black Tie Affair)*.
February 23. Seventh foal. 400,000Y. Tattersalls October Book 1. Demi O'Byrne. Closely related to the 2009 Irish 2-y-o 7f winner and Group 1 7f Moyglare Stud Stakes second Famous, to the multiple Group 1 winner (Phoenix Stakes, National Stakes, Irish 1,000 Guineas and St James's Palace Stakes) Mastercraftsman (both by Danehill Dancer) and the US Grade 3 winner Genuine Devotion (by Rock Of Gibraltar) and half-sister to the 2-y-o 6f seller winner Nordhock (by Luhuk). The dam won twice at 3 yrs in the USA and is a half-sister to 5 winners including the listed Zetland Stakes winner Matahif and the dams of the Group 1 Premio Roma winner Pressing and the Group 3 Princess Royal Stakes winner Mazuna. The second dam, Reves Celeste (by Lyphard), a quite useful 1m winner, is a three-parts sister to the Ribblesdale Stakes winner Thawakib (dam of the 'Arc' winner Sakhee) and a half-sister to the Group 2 Princess Of Wales's Stakes winner Celestial Storm. Well-liked in the yard, this filly is doing everything easily.

1284. REX ROMANORUM (IRE) ★★★
b.c. *Holy Roman Emperor – Willowbridge (Entrepreneur)*.
April 28. Fifth foal. Closely related to the quite useful triple 1m winner Willow Dancer (by Danehill Dancer) and half-brother to the fairly useful 2009 2-y-o 6f winner Aerodynamic (by Oratorio). The dam is an unraced half-sister to 6 winners including the Breeders Cup Turf winner Northern Spur and the Doncaster Cup winners Great Marquess and Kneller. The second dam, Fruition (by Rheingold), was second in the 12f Lupe Stakes and is a half-sister to 9 winners including the top-class broodmare Flame of Tara (the dam of Salsabil and Marju).

1285. RODERIC O'CONNOR (IRE) ★★★
b.c. *Galileo – Secret Garden (Danehill)*.
April 4. Fourth foal. Half-brother to the quite useful 2009 2-y-o 1m winner Burnett (by Dynaformer) and to the fairly useful 2008 2-y-o 6f winner and Group 3 6f Sirenia Stakes third Weatherstaff (by Elusive Quality). The dam, a very useful 7f listed and 8.2f winner, is a full or half-sister to 3 winners. The second dam, Chalamont (by Kris), a quite useful 2-y-o dual 6f winner, is a half-sister to 5 winners including the dual Ascot Gold Cup winner Gildoran and the French listed winner Lady Isis.

1286. RUDOLF VALENTINO ★★★
b.c. *Oasis Dream – Maganda (Sadler's Wells)*.
January 11. Third foal. 700,000Y. Tattersalls October Book 1. Demi O'Byrne. The dam, a quite useful 10f winner, is a sister to the listed winners In The Limelight and On The Nile and a half-sister to 3 winners including the German and Italian Group 1 winner Kutub. The second dam, Minnie Habit (by Habitat), an Irish 4-y-o 9f winner, is closely related to the dual Group 3 sprint winner Bermuda Classic (herself dam of the Coronation Stakes winner Shake The Yoke) and a half-sister to 6 winners.

1287. RULING (IRE) ★★★★
b.c. Footstepsinthesand – Chaturanga (Night Shift).
March 31. Ninth foal. €160,000Y. Goffs Orby. John Magnier. Half-brother to the 2009 Irish 1m placed 2-y-o Mutamaleq (by Refuse To Bend), to the fairly useful Irish 8.5f winner and Group 3 Ridgewood Pearl Stakes second Mooretown Lady (by Montjeu), the fair 11.7f winner Battledress (by In The Wings), the Irish 7f (at 2 yrs) and 6f winner Cocorica (by Croco Rouge) and the fair 9.4f all-weather winner Folaann (by Pennekamp). The dam is an unraced half-sister to 6 winners including the Irish listed 10f winner and Group 2 9.8f Prix Dollar second Strategic and the Group 2 Prix Eugene Adam winner Sobieski. The second dam, Game Plan (by Darshaan), won the Group 2 10f Pretty Polly Stakes, was second in the Oaks and is a half-sister to 10 winners including the Oaks winner Shahtoush. Pleasing his connections, he's an early type and he's doing everything nicely.

1288. SAM LORD'S CASTLE (IRE) ★★★★
b.c. Galileo – Tadkiyra (Darshaan).
April 30. Tenth foal. 550,000Y. Tattersalls October 1. John Magnier. Brother to the very useful 7f and 9f winner Chariots Of Fire, closely related to the 2-y-o Group 1 6f Phoenix Stakes and Group 2 5f Queen Mary Stakes winner Damson (by Entrepreneur) and the quite useful 7f winner Kiyra Wells (by Sadler's Wells) and half-brother to the 2-y-o Group 3 7f Prestige Stakes winner and Group 3 Musidora Stakes second Geminiani (by King Of Kings) and the quite useful 10f winner Motorway (by Night Shift). The dam won over 10f at 3 yrs in France and is a half-sister to 8 winners including the Group 3 winners Tashtiya, Tassmoun and Tashkourgan. The second dam, Tremogia (by Silver Shark), is an unraced daughter of the Prix Saint-Alary winner Tonnera.

1289. SAMUEL MORSE (IRE) ★★★★
b.br.c. Danehill Dancer – Eliza (Mt Livermore).
February 6. Twelfth foal. Half-brother to the fair 2009 2-y-o 6f winner Kilt Rock (by Giant's Causeway), to the US 2-y-o winner and Grade 2 placed Miss Doolittle (herself the dam of a stakes winner), the minor US winner of 3 races Dominique's Cat (both by Storm Cat), the fairly useful 5f and 7f 2-y-o winner and listed Chesham Stakes second Country Song (by Fusaichi Pegasus) and a minor US 3-y-o winner by Theatrical. The dam, winner of the Grade 1 Breeders Cup Juvenile Fillies and the Grade 1 Santa Anita Oaks, is a half-sister to 9 winners including the Grade 1 Santa Anita Derby winner Dinard. The second dam, Daring Bidder (by Bold Bidder), was unraced. This colt was a winner on his debut at the Curragh in mid-April.

1290. SCRIBE (IRE) ★★★
b.c. Montjeu – Crafty Example (Crafty Prospector).
February 20. Twelfth foal. Half-brother to the high-class Group 2 Queen Anne Stakes and Group 3 Diomed Stakes winner Intikhab, to the minor French 10f winner Jadarah (both by Red Ransom) and a minor winner in the USA by Bates Motel. The dam ran once unplaced and is a half-sister to 6 winners abroad. The second dam, Zienelle (by Danzig), is an unraced sister to Polish Precedent.

1291. SUN QUEEN (USA) ★★★★
ch.f. Storm Cat – Fountain Of Peace (Kris S).
February 11. The dam is an unraced half-sister to the Group 1 Prix Marcel Boussac winner Denebola, to the listed Prix Imprudence winner and US Grade 2 Revere Stakes second Glia, the US triple Grade 3 winner Snake Mountain, the Group 3 Prix de Cabourg winner Loving Kindness and to the dam of the 'Arc' winner Bago. The second dam, Coup de Genie (by Mr Prospector), won the Group 1 6f Prix Morny and the Group 1 7f Prix de la Salamandre winner and is a sister to the champion 2-y-o and top-class sire Machiavellian and a half-sister to the high-class miler Exit To Nowhere. The dam was bought for $3.1 million by John Magnier at Keeneland at the end of her 3-y-o career.

1292. TOGETHER (IRE) ★★★★
b.f. Galileo – Shadow Song (Pennekamp).
April 28. Second foal. 280,000Y. Tattersalls October 1. Demi O'Byrne. Closely related to the 2009 2-y-o Group 1 1m Criterium International winner Jan Vermeer (by Montjeu). The dam won once at 3 yrs in France and is a half-sister to 7 winners including the Group 3 May Hill Stakes winner Midnight Air (herself

dam of the Group 3 and subsequent US Grade 2 winner Midnight Line) and to the placed dam of the Group 1 Prix de l'Abbaye winner Imperial Beauty. The second dam, Evening Air (by J O Tobin), is an unraced half-sister to 5 winners including the Irish Derby Trial second Ancient Times.

1293. TOM SAWYER ★★★
b.c. Dansili – Cayman Sunset (Night Shift).
March 22. Fifth foal. £200,000Y. Doncaster St Leger. M V Magnier. Half-brother to the 2009 French 2-y-o 1m winner Kartica (by Rainbow Quest) and to the fair Irish dual 1m winner Zaharath Al Bustan (by Gulch). The dam, a useful 7f and listed 9f winner, is a sister to the useful dual Irish 7f winner (including at 2 yrs) and Group 3 Beresford Stakes third Tarfaa and a half-sister to 4 winners. The second dam, Robinia (by Roberto), a fairly useful 2-y-o 7f winner, is a half-sister to 5 winners here and abroad.

1294. WHY (IRE) ★★★★
b.f. Galileo – Rumplestiltskin (Danehill).
January 20. First foal. The dam won the Group 1 Prix Marcel Boussac and the Group 1 Moyglare Stud Stakes and is a full or half-sister to 3 winners. The second dam, Monevassia (by Mr Prospector), is a placed sister to the French 2,000 Guineas, the St James's Palace Stakes and Prix du Moulin winner Kingmambo and to the smart Group 3 6f Prix de Ris-Oranges winner Miesque's Son and a half-sister to the high-class French 1,000 Guineas, Prix de Diane and Prix Jacques le Marois winner East of the Moon.

1295. WONDER OF WONDERS (USA) ★★★★
b.f. Kingmambo – All Too Beautiful (Sadler's Wells).
February 1. Second foal. The dam, a Group 3 10.5f Middleton Stakes and listed 10f winner, is a sister to the Derby, Irish Derby and King George VI and Queen Elizabeth Diamond Stakes winner Galileo, the Group 1 12f Gran Premio del Jockey Club and Group 1 10.5f Tattersalls Gold Cup winner Black Sam Bellamy and a half-sister to the outstanding colt Sea The Stars (2,000 Guineas, Derby, Prix de l'Arc Triomphe, Champion Stakes etc), the US dual

Grade 2 8.5f winner My Typhoon, the smart listed 10f Pretty Polly Stakes winner and Oaks third Melikah and the smart 1m (at 2 yrs) and Group 2 10f Gallinule Stakes winner Urban Ocean. The dam, a top-class winner of 8 races from 1m (at 2 yrs) to 12f including the Group 1 Prix de l'Arc de Triomphe and the Group 2 Prix d'Harcourt, is closely related to the 2,000 Guineas winner King's Best and a half-sister to numerous winners.

1296. ZOFFANY (IRE) ★★★★
b.c. Dansili – Tyranny (Machiavellian).
March 18. Fourth foal. 220,000Y. Tattersalls October Book 1. John Magnier. The dam, a fairly useful dual 7f winner, is a half-sister to the listed 1m and subsequent US Grade 2 winner Spotlight. The second dam, Dust Dancer (by Suave Dancer), won 4 races including the Group 3 10f Prix de la Nonette and is a half-sister to 6 winners including the Group 3 7.3f Fred Darling Stakes winner Bulaxie (herself dam of the Group 2 winner Claxon) and the dual French listed winner Zimzalabim. This colt won on his debut at Leopardstown in mid-April and was described previously as a grand colt that was working well at home.

1297. UNNAMED ★★★★
b.f. Kingmambo – Imagine (Sadler's Wells).
February 27. Half-sister to the 2009 Irish listed 7f winner and Group 2 Champagne Stakes second Viscount Nelson (by Giant's Causeway), to the 2-y-o Group 1 7f Prix Jean Luc Lagardere winner Horatio Nelson (by Danehill), the 2-y-o Group 2 7f Rockfel Stakes winner Kitty Matcham and the Irish 10f winner and Group 1 placed Red Rock Canyon (both by Rock Of Gibraltar). The dam, winner of the Irish 1,000 Guineas and Epsom Oaks, is a half-sister to Generous, winner of the Derby, the Irish Derby, the King George VI and Queen Elizabeth Diamond Stakes and the Dewhurst Stakes. The second dam, Doff The Derby (by Master Derby), is an unraced half-sister to the Prix Ganay winner Trillion (herself dam of the outstanding racemare Triptych).

1298. UNNAMED ★★★★
b.f. Danehill Dancer – Queen Cleopatra (Kingmambo).
January 14. First foal. The dam, winner of the

Group 3 Irish 1,000 Guineas Trial, was third in the Irish 1,000 Guineas and the Prix de Diane and is a sister to the 2,000 Guineas, Irish 2,000 Guineas, St James's Palace Stakes and Sussex Stakes winner Henrythenavigator. The second dam, Sequoyah (by Sadler's Wells), winner of the Group 1 7f Moyglare Stud Stakes, is a sister to the 2-y-o Group 1 Fillies' Mile winner Listen and a half-sister to the Irish listed 5.6f winner and Group 3 7f placed Oyster Catcher.

1299. UNNAMED ★★★★
b.c. Galileo – Warrior Queen (Quiet American).
March 2. Half-sister to the fairly useful 2009 2-y-o 5f winner Queen Of Troy (by Storm Cat) and to the US dual Grade 2 8.5f winner A P Warrior (by A P Indy). The dam won the listed 6f Round Tower Stakes in Ireland and was third in the Group 3 5f Queen Mary Stakes. She is a half-sister to the Group 3 Debutante Stakes placed Rapid Ransom out of the unraced Call Me Fleet (by Afleet).

JEDD O'KEEFFE
1300. DUBAI CELEBRATION ★★★★
b.c. Dubai Destination – Pretty Poppy (Song).
February 23. Fifteenth foal. £17,000Y. Doncaster St Leger Festival. Jedd O'Keeffe. Half-brother to the top-class Group 1 5f Nunthorpe Stakes winner and sire Kyllachy, to the modest triple 6f winner Tadlil (both by Pivotal), the very useful triple 5f winner Borders (by Selkirk), the useful 5f winner of 4 races Speed On, the quite useful 2-y-o 5f winner Loving And Giving (both by Sharpo), the fairly useful dual 5f winner Follow Flanders, the quite useful 2-y-o 5f and 6f winner High Curragh (both by Pursuit Of Love), the quite useful 7f winner Ela Paparouna (by Vettori) and the fair dual 5f winners (including at 2 yrs) Pretty Miss (by Averti) and Poppy's Song (by Owington). The dam, a modest 2-y-o 5f winner, stayed 7.6f and is a half-sister to 4 winners including the Criterium de Maisons-Laffitte winner Corviglia. The second dam, Moonlight Serenade (by Crooner), is a placed sister to the winner and Group 3 5f Duke Of York Stakes third Blackbird. (A Walker). *"He was in the second part of the St Leger sales and some reason there were very few people around at the time, so I think I may have got him at a good price. He goes very well, we think* he's above average and he's one of the nicer ones I've trained. A nice, big horse that'll get stronger by the end of the season. He'll stay six furlongs later on but I'm quite surprised how sharp he is." TRAINERS' BARGAIN BUY

1301. KALKAN BAY ★★
b.g. Pastoral Pursuits – Gibraltar Bay (Cape Cross).
February 5. First foal. £24,000Y. Doncaster St Leger. J O'Keeffe. The dam, a fair 9f and 12f winner, is a half-sister to 4 winners. The second dam, Secrets Of Honour (by Belmez), is an unraced half-sister to 6 winners including the Group 1 July Cup winner Mr Brooks. (Ken & Delia Shaw-KGS Consulting LLP). *"A big horse, we haven't done an awful lot with him yet and I don't think we'll see him out before mid-summer, probably over seven furlongs. A big, powerful galloper."*

1302. LADY KILDARE (IRE) ★★★
br.f. Bachelor Duke – Teodora (Fairy King).
April 25. Half-sister to the fairly useful 2009 2-y-o triple 5f winner Duchess Dora, to the quite useful 2-y-o 7f winner Fadhb Ar Bith (both by Tagula), the fair 2-y-o 7f winner Feeling Wonderful and the useful 2-y-o dual 7f winner Prince Of Love (both by Fruits Of Love). The dam, a fairly useful 2-y-o 6f winner, was fourth in the Group 3 6f Princess Margaret Stakes and is a half-sister to 4 winners. The second dam, Pinta (by Ahonoora), won over 5f in Ireland and a listed event in Italy over 7.5f and is a half-sister to 6 winners. *"We got her on a free lease from Ireland. She's doing well, she's pretty sharp and I can see her being out in May over five furlongs. We're pleased with her."*

1303. SCOTTISH LAKE ★★
b.c. Bertolini – Diabaig (Precocious).
February 19. Third foal. 8,000foal. Tattersalls December. Not sold. Half-brother to the unplaced 2010 2-y-o Irish Eyes (by Mark of Esteem), to the fairly useful 1m winner of 5 races Ailincala (by Pursuit Of Love), the fair 10f winners Highland Love and Wester Ross (both by Fruits Of Love) and 2 hurdles winners by Bin Ajwaad and Victory Note. The dam, a fair 1m winner, is a half-sister to 4 minor winners. The second dam, Silka (by Lypheor), won once at 2 yrs in Italy and is a half-sister to 4 other minor

winners. (Ken & Delia Shaw-KGS Consulting LLP). *"We've got two of his half-brothers in the yard at the moment. This is a really powerful colt, we broke him in a bit later than the others because of his size and he probably wouldn't be out until July or August."*

1304. WITZEND (IRE) ★★★
b.c. *Footstepsinthesand – Spring Easy (Alzao)*.
April 7. Brother to the modest 2009 7f placed 2-y-o Scarboro Warning and half-brother to the Irish 11f winner Spring Opera (by Sadler's Wells), to the Italian 3-y-o winner of 7 races Picasso Blu (by Peintre Celebre) and two minor winners abroad by Galileo. The dam, unplaced in one start, is a half-sister to 8 winners including the Group 3 10.5f Prix de Royaumont winner Legend Maker and the very useful Group 2 12f King Edward VII Stakes winner Amfortas. The second dam, High Spirited (by Shirley Heights), won over 14f and 2m and is a sister to the Premio Roma winner High Hawk (herself dam of the Breeders Cup Turf winner In the Wings) and a half-sister to the dams of the Derby winner High-Rise and the Rothmans International winner Infamy. *"He's shaping up very nicely and he could well be out in late May over six furlongs. A good-bodied, medium-sized colt with a good temperament. I really like him and he's showing plenty."*

1305. UNNAMED ★★
b.c. *Whipper – Desert Royalty (Alhaarth)*.
March 28. Third foal. 17,000Y. Tattersalls October Book 2. Jedd O'Keeffe. Half-brother to Rebel Chieftain (by Dansili), unplaced in one start at 2 yrs in 2009 and to the modest 7f winner Princess Zohra (by Royal Applause). The dam, a fairly useful winner of 4 races from 1m to 12f, was listed-placed twice and is a half-sister to 2 winners. The second dam, Buraida (by Balidar), a modest 3-y-o 6f winner, is a sister to the smart sprinter Carol's Treasure and a half-sister to 4 other winners. (A Walker). *"A lovely, powerful colt, he's a really good mover and a classy-looking horse. I'm very happy with hi but he is quite tall, quite big and he's going to need a bit of time. He'll have a few runs this time but he'll be a better three-year-old."*

1306. UNNAMED ★★
b.c. *Araafa – Mount Street (Pennekamp)*.

March 25. Fourth foal. 8,000Y. Tattersalls October Book 2. Jedd O'Keeffe. The dam, a quite useful 10f winner, is a half-sister to 6 winners including the 2,000 Guineas and King George VI and Queen Elizabeth Stakes winner Golan and the Group 2 Dante Stakes winner Tartan Bearer. The second dam, Highland Gift (by Generous), a fairly useful 10f winner, is a half-sister to 4 winners including the Group 2 12f Great Voltigeur Stakes winner Bonny Scot. (A. Walker). *"A big, strong horse, he was a bit lazy to start with but the penny's starting to drop. He's definitely one for the second half of the season and next year."*

JAMIE OSBORNE

1307. DROXFORD (USA) ★★
ch.g. *Orientate – Dixiehunt (Dixieland Band)*.
February 7. Third foal. 27,000Y. Tattersalls October Book 1. David Redvers. Half-brother to the minor US 4-y-o winner Warm Climate (by El Corredor). The dam, a minor winner in the USA, is an unraced half-sister to 9 winners including the US dual Grade 3 winner Discover. *"He's just been gelded and is more of a second half of the season horse. He was the most expensive one I bought but I don't know an awful lot about him yet. A good-looking horse ... he's quite nice."*

1308. COMMERCIAL (IRE) ★★★★
b.c. *Kodiac – Call Collect (Houmayoun)*.
April 15. First foal. 15,000Y. Tattersalls Book 3. David Redvers. The dam is an unplaced half-sister to 4 winners including the German Group 2 winner and Italian Group 2 placed Checkit. The second dam, Collected (by Taufan), is an unplaced half-sister to 4 winners. *"Keep an eye on the sire because I have three by him and they can all run. I didn't go out with the intention of majoring Kodiac but they fell through the net a bit, they're all racy and they all looked very forward. This one is a good horse. I think he'll be alright and he might be our first runner. A big horse, he would look like a three-year-old next to most two-year-olds. A lot of quality, a great mover and he's going very well without really letting the handbrake off. He'll definitely win a maiden and if he goes the right way he could be alright."*

1309. FIFTH COMMANDMENT ★★★
b.f. Holy Roman Emperor – Via Milano (Singspiel).
April 21. Second living foal. €20,000Y. Goffs Orby. David Redvers. The dam won the Group 3 1m Prix des Reservoirs at 2 yrs and is a half-sister to one winner. The second dam, Salvinaxia (by Linamix), a French listed-placed 2-y-o winner, is a half-sister to 8 winners. "She's quite sharp and she could run at the end of April. She's small to the point that I look at her now and say 'bloody hell she must have shrunk!" and I was worried until I started galloping her – and she's quick. I don't know if anything as small as her has been any good, but she can motor along, she's clocking a good time and even though she's out of her Singspiel mare five furlongs is her trip."

1310. FIFTH DIMENSION ★★★
b.c. Acclamation – Sail With The Wind (Saddlers' Hall).
May 5. Third foal. 16,000Y. Tattersalls December. David Redvers. Half-brother to Expensive Detour (by Namid), a quite useful 6f winner here and subsequently a 7f winner in France. The dam, a 10f to 12f winner of 5 races, is a sister to one winner and a half-sister to 5 winners including the useful 2-y-o 10f and Group 3 10f Sandown Classic Trial winner Shield. The second dam, Shesadelight (by Shirley Heights), was placed at up to 2m and is a sister to the Grade 1 Rothmans International winner Infamy (herself the dam of three Group winners). "He wouldn't be an out-and-out five furlong type especially as he's out of a Saddlers Hall mare and I wouldn't start him until the six furlong races, possibly seven, bit he's OK and he's goes alright."

1311. FIFTH ESTATE ★★★★
br.c. Needwood Blade – Passata (Polar Falcon).
March 24. Fourth foal. 12,000Y. Tattersalls October. Amanda Skiffington. Half-brother to the champion German 2-y-o and Group 2 Criterium de Maisons-Laffitte winner Pomellato, to the German winner and French listed-placed Pom Pom Pom (both by Big Shuffle) and the minor German 1m and subsequent jumps winner Passato (by Lando). The dam won once at 3 yrs in Germany and is a half-sister to 6 winners. The second dam, Premier Amour (by Salmon Leap), a German Group 3 winner and third in the Group 1 French Oaks, is a half-sister to 9 winners. "I'm going to firmly predict right now that I've got a Needwood Blade that can run! I absolutely loved the horse at the Sales so I took a chance and I'm so glad I did. I think he's good. He can really gallop, he's not going to be a five furlong horse, he's jet black and looks just like Polar Falcon. He'll start at six furlongs in May, I just think he's a lovely horse and if you saw him in the string you'd think he should be with Godolphin. The sire's influence might come through (I'm crossing my fingers it won't) but at the moment he looks like a mini Polar Falcon, the way he moves and gallops makes me think I haven't had a two-year-old for a few years that's excited me as much. I love him." Jamie showed me the colt in his box and I could see why he was enthusing about him. Let's hope he does the business." TRAINERS' BARGAIN BUY

1312. FIFTH IN LINE (IRE) ★★
b.f. Kodiac – Surrender To Me (Royal Anthem).
February 12. First foal. £10,000Y. Goffs Orby. David Redvers. The dam is an unraced half-sister to 3 winners including the Italian listed winner Six Hitter. The second dam, Granny Kelly (by Irish River), was placed once over 7f at 2 yrs in Ireland and is a half-sister to 4 minor winners. "A beautiful actioned filly, she'll want six furlongs at least so I might delay her start but she's nice and I like her."

1313. KODIAC STAR (IRE) ★★★
b.f. Kodiac – Grade A Star (Alzao).
May 7. Eleventh foal. 6,000Y. Tattersalls October Book 2, David Redvers. Half-sister to numerous winners including the very useful Group 3 6f Phoenix Sprint Stakes winner March Star (by Mac's Imp), the quite useful Irish 6f winner Douze Points (by Redback) and the Irish 10f winner Jimmy Swift (by Petardia). The dam, an Irish 2-y-o 1m winner, stayed 11f and is a half-sister to 2 winners. The second dam, Indian Swallow (by Indian King), is an unraced half-sister to 7 winners. "She's a bit small but she has some speed and although she was a May foal she's actually a nice early two-year-old we can kick on with."

1314. LES LANDES (IRE) ★★★
b.c. Aussie Rules – Splendid (Mujtahid).
April 26. Ninth foal. €25,000Y. Goffs Orby. David Redvers. Closely related to the quite useful 7f (at 2 yrs) and 11f winner Fanditha (by Danehill Dancer) and half-brother to the fairly useful 2009 2-y-o 7f winner and Group 3 7f Killavullan Stakes second Lord High Admiral (by Galileo), the quite useful 2-y-o 6f winner Packing Hero (by Black Minnaloushe), the US stakes-placed winner of 5 races Bohunk (by Polish Numbers) and a minor US 4-y-o winner by Rahy. The dam is a placed half-sister to 4 winners including the very useful 1m (at 2 yrs) and 12f winner Peking Opera. The second dam, Braneakins (by Sallust), won 3 races over 12f in Ireland and is a half-sister to 7 winners including the Cheveley Park Stakes winners Park Appeal (the dam of Cape Cross) and Desirable (dam of the 1,000 Guineas winner Shadayid), the Irish Oaks winner Alydaress and the unraced dam of the 1,000 Guineas winner Russian Rhythm. *"He's quite sharp and it's a pedigree that could produce a decent horse, he's not over-big and he's been gelded but he goes OK. To be at his best he probably wants seven furlongs, so we'll probably start him at six. He'll be alright, I think."*

1315. MOORLAND BOY ★★
gr.c. Proclamation – Superlove (Hector Protector).
February 16. Second foal. 10,000Y. Tattersalls October 2, David Redvers. Half-brother to 2 winners in Germany by Surako and Auenadier. The dam is an unraced half-sister to 8 winners including the US dual Grade 2 winner Battle Of Hastings and the Irish listed winner Villa Carlotta. The second dam, Subya (by Night Shift), was a very useful winner of 5 races from 5f (at 2 yrs) to 10f including the Lupe Stakes, the Masaka Stakes and the Milcars Star Stakes (all listed events). *"He's alright and he's surprised me with his strength and what he taking. I thought when I bought him he'd be one for the second half of the season but now I think he'll definitely be out by June."*

1316. RETREAT CONTENT (IRE) ★★★
b.c. Dubai Destination – Sharp Point (Royal Academy).
April 20. Ninth living foal. €20,000Y. Tattersalls Ireland. David Redvers. Half-brother to the Group 3 9f Prix Chloe and Group 3 1m Premio Sergio Cumani winner Needlecraft (by Mark Of Esteem), to the minor Irish 2-y-o 1m winner Thought (by Zafonic) and the minor French 2-y-o winner Mayfield (by Danehill). The dam, a useful Irish listed 5f winner at 3 yrs, was second in the Group 1 Heinz 57 Phoenix Stakes and is a half-sister to 3 winners including the listed winner High Target. The second dam, Nice Point (by Sharpen Up), is an unraced half-sister to 4 winners including the 2,000 Guineas winner Tirol. *"A very good-looking horse for the second half of the season and he moves great. Bred by Darley, he has a bit of quality and he's a nice type of horse. He did have an issue with his knees but I don't think that's going to be a problem now."*

1317. VALEO SI VALES (IRE) ★★★
b.c. Oratorio – Eurostorm (Storm Bird).
April 15. €15,000Y. Goffs Open. David Redvers. Half-brother to the smart 1m and 10f winner Man O'Mystery (by Diesis) and to the Irish 2-y-o 6f winner Destorm (by Dehere). The dam won 4 races in Ireland and the USA including the listed 1m Brownstown Stud Stakes and the listed 10f Diamond Stakes at the Curragh. She is a half-sister to 7 winners out of the smart Eurobird (by Ela-Mana-Mou), a winner of 4 races including the Irish St Leger and the Blandford Stakes and a half-sister to the French Derby winner Bikala and to the Irish Derby and French Derby winner Assert. *"A strong, forward colt that shows a bit of pace, he's OK and I'm going to get him out in May. He's not over-big and I'm aiming to get him out fairly early – so he wouldn't be typical of the sire."*

1318. UNNAMED ★★
b.g. Araafa – Naayla (Invincible Spirit).
February 24. First foal. 11,000Y. The dam, a quite useful 2-y-o 6f winner, is a half-sister to 7 winners including the German 2-y-o 6f winner and Group 3 placed Medina, the useful 2-y-o dual 5f winner Pike Bishop, the fairly useful 2-y-o 5f winner and Group 3 Firth Of Clyde Stakes second Broken Applause. The second dam, Pink Cashmere (by Polar Falcon), is an unraced three-parts sister to the Group 1 6f July Cup winner Owington and a half-sister

to 8 winners. *"I've gelded him as he was a cheeky little lad, but he's small, strong and forward. We'll probably start him in May over six furlongs."*

1319. UNNAMED ★★
b.f. *Exceed And Excel – Nawaji (Trempolino).*
March 14. Eighth foal. €13,000Y. Goffs Open. Brendan Bashford. Half-sister to the quite useful 2009 2-y-o 7f and 1m winner Contract Caterer (by Azamour), to the useful 2-y-o 7f winner Ahmedy (by Polish Precedent), the quite useful 9.5f winner Noticeable (by Night Shift) and fair 7f (at 2 yrs) to 10f winner Press Express (by Entrepreneur). The dam, a poor placed maiden at up to 13f, is a sister to the Group 3 10f Select Stakes winner Triarius and a half-sister to the listed Fred Archer Stakes winner Sharp Noble and the unraced dam of the Group 3 Prix des Reservoirs winner Bint Alnasr. The second dam, Noble Decretum (by Noble Decree), is an unplaced half-sister to 12 winners. *"More of a Trempolino than an Exceed And Excel now because she's done a lot of growing since the Sales, but she's a lovely mover and I see her as a second half of the season two-year-old."*

1320. UNNAMED ★★
gr.c. *Aussie Rules – Set Fair (Alleged).*
March 15. Twelfth foal. 24,000Y. Tattersalls December. David Redvers. Half-brother to the very useful listed 7f (at 2 yrs) and listed 11.4f Cheshire Oaks winner Valentine Girl (by Alzao), to the very useful 7f (including at 2 yrs) and 1m winner Cloudy Start (by Oasis Dream), the fairly useful 12.3f winner Solitary (by Sanglamore) and a minor winner of 5 races in Germany by Polish Precedent. The dam, a French 10f winner, is a sister to the smart Group 2 winning stayer Non Partisan and the Canadian Grade 3 winner Jalaajel and a half-sister to 8 winners including the useful dual 2-y-o 7f winner and Group 3 Prix d'Aumale third Suntrap (herself dam of the Group/Grade 1 winners Raintrap and Sunshack). The second dam, Sunny Bay (by Northern Bay), won 3 stakes events in the USA and was second in the Grade 1 Sorority Stakes. *"Nice but backward and one for the second half of the season. Not a beautiful horse, but he's very similar in looks to his half-brother Cloudy Start who's rated 108. A nice mover, I've not done a lot with him and he's one for much later on and next year I would say."*

JOHN OXX

1321. CAPE OF GOOD GRACE (IRE) ★★★
b.f. *Cape Cross – Daganya (Danehill Dancer).*
April 24. Fourth foal. Half-sister to the modest dual 6f winner Chasca (by Namid). The dam won 2 races including a listed 6f event in Ireland and was second in the Group 2 5f Flying Five. She is a sister to the listed 5f winner Snaefell and a half-sister to 3 winners including the quite useful 5f winner of 10 races Henry Hall. The second dam, Sovereign Grace (by Standaan), won over 5f in Ireland and is a half-sister 9 winners. (J D Clague). *"She's a nice filly, very racy and athletic. She looks reasonably precocious, she moves well and has a good temperament. I like her and I'd be disappointed if she didn't show us something this year. As a bunch, I'm very happy with my two-year-olds. They look to be as good as the very good crop I had two years ago."*

1322. CREEKSIDE ★★
b.c. *Dubai Destination – Khubza (Green Desert).*
March 1. Eleventh foal. 60,000Y. Tattersalls October Book 1. John Ferguson. Brother to fair 4-y-o 6f and 7f winner Trade Centre and half-brother to the Group 2 1m Prix du Rond-Point and Group 3 8.5f Diomed Stakes winner Trans Island, the Italian Group 3 winner Welsh Diva, the useful 2-y-o 7f winner Nothing Daunted (all by Selkirk), the quite useful 2009 Irish 2-y-o 7f winner Mujaazef (by Dubawi), the quite useful 2-y-o 6f winner Bread Of Heaven (by Machiavellian) and the fair 7f winner Welsh Cake (by Fantastic Light). The dam, a quite useful 3-y-o 7f winner, is a half-sister to 7 winners including the Group 2 winners Barrow Creek and Last Resort and the listed winners Arctic Char and Heard A Whisper. The second dam, Breadcrumb (by Final Straw), a very useful winner of 3 races at 3 yrs over 6f and 7f, is a half-sister to 4 winners including the high-class sprinter College Chapel. (Sheikh Mohammed). *"A good, strong colt that's growing at the moment, I'm not sure how precocious he's going to be but he's a nice horse."*

1323. DANCE SECRETARY (IRE) ★★★★
ch.f. *Danehill Dancer – Ball Chairman (Secretariat).*
April 15. Half-sister to the US Grade 1 Shadwell Mile and dual Grade 2 winner Perfect Soul (by Sadler's Wells) and to the US stakes-placed winner Dimontina (by Dixieland Band). The dam is a placed half-sister to several winners. The second dam, A Status Symbol (by Exclusive Native), was a stakes winner of 7 races. (Mr C Fipke). *"A really nice filly, I've had a few of her sisters who were all by Sadler's Wells but she's more precocious than they were. She wouldn't be far off starting some fast work, I like her and she should show us something from midsummer onwards."*

1324. HIS EXCELLENCY (IRE) ★★★
ch.c. *King's Best – Road Harbour (Rodrigo De Triano).*
May 6. Fifth foal. 42,000Y. Tattersalls October Book 2. R O'Gorman. Half-brother to the useful 12f to 2m 2f and hurdles winner Leg Spinner (by Intikhab), to the quite useful Irish 1m winner and listed-placed Ashka (by Catcher In The Rye) and the modest Irish dual 7f winner Tuesday Flyer (by Alhaarth). The dam is an unraced half-sister to the French 3-y-o winner and subsequent US stakes winner Dance Dreamer. The second dam, Revasser (by Riverman), won the Grade 2 Tidal Handicap in the USA and was Grade 1 placed and is a half-sister to 3 winners including the US Grade 1 winner Hometown Queen and the dam of the US Grade 1 winners Sightseek and Tates Creek. (Sheikh Mohammed). *"He's nice and although he's grown a bit recently he's well-balanced and a good mover. One for the second half of the year."*

1325. KASANKA (IRE) ★★★
b.f. *Galileo – Kassana (Shernazar).*
March 4. Half-sister to the Group 1 Irish St Leger winner Kastoria (by Selkirk), to the fairly useful Irish 9f winner Kassna (by Ashkalani), the quite useful Irish 12f winner Kassabat (by Entrepreneur) and the minor French 12f winner Kasrawad (by Barathea). The dam, winner of the Group 3 12.5f Prix Minerve, is a half-sister to the Group 2 15f Prix Kergorlay winner Kassani. The second dam, Kassiyda (by Mill Reef), a useful dual 10f winner, is a half-sister to the Epsom and Irish Derby winner Kahyasi and the St Simon Stakes winner Kaliana. (H H Aga Khan). *"A very, very nice horse but obviously not bred to be precocious so we can't expect her to be out until the autumn, when she'll have a run or two. But she's really nice – you couldn't ask for nicer."*

1326. DUBAWI STAR ★★★★
b.c. *Dubawi – Cloud Hill (Danehill).*
February 26. Fifth foal. 75,000Y. Tattersalls October Book 2. Rabbah Bloodstock. Half-brother to the fair 10f and 12f winner Mista Rossa (by Red Ransom) and a winner in Greece by Inchinor. The dam is an unraced half-sister to 3 winners including the Cheshire Oaks winner and Yorkshire Oaks and St Leger second High And Low and to the unraced dam of the triple Group 1 winner American Post. The second dam, Cruising Height (by Shirley Heights), a very useful 10.6f and 12.2f winner, was second in the Group 3 Lancashire Oaks and is a half-sister to the Park Hill Stakes winner Trampship. (Sultan Ali). *"He's very typical of the Dubawi's that you see, they're sharp-looking – like he was himself. A very nice, racy colt that'll shortly start some fast work. He's done very well over the last few months."*

1327. KAYALAR (IRE) ★★★
b.c. *Noverre – Katiykha (Darshaan).*
April 7. Half-brother to the 7f (at 2 yrs) and Group 2 10f Blandford Stakes winner Katiyra (by Peintre Celebre), to the quite useful Irish 7f winner Katirisa (by Spinning World) and an Irish hurdles winner by Desert Prince. The dam, a smart Irish listed 12f and 14f winner, is a half-sister to 6 winners. The second dam, Katiyfa (by Auction Ring), won the listed 1m Prix de la Calonne and is a half-sister to 3 winners. (H H Aga Khan). *"A lovely colt, but he's had a little setback and had to go home. I'm not sure how long he'll be away but he's particularly nice and a beautiful mover. Hopefully he'll be back in the autumn."*

1328. KILBIRNIE ★★★★
b.c. *Pivotal – Blue Symphony (Darshaan).*
March 4. Fourth foal. 450,000Y. Tattersalls October Book 1. M H Goodbody. Half-brother to the 2009 7f placed 2-y-o Pink Symphony (by Montjeu), to the very smart

Group 3 7f Prestige Stakes (at 2 yrs) and Group 3 Nell Gwyn Stakes winner and dual Group 1 placed Fantasia (by Sadler's Wells) and the fair 2-y-o 7f winner Blue Rhapsody (by Cape Cross). The dam, a fair 10f winner, is a half-sister to one winner. The second dam, Blue Duster (by Danzig), winner of the Group 1 6f Cheveley Park Stakes, the Group 3 6f Princess Margaret Stakes and the Group 3 5f Queen Mary Stakes, is a sister to the smart Group 1 6f Middle Park Stakes and Group 2 7f Challenge Stakes winner Zieten and a half-sister to 9 winners. (Mr T Barr). *"A nice horse that cost a lot of money at the Sales. He's big but he's very mature mentally and we ought to be putting him into fast work shortly. He's promising and it's a speedy family so I'd say he'd start at six furlongs."*

1329. LABBA ★★
b.f. Tiger Hill – Ladeena (Dubai Millennium).
February 5. Second foal. 70,000Y. Tattersalls October Book 1. Rabbah Bloodstock. Half-sister to the useful 2009 2-y-o 6f winner and 7f listed placed Atlantis Star (by Cape Cross). The dam, a fair 7f winner at 3 yrs, is a half-sister to 2 winners. The second dam, Aqaarid (by Nashwan), a smart winner of the Group 1 Fillies Mile and the Group 3 7.3f Fred Darling Stakes, was second in the 1,000 Guineas and is a half-sister to 2 winners. (Sultan Ali). *"Quite big and backward. A lovely filly but she's unlikely to make a two-year-old."*

1330. LONG JOURNEY HOME (IRE) ★★
b.c. Dansili – Quest For Eternity (Sadler's Wells).
January 29. First foal. The dam is an unraced sister to the smart 10f winner and Group 1 Irish Oaks second Roses For The Lady. The second dam, Head In The Clouds (by Rainbow Quest), won the Group 3 12f Princess Royal Stakes and is a sister to the high-class St Leger, Chester Vase and Jockey Club Stakes winner Millenary and a half-sister to the very smart 1m (at 2 yrs) and 10f winner and Derby third Let The Lion Roar. (Mr N Jones). *"He's still in pre-training because he's backward. I've seen him and he's nice but he'd be one for the end of the year."*

1331. MANIEREE (IRE) ★★
b.f. Medicean – Sheer Spirit (Caerleon).
February 1. Half-sister to the fairly useful 10f winner and listed-placed Bold Choice (by Dubai Destination), to the useful 6f (at 2 yrs) and 7f winner River Bravo (by Indian Ridge), the fairly useful 2-y-o 6f to 1m winner Solid Rock (by Rock Of Gibraltar) and the fair 12f to 14f all-weather winner Sovereign Spirit (by Desert Prince). The dam won over 12f at 3 yrs and is a half-sister to 9 winners including the Derby winner Oath and the triple Group 1 winner Pelder. The second dam, Sheer Audacity (by Troy), was placed twice in Italy and is closely related to the Ribblesdale Stakes winner and good broodmare Miss Petard. (Mr Max Morris). *"Quite a nice filly but a little bit behind the others, she's a good-moving filly. Maybe not the most precocious-looking but she'll be OK later in the year."*

1332. MINSK (IRE) ★★
b.c. Dalakhani – Penza (Soviet Star).
April 10. Sixth foal. €160,000Y. Goffs Orby. BBA (Ire). Half-brother to the German 6f (including at 2 yrs) to 9f and subsequent Doncaster 12f winner Valmari (by Kalanisi) and the quite useful 11f winner and German listed-placed Trullitti (by Bahri). The dam is a placed half-sister to 5 winners including the Group 1 12f Italian Derby winner and 'King George' second White Muzzle, the Group 2 German St Leger winner Fair Question and the listed winner Elfaslah (dam of the Dubai World Cup winner Almutawakel). The second dam, Fair of the Furze (by Ela-Mana-Mou), won the Group 2 10f Tattersalls Rogers Gold Cup and is a half-sister to the listed winners Majestic Role, Norman Style, Proconsular and Supreme Commander. (Airlie Stud). *"A tall, leggy, backward horse and one for later in the year. He hasn't put a foot wrong, but to look at him you'd think he'd take time. He'll have a couple of runs this year, he's been cantering away all winter, hasn't missed a beat and he's done as much as any of them."*

1333. MISSY O'GWAUN (IRE) ★★★
b.f. King's Best – Angel Of The Gwaun (Sadler's Wells).
May 13. Fifth foal. Sister to the fairly useful 2-y-o 7f winner Angelonmyshoulder and half-sister to the 7f (at 2 yrs) and Group 3 10f Blue Wind Stakes winner Beauty O'Gwaun (by

Rainbow Quest). The dam is an unraced sister to the Derby third Let The Lion Roar and a half-sister to the St Leger winner Millenary. The second dam, Ballerina (by Dancing Brave), a quite useful 2-y-o 7f winner, is a half-sister to the Group 3 12f Princess Royal Stakes winner Dancing Bloom and the good French 2-y-o 5f winner and 1,000 Guineas third River Dancer (herself dam of the Champion Stakes winner Spectrum). (Mr N Jones). *"She's a nice filly that should show something in the second half of the year. A very good looker and a good mover, she's mature and although on pedigree you wouldn't want to push her early, at the same time the way she's built she'll show something this year. She doesn't look like a mid-May foal."*

1334. MOUNTAIN WOMAN (IRE) ★★★
b.f. Montjeu – Preseli (Caerleon).
February 16. Closely related to the fair 2-y-o 7f winner A Girl (by Sadler's Wells) and half-sister to the quite useful 7f and 1m winner Arizona John (by Rahy). The dam, the smart 2-y-o Group 1 7f Moyglare Stud Stakes winner, is a sister to one winner and a half-sister to the Group 3 Lingfield Derby Trial winner Kong, the useful listed 14f winner Mount Kilimanjaro and the smart 7f winner and 1,000 Guineas second Snowfire. The second dam, Hill Of Snow (by Reference Point), an Irish 10f winner, is a half-sister to the smart Group 2 Prix de Pomone winner Whitehaven. (Mr N Jones). *"A nice filly and like her dam she's not too big – so she's more like Preseli than Montjeu. Preseli was precocious enough, so I'm hopeful she'll make a two-year-old in the second half of the season."*

1335. NARJAWA (IRE) ★★
b.f. Marju – Narmina (Alhaarth).
March 5. The dam is a half-sister to 4 winners including the smart Group 3 12f Princess Royal Stakes winner Narwala and the fairly useful, tough and genuine middle-distance handicapper Noukari. The second dam, Noufiyla (by Top Ville), was placed over middle-distances and is a half-sister to the Cherry Hinton Stakes winner Nasseem. (H H Aga Khan). *"She's very big and backward, I don't know what she'll do at two. Much more of a three-year-old type."*

1336. NATALISA (IRE) ★★★★
b.f. Green Desert – Noelani (Indian Ridge).
March 18. First foal. The dam, a Group 3 6f and Group 3 7f in Ireland, is a sister to the Group 1 5f Prix de l'Abbaye winner and smart sire Namid and to the very useful Group 3 6f and 7.5f winner Noelani and a half-sister to the useful Irish 2-y-o 7f winner and dual Group placed Natalis. The second dam, Dawnsio (by Tate Gallery), a useful winner of the listed Topaz Sprint Stakes in Ireland, is a half-sister to 3 winners including the Cherry Hinton Stakes third Miss Bluebird. (Lady Clague). *"She's not too big, she's sharp looking and a good mover and obviously should do something as a two-year-old. We're hoping she'll be around from June onwards and she's a nice filly – so far, so good."*

1337. RED CALIMA (IRE) ★★★
b.c. Shirocco – So Well Red (by Sadler's Wells).
January 14. First foal. The dam, a quite useful Irish 1m winner, is a half-sister to the useful dual 6f (at 2 yrs) and 7f winner Red Liason and to the very useful Group 3 7f Brownstown Stakes winner Redstone Dancer. The second dam, Red Affair (by Generous), an Irish listed 10f winner, is a half-sister to the smart 7.6f to 10f winner Brilliant Red and to the useful 12f to 14f winner and Group 3 2m Queens Vase third Kassab (by Caerleon). (Lady Clague). *"A very nice colt, obviously he'll need some time going off the pedigree but he's quite mature looking and he's really developed over the last few months into a really nice horse. I think he'll do something at two."*

1338. REDSKIN DANCER ★★★
b.f. Namid – Red Affair (Generous).
April 11. Sister to the smart Group 3 7f Brownstown Stakes and Group 3 7f Minstrel Stakes winner Redstone Dancer and half-sister to the useful dual 6f (at 2 yrs) and listed 7f winner Red Liason (by Selkirk) and the quite useful Irish 1m winner So Well Red (by Sadler's Wells). The dam, an Irish listed 10f winner, is a half-sister to the smart 7.6f to 10f winner Brilliant Red and to the useful 12f to 14f winner and Group 3 2m Queens Vase third Kassab (by Caerleon). The second dam, Red Comes Up (by Blushing Groom), was placed 6 times in France and is a sister to Rainbow Quest. (Lady

Clague). *"She's a nice filly, her sister Redstone Dancer came into her own as a four-year-old but hopefully she'll come to hand earlier than that. There's nothing wrong with her at all and hopefully we'll see a result this year."*

1339. SHARESTAN (IRE) ★★★★
b.c. Shamardal – Sharesha (Ashkalani).
April 9. Fourth foal. Half-brother to the fair 2009 Irish 7f placed 2-y-o Shareen (by Bahri) and to the useful 6f (at 2 yrs) and 7f winner and listed-placed Sharleez (by Marju). The dam was a fairly useful Irish 10f winner out of Sharemata (by Doyoun). (H H Aga Khan). *"A nice, precocious-looking colt, he's well-grown so I'd hope that by mid-season we could start him."*

1340. THE HIGH MAN ★★★
ch.c. Medicean – Excellent (Grand Lodge).
March 20. First foal. £120,000Y. Doncaster St Leger. Peter Doyle. The dam ran unplaced twice and is a half-sister to the Group 1 1m Matron Stakes winner Echelon and the dual Group 2 1m winner Chic. The second dam, Exclusive (by Polar Falcon), winner of the Group 1 1m Coronation Stakes, is a half-sister to the 2,000 Guineas winner and Derby fourth Entrepreneur, the smart Cheshire Oaks winner and Epsom Oaks second Dance a Dream, the very useful middle-distance listed winner Sadler's Image and the useful French 2-y-o listed 7f winner Irish Order. (Mr W P Drew). *"He's quite a nice horse and we'll start him in some fast work soon, he hasn't put a foot wrong yet and I'd definitely hope he'd be out from July onwards."*

1341. TROPICAL SPIRIT (IRE) ★★★★
b.c. Invincible Spirit – Tropical Lady (Sri Pekan).
January 25. First foal. 27,000foal. Tattersalls December. Not sold. The dam won 8 races including the Group 2 10f Royal Whip Stakes, the Group 3 10f Meld Stakes and the Group 3 7f Brownstown Stakes. The second dam, Tropical Lake (by Lomond), won 6 races on the flat from 1m to 2m and 4 races over hurdles including a Group 2 event. (Mr G Kent). *"A very nice colt, he's good-looking and he's about to start some fast work now. A nicely bred horse and a good looker that should be starting at six furlongs."*

1342. TUGBOAT (IRE) ★★
b.c. Galileo – Alleluia (Caerleon).
April 23. Sixth foal. 300,000Y. Tattersalls October Book 1. M H Goodbody. Brother to the Group 1 Prix Royal Oak and multiple Group 2 winner Allegretto and half-brother to the quite useful dual 14f winner Alleviate and the fair 9f winner King's Song (both by Indian Ridge). The dam, winner of the Group 3 Doncaster Cup, is a half-sister to 7 winners including the Nassau Stakes and Sun Chariot Stakes winner Last Second (dam of the French 2,000 Guineas winner Aussie Rules), the Moyglare Stud Stakes third Alouette (dam of the dual Champion Stakes winner Alborada and the triple German Group 1 winner Albanova) and to the placed dam of the Group 1 winners Yesterday and Quarter Moon. The second dam, Alruccaba (by Crystal Palace), a quite useful 2-y-o 6f winner, is out of a half-sister to the dams of Aliysa and Nishapour. (Mr T Barr). *"A lovely-looking, well-balanced horse that cost a fair bit of money at the Sales. He's not bred to be precocious and if he was capable of winning a maiden at the end of the season you'd have plenty to look forward to, because he's bred to improve."*

1343. VELESGO (IRE) ★★★★
b.c. Dansili – Cassandra Go (Indian Ridge).
April 30. Closely related to the Group 3 6f Summer Stakes winner Theann (by Rock Of Gibraltar) and half-brother to Irish 1,000 Guineas, Nassau Stakes and Sun Chariot Stakes winner Halfway To Heaven (by Pivotal), the fairly useful dual 5f winner Neverletme Go and the fair 5f winner Mannikko (both by Green Desert). The dam, a very smart winner of the Group 2 5f Kings Stand Stakes, is a full or half-sister to 7 winners including the smart Group 3 6f Coventry Stakes winner and Irish 2,000 Guineas second Verglas. The second dam, Rahaam (by Secreto), a fairly useful 3-y-o 7f winner, is a half-sister to 8 winners including the French 2,000 Guineas third Glory Forever. (Mr T Stewart). *"He's a very nice colt, there's nothing wrong with him, he's correct and a good mover with a good temperament. He's coming along on well, I like him and he's a very nice horse. He should be doing some fast work soon and he'll be a two-year-old in the middle-to-second half of the season. A good sort."*

1344. UNNAMED ★★★
ch.f. *Dubai Destination – Alasha (Barathea)*.
March 13. Fourth foal. The dam, a useful 7f (at 2 yrs) and listed 1m winner, is a half-sister to several winners. The second dam, Alasana (by Darshaan), won twice in France over 1m and 9f and is a half-sister to the Prix Maurice de Nieuil winner Altayan and the Grand Prix de Vichy winner Altashar. (HH Aga Khan). *"The dam hasn't done a lot yet, for such a good filly she's been a little disappointing at stud so far, but this is a nice filly. She's quite racy-looking and a two-year-old type, so despite a couple of minor setbacks lately she's done plenty and is fairly forward."*

1345. UNNAMED ★★★★
b.c. *Azamour – Alaya (Ela-Mana-Mou)*.
April 2. Half-brother to the dual 7f (at 2 yrs) and Group 3 10f Mooresbridge Stakes winner Alayan (by Sri Pekan), to the very useful listed 12f winner Alaivan (by Kalanisi) and the useful 2-y-o 1m winner and Group 2 10f Royal Whip Stakes second Alarazi (by Spectrum). The dam won over 12f in Ireland and is a half-sister to the Irish Derby and King George winner Alamshar. The second dam, Alaiyda (by Shahrastani), a minor Irish 3-y-o 10f winner, is a half-sister to the smart Group 3 1m Craven Stakes winner and Group 2 10.4f Dante Stakes second Desert Story (by Green Desert). (H H Aga Khan). *"A very nice horse. Alaya has been a good mare and she seems to be able to breed good winners even to unsuccessful stallions. I'd be very hopeful for him, he's very racy looking and he looks like he'll make a good two-year-old from mid-season onwards. He's better looking than some of the mare's other foals because she doesn't always get good-lookers, but they can run. This colt is medium-sized, well-balanced, not too big but a nice length."*

1346. UNNAMED ★★
b.f. *Barathea – Handaza (Be My Guest)*.
January 9. Half-sister to the Irish Group 3 7.5f Concorde Stakes winner Hamairi (by Spectrum), to the Irish 5f (at 2 yrs) and 3-y-o listed 6f winner Hanabad (by Cadeaux Genereux), the quite useful Irish 12f winner Hadarama (by Sinndar) and the modest Irish 10f winner Hannda (by Dr Devious). The dam, a 1m winner at 3 yrs in Ireland, is out of Hazaradjat (by Darshaan), herself a half-sister to the Middle Park Stakes winner Hittite Glory. (H H Aga Khan). *"She's quite a nice filly that's going to take time because she's growing at the moment. She looks a bit immature and is one for the autumn."*

1347. UNNAMED ★★★★
b.f. *Halling – Hazariya (Xaar)*.
March 21. Second foal. Half-sister to the fair 2010 Irish 10f winner Hazarafa (by Daylami). The dam, winner of the Group 3 7f Athasi Stakes and a listed event over 7f, is a half-sister to the Group 3 Blue Wind Stakes winner Hazarista and a half-sister to numerous minor winners. The second dam, Hazaradjat (by Darshaan), won twice at 2 and 3 yrs and is a half-sister to 10 winners including the Group 1 Flying Childers Stakes winner Hittite Glory. (H H Aga Khan). *"This is a particularly nice filly. The dam was good and she should be capable of producing something nice. She should be able to show something this year I think."*

1348. UNNAMED ★★★
b.f. *Azamour – Mouramara (Kahyasi)*.
February 7. Half-sister to the very smart 2-y-o listed 9f winner and Irish Derby third Mourayan (by Alhaarth), to the very smart listed 14f winner and Melbourne Cup third Mourilyan (by Desert Prince) and the useful 12f, 13f and hurdles winner Mourad (by Sinndar). The dam, winner of the Group 2 12.5f Prix de Royallieu, is a half-sister to several winners in France and Germany. The second dam, Mamoura (by Lomond), won over 10f and 12f in Ireland and is a half-sister to 5 winners including the Group 3 12f Meld Stakes third Mirana (herself dam of the Group 3 Prix de Flore winner Miliana). (HH Aga Khan). *"A lovely filly out of a lovely mare who has bred good horses for us and this is another nice produce. We'd be hopeful for her, although it's not a family that usually does well at two, but she's nice and she's well-behaved so I'm hoping she'll be a second half of the season two-year-old."*

1349. UNNAMED ★★★★
b.c. *Red Ransom – Sinndiya (Pharly)*.
May 10. Half-brother to the fairly useful 7f (at 2 yrs) and listed 11f winner Sindirana (by Kalanisi) and to the French 11f winner Sindajan (by Medicean). The dam, a minor Irish 12f

winner, is a half-sister to the top-class middle-distance colt Sinndar, winner of the Derby, the Irish Derby and the Prix de l'Arc de Triomphe. The second dam, Sinntara (by Lashkari), won 4 races in Ireland at up to 2m. (H H Aga Khan). *"A particularly nice-looking horse. He's in need of a bit of time and he's had one or two setbacks along the way, but he's a great mover and we like him. There's plenty of stamina in the pedigree, so you'd be looking at seven furlongs for him."*

1350. UNNAMED ★★★★
b.c. Invincible Spirit – Zalaiyma
(Rainbow Quest).
February 3. The dam, a French 3-y-o dual 1m winner, was listed-placed. The second dam, Zalaiyka (by Royal Academy), won the Group 1 1m French 1,000 Guineas, the Group 3 1m Prix de la Grotte and the Group 3 1m Prix des Reservoirs. (H H Aga Khan). *"He's a nice, precocious, well put-together sort of horse about to start fast work. He's particularly nice and a racy sort."*

AMANDA PERRETT

1351. AROUND THE CLOCK (USA)
★★★★♣
b.br.c. Bernardini – Plenty Of Light
(Colony Light).
March 4. Fifth foal. $320,000Y. Keeneland September. A Perrett. Half-brother to 3 winners including one in Japan by Gone West. The dam won 5 races including the Grade 1 Spinster Stakes and is a half-sister to one stakes winner. The second dam, Iceycindy (by Northrop), a US stakes winner of 7 races at 2 and 4 yrs, is a half-sister to 7 winners. (A D Spence). *"He's by a first season stallion who was a top class racehorse and the dam was a Grade 1 winning mare. A beautiful horse and well-balanced, he does his work nicely but he'll want seven furlongs minimum. I'm very pleased with what I've seen so far, he's 16 hands and more of a three-year-old type but we'll be looking to start him in a maiden at the Glorious Goodwood meeting. The Bernardini yearlings were the most outstanding individuals at Keeneland last year."*

1352. BLUE DAZZLER (IRE) ★★★
b.c. Dalakhani – Lady Ragazza (Bering).

February 16. Second foal. 65,000Y. Tattersalls October Book 1. Amanda Perrett. The dam, placed once at 2 yrs in France, is a half-sister to 6 winners including the French Group 3 winner Tripat. The second dam, Mrs Ting (by Lyphard), is an unplaced sister to the Group 1 Prix d'Ispahan winner Al Nasr and a half-sister to 7 winners. (The Green Dot Partnership). *"He's bred for middle distances but he's a February foal and he's been showing speed on the gallops at home, so I think he'll be having a run over six furlongs in May. A powerful little horse, he's professional and wants to do his job and he's been bought for a syndicate so I'm pleased that he's a bit speedier than his pedigree suggests."*

1353. DARE TO BARE (IRE) ★★★★
b.c. Byron – Naked Poser (Night Shift).
February 7. Eighth foal. 26,000Y. Tattersalls October Book 2. Amanda Perrett. Half-brother to the quite useful 2-y-o 6f winner Wilson Star (by Tagula), to the quite useful Irish 7f and 1m winner Artist's Muse (by Cape Cross), the fair 2-y-o 6f winner Twenty Seven (by Efisio) and the modest 2-y-o 5f winner First Eclipse (by Fayruz). The dam, a quite useful 2-y-o 6f winner, is a half-sister to 4 winners including the useful sprinter Damalis. The second dam, Art Age (by Artaius), is an unraced half-sister to 9 winners. (F Cotton, Mrs S Conway). *"This colt is 16 hands and he's a big, brute of a horse. I haven't done much with him but I should imagine we'll start him over six furlongs. The dam has done incredibly well so far and this colt looks like a sprinter, he's very powerful and as broad and he's tall. I don't usually buy them in the ring, but he was such an impressive walker that he caught my eye. It's good to see that the sire has had his first winner already."* TRAINERS' BARGAIN BUY

1354. DISTURBIA (IRE) ★★★
b.f. Dubai Destination – Eoz
(Sadler's Wells).
March 14. Fourth foal. Half-sister to the fair 2009 2-y-o 7f winner Cat Hunter (by One Cool Cat). The dam won over 12f on the all-weather and is a half-sister to 2 winners. The second dam, Greek Moon (by Shirley Heights), is an unraced half-sister to 8 winners. *"She's quite sharp and she looks like she'll be pinging a bit."*

1355. FOUR NATIONS (USA) ★★★
ch.c. Langfuhr – Kiswahili (Selkirk).
February 25. First foal. 75,000Y. Tattersalls October Book 1. James Delahooke. The dam won 4 races including a listed 14f event in Germany and is a half-sister to 3 winners. The second dam, Kiliniski (by Niniski), a very smart winner of the Group 3 12f Lingfield Oaks Trial, was second in the Yorkshire Oaks and fourth in the Epsom Oaks and is a half-sister to 5 winners including the dam of the US Grade 2 winner Bienamado. (G D P Materna). *"He's out of a Selkirk mare and the pedigree is pretty stout on the dam's side. He's 15.3 hands, so he has a bit of size and scope and I've been lucky with his sire – I haven't had a bad one yet. He's done some swinging canters but he's one for seven furlongs from the middle of the season onwards."*

1356. GLENAVON ★★★♣
b.c. Nayef – Corndavon (Sheikh Albadou).
April 19. Seventh living foal. 45,000Y. Tattersalls October Book 1. James Delahooke. Half-brother to the modest 2009 7f placed 2-y-o Kilmanseck, to the smart 2-y-o Group 2 6f July Stakes winner Nevisian Lad (both by Royal Applause), the fairly useful 5f (at 2 yrs) and 6f winner and listed-placed Woodnook and the quite useful dual 7f winner Windermere Island (both by Cadeaux Genereux). The dam, a fairly useful 6f winner of 3 races, is a sister to the listed-placed winner Injaaz and a half-sister to the US sprint winner of 13 races and listed-placed Hardball. The second dam, Ferber's Follies (by Saratoga Six), a winning 2-y-o sprinter, was third in the Grade 2 6f Adirondack Stakes and is a half-sister to 11 winners including the US 2-y-o Grade 2 6f winner Blue Jean Baby. (Mr J H Richmond-Watson & Mrs J E Bodie). *"A very bonny little horse, he's not very big but he looks like he's going to grow because he's about three inches taller behind than in front. Very athletic, he's been bought to run in the two-year-old races and we'll start him at six furlongs before stepping him up."*

1357. GREEN FUTURE (USA) ★★★
b.br.c. Arch – Saturday's Child (Storm Cat).
March 31. Fifth foal. $75,000Y. Keeneland September. James Delahooke. Half-brother to a minor winner in the USA by Broken Vow. The dam, a minor US stakes winner at 2 yrs, is a full or half-sister to 8 winners. The second dam, Bashful Charmer (by Capote), a minor US 2-y-o stakes winner, is a half-sister to 5 winners in the USA. (The Green Dot Partnership). *"He is a lovely horse, 16 hands already but not heavy – he's very light on his feet. It's a sire we've had some luck with and he's going to be a seven furlong horse in mid-season."*

1358. HOOFPRINTSINTHESNOW ★★
b.c. Footstepsinthesand – Spring Snowdrop (Danehill Dancer).
March 10. First foal. 14,500Y. Tattersalls December. Not sold. The dam was a quite useful Irish 3-y-o 7f winner. The second dam, Sao Gabriel (by Persian Bold), is an unraced half-sister to 6 winners including the Champion Stakes winner Legal Case and the dam of the Oaks winner Love Divine. *"He's not a bad sort, he's been quite immature through his knees so I haven't done much with him, but he's just started to come to hand now. The stallion's done so well up to now and it's a nice young mare, so I think we ought to give this colt a mention."*

1359. INIMITABLE ROMANEE (USA) ★★★★
gr.f. Maria's Mon – Cellars Shiraz (Kissin Kris).
April 3. $210,000Y. Saratoga August. Bradley Thoroughbred Brokerage. Half-sister to the fairly useful dual 1m (at 2 yrs) and dual 12f winner Classic Vintage (by El Prado). The dam won 10 races in the USA including a Grade 3 stakes and is a full or half-sister to 5 winners. The second dam, Cellar's Best (by Band Practice), won 10 races including a minor stakes in the USA. (Mrs M Brody). *"An absolutely beautiful filly. She arrived in a snowstorm just before Christmas at two o'clock in the morning and we had to lead her halfway across the gallops in the snow! I would think that as she's a big filly she'll be suited by a mile later in the season and I'd have to say she's every TRAINERS' dream."*

1360. KELINNI ★★
b.c. Refuse To Bend – Orinoco (Darshaan).
April 7. Half-brother to the fairly useful 10f and 12f winner Bandama (by Green Desert), to the quite useful dual 12f winner Intiquilla (by Galileo) and the fair 10f winner Riverscape

(by Peintre Celebre). The dam was unplaced in one start and is a full or half-sister to 6 winners including the very smart 7f (at 2 yrs) and Group 1 12f Irish Oaks winner Winona. The second dam, My Potters (by Irish River), an Irish 3-y-o 1m handicap winner, is a half-sister to numerous winners including the champion US sprinter My Juliet (herself the dam of two Grade 1 winners) and the good middle-distance colt Lyphard's Special. (Lady Clague). *"I don't know much about the sire except to say that I loved him at the stallion parade at Newmarket. This is a beautiful, athletic horse and he's been going nicely, so we should give him a mention in the book."*

1361. MINKIE MOON (IRE) ★★★
b.c. Danehill Dancer – Minkova
(Sadler's Wells).
February 17. First foal. 22,000Y. Tattersalls October Book 1. Amanda Perrett. The dam is an unraced daughter of the Irish listed winner and Irish Oaks and Breeders Cup Filly & Mare Turf second L'Ancresse (by Darshaan), herself a sister to the Group 1 Prix Saint-Alary winner Cerulean Sky and a half-sister to the Irish Oaks winner Moonstone. (Ms O L Griffith). *"A very well-bred colt, he's going to need some time as he's quite a long horse that will want a trip, so he won't be rushed. August or September time over seven furlongs should be right for him."*

1362. OLIVER'S GOLD ★★★
b.c. Danehill Dancer – Gemini Gold
(King's Best).
March 13. First foal. 85,000Y. Tattersalls October Book 1. Amanda Perrett. The dam, a fairly useful Irish 7f winner, was third in the Group 3 Park Express Stakes and is a half-sister to 6 winners. The second dam, Wakria (by Sadler's Wells), won 3 races including the listed 1m Prix de Saint-Cyr and is a half-sister to 3 minor winners. (J P Connolly). *"He's ready to roll already, the dam won over seven at the Curragh and he's bonny and compact. All being well he'll start off at Goodwood in early May."*

1363. PIVOTMAN ★★★
ch.c. Pivotal – Grandalea (Grand Lodge).
April 26. Third foal. 190,000Y. Tattersalls December. Amanda Perrett. Half-brother to the fair 2009 5f and 6f placed 2-y-o Saddlers Lodge (by Motivator). The dam, a quite useful 7f winner, is a half-sister to 2 winners including the Group 3 7f Prestige Stakes third Red Peony. The second dam, Red Azalea (by Shirley Heights), a fairly useful 7f (at 2 yrs) and 10f winner, is a half-sister to 4 winners including the Group 3 Prestige Stakes winner and French 1,000 Guineas third Red Camellia (herself dam of the Fillies Mile winner Red Bloom). (J P Connolly). *"A very big horse that's going to want time but he's a very nice individual by a good stallion. He really took my eye at the sales, we're going to have to wait a bit for him but I think it'll be worth waiting for."*

1364. PRESTO VOLANTE (IRE) ★★★
b.c. Oratorio – Very Racy (Sri Pekan).
April 12. Fifth foal. 65,000Y. Tattersalls October Book 2. Amanda Perrett. Half-brother to the minor US winners Sandy Beach (by Clure) and An Hez Racy (by Anziyan). The dam, a minor winner in the USA, is a half-sister to 3 winners including the US Grade 2 placed Dianehill. The second dam, Very Subtle (by Hoist The Silver), won four races including the 6f Breeders Cup Sprint, the 1m Hollywood Starlet Stakes and the 8.5f Fantasy Stakes (all Grade 1 events) and is a half-sister to the stakes winner Schematic. (Mrs S Conway, Mr & Mrs Swayne, Mr R Brooks, Mrs R Doel). *"A very nice colt and we bought him just before the sire had the winner of the Dewhurst when everyone was saying you don't want an Oratorio. Well, he's everything you do want – he's well-balanced, he's got plenty of energy and he'll starting over six furlongs with a view to going seven. There's a lot to like about him and I'm very sad that our Rathbarry man won't be around to see him."*

1365. UNNAMED ★★★
b.f. Shirocco – Bright Spells (Alleged).
April 29. Half-sister to the very smart 2-y-o Group 3 7f Horris Hill Stakes winner and French 2,000 Guineas second Clearing and to the useful dual 7f winner (including at 2 yrs) Blazing Thunder (both by Zafonic). The dam, a French 12f winner, is a half-sister to the Group 2 German winner Non Partisan, the Grade 3 Canadian stakes winner Jalaajel and the useful dual 2-y-o 7f winner and Group

3 Prix d'Aumale third Suntrap (herself dam of the Grade/Group 1 winners Raintrap and Sunshack). The second dam, Sunny Bay (by Northern Bay), won 3 stakes events in the USA and was second in the Grade 1 Sorority Stakes. (Khalid Abdulla). *"A nice, compact filly for seven furlongs or a mile this year and middle-distances as a three-year-old, she's athletic and her sire was a hell of a racehorse, so she's definitely worth a mention."*

1366. UNNAMED ★★
b.c. *Malibu Moon – Capilla Bonita (Pleasant Colony).*
March 17. Third foal. $80,000Y. Keeneland September. James Delahooke. Half-brother to a minor winner in the USA by Dove Hunt. The dam is an unraced half-sister to several winners and to the dams of the Group/Grade 1 winners Crowded House and Ticker Tape. The second dam, Chapel Of Dreams (by Northern Dancer), won the Grade 2 Palomar Handicap, the Grade 2 Wilshire Handicap and the Grade 3 Golden Poppy Handicap, was Grade 1 placed and is a half-sister to the outstanding sire Storm Cat. *"He still doesn't have an owner. He stands 16.1 hands and is a nice, rangy horse for a bit later on in the year. The sire has very good two-year-old statistics but I think considering this colt's size and his general physique he'll need a bit more time and he won't be rushed."*

1367. UNNAMED ★★★
b.f. *Oasis Dream – Cochin (Swain).*
March 9. Third foal. The dam, a 3-y-o winner in France, stayed middle-distances and is a half-sister to 6 winners including the US dual Grade 1 winner Senure. The second dam, Diese (by Diesis), won 3 races in France including the Group 3 10.5f Prix Corrida and a listed 10f event, is a half-sister to 13 winners including the champion European 2-y-o Xaar. *"A nice, rangy filly and they liked her at the stud. She goes well and she'll probably have the speed to run over six furlongs."*

1368. UNNAMED ★★★
b.br.c. *Aptitude – Palisade (Gone West).*
April 28. Half-brother to the US Grade 3 7f and Grade 3 1m winner Jibboom (by Mizzen Mast), to the useful 7f and 1m winner (including at 2 yrs) Self Evident (by Known Fact) and a jumps winner by With Approval. The dam, a quite useful 2-y-o 7f winner, is a half-sister to the useful 3-y-o 1m winner Emplane and to the useful 2-y-o 1m winner Boatman. The second dam, Peplum (by Nijinsky), a useful winner of the listed 11.3f Cheshire Oaks, is a half-sister to the top class filly Al Bahathri, winner of the 1,000 Guineas and the Coronation Stakes. (Khalid Abdulla). *"A half-brother to Self Evident who won on Guineas day for us a few years ago. A nice, rangy individual from a mare we've been lucky with, he did quite a nice bit of work earlier in the year, he's growing and he'll be a nice colt over seven furlongs in mid-season."*

JON PORTMAN

1369. ADAEZE (IRE) ★★★
b.f. *Footstepsinthesand – Ringmoor Down (Pivotal).*
April 12. Second foal. 42,000Y. Tattersalls October Book 1. Not sold. Half-sister to the unplaced 2009 2-y-o Cuckoo Rock (by Refuse To Bend). The dam won 6 races from 2 to 5 yrs including the Group 3 5f King George Stakes and the Group 3 Flying Five and is a half-sister to 6 winners. The second dam, Floppie (by Law Society), a minor 3-y-o winner in France, is a sister to a listed-placed winner there and a half-sister to 4 winners including the French listed winner Love Shack. (Prof C D Green). *"We haven't done much with her, but in the little she's done she's shown speed. She's a very nervous type though, so temperament would be a issue and she won't be early but she does show potential. I like her, we'll take our time but she's nice and she looks like a sprinter."*

1370. ATIA ★★★
b.f. *Royal Applause – Chrysalis (Soviet Star).*
February 20. Seventh foal. Tattersalls October Book 2. 19,000Y. Not sold. Sister to the smart 2-y-o 6f listed and subsequent US Grade 3 6.5f winner Moth Ball and half-sister to the fair 5f (at 2 yrs) to 10f winner of 11 races Western Roots (by Dr Fong) and the quite useful 6f all-weather (at 2 yrs) and 7f winner Just Fly (by Efisio). The dam, a modest maiden, stayed 1m and is a half-sister to 4 winners. The second dam, Vivienda (by Known Fact), won 3 races at 2 yrs and is a half-sister to 5 winners including the Arc winner Saumarez. (Prof C D Green). *"She's small and a bit lazy*

but reasonably forward. She'll be able to run in May and will be better over six furlongs than five. She doesn't try very hard at home, but I think she hides her light under a bushel a bit, but I think there's a glow somewhere so I'm not worried."

1371. FASTADA (IRE) ★★★
b.f. *Holy Roman Emperor – Mellow Park (In The Wings).*
February 26. Fourth foal. 17,000Y. Tattersalls October Book 2. A Skiffington/J Portman.
The dam won the Group 3 12f Lancashire Oaks and the listed 10f Lupe Stakes and is a sister to the Group 1 12f Italian Derby, Group 2 7f Lanson Champagne Stakes and German Group 2 12f winner Central Park and a half-sister to the very useful Group 2 6f Lowther Stakes and listed 10f winner Velvet Moon (herself dam of the Dante Stakes winner Moon Ballad. The second dam, Park Special (by Relkino) won over 10f at 3 yrs in Ireland and is a half-sister to the Group 3 winners Careafolie and Gouriev and the smart French 2-y-o winner Pantile. (A H Robinson). *"She came to hand well and she's good in her coat but she's not a sprinter. She'll need seven furlongs and I can see her winning this year without being out of the top drawer."*

1372. FOLLY DROVE ★★★
b.f. *Bahri – Zoena (Emarati).*
February 9. £10,000Y. Ascot October. Not sold. Half-sister to the fair 7f winner Miss Patricia (by Mister Baileys) and to a winner in Spain by Efisio. The dam, a modest all-weather 5f and 6f winner, is a sister to the fairly useful 2-y-o 5f winner Threezedzz and a half-sister to several winners. The second dam, Exotic Forest (by Dominion), a modest 3-y-o 1m winner, is a half-sister to 5 winners including the listed October Stakes winner Toffee Nosed. (Mrs J N Edwards-Heathcote). *"I trained the dam to win a couple of sprint races, despite the fact she was a nightmare, and this filly is quite nice. She might have a run over five furlongs in April but she'll be better over six. I can see her winning as a two-year-old."*

1373. UNNAMED ★★★
b.c. *Camacho – Dear Catch (Bluebird).*
April 11. Fifth foal. 17,000Y. Tattersalls October Book 2. A Skiffington/J Portman.
Brother to the 2009 unplaced 2-y-o Choc 'a' Moca and half-brother to the quite useful 2-y-o 6f winner Golden Destiny (by Captain Rio). The dam, a 9f winner in Ireland, is a sister to the Group 3 5f Ballyogan Stakes winner and Group 1 Haydock Park Sprint Cup third Catch The Blues and a half-sister to 6 winners. The second dam, Dear Lorraine (by Nonoalco), won over 10f in France and is a half-sister to 4 winners. *"He's nice and I'm looking for an owner for him! Camacho is doing well and this colt looks the part. I had a work rider here today and he commented that he's one of my nicer ones and he's right. I'd say he'd be better over six than five and he's quite forward and mature, so he's ready to go."*

1374. UNNAMED
b.c. *Balmont – Presently (Cadeaux Genereux).*
April 23. £3,000Y. Doncaster St Leger Festival. G Howson. Half-brother to the fair 2-y-o 5f winner Ace Club (by Indian Rocket), to the fair 2-y-o 6f winner The Mighty One (by Mujadil), the modest 5f and 6f winner Brioso (by Victory Note) and the Italian 1m to 11.5f winner of 6 races Breakthru (by Ezzoud). The dam, a moderate 5f winner at 3 yrs, is a half-sister to 4 winners including the Group 2 5f Flying Childers Stakes winner Sizzling Melody. The second dam, Mrs Bacon (by Balliol), a quite useful 2-y-o 5f winner, is a half-sister to the dam of the Group 3 5f Greenlands Stakes winner Puissance. *"He looks very fast and yet he was bought for peanuts. He's not particularly early but he looks a fun horse and he's not sold. It's an honest family and they all try."* TRAINERS' BARGAIN BUY

KEVIN PRENDERGAST
1375. ANSAAB ★★
b.c. *Cape Cross – Dawn Raid (Docksider).*
March 14. Second foal. €150,000Y. Goffs Orby. Shadwell Estate Co. Half-brother to Dance Hall Girl (by Dansili), placed second in Ireland on all three of her starts at 2 yrs in 2009. The dam, a quite useful Irish 3-y-o 7f winner, is a half-sister to 7 winners including the French and Irish 2,000 Guineas and Richmond Stakes winner Bachir, to the smart 7f (at 2 yrs) to 10f and hurdles winner Albuhera and the useful 2-y-o listed 7f winner Elliots World. The second dam, Morning Welcome (by Be My Guest),

placed once over 12f at 3 yrs in Ireland, is a half-sister to 9 winners including the Irish listed Debutante Stakes and subsequent US Grade 3 winner Down Again. (Hamdan Al Maktoum). *"A very nice horse, he only arrived with me a few weeks ago because he was backward. We like him a lot but he's one for the back-end of the season."*

1376. ASHEERAH ★★★★
b.f. Shamardal – Adaala (Sahm).
April 27. Second foal. Half-sister to the useful 2009 Irish 2-y-o 6f winner and Group 3 7f Silver Flash Stakes third Alshahbaa (by Alhaarth). The dam, an Irish 7f (at 2 yrs) and listed 9f winner, is a half-sister to the Irish listed 9f winner Adaala. The second dam, Alshoowg (by Riverman), is an unraced half-sister to 4 winners. (Hamdan Al Maktoum). *"We like her a lot, she's a bigger and stronger filly than her half-sister of last year, the sire is very good and I'd say this filly will start her at six before we move her up in trip."*

1377. BLUE CANNON (IRE) ★★
b.c. High Chaparral – Blushing Barada (Blushing Groom).
April 29. Tenth foal. €50,000Y. Goffs Orby. Kevin Ross. Half-brother to the dual Group 3 Diomed Stakes winner of 10 races Blythe Knight (by Selkirk), to the quite useful staying winners High Topper (by Wolfhound) and Bid Me Welcome (by Alzao), the fair 9f and 10f winner Bubbling Fun (by Marju), the fair 2-y-o 1m winner Call Of Duty (by Storming Home), the modest 9f and 10f winner Barbirolli (by Machiavellian) and two minor winners abroad by Anabaa. The dam is a placed full or half-sister to 5 winners including the Irish St Leger winner Authaal. The second dam, Galletto (by Nijinsky), a smart listed Galtres Stakes winner, is a half-sister to 2 winners. (P Sloan). *"He's not a forward horse but he's done very well since he came here and he's a very good mover. Quite a tidy horse, about 15.1 hands, he's one for the back-end of the season over seven furlongs plus."*

1378. BRAZILIAN BREEZE (IRE) ★★★
b.f. Invincible Spirit – Brazilian Bride (Pivotal).
March 27. First foal. The dam won the Group 3 6f Swordlestown Stakes and is a half-sister to several winners the 2-y-o 7.5f winner and Group 3 7f second Brazilian Star. The second dam, Braziliz (by Kingmambo), placed fourth once over 5f at 2 yrs, is a half-sister to 8 winners including Or Vision (dam of the Irish 2,000 Guineas winner Saffron Walden, the Grade 1 E P Taylor Stakes winner Insight and the Group 1 7f Prix de la Foret winner Dolphin Street). (Lady O'Reilly). *"Not a big filly, she's gone home for a break, she's one for the second half of the season and we like her."*

1379. BROWN BUTTERFLY ★★★
b.f. Medicean – Auspicious (Shirley Heights).
May 8. Seventh foal. €65,000Y. Goffs Orby. Frank Barry. Half-sister to the fair 2009 2-y-o 1m winner Perfect Vision (by Starcraft), to the fairly useful 2-y-o 7f and 1m winner Doctrine (by Barathea), to the quite useful 2-y-o 1m winner Australian (by Danzero) and the quite useful 1m to 10f winner Prince Picasso (by Lomitas). The dam, a fairly useful 10.2f winner, is a sister to the smart Group 2 11.9f Great Voltigeur Stakes winner Sacrament and a half-sister to 5 winners and to the dam of the Group 1 winner Chorist. The second dam, Blessed Event (by Kings Lake), winner of the listed 10f Ballymacoll Stud Stakes and placed in the Yorkshire Oaks and the Champion Stakes, is a half-sister to 4 winners. (John Foley). *"A nice filly but a late foal, we're giving her some time but she goes well. One for the middle of the season, she's a nice, good-sized, quality filly."*

1380. DAZZLING DREAM (IRE) ★★★★
ch.f. Hernando – Dazzling Dancer (Nashwan).
March 17. Third foal. Sister to the fairly useful 2009 Irish 2-y-o 7f winner Dazzling Day and half-sister to the Irish listed-placed 2-y-o 7f winner and subsequent US 1m winner and Grade 3 placed Driving Snow (by Verglas). The dam, a quite useful Irish 12f winner, is a half-sister to one winner. The second dam, Danse Classique (by Night Shift), a listed-placed winner in Ireland, is a half-sister to the triple Group 1 winner Petrushka. *"A nice, big filly, I like her a lot but she won't be out until towards the back-end of the season. Her sister won over seven last year and I'd expect this filly to do likewise."*

1381. EMOTIONAL DREAM ★★★
b.f. Shirocco – Tricoteuse (Kris).
March 19. Fourth foal. 57,000Y. Tattersalls October Book 2. F Barry. Half-sister to the French 2-y-o 9f winner Boudin (by Peintre Celebre), to the fair 11f to 2m and hurdles winner Riguez Dancer (by Dansili). The dam is an unraced daughter of the quite useful 11f and 12f winner of 4 races Dear Life (by Lear Fan), herself a half-sister to 6 winners including the Group winners Kingfisher Mill and Wellbeing. *"I like her a lot, she's a nice, big filly but being by Shirocco I'd expect her to want seven furlongs to begin with. The sire is getting good-lookers and this one is the same – she's a smashing looking filly."*

1382. ESTITHMAAR (IRE) ★★★
ch.c. Pivotal – Walayef (Danzig).
May 10. Fourth foal. Half-brother to the fairly useful 2009 Irish 2-y-o 6f and 7f winner Jamaayel (by Shamardal) and to the quite useful Irish 2-y-o 7f winner Reyaada (by Daylami). The dam, a listed 6f (at 2 yrs) and Group 3 7f Athasi Stakes winner, is a sister to the smart 2-y-o 6f winner Haatef and to the Irish dual listed 6f winner Ulfah. The second dam, Sayedat Alhadh (by Mr Prospector), a US 7f winner, is a sister to the US Grade 2 7f winner Kayrawan and a half-sister to the useful winners Amaniy, Elsaamri and Mathkurh. (Hamdan Al Maktoum). *"A backward horse and we won't see him until the back-end of the season."*

1383. GEMMA'S PEARL (IRE) ★★★
b.f. Marju – Royals Special (Caerleon).
February 22. Fifth foal. €55,000Y. Goffs Orby. Frank Barry. Half-sister to the modest 2009 triple 7f placed 2-y-o Bandear (by Royal Applause) and to the fairly useful 9f and 14f winner Yes Mr President (by Montjeu). The dam is an unplaced half-sister to 5 winners including Ezzoud, winner of the Eclipse Stakes and the Juddmonte International Stakes (twice) and Distant Relative, winner of the Sussex Stakes and the Prix du Moulin. The second dam, Royal Sister II (by Claude), a winner over 10f at 4 yrs in Ireland, also won 7 races in Italy from 3 to 5 yrs and is a half-sister to 4 winners. (P O'Grady). *"A very nice filly owned by Pat O'Grady who had King Ledley last year – a colt that ended up running in the Breeders Cup. We like this filly a lot, she's out of a Caerleon mare and she's a big filly that will want six furlongs in June."*

1384. GLENDARAGH (IRE) ★★★
b.c. Ad Valorem – Happy Flight (Titus Livius).
April 7. Third foal. €48,000Y. Tattersalls Ireland. Frank Barry. Half-brother to the Italian dual winner and 2-y-o listed 1m placed Red Kimi (by Denon). The dam won 4 races at 2 and 3 yrs in Italy and is a half-sister to 4 other minor winners abroad. The second dam, Gezalle (by Shareef Dancer), won over 1m and 9f in Ireland at 3 yrs and is a half-sister to 6 winners. (Mr N Ormiston). *"A nice horse, he would have been out by now but he got a bit of mucus in his neck. He'll be racing in the next three weeks and he'll go five furlongs but I'd say he'll be better over six."*

1385. HANDASSA ★★★
br.f. Dubawi – Starstone (Diktat).
March 28. Second foal. 100,000Y. Tattersalls October Book 1. Shadwell Estate Co. Sister to the fair 2009 2-y-o 6f winner Emirates Hills. The dam is an unraced half-sister to the Group 1 July Cup winner Pastoral Pursuits and the Group 1 Haydock Park Sprint Cup winner Goodricke. The second dam, Star (by Most Welcome), a quite useful 5f winner, is a half-sister to 7 winners including the useful 2-y-o listed 5f winner Four-Legged-Friend and the US Grade 3 7f winner Superstrike. (Hamdan Al Maktoum). *"A big filly, she'll take a bit of time but we like her. One for seven furlongs plus and from August onwards."*

1386. KISSABLE (IRE) ★★★
b.f. Danehill Dancer – Kitty O'Shea (Sadler's Wells).
March 14. Second foal. 90,000Y. Tattersalls October Book 1. BBA (Ire). The dam ran twice and won both races over 1m (including at 2 yrs and a listed event at 3 yrs). She is a sister to the Group 1 Racing Post Trophy and Group 1 St Leger winner Brian Boru and a half-sister to the Group 3 12.5f Prix de Royallieu winner Moon Search. The second dam, Eva Luna (by Alleged), won the Group 3 14.6f Park Hill Stakes and is a half-sister to 5 winners including the US listed winner Rougeur (herself dam of the US Grade

1 winner Flute). (Lady O'Reilly). *"She's out of a Sadler's Wells mare so she's going to take a bit of time but I could see her out in August. She's a tall, angular filly."*

1387. LONGHUNTER ★★★★
b.c. Halling – Dawnus (Night Shift).
January 31. Third foal. 60,000Y. Tattersalls October Book 2. F Berry. The dam, a useful listed 10f winner, is out of the French 1m winner Dame's Violet (by Groom Dancer), herself a full or half-sister to 6 winners including the Group 2 Princess Of Wales's Stakes winner Wagon Master. (Mr & Mrs Hamilton). *"He's a very nice horse and he just might make his debut in a six furlong race at Leopardstown in April. Very well-developed, he's a nice horse and we like him a lot. He's out of a Night Shift mare and despite being by Halling he'll make an early two-year-old. He goes very well."*

1388. MADEIRA MAN (IRE) ★★★
gr.c. Verglas – Lingering Melody (Nordico).
March 4. Eighth foal. €14,000Y. Tattersalls Ireland. Frank Barry. Half-brother to the smart 3-y-o listed 5f winner Indian Prince (by Indian Ridge), to the quite useful dual 7f winner (including at 2 yrs) Rainbow Melody (by Rainbows For Life), the Irish 2-y-o 6f winner Melody Island (by Turtle Island), the quite useful 6f (at 2 yrs) and 1m winner B Major (by Key Of Luck), the quite useful 12f and hurdles winner Define (by Definite Article) and the fair 1m and 10f winner Dusty Trail (by Indian Danehill). The dam was placed at up to 1m in Ireland and is a half-sister to the Group 2 Queen Anne Stakes and the Group 2 Sea World International Stakes winner Alflora. The second dam, Adrana (by Bold Lad, Ire), won over 5f at 2 yrs on her only start and is a half-sister to the top-class middle-distance stayer Ardross. *"A forward sort of horse, he's not a big colt and he's had one run already. He'll probably run again in April because he's an early, racy type and a very well-muscled horse that looks a two-year-old."*

1389. OBLIGADA (IRE) ★★★★
ch.f. Beat Hollow – Oblique (Giant's Causeway).
February 6. Second foal. The dam, a fairly useful 9f, 10f and listed 12f winner, is a half-sister to 4 winners including the useful 12f to 15.4f winner One Off. The second dam, On Call (by Alleged), a useful winner of 7 races at up to 2m, is a half-sister to 6 winners including the useful 9f and 10f winner Medico, the fairly useful 7f winner Bi Polar and the fairly useful 5.2f (at 2 yrs) and 6f winner Doctor's Glory. (Lady O'Reilly). *"A very nice filly, she's goes really well and we like her a lot. Six furlongs plus at the end of May or early June should be fine for her."*

1390. RISING WIND (IRE) ★★★★
b.f. Shirocco – Right Key (Key Of Luck).
January 26. Second foal. Half-sister to the fair 2009 Irish 2-y-o 1m winner Rightside (by High Chaparral). The dam, a very useful Irish 7f (at 2 yrs) and Group 3 10f and 12f winner, is a sister to several winners including the Irish dual 7f (at 2 yrs) and listed 1m winner and dual Group 2 placed Wrong Key. The second dam, Sarifa (by Kahyasi), is an unraced half-sister to the Group 3 Prix du Palais Royale winner Saratan. (Lady O'Reilly). *"I like her a lot, six or seven furlongs will suit her and she goes well but she does need a bit of time. An attractive filly, she's light framed but the family are like that."*

1391. ROSE BONHEUR ★★★
b.f. Danehill Dancer – Red Feather (Marju).
February 5. The dam, a Group 3 1m winner in Ireland, is a half-sister to the smart dual 10f winner and dual Group 3 12f placed Frankies Dream. The second dam, Galyph (by Lyphard), a modest Irish 10f winner at 4 yrs, is a half-sister to 2 minor winners. (Lady O'Reilly). *"At home at the moment with a bit of a muscular issue but she's back in next week and we like her a lot. Not over-big, but nice and we'll be looking at six/seven furlongs with her."*

1392. SNOW WATCH (IRE) ★★★
gr.c. Verglas – Pitrizza (Machiavellian).
March 30. Sixth foal. €75,000Y. Goffs Orby. Ben McElroy. Brother to the useful Irish 2-y-o 6f winner and listed placed Vilasol and half-brother to the fair 6f and 7f winner of 4 races Perfect Treasure (by Night Shift) and a minor winner abroad by Sinndar. The dam won once over 12f in France and is a half-sister to 4 other minor winners. The second dam, Unopposed (by Sadler's Wells), is an unraced half-sister

to 11 winners including the dam of the dual Group 2 winner and sire Titus Livius. (Mr & Mrs Hamilton). *"He was to be our first runner but he got a bruise on a heel after kicking a wall. He's back cantering again and although he's a precocious type he'll get seven furlongs alright."*

1393. TARKHEES ★★★
b.f. Haafhd – Alshakr (Bahri).
March 29. Sixth foal. Half-sister to the fairly useful Irish dual 7f (at 2 yrs) and 10f winner Nafaath (by Nayef) and to the quite useful Irish 14f winner Sufad (by Alhaarth). The dam, a very useful winner of the Group 2 1m Falmouth Stakes, is a half-sister to the dam of the 1,000 Guineas winner Harayir. The second dam, Give Thanks (by Relko), won the Irish Oaks, the Lancashire Oaks and the Musidora Stakes. (Hamdan Al Maktoum). *"A tidy filly, she's not over-big but she should be ready to run at the end of May over six furlongs."*

1394. TASHQEEL ★★★★★
b.c. Medicean – Ulfah (Danzig).
March 2. Third foal. The dam, an Irish dual listed 6f winner, is a sister to the Group 2 6f Diadem Stakes winner Haatef, to the listed winner and Group 1 Moyglare Stud Stakes second Shimah and the listed 6f (at 2 yrs) and Group 3 7f Athasi Stakes winner Waleyef. The second dam, Sayedat Alhadh (by Mr Prospector), a US 7f winner, is a sister to the US Grade 2 7f winner Kayrawan and a half-sister to the useful winners Amaniy, Elsaamri and Mathkurh. (Hamdan Al Maktoum). *"A very nice horse, six furlongs will do nicely for him and he's out of Ulfah – a good mare that we had. It's been a good family for us and this is a very strong colt, not tall but very muscular. One to look out for."*

1395. TAZAAMUN (IRE) ★★
b.c. Shirocco – Glorious (Nashwan).
March 15. Ninth foal. €80,000Y. Goffs Orby. Shadwell Estate Co. Half-brother to the moderate 2009 2-y-o 8.3f seller winner Miss Whippy (by Whipper), to the fairly useful triple 10f winner Closertobelieving (by Xaar), the fairly useful 2-y-o 7f winner Abundant (by Zafonic), the fair all-weather 3-y-o 7f and 1m winner Athboy (by Entrepreneur), the fair 9f winner of 4 races Plush (by Medicean) and a winner in Greece by Danzero. The dam is an unraced half-sister to 7 winners including the smart 8.2f winner and Group 1 St James's Palace Stakes fourth Killer Instinct and the very useful 2-y-o 7f winner and Group 1 Hoover Fillies Mile second Pick of the Pops. The second dam, Rappa Tap Tap (by Tap On Wood), a useful 6f Blue Seal Stakes winner, is a half-sister to the Irish Oaks winner Colorspin (herself the dam of Opera House, Kayf Tara and Zee Zee Top), to the Group 2 Prix de l'Opera winner Bella Colora (dam of the high-class colt Stagecraft) and the Irish Champion Stakes winner Cezanne. (Hamdan Al Maktoum). *"I saw him at the Sales but he's in Dubai with two others they'll be sending me in mid-April. If you look at their pedigrees and remember that hitting a new climate will probably set them back a bit, you'd have to think they'll be back-end type two-year-olds."*

1396. TELL THE WIND (IRE) ★★
b.f. Mujadil – Fantastic Account (Fantastic Light).
March 23. Second foal. €62,000Y. Tattersalls Ireland. Frank Barry. The dam is an unraced half-sister to 3 minor winners. The second dam, Fabulous Account (by Private Account), is a placed half-sister to 9 winners including the US Grade 1 winner Joyeux Danseur and the Group 3 placed Danseur Fabuleux (dam of the outstanding 2-y-o Arazi and the Sussex Stakes winner Noverre). (Mr J M McGrath). *"A nice filly, but she's still growing and we'll take our time with her."*

1397. THAWAABET ★★★
b.br.f. Dansili – Nasheed (Riverman).
January 16. Sixth foal. Half-sister to the useful Irish 7f and 1m winner Tamazug, to the quite useful Irish 7f to 10f winner Mutadarek (both by Machiavellian) and the modest 11f and 14f winner Al Azy (by Nayef). The dam, a useful 7f (at 2 yrs) and 10f winner, is a half-sister to the high-class Prix de l'Arc de Triomphe and Juddmonte International winner Sakhee. The second dam, Thawakib (by Sadler's Wells), a useful dual 7f (at 2 yrs) and Group 2 12f Ribblesdale Stakes winner, is a half-sister to numerous winners including the top-class middle-distance colt Celestial Storm

(winner of the Group 2 Princess of Wales's Stakes). (Hamdan Al Maktoum). *"A nice filly, she got a touch of sore shins so I sent her home to Derrinstown Stud but she'll be back in this week. Quite attractive, not a big filly but a racy type that will make a two-year-old."*

1398. UNNAMED ★★
ch.c. Refuse To Bend – Green Lassy (Green Tune).
March 21. Fourth foal. €30,000Y. Goffs Orby. Frank Barry. Half-brother to the fair Irish 3-y-o 1m winner Gleaming Silver (by Dalakhani). The dam won over 13f and 14f at 4 yrs in Ireland and is a half-sister to 3 winners including the French dual Group 2 winner (over 15f and 2m) Cut Quartz. The second dam, Cutlass (by Sure Blade), is a placed half-sister to 3 stakes winners. (Kevin Ross). *"He's a nice enough horse, but one for the second half of the season. I have a Refuse To Bend three-year-old that was just beaten a neck yesterday and he's been placed in all four of his starts now, so I hope it's not a case of 'Refuse To Win'!"*

1399. UNNAMED ★★★
b.f. Pivotal – Nebraas (Green Desert).
April 19. Fourth foal. €90,000Y. Goffs Orby. Frank Barry. Half-sister to the quite useful 7f (at 2 yrs) and 6f winner My Kingdom and the quite useful 7f winner Royalist (both by King's Best). The dam is an unraced three-parts sister to the very useful 6f winner (including at 2 yrs) Mutaakkid and a half-sister to 4 winners including the Group 1 Golden Jubilee Stakes winner Malhub. The second dam, Arjuzah (by Ahonoora), a useful winner of the listed 7f Sceptre Stakes, is a half-sister to the Irish listed winner Ormsby. (Mr N Ormiston). *"A very nice filly, she has a nice pedigree but she's grown a fair bit. She has a good way of going, we like her a lot, but she's a good-sized filly that will take a bit of time."*

1400. UNNAMED ★★★★
b.f. High Chaparral – Ugo Fire (Bluebird).
April 28. First foal. 36,000Y. Tattersalls December. Not sold. The dam, a 2-y-o Group 3 7f C L Weld Park Stakes and 3-y-o 6f listed winner, was second in the Group 1 7f Moyglare Stud Stakes second and is a half-sister to one winner. The second dam, Quiet Mouse (by Quiet American), is an unraced half-sister to 6 winners including the fairly useful 2-y-o 6f and 7f winner and smart broodmare Witch Of Fife. (Mr N Ormiston). *"A very nice filly that has a bit of class. The dam was good and this filly is a good size for a first foal."*

SIR MARK PRESCOTT

1401. ALBARAKA ★★★
gr.f. Selkirk – Alborada (Alzao).
January 25. Fifth foal. Sister to the French listed 10.5f winner Alvarita. The dam was a high-class winner of the Champion Stakes (twice), Nassau Stakes and Pretty Polly Stakes and is a sister to the smart listed 10.2f winner Albanova and a half-sister to the fairly useful dual middle-distance winner Alakananda. The second dam, Alouette (by Darshaan), a useful 1m (at 2 yrs) and listed 12f winner, is a sister to the listed winner and Irish Oaks third Arrikala and to the placed Jude (dam of the Group 1 winners Yesterday and Quarter Moon) and a half-sister to the Nassau Stakes and Sun Chariot Stakes winner Last Second (dam of the French 2,000 Guineas winner Aussie Rules). (Miss K Rausing). *"She'll take a bit of time. I trained her listed-winning half-sister Alvarita and she didn't run at two. This filly should be seen out over seven furlongs or a mile in the autumn and she's bigger than Alvarita who was a small filly."*

1402. ALL MY HEART ★★
gr.f. Sadler's Wells – Alba Stella (Nashwan).
February 21. Third foal. €300,000Y. Goffs Orby. R Frisby. Half-sister to the quite useful 10f to 12f winner of 6 races at 3 and 4 yrs Aleatricis (by Kingmambo) and to the fair dual 11f winner Alicante (by Pivotal). The dam, a fairly useful dual 12f winner, is a half-sister to 7 winners including the high-class dual Champion Stakes winner Alborada, the triple German Group 1 winner Albanova and the dam of the Epsom Derby second Dragon Dancer. The second dam, Alouette (by Darshaan), a useful 1m (at 2 yrs) and listed 12f winner, is a sister to the listed winner and Irish Oaks third Arrikala and a half-sister to the Nassau Stakes and Sun Chariot Stakes winner Last Second (dam of the French 2,000 Guineas winner Aussie Rules), the Doncaster Cup

winner Alleluia (dam of the Group 1 winner Allegretto) and the placed dam of the Group 1 winners Quarter Moon and Yesterday. (Miss K Rausing). *"She won't race until the autumn but she looks quite a nice filly. We turned her out and being by Sadler's Wells she'll probably want a bit of cut in the ground."*

1403. APPEALING (IRE) ★★
b.f. Selkirk – Amenixa (Linamix).
May 2. Eighth foal. 200,000Y. Tattersalls October Book 1. Denford Stud. Half-sister to the 2-y-o Group 2 6f Criterium de Maisons-Laffitte and Group 3 Prix Eclipse winner Zinziberene (by Zieten) and to the quite useful 2-y-o 7f and 1m winner Palm Court (by Green Desert). The dam, a 4-y-o 10f winner, is a sister to the dual Group 1 Prix Royal-Oak winner Amilynx and the listed winner Amie De Mix and a half-sister to the Group 2 Criterium de Maisons-Laffitte winner Amiwain. The second dam, Amen (by Alydar), was a Grade 3 placed winner of 5 races in the USA and a half-sister to 4 winners. (Denford Stud). *"She's turned out in a field and she won't run until ten furlongs in the autumn."*

1404. ARABIAN HEIGHTS ★★★
gr.c. Araafa – Makhsusah (Darshaan).
April 18. Fifth foal. 35,000Y. Tattersalls October Book 2. Sir Mark Prescott. Half-brother to the quite useful 2009 2-y-o 1m and 9f winner Wild Rose (by Doyen), to the useful 2-y-o 6f and 7f and subsequent US stakes winner Market Day (by Tobougg) and the modest 6f winner Motivated Choice (by Compton Place). The dam is an unraced half-sister to 4 winners abroad. The second dam, Zephyrine (by Highest Honor), is an unraced half-sister to 3 winners including Mutamam (Grade 1 Canadian International). (W E Sturt-Osborne House II). *"From the sire's first crop, for a big horse he goes alright and I suppose he'll be out in June or July, probably over seven furlongs. He's more mature than his pedigree would indicate."*

1405. CAFÉ ELEKTRIC ★★★★
ch.c. Pivotal – Shanghai Lily (King's Best).
February 14. First foal. The dam, a very useful 6f and 7f 2-y-o winner, is a half-sister to the very useful dual 1m winner (including at 2 yrs) and listed-placed General Eliott and the useful 7f (at 2 yrs) and 1m winner Eden Rock. The second dam, Marlene-D (Selkirk), a minor Irish 3-y-o 9f winner, is a half-sister to 7 winners including the useful Queen's Vase winner Arden and the French listed winner Kerulen and to the placed dam of the US Grade 1 winner Kiri's Clown. (Cheveley Park Stud). *"A family that Sir Michael has done well with, this colt would be suited by six or seven furlongs in mid-season. He's not over-big and he's a solid individual."*

1406. CLINICAL ★★★★
b.f. Motivator – Doctor's Glory (Elmaamul).
April 29. Half-sister to the smart Group 3 7f Horris Hill Stakes winner Cupid's Glory, to the fairly useful 7f (at 2 yrs) and listed 1m and 10f winner Courting, the fair 13f and hurdles winner Dolzago (all by Pursuit Of Love), the fairly useful 6f winner of 4 races Prescription (by Pivotal), the quite useful 1m winner Instructor and the fair 2-y-o dual 5f winner Bridal Path (both by Groom Dancer). The dam, a fairly useful 5.2f (at 2 yrs) and 6f winner, is a half-sister to 4 winners including the useful On Call, a winner of 7 races at up to 2m. The second dam, Doctor Bid (by Spectacular Bid), is an unraced half-sister to 9 winners including the smart Group 3 Prix Thomas Bryon winner Glory Forever and the dam of the Group winners Verglas and Cassandra Go. (Cheveley Park Stud). *"The family have done me jolly well and they normally come at two, so I would think she'd run in mid-season over six/seven furlongs. Despite being by Motivator, there are plenty of quick ones in the family."*

1407. COEUS ★★★★♣
gr.c. Ishiguru – Lady Georgia (Arazi).
March 11. Seventh foal. £40,000Y. Doncaster St Leger. W Charnley. Half-brother to the fairly useful dual 5f winner (including at 2 yrs) and Group 2 5f Queen Mary Stakes fourth Sparkling Eyes (by Lujain), to the quite useful triple 6f winner Harbour Blues (by Best Of The Bests) and a winner in Greece by Bien Bien. The dam, a useful 3-y-o 7.8f winner, was fourth in the Group 3 7f Prestige Stakes at 2 yrs. The second dam, Petillante (by Petong), won the Group 3 Norfolk Stakes at 2 yrs and is a half-sister to 8 winners. (William Charnley &

Richard Pegum). *"He'll be out in June I should think and he's bred to be a six furlong two-year-old. A strong, medium-sized colt."*

1408. DANCE TO THE STARS ★★
b.c. Montjeu – Dancingintheclouds (Rainbow Quest).
March 11. Second foal. €90,000Y. Goffs Orby. Not sold. The dam is an unplaced sister to a high-class St Leger, Chester Vase and Jockey Club Stakes winner Millenary and to the smart Group 3 12f Princess Royal Stakes winner Head In The Clouds and a half-sister to the very smart 1m (at 2 yrs) and 10f winner and Derby third Let The Lion Roar. The second dam, Ballerina (by Dancing Brave), a quite useful 2-y-o 7f winner, is a half-sister to 5 winners including the very useful 6f (at 2 yrs) and Group 3 12f Princess Royal Stakes winner Dancing Bloom and the listed winner River Dancer (dam of the Champion Stakes winner Spectrum). (W E Sturt – Osborne House). *"He's still in a field benefiting from the spring grass. A medium-sized, light framed horse for the back-end of the season."*

1409. DUCAL ★★
b.c. Iceman – Noble Lady (Primo Dominie).
March 24. Fourth foal. Half-brother to the modest 6f winner Royal Crest (by Royal Applause). The dam, a fair 3-y-o all-weather dual 6f winner, is a full or half-sister to 6 winners including the useful dual 5f winner Noble One (herself dam of the dual Group 1 winner Peeress). The second dam, Noble Destiny (by Final Straw), was a fairly useful 2-y-o 7f winner. (Cheveley Park Stud). *"He's having a break and will come back into me soon. He doesn't look particularly like a two-year-old type, despite the sire."*

1410. EL DJEBENA ★★
ch.c. Invincible Spirit – Sun Seasons (Salse).
May 14. Third foal. €26,000Y. Goffs Orby. Sir Mark Prescott. The dam, a fairly useful Irish 2-y-o 7f winner, is a half-sister to 9 winners including the Group 2 11f Blandford Stakes and Grade 2 Orchid Handicap winner Lisieux Rose. The second dam, Epicure's Garden (by Affirmed), a useful Irish 7f (at 2 yrs) to 9f winner, was Group 3 placed three times and is a sister to the Irish 1,000 Guineas winner Trusted Partner (dam of the high-class filly Dress To Thrill) and a half-sister to the Group 2 winner Easy To Copy (the dam of 3 stakes winners). (Ne'er Do Wells III). *"A late foal, he'll run in August/September time and he looks as if he'll be a better three-year-old. We'll see how he goes, he had been turned out but came out of his field last week!"*

1411. FIRE FIGHTER (IRE) ★★
b.c. Tiger Hill – Firecrest (Darshaan).
March 2. Sixth foal. 48,000Y. Tattersalls October Book 1. Sir Mark Prescott. Half-brother to the quite useful 7f (at 2 yrs) to 12f winner of 4 races Phoenix Flight (by Hawk Wing), to the quite useful 12.4f winner Grey Plover (by Alzao), the fair 9f winner La De Two (by Galileo) and the fair 9f and 12f winner Lady Songbird (by Selkirk). The dam won 5 races at around 12f including the listed Galtres Stakes and is a half-sister to 4 minor winners. The second dam, Trefoil (by Blakeney), won 3 races in France and is a half-sister to 6 winners including the French Group 2 First Prayer, the US Grade 3 winner Water Lily (herself dam of the Grade 1 winner Talinum) and the dam of the Melbourne Cup winner Jeune. (J E Fishpool-Osborne House). *"He's in a field he'll come back to us on the 15th May and he'll run in September. More of a three-year-old I type, as his pedigree would suggest, but he's not that backward."*

1412. HOORAY ★★★★
b.f. Invincible Spirit – Hypnotize (Machiavellian).
March 7. Sixth foal. Half-sister to the fairly useful 2009 2-y-o 1m winner Notorize (by Hernando), to the useful 2-y-o listed 8.3f winner of 7 races Hypnotic (by Lomitas), to the quite useful 2-y-o 6f winner Hip (by Pivotal) and the quite useful dual 7f winner Macedon (by Dansili). The dam, a useful 2-y-o dual 7f winner, is closely related to 2 winners including the Group 3 6f Cherry Hinton Stakes winner Dazzle and a half-sister to 5 winners including the useful 7f (at 2 yrs) and 1m listed winner Fantazise and to the placed dam of the Group 2 winning sprinter Danehurst. The second dam, Belle et Deluree (by The Minstrel), won over 1m (at 2 yrs) and 10f in France and is a half-sister to the very useful 6f and 1m winner and Cheveley Park Stakes second Dancing

Tribute (herself dam of the Group/Grade 2 winners Souvenir Copy and Dance Sequence). (Cheveley Park Stud). *"She'll be ready to work at the end of April and ready to run in late May/ early June if all went well. Being by Invincible Spirit I suppose she'd be a firm ground filly and the dam has already bred me a listed winning two-year-old, so there's a chance of her doing something this year. I would say she'd make a six furlong two-year-old."*

1413. KEPLER'S LAW ★★
b.c. Galileo – Tina Heights (Shirley Heights).
April 3. Seventh foal. 70,000Y. Tattersalls October Book 1. Sir Mark Prescott. Brother to the fairly useful 10f and 12f winner Bashkirov and half-brother to the 2-y-o Group 3 1m May Hill Stakes winner, Sun Chariot second, Oaks third and Yorkshire Oaks third Summitville (by Grand Lodge), the fairly useful Irish 1m to 10f winner Worldly Wise (by Namid) and the fair 10f winner Deportment (by Barathea). The dam, a quite useful 10f winner of her only start, is a half-sister to 3 winners including the useful 12f winner and listed-placed Tinashaan. The second dam, Catina (by Nureyev), a useful Irish 2-y-o 6f winner, was listed-placed and is a half-sister to 7 winners including the Group 1 Premio Regina Elena winner Rosananti. (Rectory Racing). *"He's another one for seven furlongs or a mile from September onwards."*

1414. KRYPTON FACTOR ★★★★
b.br.c. Kyllachy – Cool Question (Polar Falcon).
February 19. Fourth foal. 20,000Y. Tattersalls October Book 2. Sir Mark Prescott. Half-brother to the quite useful dual 5f winner (including at 2 yrs) Fairfield Princess (by Inchinor), to the quite useful 2-y-o dual 6f winner Haven't A Clue (by Red Ransom) and a winner in Sweden by Diktat. The dam, a useful 2-y-o 5f and listed 6f winner, is a half-sister to 3 winners. The second dam, Quiz Time (Efisio), a fairly useful 2-y-o 5f winner, was second in the listed St Hugh's Stakes and is a half-sister to 6 winners including the Group 3 Premio Dormello winner Brockette. (Lady Fairhaven & The Hon. C & H Broughton). *"It's a two-year-old family and he'll be out in June. I would think five or six furlongs will do and he won't get much further because it's a fast family. A stocky, full-square colt."*

1415. LION COURT (IRE) ★★
ch.c. Iffraaj – Spanish Falls (Belmez).
February 19. Seventh living foal. 40,000Y. Tattersalls October Book 2. Sir Mark Prescott. Half-brother to the fair 2-y-o 1m winner Tawahoj (by Zafonic) and to a minor winner in the USA by Elusive Quality. The dam, winner of the Group 2 12f Prix de Royaumont, is a half-sister to 5 winners including the St James's Palace Stakes and Prix Jean Prat winner Starborough and Group 1 1m Racing Post Trophy winner Aristotle. The second dam, Flamenco Wave (by Desert Wine), won the Group 1 6f Moyglare Stud Stakes and is a half-sister to 3 winners. (Mr & Mrs Arthur Finn). *"In a field at the moment and he wouldn't be a factor until he's three. He's out of a Belmez mare and I would think there's more Belmez in him than Iffraaj, so he's one to have the odd run as a two-year-old."*

1416. MAGGIE R (USA) ★★★
b.f. Rainbow Quest – Silver Rhapsody (Silver Hawk).
March 8. Second foal. Half-sister to the Italian middle-distance winner Algernon Talmage (by Diesis). The dam won the Group 3 12f Princess Royal Stakes, was third in the Group 1 Yorkshire Oaks and is a half-sister to 5 winners out of the minor US winner Sister Chryss (by Fit To Fight), herself a half-sister to 8 winners including the dual US Grade 2 winner Coolawin. (Timothy Rooney). *"She went lame early on but she's back here now. During her break she's grown a bit, so she's not small and will make a two-year-old later on."*

1417. MEMORY LANE ★★
b.f. With Approval – Miss Prism (Niniski).
February 11. Half-sister to the very useful 1m winner of 4 races Island Light (by Inchinor) and to the Swedish winner of 6 races, including at 2 yrs, Royal Gold (by Emarati). The dam, a maiden who stayed 2m, is a half-sister to 5 winners here and abroad. The second dam, Reflected Glory (by Relko), is a placed half-sister to 4 minor winners. (Miss K Rausing). *"A seven furlong filly in July or August, she's quite light-framed and growing a lot at the moment. She'll stay as far as you want, but she isn't a backward two-year-old."*

1418. MISS CLAIRTON ★★★
b.br.f. Marju – Spirito Libro (Lear Fan).
March 1. Eighth foal. 26,000Y. Tattersalls December. J R Collins. Sister to the useful listed 6f winner of 7 races Prince Aaron and half-sister to the modest 7f winner Memphis Marie (by Desert Sun). The dam, a fairly useful 5f (at 2 yrs) to 10f winner of 4 races, is a half-sister to 4 winners including the Irish sprint winner and Group 3 Phoenix Sprint Stakes second Conormara. The second dam, Teeming Shore (by L'Emigrant), was a very useful winner of 6 races over 5f and 6f. (Mrs June Rooney). *"She'll be working from late April onwards, I trained her grandam and she was good. This filly should make a two-year-old alright."*

1419. MOTIVADO ★★★
b.c. Motivator – Tamise (Time For A Change).
February 20. Seventh foal. 65,000Y. Tattersalls October Book 2. Highflyer Bloodstock. Half-brother to the quite useful 1m winners Love In Seattle (by Seattle Slew) and Taminos Love (by Lomitas). The dam won 4 races including the Group 3 10.5f Prix de Flore and is a half-sister to 10 winners including the US 8.5f stakes winner and Grade 1 placed Luthier's Launch. The second dam, Tanapa (by Luthier), won once in France at 2 yrs, was fourth in the Group 1 10f Premio Lydia Tesio and is a half-sister to 9 winners including the Group 3 6f winner Big John. (Syndicate 2009). *"Still biding his time in a field, he's a very tall, deep-girthed colt and a good mover, he'll be running in September."*

1420. PIZZETTI (IRE) ★★
b.c. Singspiel – Mazuna (Cape Cross).
February 17. Second foal. 32,000Y. Tattersalls October Book 1. G D Waters. Half-brother to the unplaced 2009 2-y-o Slasl (by Dubawi). The dam, winner of the Group 3 12f Princess Royal Stakes and second in the Group 2 Park Hill Stakes, is a half-sister to 6 winners. The second dam, Keswa (by King's Lake), a fairly useful 1m (at 2 yrs) and 12f winner, is a half-sister to 5 winners including the listed Zetland Stakes winner Matahif and the dam of the multiple Group 1 winner Mastercraftsman. (G D Waters). *"He'll make a seven furlong/mile two-year-old in September I would think."*

1421. RED OLEANDER ★★
b.f. Pivotal – Red Peony (Montjeu).
March 19. Second foal. The dam, a useful 7f (at 2 yrs) and 12f winner and Group 3 7f Prestige Stakes third, is a half-sister to 3 winners. The second dam, Red Azalea (by Shirley Heights), a fairly useful 7f (at 2 yrs) and 10f winner, is a half-sister to 4 winners including the Group 3 Prestige Stakes winner and French 1,000 Guineas third Red Camellia (herself dam of the Fillies Mile winner Red Bloom). (Cheveley Park Stud). *"She's weak at present, I trained the mother who was a goodish two-year-old and the first black type horse sired by Montjeu. This filly should be out in July over seven furlongs."*

1422. SNOW RIDGE ★★
ch.c. Iceman – Confetti (Groom Dancer).
January 28. Second foal. Closely related to the quite useful 2-y-o 6f winner Wedding List (by Pivotal). The dam was unplaced in two starts. The second dam, Fabulous (by Fabulous Dancer), is an unraced sister to the French 2-y-o 7.5f winner and US 1m stakes winner La Piaf and to the French listed-placed winner Legendary and a half-sister to several winners including the triple US Grade 1 winner Golden Apples and the Group 3 Park Hill Stakes winner Alexander Three D. (Cheveley Park Stud). *"He's at home and despite being by Iceman he looked like he needed time. A good, solid type, I shouldn't think he'd be effective until he's three."*

1423. SOIE DE CHINE ★★★
ch.f. Selkirk – Robe Chinoise (Robellino).
February 15. Third foal. Sister to the fair 1m (at 2 yrs) and 12f winner Mannlichen. The dam, a quite useful 10f and 12f winner, is a half-sister to 3 winners. The second dam, Kiliniski (by Niniski), winner of the Group 3 12f Lingfield Oaks Trial, was second in the Yorkshire Oaks and fourth in the Epsom Oaks and is a half-sister to 5 winners including the dam of the US triple Grade 1 winner Bienamado. (Miss K Rausing). *"She'll be a mile filly around August time. She's tall, narrow and athletic."*

1424. STATE SENATOR (USA) ★★★♣
b.br.c. Mr Greeley – Summer Night (Nashwan).
January 28. Seventh foal. 70,000Y. Tattersalls October Book 1. Sir Mark Prescott. Half-

brother to the 2-y-o Group 3 1m Prix des Reservoirs winner Songerie, to the fairly useful 2-y-o 7.2f winner and Group 3 1m Prix des Reservoirs third Souvenance (both by Hernando), the useful listed 9.5f winner of 3 races Soft Morning (by Pivotal), the fairly useful 7f (at 2 yrs) and Scandinavian listed 8.5f winner Sourire (by Domedriver) and a minor winner of 6 races in Italy by Selkirk. The dam, a fairly useful 3-y-o 6f winner, is a half-sister to 6 winners including the Group 3 Prix d'Arenburg winner Starlit Sands and the listed 6f winner Sea Dane. The second dam, Shimmering Sea (by Slip Anchor), a fairly useful Irish 2-y-o 5f and 7f winner and third in the Group 3 Silken Glider Stakes, is a half-sister to 5 winners including the King George VI and Queen Elizabeth Stakes winner Petoski. (Charles C Walker-Osborne II). *"He'll be back in the yard in mid-May and the dam is a good mare but they usually come late in the season. A January foal, he could make a two-year-old by August/September time."*

1425. TENBY LADY (USA) ★★
b.f. Anabaa – Bluebird Day (Sadler's Wells).
March 26. Third foal. €70,000Y. Arqana Deauville August. Blandford Bloodstock. Half-sister to a minor winner in the USA by Gulch. The dam, a minor US 3-y-o winner, is a half-sister to 6 winners including the dual Group 3 placed Distant Mirage. The second dam, Desert Bluebell (by Kalaglow), is a placed half-sister to 10 winners including the Group 3 Solario Stakes winner Shining Waters (herself dam of the Group 1 Grand Criterium winner Tenby). (David O'Rourke). *"A small, scopey filly, she's with the breeders and will come back in May. She cantered well but will be a three-year-old."*

1426. WALTZING CAT (USA) ★★★
ch.f. More Than Ready – Hopeful Sign (Warning).
May 20. Fifth foal. Half-sister to the useful 7f (at 2 yrs) and listed 1m winner and Group 3 Prix du Calvados second Londonnetcom (by Night Shift). The dam ran once unplaced and is closely related to the 5-time winner and St James's Palace Stakes second Greensmith and a half-sister to 7 winners including the Group 3 winners Ecologist, Infrasonic and Green Reef.

The second dam, Infra Green (by Laser Light), won the Group 1 Prix Ganay. (Timothy Rooney). *"She came back to us last week and will run around August time. She's an attractive filly with a strong, rounded action."*

MICHAEL QUINLAN

1427. BISHOPS MOON ★★★★
b.f. Araafa – Shirley Moon (by Montjeu).
March 18. Second foal. Tattersalls October 2. No bid. Half-sister to the unplaced 2009 2-y-o Noverre Over There (by Noverre). The dam is an unraced half-sister to 3 minor winners. The second dam, Greek Moon (by Shirley Heights), is an unraced half-sister to 8 winners including the US stakes winner Nash Terrace. *"This is a proper filly, she'll be racing in April and at the moment she's doing really well. More than capable of winning."*

1428. FOR THE REASON (IRE) ★★
b.c. Medicean – Jamrah (Danehill).
February 17. First foal. The unraced dam is closely related to the Group 3 Anglesey Stakes winner Walk On Bye. The second dam, Pipalong (by Pips Pride), won 10 races including the Group 1 6f Haydock Park Sprint Cup, the Group 3 Duke Of York Stakes and the Group 3 Palace House Stakes and is a half-sister to 5 winners including the fairly useful 2-y-o 6f listed winner Out Of Africa. The second dam, Limpopo (by Green Desert), a poor 5f placed 2-y-o, is a half-sister to 6 winners here and abroad. *"He has a lovely pedigree and although he's not as good as some other members of his family he'll win. We might have to put blinkers on him the first time he runs because he's a bit timid and he backs off a bit. He's not ungenuine but he was very skittish when he first arrived."*

1429. MISS BOOPS (IRE) ★★★
b.f. Johannesburg – Sky Bird (Galileo).
February 16. Second foal. 14,000Y. Tattersalls December. Not sold. The dam is an unraced half-sister to 4 winners including the smart listed 9f Strensall Stakes winner and dual Group 1 third Gold Academy. The second dam, Soha (by Dancing Brave), a modest 12f placed 3-y-o, is a half-sister to one winner. *"She's quite forward, she's strong and goes well. I can see her being out in May over six furlongs. She's quite strong-minded, so I need*

to have the right rider on her, but after being a bit difficult in the first week she settled down. I think she'll be alright and I'm happy with her."

1430. UNNAMED ★★★
b.c. Danehill Dancer – Dinka Raja (Woodman). **May 8. Eighth foal. 78,000Y. Tattersalls October 1. Not sold.** Half-brother to the useful 2009 2-y-o 7f winner Hanson'D (by Pivotal), to the Group 1 6f Cheveley Park Stakes and Group 2 6f Lowther Stakes winner Carry On Katie (by Fasliyev), the 2-y-o 6f all-weather winner Pinkabout (by Desert Style) and the minor US 3-y-o winner Geebeekay (by Peintre Celebre). The dam, a minor French 3-y-o 1m winner, is a half-sister to 4 winners. The second dam, Miss Profile (by Sadler's Wells), is an unraced half-sister to 4 stakes winners including the Group 1 Prix Saint-Alary winner Grise Mine and the triple US Grade 1 winner Kostroma. "He was showing us plenty but got a little cut on the pad of the walker which needed stitches and that meant we had to hold him up. Actually we were delighted about that because he was coming forward too quickly. He became unfurnished but he's back walking and cantering now and potentially he's a lovely horse."

1431. UNNAMED ★★
b.f. Dubawi – Dixie Belle (Diktat). **February 21. First foal.** The dam, a Group 3 5f and listed 6f winner, is a half-sister to one winner. The second dam, Inspiring (by Anabaa), is an unraced half-sister to 3 minor winners. "The Dubawi's didn't come good until August last year, so we'll give her a bit of time. If she didn't have the pedigree she has then she'd be further down my list because at the moment she doesn't excite me too much, but at some point in the next few weeks she might just come good."

1432. UNNAMED ★★♣
b.f. Noverre – Lady Miletrian (Barathea). **April 5. Fifth living foal. 11,500 2-y-o. Kempton Breeze-Up. D McGreavy.** Half-sister to the useful 2-y-o 6f winner and Group 2 Coventry Stakes fourth Himalya (by Danehill) and to the quite useful 6f all-weather winner Dama'a (by Green Desert). The dam, a useful 1m winner and fourth in the Group 3 Fred Darling Stakes, is a sister to the listed winning 2-y-o Duty Paid and a half-sister to 3 winners. The second dam, Local Custom (by Be My Native), was placed at up to 7f at 2 yrs and is a sister to the listed winner Tribal Rite and a half-sister to the Middle Park Stakes winner Balla Cove. "Bought out of the Kempton breeze-up, she skipped along nicely there and she's having a little break at the stud, so I don't know much about her yet."

1433. UNNAMED ★★★
b.f. Araafa – Pink Stone (Bigstone). **March 20. Sixth foal. 45,000Y. Tattersalls October 1. Pier House Stud.** Half-sister to the fair 2009 1m placed 2-y-o Battleoftrafalgar (by Galileo), to the useful but ill-fated 2-y-o 7f winner Tiger Eye (by Danehill Dancer), the quite useful 2-y-o 8.3f winner Alright My Son (by Pennekamp) and a minor winner abroad by Agnes World. The dam was placed three times in France and stayed 10f and is a half-sister to 8 winners including the triple Group 3 winner Pink and the French listed winners Ring Pink and Lypink. The second dam, Pink Valley (by Never Bend), won the listed Prix d'Aumale and is a half-sister to 12 winners including the French 2,000 Guineas winner and sire Green Dancer. "I won't be rushing her – her half-sister Tiger Eye was potentially very smart but sadly died – so this filly has a chance of being decent."

1434. UNNAMED ★★★
b.c. Dr Fong – Query (Distant View). **February 12. First foal. £3,000Y. Doncaster St Leger Festival. Not sold.** The dam is an unraced half-sister to 5 minor winners here and abroad. a useful winner at around 1m, is a half-sister to 2 winners including the listed 10f winner Zante. The second dam, Questonia (by Rainbow Quest), a useful winner at around 1m, is a half-sister to 2 winners including the listed 10f winner Zante. "When he came in he was just a big, ordinary horse, but he's pleased us every day since, so I have to say that I do like him. An easy horse to train – he doesn't sweat up or pull. Probably one for late May or June."

KEVIN RYAN

1435. CANUKEEPASECRET ★★★
b.f. Mind Games – Our Little Secret (Rossini).

April 4. First foal. The dam, a useful listed 5f winner of 6 races, is a half-sister to 2 winners. The second dam, Sports Post Lady (by M Double M), a fair 5f winner of 4 races, is a half-sister to the useful sprinter Palacegate Episode (a winner of 11 races here and abroad including a Group 3 race in Italy and numerous listed events), to the fair sprinter Another Episode (a winner of 11 races and second in the Group 3 Molecomb Stakes) and the useful sprinter Palacegate Jack (also a winner of 11 races including listed events).

1436. COPEX ★★★
ch.f. Compton Place – May Light (Midyan).
April 16. £12,000Y. Doncaster St Leger. Stephen Hillen. Half-sister to the smart Group 3 6f Bentinck Stakes winner of 6 races Bygone Days (by Desert King), to the fairly useful 2-y-o 1m winner Trio (by Cyrano de Bergerac) and the moderate 5f (at 2 yrs) and 12f winner Well Informed (by Averti). The dam, a modest 7f placed maiden, is a half-sister to 10 winners including the Group 3 Prix de Flore winner Lighted Glory (herself the dam of 3 Group winners), the Group 2 Prix Kergorlay winner King Luthier and the dam of the US Grade 1 winner Cool. The second dam, Lighted Lamp (by Sir Gaylord), was placed in the USA and is a half-sister to 7 winners including the Middle Park Stakes winner Crocket.

1437. COUNTRYWIDE FLAME ★★★
b.c. Haafhd – Third Party (Terimon).
March 25. Eighth foal. £36,000Y. Doncaster St Leger Festival. K Ryan. Half-brother to the very useful 7f (at 2 yrs) and listed 7f and 1m all-weather winner Party Boss (by Silver Patriarch), to the fair 7f and 1m winner Best In Class (by Best Of The Bests) and the modest 7f winner Party Turn (by Pivotal). The dam, a modest 3-y-o 6f winner, is a half-sister to 6 winners including the German Group 3 winning sprinter Passion For Life and the fairly useful sprint winner of 13 races Very Dicey. The second dam, Party Game (by Red Alert), a fair 6f winner at 3 yrs, is a half-sister to 5 minor winners.

1438. FLEET CAPTAIN ★★★
b.c. Compton Place – Mrs Brown (Royal Applause).
February 2. Third foal. £40,000Y. Doncaster St Leger. Not sold. Brother to the quite useful 2009 2-y-o 5f winner Kings Of Leo. The dam, a moderate 7f placed 3-y-o, is a half-sister to 5 winners including the Italian Group 3 winner Shifting Place. The second dam, Shifting Mist (by Night Shift), a modest 10f to 14f winner of 5 races, is a half-sister to 7 winners including the dam of the Group/Grade 3 winner Needwood Blade.

1439. FORMIDABLE GIRL (USA) ★★★
b.br.f. Roman Ruler – Gracility (Known Fact).
April 2. Second foal. $100,000Y. Fasig-Tipton Kentucky. Stephen Hillen. The dam, a minor US stakes winner, is a half-sister to one stakes winner. The second dam, Kuma (by Naevus), a minor stakes-placed winner of 15 races, is a half-sister to 7 winners.

1440. GEESALA (USA) ★★★★
ch.f. Barathea – Shivaree (Rahy).
March 17. Second foal. €33,000Y. Tattersalls Ireland. Stephen Hillen. Half-sister to the fair 2009 2-y-o 5f winner Tomintoul Singer (by Johannesburg). The dam, a fair 2-y-o 6f winner, is a half-sister to one winner. The second dam, Shmoose (by Caerleon), a useful 6f winner at 2 yrs and third in the Group 3 6f Prix de Seine-et-Oise, is a half-sister to 6 winners and to the good broodmare June Moon. A winner at the first attempt, at Pontefract on the 19th April.

1441. GO MAGGIE GO (IRE) ★★★
b.f. Kheleyf – Born To Glamour (Ajdal).
March 2. Eleventh foal. €17,000Y. Goffs Open. J Brummitt. Half-sister to the Irish 2-y-o 5.8f winner Lady Meagan (by Val Royal), the useful 2-y-o 5f winner and Group 2 6f Gimcrack Stakes second Sailing Shoes (by Lahib), the fairly useful Irish 10f winner Tarbaan, the Italian 3-y-o winner Dazzling Dawn (both by Nashwan), the quite useful 2-y-o 1m winner and Group 3 Prix des Chenes third Canwinn (by Refuse To Bend), the quite useful 2-y-o 6f winner Encanto (by Bahhare), the Irish 2-y-o 7f and subsequent US winner Hot Trotter (by Halling) and the quite useful 6f and 7f winner Pawan (by Cadeaux Genereux). The dam, a winner over 6f in Ireland at 2 yrs, is a half-sister to 8 winners including the French listed winner North Haneena. The second dam, the French winner Haneena (by Habitat), was fourth in

the Cheveley Park Stakes and is a half-sister to 6 winners including the Jersey Stakes winner Gwent.

1442. KING OF AQUITAINE (IRE) ★★★
b.c. Holy Roman Emperor – Plume Rouge (Pivotal).
April 3. Second foal. €35,000Y. Goffs Orby. Stephen Hillen. Half-brother to the quite useful 7f winner Mean Lae (by Johannesburg). The dam, a useful 2-y-o 6f and 3-y-o listed 7.5f winner in Ireland, is a half-sister to one winner. The second dam, Classic Fan (by Lear Fan), is a placed half-sister to 3 winners.

1443. LOUIS THE PIOUS ★★★
b.br.c. Holy Roman Emperor – Whole Grain (Polish Precedent).
April 13. Second foal. 57,000Y. Tattersalls October Book 1. Stephen Hillen. The dam was last of 3 runners twice over 12f and 2m in France but is a sister to 2 winners including Pure Grain, winner of the Group 3 7f Prestige Stakes at 2 yrs and the Group 1 12f Irish Oaks and Group 1 12f Yorkshire Oaks at 3 yrs, and a half-sister to 6 winners. The second dam, Mill Line (by Mill Reef), a fair 14.6f winner at 3 yrs, is a half-sister to 6 winners.

1444. NASHARRA (IRE) ★★★
ch.c. Iffraaj – There With Me (Distant View).
March 8. Third foal. £37,000Y. Doncaster St Leger. Three Ways Bloodstock. Half-brother to the fairly useful 2-y-o triple 5f winner and listed placed Give Me The Night (by Night Shift) and to the quite useful 6f winner Prime Mood (by Choisir). The dam, a 6f winner at 4 yrs, is a half-sister to 9 winners. The second dam, Breeze Lass (by It's Freezing), a minor winner at 2 yrs in the USA, is a half-sister to 7 winners.

1445. PRITZKER PRIZE ★★★
b.c. Pastoral Pursuits – Grand Design (Danzero).
February 24. First foal. £20,000Y. Doncaster St Leger. J Fretwell. The dam, placed fourth twice over 7f, is a half-sister to 6 winners including the listed 10.4f Middleton Stakes winner Jalousie. The second dam, Duende (by High Top), a fair 2-y-o 6f winner, is a half-sister to 8 winners including the French listed winner Blushing All Over.

DAVID SIMCOCK

1446. AGADIR SUMMER ★★★♣
b.f. Cape Cross – Easy To Love (Diesis).
March 27. Seventh foal. 30,000Y. Tattersalls October 1. Rabbah Bloodstock. Half-sister to the fairly useful 2-y-o 7f and 1m winner and listed-placed Easy Lover (by Pivotal) and to the fair 2-y-o 7f winner Pezula Bay (by Oasis Dream). The dam, a quite useful 4-y-o 11.5f winner, is a sister to the Oaks winner Love Divine (herself dam of the St Leger winner Sixties Icon) and a half-sister to 3 winners including the listed 12f winner Floreeda. The second dam, La Sky (by Law Society), a useful 10f winner and second in the Group 3 Lancashire Oaks, is closely related to the Champion Stakes winner Legal Case and a half-sister to 4 winners. "A scopey, good-actioned filly, she's very natural, has a good attitude and a very nice way of going. She'll start off at seven furlongs and she's just a very likeable filly."

1447. AJABNY ALZAIN (IRE) ★★★
b.c. Acclamation – Ink Pot (Green Dancer).
April 16. Tenth living foal. 70,000Y. Tattersalls October Book 1. Rabbah Bloodstock. Half-brother to the fairly useful 6f, 7f and Hong Kong winner Quink (by Selkirk), the fair 3-y-o 7f winner Calligraphy (by Kris), the fair 7f (at 2 yrs) and 10f winner Joinedupwriting (by Desert Style), the moderate 2-y-o 6f winner Monte Mayor Eagle (by Captain Rio) and a winner in New Zealand by Medicean. The dam was placed twice at 2 yrs and is a half-sister to 7 winners including the fairly useful 2-y-o 7f winner Spurned (herself dam of the Group winners Hidden Meadow and Scorned) and the 1995 German champion 2-y-o and subsequent US Grade 2 placed Winter Quarters. The second dam, Refill (by Mill Reef), placed fourth in the Group 3 6f Cherry Hinton Stakes at 2 yrs, subsequently won 4 races at up to 11f in the USA and is a half-sister to 9 winners including the dam of the Group 2 5f Kings Stand Stakes winner Don't Worry Me. "The mare has produced one decent horse. This colt is very likeable, very attractive and quite a big horse. He's just grown on me slightly and may want a bit more time."

1448. AJEEB (USA) ★★
b.c. Harlan's Holiday – Fair Settlement
(Easy Goer).
May 13. Tenth foal. $50,000Y. Keeneland September. Rabbah Bloodstock. Half-brother to 4 winners including the minor US stakes-placed Mustang Jock (by Wild Again). The dam is an unraced half-sister to 8 winners including the US Grade 3 winner Party Manners. The second dam, Duty Dance (by Nijinsky), a US Grade 2 and Grade 3 winner, is a half-sister to the US Grade 1 winner Squander. *"He's not bad at all, I wouldn't be rushing him because he's a big, scopey horse and he was a late foal. One for July perhaps, but he's likeable."*

1449. AL BIRRWAZ ★★
b.c. Cape Cross – Bezzaaf (Machiavellian).
March 3. Sixth foal. 52,000Y. Tattersalls October Book 1. Rabbah Bloodstock. Half-brother to the fairly useful 6f, 1m (both at 2 yrs) and 10f winner and listed-placed Zaskar (by Anabaa), to the useful 6f (at 2 yrs) and subsequent listed 7f Abu Dhabi winner Ans Bach (by Green Desert), the modest 2-y-o 7f winner Zefooha (by Lomitas) and a winner in Greece by Bachir. The dam, a fairly useful 3-y-o 10f winner, is a half-sister to 5 winners. The second dam, Maid Of Kashmir (by Dancing Brave), a fairly useful Irish 10f winner and third in the listed Oaks Trial, is a half-sister to 7 winners. *"Not over big, but he's progressing nicely. He won't be massively early but he'll be a mid-season two-year-old."*

1450. ALEMARATIYA ★★★
b.f. Dalakhani – Marannatha
(Pursuit Of Love).
April 27. April 27. Second foal. 10,000Y. Tattersalls October Book 1. Rabbah Bloodstock. The dam, a fair Irish 7f 2-y-o winner, is a half-sister to 5 winners including the Italian Group 3 winner Uruk. The second dam, Lili Cup (by Fabulous Dancer), is an unraced half-sister to 10 winners including the Irish Group 3 winner Nysaean. *"She's got a terribly dipped back, which is why she only cost Ten Grand, but she's very natural. She shows a bit of attitude and can be quite naughty, but I love the way she goes. Being by Dalakhani that surprises me, but seven furlongs in June should be her starting point and she should be easy to place in a maiden auction."* TRAINERS' BARGAIN BUY

1451. AL MAYASAH (IRE) ★★★
b.f. Shamardal – Mia Mambo (Affirmed).
April 23. Fourth foal. 48,000Y. Tattersalls October Book 1. Rabbah Bloodstock. Half-sister to the fair 1m and 9f winner Candy Ride (by Pivotal) and to a minor winner in Greece by Gulch. The dam is an unraced half-sister to 5 winners including the dual listed winner Byzantium. The second dam, Bravemie (by Nureyev), is an unraced sister to the outstanding filly and broodmare Miesque. *"This filly has turned round, she goes well, is very natural and quicker than I thought she'd be. She was a fairly late foal and she needs to furnish a touch, but she does everything asked."*

1452. BINT ELNADIM (IRE) ★★
b.f. Elnadim – Redrightreturning (Diktat).
April 5. Second foal. 18,000Y. Tattersalls October Book 3. David Simcock. The dam, a quite useful Irish 2-y-o 7f winner, is a half-sister to 2 winners. The second dam, Wars (by Green Desert), is a placed sister to the very smart 7f and 1m performer Gabr and a half-sister to 4 winners including the smart middle-distance horse Kutta. *"Cheap and cheerful, she shows enough and although she isn't going to be a star she's likeable."*

1453. BRETON STAR ★★★
b.c. Medicean – Wannabe Grand
(Danehill).
May 3. 22,000Y. Tattersalls December. Mr J Cook. Half-brother to the useful 7f to 10f winner King Of Argos (by Sadler's Wells), to the useful 7f (at 2 yrs) to 9f winner of Wannabe King (by King's Best), the fairly useful triple 7f winner (including at 2 yrs) and subsequent Hong Kong winner Walkonthewildside (by Giant's Causeway), the fairly useful 2-y-o 5f winner Bachelor Of Arts (by Stravinsky), the quite useful 10.2f winner King Of Argos (by Sadler's Wells) and a winner in Japan by Selkirk. The dam won the Group 1 6f Cheveley Park Stakes and the Group 3 6f Cherry Hinton Stakes and is a half-sister to 3 winners including the useful 2-y-o dual 1m winner and Group 3 second. The second dam, Wannabe (by Shirley

Heights), a quite useful 1m and 10f winner, is a half-sister to 3 winners including the Group 1 Cheveley Park Stakes second Tanami. *"I like this horse, he was inexpensive, not particularly pretty in front but from a great producing mare. He's going to be a seven furlong/miler and he has a very likeable attitude and a likeable way of cantering."*

1454. CHESNUT COFFEE ★★
ch.f. *Nayef – Culture Queen (King's Best).*
March 28. First foal. 38,000Y. Tattersalls October Book 2. Gill Richardson. The dam, a quite useful 2-y-o 6f winner, is a half-sister to 4 winners. The second dam, Cultured Pearl (by Lammtarra), was placed once over 8.2f at 3 yrs and is a half-sister to one winner. *"Not overly-big, but she has quite a nice action. Not particularly early."*

1455. DUJA ALLAYL (USA) ★★★
ch.f. *Silver Train – East Cape (Mr Prospector).*
February 17. Seventh foal. $50,000Y. Keeneland September. Blandford Bloodstock. Half-sister to 5 winners including the useful 2009 2-y-o 7f winner and listed-placed Dubai Miracle (by Consolidator), the US stakes-placed Ottawa Chief and the minor US winner Powerstown (both by Forestry). The dam is an unraced half-sister to 6 winners including the US Grade 1 Nassau County Handicap winner West By West (by Gone West). The second dam, West Turn (by Cox's Ridge), is a placed sister to the US Grade 1 Brooklyn Handicap winner Little Missouri. *"Bought in America, she's coming along nicely and is likely to be a mid-season two-year-old over seven furlongs."*

1456. GEBLAH (IRE) ★★★★
b.f. *Green Desert – Cedar Sea (Persian Bold).*
March 1. Fourth foal. 32,000Y. Tattersalls October Book 2. Blandford Bloodstock. Closely related to the fair 2009 2-y-o 1m winner Corsica (by Cape Cross). The dam, a French 1m winner and second in the listed Prix Yacowlef, is a half-sister to 3 winners including the Group 3 6f Coventry Stakes winner CD Europe. The second dam, Woodland Orchid (by Woodman), is an unplaced half-sister to the Group 3 Derrinstown Stud Derby Trial winner Truth Or Dare, the UAE Group3 winner D'Anjou and the listed winner Sandstone. *"She should be starting over six furlongs in May, she has a good attitude and is very likeable. She wouldn't want the ground too quick I shouldn't think, but I'm very happy with her."*

1457. GOLD TOBOUGG ★★★
b.f. *Tobougg – Maristax (Reprimand).*
March 9. Seventh foal. 54,000Y. Tattersalls October Book 1. Gill Richardson. Sister to the smart listed 1m and listed 10f winner of 6 races and Group 3 Musidora Stakes second Sweet Lilly and half-sister to the useful 9f and 10f winner of 7 races Ofaraby (by Sheikh Albadou) and the moderate 1m and 10f winner Circadian Rhythm (by Lujain). The dam, a fair 2-y-o 7f winner, is closely related to the useful 2-y-o listed 5f winner Four-Legged-Friend and a half-sister to 6 winners including the dual US Grade 3 winner Superstrike and the dam of the Group 1 winning sprinters Goodricke and Pastoral Pursuits. The second dam, Marista (by Mansingh), ran twice unplaced at 2 yrs and is a half-sister to 3 winners. *"She's a bit like her sister Sweet Lilly in that she can show plenty of attitude and can be quite naughty, but she's very likeable, not overly-big and very mature. She'll start off at seven furlongs but a mile will be right up her street."*

1458. HO YA MAL (IRE) ★★★
ch.c. *Shamardal – Ridotto (Salse).*
February 8. Seventh foal. 50,000Y. Tattersalls October Book 3. Blandford Bloodstock. Half-brother to the fairly useful 2009 2-y-o 7f winner Rock Of Love (by Rock Of Gibraltar), to the useful 2-y-o 5f winner and Group 2 Lowther Stakes and Group 2 Cherry Hinton Stakes winner Salsa Brava (by Almutawakel), the fair 2-y-o 1m winner Love Valentine (by Fruits Of Love) and the fair 2-y-o 7f and hurdles winner Stagehand (by Lend A Hand). The dam was placed twice at 3 yrs in France. The second dam, Carnival Appeal (by Valid Appeal), a minor dual winner in the USA, is a full or half-sister to 6 winners. *"He was quite expensive and he's a big horse that hasn't done a massive amount yet because he'll need a bit of time. But he has a very likeable character."*

1459. LOOK TWICE ★★★
b.f. *Royal Applause – Exchanging Glances (Diktat).*
February 14. First foal. 22,000Y. Tattersalls October Book 2. Blandford Bloodstock. The dam is an unraced half-sister to one winner. The second dam, Princess Miletrian (by Danehill), a fair 3-y-o 8.2f winner, is a half-sister to 6 winners including the German Group 3 1m winner Sinyar and to the unraced dam of the US Grade 2 winner Ventiquattrofogli. *"A sharp little filly, she'll probably be our first two-year-old filly to run. She goes well, has a good attitude and a good action. Quite likeable and well put-together."*

1460. MAHER (USA) ★★★
b.c. *Medaglia d'Oro – Bourbon Blues (Seeking The Gold).*
March 19. Seventh foal. $70,000Y. Keeneland September. Rabbah Bloodstock. Half-brother to 5 winners including the US stakes-placed Old Fashion Girl (by Arch) and 2 minor US winners by Lion Heart and Johannesburg. The dam, a minor US 2-y-o winner, is out of the Grade 2 Del Mar Debutante Stakes winner Beal Street Blues (by Dixieland Band), herself a sister to the US Grade 2 winner Dixieland Brass. *"A very natural horse, he's related to one I had three seasons ago called Wolf River. This colt was relatively cheap for a son of such a good stallion and he's very likeable, very forward and doing everything I ask really well."*

1461. MARHABA MALYOON (IRE) ★★
b.c. *Tiger Hill – Mamonta (Fantastic Light).*
March 4. First foal. 40,000Y. Tattersalls October Book 1. Rabbah Bloodstock. The dam, placed once over 2m, is a half-sister to 5 winners including the Group 2 12.5f Prix de Royallieu winner Mouramara. The second dam, Mamoura (by Lomond), won over 10f and 12f in Ireland and is a half-sister to 5 winners. *"I trained the mare but she wasn't very fast. He reminds us of Darley Sun to a certain extent in the sense that he'll need a lot of time and a trip. From a good Aga Khan family, he's a stayer for the future."*

1462. MAYFAIR LADY ★★
ch.c. *Bertolini – Flower Market (Cadeaux Genereux).*
March 22. Second foal. 13,000Y. Tattersalls October Book 2. D Simcock. Half-brother to the fairly useful 2009 5f listed-placed 2-y-o Aalsmeer (by Invincible Spirit). The dam, a fair 2-y-o 6f winner, is a half-sister to 7 winners including the fairly useful 2-y-o 6f winner Medley. The second dam, Marl (by Lycius), a fairly useful 2-y-o 5.2f winner, is a half-sister to 4 winners including the very useful 2-y-o listed 5f National Stakes winner Rowaasi. *"He hasn't been with us long so we haven't found out much about him, but he goes OK and he's not a bad little horse."*

1463. MEINAAWI (USA) ★★★★
b.c. *Bernstein – Brocatelle (Green Desert).*
April 13. Eighth foal. $60,000Y. Keeneland September. Rabbah Bloodstock. Half-brother to the Japanese winner of 6 races from 2 to 5 yrs and listed-placed Fusaichi Hokutosei (by Machiavellian). The dam, a modest 7f placed maiden, is a half-sister to 8 winners including the top-class milers Barathea and Gossamer (dam of the Group 1 winner Ibn Khaldun) and the Group 3 winners Zabar and Free At Last (herself dam of the multiple Graded stakes winner Coretta). The second dam, Brocade (by Habitat), was a high-class filly at up to 1m, winning five races including the Group 1 7f Prix de la Foret and is a half-sister to 7 winners. *"He's showing up well, he should start off at six furlongs in mid-May and he'll be a very nice six/seven furlong horse in the future. He goes well, he's a very likeable, scopey horse and it's a family that does surprisingly well at two."*

1464. MUBTADI ★★★
b.c. *Dr Fong – Noble Peregrine (Lomond).*
March 5. Eleventh foal. 40,000Y. Tattersalls October Book 1. Rabbah Bloodstock. Brother to the 6f (at 2 yrs) and triple listed winner Dubai's Touch and half-brother to the quite useful 2009 2-y-o 6f winner Arabian Pride (by Cadeaux Genereux), the smart 8.5f and 9f winner and Group 3 Diomed Stakes third Wannabe Around (by Primo Dominie), the useful triple 6f winner (including at 2 yrs) and subsequent Abu Dhabi listed winner Grantley Adams (by Dansili), the useful 7.5f to 10f winner and French Group 3 1m third Nobelist (by Bering) and the fairly useful 7f (at

2 yrs) and 1m winner Noble Pursuit (by Pursuit Of Love). The dam, an Italian 10f winner, is closely related to the French 2-y-o listed 10f winner Noble Ballerina and a half-sister to 6 winners. The second dam, Noble Dust (by Dust Commander), is an unraced half-sister to 6 winners. "We had the half-brother Arabian Pride last year who was half the size of this fellow and lacking in scope. This colt has loads of scope and he's a better actioned horse with a better attitude. For a big horse he's extremely natural and for what he cost he'll do very well. A mid-season two-year-old."

1465. MUTAWEL AL GAIBA ★★★
b.c. Royal Applause – Shaken And Stirred (Cadeaux Genereux).
February 29. Third foal. £40,000Y. Doncaster St Leger. Blandford Bloodstock.
Half-brother to the fairly useful 2009 5f and 6f winner and Group 3 Firth Of Clyde Stakes second Midnight Martini (by Night Shift). The dam is an unraced half-sister to 3 winners including the Group 3 Musidora Stakes third Sues Surprise. The second dam, My Micheline (by Lion Cavern), is an unraced half-sister to 4 winners including the listed winner Well Beyond (herself dam of the US Grade 3 winner Out Of Reach). "He's not a particularly forward horse, but he's likeable, big and he'll want a bit of time."

1466. ON ALERT ★★
b.c. Deploy – Morina (Lyphard).
February 25. Eleventh foal. 38,000Y. Tattersalls October Book 2. M Crossman.
Brother to the very smart Group 2 1m Royal Lodge Stakes winner Mons and to the smart 10f winner and Irish Oaks third Inforapenny and half-brother to the quite useful 14f winner Teresa (by Darshaan), the quite useful 1m all-weather winner Yo Pedro (by Mark Of Esteem), the quite useful 10f and 12f winner Funday, the hurdles winner Pigeon Island (both by Daylami) and the fair 10f winner Lomapamar (by Nashwan). The dam won over 11f in France and is a half-sister to 10 winners including the US stakes winner Have Fun. The second dam, Arewehavingfunyet (by Sham), won the Grade 1 Oak Leaf Stakes and the Grade 2 Del Mar Debutante Stakes and is a half-sister to 6 winners. "A full-brother to Mons, so he's out of an old mare, but he's likeable and relatively mature. He's not backward, not overly-big and I like him."

1467. RUTLAND BOY ★★
ch.c. Bertolini – Israar (Machiavellian).
March 30. Second foal. 15,000Y. Tattersalls October Book 3. Blandford Bloodstock.
Half-brother to the moderate 2010 3-y-o 5f winner Exceed Power (by Exceed And Excel). The dam is an unraced half-sister to 3 minor winners. The second dam, El Opera (by Sadler's Wells), a useful dual 7f winner, is a half-sister to 8 winners including the very useful Group 1 6f Heinz "57" Phoenix Stakes winner Pharaoh's Delight. "Relatively inexpensive and quite precocious, he's a half-brother to a filly I've got called Exceed Power. I don't dislike him at all – he's quite workmanlike."

1468. SAR POOT (IRE) ★★
b.c. Iffraaj – Vampire Queen (General Monash).
March 20. Fourth foal. 25,000Y. Tattersalls October Book 2. Rabbah Bloodstock. Half-brother to a minor winner in Italy by Bertolini. The dam, a modest 3-y-o 6f winner, is a full or half-sister to 5 winners. The second dam, Taniokey (by Grundy), won at 3 yrs and is a half-sister to 5 winners including Kittyhawk (Group 3 Lowther Stakes). "A horse that's very natural but he's grown and grown. Wasn't overly expensive but he has a very likeable attitude. He was 'cheap and cheerful' but as an individual he's very attractive."

1469. SEEKING GLORY ★★
b.c. King's Best – Ataba (Anabaa).
April 7. Fifth living foal. 23,000Y. Tattersalls October Book 2. Blandford Bloodstock.
Half-brother to the quite useful 7f and 1m winner Atabaas Allure (by Alhaarth) and to the quite useful 2-y-o 6f winner Atabaas Pride (by Pivotal). The dam, a listed 1m winner in France, is a half-sister to 4 winners including the French listed winner Paix Blanche. The second dam, Alma Ata (by Rheffic), won a listed race in France and is a half-sister to 5 winners. "A big horse, he isn't terribly forward but he is a good-actioned horse. Not one of the early two-year-olds."

1470. UNNAMED ★★★★
br.c. Cape Cross – Bradamante (Sadler's Wells).
February 14. Second foal. 50,000Y. Tattersalls October 1. Rabbah Bloodstock. The dam, a French 2-y-o 1m winner, is a half-sister to 3 winners including the listed Godolphin Stakes winner and Group 2 placed Galactic Star. The second dam, Balisada (by Kris), won the Group 1 1m Coronation Stakes and is a half-sister to 2 winners. *"Quite an attractive horse, he's one for the middle of the season and he has a good action and a good attitude. Quite mature and well put-together, he's very much like his sire Cape Cross."*

1471. UNNAMED ★★★★
b.f. Red Ransom – Capistrano Day (Diesis).
February 8. Fifth foal. 40,000Y. Tattersalls October Book 2. Blandford Bloodstock. Sister to the useful 6f (at 2 yrs) to 1m winner and Group 3 Supreme Stakes third Sabbeeh and half-sister to the fairly useful 2-y-o 6f winner and Group 3 Nell Gwyn Stakes second Dream Day (by Oasis Dream), the fair 7f and 1m winner of 4 races Green Agenda (by Anabaa) and a winner in Greece by Green Desert. The dam, a smart listed 7f winner, was fourth in the 1,000 Guineas and is a full or half-sister to 5 winners. The second dam, Alcando (by Alzao), a smart 5f (at 2 yrs) to 10f winner here, subsequently won the Grade 1 9f Beverly Hills Handicap in the USA and is a half-sister to 5 winners. *"A nice big filly with plenty of size and scope. She has a good action and everything she's done so far has been good. Very likeable."*

1472. UNNAMED ★★★
b.c. Iffraaj – Heckle (In The Wings).
March 28. Seventh foal. 50,000Y. Tattersalls October Book 1. Rabbah Bloodstock. Half-brother to the fairly useful 2-y-o triple 6f and subsequent Hong Kong Chairman's Sprint Prize winner Algol (by Kyllachy) and to the moderate 4-y-o 6f winner Pintano (by Dr Fong). The dam was placed fourth once over 6f at 2 yrs and is a half-sister to 4 winners including the Irish listed sprint winner Mitsubishi Vision. The second dam, Valiant Cry (by Town Crier), won over 9f at 4 yrs in France and is a half-sister to 2 winners. *"Probably the most forward of my two-year-olds, he's very likeable, very forward and workmanlike. He wouldn't want the ground too quick and I would expect him out around May time."*

1473. UNNAMED ★★★
b.c. Motivator – Soliza (Intikhab).
February 4. Second foal. 27,000Y. Tattersalls October Book 2. Rabbah Bloodstock. Brother to Domination, placed fourth once over 9f at 2 yrs in 2009. The dam, a quite useful Irish 10f winner of 3 races over 10f, is a half-sister to 5 winners including the multiple listed winner Salford Mill and the very useful 10f and 12f winner Ovambo. The second dam, Razana (by Kahyasi), a fair 10f winner here, later won at up to 12f in France and is a half-sister to 5 winners and to the unplaced dam of the Group 1 Prix de l'Opera winner Kinnaird. *"A cheap horse, he's not overly big but he's surprisingly forward and his brain is pretty good for a Motivator. He's doing plenty and he'll start off in the early seven furlong races in June."*

1474. UNNAMED ★★★
b.c. Cadeaux Genereux – Tahirah (Green Desert).
March 13. Third foal. The dam, a useful 3-y-o 7f and 1m winner, is a half-sister to 4 winners including the fairly useful 6f to 1m winner Suruor. The second dam, Kismah (by Machiavellian), a very useful dual 1m winner, is a half-sister to 8 winners. *"A very attractive colt from the family of Suruor who did well for us last year. This colt had a problem at the stud early doors so he hasn't been with us long, but he's a very likeable colt."*

TOMMY STACK

1475. FROZEN FRONTIER (IRE) ★★★
b.c. Kodiac – Shining Desert (Green Desert).
March 14. Eighth foal. €42,000Y. Goffs Orby. DeBurgh Equine. Half-brother to the Italian winner of 13 races from 2 to 6 yrs Bryan Gold (by Bahhare), to the quite useful 9f, 10f and 11f winner Mid Mon Lady (Danetime), the modest 6f winner of 4 races Maison Dieu (by King Charlemagne) and the Italian winner (including at 2 yrs), Compton Flowers (by Compton Place). The dam, a quite useful 2-y-o 5f winner, is a half-sister to 2 winners. The second dam, Riyoom (by Vaguely Noble), won over 1m in Ireland at 2 yrs, is a half-sister

to 5 winners including the US triple Grade 3 winner Lt Lao. *"He's a big colt with a bit of a knee action, so he might need some ease in the ground. He'll probably take a bit of time and he's a six/seven furlong horse."*

1476. GREAT HUZZAR (IRE) ★★★
b.c. Danehill Dancer – Labrusca (Grand Lodge).
February 28. Fifth foal. €130,000Y. Goffs Orby. C McCormack. The dam was third over 10f on her only start and is a half-sister to 9 winners including the high-class Group 1 12f Yorkshire Oaks and Group 3 12f Lancashire Oaks winner Catchascatchcan (herself dam of the very smart miler Antonius Pius), the listed 10f winner Licorne and the dam of the Australian Group winners Tall Timbers and Taken. The second dam, Catawba (by Mill Reef), a useful 10.5f winner, is a half-sister to 7 winners including the Ribblesdale Stakes winner Strigida. *"A big, strong, good-looking colt. He'll probably be a seven furlong/mile horse this season. He should be out at the end of May and we're pleased with what he's done."*

1477. HIGH AWARD (IRE) ★★★★
b.c. Holy Roman Emperor – Tarascon (Tirol).
April 2. Sixth foal. 425,000foal. Tattersalls December. Demi O'Byrne. Closely related to the French dual 7f winner (including at 2 yrs) and listed-placed Mayano Sophia (by Rock Of Gibraltar) and half-brother to the quite useful Irish 10f winner Estephe (by Sadler's Wells), the Irish dual 9f Beucaire (by Entrepreneur) and the Irish 12f winner Perfecto (by Peintre Celebre). The dam, winner of the 7f Moyglare Stud Stakes and the Irish 1,000 Guineas, is a half-sister to the Group 2 Prix Guillaume d'Ornano winner Mister Monet and to the very useful 5f winner and Moyglare Stud Stakes and Cheveley Park Stakes placed Mala Mala. The second dam, Breyani (by Commanche Run), a useful winner at up to 2m, is a half-sister to 4 winners. *"He won the first two-year-old race of the season, at the Curragh in mid-March, he'll go to Cork next, then the Marble Hill and hopefully Royal Ascot after that. He has plenty of speed, he isn't over-big but I suppose that's the sire's influence. A good, strong, tough horse."*

1478. HIGHLY COMPOSED ★★★
b.f. Oratorio – Kanisfluh (Pivotal).
March 18. Third foal. 21,000Y. Doncaster St Leger. Ms L Foster. Half-sister to the fairly useful 2009 2-y-o 6f winner Bond Fastrac (by Monsieur Bond). The dam won 2 races over 6f and 7f at 2 yrs including the listed Flame Of Tara Stakes and is a half-sister on tone winner. The second dam, Kahina (by Warning), won 3 races at 3 yrs in Germany and is a half-sister to 3 winners. *"A good, strong filly that's done a few bits of work. She'd prefer quickish ground and I'd say she'd go six at the end of May but she's more of a seven furlong filly."*

1479. KUCHAROVA (IRE) ★★★
b.f. Danehill Dancer – Gates Of Eden (Kingmambo).
February 10. First foal. 68,000Y. Tattersalls October Book 1. Cormac McCormack. The dam, a modest 7f placed 2-y-o, is a half-sister to 3 minor winners here and abroad. The second dam, Amethyst (by Sadler's Wells), won the listed Irish 1,000 Guineas Trial, was second in the Irish 1,000 Guineas and is a sister to the Group 1 National Stakes and 2,000 Guineas winner King Of Kings and the Group 3 winner Lucky and a half-sister to 4 winners including the Group 2 Prix Robert Papin winner General Monash. The second dam, Zummerudd (by Habitat), is an unplaced sister to the Irish Group 3 and US Grade 3 winner Ancestral. *"She's quite a sharp filly and probably a sprinting two-year-old. She'd want fast ground and she should be racing in May. Not over-big, but strong."*

1480. MACHAPUTO (IRE) ★★★
b.c. Elusive City – Free Lance (Grand Lodge).
March 4. First foal. 56,000Y. Tattersalls October Book 2. De Burgh Equine. The dam is an unplaced half-sister to 3 winners including the Irish listed winner Flash McGahon. The second dam, Astuti (by Waajib), a quite useful 2-y-o 6f winner, is a half-sister to 6 winners including the Group 2 Kings Stand Stakes and Group 3 5f King George V Stakes winner The Tatling and the fairly useful 5.2f listed and 6f Tattersalls Breeders Stakes winner Amazing Dream. *"He looks very sharp and strong. A real two-year-old, he wants goodish ground and once he's got his ground we should be alright."*

1481. MR MOJITO (IRE) ★★★
ch.c. Danehill Dancer – Pina Colada
(Sabrehill).
April 19. Fourth foal. £44,000Y. Doncaster St Leger. F Stack. Brother to the fair 2009 7f placed 2-y-o Colonel Carter. The dam, a winner of 3 races here and in the USA including a minor stakes, was Grade 2 placed and is a half-sister 4 winners. The second dam, Drei (by Lyphard), is a placed full or half-sister to 3 winners. *"We quite like him, he seems to be sharp and his mother was quite fast. He'd want goodish ground, he's quite professional and five furlongs should suit him."* This colt won on his debut at Tipperary in mid-April.

1482. NUCALS STAR (IRE) ★★★
b.c. Danehill Dancer – May Kiersey
(Sadler's Wells).
January 20. First foal. 110,000Y. Tattersalls October Book 1. C McCormack. The dam is an unraced sister to the Group 3 Prix des Reservoirs winner and Group 1 French and Irish Oaks placed Gagnoa. The second dam, Gwynn (by Darshaan), is an unraced half-sister to 2 minor winners. *"He goes quite nicely, he wants ease in the ground and I'll set him off over six furlongs but he'll end up wanting seven furlongs or a mile. Quite a nice horse with a fair bit of size and scope."*

1483. WAVE OF APPLAUSE ★★★★
b.f. Royal Applause – Making Waves
(Danehill).
February 19. Third foal. £19,000Y. Doncaster St Leger. F Stack. Half-sister to the moderate 2-y-o 6f winner Top Flight Queen (by Bertolini). The dam is an unplaced half-sister to the French winner and Group 2 Prix de Malleret second Buoyant. The second dam, Wavey (by Kris), a quite useful 2-y-o 7f winner here, subsequently won a listed event in France and is a half-sister to 5 winners including two French listed winners. *"She's a very good mover, she's been going nicely and although she's probably got the speed to win over five we're more than likely going to start her at six. She should be quite nice, she's a big, strong, very mature filly with plenty of size and scope and we're very happy with her progress."*
TRAINERS' BARGAIN BUY

1484. UNNAMED ★★★
b.c. Piccolo – Alhufoof (Dayjur).
April 6. Seventh foal. 90,000Y. Tattersalls October Book 2. J O'Byrne. Half-brother to the Group 2 7f Lennox Stakes and 2-y-o Group 3 5f Molecomb Stakes winner Finjaan and to the fair 7f winner Fustaan (both by Royal Applause). The dam, a fairly useful 2-y-o 6f winner, was fourth in the Group 3 7f Nell Gwyn Stakes and is a half-sister to 5 winners including the dam of the 1,000 Guineas winner Lahan. The second dam, Cheval Volant (by Kris S), won 5 races from 5.5f to 8.5f in the USA including the Hollywood Starlet Stakes and the Las Virgines Stakes (both Grade 1 1m events). *"She's only just arrived in the yard, so it's too early to assess her."*

1485. UNNAMED ★★★
ch.f. Danehill Dancer – Lac Dessert
(Lac Ouimet).
April 9. Sixth foal. €120,000Y. Goffs Orby. C McCormack. Half-sister to the fair 1m and 12f winner Exclusive Air (by Affirmed). The dam, a dual 2-y-o 7f winner and subsequently a US stakes winner, is a half-sister to one winner. The second dam, Tiramisu (by Roberto), won at 3 yrs in France and is a half-sister to 7 winners including the dam of the Group 1 winners Pas de Reponse and Green Tune. *"A good-moving filly that'll take a bit of time, she's a good-bodied filly with plenty of size and scope. Hopefully she'll be in action in mid-summer and we're happy with what she's done so far."*

1486. UNNAMED ★★
b.c. Encosta De Lago – Mosaique Bleue
(Shirley Heights).
April 29. Thirteenth foal. €80,000Y. Goffs Orby. Form Bloodstock. Half-brother to the US Grade 1 Gulfstream Park Breeders Cup Handicap and Group 2 King Edward VII Stakes winner Subtle Power, to the quite useful 12f winner Make Haste, the minor Irish 13f winner Mosaique Beauty (all by Sadler's Wells), the useful 1m winner and listed-placed Arhaaf (by Danehill), the useful dual 7f winner Liberation (by Refuse To Bend), the fairly useful Irish 7f to 9f winner Almazhar (by Last Tycoon) and the quite useful 9f winner Poker School (by Night Shift). The dam is an unraced half-sister to the

Prix Royal-Oak winner Mersey and to the 10f Prix Saint-Alary winner Muncie. The second dam, Martingale (by Luthier), won twice over 1m at 3 yrs and is a half-sister to the Group 1 winners Mount Hagen and Madelia (herself dam of the Prix Saint-Alary winner Moonlight Dance). "He's a big horse for the second half of the year. He has quite a good action and a great temperament, but he'll definitely take a bit of time to mature."

1487. UNNAMED ★★
b.f. High Chaparral – Mystery Hill (Danehill).
March 4. Sixth foal. 34,000Y. Tattersalls October Book 2. J O'Byrne. Half-sister to the fairly useful 9f (at 2 yrs) and 10f winner Mystery Star (by Kris Kin), to the fair 5f and 6f winner Lilly Be (by Titus Livius), the fair 2-y-o 6f winner Shebang (by Trans Island) and the moderate 2-y-o 6f seller winner Flawless Diamond (by Indian Haven). The dam won once at 4 yrs in the UAE and is a half-sister to 3 other minor winners. The second dam, Tendermark (by Prince Tenderfoot), won over 1m (at 2 yrs) and 7f in Ireland and is a sister to the Group 3 Athasi Stakes winner Kemago and a half-sister to 4 winners. "She's not over-big, which makes her look more of a two-year-old than some of the High Chaparral's and she's cantering away, but knowing the sire she'll probably want seven furlongs or a mile. We're happy with her so far."

1488. UNNAMED ★★★
b.c. Ad Valorem – Non Dimenticar Me (Don't Forget Me).
April 26. Tenth foal. 38,000Y. Tattersalls October Book 2. De Burgh Equine. Half-brother to the useful 1m (including at 2 yrs) and listed 6f winner and Irish 1,000 Guineas second Dimenticata (by Danetime), to the useful listed 6f winner Master Fay, the fair 2-y-o 5f winner Louvolite (both by Fayruz), the useful 7f winner Zarin (by Inzar), the quite useful triple 6f winner Didn't We and the German winner at up to 11f Sambucan Daze (both by Mujadil). The dam, a modest 3-y-o 5f winner, stayed 7f and is a half-sister to 7 winners. The second dam, Amboselli (by Raga Navarro), was a fair 5f placed 2-y-o and a half-sister to 9 winners. "Quite a big horse that's thrived of late, he's quite a good mover and although he hasn't done any serious work yet he's pleased us with what we've seen to date."

SIR MICHAEL STOUTE

1489. ALBAASIL (IRE) ★★★★
b.c. Dansili – Wrong Key (Key Of Luck).
March 23. Third living foal. 320,000Y. Tattersalls October Book 1. Shadwell Estate Co. Half-brother to the useful 2009 2-y-o listed 5f Marble Hill Stakes winner Wrong Answer (by Verglas) and to the quite useful Irish 2-y-o 1m winner Wrong Number (by King's Best). The dam, an Irish 7f (at 2 yrs) and listed 1m winner, was placed in the Group 2 1m Goffs International Stakes and the Group 2 10f Pretty Polly Stakes and is a sister to the 7f (at 2 yrs) and Group 3 10f and 12f winner Right Key. The second dam, Sarifa (by Kahyasi), is an unraced half-sister to the Group 3 Prix du Palais Royal winner Saratan. (Hamdan Al Maktoum).

1490. APACE (IRE) ★★★★♣
b.f. Oasis Dream – Much Faster (Fasliyev).
April 6. Third foal. 350,000Y. Tattersalls October Book 1. Cheveley Park Stud. Sister to the useful Irish 2-y-o 5f winner Sugar Free. The dam won 4 races including the Group 2 6f Prix Robert Papin and the Group 3 5f Prix du Bois and was second in the Group 1 Prix Morny. The second dam, Interruption (by Zafonic), is an unraced half-sister to the Grade 2 La Prevoyante Handicap winner Interim and the Group 2 Prix Maurice de Gheest winner and smart broodmare Interval. (Cheveley Park Stud).

1491. AUDACIOUS ★★★
b.c. Motivator – Flash Of Gold (Darshaan).
February 13. Third foal. Half-brother to the fairly useful dual 7f winner (including at 2 yrs) Firestreak (by Green Desert) and to the fair 12f winner Going For Gold (by Motivator). The dam, a fair 12f placed maiden, is a half-sister to 4 winners including the smart Group 2 12f Ribblesdale Stakes and Group 2 13.3f Geoffrey Freer Stakes winner Phantom Gold. The second dam, Trying For Gold (by Northern Baby), was a useful 12f and 12.5f winner at 3 yrs. (The Queen).

1492. BUTTONHOLE ★★
b.f. Montjeu – Red Camellia (Polar Falcon).
May 31. Half-sister to the smart Group 1 Fillies' Mile and Group 2 10f Blandford Stakes winner Red Bloom, to the quite useful 2009 2-y-o 1m winner Botanist (both by Selkirk), the smart 10f, 12f and listed 13f winner Red Gala (by Sinndar) and the fair 9f winner Red Blossom by Green Desert). The dam, winner of the Group 3 7f Prestige Stakes and third in the French 1,000 Guineas, is a half-sister to the German middle-distance winner Red Bouquet. The second dam, Cerise Bouquet (by Mummy's Pet), a fair 2-y-o 5f winner, is a half-sister to the Irish St Leger winner and Breeders Cup Classic second Ibn Bey and to the Yorkshire Oaks winner Roseate Tern. (Cheveley Park Stud).

1493. CHILLED ★★★♣
b.c. Iceman – Irresistible (Cadeaux Genereux).
March 28. Fourth foal. Closely related to the quite useful 2009 2-y-o 7f winner Thrill and to the very smart 7f (at 2 yrs) and Group 3 7f Nell Gwyn Stakes winner and Coronation Stakes and Falmouth Stakes second Infallible (by Pivotal). The dam was a fairly useful 5f (at 2 yrs) and listed 6f winner and is a half-sister to one winner. The second dam, Polish Romance (by Danzig), a minor 7f winner in the USA, is a sister to the US stakes winner Polish Love and a half-sister to 3 minor winners. (Cheveley Park Stud).

1494. CRYSTAL ETOILE ★★★
b.f. Dansili – Crystal Star (Mark Of Esteem).
April 29. Fourth foal. Half-sister to the smart Group 2 12f Pride Stakes and Group 3 10.3f Middleton Stakes winner Crystal Capella (by Cape Cross) and to the fairly useful 1m and 10f winner Sandor (by Fantastic Light). The dam, winner of the listed Radley Stakes and second in the Group 3 Fred Darling Stakes, is a half-sister to 5 winners. The second dam, Crystal Cavern (by Be My Guest), a fairly useful 2-y-o 7f winner here and subsequently a dual winner in Canada, is a half-sister to 5 winners including the French 1,000 Guineas winner Rose Gypsy.

1495. DENY ★★★♣
ch.c. Mr Greeley – Sulk (Selkirk).
April 22. Fifth foal. 150,000Y. Tattersalls October Book 1. John Warren. Half-brother to the UAE dual 7f winner Ibn Battuta (by Seeking The Gold) and a minor winner abroad by Kingmambo. The dam, a smart winner of the Group 1 1m Prix Marcel Boussac and the Group 1 10f Nassau Stakes, is a half-sister to 4 winners including the Group 1 Hong Kong Cup and Group 2 Beresford Stakes winner Eagle Mountain and the smart 1m listed winner Wallace. The second dam, Masskana (by Darshaan), a minor 9f and 10f winner in France, is a half-sister to 3 winners including the US Grade 3 Arcadia Handicap winner Madjaristan and the Group 2 Gallinule Stakes winner Massyar. (Highclere Thoroughbreds).

1496. DE RIGUEUR ★★★
b.c. Montjeu – Exclusive (Polar Falcon).
March 30. Seventh foal. Half-brother to the Group 1 1m Matron Stakes and Group 2 Celebration Mile winner Echelon (by Danehill), to the dual Group 2 1m winner Chic (by Machiavellian) and the fair 9f winner Expressive (by Falbrav). The dam, winner of the Group 1 1m Coronation Stakes, is a half-sister to the 2,000 Guineas winner and Derby fourth Entrepreneur, the smart Cheshire Oaks winner and Epsom Oaks second Dance a Dream, the very useful middle-distance listed winner Sadler's Image and the useful French 2-y-o listed 7f winner Irish Order. The second dam, Exclusive Order (by Exclusive Native), won 4 races in France including the Group 2 6.5f Prix Maurice de Gheest and the Group 3 7f Prix de la Porte Maillot. (Cheveley Park Stud).

1497. DUMBARTON (IRE) ★★★
br.c. Danehill Dancer – Scottish Stage (Selkirk).
February 9. First foal. The dam, a listed 10f winner, was second in the Group 1 12f Irish Oaks and is a half-sister to 3 winners including the fairly useful 10f winner and Group 3 placed Voice Coach. The second dam, Drama Class (by Caerleon), a useful 10.2f winner, is a half-sister to the Group 2 10.3f winner Stage Gift. (Ballymacoll Stud Farm Ltd).

1498. ELAN ★★★★
b.f. Dansili – Chic (Machiavellian).
February 8. First foal. The dam won the dual Group 2 1m Celebration Mile twice and is a half-sister to the Group 1 1m Matron Stakes winner Echelon. The second dam, Exclusive

(Polar Falcon) winner of the Group 1 1m Coronation Stakes, is a half-sister to the 2,000 Guineas winner and Derby fourth Entrepreneur, the smart Cheshire Oaks winner and Epsom Oaks second Dance a Dream, the very useful middle-distance listed winner Sadler's Image and the useful French 2-y-o listed 7f winner Irish Order. (Cheveley Park Stud).

1499. FIORENTE (IRE) ★★★
br.c. Monsun – Desert Bloom (Pilsudski).
February 26. Half-brother to the fairly useful 5f (at 2 yrs) and dual 6f winner Masada (by Key Of Luck) and to the quite useful 2-y-o 6f winner Rashanak (by Spinning World). The dam is an unraced half-sister to a winner in Japan. The second dam, Desert Beauty (by Green Desert), a fairly useful 7f and 1m winner, is a half-sister to the top-class filly Islington. (Ballymacoll Stud Farm Ltd).

1500. FIRST BATTALION (IRE) ★★
b.c. Sadler's Wells – Mubkera (Nashwan)
April 11. Half-brother to the useful 1m (at 2 yrs) and 10f winner Aqwaal (by Red Ransom) and to the minor French 12f winner Manjam (by Almutawakel). The dam, a quite useful 1m winner (at 2 yrs) and listed 10f placed, is a half-sister to several winners. The second dam, Na Ayim (by Shirley Heights), a modest 2-y-o 6f winner, is a half-sister to several winners out of a half-sister to the dam of Rainbow Quest and Slightly Dangerous.

1501. FLAMING ARROW (IRE) ★★
b.c. Sadler's Wells – Pescia (Darshaan).
April 19. Sixth foal. Closely related to the useful 10f winner and listed-placed Stately Home (by Montjeu). The dam, a winner over 10f and 12f in France, was Group 3 placed and is a half-sister to 4 winners. The second dam, Lambada (by Lyphard), won once at 3 yrs in France and was listed-placed and is a half-sister to 4 winners including the champion 2-y-o Tobougg.

1502. FOCAL ★★★
b.f. Pivotal – Coy (Danehill).
February 18. Third foal. Sister to the unplaced 2009 2-y-o Redden. The dam won over 6f (at 2 yrs) and the listed 1m Valiant Stakes and is a sister to the fairly useful triple 7f winner Presumptive and a half-sister to the very useful dual listed winner Il Warrd (by Pivotal). The second dam, Demure (by Machiavellian), is an unraced half-sister to the very smart colt Diffident, winner of the Group 3 6f Diadem Stakes, the Group 3 6f Prix de Ris-Orangis and the listed 7f European Free Handicap. (Cheveley Park Stud).

1503. HAYMANA (IRE) ★★★
b.f. Pivotal – Briolette (Sadler's Wells).
February 18. Second foal. 650,000Y. Tattersalls October Book 1. Shadwell Estate Co. The dam won the listed 10f Trigo Stakes, was second in the Group 3 12f Princess Royal Stakes and is a sister to the Irish listed winner Peach Out Of Reach and a half-sister to 6 winners including the Grade 1 12f Breeders Cup Turf, Grade 1 12f Japan Cup, Group 1 10f Grosser Preis von Baden and Group 1 10f Coral-Eclipse Stakes winner Pilsudski and the champion Japanese filly Fine Motion. The second dam, Cocotte (by Troy), a very useful 10.2f winner, was second in the Group 3 Prix de Psyche, fourth in the Group 2 10f Nassau Stakes and is a half-sister to the listed winner Gay Captain. (Hamdan Al Maktoum).

1504. HOT TICKET (IRE) ★★★
ch.f. Selkirk – Drama Class (Caerleon).
March 22. Sister to the listed 10f winner and Group 1 12f Irish Oaks second Scottish Stage and half-sister to the fair 2009 2-y-o 1m winner Eleanora Duse (by Azamour), the fairly useful 10f winner Voice Coach (by Alhaarth) and the quite useful 10f winner Namibian Orator (by Cape Cross). The dam, a useful 10.2f winner, is a half-sister to the Group 2 10.3f winner Stage Gift. The second dam, Stage Struck (by Sadler's Wells), a quite useful 12f winner, is a sister to the high-class Group 1 7f Dewhurst Stakes winner (in a dead-heat) Prince of Dance and to the useful middle-distance winners Ballet Prince and Golden Ball. (Ballymacoll Stud Farm).

1505. JUSTLOOKDONTTOUCH (IRE) ★★
ch.f. Galileo – Hellenic (Darshaan).
May 17. Closely related to 6 winners by Sadler's Wells including the high-class Grade 1 Breeders Cup Filly & Mare Turf, Group 1 1m Nassau Stakes and Group 1 Yorkshire Oaks

winner Islington, the very smart 10f performer Greek Dance, the smart stayer Election Day and the very useful listed 10f winner New Morning and half-brother to the useful 7f and 1m winner Desert Beauty (by Green Desert) and the useful 10.3f winner Mountain High (by Danehill). The dam won the Yorkshire Oaks and was second in the St Leger. She is a half-sister to numerous winners including the Group 2 Lanson Champagne Vintage Stakes second Golden Wave. The second dam, Grecian Sea (by Homeric), won once in France, was fourth in the Group 3 7f Prix du Calvados and is a half-sister to 8 winners. (Ballymacoll Stud Farm).

1506. LEVITATE ★★★★
ch.c. *Pivotal – Soar (Danzero).*
March 19. Second foal. Half-brother to the quite useful 2009 2-y-o 6f winner Racy (by Medicean). The dam, winner of the Group 2 6f Lowther Stakes and the Group 3 Princess Margaret Stakes at 2 yrs, is a half-sister to numerous winners including the very smart 6f and 7f winner of 7 races Feet So Fast. The second dam, Splice (by Sharpo), a smart winner of the listed 6f Abernant Stakes, is a full or half-sister to several winners including the fairly useful 1m winner and subsequent Italian winner Alfujairah. (Cheveley Park Stud).

1507. LINDORAS GRACE ★★★
b.f. *Galileo – Lines Of Beauty (Line In The Sand).*
March 15. €220,000Y. Arqana Deauville August. C de Moubray. Half-sister to the smart 8.5f (at 2 yrs), 10f, 12f and listed 14f winner Linas Selection (by Selkirk). The dam won 9 races at 2 to 5 yrs in the USA including the Grade 3 9f Gardenia Stakes and is a half-sister to the US stakes winner Superduper Miss. The second dam, Duper (by Garthorn), is an unraced half-sister to 5 winners.

1508. MAJOUNES DREAM ★★★
b.f. *Oasis Dream – Majoune (Take Risks).*
April 16. Sixth foal. 100,000Y. Tattersalls October Book 1. Not sold. Half-sister to the 7f (at 2 yrs) and German Group 3 11f winner Majoune's Song (by Singspiel), to the fair 10.2f winner and German listed-placed Maria's Magic and the fair 12f winner Magic Moth (both by Mtoto). The dam won 4 races including the Group 3 11f Prix Corrida and is a half-sister to 8 winners including the Group 3 1m Prix des Reservoirs winner and Group 1 10.5f Prix de Diane second Mousse Glacee. The second dam, Madame Est Sortie (by Longleat), won the Group 3 10.5f Prix Penelope and is a half-sister to 5 winners.

1509. MAKE LIGHT (USA) ★★★
b.f. *Empire Maker – Light Jig (Danehill).*
April 19. Third foal. Half-sister to the quite useful 2-y-o 7f winner Treble Jig (by Gone West). The dam, a US Grade 1 10f Yellow Ribbon Stakes winner, is a half-sister to numerous winners including the very useful French 2-y-o listed 1m winner Battle Dore. The second dam, Nashmeel (by Blushing Groom), was a very smart winner of three races over 1m including the Group 2 Prix d'Astarte and was second in the Prix Jacques le Marois (to Miesque), the Yellow Ribbon Invitational and the Matriarch Stakes. (Khalid Abdulla).

1510. MOONSCAPE ★★★★
ch.c. *Pivotal – Moon Goddess (Rainbow Quest).*
April 5. Fifth foal. The dam, a fairly useful 1m winner, is a half-sister to the Group 1 Eclipse Stakes and Group 1 Lockinge Stakes winner and sire Medicean. The second dam, Mystic Goddess (by Storm Bird), a fairly useful winner of the listed 7f Sweet Solera Stakes at 2 yrs, was placed in the Queen Mary Stakes, the Cherry Hinton Stakes and the Rockfel Stakes and is a half-sister to the smart Group 1 Gran Criterium winner Sanam and to the South African Grade 2 winner Shaybani. (Cheveley Park Stud).

1511. MUTAYASER ★★
b.c. *Shamardal – Borgia (Acatenango).*
March 20. Seventh foal. 230,000Y. Tattersalls October Book 1. Shadwell Estate Co. Half-brother to the quite useful French 12f winner Bahama Bay (by Dansili), to the quite useful 14f winner Bora Blues (by Peintre Celebre), the fair 14f winner Born Wild (by Sadler's Wells) and the minor dual German winner Boreas Rush (by Green Desert). The dam was a high-class winner of the Group 1 German Derby, the Group 1 Grosser Preis von Baden and the Hong Kong Vase (all 12f events). The second dam, Britannia (by Tarim), won the Group

2 11f German St Leger and the Group 3 2m Oleander Rennen. (Hamdan Al Maktoum).

1512. PIECE D'OR (IRE) ★★★
gr.f. Verglas – Gold Bar (Barathea).
March 18. The dam, a 10f placed maiden, is closely related to the high-class Group 1 7f Dewhurst Stakes dead-heater Prince of Dance and to the Group 2 Scottish Derby winner Princely Venture. The second dam, Sun Princess (by English Prince), a top-class winner of the Oaks, the St Leger and the Yorkshire Oaks, is a half-sister to the high-class middle-distance colt Saddlers Hall. (Ballymacoll Stud Farm).

1513. POPE LEO (IRE) ★★★
ch.c. Medicean – Frizzante (Efisio).
April 22. Half-brother to the fair 2009 6f placed 2-y-o Pin Cushion (by Pivotal) and to the quite useful 2-y-o 7f winner Greensward (by Green Desert). The dam won 7 races including the Group 1 July Cup and is a half-sister to 4 winners including the Stewards Cup winner Zidane and the dual 6f listed winner Firenze. The second dam, Juliet Bravo (by Glow), a modest 2-y-o 5f winner, is a half-sister to the very smart filly Donna Viola, a winner of 11 races here and abroad including the Grade 1 Yellow Ribbon Handicap, the Grade 1 Gamely Handicap and the Group 2 Prix de l'Opera.

1514. PROFONDO ROSSO (IRE) ★★★
b.c. Red Ransom – Desert Beauty (Green Desert).
March 24. Brother to the useful 7f and 1m winner and listed-placed Red Dune and half-brother to the quite useful 7f (at 2 yrs) and 10f winner Rose Of Petra (by Golan) and to a winner in Japan by Machiavellian. The dam, a useful 7f and 1m winner, is a half-sister to the Yorkshire Oaks and Nassau Stakes winner Islington, to the smart stayer Election Day and the smart 10f performer Greek Dance. The second dam, Hellenic (by Darshaan), won the Yorkshire Oaks and the Ribblesdale Stakes and is a half-sister to 8 winners.

1515. PURSUITOFEXCELLENCE (IRE) ★★★
b.c. Galileo – Lila (Zafonic).
February 25. Third foal. 550,000Y. Tattersalls October Book 1. Sir Robert Ogden. The dam, a 3-y-o 1m winner, is a sister to the 2-y-o 1m winner and Group 2 King Edward VII Stakes second Zafonium and a half-sister to 7 winners including the very useful winner of 7 races (including the Group 3 10f Gran Premio Citta di Napoli) Revere. The second dam, Bint Pasha (by Affirmed), won the Group 1 12f Yorkshire Oaks, the Group 1 12f Prix Vermeille and the Group 2 10f Pretty Polly Stakes.

1516. QUIXOTIC ★★★★
ch.f. Pivotal – Virtuous (Exit To Nowhere).
April 30. Sister to the Group 1 1m Lockinge Stakes and dual listed winner Virtual and to the quite useful 10f winner Virtuosity, closely related to the very smart 2-y-o Group 2 6f Coventry Stakes winner and Group 1 6f Middle Park Stakes third Iceman (by Polar Falcon) and half-sister to the quite useful 10f winner Peace (by Sadler's Wells) and the fair 2-y-o 6f winner Liberty (by Singspiel). The dam, a fairly useful 2-y-o 1m winner, was third in the listed 11.5f Oaks Trial and is a sister to one winner. The second dam, Exclusive Virtue (by Shadeed), a fairly useful 2-y-o 7f winner, stayed 12f and is a half-sister to 8 winners including the 2,000 Guineas winner and Derby fourth Entrepreneur and the Coronation Stakes winner Exclusive. (Cheveley Park Stud).

1517. RAAHIN (IRE) ★★★
b.c. Oasis Dream – Sparkle Of Stones (Sadler's Wells).
March 24. Second foal. 200,000Y. Tattersalls October Book 1. Shadwell Estate Co. The dam is an unraced sister to the useful French 1m and 11f winner Synergetic and a half-sister to 6 winners including the very smart Group 3 7f Greenham Stakes winner and 2,000 Guineas second Enrique and the smart sprinter/miler Piperi. The second dam, Gwydion (by Raise A Cup), won the Group 3 5f Queen Mary Stakes, the listed 6f Hackwood Stakes and the listed 5f Bentinck Stakes and is a half-sister to 5 winners. (Hamdan Al Maktoum).

1518. REGAL HEIRESS ★★★★★
b.f. Pivotal – Regal Rose (Danehill).
March 5. Fourth foal. Half-sister to the fairly useful 2-y-o 6f winner Regal Royale and to the fair 6f (including at 2 yrs) and 5f winner of 7 races Regal Riband (by Fantastic Light). The dam won both her starts including the Group

1 6f Cheveley Park Stakes. She is a sister to the Japanese 10f stakes winner Generalist and a half-sister to 7 winners including the very useful listed-placed Regal Flush. The second dam, Ruthless Rose (by Conquistador Cielo), ran twice unplaced and is a half-sister to 9 winners including the high-class miler Shaadi. (Cheveley Park Stud).

1519. STAR OF DANCE (IRE) ★★★★
b.c. *Danehill Dancer – Miss Honorine (Highest Honor).*
April 16. Fourth foal. 370,000Y. Tattersalls October Book 1. Sir Robert Ogden. Half-brother to the quite useful 2009 2-y-o 7f winner Admire The View (by Dubawi) and to the fairly useful 2-y-o 6f winner Master Chef (by Oasis Dream). The dam won 4 races at 3 and 4 yrs in Ireland including three listed events from 1m to 10f and is a half-sister to 7 winners. The second dam, Nini Princesse (by Niniski), won 6 races from 2 to 4 yrs in France and is a sister to the US Grade 1 winner Louis Cyphre and a half-sister to 7 winners including the Group 2 winner Psychobabble.

1520. STAR VALUE (IRE) ★★
b.f. *Danehill Dancer – Shemaka (Nishapour).*
February 9. Closely related to the French listed 10f winner Shemala (by Danehill) and half-sister to the French Group 3 10f and Group 3 15f winner Shemima (by Dalakhani), the French 9f winner and listed-placed Shediyama (by Red Ransom) and a hurdles winner by Unfuwain. The dam was a smart filly and winner of the Group 1 10.5f Prix de Diane, the Group 3 10f Prix de la Nonette and the Group 3 9f Prix de Conde. The second dam, Shashna (by Blakeney), was unplaced in both her races (over 10f) and is a half-sister to the Grade 1 11f Bowling Green Handicap winner Sharannpour, the Group 1 12f Grand Prix de Saint-Cloud winner Shakapour and to the dam of the dual Derby winner Shahrastani. (The Queen).

1521. STRIKING VEIL (USA) ★★
b.f. *Smart Strike – Yashmak (Danzig).*
April 22. Half-sister to the quite useful 7f to 10f and subsequent Australian 7f winner Sound Of Nature (by Chester House) and to the useful 3-y-o 1m winner (on her only start) Eyes Only (by Distant View). The dam, winner of the Grade 1 10f Flower Bowl Invitational Handicap and the Group 2 12f Ribblesdale Stakes, is a sister to the Great Voltigeur Stakes winner Dushyantor and a half-sister to the Epsom Derby and Irish Derby winner Commander in Chief, the champion 2-y-o and miler Warning and the Irish Derby second Deploy. The second dam, Slightly Dangerous (by Roberto), a very smart filly and winner of the 7.3f Fred Darling Stakes, was second in the Oaks to Time Charter and is a half-sister to the dams of the Arc winner and top class sire Rainbow Quest and the Dewhurst Stakes dead-heater Scenic. (Khalid Abdulla).

1522. THE MONGOOSE ★★★
b.c. *Montjeu – Angara (Alzao).*
January 27. The dam, winner of Grade 1 10f Beverly D Stakes and Grade 1 9f Diana Stakes in the USA, is a half-sister to numerous winners including the French Group 2 Prix Corrida winner Actrice. The second dam, Ange Bleu (by Alleged), was placed at 3 yrs in France and is a half-sister to 10 winners including the Group 3 Prix de Psyche winner and French 1,000 Guineas and French Oaks placed Agathe (herself dam of the Grade/Group 1 winners Artiste Royale and Aquarelliste), to the Breeders Cup Classic winner Arcangues and the dam of the 1,000 Guineas winner Cape Verdi.

1523. ZYKINA ★★★★
ch.f. *Pivotal – Russian Rhythm (Kingmambo).*
February 6. Third foal. Sister to Safina, placed third over 7f on her only start at 2 yrs in 2009. The dam won the 1,000 Guineas, Coronation Stakes, Nassau Stakes and Lockinge Stakes and is a half-sister to several winners including the 2-y-o Group 2 1m Royal Lodge Stakes winner Perfectperformance. The second dam, Balistroika (Nijinsky), is an unraced half-sister to numerous winners including Park Appeal (winner of the Cheveley Park Stakes and the Moyglare Stud Stakes and the dam of Cape Cross), Alydaress (Irish Oaks) and Desirable (winner of the Cheveley Park Stakes and the dam of Shadayid). (Cheveley Park Stud).

1524. UNNAMED ★★★★
b.f. *Street Cry – Camlet (Green Desert).*
March 7. Half-sister to the quite useful 2-y-o 6f winner Cheviot (by Rahy). The dam, a fairly

useful dual 6f (including at 2 yrs), is a half-sister to the Group 1 Fillies Mile and Irish 1,000 Guineas winner Gossamer, to the high-class Breeders Cup Mile, Irish 2,000 Guineas and Queen Anne Stakes winner Barathea and the smart colt Zabar, winner of the Prix du Chemin de Fer du Nord, the Prix du Muguet and the Prix Perth – all Group 3 1m events. The second dam, Brocade (by Habitat), was a high-class filly at up to 1m, winning five races including the Group 1 7f Prix de la Foret and the Group 3 7f Bisquit Cognac Challenge Stakes. She is a sister to the very useful 2-y-o Cause Celebre and a half-sister to 5 winners.

1525. UNNAMED ★★★
b.f. *King's Best – Contiguous (Danzig).*
March 7. Sister to the French 3-y-o listed-placed 10f winner Nearby and half-sister to the very smart 7f (at 2 yrs) and Group 3 1m winner Confront (by Nayef). The dam is an unraced three-parts sister to Reams of Verse, winner of the Oaks and the Group 1 Fillies Mile and a half-sister to the Group 1 10f Coral Eclipse Stakes and Group 1 10f Phoenix Champion Stakes winner Elmaamul. The second dam, Modena (by Roberto), is an unraced half-sister to the smart 2-y-o 7f winner and Queen Elizabeth II Stakes third Zaizafon – herself dam of Zafonic. (Khalid Abdulla).

1526. UNNAMED ★★★
ch.c. *Shamardal – Dynacam (Dynaformer).*
May 3. The dam, a quite useful 2-y-o 10f winner, is a half-sister to the champion US 2-y-o colt and Breeders Cup Juvenile winner Action This Day. The second dam, Najecam (by Trempolino), a winner over 6f at 2 yrs here and later a smart US 1m/9f winner, was placed in two Grade 2 events in the USA, is a sister to the listed-placed winner Lady Ilsley (herself dam of the Irish Group 3 and UAE Group 2 winner Lord Admiral) and a half-sister to 5 winners.

1527. UNNAMED ★★★★
b.f. *Hurricane Run – Ithaca (Distant View).*
April 3. Second foal. Half-sister to the high-class 7f (at 2 yrs) and Group 2 Celebration Mile winner and Group 1 Queen Elizabeth II Stakes second Zacinto (by Dansili). The dam, a useful 2-y-o 7f winner and second in the Group 3 7f Prestige Stakes, is a half-sister to several winners including the useful dual 10f winner Many Volumes. The second dam, Reams Of Verse (by Nureyev), won the Oaks, the Fillies Mile, the Musidora Stakes and the May Hill Stakes and is a half-sister to numerous winners including the high-class Group 1 10f Coral Eclipse Stakes and Group 1 10f Phoenix Champion Stakes winner Elmaamul. (Khalid Abdulla).

1528. UNNAMED ★★★
b.c. *Araafa – Majestic Sakeena (King's Best).*
February 12. Second foal. Half-brother to Nouriya (by Danehill Dancer), placed fourth over 1m on her only start at 2 yrs in 2009. The dam is an unraced half-sister to the German listed sprint winner Shy Lady (herself dam of the St James's Palace Stakes winner Zafeen) and to the French listed winner Sweet Story. The second dam, Shy Danceuse (by Groom Dancer), a minor French 1m winner, is a half-sister to the very smart colt Diffident, winner of the Group 3 6f Diadem Stakes, the Group 3 6f Prix de Ris-Orangis and the listed 7f European Free Handicap.

1529. UNNAMED ★★★
b.c *Arch – Quickfire (Dubai Millennium).*
February 9. The dam, a useful 2-y-o 7f winner, was second in the Group 3 Musidora Stakes and the Group 3 7f Oak Tree Stakes and is a half-sister to 2 winners. The second dam, Daring Miss (by Sadler's Wells), won 4 races in France including the Group 2 12f Grand Prix de Chantilly and is a half-sister to several winners including the Group 3 12f Prix de Royaumont winner Apogee. (Khalid Abdulla).

1530. UNNAMED ★★★
b.f. *Dansili – Quiff (Sadler's Wells).*
January 8. First foal. The dam won the Group 1 12f Yorkshire Oaks and was second in the St Leger and is a sister to the very useful 10f winner and Group 3 placed Arabian Gulf. The second dam, Wince (by Selkirk), won the 1,000 Guineas and the Group 3 Fred Darling Stakes and is a half-sister to the very smart middle-distance winner Ulundi, the fairly useful 10f winner Flitwick and the French 10f winner Fleeting Glimpse.

1531. UNNAMED ★★
gr.f. Dalakhani – Soviet Moon (Sadler's Wells).
March 6. Fourth foal. Half-sister to Workforce (by King's Best), a promising 7f winner on his only start at 2 yrs in 2009. The dam is an unraced sister to 3 winners including the Group 1 Racing Post Trophy and Group 1 St Leger winner Brian Boru and the listed 1m winner Kitty O'Shea and a half-sister to the Group 3 12.5f Prix de Royallieu winner Moon Search. The second dam, Eva Luna (by Alleged), won the Group 3 14.6f Park Hill Stakes and is a half-sister to several winners.

1532. UNNAMED ★★★
b.c. Street Cry – Talented (Bustino).
April 30. Half-brother to the very useful French 1m (at 2 yrs) and triple listed winner at up 10 15f and Group 1 Criterium International fourth Friston Forest (by Barathea), to the 7f and 1m winner Flawed Genius (by Fasliyev), the 2-y-o 5f winner Secret Pride (by Green Desert) and the 2-y-o 7f winner Zaeema (by Zafonic) – all 3 fairly useful. The dam, a very useful filly, won three races including the Group 2 10f Sun Chariot Stakes, was second in the Ribblesdale Stakes and is a half-sister to 6 winners. The second dam, Triple Reef (by Mill Reef), is an unraced half-sister to 13 winners including the smart middle-distance winners Maysoon, Richard of York, Three Tails (dam of the high-class middle-distance colt Tamure) and Third Watch.

1533. UNNAMED ★★★
b.c. Dansili – Tarocchi (Affirmed).
February 10. Brother to the French 2-y-o 7f and subsequent US Grade 1 1m Matriarch Stakes winner Price Tag and half-sister to the French 9f winner Perfect Hand (by Barathea) and the modest 9f winner Eagle Nebula (by Observatory). The dam, a minor French 10.5f winner, is a half-sister to numerous winners including the very useful Group 2 12f Prix de Malleret winner Privity and the Group 3 9f Prix Saint Roman winner Zindari. The second dam, Sylph (by Alleged), was a very useful winner of the Group 3 12f Princess Royal Stakes, is a sister to the Irish St Leger winner Leading Counsel and closely related to the very useful middle-distance stakes winner Present The Colors. (Khalid Abdulla).

1534. UNNAMED ★★★★
b.c. Dansili – Valencia (Kenmare).
February 18. Brother to the useful 2-y-o 6f winner and Group 3 7f placed Cantabria and half-brother to the useful 2-y-o 5f and listed 6f winner Deportivo (by Night Shift), the useful 2-y-o listed 5f winner Irish Vale (by Wolfhound), the fairly useful 2-y-o 7f and 7.6f winner La Coruna (by Deploy), the quite useful dual 5f (including at 2 yrs) Affluent (by Oasis Dream) and the fair 7f winner Subadar (by Zamindar). The dam, placed over 1m at 2 yrs on her only start, is a half-sister to numerous winners including the dual US Grade 1 winner Wandesta, the Group 2 12f winner De Quest and the smart 10f to 15f winner Turners Hill. The second dam, De Stael (by Nijinsky), a fairly useful dual 7f winner at 2 yrs, is a sister to the high-class middle-distance colts Peacetime and Quiet Fling. (Khalid Abdulla).

TOM TATE

1535. BREATHLESS STORM (USA) ★★★★
ch.c. Storm Cat – Takesmybreathaway (Gone West).
February 29. Fifth foal. $300,000Y. Keeneland September. Tom Tate. Closely related to the Irish 2-y-o Group 3 Killavullan Stakes, 3-y-o Group 3 10f Kilternan Stakes and subsequent US Grade 1 10f Suburban Handicap winner Frost Giant (by Giant's Causeway). The dam is an unplaced half-sister to 5 winners including the listed John Of Gaunt Stakes winner and Grade 2 placed Mutakddim. The second dam, Oscillate (by Seattle Slew), a sprint winner of one race in the USA, is a half-sister to the Grade 1 Breeders Cup Juvenile winner Rhythm, to the US Grade 3 Affectionately Handicap winner Get Lucky and the US Grade 1 placed Offbeat. (Mrs F H Hay). *"He's a progressive type and he should be racing reasonably early. A good, big sort, he's got scope but I should think he'll do something in the first half of the season."*

1536. DEFENCE OF DURESS (IRE) ★★★★
b.c. Motivator – Ultra Finesse (Rahy).
February 13. €230,000Y. Goffs Orby. Tenth foal. Tom Tate. Half-sister to the useful 2-y-o 6f winner and listed placed Proceed With Care (by Danehill), the useful 6f and 7f winner and listed-placed Dramatic Quest (by Zafonic), the fair 7f (at 2 yrs) and 1m winner Debonnaire

(by Anabaa) and a minor 4-y-o winner in the USA by Sunday Silence. The dam, a useful French 8.5f and 10f winner, was second in the Group 2 12f Prix de Malleret and is a half-sister to 6 winners including the top-class colt Suave Dancer (winner of the Prix de l'Arc de Triomphe, the Prix du Jockey Club and the Phoenix Champion Stakes) and Suave Tern (Gran Premio d'Italia second and French 10f listed winner). The second dam, Suavite (by Alleged), a winner of four races and second in the Grade 3 7f Comely Stakes, is a half-sister to 4 winners. (Mrs F H Hay). *"A nice-moving, staying type of horse who will mature into a nice three-year-old but nevertheless he should be running in the second half of the season. A very nice, good-sized, quality horse."*

1537. EAGLE ROCK (IRE) ★★★
b.c. High Chaparral – Silk Fan (Unfuwain).
April 4. Second foal. 36,000Y. Tattersalls October Book 1. Tom Tate. The dam, a fairly useful triple 7f winner (including at 2 yrs), is a half-sister to 2 winners. The second dam, Alikhlas (by Lahib), a fair 3-y-o 1m winner, is a half-sister to 3 winners including the listed winner and Group 2 Lancashire Oaks second Sahool. (The Ivy Syndicate). *"He's similar to the previous two-year-old Defence of Duress in that he's a quality mover and a good size, he'll be a late two-year-old but he should make up into a better three-year-old."*

1538. ELAND ALLY ★★
b.c. Striking Ambition – Dream Rose (Anabaa).
February 13. First foal. £13,000Y. Doncaster St Leger. Tom Tate. The dam was a quite useful 1m winner. The second dam, Hiddnah (by Affirmed), a fairly useful 2-y-o 7f winner, was listed-placed three times and is a half-sister to 5 winners including the Group 1 Sun Chariot Stakes winner Majestic Roi and the US 2-y-o winner and Grade 3 third Heza Gone West. (The Ivy Syndicate). *"A good-sized colt that's a bit behind the others but I think he'll catch them up. It wouldn't surprise me if he doesn't get going by the middle of summer. He's not without ability."*

1539. HOBBESIAN WAR ★★★
b.c. Danehill Dancer – Bold Classic (Pembroke).
May 2. Second foal. 52,000Y. Tattersalls December. Paul Moulton. Half-brother to the unplaced 2009 2-y-o New World Symphony (by War Chant). The dam, a minor US winner of 6 races, is a half-sister to the 1,000 Guineas and Group 2 Rockfel Stakes winner Speciosa and a half-sister to the US Grade 3 stakes winner of 11 races and Grade 1 placed Major Rhythm. The second dam, Specifically (by Sky Classic), won once at 2 yrs in the USA and is a half-sister to 7 winners including the Group 1 Champion Stakes, Grand Prix de Saint-Cloud and Hong Kong Cup winner Pride. (Mr P Moulton). *"A big, strong horse who is coming together well. One for the middle of the season and he'll have the speed for six furlongs."*

1540. LOOSE QUALITY (USA) ★★★★
b.c. Elusive Quality – Djebel Amour (Mt Livermore).
April 15. Fourth foal. $160,000Y. Keeneland September. Tom Tate. Closely related to the useful 2-y-o 6f winner Dodge City (by Gone West) and half-brother to the Irish 2-y-o 7f winner and Group 3 Irish 1,000 Guineas second Smart Coco (by Smarty Jones). The dam, a 1m winner in the USA, is a half-sister to the smart 2-y-o Group 2 7f Champagne Stakes winner Almushahar. The second dam, Sayyedati (by Shadeed), won the Group 1 7f Moyglare Stud Stakes and the Group 1 6f Cheveley Park Stakes at 2 yrs, the 1,000 Guineas and Prix Jacques le Marois at 3 yrs and the Sussex Stakes at 5 yrs. She is a full or half-sister to numerous winners including the multiple Group 1 winner Golden Snake. (Mrs F H Hay). *"As his name suggests he's a quality horse who will be showing class and ability from the middle of the season onwards and over six and seven furlongs."*

1541. MY SINGLE MALT (IRE) ★★★★
b.c. Danehill Dancer – Slip Dance (Celtic Swing).
January 22. First foal. €175,000Y. Arqana Deauville August. Not sold. The dam, a dual sprint listed winner, was second in the Group 3 7f Sweet Solera Stakes and is a half-sister to 5 winners including the listed 6f (at 2 yrs) and listed 7f winner and Group 3 placed Misu Bond. The second dam, Hawala (by Warning), a useful 8.3f winner, is a half-sister to the French Group 3 winner Afaf. (Mrs F H Hay). *"A big, strong, progressive type who should be ready*

early. He's a powerful horse with quality who I see as a miler later on, but he'll have enough speed for early two-year-old races."

1542. ON THE HIGH TOPS (IRE) ★★★
b.c. Kheleyf – Diplomats Daughter (Unfuwain).
February 25. Second foal. £34,000Y. Doncaster St Leger. Tom Tate. The dam, a quite useful Irish 3-y-o 10f winner, is a half-sister to 6 winners here and abroad. The second dam, Quest Of Fire (by Rainbow Quest), won once at 3 yrs in France and is a half-sister to the Group 3 Prix Cleopatre winner and smart broodmare Brooklyn's Dance and the dams of the Derby winner Authorized and the Group 1 Grand Criterium winner Okawango. (The Ivy Syndicate). *"An early two-year-old showing plenty of ability, he's medium-sized and he'll start off at five furlongs."*

1543. PINK DIVA (IRE) ★★★★
ch.f. Giant's Causeway – Saoire (Pivotal).
January 30. Second foal. €475,000Y. Goffs Orby. Hugo Merry for Tom Tate. The dam, winner of the Irish 1,000 Guineas and third in the Group 1 Moyglare Stud Stakes, is a half-sister to 5 winners. The second dam, Polish Descent (by Danehill), is an unraced half-sister to 4 winners. (Mrs F H Hay). *"She's a very powerful, medium-sized mare with a lot of class. She'll make a two-year-old from the middle of the season onwards over seven furlongs. A quality individual."*

1544. WILD HYSTERIA (IRE) ★★★
gr.c. Verglas – White Wisteria (Ahonoora).
April 4. £6,000Y. Doncaster St Leger. Tom Tate. Half-brother to the very useful 2-y-o listed 5f winner and Group 2 Richmond Stakes third Bodyguard (by Zafonic), to the Italian winner of 19 races (including a listed event) White Gulch (by Gulch) and the minor US winner of 4 races Hikes (by Java Gold). The dam is an unraced half-sister to 6 winners including the dam of the Irish 2,000 Guineas winner Bachelor Duke. The second dam, Lisaleen (by Northern Dancer), won twice at 3 yrs and was third in the Group 3 Gilltown Stud Stakes and is a half-sister to the Group 1 National Stakes winner Fatherland. (Miss Nuala Cassidy). *"Quite progressive and tough, he's showing* some ability and he'll be running early doors."

1545. UNNAMED ★★★
b.c. Librettist – Fiveofive (Fairy King).
May 2. Twelfth foal. 15,500Y. Tattersalls December. Tom Tate. Half-brother to Medici Code (by Medicean), a quite useful 1m and 9f winner here and subsequently a Grade 2 winner in the USA, to the quite useful 2-y-o 5f and 6f winner and listed-placed Polly Alexander (by Foxhound), the fair and 1m and 10f winner Lilli Marlene (by Sri Pekan), the fair 2-y-o 7f winner My Only Sunshine (by First Trump) and the fair 12f winner Sweet Angeline (by Deploy). The dam, a modest 5f (at 2 yrs) and 1m winner, is a half-sister to 4 winners including the Group 3 6f July Stakes third The Old Firm. The second dam, North Hut (by Northfields), ran twice unplaced and is a half-sister to 4 winners. *"Quite forward, he's a medium sized colt that shows a reasonable amount of ability and he still wants an owner."*
TRAINERS' BARGAIN BUY

MARK TOMPKINS
1546. ASTROMAGICK ★★
b.f. Rainbow Quest – Astrocharm
(Charnwood Forest).
April 10. First foal. The dam, a useful winner of 7 races including the Group 3 14f Lily Langtry Stakes, is a half-sister to several winners including the Group 3 placed Nehaam. The second dam, Charm The Stars (by Roi Danzig), ran twice unplaced and is a half-sister to 2 minor winners. (Mystic Meg Ltd). *"The dam was as game as a pebble. This filly is quite compact and has a good attitude and we like everything she's done. One for the seven furlongs/mile maidens at the back-end of the season."*

1547. ASTROVERDI ★★★
b.c. Green Desert – Nutmeg
(Lake Coniston).
April 13. Fourth foal. Half-brother to a winner in Spain by Medicean. The dam, a fair 7f winner at 5 yrs, is a half-sister to 9 winners here and abroad. The second dam, Overdue Reaction (by Be My Guest), is an unplaced half-sister to 7 winners including the US Grade 2 winner Wait Till Monday. (Mystic Meg Ltd).

"A big, strong colt by a good sire, he moves alright and goes well enough at the moment. I won't be in a rush with him and I would think he'd be one for the mid-season onwards over six furlongs."

1548. BAWRICH ★★
b.c. Beat Hollow – Tenpence (Bob Back).
April 13. Fourth foal. Half-brother to Zenarinda (by Zamindar), placed fourth on both her outings at 2 yrs over 6f and 1m in 2009. The dam, unplaced in two starts, is a sister to the 2-y-o 1m winner and Group 3 Prix Saint-Roman second Ten Bob I and a half-sister to one winner. The second dam, Tiempo (by King Of Spain), was unplaced. "He's a well-grown, strong colt and we like him quite a bit. One for the mid-season onwards and he's no mug."

1549. COMRADE BOND ★★★
ch.c. Monsieur Bond – Eurolink Café (Grand Lodge).
February 18. Sixth foal. 3,500Y. Tattersalls October 3. M Tompkins. Half-brother to the modest dual 7f winner (including at 2 yrs) Autumn Charm (by Reel Buddy) and a winner in Greece by Averti. The dam is an unraced half-sister to 3 winners. The second dam, North Kildare (by Northjet), is an unraced half-sister to 7 winners including the US Grade 1 winner Labeeb, the Grade 2 winner Fanmore and the Group 2 winner Alrassaam. (Raceworld). "A real two-year-old type, he's strong and a great mover. Could be one of the first runners for the yard." TRAINERS' BARGAIN BUY

1550. DICTATE ★★★
ch.c. Araafa – Navajo Love Song (Dancing Brave).
April 13. Tenth living foal. 16,000Y. Tattersalls October Book 2. M Tompkins. Half-brother to the 2-y-o Group 1 1m National Stakes winner Mus-If (by Lahib), to the very smart 1m (at 2 yrs) and 10f winner Jammaal (by Robellino), the quite useful 12f winner Navajo Chieftain (by Sinndar) and the minor Irish 11f winner Daqtora (by Dr Devious). The dam, placed once at 4 yrs, is a half-sister to 4 minor winners in France and Italy. The second dam, Marquina (by Posse), won over 10.5f in France and is a half-sister to 7 winners including the French listed winners Fabulous Queen, Fabulous Teaser, Kopelman and Quemora. (Mrs B M Lockley). "He's a big, strong type, a bit backward at the moment but I'm sure he'll be alright from the middle of the season onwards. He goes well enough and I think he was well-bought."

1551. ICE MAGIC ★★★
b.c. Iceman – Naomi Wildman (Kingmambo).
March 12. Fourth foal. 12,500Y. Tattersalls October Book 2. M Tompkins. Half-brother to the fair 2009 2-y-o 7f winner Exceedthewildman (by Exceed And Excel), to the fair 11f and 13f winner Sherman McCoy (by Reset) and a winner over jumps in France by Red Ransom. The dam is an unplaced half-sister to 4 winners in France including the listed winner Mondovino. The second dam, Divinite (by Alleged), won twice at 3 yrs in France and is a half-sister to 5 winners. (Kenneth MacPherson). "A nice, strong horse by a first season sire and he's a well put-together colt that's never done anything wrong. I like him, he's just starting to do a bit of work now and I should think he'll be out from May onwards."

1552. LADY CHLOE ★★★
b.f. Noverre – Iwunder (King's Best).
March 6. First foal. 30,000Y. Tattersalls December. M Tompkins. The dam, a modest 1m placed maiden, is a half-sister to 3 winners including the Irish listed winner Molly-O. The second dam, Sweetest Thing (by Prince Rupert), won over 7f and 10f in Ireland and is a half-sister to 3 winners including the listed City Of York Stakes winner Reported. (The Wiggins Family). "A very strong filly and a great walker with an unbelievably good temperament. She was backward in her coat and is just coming to hand now, so she's one for the middle of the season onwards. I quite like her."

1553. PICCARELLO ★★
b.c. Piccolo – Latina (King's Theatre).
January 13. Sixth foal. 7,000Y. Tattersalls October 3. M Tompkins. The dam won twice at 2 yrs in France, including over 6f, and is a half-sister to 4 winners including an Italian listed winner. The second dam, Peralta (by Green Desert), is an unraced half-sister to 6 winners including the Group 3 winner

Caprarola and the listed winners Bormio and Cortona. (Roalco Ltd). *"He's a strong horse, a January foal and he goes well enough. He'll be out in late April/early May. Five or six furlongs will suit."*

1554. PRINCE FREDDIE ★★★
b.c. Red Ransom – Pitcroy (Unfuwain).
March 5. Seventh living foal. 37,000Y. Tattersalls December. Mark Tompkins. Half-brother to the useful 3-y-o listed 10f winner Succinct (by Hector Protector), to the fairly useful 7f and 1m (including at 2 yrs) and German listed 1m winner Succession (by Groom Dancer) and a winner in Greece by Mark Of Esteem. The dam, a useful 10f winner, is a half-sister to 8 winners including the very useful Group 3 7f Jersey Stakes winner Ardkinglass. The second dam, Reuval (by Sharpen Up), a useful winner of 2 races over 1m at 3 yrs, is closely related to the dams of the Group 2 winners Ozone Friendly, Reprimand and Wiorno. (The Wiggins Family). *"A well-grown, strong colt, we can't get to the bottom of him. A half-brother to one or two good horses, he could easily be alright, and he'll be a mid-season two-year-old."*

1555. PRINCESS IZZY ★★
gr.f. Tale Of The Cat – Victory Spirit (Alphabet Soup).
March 31. First foal. 17,000Y. Tattersalls December. M Tompkins. The dam won 2 minor races in the USA at 3 and 4 yrs and is a half-sister to 8 winners including the Canadian Grade 2 winner Super Red. The second dam, Regal Victress (by Diamond Prospect), won the Grade 2 First Flight Handicap and is a full or half-sister to 5 winners. (The Wiggins Family). *"She's a sharp little filly. She was only small when we bought her but she's grown well and thickened out, so we're quite happy with her. She loves to go alright, and she may be the first of the fillies to run – possibly in May."*

1556. STAR COMMANDER ★★★
b.c. Desert Style – Barakat (Bustino).
March 5. Thirteenth foal. 27,000Y. Tattersalls October Book 3. M Tompkins. Half-brother to the 10.3f and US stakes winner and Grade 2 placed Mabadi (by Sahm), to the useful 10f winner and listed-placed Ta Awun (by Housebuster), the fairly useful 10f winner Mudalal (by Dixieland Band), the fairly useful middle-distance winner Mumaris (by Capote), the quite useful 11.7f winner Mabrooka (by Bahri), the quite useful dual 12f winner Killcara Boy (by Tobougg), the fair 8.5f winner Tadawul (by Diesis) and the fair 7f winner Fakih (by Zilzal). The dam, a fairly useful 14.6f winner, is a half-sister to the Group 1 winners Ibn Bey and Roseate Tern. The second dam, the useful 7.5f and 1m winner Rosia Bay (by High Top), is a half-sister to 5 winners including the Queen Elizabeth II Stakes and Arlington Million winner Teleprompter. (J Brenchley). *"I like him a lot – he's a nice horse that's related to a couple of decent horses and he goes well. Another one with a good temperament and a great mover, I think he'll make a two-year-old from May onwards."*

1557. TOPARICHI ★★★
ch.c. Bahamian Bounty – Topatori (Topanoora).
April 4. Brother to the Group 3 10.3f winner Topatoo and half-brother to the quite useful 1m to 14f winner Toparudi (by Rudimentary), the fair dual 1m winner Top Shot (by College Chapel) and the fair 1m winner Top Tiger (by Mtoto). The dam was a quite useful 7f to 11f winner of 4 races. The second dam, Partygoer (by Cadeaux Genereux), was unplaced. (P Bowring). *"I love him – he's lovely and his mare always breeds nice horses. He's strong, attractive, moves well and hopefully he'll be as good as his sister Topatori who won four times – all at York."*

MARCUS TREGONING
1558. AKTAAF ★★
ch.c. Haafhd – Inaaq (Lammtarra).
April 18. Half-brother to the modest 1m (at 2 yrs) to 12f winner of 4 races Mayadeen (by King's Best). The dam, a smart 10f winner, was third in the Group 3 12f Princess Royal Stakes and is a half-sister to the high-class Dubai World Cup and Prix Jean Prat winner Almutawakel and to the UAE 1,000 Guineas winner and Newmarket 1,000 Guineas second Muwakleh. The second dam, Elfaslah (by Green Desert), a listed winner of three races from 10f to 10.4f, is a half-sister to the Group 1 12f Italian Derby winner and 'King George'

second White Muzzle. (Hamdan Al Maktoum). "Still in Dubai, when I saw him he seemed to be a reasonable mover. Maybe one for later on this year. The Dubai horses will be coming over in mid-April."

1559. ASKER (IRE) ★★★★
b.c. High Chaparral – Pay The Bank (High Top). **April 23. Twelfth foal. 125,000Y. Tattersalls October Book 2. M Tregoning.** Half-brother to the listed 6f and listed 7f winner and 1,000 Guineas fourth My Branch (herself dam of the Group 1 Haydock Park Sprint Cup winner Tante Rose), to the smart 10f winner, Chester Vase third and high-class jumper Celestial Halo (by Galileo), the quite useful 7f all-weather and 1m winner Guaranteed, a winner in Hong Kong (all by Distant Relative), the fairly useful 12f winner Banco Suivi (by Nashwan) and the 2m and hurdles winner High Prospect (by Lycius). The dam, a quite useful 2-y-o 1m winner, stayed 10f and is a half-sister to 4 winners. The second dam, Zebra Grass (by Run The Gantlet), was a quite useful 2-y-o 6f and 7f winner and a half-sister to 2 minor winners. (N Bizakov). "He's in full work – and you wouldn't expect that because on pedigree you'd think he'd be one for seven furlongs and a mile. He took it all so well in the spring we just let him get on with it and he goes nicely. While the ground's still good we'll get him up to speed so he's ready when the seven furlong races come in. He's done very well, we're very happy with him, his work is nice and I think he's a really nice colt by a very good stallion. He has a very good action, a good temperament and he could be anything. He certainly looks the part to me."

1560. ASPANTAU (IRE) ★★★
b.c. Encosta De Lago – Jabali (Shirley Heights). **March 22. Eleventh foal. 110,000Y. Tattersalls October Book 2. M Tregoning.** Half-brother to 6 minor winners in France by Caerleon, Grand Lodge, Green Desert, Linamix, Sanglamore and Vettori. The dam is an unplaced half-sister to 4 winners including the French Group winners Dadarissime and Floripedes (the dam of Montjeu). The second dam, Toute Cy (by Tennyson), is a placed full or half-sister to 4 winners including the Grade 1 Arlington Million winner Dear Doctor. (N Bizakov). "I must admit I went through a patch where I thought he was a bit heavy but he's fined down a lot and maybe the sire Encosta De Lago (being by Danehill) has helped because there's plenty of speed in that line. He goes well enough, he might have enough speed for six furlongs and he's very strong with a pretty good temperament. Quite a nice two-year-old, he'll win."

1561. ATRAAF (IRE) ★★
b.c. Intikhab – Kismah (Machiavellian). **May 15.** Brother to the quite useful 2009 6f placed 2-y-o King Of Windsor and to the fairly useful 6f (at 2 yrs) to 1m winner of 4 races Suruor and half-brother to the useful 7f and 1m winner Tahirah, the modest 10f to 12f winner Eijaaz (both by Green Desert), the quite useful dual 6f winner Tawzeea (by Cadeaux Genereux) and the fair Irish 12f winner Honey Run (by Sinndar). The dam, a very useful dual 1m winner, is a half-sister to 3 winners including the fairly useful 7f winner Tawaaded. The second dam, Thaidah (by Vice Regent), was a useful winner from 5f (at 2yrs) to 7f and is a half-sister to the champion US 2-y-o Devil's Bag and to the top-class filly Glorious Song (the dam of Singspiel and Rahy). (Hamdan Al Maktoum). "He was a late foal and he came in very late, so he's very backward. He's a very good shape, he's a good mover with a very good temperament, but he's one for later in the year."

1562. AWAROA (IRE) ★★★★
b.f. Cape Cross – For Evva Silca (Piccolo). **March 1. Fourth foal. 50,000Y. Tattersalls October Book 1. McKeever St Lawrence.** Half-sister to the very useful Irish listed 5f (at 2 yrs), 6f and UAE 7f winner Warsaw (by Danehill Dancer). The dam, placed once at 2 yrs, is a half-sister to 7 winners including the 2-y-o Group 1 6f Prix Morny winner Silca's Sister, the Group 2 6f Mill Reef Stakes and German Group 2 winner and Group 1 placed Golden Silca and the very useful 5f winner and listed 6f winner of 12 races (including at 2 yrs) Green Manalishi. The second dam, Silca-Cisa (by Hallgate), a fairly useful dual 5f winner, was listed placed over 5f at 4 yrs and is a half-sister to the Group 3 placed sprinter Azizzi. (Mr G C B Brook). "I was really quite keen to get into this 'Mick Channon' family. I think the dam was a bit

incorrect but there's nothing wrong with the conformation of this filly. I'm really excited by her, she's very nice, has a typical 'Cape Cross' head and I'm very pleased with her. Luckily, the combination seems alright because she has plenty of speed and looks well forward. I'd expect to see her out in early May, she has a brilliant temperament, not over-big but she's going to grow a bit. I really do like her."

1563. BLUE VINNEY ★★
gr.c. Proclamation – Easy Mover (Bluebird).
February 16. Second foal. £5,000Y. Doncaster Festival. M Tregoning. Half-brother to the fair 2009 2-y-o 5f winner Dispol Keasha (by Kheleyf). The dam, a fair 2-y-o 7f winner, is a half-sister to one winner. The second dam, Top Brex (by Top Ville), won once at 3 yrs in France and is a half-sister to 6 winners including the Italian Group 3 Premio Ambrosiano winner Charlo Mio.(Park Walk Racing). *"He was incredibly cheap as a yearling but he's by a son of King's Best and he very much has the good shape of a King's Best. He's no beauty, in fact he's quite plain, but I like his spirit and he'll be going early. If we can we'll try for the Sales Bonus which I think is a great attraction."*

1564. CHATTERER (IRE) ★★★
b.f. Alhaarth – Miss Bellbird (Danehill).
April 20. Third foal. €24,000Y. Goffs Orby. Not sold. The dam is an unraced half-sister to 8 winners including the Group 2 12f King Edward VII Stakes winner Amfortas and the Group 3 10.5f Prix de Royaumont winner Legend Maker (herself dam of the 1,000 Guineas winner Virginia Water). The second dam, High Spirited (by Shirley Heights), was quite useful and won two of her seven races over 14f and 2m at 3 yrs. She is a sister to the Premio Roma, Ribblesdale Stakes and Park Hill Stakes winner High Hawk (herself dam of the Breeders Cup Turf winner In the Wings) and a half-sister to the dams of the Derby winner High Rise and the Rothmans International winner Infamy. (Horne, Hoare, Gaskell & Partners). *"She has a really good pedigree and I'm pleased to have her. The sire has been very good to us and I think the Danehill bit will help us because it might add a bit of speed. She's a perfect size and a well-grown filly in full work that shows*

some nice pace. I'm pleased with her, she's a filly with a lot of quality and presence, very straightforward and good-tempered. I picked her up for 25k outside the ring because she didn't sell and I'd be very disappointed if she can't win races. If she does do well we'll be laughing, considering her potential as a broodmare." TRAINERS' BARGAIN BUY

1565. DARAJAAT ★★★
b.f. Elusive Quality – Misterah (Alhaarth).
March 5. Half-sister to the useful 6f (at 2 yrs) and listed 1m winner and Group 3 7f Oak Tree Stakes third Shabiba. The dam, a very useful listed 6f (at 2 yrs) and Group 3 7f Nell Gwyn Stakes winner, is sister to one winner and a half-sister to the useful 2-y-o 6f winner Muqtarb. The second dam, Jasarah (by Green Desert), was a fair 7f placed maiden. (Hamdan Al Maktoum). *"She's in Dubai but I've had a good look at her. She's quite nice and a similar build to her mother, so let's hope she's as good."*

1566. ELFAATEN (USA) ★★★
b.c. Forestry – Thaminah (Danzig).
February 20. Second foal. Half-brother to the fair 1m winner Sahaal (by Rahy). The dam, a quite useful 2-y-o 6f winner, is a half-sister to 4 winners including the fairly useful dual 1m winner Mosayter. The second dam, Bashayer (by Mr Prospector), a useful dual 1m winner, is a sister to the useful 1m and 10.4f winner Wijdan and the useful 10f listed winner Sarayir and a half-sister to several winners including Nashwan and Unfuwain. (Hamdan Al Maktoum). *"We saw him in Dubai and thought he was nice. He's a big, strong colt and I've had the dam and a lot of this family. I think the jury's out as regards the stallion but this colt is a nice type and one of the better looking ones."*

1567. ELWAZEER (USA) ★★★
b.c. Oasis Dream – Hazimah (Gone West).
March 13. Fifth foal. The dam, a fair 7f and 1m placed maiden, is a half-sister to numerous winners including the high-class 2-y-o Mujahid, winner of the Group 1 7f Dewhurst Stakes and subsequently third in the 2,000 Guineas. The second dam, Elrafa Ah (by Storm Cat), was a useful winner of 3 races over 5f and 6f including

the listed Bentinck Stakes. The second dam, Bubbles Darlene (by Fappiano), won twice at up to 1m. (Hamdan Al Maktoum). *"Quite a nice horse, he's still in Dubai and he's a bit on the small side which I don't mind at all. The sire is an all-round star stallion at any distance."*

1568. ESTILAAM (IRE) ★★★
b.c. Alhaarth – Elutrah (Darshaan).
February 7. Half-brother to the quite useful 2009 2-y-o 1m winner Multames (by Cape Cross). The dam is an unraced sister to the very useful Group 2 7f Rockfel Stakes winner Sayedah and a half-sister to 4 winners. The second dam, Balaabel (by Sadler's Wells), a quite useful 1m winner, is a half-sister to 3 winners including the US Grade 2 7f winner Kayrawan. (Hamdan Al Maktoum). *"I'm always pleased to get an Alhaarth because he keeps getting good horses. This is a nice sort of horse, he's a reasonable mover and I know the family well. Not a bad sort, he's still in Dubai."*

1569. IRTIDAA (USA) ★★★
b.f. Elusive Quality – Irtahal (Swain).
March 25. Fourth foal. Half-sister to the quite useful 11f and 12f winner Qelaan (by Dynaformer) and the fair French 7f and 10f winner Nasaq (by Gulch). The dam, a fairly useful 1m winner, was third in the Group 3 Musidora Stakes and is a half-sister to several winners. The second dam, Elhasna (by Danzig), a quite useful 3-y-o 6f winner, is a sister to the outstanding sprinter Dayjur and closely related to the dual US Grade 1 winner Maplejinsky. (Hamdan Al Maktoum). *"This is one I really liked when I saw her in Dubai. She's a nice moving sort, a reasonable size and not a bad filly at all. Having said that she's yet to come over from Dubai so it's hard to say any more than that."*

1570. JADHWAH ★★★
b.f. Nayef – Dhelaal (Green Desert).
March 27. Second foal. The dam is an unraced half-sister to 7 winners including the champion 2-y-o Alhaarth, winner of the Dewhurst Stakes, the Laurent Perrier Champagne Stakes, the Prix Dollar, the Budweiser American Bowl International Stakes and the Prix du Rond-Point and a half-sister to the very useful 2-y-o Group 3 7f Prix du Calvados winner Green Pola. The second dam, Irish Valley (by Irish River), is an unplaced half-sister to 10 winners, notably the Observer Gold Cup, French 2,000 Guineas and 10.5f Prix Lupin winner and good sire Green Dancer, the US Grade 3 winner Ercolano and the US Graded stakes winner Val Danseur. (Hamdan Al Maktoum). *"This filly is very nice, she's certainly deep enough, very sensible, good natured and a very sound horse – as I would hope considering she's by Nayef because he was incredibly sound. She's done a little bit and in May I'll do a bit more with her. I haven't rushed her because she's one for a bit later on. A nice type."*

1571. JUHD (IRE) ★★
br.c. Nayef – Norfolk Lavender (Ascot Knight).
February 12. Ninth foal. €130,000Y. Arqana Deauville August. Shadwell Estate Co. Half-brother to the modest 2009 2-y-o 1m winner Cherry Bee (by Acclamation), to the useful 8.3f to 12f winner of 5 races Celtic Mission (by Cozzene), the quite useful 7f and 1m winner In The Pink (by Indian Ridge), the quite useful Irish 10f winner Takween (by Nayef) and the fair 2-y-o 6f winner Fragrant Star (by Soviet Star). The dam, a modest 1m all-weather winner here, subsequently won a stakes event in the USA and was Grade 3 placed. She is a half-sister to 5 winners including the US stakes winner Concordene out of the 1,000 Guineas winner Nocturnal Spree (by Supreme Sovereign), herself a half-sister to the Prix Saint-Alary winner Tootens and to the dam of the St Leger winner Moonax. (Hamdan Al Maktoum). *"A very big horse and a seven furlong/mile horse for the back-end. He's good tempered and a good mover."*

1572. KONSTANTIN (IRE) ★★★
b.c. Balmont – Manuka Magic (Key Of Luck).
March 30. Third foal. 115,000Y. Tattersalls October Book 1. Peter Doyle. Half-brother to the smart 2009 2-y-o Group 3 6f Firth Of Clyde Stakes winner and Group 1 6f Cheveley Park Stakes second Aspen Darlin (by Indian Haven). The dam is an unraced half-sister to 3 winners. The second dam, Magic Garter (by Precocious), is an unraced half-sister to 7 winners and to the unraced dam of Grand

Lodge. (Lady Tennant). *"He was the sire's most expensive yearling, expertly bought by Peter Doyle! We've had some good horses together with Lady Tennant and we have to hope this is another one. A lovely-moving horse, he's quite backward and will need time but I do like him, he's got a lovely nature and is a nice type for the back-end of the season."*

1573. LADY ROSAMUNDE ★★★
gr.f. *Maria's Mon – String Quartet (Sadler's Wells).*
April 1. Sixth foal. Half-sister to the fair 2009 7f and 1m placed 2-y-o Meeznah (by Dynaformer), to the smart 1m winner (at 2 yrs) and Group 2 12f Princess Of Wales's Stakes second Shahin (by Kingmambo) and the moderate 7f winner Lyric Art (by Red Ransom). The dam, a 12.5f listed winner in France and third in the Group 3 Lancashire Oaks, is a sister to the Irish listed 10f winner Casey Tibbs and a half-sister to 4 winners. The second dam, Fleur Royale (by Mill Reef), won the Group 2 Pretty Polly Stakes, was second in the Irish Oaks and is a half-sister to 4 winners. (Mr & Mrs A E Pakenham). *"She's a nicer type in terms of her temperament than her half-brother Shahin. A very kind filly, I did a little bit with her early on and that went very well, but she went a bit weak so I gave her some time. I suspect she's one for the mid-summer onwards but she's a nice type, definitely."*

1574. MISS THEA ★★
ch.f. *Barathea – Misplace (Green Desert).*
February 13. Half-sister to the French 1m to 10f winner and Group 3 third Mayweather (by Nayef), to the French 2-y-o 1m winner and Group 3 fourth Mistaken Identity (by Vettori) and the minor French 7f winner Milhaarth (by Alhaarth) and to the unraced dam of the Group 1 1m Falmouth Stakes and Group 2 6f Lowther Stakes winner Nahoodh. The dam ran once unplaced and is a half-sister to 6 winners including the French Group 3 winner Not Just Swing and the French listed winner Minoa. The second dam, Misbegotten (by Baillamont), a French listed 1m Prix Finlande winner, was second in the Group 2 Prix de l'Opera and is a half-sister to 4 winners. (Miss S M Sharp). *"She's not from a very precocious family, so I'll just feel my way with her. Quite a tall filly, but she's not too big and we just need to give her a bit more time. One for the mid-summer."*

1575. MONTEGONIAN (USA) ★★
gr.c. *Maria's Mon – Nadeszhda (Nashwan).*
March 31. The dam, a quite useful triple 12f winner, is a half-sister to the useful 2-y-o 6f winner and 7f Group 3 placed Nataliya. The second dam, Ninotchka (by Nijinsky), a listed winner in Italy and third in the Group 3 12f Lancashire Oaks and the Group 3 12f Princess Royal Stakes, is a half-sister to 5 winners. (Miss K Rausing). *"A very big horse, he's very nice natured and a perfectly good mover but he will take time. I expect to see him out in the autumn."*

1576. MULAQEN ★★★
ch.c. *Haafhd – Burqa (Nashwan).*
March 21. 30,000foal. Tattersalls December. Shadwell Estate Co. Third foal. Half-brother to the fair Irish 6f and 7f winner Boule Masquee (by Compton Place). The dam is an unraced half-sister to several winners including the Group 3 10f Prix Exbury winner and Group 1 Premio Presidente della Repubblica third Barbola. The second dam, Barboukh (by Night Shift), a fairly useful winner of the 1m listed Fern Hill Stakes, is a half-sister to 3 winners. (Hamdan Al Maktoum). *"A big horse but not too big, he's a good mover, seems to have a nice temperament and he's done plenty of sharp canters. I suspect he's more of a seven furlong/mile horse and the likelihood is we'll have to wait until later on, but you never know we might go for a race like the Haynes, Hanson and Clark Stakes. A good-looking type and he's straightforward. A nice sort."*

1577. MUNAAWIB ★★★
b.c. *Haafhd – Mouwadh (Nureyev).*
March 30. Closely related to the fair 2-y-o 7f winner Malaath (by Green Desert) and half-brother to the quite useful 11f winner Mathaaq (by Nayef). The dam, unplaced in both her starts, is a half-sister to numerous winners including the smart 10f, 12f and UAE listed winner Mutasallil and the dual winner and Group 3 placed Ajhar. The second dam, Min Alhawa (by Riverman), a useful 7f (at 2 yrs) to 10f winner, is a sister to the 1,000 Guineas

winner Harayir. (Hamdan Al Maktoum). *"Quite a nice type, he's not too backward and is just starting to do sharp canters. As a type, he's the perfect size you'd want for a two-year-old."*

1578. MUNTASIB ★★
ch.c. Mr Greeley – Halo River (Irish River).
March 4. Eighth foal. $375,000Y. Keeneland September. Shadwell Estate Co. Half-brother to 4 winners including the North American Grade 3 Cliff Hanger Stakes winner and Grade 2 placed Old Forester (by Forestry) and the minor US 3-y-o winner Possessive (by Belong To Me). The dam, a minor US sakes winner of 3 races and 2 and 3 yrs, is s half-sister to 4 minor winners. The second dam, All Hallows (by Halo), a minor US 2-y-o winner, is a half-sister to the Irish 1,00 Guineas and Group 2 Mill Reef Stakes winner Forest Flower and the stakes winner Scoop The Gold (dam of the US Grade 1 winner High Yield). (Hamdan Al Maktoum). *"In Dubai still, he's quite a big, solid horse. I thought he looked a nice type when I saw him and he appeared to move well – although we were only watching him on the sand. He seems like a nice horse but I haven't had one of the better Mr Greeleys yet!"*

1579. OPERA BOX ★★
b.f. Singspiel – Annex (Anabaa).
March 17. Fifth foal. 25,000Y. Tattersalls October Book 1. M Tregoning. Half-sister to the French 7f (at 2 yrs) and 1m winner and listed-placed Alsace (by King's Best). The dam, a 7f winner at 3 yrs in Deauville, is a half-sister to 4 winners including the US Grade 2 1m and Group 3 1m Prix Quincey winner Bon Point. The second dam, Twixt (by Kings Lake), won over 7f in France and is a half-sister to 5 winners including the Group 2 Maurice de Gheest winner Interval, to the Grade 2 La Prevoyante Handicap winner Interim (dam of the US Grade 1 winner Midships) and to the dam of the Hoover Fillies Mile winner Invited Guest. (Efemera Stud). *"This is a nice type and a very good-looking filly although for some reason she didn't make her reserve, but that's good for me because I've got her. She basically needs more time but I'm happy with her and it's a nice pedigree."*

1580. RUMOOZ ★★★
b.f. Cape Cross – Esloob (Diesis).
February 19. Fourth foal. Half-sister to the fair 2009 2-y-o 7f winner Huroof (by Pivotal). The dam, a 7f (at 2 yrs) and listed Pretty Polly Stakes winner, was third in the Fillies' Mile and is a half-sister to the Pretty Polly Stakes winner Siyadah. The second dam, Roseate Tern (by Blakeney), a very smart winner of the Group 1 12f Yorkshire Oaks and the Group 2 12f Jockey Club Stakes was second in the Epsom Oaks and third in the St Leger and is a half-sister to the high-class middle-distance stayer Ibn Bey. (Hamdan Al Maktoum). *"Still in Dubai until mid-April, she appeared to move well when I saw her and seemed a nice type. I'm delighted to have another Cape Cross and the dam was a decent filly, so you'd have to be hopeful."*

1581. RUSOOM ★★
b.f. Dalakhani – Itqaan (Danzig).
April 10. Second foal. The dam, a fair 1m winner, is a sister to useful dual 1m winner Mawatheeq and a half-sister to 3 winners. The second dam, Sarayir (by Mr Prospector), winner of a 1m listed event, is closely related to the top-class Champion Stakes winner Nayef and a half-sister to numerous winners including the Two Thousand Guineas, Eclipse, Derby and King George winner Nashwan and the high-class middle distance colt Unfuwain. (Hamdan Al Maktoum). *"Quite tall and rangy and more of a three-year-old type."*

1582. SEA THE FLAMES (IRE) ★★★
b.c. Chineur – Flames (Blushing Flame).
May 14. Sixth foal. €23,000Y. Goffs Orby. M Tregoning. Half-brother to Pink Flames, unplaced in one start at 2 yrs in 2009, to the 2-y-o Group 2 6f Rockfel Stakes and 3-y-o Grade 1 10f E P Taylor Stakes winner Lahaleeb (both by Redback) and the fairly useful dual 6f (at 2 yrs) and listed 1m Masaka Stakes winner Precocious Star (by Bold Fact). The dam is an unraced half-sister to 4 winners including the listed winner Dance Partner. The second dam, Dancing Debut (by Polar Falcon), is a placed half-sister to 4 winners including Virtuous (dam of the Group 1 Lockinge Stakes winner Virtual and the Group 2 Coventry Stakes winner Iceman). (David & Gwyn Joseph). *"I'm very pleased to have bought him because that*

was a coup. After the sale Mick Channon's filly won the Grade 1 in Canada which was very exciting for us, especially as we didn't pay a lot for this colt. He's got very nice owners and he was a late foal so after a few sharp canters we backed off him. He's a two-year-old alright, we'll probably start him in mid-summer and he could be quite nice. The sire can get speedy ones and this family seem to be able to run."

1583. SHAQIRA ★★
b.br.f. Redoute's Choice – Hammiya (Darshaan).
February 21. Third foal. Half-brother to the useful 7f winner Masaalek (by Green Desert). The dam, a useful 11.4f listed Cheshire Oaks winner, is a half-sister to the useful 2-y-o 1m winner Achill Bay. The second dam, Albacora (by Fairy King), winner of the listed 1m Prix Herod, is closely related to the Prix de Saint-Georges winner and French 1,000 Guineas second Pont-Aven (herself dam of the Gimcrack Stakes winner Josr Algharoud and the dual Group winner Saint Marine). (Hamdan Al Maktoum). *"We did a bit of work with he early on and she showed enough pace to suggest she might hopefully win this year, but I backed off her because I felt she needed a bit more time. We won't be in a rush with her and we'll probably aim for seven furlongs with her this year."*

1584. SHAQRAA ★★★
ch.f. Mr Greeley – Saintly Persuasion (Saint Ballado).
March 15. Third foal. The dam was a stakes-placed winner in the USA. The second dam, Private Persuasion (by Pirate's Bounty), won the Grade 1 Vanity Handicap and is a half-sister to 2 winners. (Hamdan Al Maktoum). *"She's in Dubai and there's something very nice about her. They say she doesn't behave too well which is interesting because I quite like that, because if she's misbehaving then she's strong enough. They say it takes their best rider and all that sort of thing. She's nice, a lovely size and a very nice type. One of the nicest I saw out there."*

1585. TARJEYH (IRE) ★★★★
b.c. Medicean – Navajo Rainbow (Rainbow Quest).
February 18. Fourth foal. 220,000Y. Tattersalls October Book 2. Shadwell Estate Co. Half-brother to the quite useful 2009 2-y-o 5f winner an listed placed Navajo Chief (by King's Best) and to a winner in Italy by Dr Fong. The dam is an unraced half-sister to 4 winners including the Group 1 National Stakes winner Mus-If and the triple Irish listed winner Jammaal. The second dam, Navajo Love Song (by Dancing Brave), placed once at 4 yrs, is a half-sister to 5 minor winners in France and Italy. (Sheikh Ahmed Al Maktoum). *"He's in full work and he's a big, strong, bull of a horse, but he shows enough ability to be able to work with. I'd say my nicest two-year-olds at the moment are the colts. He's able to do it so I quite fancy him, he'll be a mid-summer horse and he's a good mover with a good temperament. At this stage I would say he's a nice sort and he might be alright to start at six furlongs before moving him up in trip."*

1586. TAWSEEF (IRE) ★★★★
b.c. Monsun – Sahool (Unfuwain).
April 30. Third foal. Half-brother to Latansaa (by Indian Ridge), a promising third over 1m on his only start at 2 yrs in 2009 and to the very useful 10f winner Arwaah (by Dalakhani). The dam, a 1m (at 2 yrs) and listed 12f winner, was second in the Group 2 Lancashire Oaks and is a half-sister to 2 winners. The second dam, Mathaayl (by Shadeed), a quite useful 6f and 10f winner, is a half-sister to 3 winners including the dams of the Group/Graded stakes winners Kayrawan, Asfurah and Istintaj. (Hamdan Al Maktoum). *"I like him, he's not very big but he's lovely and I quite fancy the mare to do well. It was really disappointing that his half-sister Arwaah didn't do well because nothing went right for her. Being by Monsun he's only just started doing sharp canters but he just does everything very nicely and sensibly. I can see him winning two-year-old races, definitely."*

1587. WATERED SILK ★★★★
gr.c. Encosta De Lago – Tussah (Daylami).
April 19. The dam is an unraced half-sister to 6 winners including the very promising 2009 2-y-o 7f winner Seta, the Group 2 13f Prix de Pomone winner Armure, the very useful listed 11f and 12f winner Gravitas and the listed 2m winner Affirmative Action. The second dam,

Bombazine (by Generous), a useful 10f winner, is a half-sister to the Breeders Cup Mile, Irish 2,000 Guineas and Queen Anne Stakes winner Barathea, to the Fillies Mile and Irish 1,000 Guineas winner Gossamer and the triple Group winner Zabar. (Mr & Mrs A Pakenham). *"I like this horse a lot – I must say. I've got two by the sire and they're both promising. This one I like a lot, I think he's a nice horse with a really decent pedigree. If this one comes out and does some good it will be important for the mare. I might start him at six furlongs because he looks like having the speed for it before progressing to seven. He's very good natured, powerful and he gallops really well, so we're very pleased with him."*

1588. UNNAMED ★★★
b.c. Camacho – Berenica (College Chapel).
May 4. £14,000 2-y-o. Goffs Kempton Breeze Up. M Tregoning. Half-brother to the quite useful triple 6f winner (including at 2 yrs) Kingswinford (by Noverre). The dam, a dual Irish 6f winner (including at 2 yrs) was listed-placed and is half-sister to numerous winners including the fairly useful 5f winner of 4 races and listed-placed Gaelic Princess. The second dam, Berenice (by Marouble), was unraced. *"He doesn't have the flashiest pedigree but the sire is firing in the winners. I'm very pleased with Camacho because they seem to be sensible horses and they keep winning. This is a cheap horse that was well broken in by Trickledown Stud and he's ready to go, so he's a good buy."*

ED VAUGHAN
1589. SCARBOROUGH LILY ★★★
b.f. Dansili – Queen Isabella (El Prado).
March 19. First foal. €28,000Y. Goffs Orby. Not sold. The dam is an unplaced half-sister to 8 winners including the smart 2-y-o Group 2 July Stakes winner Strategic Prince and the very useful 1m (at 2 yrs) and 13.3f winner Yorkshire. The second dam, Ausherra (by Diesis), won the listed 12f Lingfield Oaks Trial and is a full or half-sister to 9 winners including the Oaks, Irish Oaks and Yorkshire Oaks winner Ramruma. (A M Pickering). *"A nice, big filly that'll take plenty of time. She reminds me a lot of a nice filly we had called Eloquently – which is why we bought her. An athletic, well-grown filly, I won't be doing too much too soon with her but she'll probably be suited by seven furlongs in August."*

1590. STORMY THUNDER ★★
ch.c. Shamardal – Blue Lightning (Machiavellian).
March 2. Third foal. The dam is an unraced sister to the smart Group 3 7f Solario Stakes (at 2 yrs) and Group 1 Prix Jean Prat winner Best Of The Bests and a half-sister to several winners including the smart 6f (at 2 yrs) and 9f winner and Group 2 Dante Stakes third Dunhill Star. The second dam, Sueboog (by Darshaan), a half-sister to 3 winners, was a very useful winner of the Group 3 7.3f Fred Darling Stakes, was third in the Musidora Stakes and the Nassau Stakes and fourth in the Oaks. The second dam, Nordica (by Northfields), was a useful 6f (a listed event in Ireland) and 1m winner and stayed 10f. (Mohammed Obaida). *"A colt that's very unfurnished and backward, he has to grow a lot and I don't think we'll see him out until late summer over seven furlongs, but I do like him."*

1591. WHITBY JET (IRE) ★★★
b.c. Mujadil – Anazah (Diesis).
March 16. Second foal. 20,000Y. Tattersalls October Book 3. Blandford Bloodstock. Half-brother to the quite useful 2009 2-y-o 7f winner Thrust Control (by Fath). The dam is an unplaced half-sister to Canadian winner at 2 and 4 yrs and stakes-placed Faswiga (by Fasliyev). The second dam, Tadwiga (by Fairy King), winner of the Group 3 Matron Stakes in Ireland and second in the Group 3 Rockfel Stakes (at 2 yrs), is a sister to the useful Irish 2-y-o listed 7f Orby Stakes winner and Group 2 Premio Ribot fourth Bartok. (A M Pickering). *"Probably our first 2-y-o runner, he's likely to be out in May and he looks an out-and-out 2-y-o. He'd want soft ground I should imagine and will be a five/six furlong type."*

1592. UNNAMED ★★
b.f. Librettist – Cal Norma's Lady (Lyphard's Special).
April 22. Eleventh foal. 60,000Y. Tattersalls October Book 1. Rabbah Bloodstock. Half-sister to Lion Mountain (by Tiger Hill), second over 1m on his only start at 2 yrs in 2009, to

the Group 1 6f Cheveley Park Stakes and Group 2 6f Cherry Hinton Stakes winner Donna Blini (by Bertolini), the quite useful 2-y-o 6f winner and subsequent US Grade 3 8.5f Will Rogers Handicap winner Magical, the fair all-weather 7f winner Dundonald (both by Magic Ring), the quite useful 2-y-o 5f winner Sabre Lady (by Sabrehill), the fair all-weather 7f and 9f winner Bijou Dan (by Bijou d'Inde), the fair 8.5f and 9f winner Jordan's Elect (by Fleetwood) and the modest 2-y-o 5f winner Under Pressure (by Keen). The dam, a quite useful 2-y-o 6f and 7f winner, is out of the unraced June Darling (by Junius), herself a half-sister to 8 winners. (A Saeed). *"She doesn't altogether look like making a 2-y-o, except maybe much later in the season. She's gone "high behind" and her action suggests she won't be anything like her smart half-sister Donna Blini."*

1593. UNNAMED ★★★
b.c. *Invincible Spirit – Lady High Havens (Bluebird).*
April 4. Fourth foal. 78,000Y. Tattersalls October Book 1. Rabbah Bloodstock. Half-brother to Nurai (by Danehill Dancer), unplaced in two starts at 2 yrs in 2009. The dam, a useful 2-y-o 6f and 7f winner and second in the Group 2 6f Cherry Hinton Stakes, is a half-sister to 4 winners including the smart dual 1m winner and Group 3 Desmond Stakes third Middlemarch. The second dam, Blanche Dubois (by Nashwan), is an unraced half-sister to 7 winners including the Irish 2,000 Guineas winner Indian Haven and the Group 1 Gran Criterium winner Count Dubois. (A Saeed). *"A nice colt, I like him a lot. He has a very good action and looks like a six/seven furlong 2-y-o. Very nice physically, he looks like a top of the ground horse and although he's gone quite high behind when he furnishes he'll be quite nice."*

1594. UNNAMED ★★★
ch.f. *More Than Ready – Maybe In May (Miswaki).*
February 7. Seventh foal. 20,000Y. Tattersalls October. Rabbah Bloodstock. Sister to the useful 2-y-o 6f and 7f winner and Group 3 7f Acomb Stakes third Ready For Spring and to two minor winners in the USA and half-sister to another minor US winner by Mecke. The dam is an unplaced half-sister to 6 winners. The second dam, Sunrise Symphony (Secretariat), was an unplaced half-sister to 3 winners. (A Saeed). *"The sire is phenomenal and this is a nice filly that moves well, she's just very slow to eat because she's a little bit of a worrier. She's just doing two canters for now but she should make a 2-y-o. I just want her to pick up and eat more before I do more with her."*

1595. UNNAMED ★★
b.c. *Tiger Hill – Silver Bracelet (Machiavellian).*
March 19. Fifth foal. Half-brother to the fairly useful triple 1m winner Stoic (by Green Desert) and to the minor French 1m winner Dark Beauty (by Singspiel). The dam, a fairly useful 8.3f winner, was third in the listed Masaka Stakes and is a half-sister to one winner out of the very useful 2-y-o Group 3 7f Prestige Stakes winner and Group 1 Prix Marcel Boussac third Love Of Silver (by Arctic Tern) – herself a half-sister to 6 winners. (Ali Saeed). *"A colt with a lot of quality and despite his pedigree he doesn't altogether look as if he needs another year. A strong-topped horse, he looks as if he could make a 2-y-o over seven furlongs."*

1596. UNNAMED ★★★
b.f. *Red Ransom – Shersha (Priolo).*
March 10. Fourth foal. 20,000Y. Tattersalls October Book 2. Not sold. The dam, a useful Irish 6f (listed) and dual 1m winner at 3 and 6 yrs, is a half-sister to 2 winners. The second dam, Sheriya (by Green Dancer), was an unraced half-sister to 2 winners. (A Saeed). *"A nice, big filly that goes well. She was an inexpensive purchase because she's a little bit faulty in the knees but I think she was well-bought. I do like her, she's done well and I should imagine I'll start her off at six furlongs but she'll be better at seven."*

1597. UNNAMED ★★★
b.c. *Kyllachy – Topkamp (Pennekamp).*
March 8. Third foal. 27,000Y. Tattersalls October Book 2. Rabbah Bloodstock. Half-brother to Tell Halaf (by Oasis Dream), unplaced in two starts at 2 yrs in 2009 and to the quite useful 7f and 1m winner of 5 races Topazes (by Cadeaux Genereux). The dam, a useful 5f (at 2 yrs) and 6f listed winner, was Group 3 placed

in Ireland Germany and is a half-sister to the listed winning sprinter Morinqua. The second dam, Victoria Regia (by Lomond), a stakes winner of 3 races from 6f to 1m here and in the USA, is a half-sister to 9 winners. (A Saeed). *"A nice colt, the dam was pretty useful and we'll probably start this colt off at six furlongs. A real, strong 2-y-o type with a good action and I see him starting off in May. He's just looks a tough, TRAINERS' type of horse that you can get stuck into."*

1598. UNNAMED ★★★★
b.f. Dynaformer – Zuppardo Ardo (Zuppardo's Prince).
January 26. Fifth foal. $75,000Y. Keeneland September. Rabbah Bloodstock. Half-brother to 2 winners including the minor US 4-y-o winner Woodford Gale (by Distorted Humor). The dam won 14 races including the Grade 2 Humana Distaff Handicap and is a half-sister to 8 winners. The second dam, Alice Petite (by Ramirez) was a minor 2-y-o winner. (A Saeed). *"For a Dynaformer she came to hand quite quickly and she's done a few bits of work. A really nice type of filly, she goes well, I like her a lot and I think she looks fast enough for six furlongs. Seems to go better on the grass than the all-weather and she wouldn't mind a bit of juice. Hopefully she'll start off in the first six furlong fillies maiden here at Newmarket in May. She'd be nearly the pick of the fillies at the moment – she's the most forward-going anyway."*

CHRIS WALL
1599. DARSAN (IRE) ★★★
ch.f. Iffraaj – Coolrain Lady (Common Grounds).
April 14. Twelfth foal. €22,000foal. Goffs. Not sold. Half-sister to the 2-y-o listed 1m winner and Group 3 Prix Saint-Roman second La Vita E Bella (by Definite Article), to the 2-y-o dual listed 5f winner and Group 2 Criterium de Maisons-Laffitte third Bella Tusa (by Sri Pekan), the fairly useful 2-y-o dual 5f winner Light The Rocket (by Pips Pride) and the fair 2-y-o dual 7f winner Princess Petardia. The dam was placed 12 times in Ireland from 1m to 10f and is a half-sister to 4 minor winners. The second dam, Moneycashen (by Hook Money), won once at 3 yrs and over hurdles. (Ne'er Do Wells III). *"This is a family we know quite well as we've trained two of the half-sisters. This filly doesn't appear to be as sharp as Bella Tusa and I'd say she's likely to want six furlongs and that she may even want seven. She's a nice filly and sharp enough to make a two-year-old and we'll hopefully have a decent season with her. I wouldn't be rushing to get her out but hopefully she'll be racing in mid-summer. As a bunch of two-year-olds, these are as nice a group as I've had for some time."*

1600. FLASH FORWARD ★★★
gr.c. Haafhd – Regrette Rien (Unbridled's Song).
January 16. Third foal. 110,000Y. Tattersalls October Book 1. Not sold. Brother to the smart 2009 2-y-o Group 2 7f Superlative Stakes winner Silver Grecian and to the fair Irish 12f and hurdles winner Chebona Bula. The dam, unplaced in France at 2 yrs, is a half-sister to 6 winners including the US stakes winner Salty Sea. The second dam, Rose Indien (by Crystal Glitters), a winner of 5 races including the listed 6f Hopeful Stakes, is a half-sister to 8 winners including the French Group 2 12f winners America and Majorien. (Ms S Fustoq). *"A home-bred colt and he looks pretty similar to his brother Silver Grecian. The two of them are like two peas out of a pod in many regards, but whether this one will be as good as his half-brother we'll have to wait and see. He had an issue with a muscle problem early on so we don't know too much about him yet, but he's a nice solid sort of a colt that should be running as a two-year-old in mid-summer."*

1601. GOLDEN CITY (IRE) ★★
b.f. Azamour – Generous Lady (Generous).
April 30. Ninth foal. Sister to the unplaced 2009 2-y-o Azaday and half-sister to the very smart 7f (at 2 yrs), Group 2 12f King Edward VII Stakes and dual Group 3 12f Cumberland Lodge Stakes winner High Accolade (by Mark Of Esteem), to the useful 9f (at 2 yrs) and 13f winner Oasis Knight (by Oasis Dream), the quite useful 12f to 2m winner Highland Legacy (by Selkirk), the quite useful 12f all-weather winner Summer Wine (by Desert King) and the fair 12f winner Mango Lady (by Dalakhani). The dam, a middle-distance winner of 4 races in Ireland including a listed event, is a half-sister to 6 winners including the Group 2 Premio Guido

Beradelli and Group 3 St Leger Italiano winner Jape. The second dam, Northern Blossom (by Snow Knight), was a champion 3-y-o filly in Canada and won two Graded stakes events. (Ms S Fustoq). *"We've had quite a few out of this mare, although the two best ones were colts and they were sold. Generally they stay quite well, but that said we've had a couple that were sharper, running over a mile. This filly has a bit of scope but she'll take a bit of time to develop."*

1602. GOSPEL MUSIC ★★★
b.f. Beat Hollow – Bible Box (Bin Ajwaad).
February 23. Fourth foal. Half-sister to the French 2-y-o 9f listed-placed Bahamian Box, to the fairly useful triple 6f winner (including at 2 yrs) Bounty Box (both by Bahamian Bounty) and the fairly useful 2-y-o 6f winner and listed-placed Vive Les Rouges (by Bin Ajwaad). The dam, a quite useful 7f to 9f winner of 3 races, is out of the 2-y-o 1m seller winner Addie Pray (by Great Commotion), herself a half-sister to 7 winners. (Mr M Sinclair). *"The dam's pedigree is nothing to get too excited about but she was a decent filly herself and her first three foals have all been above average. This is a nice filly, quite well-grown and scopey, so probably not as precocious as the other two fillies I've had. I'd like to think she'll be running in the summer."*

1603. HEIGHT OF SUMMER (IRE) ★★
b.f. Alhaarth – Summer Dreams (Sadler's Wells).
March 12. Fifth foal. 35,000Y. Tattersalls October Book 1. Chris Wall. Half-sister to the fairly useful 2-y-o 7f winner and Group 3 1m Autumn Stakes third Moudez (by Xaar). The dam was placed at up to 14f and is a half-sister to 5 winners including the German Derby winner All My Dreams. The second dam, Marie de Beaujeu (by Kenmare), won twice and was listed placed in France and is a half-sister to 4 winners. (Hughes, Gibson & Scott). *"A nice, athletic filly. There are mixed messages from her pedigree in that there are bits that suggest she'll stay well and other bits that say she might be a bit speedier. She's not over-big and certainly looks like making her mark at two before training on."*

1604. LILAC SONG (IRE) ★★
b.f. Oratorio – Ivy League Star (Sadler's Wells).
February 29. The dam is an unplaced sister to the fillies Ivrea and Iziva, both 2-y-o 7f winners and second in the Ribblesdale Stakes and a half-sister to 3 winners including the very useful Ivyanna, a winner of two races over 1m (at 2 yrs) and the Group 1 12f Italian Oaks. The second dam, Ivy (by Sir Ivor), was placed twice at 2 yrs in the USA, is a sister to the dam of a stakes winner and a half-sister to 12 winners including the Graded stakes winners An Act, Din and Sarsar and to the dam of the Grade 2 winner Herat. (Ms S Fustoq). *"This is a nice enough filly but she looks destined to be much more of a three-year-old than a filly for this year."*

1605. MIDNIGHT RIDER (IRE) ★★★
b.c. Red Ransom – Foreplay (Lujain).
February 10. First foal. 28,000Y. Tattersalls October Book 2. Chris Wall. The dam, a fair 6f (at 2 yrs) and 7f winner, is a half-sister to the smart listed 9f and listed 10f winner and Group 1 Prix Jean Prat third Rocamadour and to the Irish 2-y-o 5f winner and listed-placed Church Cross. The second dam, Watch Me (by Green Desert), a useful 6f winner and third in the Group 3 6f Cork And Orrery Stakes, is a half-sister to 3 winners here and abroad. (The Leap Year Partnership). *"A nice colt that looks like making a summer two-year-old over six or seven furlongs and he might even stay a mile later on. One of our earlier ones."*

1606. MOONLIGHT MYSTERY ★★★
ch.f. Pivotal – Mauri Moon (Green Desert).
March 31. Fifth foal. 72,000Y. Tattersalls October Book 1. Not sold. Sister to the fairly useful 2009 2-y-o dual 7f winner Karaka Jack and to the quite useful 2-y-o 7f winner Shamayel and half-sister to the fair 2-y-o 1m winner Kiwi Moon (by Nayef) and the fair 2-y-o 7f all-weather winner Capannina (by Grand Lodge). The dam won 4 races including the listed Oak Tree Stakes and is a half-sister to 5 winners including the Singapore Derby winner Kimbridge Knight. The second dam, Dazzling Heights (by Shirley Heights), a useful winner of 4 races from 7f (at 2 yrs) to 11f including a listed (event in France, is a full or half-sister to 6 winners. (Tarworth Bloodstock Investment).

"Obviously a well-bred filly, I think she missed her slot at the Sales because she had a problem at the time so the owner Mr Pritchard retained her. Out of a mare who was a bit tricky on the racecourse but won a listed race, this filly's half-brothers and sisters have all done alright. She's not particularly precocious, she's quite well-grown and has some developing to do yet, but she's done nothing wrong so far."

1607. PRECOCIOUS KID (IRE) ★★★
b.c. Whipper – Valley Lights (Dance Of Life).
April 6. 13,000Y. Tattersalls October Book 2. C Wall. Half-brother to the useful triple 6f winner (including at 2 yrs) Masha-il (by Danehill), to the fairly useful dual 2-y-o 7f winner and subsequent US winner Il Colosseo (by Spectrum), the fairly useful 10f to 2m winner Mumbling (by Dr Devious), the quite useful 6f (at 2 yrs) and 7f winner of 4 races Niran (by Captain Rio) and a winner in Hong Kong by Bigstone. The dam was placed once (fourth of five) over 1m in Ireland and is a half-sister to 7 winners including the high-class miler Then Again. The second dam, New Light (by Reform), won over 10f and is a half-sister to the dam of the top-class Oaks and St Leger winner Sun Princess and the Coronation Cup winner Saddlers Hall. (D M Thurlby). "Being by Whipper he ought to be a two-year-old. He's a little bit 'on the leg' at the moment but he's developing all the time. Unlike his sire he's got a bit of size about him, so I would hope he'd make a summer two-year-old and given his purchase price he'll hopefully be competitive in the auction races." TRAINERS' BARGAIN BUY

DERMOT WELD

1608. ACOUSTIC CHEER (USA) ★★★
b.br.f. Arch – Hymn Of Love (Barathea).
January 15. The dam, an Irish listed 1m winner, is a half-sister to several winners including the Irish 6f and subsequent US winner Still As Sweet. The second dam, Perils Of Joy (by Rainbow Quest), a 3-y-o 1m winner in Ireland, is a half-sister to 5 winners including the Italian Group 3 winner Sweetened Offer. (Moyglare Stud Farm).

1609. ACTS OUT LOUD (USA) ★★★
ch.f. Mr Greeley – Burren Rose (Storm Cat).
February 21. The dam, a useful Irish 1m, 10f and listed 12f winner, is a half-sister to one winner. The second dam, Lisieux Rose (by Generous), won the Group 2 11f Blandford Stakes and is a half-sister to 2 winners. (Moyglare Stud Farm).

1610. A WORD APART (IRE) ★★★
b.c. Desert Style – Lady Luck (Kris).
April 23. Half-brother to the very smart 7f (at 2 yrs) and Group 2 10f Leopardstown Derby Trial winner and dual Derby placed Casual Conquest (by Hernando), to the Irish 2-y-o listed 7f winner Elusive Double (by Grand Lodge), the Irish 7f winner Moving Heart (by Anabaa) and the quite useful Irish 9f winner Media Asset (by Polish Precedent). The dam won over 1m in Ireland and is a half-sister to several winners including the Irish Group 3 Boland Stakes winner Social Harmony. The second dam, Latest Chapter (by Ahonoora), is an unraced half-sister to the Grade 1 Belmont Stakes winner Go And Go. (Moyglare Stud Farm).

1611. DUBAI PRINCE (IRE) ★★★
b.c. Shamardal – Desert Frolic (Persian Bold).
February 15. 48,000foal. Tattersalls December. John Ferguson. Half-brother to the useful 9f (at 2 yrs), 1m and 12f winner and listed-placed Jakarta Jade (by Royal Abjar) and the fairly useful 7f and 1m winner Cadre (by King's Best). The dam, a fairly useful 11f to 13f winner, is a half-sister to 3 winners including the Group 2 12f King Edward VII Stakes winner Storming Home. The second dam, Try To Catch Me (by Shareef Dancer), won once over 1m at 3 yrs in France, is closely related to the US stakes winner Air Dancer and a half-sister to the Group 2 Criterium de Maisons-Laffitte winner Bitooh and the dam of the Group 2 winner Slip Stream. (Darley Stud Management).

1612. ETERNAL YOUTH (IRE) ★★★
ch.c. Intikhab – Endless Peace
(Russian Revival).
March 16. Second foal. 55,000Y. Tattersalls October Book 2. Bobby O'Ryan. Half-brother to the modest 2009 2-y-o 5f winner Zelos Dream (by Redback). The dam, a modest 6f (at 2 yrs) to 8.7f placed maiden, is a half-sister to 6 winners including the smart Group 3 winning sprinter and 2-y-o Group 2 placed Hoh Mike

and the very useful sprinter Hogmaneigh. The second dam, Magical Peace (by Magical Wonder), a quite useful Irish 6f winner, is a half-sister to one winner. (Dr R Lambe)

1613. ENTIKAAL ★★★★
b.c. *Royal Applause – Notjustaprettyface (Red Ransom).*
March 15. Second foal. 160,000Y. Tattersalls October Book 1. Shadwell Estate Co. Half-brother to the quite useful 2009 2-y-o 5f winner Tropical Treat (by Bahamian Bounty). The dam, a fairly useful 2-y-o 5f winner, was listed-placed twice and fourth in the Group 2 Lowther Stakes and is a half-sister to a winner in the UAE. The second dam, Maudie May (by Gilded Time), won over 8.5f in the USA and is a half-sister to 6 winners including Sri Pekan. (Hamdan Al Maktoum)

1614. HARANGUE (IRE) ★★★
b.c. *Street Cry – Splendeur (Desert King).*
April 18. Third foal. €100,000Y. Goffs Orby. John Ferguson. The dam won twice in France including over 11f and is a half-sister to 4 winners including the Group 1 Italian Derby winner Gentlewave. The second dam, Saumareine (by Saumarez), won two minor races in France at 3 and 4 yrs and is a half-sister to 7 winners including Charming Duke (Grade 1 Hollywood Derby). (Darley Stud Management)

1615. HILL OF CONTENT (IRE) ★★
b.c. *Westerner – Delphinium (Dr Massini).*
May 3. Third foal. €60,000Y. Goffs Orby. Bobby O'Ryan. Half-brother to the useful 7f (at 2 yrs) and Group 3 11f Gallinule Stakes winner Hebridean (by Bach). The dam is an unplaced half-sister to 4 winners. The second dam, Lunulae (by Tumble Wind), won at 2 yrs and over hurdles and is a half-sister to 3 winners. (Dr R Lambe)

1616. FLIC FLAC (IRE) ★★
ch.c. *Dubawi – Polite Reply (With Approval).*
March 16. Second foal. 20,000Y. Tattersalls October Book 3. R O'Gorman. The dam ran once unplaced and is a half-sister to the Italian dual Group 3 winner and Group 1 placed Exhibit One. The second dam, Tsar's Pride (by Sadler's Wells), a winner over 12f in France and listed-placed over 10f, is a half-sister to 3 winners. (Moyglare Stud Farm)

1617. MALAYAN MIST (IRE) ★★
b.f. *Dansili – Misty Heights (Fasliyev).*
April 20. Second foal. Half-sister to the fair 1m winner Greyfriarschorista (by King's Best). The dam, an Irish listed 9f winner, is a half-sister to 4 winners. The second dam, Mountains Of Mist (by Shirley Heights), a quite useful 10f winner, is a half-sister to the 2-y-o Group 2 6f Lowther Stakes winner Enthused. (Lady O'Reilly)

1618. MIDNIGHT MUSIC (IRE) ★★★
ch.f. *Dubawi – Midnight Mist (Green Desert).*
March 9. The dam, a fair Irish 7f and 1m winner, is a half-sister to the Canadian Grade 3 winner Madeira Mist, to the listed 8.5f winner and Group 1 7f Moyglare Stud Stakes fourth Misty Heights (by Fasliyev), the Irish 2-y-o 7f winner Mountain Snow (by Barathea), the quite useful 1m, 10f and hurdles winner Fortune Point (by Cadeaux Genereux) and the Irish dual 12f winner Mist Of Magic (by Caerleon). The second dam, Mountains Of Mist (by Shirley Heights), a quite useful 10f winner, is a half-sister to 7 winners including the Group 2 Lowther Stakes winner Enthused and the listed 12f Prix Vulcain winner From Beyond. (Lady O'Reilly)

1619. FARAWAY MOUNTAIN (IRE) ★★★
ch.c. *Indian Haven – Muschana (Deploy).*
April 25. Sixth living foal. €40,000Y. Goffs Orby. Bobby O'Ryan. Half-brother to the useful 2009 Irish 7f placed Senior (by Medicean), to the quite useful 2-y-o 7f winner Montagne d'Or (by Montjeu), the quite useful 2-y-o 7f winner Peace And Love (by Fantastic Light) and the fair 12f and 13f winner Mpenzi (by Groom Dancer). The dam, a quite useful dual 10f winner, is a half-sister to 4 winners including Jeune, winner of the Group 2 12f Hardwicke Stakes here and the Melbourne Cup in Australia and the very useful Group 2 12f King Edward VII Stakes winner Beneficial. The second dam, Youthful (by Green Dancer), won over 12f and is a half-sister to the Group 2 Grand Prix de Deauville winner First Prayer and the US Grade winner Water Lily (dam of the Grade 1 Flamingo Stakes winner Talinum).

1620. NAASEH ★★★
b.c. Medicean – Tiriana (Common Grounds).
April 30. Eighth foal. €270,000Y. Goffs Orby. Shadwell Estate Co. Half-sister to the useful Group 3 7f Dubai Duty Free (Fred Darling Stakes) and 2-y-o 7f listed winner and Irish 1,000 Guineas second Penkenna Princess (by Pivotal), the quite useful 2-y-o 5f winner and listed placed Mystery Ocean (by Dr Fong), the quite useful 7f winner Divine Power (by Kyllachy), the fair winner of 3 races at around 1m Madamoiselle Jones (by Emperor Jones) and the moderate 10f and 2m winner Salut Saint Cloud (by Primo Dominie). The dam is a placed half-sister to 4 winners including the 2-y-o listed 5.2f winner Head Over Heels. The second dam, Proudfoot (by Shareef Dancer), won over 14f in Ireland and is a full or half-sister to 7 winners. (Hamdan Al Maktoum)

1621. NOTABLE GRADUATE (IRE) ★★★★
b.c. Galileo – Market Slide (Gulch).
March 11. Closely related to Refuse To Bend, a top-class winner of four Group 1 races from 7f (at 2 yrs) to 10f, to the very useful 2-y-o 7f winner and Group 2 Beresford Stakes second Domestic Fund and the fairly useful Irish 12f winner Ripple Of Pride (all by Sadler's Wells) and half-sister to the Melbourne Cup winner Media Puzzle (by Theatrical). The dam, an Irish 6f (at 2 yrs) and 6.5f winner, is closely related to the minor Irish 7f winner First Breeze and a half-sister to the Breeders Cup Classic second Twilight Agenda and the minor Irish 7f winner Early Memory. (Moyglare Stud Farm).

1622. NUBA (IRE) ★★
b.f. Exceed And Excel – Little Doll (Gulch).
February 7. First foal. £74,000Y. Doncaster St Leger. Shadwell Estate Co. The dam is an unraced half-sister to one winner. The second dam, Showlady (by Theatrical), a US Grade 3 winner, is a sister to the Group 2 Blandford Stakes winner Humbel and a half-sister to the US multiple Grade 1 winner Escena. (Hamdan Al Maktoum)

1623. OLFA ★★★
b.f. Dubawi – Shahaamah (Red Ransom).
February 10. Fourth foal. Half-sister to the quite useful 2009 6f and 7f placed 2-y-o Mutafajer (by Oasis Dream), to the fairly useful 2-y-o 7f winner Zakhaaref (by Daylami) and the fair 2-y-o 5f winner Azwa (by Haafhd). The dam is an unraced half-sister to 4 winners including the very useful 2-y-o 6f winner and Group 2 6f Lowther Stakes second Khulan and the useful 7f (at 2 yrs) and 1m winner Thajja. The second dam, Jawlaat (by Dayjur), a fairly useful dual 6f winner, is closely related to the July Cup winner Elnadim and a half-sister to the Irish 1,000 Guineas winner Mehthaaf. (Hamdan Al Maktoum).

1624. OLYMPIAD (IRE) ★★★★
b.c. Galileo – Caumshinaun (Indian Ridge).
March 9. Sixth foal. 650,000Y. Tattersalls October Book 1. Sir Robert Ogden. Brother to the Group 1 Irish 1,000 Guineas winner Nightime and half-brother to the Irish 2-y-o 1m winner and listed-placed Mermaid Island (by Mujadil) and the fairly useful dual 7f winner Gunga Din (by Green Desert). The dam won 5 races from 6f to 1m in Ireland at 3 and 4 yrs including a listed event and was Group 3 placed. She is a half-sister to one winner out of the Irish 2-y-o 6f winner Ridge Pool (by Bluebird). (Sir Robert Ogden CBE LLD)

1625. HISAABAAT (IRE) ★★★
b.c. Dubawi – Phariseek (Rainbow Quest).
April 10. Fifth foal. €140,000Y. Goffs Orby. Shadwell Estate Co. Half-brother to the unplaced 2009 2-y-o The Caped Crusader (by Cape Cross), to the fair Irish 1m winner Young Lochinvar (by Pivotal) and the fair Irish 6f winner Toberanthawn (by Danehill Dancer). The dam, an Irish 2-y-o 7f winner, was listed-placed twice and is a half-sister to 5 winners including the Irish 2-y-o listed 6f winner Pharmacist (herself dam of the Breeders Cup Turf winner Red Rocks). The second dam, Pharaoh's Delight (by Fairy King), a half-sister to 8 winners, won the 2-y-o Group 1 5f Phoenix Stakes. (Hamdan Al Maktoum)

1626. PRIMADONA (IRE) ★★★
b.f. Galileo – Dress To Thrill (Danehill).
April 1. Fourth foal. The dam won Grade 1 9f Matriarch Stakes and Group 2 1m Sun Chariot Stakes and is a sister to 2 winners and a half-sister to 6 winners. The second dam, Trusted Partner (by Affirmed), winner of the Group 3 7f C.L. Weld Park Stakes (at 2 yrs) and the Irish

1,000 Guineas, is a sister to the useful middle distance performers Easy to Copy and Epicure's Garden. (Moyglare Stud Farm).

1627. PROVIDE (IRE) ★★
b.c. *Holy Roman Emperor – Uliana (Darshaan).*
April 29. Sixth foal. €34,000Y. Goffs Orby. Not sold. Half-brother to the minor Irish 2-y-o 1m and subsequent US winner So Amazing (by Galileo) and to the Irish 1m winner and Group 3 Blue Wind Stakes second Festival Princess (by Barathea). The dam, an Irish 10f winner, is a half-sister to 3 winners including the 1m 2-y-o and subsequent German Group 1 10f winner Ransom O'War. The second dam, Sombreffe (by Polish Precedent), a fair 7f all-weather winner, is a half-sister to 11 winners including the Group 2 winners Russian Bond and Snaadee. (B R Firestone)

1628. QUBUH (IRE) ★★★
b.c. *Invincible Spirit – Chica Roca (Woodman).*
February 23. Third foal. €95,000Y. Goffs Orby. Shadwell Estate Co. Half-brother to the fair Irish 6f (at 2 yrs) and 7f winner Chibcha (by High Chaparral). The dam, placed twice at 2 yrs in France, is a half-sister to the Group 2 Criterium de Maisons-Laffitte winner Zinziberine. The second dam, Amenixa (by Linamix), a 4-y-o 10f winner, is a sister to the dual Group 1 Prix Royal-Oak winner Amilynx and the listed winner Amie De Mix and a half-sister to the Group 2 Criterium de Maisons-Laffitte winner Amiwain. (Hamdan Al Maktoum)

1629. REGAL TRAMP (USA) ★★★
b.f. *Street Cry – Unique Pose (Sadler's Wells).*
March 25. Second foal. The dam, an Irish 6f (at 2 yrs) and 10f winner, was listed-placed and is a sister to the Irish 3-y-o 7f winner and 2-y-o Group 3 7f C L Weld Park Stakes third Easy Sunshine. The second dam, Desert Ease (by Green Desert), an Irish 2-y-o listed 6f winner, is a half-sister to several winners including the Group 3 Tetrarch Stakes and Group 3 7f Concorde Stakes winner Two-Twenty-Two. (Moyglare Stud Farm).

1630. RICH TAPESTRY (IRE) ★★★
b.c. *Holy Roman Emperor – Genuine Charm (Sadler's Wells).*

March 26. Second foal. Half-brother to the quite useful Irish 1m winner Anywaysmile (by Indian Ridge). The dam is a placed sister to 3 winners including the top-class winner of four Group 1 races from 7f (at 2 yrs) to 10f Refuse To Bend and a half-sister to the Melbourne Cup winner Media Puzzle. The second dam, Market Slide (by Gulch), an Irish 6f (at 2 yrs) and 6.5f winner, is a half-sister to the Breeders Cup Classic second Twilight Agenda. (Moyglare Stud Farm).

1631. SANADAAT ★★★
b.br.f. *Green Desert – Manayer (Sadler's Wells).*
March 21. The dam is an unraced full or half-sister to 2 winners. The second dam, Dazzling Park (by Warning), a very smart winner of the Group 3 1m Matron Stakes and a listed 9f event, was placed in the Group 1 Irish Champion Stakes and the Irish 1,000 Guineas. She is a half-sister to 7 winners including the Derby, Champion Stakes, Dewhurst Stakes and National Stakes winner New Approach. (Hamdan Al Maktoum).

1632. SAPPHIRE (IRE) ★★★
b.f. *Medicean – Polished Gem (Danehill).*
February 2. First foal. The dam, an Irish 2-y-o 7f winner, is a sister to 2 winners including the Grade 1 9f Matriarch Stakes and Group 2 1m Sun Chariot Stakes winner Dress To Thrill and a half-sister to 6 winners. The second dam, Trusted Partner (by Affirmed), was a very useful winner of the Group 3 7f C.L. Weld Park Stakes (at 2 yrs) and the Irish 1,000 Guineas and is a sister to the useful middle distance performers Easy to Copy and Epicure's Garden and to the useful Irish 7f listed and US Grade 3 winner Low Key Affair. (Moyglare Stud Farm).

1633. SAQIL (USA) ★★
b.c. *El Prado – Rumansy (Theatrical).*
April 20. Half-brother to the quite useful Irish 2-y-o 7f winner Labaqa (by Rahy). The dam is a placed sister to the US Grade 3 Generous Stakes winner Startac. The second dam, Uenga (Mr Prospector), won a minor event at 2 yrs in France and is a half-sister to 5 winners including the US Grade 2 winner Jade Flush. (Hamdan Al Maktoum).

1634. TAFJEER (USA) ★★
b.f. *Elusive Quality – Nuzooa (by A P Indy)*.
January 1. Second foal. The dam, a fairly useful 10f and 12f winner, is a half-sister to 3 winners including the smart 10f, 12f and UAE listed winner Mutasallil. The second dam, Min Alhawa (by Riverman), a useful 7f (at 2 yrs) to 10f winner, is a sister to the very smart One Thousand Guineas and Tripleprint Celebration Mile winner Harayir. (Hamdan Al Maktoum).

1635. TENUOUS LINK (IRE) ★★★
b.c. *Oasis Dream – Summer Trysting (Alleged)*.
April 27. Tenth foal. Half-brother to the Irish 2-y-o 7f listed and subsequent US Grade 2 9.5f Arlington Derby winner Simple Exchange (by Danehill), to the Irish 7f (at 2 yrs), Group 3 Brigadier Gerard Stakes and Group 3 Newbury Dubai Duty Free 'Arc' Trial winner Sights On Gold, the fairly useful Irish 8.5f winner Romantic Venture (both by Indian Ridge), the fairly useful Irish 9f winner Beat The Heat (by Salse) and the fair Irish 12f winner Tempting Paradise (by Grand Lodge). The dam was placed at up to 12f in Ireland and is a half-sister to the smart performer at up to 10f Smooth Performance. The second dam, Seasonal Pickup (by The Minstrel), won four listed races in Ireland and is a half-sister to the dam of Grey Swallow. (Moyglare Stud Farm).

1636. TRAIN OF THOUGHT (IRE) ★★
b.c. *Sadler's Wells – Cool Clarity (Indian Ridge)*.
April 19. Fourth foal. €200,000Y. Goffs Orby. Bobby O'Ryan. The dam, an Irish listed 7f winner, is a half-sister to 6 winners including the 2-y-o listed 7f Tyros Stakes winner and Group 3 7f Boland Stakes second Artistic Blue and the Irish listed 7.5f winner Queen Of Palms. The second dam, Tapolite (by Tap On Wood), won the listed 7f Tyros Stakes, is a sister to the 2-y-o Group 3 1m Killavullen Stakes winner Sedulous and a half-sister to 4 winners. (Dr R Lambe).

1637. TRIPLE EIGHT (IRE) ★★★
b.c. *Royal Applause – Hidden Charm (by Big Shuffle)*.
February 8. First foal. The dam, a quite useful 5f and 6f winner, is a half-sister to one winner. The second dam, Polite Reply (by Be My Guest), a quite useful Irish 7f and 1m winner, is a half-sister to 2 winners. (Moyglare Stud Farm).

1638. UNCUT STONE (IRE) ★★★
b.c. *Awesome Again – Suitably Discreet (Mr Prospector)*.
March 8. Half-brother to the Irish 2-y-o 7f winner and Group 2 1m Beresford Stakes second Capital Exposure and to the quite useful Irish 9f and 11f winner Designated Decoy (both by Danzig). The dam is an unraced half-sister to the Group 2 1m Goffs International Stakes and US Grade 2 Arcadia Handicap winner Century City. The second dam, Alywow (by Alysheba), a champion filly in Canada, won 7 races including the Grade 3 8.5f Nijana Stakes and was second in the Grade 1 Rothmans International and the Grade 1 Flower Bowl Invitational. (Moyglare Stud Farm)

1639. WALKING ON WATER (IRE) ★★★
b.f. *Galileo – Treasure The Lady (Indian Ridge)*.
March 4. Third foal. The dam won once in Ireland at 2 yrs over 7f and was listed-placed and is a half-sister to 6 winners including High Chaparral. The second dam, Kasora (by Darshaan), is an unraced full or half-sister to 8 winners. (Mrs A Coughlan)

1640. UNNAMED ★★★
b.c. *Invincible Spirit – Anna Frid (Big Shuffle)*.
February 27. Third foal. 115,000Y. Tattersalls October Book 1. Not sold. Half-brother to the fairly useful 2-y-o 5f winner Sharp Bullet (by Royal Applause). The dam, a useful Irish listed 5f winner, is a sister to the smart winner of the Group 3 5f King George 200th Anniversary Stakes winner Agnetha and to the smart German Group 2 sprint winner Areion and a half-sister to 5 winners. The second dam, Aerleona (by Caerleon), a German 2-y-o 6f winner, is a half-sister to 5 winners including the Fillies' Mile winner Nepula.(J Higgins)

1641. UNNAMED ★★★
b.f. *Zamindar – Fame At Last (Quest For Fame)*.
March 18. Sister to the fair French 1m winner Everlasting Fame, closely related to the quite useful 6f winner Anchor Date (by Zafonic) and half-sister to the very smart 6f (at 2 yrs), Group 3 Irish 2,000 Guineas Trial, Group 3 9f

International Stakes and Group 3 1m Desmond Stakes winner Famous Name (by Dansili) and the fair 1m winner Final Esteem (by Lomitas). The dam, a fairly useful 2-y-o 7f winner, is a half-sister to one winner. The second dam, Ranales (by Majestic Light), a minor 2-y-o 1m winner in the USA, is a half-sister to 9 winners including the listed 10f Virginia Stakes winner Rambushka and the Group 2 7f Laurent Perrier Champagne Stakes second Arokat. (Khalid Abdulla).

1642. UNNAMED ★★★
b.f. *Royal Applause – Grizel (Lion Cavern).*
January 20. Third foal. Sister to the Irish 2-y-o 7f and subsequent US Grade 2 1m and 9f winner Whatsthescript. The dam, a fair 5f and 6f all-weather winner of 3 races, is a half-sister to very useful 2-y-o listed 7f winner and Group 2 1m May Hill Stakes second Queen Of Poland and to the useful 2-y-o dual 7f winner White Hawk. The second dam, Polska (by Danzig), a useful winner over 6f at 2 yrs, is closely related to the useful filly Millstream, a winner of five races over 5f including the Group 3 Ballyogan Stakes and the Group 3 Cornwallis Stakes. (C McHale).

1643. UNNAMED ★★★
b.c. *Oasis Dream – Musical Horizon (Distant View).*
February 24. First foal. The dam is an unplaced sister to the champion 2-y-o Distant Music (winner of the Group 1 7f Dewhurst Stakes, the Group 2 7f Champagne Stakes and the Group 2 9f Goffs International Stakes) and a half-sister to several winners including the useful 10f winner and Group 3 Lancashire Oaks third New Orchid (herself dam of the Group 1 6f Haydock Sprint Cup winner African Rose). The second dam, Musicanti (by Nijinsky), a French 14.5f winner, is a half-sister to the top-class American middle-distance colt Vanlandingham, winner of the Washington D.C. International, the Jockey Club Gold Cup and the Suburban Handicap. (Khalid Abdulla).

1644. UNNAMED ★★
b.f. *Cacique – Neath (Rainbow Quest).*
March 5. The dam, a fair 10f placed maiden, is a sister to the 1m (at 2 yrs) and 9f winner and listed-placed Rainwashed Gold and a half-sister to 3 winners. The second dam, Welsh Autumn (by Tenby), a French listed winner and second in the Group 3 10.5f Prix Penelope, is a half-sister to 3 winners. (Khalid Abdulla).

1645. UNNAMED ★★★★
b.c. *King's Best – Return (Sadler's Wells).*
April 4. Brother to the useful 2-y-o 6f winner and subsequent US Graded stakes placed To Sender and half-brother to the fair 2009 Irish 2-y-o 1m winner Address Unknown (by Oasis Dream) and the quite useful 10f winner Coming Back (by Fantastic Light). The dam, a quite useful 12f winner, is a sister to the Group 2 Great Voltigeur Stakes winner Dushyantor, closely related to the Grade 1 10f Flower Bowl Invitational Handicap winner Yashmak and a half-sister to Commander in Chief, Warning and Deploy. The second dam, Slightly Dangerous (by Roberto), a very smart filly and winner of the 7.3f Fred Darling Stakes, was second in the Oaks to Time Charter and is a half-sister to the dams of the Arc winner and top class sire Rainbow Quest and the Dewhurst Stakes dead-heater Scenic. (Khalid Abdulla).

1646. UNNAMED ★★★
br.c. *Dansili – Verbose (Storm Bird).*
February 5. Brother to the smart Group 3 7f Somerville Tattersall Stakes winner Thousand Words and half-brother to the fair 1m and 9f placed 2-y-o Chinese Puzzle (by Dr Fong). The dam, a fairly useful listed-placed 1m winner, is a half-sister to the useful 9f and 10f winner and subsequent US Grade 2 placed Exterior. The second dam, Alvernia (by Alydar), a winner over 8.5f and 9f in the USA, is a half-sister to the dam of the French 1,000 Guineas winner Matiara. (Khalid Abdulla).

1647. UNNAMED ★★
b.c. *Cacique – Zorleni (Zafonic).*
March 12. Half-brother to the modest 6f (at 2 yrs) to 1m winner of 4 races Bucharest (by Barathea). The dam is an unplaced half-sister to 5 winners including the very useful Prix d'Aumale, Prix Vanteaux and Prix de Malleret winner Bonash. The second dam, Sky Love (by Nijinsky), a fairly useful 10f winner, is a half-sister to the high-class Prix de la Cote Normande winner Raft. (Khalid Abdulla).

PETER WINKWORTH

I have Assistant Trainer Anton Pearson to thank once again for helping me out with the comments.

1648. DARK AND DANGEROUS (IRE) ★★★
b.c. Cacique – Gilah (Saddler's Hall).
January 22. Fifth foal. 62,000Y. Tattersalls October Book 1. N H Bloodstock. Half-brother to the fairly useful 2-y-o dual 1m winner Night Of Joy (by King's Best), to the quite useful 10f to 2m and hurdles winner Ainama (by Desert Prince) and the quite useful 2-y-o 8.3f winner Congressional (by Grand Lodge). The dam is an unraced half-sister to 7 winners including the very useful 10.2f winner Cocotte (the dam of 5 stakes winners including the top-class colt Pilsudski). The second dam, Gay Milly (by Mill Reef), a fair 3-y-o 1m winner, is out of the Irish 1,000 Guineas winner Gaily. (North South Alliance). "The sire doesn't have many too many on the ground because he isn't very fertile, but this is a nice individual and apart from being slightly weak behind he's a lovely colt to look at. Fairly backward, despite having an early foaling date, he'll be looked after in the first half of the season and he's one for seven furlongs to begin with. A strong, fairly correct individual."

1649. DIRECTOR'S DREAM (IRE) ★★
gr.f. Act One – Najayeb (Silver Hawk).
February 7. Fifth foal. 24,000Y. Tattersalls December. David Redvers. Half-sister to the smart 2009 1m winner and Group 2 Royal Lodge Stakes second Waseet (by Selkirk) and to the quite useful 2-y-o 1m winner Mutadarrej (by Fantastic Light). The dam is an unraced half-sister to 6 winners including the high-class Prix de l'Arc de Triomphe and Juddmonte International winner Sakhee and the useful 7f (at 2 yrs) and listed 10f winner Nasheed. The second dam, Thawakib (by Sadler's Wells), a useful dual 7f (at 2 yrs) and Group 2 12f Ribblesdale Stakes winner, is a half-sister to 9 winners including the top-class middle-distance colt Celestial Storm (winner of the Group 2 Princess of Wales's Stakes). (Kennet Valley Thoroughbreds). "Very backward, it's a lovely family but the sire isn't popular and she's very tall and weak."

1650. DRUMMER BOY ★★★
ch.c. Haafhd – Largo (Selkirk).
January 23. Fourth foal. Half-brother to a minor winner abroad by Dubai Destination. The dam, a fairly useful dual 12f winner, is a half-sister to 3 winners including the useful 1m (at 2 yrs) and 2m winner Coventina. The second dam, Lady Of The Lake (by Caerleon), a useful 2m listed winner of 4 races, is a half-sister to 5 winners including the Italian Group 3 winner Guest Connections. (Mrs Katie Warr & Mrs Jessica Muddle). "I really like this colt. The sire hasn't set the world alight even though he's had winners but this is a dead ringer for him. Right from day one it was like having a ten year old in the yard, because he was broken easily, he wandered into the gate and shot out – everything was easy for him. But the thing I like about him is – every time you ask him for a bit more, or ask him to go a bit quicker, he responds. He's a January foal and yet he's still a bit backward, but he could well be alright."

1651. FOXTROT HOTEL (IRE) ★★★
b.c. Majestic Missile – Opalescent (Polish Precedent).
April 9. Third foal. 11,000Y. Tattersalls October Book 3. Highflyer Bloodstock. Half-brother to the modest 6f winner of 4 races Fyelehk (by Kheleyf). The dam is an unraced half-sister to 3 winners including the Group 1 Phoenix Stakes third Polar Force. The second dam, Irish Light (by Irish River), won twice at 3 yrs and is a half-sister to 5 winners. (Foxtrot Racing Partnership IV). "He was a cheap individual, he's very tall, 'on the leg' and is still growing. He wasn't an early foal so he's every right to be backward and I'm pleased with the bit he's done so far. He could well be alright."

1652. OFFBEAT SAFARIS (IRE) ★★★
b.c. Le Vie Dei Colori – Baywood (Emarati).
March 1. Fifth foal. £22,000Y. Doncaster St Leger. David Redvers. Half-brother to the moderate 6f winner Left Nostril (by Beckett). The dam is an unplaced half-sister to the listed-placed winners Baize and Bayleaf. The second dam, Bayonne (by Bay Express), won twice at 3 yrs and is a half-sister to 7 winners. (P Winkworth). "The sire usually gets wiry, athletic types that like to play around. This colt is the nicest one by the sire I've ever seen –

1653. TULLIUS (IRE) ★★★★♣
ch.c. Le Vie Dei Colori – Whipped Queen (Kingmambo).
April 23. Seventh foal. 20,000Y. Tattersalls October Book 2. David Redvers. Half-brother to the useful 2-y-o 7f and 9f winner Poster (by Johannesburg) and to a minor US 4-y-o winner by Black Minnaloushe. The dam won 2 minor races at 3 and 4 yrs in the USA and is a half-sister to 10 winners including the Group 1 Prix Jean Prat placed Monsagem and the US Grade 3 winner Pie In Your Eye. The second dam, Meringue Pie (by Silent Screen), was a stakes winner of 14 races in the USA. (Kennet Valley Thoroughbreds IV). *"He was quite a late foal but he's a very athletic individual. He was broken in by Grace Muir who does a fantastic job – I really can't thank her enough and whatever information she gives you is always spot on. She raved about this horse, but when he came to me I thought he was horrible! But saying that, he's begun to thicken and mature and although you won't see him until May he's one of the most forward I've got, despite his foaling date. He'll definitely win races, but quite how good he'll be I don't know. He doesn't have the substance and size of the one we had by this sire last year which was sold to Hong Kong."* TRAINERS' BARGAIN BUY

1654. VAL O'HARA (IRE) ★★
ch.f. Ad Valorem – Lady Scarlett (Woodman).
April 23. Sixth foal. 12,000Y. Tattersalls October Book 2. Not sold. Half-sister to the quite useful 2009 2-y-o 1m winner Whistleinthewind (by Oratorio), to the useful 5f and 6f winner of 5 races and listed-placed Sunrise Safari (by Mozart) and a winner over hurdles by High Chaparral. The dam is an unraced half-sister to 5 winners including the listed Sha Tin Trophy winner and Irish Derby third Desert Fox and the US Grade 3 winners Poolesta and Home Of The Free and to the unplaced dam of the US Grade 1 winner Grand Couturier. The second dam, Radiant (by Foolish Pleasure), won once at 3 yrs and is a half-sister to the triple Grade 1 winner Gold And Ivory and to the dams of the Group/Graded stakes winners Heart Of Darkness, Anees, Elusive Quality and Rossini. (Mr M Stewkesbury). *"I had this filly's half-brother Sunrise Safari who was a good racehorse but this is a different sort altogether – she's a big, plain, strapping individual. It's too early to say anything about her, I can't condemn her in any way, but she's huge. One for the back-end of the season."*

1655. UNNAMED ★★
b.c. Pleasantly Perfect – Perfectly Clear (Woodman).
April 15. Sixth foal. €36,000Y. Tattersalls Ireland. David Redvers. Half-sister to the US stakes-placed winner of 3 races at 2 and 3 yrs Perfectly Quiet (by Quiet American) and to 2 minor winners in the USA by Orientate and Touch Gold. The dam, a listed stakes winner of 5 races at 3 to 5 yrs, is a half-sister to 8 winners. The second dam, Crystal Cream (by Secretariat), won twice at 3 yrs in the USA and is a half-sister to 6 winners. *"He's a gorgeous individual, but he's very big and backward and he's had a touch of sore shins. Hopefully he'll be out in the second half of the season but I've not worked him yet."*

Stallion Reference

This section deals with the vast majority of sires with two-year-old representatives in the book. Amongst the stallions listed are most of the best sires of America and Europe, horses like the US-based sires Distorted Humor, Dynaformer, Elusive Quality, Giant's Causeway, Gone West, Kingmambo, Medaglia d'Oro, Seeking The Gold, Smart Strike, Storm Cat, and Street Cry.

The top European sires with two-year-olds in the book include Cape Cross, Dalakhani, Danehill Dancer, Dansili, Galileo, Green Desert, Invincible Spirit, Montjeu, Oasis Dream, Pivotal, Sadler's Wells and Selkirk. In addition, you should look out for successful two-year-old sires like Acclamation, Bahamian Bounty, Bertolini, Dubawi, Exceed And Excel, Kheleyf and Shamardal.

ACCLAMATION 2000 *Royal Applause – Princess Athena (Ahonoora)* **Racing record:** Won 6 times, including Diadem Stakes. Also placed in King's Stand and Nunthorpe. **Stud record:** First crop now five-year-olds, he was an instant hit with his first crop in 2007, notably with his Group 1 winner Dark Angel. His subsequent good winners include the Group 1 King's Stand winner Equiano and the King's Sand third Angelzarke. His 2009 two-year-olds won 14 races. Standing at Rathbarry Stud, Ireland. **2010 fee:** Private (was €20,000 in 2009).

AD VALOREM 2002 *Danzig – Classy Women (Relaunch)* **Racing record:** Won 4 races including Middle Park Stakes (6f at 2 yrs) & Queen Anne Stakes (1m). **Stud record:** First runners 2010. Standing at Coolmore Stud, Ireland. **2010 fee:** €5,000.

AFLEET ALEX 2002 *Northern Afleet – Maggy Hawk (Hawkster)* **Racing record:** Won 8 races including Hopeful Stakes and Sanford Stakes at 2yrs. Preakness Stakes and Belmont Stakes. **Stud record:** First runners 2010. Standing at Gainesway Farm, Kentucky. **2010 fee:** $15,000.

ALHAARTH 1993 *Unfuwain – Irish Valley (Irish River)* **Racing record:** Champion 2-y-o of 1995 when winner of 4 group races, notably Dewhurst Stakes. Showed very smart form up to 10f at 3/4 yrs, winning three Group 2 events. **Stud record:** First runners in 2001. Sire of Awzaan (2009 2-y-o Group 1 6f Middle Park Stakes), Haafhd (2000 Guineas and Champion Stakes), Bandari and Phoenix Reach (Canadian International, Hong Kong Vase and Dubai Sheema Classic) and the smart performers Bouguereau, Dominica, Hoh Buzzard, Maharib, Mourayan and Mutajarred. Standing at Derrinstown Stud, Ireland. **2010 fee:** €7,000.

ANABAA 1992 *Danzig – Balbonella (Gay Mecene)* **Racing record:** Won 8 races including the July Cup and the Prix Maurice de Gheest. **Stud record:** First runners in 2000. Sire of the top-class filly Goldikova, Anabaa Blue (Prix du Jockey Club), Martillo (multiple German Group 2 winner), Precision (Hong Kong Cup) and the smart performers Amonita, Ana Marie, Celtic Slipper, Blue Ksar, Loup Breton, Marshall, Miss Anabaa, Morana, Passager, Rouvres, Shaard, Tarzan City and Victorieux. Dead.

ANTONIUS PIUS 2001 *Danzig – Catchascatchcan (Pursuit of Love)* **Racing record:** Won the Group 2 Railway Stakes at 2 yrs. Placed in the French 2,000 Guineas, St James's Palace Stakes and Breeders Cup Mile. **Stud record:** First European runners in 2009 and sire of 15 winners (but no stakes winners to date). Standing at Coolmore Stud, Ireland. **2010 fee:** €5,000.

ARAAFA 2003 *Mull of Kintyre – Resurgence (Polar Falcon)* **Racing record:** Won 3 races including the St James's Palace Stakes and the Irish 2,000 Guineas. **Stud record:** First runners 2010. Standing at Plantation Stud, Newmarket. **2010 fee:** £7,000.

ARAKAN 2000 *Nureyev – Far Across (Common Grounds)* **Racing record:** Won 6 races including the Group 3 Criterion Stakes, the Group 3 Supreme Stakes (both 7f), the listed Abernant Stakes and the City Of York Stakes (both 6f). **Stud record:** His first runners appeared in 2009 and his 8 winners included the Group 2 Richmond Stakes and Tattersalls Ireland Sales Race winner Dick Turpin. Standing at Ballyhane Stud. **2010 fee:** €3,000.

ARCH 1995 *Kris S – Aurora (Danzig)* **Racing record:** 5 wins including Super Derby and Fayette Stakes. **Stud record:** Sire of Arravale (Grade 1 Del Mar Oaks), Les Arcs (Golden Jubilee Stakes and July Cup), Pine Island (dual US Grade 1 winner), Overarching (South African Group 1 winner), Prince Arch (US Grade 1 winner) and Montgomery's Arch (Group 2 Richmond Stakes). Standing at Claiborne Farm, Kentucky. **2010 fee:** $25,000.

AUCTION HOUSE 1996 *Exbourne – Fast Flow (Riverman)* **Racing record:** Won 4 Group races Including Champagne Stakes, Acomb Stakes **Stud record:** His first runners 2007. Amongst his winners Bid For Glory, Fratellino and Ghetto. Standing at Llety Farms. **2010 fee:** £4,000

AUSSIE RULES 2003 *Danehill – Last Second (Alzao)* **Racing record:** Won 4 races including the Shadwell Turf Mile and the French 2,000 Guineas. **Stud record:** First runners 2010. Standing at Coolmore Stud, Ireland. **2010 fee:** €6,000.

AVONBRIDGE 2000 *Averti – Alessia (Caerleon)* **Racing record:** Won the Prix de l'Abbaye and the Palace House Stakes, second in the July Cup. **Stud record:** 19 winners among his first runners in 2009 including the smart listed 5f winner Iver Bridge Lad. Standing at Whitsbury Manor Stud. **2010 fee:** £3,500.

AZAMOUR 2001 *Night Shift – Azmara (Lear Fan)* **Race record:** Won St James's Palace Stakes, Irish Champion Stakes, Prince of Wales's Stakes and King George VI and Queen Elizabeth Diamond Stakes. **Stud record:** 10 winners among his first runners in 2009 including the listed winner Azmeel. Standing at Gilltown Stud, Ireland. **2010 fee:** €15,000.

BACHELOR DUKE 2001 *Miswaki – Gossamer (Seattle Slew)* **Racing record:** Won Irish 2,000 Guineas. **Stud record:** His first two crops of runners included the New Zealand dual Group 2 winner Keyora and the Group 3 Silver Flash Stakes winner Luminous Eyes. Standing at Ballylynch Stud, Ireland. **2010 fee:** Private (was €7,500 in 2009).

BAGO 2001 *Nashwan – Moonlight's Box (Nureyev)* **Racing record:** Prix de L'Arc de Triomphe 2004, Prix Jean Prat, Grand Prix de Paris & Prix Ganay. **Stud record:** Oken Sakura, Flower Cup G3, 9f. Standing at JBBA Shizunai Stallion Station. Japan. **2010 fee:** Private

BAHAMIAN BOUNTY 1994 *Cadeaux Genereux – Clarentia (Ballad Rock)* **Racing record:** Winner of 3 races at 2 yrs, notably Prix Morny and Middle Park. Also fourth in July Cup at 3 yrs. **Stud record:** First runners in 2001. Sire of high-class performer Pastoral Pursuits (July Cup), very smart Goodricke (Sprint Cup) and Mister Napper Tandy (US Grade 2) and smart performers Gallagher, Babodana, Dubaian Gift, Naahy, Paradise Isle and Topatoo. Standing at the National Stud, Newmarket. **2010 fee:** £10,000.

BALMONT 2001 *Stravinsky – Aldebaran Light (Seattle Slew)* **Racing record:** Won 4 races at 2 yrs including the Group 1 Middle Park Stakes (6f) and the Group 2 Gimcrack Stakes (6f). **Stud record:** First runners 2010. Standing at Tara Stud, Ireland. **2010 fee:** €5,000

BARATHEA 1990 *Sadler's Wells – Brocade (Habitat)* **Racing record:** 5 wins, notably Breeders Cup Mile and Irish 2000 Guineas. **Stud record:** First runners in 1998. Sire of high-class Tobougg (Prix de la Salamandre and Dewhurst) and Tante Rose (Sprint Cup), and numerous smart performers including Alasha, Apsis, Barathea Guest, Barshiba, Cornelius, Enrique, Hazarista, Jumbajukiba, Lost Soldier Three, One Off, Opera Cape, Pongee, Port Vila, Raincoat, Sanaya, Shield, Sina Cova and Stotsfold. Barathea died in 2009.

BEAT HOLLOW 1997 *Sadler's Wells – Wemyss Bight (Dancing Brave)* **Racing record:** Won 7 races Grand Prix de Paris, Arlington Million, Woodford Reserve Turf Classic. **Stud record:** To stud 2003. Sire of 5 stakes winners including Proportional (Group 1 Prix Marcel Boussac). Standing at Banstead Manor Stud, Newmarket. **2010 fee:** £6,000

BERNARDINI 2003 *A P Indy – Cara Rafaela (Quiet American)* **Racing record:** Won 5 Grade 1 events in the USA including the 1mWithers

Stakes, the 9.5f Preakness Stakes, the 9f Jim Dandy Stakes, the 10f Jockey Club Gold Cup and the 10f Travers Stakes. **Stud record:** First runners 2010. Standing at Darley Stud, Kentucky. **2010 fee:** $60,000.

BERTOLINI 1996 *Danzig – Aquilega (Alydar)* Racing record: Won 2 races, including July Stakes at 2 yrs, and placed in July Cup, Sprint Cup and Nunthorpe Stakes. **Stud record:** First runners in 2005. Sire of the smart winners Moorhouse Lad and Prime Defender and the useful performers Blades Girl, Bobs Surprise, Come Out Fighting, Donna Blini (Cheveley Park), Mac Gille Eoin, Medic Power (in Hong Kong), Signor Peltro, Suits Me and Tabaret. He has sired 113 two-year-old winners in five crops. Standing at Overbury Stud, Gloucestershire. **2010 fee:** £4,000.

BYRON 2001 *Green Desert – Gay Gallanta (Woodman)* **Racing record:** Won 3 races including the Group 2 6f Mill Reef Stakes (at 2 yrs) and the Group 2 7f Betfair Cup (Lennox Stakes). **Stud record:** First runners 2010. Standing at Dalham Hall Stud, Newmarket. **2010 fee:** £4,000.

CADEAUX GENEREUX 1985 *Young Generation – Smarten Up (Sharpen Up)* **Racing record:** 7 wins notably July Cup and William Hill Sprint Championship. **Stud record:** Best winners include high-class Bijou d'Inde (Group 1 St James's Palace Stakes), Donativum (Grade 1 Breeders Cup Juvenile) and Touch of The Blues (Atto Mile in Canada) and numerous smart performers including Bahamian Bounty (Group 1 Middle Park Stakes), Desert Deer (Group 2 Sandown Mile), Embassy (Group 1 Cheveley Park Stakes), Hoh Magic (Prix Morny), Land Of Dreams (Group 2 Flying Childers Stakes), Major Cadeaux (Group 2 Sandown Mile), Stage Gift (Group 2 York Stakes) and Toylsome (Group 1 Prix de la Foret). Standing at Whitsbury Manor Stud, Hampshire. **2010 fee:** Private (was £10,000 in 2009).

CAMACHO 2002 *Danehill – Arabesque (Zafonic)* **Racing record:** Won a listed race over 6f and was second in the Group 3 7f Jersey Stakes. **Stud record:** Had his first runners in 2009 when his 7 winners included the tough listed winner Star Rover and the subsequent 2010 Fred Darling Stakes winner Puff. Standing at Morristown Lattin Stud, Ireland. **2010 fee:** €4,000.

CAPE CROSS 1994 *Green Desert – Park Appeal (Ahonoora)* **Racing record:** Won 4 races, including Lockinge Stakes, Queen Anne Stakes and Celebration Mile. **Stud record:** First runners in 2003. Sire of the outstanding colt Sea The Stars (2,000 Guineas, Derby, Prix de l'Arc de Triomphe etc,), top-class Ouija Board (7 Group 1 wins including the Oaks & the Breeders' Cup Filly and Mare Turf), Hong Kong Group 1 winner Able One and numerous smart performers including Borthwick Girl, Cape Fear, Castleton, Charlie Farnsbarns, Crossing The Line, Crosspeace, Crystal Capella, Halicarnassus, Hatta Fort, Hazyview, Mac Love, Madid, Mazuna, Musicanna, Privy Seal and Russian Cross. Standing at Kildangan Stud, Ireland. **2010 fee:** €35,000.

CAPTAIN RIO 2000 *Pivotal – Beloved Visitor (Miswaki)* **Racing record:** Won 4 times, including Criterium de Maisons-Laffitte at 2 yrs. **Stud record:** From 3 crops racing sire of the New Zealand Grade 1 winner Il Quello Veloce, Group 3 Tetrarch Stakes winner Energizer, the smart Capt Chaos and Captain Dunne and the Group 3 Sirenia Stakes winner Philario. 20 individual two-year-old winners in England and Ireland last year. Standing at Ballyhane Stud, Ireland. **2010 fee:** €5,000.

CHINEUR 2001 *Fasliyev – Wardara (Sharpo)* **Race record:** Won Kings Stand Stakes and Prix de Saint-Georges. **Stud record:** His first runners in 2009 yielded ten winners including the useful colts Roi de Vitesse, Singeur and En Un Clin D'Oeil and the Group 3 placed filly Silver Grey. Standing at Haras Des Granges, France. **2010 fee:** €3,000.

CHOISIR 2000 *Danehill Dancer – Great Selection (Lunchtime)* **Racing record:** Group 1 winner in both Australia and Britain, including King's Stand Stakes and Golden Jubilee Stakes. **Stud record:** His winners include the Australian dual Group 1 winner Starspangledbanner, Group 2 Challenge Stakes winner Stimulation, Australian Group 2 winners Dreamscape, Gold Water and Hurried Choice, Group 3 Somerville Tattersalls Stakes Sir Parky, Group 3 C L Weld Park Stakes winner

Lady Springbank and the listed winners Choose Me, Fat Boy, Luna Nel Pozz, Meydan Princess, Porto Marmay and Prime Champion. Standing at Coolmore Stud, Ireland. **2010 fee:** £6,000.

CLODOVIL 2001 *Danehill – Clodora (Linamix)* **Racing record:** Won 5 races, including Poule d'Essai des Poulains. **Stud record:** His first crop were two-year-olds in 2007 and from relatively small crops his best winners to date are the Group 1 Falmouth Stakes winner Nahoodh and the very useful Beacon Lodge (Group 3 Horris Hill Stakes) and the Group 3 placed Dovil Boy. Standing at Rathasker Stud, Ireland. **2010 fee:** €9,000.

COMPTON PLACE 1994 *Indian Ridge – Nosey (Nebbiolo)* **Racing record:** Won 3 races, notably July Cup. **Stud record:** First runners in 2002. Sire of the Group 1 Nunthorpe Stakes winner Borderlescott, the smart Boogie Street and Intrepid Jack, US Grade 2 winner Passified, the Group 2 winners Godfrey Street and Prolific, and numerous useful performers including Compton's Eleven, If Paradise, Judd Street, Hunter Street and Pacific Pride. Standing at Whitsbury Manor Stud, Hampshire. **2010 fee:** £6,000.

CONGAREE 1998 *Arazi – Mari's Sheba (Maria's Book)* **Racing record:** twelve races, notably Swaps Stakes and Wood Memorial. At four won Cigar Mile (G1) twice, 8f by 5½ lengths. Del Mar Breeders Cup Handicap G3, Hollywood Gold Cup G1, 10f. **Stud record:** Jeranimo, Strub Stakes, Mythical Power, Lone Star Derby, Maoineach, Leopardstown 1,000 Guineas Trial. Standing at Highcliff Farm, NY. **2010 fee:** $7,500

COUNTRY REEL 2000 *Danzig – Country Belle (Seattle Slew)* **Racing record:** Won Scottish Equitable Stakes, 6f, Chipchase Stakes at Newcastle and Bentinck Stakes at Newmarket at 4 yrs. **Stud record:** Sire of the listed winners Baine, and Go Country. Standing at Haras de Logis, **2010 fee:** €4,500.

DALAKHANI 2001 *Darshaan – Daltawa (Miswaki)* **Racing record:** Won 8 of 9 starts, including Prix du Jockey Club and Arc. **Stud record:** First crop were two-year-olds in 2007. €50,000. Sire of 2 classic winners from his first crop in Conduit (St Leger, Breeders Cup Turf (twice), King George VI & Queen Elizabeth Stakes) and Moonstone (Irish Oaks) and also worthy of note are the Group 2 winners Centennial, Chinese White, Armure and Democratie. With just three crops racing he's had an excellent start. Standing at Gilltown Stud, Ireland. **2010 fee:** €50,000.

DANBIRD 2000 *Danehill – Fitting (Marcay)* **Racing record:** Won six races including the Pago Pago Stakes G2, at 4 won the Counties RC Counties Bowl Handicap. Stands in Australia at Eliza Park. **2010 fee:** $5,500 Au.

DANEHILL DANCER 1993 *Danehill – Mira Adonde (Sharpen Up)* **Racing record:** Winner of 4 races, including Heinz 57 Phoenix Stakes and National Stakes at 2 yrs and Greenham at 3. **Stud record:** First runners in 2001. Sire of high-class performer Choisir (Golden Jubilee Stakes), multiple Group 1 winner Mastercraftsman, Irish 1,000 Guineas and Moyglare Stud Stakes winner Again, the US Grade 1 Garden City Stakes winner Alexander Tango, Queen Elizabeth II Stakes winner Where Or When, 1,000 Guineas winner Speciosa, dual Group 3 winner Indesatchel & numerous smart performers including Alexander Tango, Anna Pavlova, Blue Sky Thinking, Express Wish, Fast Company, Ice Queen, Jeremy, Lady Dominatrix, Lizard Island, Medicine Path, Miss Beatrix, Monsieur Bond, Pride Of Nation and Snaefell. Standing at Coolmore Stud, Ireland. **2010 fee:** Private.

DANROAD 1999 *Danehill – Strawberry Girl (Strawberry Road)* **Racing record:** Won 6 races over 6f in New Zealand, including a Group 2 and was Group 1 placed. **Stud record:** Had a two-year-old Group 1 winner in Australia (Rockdale) and a Group1 placed in New Zealand (Down The Road) in his first crop and his first European crop were runners in 2009. Standing at Rathmuck Stud, Ireland. **2010 fee:** €3,000.

DANSILI 1996 *Danehill – Hasili (Kahyasi)* **Racing record:** Won 5 races in France, and placed in six Group/Grade 1 events including Sussex Stakes and Breeders' Cup Mile. **Stud record:** First runners in 2004. Sire of top-class Rail Link (Arc, Grand Prix de Paris), Zambezi Sun (Group 1 Grand Prix de Paris), Zacinto (Group 2 Celebration Mile) and numerous very smart performers including Dansant, Delegator, Famous Name, Grecian Dancer, Home Affairs, Illustrious Blue, Passage Of Time, Price Tag (US Grade 1 winner and first past post in Poule d'Essai des Pouliches), Proviso, Sense Of Joy, Shaweel (Gimcrack Stakes), Silver Touch and Strategic Prince. Standing at Banstead Manor Stud, Newmarket. **2010 fee:** £65,000.

DEPORTIVO 2000 *Night Shift – Valencia (Kenmare)* **Racing record:** Won Flying Five Stakes at The Curragh, Rose Bowl Stakes at Newbury, Balmoral Handicap at Royal Ascot. Standing at Walton Fields stud. **2010 fee:** £3,000.

DESERT STYLE 1992 *Green Desert – Organza (High Top)* **Racing record:** Won Tetrarch Stakes 7f, Ballycorus St, G3. Phoenix Sprint Stakes, **Stud record:** Caradak – Prix de la Foret 7f, Celebration Mile, Cool Creek – Mill Reef Stakes, Next Desert Oppenheim Union-Rennen, 11f, German Derby. Standing at Haras du Hugenet **2010 fee:** €3,000

DIAMOND GREEN 2001 *Green Desert – Diamonaka (Akarad)* **Racing record:** Won 3 races including the Group 3 7f Prix la Rochette. First runners 2010. Standing at Ballyhane Stud, Carlow, Ireland. **2010 fee:** €8,000.

DIKTAT 1995 *Warning – (Sadler's Wells)* **Racing record:** Jersey Stakes, Shergar Cup 7f, Van Gheest Criterion Stakes, Prix Maurice de Gheest G1, Sprint Cup, 6f. **Stud record:** His best winners include Formal Decree, Shirt Skirt, Lady Gloria and Rajeem. Standing at Dehesa de Milagro, Spain

DISTORTED HUMOR 1993 *Forty Niner – Danzig's Beauty (Danzig)* **Racing record:** Won 11 races in the USA including the Champagne Stakes, Futurity Stakes, Haskell Invitational and Travers Stakes (all Grade 1). Champion 2-y-o. **Stud record:** Sire of a host of Grade 1 winners including Any Given Saturday, Commentator, Coronado's Quest, Ecton Park, Editor's Note, Flower Alley, Funny Cide, Gold Fever, Marley Vale & Nine Keys. Standing at Win Star Farm, Kentucky. **2010 fee:** $100,000.

DIXIE UNION 1997 *Dixieland Band – She's Tops (Capote)* **Racing record:** Won 7 races including the Haskell Invitational and the Malibu Stakes (both Grade 1 events in the USA). **Stud record:** Sire of the US Grade 1 winners Dixie Chatter and Hot Dixie Chick, the Group 2 Cherry Hinton Stakes winner Sander Camillo and the US Grade 2 winners Justwhistledixie, Most Distinguished and Nothing But Fun. Standing at Standing at Lane's End Farm, Kentucky. **2010 fee:** $35,000.

DOYEN 2000 *Sadler's Wells – Moon Cactus (Kris)* **Racing record:** Won the King George VI and Queen Elizabeth Diamond Stakes, Hardwicke Stakes. **Stud record:** His first runners appeared in 2009 and he had 12 winners but no stakes horses – hardly surprising as his pedigree and race record show they'll improve with age. Standing at Gestut Auenquelle in Germany. **2010 fee:** €5,000.

DR FONG 1995 *Kris S – Spring Flight (Miswaki)* **Racing record:** Won 5 races, including St James's Palace Stakes. **Stud record:** First runners in 2003. Sire of the US Grade 1 winner Shamdinan and the Group 1 Prix Saint-Alary winner Ask For The Moon, the smart performers Andronikos, Celimene, Doctor Brown, Dubai's Touch, Fong's Thong, Forward Move, Group Captain, Metropolitan Man and Spotlight, and of numerous very useful performers. Standing at Haras Du Thenney, France. **2010 fee:** €5,000.

DUBAI DESTINATION 1999 *Kingmambo – Mysterial (Alleged)* **Racing record:** Won 4 times, including Champagne Stakes and Queen Anne Stakes. **Stud record:** First crop were two-year-olds in 2007 and included the Group 1 winner Ibn Khaldun and the smart gelding Charm School. Subsequently, his best has been the smart colt Firebet. Standing at Glenview Stud, Ireland. **2010 fee:** £3,500.

DUBAWI 2002 *Dubai Millennium – Zomaradah (Deploy)* **Race record:** Won the National Stakes at 2 and the Irish 2,000 Guineas and Prix Jacques le Marois at 3. Third in the Derby. **Stud record:** His first runners appeared in 2009 and he was the leading first-crop sire by number of winners. They included the Group 2 winners Poet's Voice and Sand Vixen. He also had the New Zealand Group 2 winner Cellarmaster and the smart Group 2 placed maiden Dubawi Heights.

Standing at Dalham Hall Stud, Newmarket. **2010 fee:** €20,000.

D'WILDCAT 1998 *Forest Wildcat – D'Enough (D'Accord)* **Racing record:** Swale Stakes, 7f, Frank de Francis Memorial Dash, G1, 6f, Churchill Downs Handicap G2, **Stud record:** D'Funnybone Swale Stakes, Hutcheson Stakes, D'Wild Ride, Regret Stakes. Standing at Vinery, Florida. **2010 fee:** $10,000

DYNAFORMER 1985 *Roberto – Andover Way (His Majesty)* **Racing record:** 7 wins in USA including Grade 2 Florida Derby and Grade 2 Discovery Handicap. **Stud record:** Best winners include the Group 1 winner Lucarno, the 2008 Group 1 Fillies' Mile winner Rainbow View, Group 2 Ribblesdale winner Michita, the very smart Beat All and (in USA) Grade 1 winners Barbaro, Dynaforce, Film Maker, Perfect Drift and Starrer, and numerous smart performers including Dynever, Ocean Silk, Sharp Susan and Spanish John. Standing at Three Chimneys Farm, Kentucky. **2010 fee:** $150,000.

ELNADIM 1994 *Danzig – Elle Seule (Exclusive Native)* **Racing record:** Won 5 races, notably Diadem Stakes and July Cup. **Stud record:** First runners in 2004, first European runners in 2005. Sire of smart performers Al Qasi (Group 3 Phoenix Stakes), Caldra (Group 3 Autumn Stakes), Culminate (New Zealand Group 1), Elletelle (Group 2 Queen Mary Stakes), Elnawin (Group 3 Sirenia Stakes) and Wi Dud (Group 2 Gimcrack Stakes). Standing at Derrinstown Stud, Ireland. **2010 fee:** €6,000.

EL PRADO 1989 *Sadler's Wells – Lady Capulet (Sir Ivor)* **Racing record:** National Stakes G1 8f, Beresford Stakes 8f G2. Railway Stakes, G3. Dead. Best winners include Borrego, Medaglia d'Oro, Kitten's Joy, Artie Schiller and Spanish Moon.

ELUSIVE CITY 2000 *Elusive Quality – Star of Paris (Dayjur)* **Racing record:** Won Group 1 Prix Morny and Group 2 Richmond Stakes. Also placed in Middle Park. **Stud record:** First crop were two-year-olds in 2008. His best winners include Elusive Wave (French 2,000 Guineas), Soul City (Group 3 Prix La Rochette and Goffs Million) and multiple listed winner Nashmiah. Standing at Haras D'Etreham. **2010 fee:** €20,000.

ELUSIVE QUALITY 1993 *Gone West – Touch of Greatness (Hero's Honor)* **Racing record:** Won 9 races in USA, including Grade 3 events at 7f/1m. **Stud record:** Sire of top-class Kentucky Derby/Preakness Stakes winner Smarty Jones, Breeders Cup Classic and Queen Elizabeth II Stakes winner Raven's Pass, Prix Morny winner Elusive City and numerous US graded stakes winners including Chimichurri, Elusive Diva, Girl Warrior, Maryfield, Omega Code, Quality Road, Royal Michele and True Quality, the smart dual listed winner Baharah and the Group 3 winning two-year-olds Elusive Pimpernel and Evasive. Standing at Darley Jonabell Farm Kentucky. **2010 fee:** $75,000.

EMPIRE MAKER 2000 *Unbridled – Toussaud (El Gran Senor)* **Racing record:** Belmont Stakes. Florida Derby, Wood Memorial Stakes. Jim Dandy Stakes. **Stud record:** US Grade 1 winners Battle Plan, Mushka, Icon Project, Country Star and Pioneerofthe Nile. Standing at Juddmonte Farms. **2010 fee:** $50,000

ENCOSTA DE LAGO 1993 *Fairy King – Shoal Creek (Star Way)* **Racing record:** At 3 yrs won a Group 1 7f event and two Group 2 events in Australia. **Stud record:** Sire of 16 individual Group 1 winners including the multiple Group 1 winners Sacred Kingdom (in Hong Kong), Alinghi, Sirmione and Racing To Win (all in Australia). Standing at Coolmore Stud, Australia. **2010 fee:** $220,000AUS.

EXCEED AND EXCEL 2000 *Danehill – Patrona (Lomond)* **Racing record:** Champion sprinter in Australia, won 7 races including the Grade 1 Newmarket H'cap, the Grade 1 Dubai Racing Club Cup and the Grade 2 Todman Stakes. **Stud record:** First northern hemisphere runners in 2008. His best winners include Infamous Angel (Lowther Stakes) and the Royal Ascot winner Flashmans Papers. His Australasian winners include the Group 1 winner Reward For Effort, Group 2 winner Wilander and the Group 3 winners Exceedingly Good, Sugar Babe and Believe 'n' Succeed. The leading sire of juveniles in Britain and Ireland in 2009, with 31 winners. Standing at Dalham Hall Stud, Newmarket. **2010 fee:** £12,000.

FASLIYEV 1997 *Nureyev – Mr P'S Princess (Mr Prospector)* **Racing record:** Unbeaten in 5 starts at 2 yrs (only season to race), including Coventry Stakes, Heinz 57 Phoenix Stakes and Prix Morny. **Stud record:** First runners in 2003. Sire of Carry On Katie (Cheveley Park Stakes), very smart Group 2 and Group 3 winner Chineur, smart performers Fyodor, City Leader, Kings Point, Lady Deauville, Much Faster, Russian Valour, Russki and Steppe Dancer and numerous useful performers. Now standing in Japan.

FIREBREAK 1999 *Charnwood Forest – Breakaway (Song)* **Racing record:** Won the Godolphin Mile in Dubai (twice), Challenge Stakes and Hong Kong Mile. **Stud record:** From a small first crop in 2009 his runners included the Group 1 Gran Criterium winner Hearts Of Fire and the listed Radley Stakes winner Electric Feel. Standing at Bearstone Stud. **2010 fee:** £3000.

FOOTSTEPSINTHESAND 2002 *Giant's Causeway – Glatisant (Rainbow Quest)* **Racing record:** Won all 3 of his starts, notably the 2,000 Guineas. **Stud record:** His first European runners in 2009 included the Dewhurst Stakes fourth Steinbeck, the Group 3 Prestige Stakes winner Sent From Heaven and the listed winner Song Of My Heart. Standing at Coolmore Stud, Ireland. **2010 fee:** €12,500.

GALILEO 1998 *Sadler's Wells – Urban Sea (Miswaki)* **Racing record:** Won 6 races, including Derby, Irish Derby and King George And Queen Elizabeth Stakes. **Stud record:** First runners in 2005. Sire of champion 2-y-o's Teofilo and New Approach (subsequent Derby, Champion Stakes and Irish Champion Stakes winner) and of the top-class double Group 1 winner Rip Van Winkle, Sixties Icon (St Leger), Red Rocks (Breeders' Cup Turf), Allegretto (Prix Royal-Oak), Lush Lashes (Coronation Stakes and Sun Chariot Stakes), Soldier Of Fortune (Irish Derby) and Nightime (Irish 1000 Guineas). Standing at Coolmore Stud, Ireland. **2010 fee:** Private (was €150,000).

GHOSTZAPPER 2000 *Awesome Again – Baby Zip (Relaunch)* **Racing record:** Vosburgh, Breeders Cup Classic, Woodward, Tom Fool, Philip Iselin Metropolitan Hcp. Horse of the Year and Champion Older Male. **Stud record:** Best winners include Stately Victor, Blue Grass Stakes, Golden Ghost, First State Dash. Standing at Adena Springs Ky. **2010 fee:** $30,000

GIANT'S CAUSEWAY 1997 *Storm Cat – Mariah's Storm (Rahy)* **Racing record:** Won 9 races, 6 of them Group 1 events, including Prix de la Salamandre, Juddmonte International and Sussex Stakes. **Stud record:** First runners in 2004. Sire of high-class Shamardal (Dewhurst Stakes, St James's Palace Stakes and Prix du Jockey Club), very smart Footstepsinthesand (2000 Guineas) and a number of very smart performers including Ghanaati (1,000 Guineas and Coronation Stakes), Aragorn (dual US Grade winner), Heatseeker (Santa Anita Handicap), Maids Causeway (Coronation Stakes), My Typhoon, Swift Temper (US Grade 1 winners), Oonagh Maccool and First Samurai (US 2-y-o Grade 1 winner). Standing at Ashford Stud, Kentucky. **2010 fee:** $100,000.

GONE WEST 1984 *Mr Prospector – Secrettame (Secretariat)* **Racing record:** 6 wins including Grade 1 Dwyer Stakes. **Stud record:** Best winners include North American performers Came Home (Pacific Classic), Commendable (Belmont Stakes), Da Hoss (Breeders' Cup Mile), Johar (Breeders' Cup Turf), Link River (John A. Morris Handicap), March Side (Canadian International), Speightstown (Breeders Cup Sprint), West By West (Nassau County Handicap) and Zaftig (Acorn Stakes), the smart Japanese horse Zafolia and in Europe the top-class colt Zafonic (4 Group 1 wins including Dewhurst Stakes and 2000 Guineas). He's also the sire of the good sires Mr Greeley and Zamindar. Standing at Mill Ridge Farm, Kentucky. **2010 fee:** $65,000.

GREEN DESERT 1983 *Danzig – Foreign Courier (Sir Ivor)* **Racing record:** 5 wins including July Cup, Vernons Sprint Cup and Flying Childers Stakes. **Stud record:** Best winners (all very smart or better) include Alkaadhem, Cape Cross (Lockinge Stakes), Desert Lord (Prix de l'Abbaye), Desert Prince (Irish 2000 Guineas, Prix du Moulin, Queen Elizabeth Stakes), Desert Style, Desert Sun, Gabr, Invincible Spirit (Haydock Sprint Cup), Oasis Dream (Middle Park, July Cup, Nunthorpe Stakes), Owington (July Cup), Sheikh Albadou (Nunthorpe Stakes/Haydock Sprint Cup), Tamarisk (Haydock Sprint Cup) and

Tropical. Standing at Nunnery Stud, Norfolk. **2010 fee:** £25,000.

GREEN TUNE 1991 *Green Dancer – Soundings (Mr Prospector)* **Racing record:** Poule d'essai des Poulains, Prix du Muguet, Prix d'Ispahan. **Stud record:** Fuisse (Prix de Mesil), Lune d'Or (Premio Lydia Tesio G1), Gold Sound (Prix de Guiche). Standing at Haras d'Etreham. **2010 fee:** €10,000

GULCH 1984 *Mr Prospector – Jameela (Rambunctious)* **Racing record:** Won or placed in 16 Grade 1 races. His wins included the Breeders Cup Sprint, the Wood Memorial and the Metropolitan Handicap. **Stud record:** Best winners include Nayef (four Group 1 wins including Champion Stakes and Prince Of Wales's Stakes), Harayir (1,000 Guineas), US Grade 1 winners Great Navigator, Thunder Gulch, The Cliff's Edge, Wallenda and Court Vision, Group 1 Prix Jean Prat winner Torrential, Japanese Grade 1 winner Eagle Café and French dual Group 3 winner Agol Lack. Now retired from stud.

HAAFHD 2001 *Alhaarth – Al Bahathri (Blushing Groom)* **Racing record:** Won 5 races, notably 2,000 Guineas and Champion Stakes. **Stud record:** First crop were two-year-olds in 2008. His best performer so far is the 2009 2-y-o Group 2 Superlative Stakes winner Silver Grecian. Standing at Nunnery Stud, Norfolk. **2010 fee:** £6,000.

HALLING 1991 *Diesis – Dance Machine (Green Dancer)* **Racing record:** Won 12 races including Coral-Eclipse Stakes (twice), Juddmonte International (twice) and Prix d'Ispahan. **Stud record:** First runners in 2000. Sire of the Group 1 Grand Prix de Paris winner Cavalryman, the high-class Norse Dancer, very smart Hala Bek and The Geezer, Group 2 King Edward VII Stakes winner Boscobel, and numerous smart performers including Bauer, Chancellor, Coastal Path, Cutlass Bay, Dandoun, Fisich, Foodbroker Fancy, Franklins Gardens, Giovani Imperatore, Harland, Hattan, Hero's Journey, Mkuzi, Nordhal, Parasol, Pinson and Vanderlin. Standing at Dalham Hall Stud, Newmarket. **2010 fee:** £10,000.

HAWK WING 2000 *Woodman – La Lorgnette (Val de l'Orne)* **Racing record:** Won 5 times, including National Stakes, Eclipse and Lockinge.

Stud record: First crop were two-year-olds in 2007. Best winners to date include the smart Stubbs Art, Feared In Flight, The Bogberry and Lucky General (Goffs Million Sprint). Standing at Coolmore Stud, Ireland. **2010 fee:** €15,000.

HENNY HUGHES 2003 *Hennessy – Meadow Flyer (Meadowlake)* **Racing record:** Won 6 races including the Grade 1 6f Vosburgh Stakes, the Grade 1 7f King's Bishop Stakes and the Grade 2 6f Saratoga Special Stakes. **Stud record:** First runners 2010. Standing at Darley Stud, Kentucky. **2010 fee:** $25,000.

HERNANDO 1990 *Niniski – Whakilyric (Miswaki)* **Racing record:** Won 7 races including Prix Lupin and Prix du Jockey Club. **Stud record:** First runners in 1999. His Group/Grade 1 winners are Look Here (Oaks), Holding Court (Prix du Jockey Club), Sulamani (Prix du Jockey Club, Arlington Million, Turf Classic Invitational, Juddmonte International) and Gitano Hernando (US Goodwood Stakes). Also responsible for the US Grade 2 winners Arvada, Atlando and Herboriste, the very smart performers Asian Heights, Casual Conquest, Foreign Affairs, Mr Combustible, Samando, Songerie and Tau Ceti and numerous smart performers. Standing at Lanwades Stud, Newmarket. **2010 fee:** £12,000.

HIGH CHAPARRAL 2000 *Sadler's Wells – Kasora (Darshaan)* **Racing record:** Won 10 races, including Derby, Irish Champion Stakes and Breeders' Cup Turf (last event twice). **Stud record:** First crop were two-year-olds in 2007. Best performers to date include Australian Grade 1 winners So You Think, Monaco Consul and Shoot Out, St Leger runner-up Unsung Heroine, Group 2 Park Hill Stakes winner The Miniver Rose and the Group 3 winners Above Average, Golden Sword, High Heeled, Joanna, Magadan and Senlis. Standing at Coolmore Stud, Ireland. **2010 fee:** €15,000.

HOLY ROMAN EMPEROR (2004) *Danehill – L'On Vite (Secretariat)* **Racing record:** Won 4 races at 2 yrs including the Group 1 7f Prix Jean-Luc Lagardere, the Group 1 6f Waterford Phoenix Stakes and Group 2 6f Railway Stakes. **Stud record:** First runners 2010. Standing at Coolmore Stud, Ireland. **2010 fee:** €17,500.

STALLION REFERENCE 333

HURRICANE RUN 2002 *Montjeu – Hold On (Surumu)* **Racing record:** Won 8 races including the Group 1 12f King George VI & Queen Elizabeth Diamond Stakes, Group 1 10.5f Tattersalls Gold Cup and Group 1 12f Prix de l'Arc de Triomphe. **Stud record:** First runners 2010. Standing at Coolmore Stud, Ireland. **2010 fee:** €17,500.

ICEMAN 2002 *Polar Falcon – Virtuous (Exit To Nowhere)* **Racing record:** Won the Group 2 6f Coventry Stakes at 2 yrs at Royal Ascot. **Stud record:** First two-year-olds appear in 2010. Dead.

IFFRAAJ 2001 *Zafonic – Pastorale (Nureyev)* **Racing record:** Won 7 races including the Group 2 7f Park Stakes (twice), Group 2 7f Betfair Cup (Lennox St) and the 6f Wokingham Stakes. **Stud record:** First runners 2010. Standing at Kildangan Stud, Ireland. **2010 fee:** €5,000.

INDESATCHEL 2002 *Danehill Dancer – Floria (Petorius)* **Racing record:** Won 4 races including the Group 3 7f Tetrarch Stakes and the Group 3 7f Greenham Stakes. **Stud record:** First runners 2010. Standing at Bearstone Stud, Shropshire. **2010 fee:** £3,000.

INDIAN HAVEN 2000 *Indian Ridge – Madame Dubois (Legend Of France)* **Racing record:** Won 3 races including the Group 1 Irish 2,000 Guineas. **Stud record:** His first crop were 2-y-o's of 2008 and included the smart Group 3 winners Ashram and Aspen Darlin. His best 2-y-o of 2009 was the Irish Group 2 placed In Some Respect. Standing at the Irish National Stud. **2010 fee:** €6,000.

IMPERIAL DANCER (1998) *Primo Dominie – Gorgeous Dancer (Nordico)* **Racing record:** Won 11 races from 65 races including Festival Stakes, Scottish Classic, Meld Stakes, St Simon Stakes. Premio Roma. **Stud record:** Sire of one listed winner – Imperial Guest. Standing at Launceston Stud. **2010 fee:** £2,000.

INTIKHAB 1994 Red *Ransom – Crafty Example (Crafty Prospector)* **Racing record:** 8 wins including Diomed and Queen Anne Stakes. **Stud record:** First runners in 2003. Sire of Red Evie (Lockinge Stakes & Matron Stakes), smart Bonnie Charlie (2008 two-year-old), Hoh Mike, Khabfair, Motashaar and Without A Prayer, and numerous very useful performers including Fine Silver, Leg Spinner, Les Fazzani, Moon Unit, Paita, Toupie and Tropical Strait. Standing at Derrinstown Stud, Ireland. **2010 fee:** €5,500.

INVINCIBLE SPIRIT 1997 *Green Desert – Rafha (Kris)* **Racing record:** 7 wins, notably Sprint Cup at 5 yrs. **Stud record:** First runners in 2006. Sire of dual Group 1 winner Lawman (French Derby & Prix Jean Prat), Fleeting Spirit (July Cup, Temple Stakes, Flying Childers Stakes and Molecomb Stakes), Grade 1 Breeders Cup Juvenile winner Vale Of York, Gimcrack Stakes and Stewards Cup winner Conquest, Group 2 Criterium de Maisons-Lafitte winner Our Jonathan, Group 2 Flying Childers winner Madame Trop Vite, the smart performers Allied Powers, Campfire Glow, Captain Marvelous and Staying On, and the useful performers Bahama Mama, Hurricane Spirit, Invincible Force and Kingship Spirit. Standing at Irish National Stud. **2010 fee:** €45,000.

ISHIGURU 1998 *Danzig – Strategic Maneuver (Cryptoclearance)* **Race record:** Won 3 races including the Group 3 Flying Five at Leopardstown and the listed Belgrave Stakes at the Curragh. **Stud record:** His best winners are Ferneley (5 wins including the Grade 2 1m Del Mar Handicap), Hellvelyn (5 wins including the Group 2 6f Coventry Stakes) and She's Our Mark (6 wins including the Group 3 10f Meld Stakes, the Group 3 1m Desmond Stakes and two listed events). Dead.

IVAN DENISOVICH 2003 *Danehill –Hollywood Wildcat (Kris S)* **Race record:** Won the Group 2 6f July Stakes (at 2 yrs) and the listed 1m Solonaway Stakes at the Curragh. Group/Grade 1 placed in the Prix Morny, St James's Palace Stakes, Secretariat Stakes and the Hollywood Derby. **Stud record:** His first crops are two-year-olds in 2010. Standing at Coolmore Stud, Ireland. **2010 fee:** €3,000.

JOHANNESBURG 1999 *Hennessy – Myth (Ogygian)* **Racing record:** Unbeaten at 2 yrs, when 7 wins included Phoenix Stakes, Prix Morny, Middle Park and Breeders' Cup Juvenile. Below form at 3 yrs. **Stud record:** First runners in 2006. Sire of the Group 1 Prix d'Ispahan winner

Sageburg, Group 2 Norfolk Stakes winner Radiohead, US Grade 1 winner Scat Daddy, US Grade 2 winners Eaton's Gift and Teuflesburg, Australian dual Group 1 winner Turffontein and the smart performers Diamond Tycoon, Hammody, Jupiter Pluvius, Rabatash and Tombi. Standing at Ashford Stud, Kentucky. **2010 fee:** $35,000.

KEY OF LUCK 1991 *Chief's Crown – Balbonella (Gay Mecene)* **Racing record:** Winner of Prix d'Arenberg at 2 yrs and Dubai Duty Free at 5 yrs, when also runner-up in US Grade 1 9.5f event. **Stud record:** First runners in 2001. Sire of top-class Alamshar (Irish Derby, King George VI and Queen Elizabeth Diamond Stakes), smart performers Miss Emma, Profit's Reality, Wrong Key and Right Key, and of numerous useful performers. Standing at Tara Stud, Ireland. **2010 fee:** €9,000.

KHELEYF 2001 *Green Desert – Society Lady (Mr Prospector)* **Racing record:** Won 3 races including the Group 3 Jersey Stakes. **Stud record:** From just two crops racing he is the sire of an exceptional 51 two-year-old winners. The best so far are Sayif (Group 2 Diadem Stakes), Percolator (Group 3 Prix du Bois) and the listed winners Captain Ramius and Playfellow and the Group 3 placed Deposer. Standing at Kildangan Stud, Newmarket. **2010 fee:** €8,000.

KINGMAMBO 1990 *Mr Prospector – Miesque (Nureyev)* **Racing record:** Won the French 2,000 Guineas, the Prix du Moulin and the St James's Palace Stakes. **Stud record:** His European Group 1 winners include the multiple Group 1 winner Henrythenavigator, King's Best (both 2,000 Guineas), Russian Rhythm, Virginia Waters (both 1,000 Guineas), Rule Of Law (St Leger), Divine Proportions, Bluemamba (both French 1,000 Guineas), Light Shift (Oaks), Malhub (Golden Jubilee Stakes), Dubai Destination, (Queen Anne Stakes) and Okawango (Grand Criterium). Also the Japan Cup and French Group 1 winner Alkaased, Belmont Stakes winner Lemon Drop Kid, the Japanese champions El Condor Pasa and Kingkamehameha and the Hong Kong Q E II Stakes winner Archipenko. Standing at Lane's End Farm, Kentucky. **2010 fee:** Private (was $250,000 in 2009).

KING'S BEST 1997 *Kingmambo – Allegretta (Lombard)* **Racing record:** Won 3 races, including 2000 Guineas. **Stud record:** First runners in 2004. Sire of the high-class Proclamation (Sussex Stakes) and Creachadoir (Lockinge Stakes), the very smart Allybar, Ancien Regime, Army Of Angels, Best Alibi, Best Name, King's Apostle (Group 1 Prix Maurice de Gheest) and Spice Route and the smart performers Dubai Surprise, Elliots World, Notability, Not Just Swing, Oiseau Rare and Runaway. Sire of 20 juvenile winners in 2009. Standing at Haras Du Logis, France. **2010 fee:** €15,000.

KODIAC 2001 *Danehill – Rafha (Kris)* **Racing record:** Won 4 races here and in the UAE over 6f and 7f including the Datel Trophy and Group 3 placed. **Stud record:** First runners 2010. Standing at Tally Ho Stud, County Westmeath, Ireland. **2010 fee:** €4,000.

KYLLACHY 1998 *Pivotal – Pretty Poppy (Song)* **Racing record:** Winner of 6 races, including Nunthorpe Stakes at 4 yrs. **Stud record:** First runners in 2006. Sire of Group 2 winners Arabian Gleam and Tariq, Hong Kong Group 1 winner Dim Sum, the very smart sprinter Corrybrough, and numerous smart performers including Awinnersgame, Befortyfour and Mood Music. Standing at Cheveley Park Stud, Newmarket. **2010 fee:** £10,000.

LEMON DROP KID (1996) *Kingmambo – Charming Lassie (Seattle Slew)* **Racing record:** Won Belmont Stakes, Whitney Hcp and Woodward Stakes. **Stud record:** Bronze Cannon (Hardwicke Stakes, Jockey Club Stakes) and US Grade 1 winners Richard's Kid, Santa Teresita, Christmas Kid, Cittronade and Lemon's Forever. Standing at Lane's End, USA. **2010 fee:** $35,000.

LE VIE DEI COLORI 2000 *Efisio – Mystic Tempo (El Gran Senor)* **Racing record:** Won 12 races in Italy (notably the Premio Parioli and the Premio Vittorio di Capua) and 2 races here including the Challenge Stakes. **Stud record:** His first runners appeared in 2009 and included some smart two-year-olds including Carnaby Street, Classic Colori, Perfect Symmetry and Za Za Zoom. Dead.

LIBRETTIST 2002 *Danzig – Mysterial (Alleged)* **Racing record:** Won 7 races including the Group

STALLION REFERENCE 335

1 Prix du Moulin and the Group 1 Prix Jacques Le Marois (both 1m). **Stud record:** First runners 2010. Standing at Haras du Logis, France. **2010 fee:** €7,000.

LION HEART 2001 *Tale Of The Cat – Satin Sunrise (Mr Leader)* **Racing record:** Won the Hollywood Futurity and the Haskell Invitational (both Grade 1 events). **Stud record:** His first crop of 2-y-o's appeared in 2008 and his best performers to date include the US Grade 2 winners Azul Leon and Soul Warrior, and the Grade 3 winners Heart Ashley, Pretty Prolific and Silent Valor. Standing at Ashford Stud, Kentucky. **2010 fee:** $12,500.

LUCKY STORY 2001 *Kris S – Spring Flight (Miswaki)* **Racing record:** Won 4 races including the Group 2 Champagne Stakes and Group 2 Vintage Stakes. **Stud record:** First crop (bred in Japan) were two-year-olds in 2007. His first two European crops include the high-class Group 1 Golden Jubilee and Group 2 Coventry Stakes winner Art Connoisseur, the listed Redcar Two-Year-Old Trophy winner Lucky Like, the Group-placed Lucky Rave and several listed-placed horses. Standing at Tweenhills Stud. **2010 fee:** £3,000.

MAJESTIC MISSILE 2003 *Royal Applause – Tshusick (Dancing Brave)* **Racing record:** Won 6 including the Molecomb Stakes, Cornwallis Stakes and Prix du Petit Couvert (all 5f events). **Stud record:** First runners 2010. Standing at Ballyhane Stud, County Carlow, Ireland. **2010 fee:** €5,000.

MARIA'S MON (1993) *Wavering Monarch – Carlotta Maria (Caro)* **Racing record:** Futurity Stakes, Champagne Stakes, **Stud record:** Paris Vegas Prix Policeman. Died 2007

MARJU 1988 *Last Tycoon – Flame of Tara (Artaius)* **Racing record:** 3 wins including St James's Palace Stakes and runner-up in Derby. **Stud record:** First runners in 1993. Sire of the high-class Soviet Song (5 Group 1 events, including Sussex Stakes), the multiple Hong Kong Group 1 winner Viva Pataca and numerous smart performers including Asset, Brunel, Marju Snip (Group 1 Australasian Oaks), My Emma (Prix Vermeille), Sil Sila (Prix de Diane) and Watar. Standing at Derrinstown Stud, Ireland. **2010 fee:** €20,000.

MEDAGLIA D'ORO (1999) *El Prado – Cappucino Bay (Bailjumper)* **Racing record:** Won the Travers Stakes, Jim Dandy, San Felipe Stakes. **Stud record:** Best winners include champion Rachel Alexandra and the US Grade 1 winner Gabby's Golden Gal and Passion For Gold. Standing at Darley, Ky, USA. **2010 fee:** $100,000

MEDICEAN 1997 *Machiavellian – Mystic Goddess (Storm Bird)* **Racing record:** 6 wins included Lockinge Stakes and Eclipse. **Stud record:** First runners in 2005. Sire of very smart Dutch Art (Prix Morny, Middle Park), the smart performer Nannina (Fillies' Mile, Coronation Stakes), the very smart miler Bankable (Dubai Group 2 1m winner), Almerita (Group 1 German Oaks), Chevron (Group 1 Raffles International Cup), German Group 3 winner Love Academy and the very smart Abigail Pett, Al Shemali, Cartimandua, Mr Medici and Medici Code. Standing at Cheveley Park Stud. **2010 fee:** £15,000.

MINGUN (2000) *A P Indy – Miesque (Nureyev)* **Racing record:** Meld Stakes, Citation Handicap. **Stud record:** Sired 13 winners so far from his first crop of 2009. Standing at Lane's End, Ky USA. **2010 fee:** $5,000

MIZZEN MAST (1998) *Cozzene – Kinema (Graustark)* **Racing record:** Malibu Stakes, Strub Stakes. **Stud record:** Best winners include Midships (Charles Whittingham St), Mast Track (Hollywood Gold Cup), Jibboom (Buena Vista Hcp), Madeo (Del Mar Derby). Standing at Juddmonte Farms Ky. **2010 fee:** $15,000

MONSIEUR BOND 2000 *Danehill Dancer – Musical Essence (Song)* **Racing record:** Won 6 races, including Valiant Fortune Stakes, Gladness Stakes, Duke of York Stakes, **Stud record:** first runners 2006. Gilt Edge Girl, Sneak Preview, Amber Sunset. Standing at Norton Grove Stud. **2010 fee:** £2,000

MONTJEU 1996 *Sadler's Wells – Floripedes (Top Ville)* **Racing record:** Won 11 races, including Prix de l'Arc de Triomphe and King George VI and Queen Elizabeth Diamond Stakes. **Stud record:** First runners in 2004. A top-class stallion son of

Sadler's Wells. Sire of top-class Hurricane Run (Irish Derby, Prix de l'Arc de Triomphe, Tattersalls Gold Cup and King George), Authorized (Racing Post Trophy, Derby & Juddmonte International), Motivator (Racing Post Trophy and Derby) and Fame And Glory (Irish Derby and Racing Post Trophy), the 2009 Group 1 winning two-year-olds Jan Vermeer and St Nicholas Abbey and the high-class Alessandro Volta, Frozen Fire, Honolulu, Corre Caminos, Jukebox Jury, Macarthur, Montmartre, Papal Bull and Scorpion. Standing at Coolmore Stud, Ireland. **2010 fee:** Private (was €125,000).

MORE THAN READY (1997) *Southern Halo – Woodman's Girl (Woodman)* **Racing record:** Won King's Bishop Stakes, Hutcheson Stakes and Sanford Stakes. **Stud record:** Sire of the Australian Group 1 winners Benicio, Sebring, Phelan Ready, Perfectly Ready, More Joyous and Carry On Cutie. Standing at Vinery Stud, USA. **2010 fee:** $30,000.

MOTIVATOR 2002 *Montjeu – Out West (Gone West)* **Racing record:** Won the Derby, the Racing Post Trophy and the Dante Stakes. **Stud record:** His first runners came in 2009 and they included the Group 2 May Hill Stakes winner Pollenator, the Italian listed winner Super Motiva and the Group 3 Autumn Stakes second Prompter. Standing at The Royal Studs. Withdrawn from stud duty 2010.

MR GREELEY 1992 *Gone West – Long Legend (Reviewer)* **Racing record:** Triple Grade 3 winner in USA and runner-up in Breeders' Cup Sprint. **Stud record:** First runners in 1999. Sire of Finsceal Beo (English & Irish 1,000 Guineas), Saoirse Abu (Phoenix Stakes, Moyglare Stud Stakes), Reel Buddy (Sussex Stakes), US Grade 1 winners El Corredor, Celtic Melody, Nonsuch Bay and Whywhywhy, the Australian Group 1 winner Miss Kournikova and numerous other Group/Graded stakes winners. Standing at Gainesway Farm, Kentucky. **2010 fee:** €50,000.

MUHTATHIR (1995) *Elmaamul – Majmu (Al Nasr)* **Racing record:** Won Hungerford Stakes, Celebration Mile, Premio Vittorio di Capua, Premio Emilio Turati, Prix Jacques Le Marois. **Stud record:** Best winners include Doctor Dino (Man O'War Stakes, Hong Kong Vase), Mauralakana (Beverley D Stakes) & Satwa Queen (Prix de l'Opera). Standing at Haras du Mezeray. **2010 fee:** €12,000.

MUJADIL 1988 *Storm Bird – Vallee Secrete (Secretariat)* **Racing record:** 3 wins (at 2 yrs) including Group 3 Cornwallis Stakes. **Stud record:** Best winners include Kingsgate Native (Group 1 Nunthorpe Stakes & Group 1 Golden Jubilee Stakes), Bouncing Bowdler (Group 2 Mill Reef Stakes), Galeota (Group 2 Mill Reef Stakes), the Group 3 winners Dancal (in Australia), Daunting Lady, Leggy Lou, Lesson In Humility, Master Plasta, Satri and Show Me The Money and 17 listed winners. Standing at Rathasker Stud, Ireland. **2010 fee:** €7,500.

NAMID 1996 *Indian Ridge – Dawnsio (Tate Gallery)* **Racing record:** Won 5 races, including Prix de l'Abbaye. **Stud record:** First runners in 2004. Sire of the Total Gallery (Group 1 Prix de l'Abbaye), Pout (Group 2 Ridgewood Pearl Stakes), Redstone Dancer (Group 3 Brownstown Stakes), Blue Dakota (Group 3 Norfolk Stakes), Belle Artiste (Group 2 Leopardstown 1,000 Guineas Trial) and the smart performers Hogmaneigh and Resplendent Glory and several useful performers including Buachaill Dona, Burning Incense, Damika, Pike Bishop and That's Hot. Standing at Haras Du Hoguenet, France. **2010 fee:** €5,000.

NAYEF 1999 *Gulch – Height of Fashion (Bustino)* **Racing record:** Won 9 races, including Champion Stakes and Juddmonte International Stakes. **Stud record:** First crop were two-year-olds in 2007. His best winners are Tamayiz (dual Group 1 winner in France), Lady Marian (Prix de l'Opera), Spacious (dual Group 2 winner and 1,000 Guineas second), the 2009 2-y-o Group 3 7f Oh So Sharp Stakes winner Tabassum, the very smart Confront (Group 3 1m Joel Stakes) and the smart Group 1 placed Top Lock. Standing at Nunnery Stud, Norfolk. **2010 fee:** £15,000.

NEEDWOOD BLADE 1998 *Pivotal – Finlaggan (Be My Chief)* **Racing record:** Won 9 races here and in the USA including the Group 3 5f Palace House Stakes and the Grade 3 9f Bay Meadows Breeders Cup Handicap. **Stud record:** His first crop were 2-y-o's in 2008 and to date he's been responsible for 15 individual winners. Standing at Mickley Stud. **2010 fee:** £3,000.

NIGHT SHIFT (1980) *Northern Dancer – Ciboulette (Chop Chop)* **Racing record:** won 1 race. **Stud record:** Although he has now retired he has sired numerous winners including Azamour, In The Groove, Deportivo, & Nicolette.

NORSE DANCER (2000) *Halling – River Patrol (Rousillon)* **Racing record:** Won 4 races including Earl of Sefton Stakes, 9f, Sovereign Stakes G3 8f. **Stud record:** This is Norse Dancer's first crop of two-year-old runners. Standing at Wood Farm Stud. **2010 fee:** £2,500.

NORTH LIGHT 2001 *Danehill – Sought Out (Rainbow Quest)* **Racing record:** Won 3 races including the Derby. **Stud record:** Standing at Adena Springs, Ky. **2010 fee:** $15,000.

NOVERRE 1998 *Rahy – Danseur Fabuleux (Northern Dancer)* **Racing record:** Won 4 races at 2 yrs, including Champagne Stakes, and Sussex Stakes at 3 yrs. Placed in 7 Group 1 events afterwards. **Stud record:** First runners in 2006. Sire of the Group 1 French Derby winner Le Havre, Group 2 Challenge Stakes winner Miss Lucifer, 2009 2-y-o Group 2 7f Rockfel Stakes winner Music Show, Group 3 Albany Stakes winner Nijoom Dubai, the very smart dual Group 3 winner Summit Surge, Group 2 Queen Mary Stakes winner Langs Lash, the smart listed winning sprinter Aahayson, Italian Group 3 winner Cottonmouth and the useful performer Elhamri. Standing at Kildangan Stud, Ireland. **2010 fee:** €15,000.

NUMEROUS (1991) *Mr Prospector – Number (Nijinsky)* **Racing record:** Ran in Preakness Stakes. **Stud record:** Best winners include German Group 1 winner Kela and US Grade 1 winner Miss Loren. Standing at Haras du Quesnay. **2010 fee:** €8,000.

OASIS DREAM 2001 *Green Desert – Hop (Dancing Brave)* **Racing record:** Won 4 races, including Middle Park Stakes, July Cup and Nunthorpe Stakes (all Group 1 events). **Stud record:** His first crop were two-year-olds in 2007 and he's built himself an outstanding reputation already with the Group 1 winners Aqlaam (Prix du Moulin), Arcano (Prix Morny), Midday (Nassau Stakes, Breeders Cup Filly & Mare Turf) and Naaqoos (Prix Jean-Luc Lagardere), along with over 10 other Group/Graded stakes winners including Captain Gerrard, Misheer, Monitor Closely, Showcasing (Gimcrack Stakes), Sri Putra, Starlit Sands, Tuscan Evening, Visit and Young Pretender. Standing at Banstead Manor Stud, Newmarket. **2010 fee:** £65,000.

OBSERVATORY 1997 *Distant View – Stellaria (Roberto)* **Racing record:** His 6 wins included the Group 1 Queen Elizabeth II Stakes and the Group 1 Prix d'Ispahan. **Stud record:** First runners in 2005. Sire of the Group 1 Sprint Cup winner African Rose, the Group 1 Champion Stakes winner Twice Over, Group 3 winning two-year-old Violette and 5 listed winners including the Group 3 placed Nidhaal. Standing at Banstead Manor Stud, Newmarket. **2010 fee:** £4,000.

OFFICER (1999) *Bertrando – St Helen's Shadow (Septieme Ciel)* **Racing record:** Best Pal Stakes, Del Mar Futurity Champagne Stakes at Belmont Stakes at two years. **Stud record:** Elite Squadron (Churchill Downs Stakes), Legal Consent, Captain Brilliance and Officer Cherrie. Standing at Taylor Made Stallions, USA. **2010 fee:** $10,000.

ONE COOL CAT 2001 *Storm Cat – Tacha (Mr Prospector)* **Racing record:** At two in Ireland won the Group 1 6f Phoenix Stakes and the Group 1 7f National Stakes. **Stud record:** First crop were two-year-olds in 2008. Best performers include the Group 3 placed Hallie's Comet, Irish Cat and One Clever Cat and the listed winners Cool Contest, Icesolator, Layla's Hero, Lungwa and Magic Cat, Sarabia and Smokey Storm. Standing at Coolmore Stud, Ireland. **2010 fee:** €9,000.

ORATORIO 2002 *Danehill – Mahrah (Vaguely Noble)* **Racing record:** Won the Prix Jean-Luc Lagardere (at 2 yrs), the Eclipse Stakes and Irish Champion Stakes. **Stud record:** His first crop were two-year-olds in 2009 and they included the first two home in the Group 1 Dewhurst Stakes, Beethoven and Fencing Master. He also had the dual listed winner Big Audio, the Group 3 fourth Blue Angel and the listed placed Mabura and Miracle Match. In March this year he had a Group 1 winning 2-y-o in New Zealand – Banchee. Standing at Coolmore Stud, Ireland. **2010 fee:** €15,000.

ORIENTATE (1998) *Mt Livermore – Dream Team (Cox's Ridge)* **Racing record:** Won ten races including, Forego Handicap, Commonwealth Handicap, A G Vanderbilt Handicap, **Stud record:** Lady Joanne, Alabama Stakes, Intangaroo, Humana Distaff. Standing at Gainesway Ky. **2010 fee:** $10,000.

ORPEN (1996) *Lure – Bonita Francita (Devil's Bag)* **Racing record:** Won two races including Prix Morny. Champion at 2 yrs. **Stud record:** Torrestrella (Poule d'Essai des Pouliches). Rocks off, War Artist (Prix de L'Abbaye). Standing at Haras du Thenney. **2010 fee:** €8,000

PASTORAL PURSUITS 2001 *Bahamian Bounty – Star (Most Welcome)* **Racing record:** Won 6 races including the July Cup, Sirenia Stakes and Park Stakes. **Stud record:** His first crop were runners in 2009 and his winners included the Group 2 Mill Reef Stakes second Angel's Pursuit and the dual winner and Group 2 fourth Rose Blossom. Standing at the National Stud. **2010 fee:** £5,000.

PEINTRE CELEBRE (1994) *Nureyev – Peinture Bleue (Alydar)* **Racing record:** Won 5 races including Prix du Jockey Club, Grand Prix de Paris, Prix de L'Arc de Triomphe. **Stud record:** Pride, Prix Jean Romanet, Prix Foy, Grand Prix de Saint Cloud, Champion Stakes, Hong Kong Gold Cup. Dai Jin whose wins included the German Derby and Valle Enchantee. Standing at Coolmore Ire. **2010 fee:** €17,500.

PHOENIX REACH (2000) *Alhaarth – Carroll's Canyon (Hatim)* **Racing record:** Wins include Sheema Classic, Hong Kong Vase, Canadian International, Gordon Stakes. **Stud record:** First crop of foals are two-year-old this year. Standing at National Stud, Newmarket. **2010 fee:** £2,500

PICCOLO 1991 *Warning – Woodwind (Whistling Wind)* **Racing record:** 4 wins including Nunthorpe Stakes and Kings Stand Stakes. **Stud record:** Sire of the Group 1 Nunthorpe Stakes winner La Cucaracha, the Australian Group 1 winner Picaday, the Group 2 winners Ajigolo, Express Air, St Trinians and Winker Watson and numerous other smart performers including Aegean Dancer, Bond Boy (Steward's Cup winner), Hoh Hoh Hoh, Hunting Lion, Lipocco, Pan Jammer and Pickle. Standing at Throckmorton Court Stud. **2010 fee:** £3,000.

PIVOTAL 1993 *Polar Falcon – Fearless Revival (Cozzene)* **Racing record:** 4 wins including the Nunthorpe Stakes and King's Stand Stakes. **Stud record:** First runners in 2000. An outstanding sire whose best winners include the high-class Excellent Art (St James's Palace Stakes), Falco (French 2,000 Guineas), Halfway To Heaven (Irish 1,00 Guineas, Nassau Stakes and Sun Chariot Stakes, Kyllachy (Nunthorpe Stakes), Sariska (Oaks and Irish Oaks), and Somnus (Sprint Cup, Prix de la Foret, Prix Maurice de Gheest), the very smart Beauty Is Truth (Group 2 Prix du Gros-Chene), Captain Rio (Group 2 Criterium des Maisons-Laffitte), Chorist (Pretty Polly Stakes), Golden Apples (triple US Grade 1 winner), Leo (Group 2 Royal Lodge Stakes), Peeress (Lockinge Stakes, Sun Chariot Stakes), Pivotal Point (Group 2 Diadem Stakes) and Virtual (Lockinge Stakes) and numerous smart performers including Falco (French 2,000 Guineas), Megahertz (2 US Grade 1 events), Regal Parade (Haydock Sprint Cup), Silvester Lady (German Oaks), Siyouni (2009 2-y-o Group 1 Prix Jean-Luc Lagardere) and Saoire (Irish 1000 Guineas). Standing at Cheveley Park Stud, Newmarket. **2010 fee:** £65,000.

PROCLAMATION 2002 *King's Best – Shamarra (Zayyani)* **Racing record:** Won 4 races including the Group 1 1m Sussex Stakes and Group 3 7f Jersey Stakes. **Stud record:** First runners 2010. Standing at Overbury Stud. **2010 fee:** £3,000.

PROUD CITIZEN 1999 *Gone West – Drums Of Freedom (Green Forest)* **Racing record:** Won 3 races including the Grade 3 Lexington Stakes and second the Kentucky Derby. **Stud record:** Retired to stud in 2004. First crop were 2-y-o's in 2007. Sire of the US dual Grade 1 winner Proud Spell, the Group 3 Somerville Tattersall Stakes winner River Proud, the US Grade 3 winner Motovato and a number of other US stakes winners. Standing at Airdrie Stud, Kentucky. **2010 fee:** $15,000.

RAHY 1985 *Blushing Groom – Glorious Song (Halo)* **Racing record:** Won 3 races in Britain including twice at 2 yrs when second in Middle Park Stakes. Later a Grade 2 1m winner in USA. Half-brother to Singspiel. **Stud record:**

Best winners include top-class Fantastic Light (7 Group/Grade 1 successes, including Irish Champion Stakes and Breeders' Cup Turf), high-class Hawksley Hill, Noverre (Sussex Stakes, also first past post in French 2000 Guineas), Rio de la Plata (Prix Jean-Luc Lagardere), Serena's Song (won 11 US Grade 1 events), US Grade 1 winners Dancing Forever, Designed For Luck, Dreaming Of Anna and Tates Creek, the US Grade 2 winners Lewis Michael and Pounced, French Group 2 winner Legerete and the 2-y-o Group 3 July Stakes winner City On A Hill. Now retired from stud.

RAINBOW QUEST (1981) *Blushing Groom – I Will Follow (Herbager)* **Racing record:** Won 3 races including Great Voltigeur Stakes, Irish Derby, Craven Stakes. **Stud record:** High-class sire. Best winners include Quest For Fame (Derby) and Nedawi (St Leger). Died 2007.

RAKTI 1999 *Polish Precedent – Ragera (Rainbow Quest)* **Racing record:** Won the Italian Derby, Champion Stakes, Prince of Wales's Stakes, Queen Elizabeth II Stakes and Lockinge Stakes. **Stud record:** His first runners appeared in 2009 and he is the sire of 9 individual 2-y-o winners. Standing at the Irish National Stud. **2010 fee:** €5,000.

REDBACK 1999 *Mark of Esteem – Patsy Western (Precocious)* **Racing record:** Won Solario Stakes and Greenham Stakes. **Stud record:** Winners include the very smart Grade 1 10f E P Taylor Stakes and Group 2 Rockfel Stakes winner Lahaleeb, the Group 2 Queen Mary Stakes winner Gilded and the listed winners Sonny Red & Redolent (also Group 1 placed). Standing at Haras De Victot, France. **2010 fee:** €3,500.

RED RANSOM 1987 *Roberto – Arabia (Damascus)* **Racing record:** 2 wins in US, at 5f and 6f, from three outings. **Stud record:** Best performers include outstanding miler Intikhab, high-class Ekraar (Group 1 Italian Derby) and Electrocutionist (Dubai World Cup, Juddmonte International), very smart performers Casual Look (Oaks), China Visit (Group 2 Prix du Rond-Point), Bail Out Becky (Del Mar Oaks), Perfect Sting (Queen Elizabeth II Challenge Cup and BC Filly and Mare Turf), Red Clubs (Haydock Park Sprint Cup), Australian Grade 1 winners Red Dazzler, Charge Forward & Typhoon Tracy (four Group 1 wins), the German Group 1 winner Ransom O'War and the dual Group 2 winning 2-y-o Sri Pekan. Standing at Dalham Hall Stud, Newmarket. **2010 fee:** £25,000.

REEL BUDDY 1998 *Mr Greeley – Rosebud (Indian Ridge)* **Racing record:** Abernant Stakes, Hungerford Stakes, Sussex Stakes. **Stud record:** Best winners include Reel Gift and Mymumsaysimthebest, Standing at Bearstone Stud, 2010 fee £3,000.

REFUSE TO BEND 2000 *Sadler's Wells – Market Slide (Gulch)* **Racing record:** Won 7 races including National Stakes, 2,000 Guineas, Eclipse Stakes & Queen Anne Stakes. **Stud record:** His first crop were two-year-olds in 2008 and his best to date include the smart dual winner Liberation, the Group 3 winners Grace O'Malley and Neon Light and the listed winners Alaiyma and Mibar. Standing at Whitsbury Manor Stud. **2010 fee:** £5,000.

ROCKPORT HARBOR (2002) *Unbridled's Song –Regal Miss (Song)* **Racing record:** Won 5 races including Remsen Stakes, Nashua Stakes, Essex Handicap. **Stud record:** His first two-year-olds will run this year. Stands at Darley Ky. **2010 fee:** $12,500.

ROMAN RULER (2002) *Fusaichi Pegasus – Silver Swan (Silver Deputy)* **Racing record:** Won 5 races including Norfolk Stakes, Best Pal Stakes. Haskell Invitational, Dwyer Stakes. Stud record. Best winners include Homeboykris (Champagne Stakes) and Roman Invasion, from his first crop. Standing at Hill N'Dale Farm Ky. **2010 fee:** $20,000.

ROYAL ACADEMY (1987) *Nijinsky – Crimson Saint (Crimson Satan)* **Racing record:** Tetrarch Stakes, July Cup, Breeders Cup Mile. **Stud record:** First runners 1994, Oscar Schindler, Val Royal, Ali Royal, Bullish Luck, Gold Academy, Standing at Ashford Stud, Ky. **2010 fee:** $15,000

ROYAL APPLAUSE 1993 *Waajib – Flying Melody (Auction Ring)* **Racing record:** Winner of 9 races, including Middle Park at 2 yrs and Haydock Park Sprint Cup at 4. **Stud record:** First runners in 2001. Sire of the US dual Grade 1 winner Ticker

Tape, Group/Grade 2 winners Acclamation, Battle Of Hastings, Finjaan, Lovelace, Mister Cosmi, Nevisian Lad, Please Sing and Whatsthescript and numerous very smart performers including Crime Scene, Majestic Missile, Peak To Creek and Prince Siegfried. Standing at The Royal Studs, Norfolk. **2010 fee:** £9,000.

SADLER'S WELLS 1981 *Northern Dancer – Fairy Bridge (Bold Reason)* **Racing record:** Winner of Irish 2,000 Guineas, Phoenix Champion Stakes and Coral-Eclipse Stakes. **Stud record:** A great sire of numerous Group/Grade 1 winners including top-class performers Doyen, Galileo, High Chaparral, Kayf Tara, Montjeu, Old Vic, Opera House, Salsabil and Yeats. Retired from stud.

SAKHEE 1997 *Bahri – Thawakib (Sadler's Wells)* **Racing record:** Won 8 races, including Juddmonte International and Prix de l'Arc de Triomphe, and runner-up in Derby. **Stud record:** First runners in 2006. Sire of the Group 1 July Cup winner Sakhee's Secret, the Hong Kong Group 1 winner Presvis and the very smart Regal Flush, Royal Rock and Samuel. Standing at Nunnery Stud, Norfolk. **2010 fee:** £6,000.

SEEKING THE GOLD 1985 *Mr Prospector – Con Game (Buckpasser)* **Racing record:** 8 wins in USA, notably Grade 1 events Dwyer Stakes and Super Derby. **Stud record:** First runners in 1993. His best winners include the outstanding Dubai Millennium (Dubai World Cup, Prix Jacques le Marois, Queen Elizabeth II Stakes), the high-class Cape Town, Heavenly Prize, Jazil (Belmont Stakes) and Pleasant Home (Breeders' Cup Distaff), the Japanese Grade 1 winner Gold Tiara and very smart Bob and John (US Grade 1 Wood Memorial), Cash Run (US Grade 1 Breeders Cup Juvenile), Dream Supreme, Flanders, Fort Dignity, Lujain (Group 1 Middle Park Stakes), Meiner Love, Quest and Seeking The Pearl (Prix Maurice de Gheest and Japanese Group 1 event). Retired from stud.

SELKIRK 1988 *Sharpen Up – Annie Edge (Nebbiolo)* **Racing record:** 6 wins including Queen Elizabeth II Stakes, Lockinge Stakes, Beefeater Gin Celebration Mile and Challenge Stakes. **Stud record:** A leading British-based stallion, he has sired 11 Group 1 winners and is the broodmare sire of 4 more. His best include Leadership (Gran Premio d'Italia), the Premio Presidente Repubblica winners Altieri and Selmis, Border Arrow, Etlaala, Favourable Terms (Nassau Stakes), Field of Hope (Prix de la Foret), Highest, Kastoria (Irish St Leger), Pipedreamer, Prince Kirk (Prix d'Ispahan), Red Bloom (Fillies' Mile), Scott's View, Squeak (Beverly Hills Handicap), Sulk (Prix Marcel Boussac), Tam Lin, The Trader, Tranquil Tiger, Trans Island, Wince (1000 Guineas) and Wordly. Standing at Lanwades Stud in Newmarket. **2010 fee:** £20,000.

SHAMARDAL 2002 *Giant's Causeway – Helsinki (Machiavellian)* **Racing record:** Won Dewhurst Stakes, French 2,000 Guineas, French Derby and St James's Palace Stakes. **Stud record:** His first European runners appeared in 2009 and he's had a very good start to his stud career. His best performers to date have been Arctic (Group 3 Round Tower Stakes), Shakespearian (Group 3 Solario Stakes winner and Group 2 placed), Zazou (third in the Group 1 Criterium de Saint-Cloud) and the listed UAE 1,000 Guineas winner Siyaadah. In Australia he's had the Group 1 winner Faint Perfume and the Group 3 winner Shamoline Warrior. Standing at Kildangan Stud, Ireland. **2010 fee:** €20,000.

SHARP HUMOR (2003) *Distorted Humor – Bellona (Hansel)* **Racing record:** Won Swale Stakes. **Stud record:** First two year olds 2010. Standing at Winstar Farm, Ky. **2010 fee:** $7,500

SILVER TRAIN (2002) *Old Trieste – Ridden in Thestars (Cormorant)* **Racing record:** Breeders Cup Sprint, Jerome Handicap, Metropolitan Hcp, Tom Fool Hcp. **Stud record:** First two year olds this year. Standing at Vinery, Ky. **2010 fee:** $12,500.

SHIROCCO 2001 *Monsun – So Sedulous (The Minstrel)* **Racing record:** Won 7 races including the German Derby, French Derby, Breeders Cup Turf and Coronation Cup (all Group 1, 12f events). **Stud record:** First runners 2010. Standing at Dalham Hall Stud. **2010 fee:** £10,000.

SINGSPIEL 1992 *In The Wings – Glorious Song (Halo)* **Racing record:** Winner of 9 races, notably Canadian International and Japan Cup at 4 yrs and Dubai World Cup, Coronation Cup and Juddmonte International at 5. **Stud record:** First runners in 2001. Sire of top-class performer Moon Ballad, US dual Grade 1 winner Lahudood, high-class Lohengrin (in Japan), very smart Asakusa Den'en (Japanese Group 1 winner), Confidential Lady (Prix de Diane), Da Re Mi (Yorkshire Oaks and Pretty Polly Stakes), Eastern Anthem (Dubai Sheema Classic), Folk Opera (E P Taylor Stakes), Lateral (Gran Criterium), Papineau (Gold Cup), Silkwood (Ribblesdale Stakes), Singhalese (Del Mar Oaks) and of numerous smart performers. Standing at Dalham Hall Stud, Newmarket. **2010 fee:** £15,000.

SINNDAR 1997 *Grand Lodge – Sinntara (Lashkari)* **Racing record:** Won 7 races, including Derby and Prix de l'Arc de Triomphe. **Stud record:** First runners in 2004. Sire of the top-class colt and multiple Group 1 winner Youmzain, the 2009 2-y-o Group 1 Prix Marcel Boussac winner Rosanara, the very smart performer Shawanda (Irish Oaks and Prix Vermeille), the smart Albahja, Aqaleem, Four Sins (Blandford Stakes), Pictavia and Visindar (Prix Greffulhe) and the very useful Gale Force, Kerashan and Red Gala. Standing at Haras du Bonneval, France. **2010 fee:** €12,500.

SLEEPING INDIAN 2001 *Indian Ridge – Las Flores (Sadler's Wells)* **Racing record:** Won 6 races including the Group 2, 7f Challenge Stakes the Group 3 7f Hungerford Stakes and three listed events. **Stud record:** First runners 2010. Standing at Tweenhills Stud. **2010 fee:** £4,000.

SMART STRIKE 1992 *Mr Prospector – Classy 'n Smart (Smarten)* **Racing record:** Won 8 races in the USA including the Grade 2 8.5f Philip H Iselin Handicap and the Grade 3 Salvator Mile. **Stud record:** Best winners include the top-class colt Curlin (Preakness Stakes, Dubai World Cup, Breeders Cup Classic), the US Grade 1 winners English Channel, Fabulous Strike, Furthest Land, Lookin At Lucky, Shadow Cast, Soaring Free and Square Eddie, and the Japan Cup winner Fleetstreet Dancer. Standing at Lane's End Farm. **2010 fee:** €75,000.

SONGANDAPRAYER (1998) *Unbridled's Song – Alizen (Premiership)* **Racing record:** Won Fountain of Youth Stakes, 2nd Blue Grass Stakes. **Stud record:** Songster (Woody Stephens Breeders Cup and Bold Ruler Stakes). What A Song, (Best Pal Stakes), Praying for Cash, He's Got Grit. Standing at Walmac Farms, Ky. **2010 fee:** $12,500.

SOVIET STAR 1984 *Nureyev – Veruschka (Venture)* **Racing record:** Trusthouse Forte Mile, July Cup, Prix Moulin de Longchamp. **Stud record:** Starcraft, Queen Elizabeth 11 Stakes, Prix du Moulin de Longchamp, Freedom Cry, Ashkalani, winner of 4 races including Prix Thomas Bryon G3, 1m, Prix de Fontainebleau, French 2,000 Guineas G1, Prix du Moulin de Longchamp, G1 Starborough, Prix Jean Prat 9f, St James's Palace Stakes G1 plus Presenting, Soviet Line and Russian Pearl. Standing at Ballylinch Stud Ireland. **2010 fee:** €8,000

SPEIGHTSTOWN (1998) *Gone West – Silken Cat (Storm Cat)* **Racing record:** Won Breeders Cup Sprint, Churchill Downs Hcp, True North Breeders Cup Hcp, Alfred Vanderbilt Handicap. **Stud record:** Best winners include Munnings & Lord Shanakill. Standing at Winstar Farm, Ky **2010 fee:** $35,000

STARCRAFT 2000 *Soviet Star – Flying Floozie (Pompeii Court)* **Racing record:** Won 9 races in Australia/New Zealand including three Group 1 events. Subsequently won the Prix du Moulin and the Queen Elizabeth II Stakes. **Stud record:** First runners appear this year. Now in Australia.

STORM CAT 1983 *Storm Bird – Terlingua (Secretariat)* **Racing record:** 4 wins from 6f to 8.5f notably Grade 1 Young America Stakes. **Stud record:** An outstanding source of speed and of classy two-year-olds. Best winners include Group/Grade 1 winners After Market, Aljabr, Black Minnaloushe, Bluegrass Cat, Cat Thief, Catinca, Desert Stormer, Forestry, Giant's Causeway, Good Reward, Hennessy, High Yield, Nebraska, One Cool Cat, Sharp Cat, Storm Flag Flying, Sweet Catomine, Tabasco Cat, Tornado and Vision And Verse. Retired from stud.

STORMING HOME (1998) *Machiavellian – Try To Catch Me (Shareef Dancer)* **Racing record:** Won the Champion Stakes, Charles Whittingham Hcp, Clement Hirsch Memorial Stakes and King Edward V11 Stakes. **Stud record:** Best winners include Flying Cloud (Ribblesdale Stakes) and Jakkalberry. Standing Darley Japan. **2010 fee:** 1m500,000yen.

STORMY ATLANTIC (1994) *Storm Cat – Hail Atlantis (Seattle Slew)* **Stud record:** Has sired 8 crops, winners include Stormello (Hollywood Futurity St, Norfolk Breeders Cup Stakes), My Princess Jess (Lake George Stakes). Standing at Hill N'Dale Farms, Ky. **2010 fee:** $35,000

STREET CRY 1998 *Machiavellian – Helen Street (Troy)* **Racing record:** 5 wins including Dubai World Cup. **Stud record:** First runners in 2006. Sire of the outstanding multiple Grade 1 winning racemare Zenyatta and the Group/Grade 1 winners Street Sense (Breeders' Cup Juvenile, Kentucky Derby, Travers Stakes), Cry And Catch Me (Oak Leaf Stakes), Majestic Roi (Sun Chariot Stakes), Street Boss (Triple Bend Invitational, Bing Crosby H'cap), Seventh Street (dual US Grade 1), Street Hero (Norfolk Stakes) and the Australian Group 1 winners Shocking (Melbourne Cup) and Whobegotyou (Caulfield Guineas and Yalumba Stakes). Standing at Jonabell Stud Farm, Kentucky. **2010 fee:** $150,000.

STRIKING AMBITION (2000) *Makbul – Lady Roxanne (Cyrano de Bergerac)* **Racing record:** Won Carnarvon Stakes at Newbury, Waterford Testimonial Stakes 6f, Prix Contessina, Woodlands Stakes, Group 3 Prix Ris-Orangis, Group 2 Golden Peitsche. First crop are two-year-olds. Standing at Longdon Stud, Staffordshire. **2010 fee:** £2,500

TAGULA 1993 *Taufan – Twin Island (Standaan)* **Racing record:** Won 4 races including the Group 1 6f Prix Morny (at 2 yrs) and the Group 3 7f Supreme Stakes. **Stud record:** Sires plenty of winners, amongst the best being the impressive 2009 2-y-o Group 2 Coventry Stakes winner Canford Cliffs, the Group 2 Prix du Gros-Chene winner Tax Free, the Group 2 Royal Lodge Stakes winner Atlantis Prince, the German Group 2 winner Tagshira, the smart Group 2 placed Beaver Patrol and the listed winners Bakewell Tart, Double Vie, Drawnfromthepast, King Orchisios, Macaroon, Pure Poetry and Red Millennium. Standing at the Rathbarry Stud. **2010 fee:** Private (was €4,000 in 2009).

TIGER HILL 1995 *Danehill – The Filly (Appiani II)* **Racing record:** Won 17 races including three Group 1 events in Germany. **Stud record:** Compiled an excellent record in Germany (including the Group 1 winners Iota and Konigstiger and a multitude of other stakes winners) prior to coming to England. His first British crop of two-year-olds appeared in 2009. In the next few years it will be fascinating to see what his offspring can achieve once they have matured and become three-year-olds and above. Standing at Dalham Hall Stud. **2010 fee:** £8,000.

TOBOUGG 1998 *Barathea – Lacovia (Majestic Light)* **Racing record:** Won three times at 2 yrs including the Dewhurst Stakes and was subsequently placed in four other Group 1 events including Derby and Eclipse. **Stud record:** He had his first runners in 2006 when he was the leading British-based first season sire. Sire of the Grade 1 New Zealand 1,000 Guineas winner The Pooka, the very smart Group 2 German 1,000 Guineas winner Penny's Gift, Sweet Lilly (three listed wins), the Group 3 winners Lady Alida, Distinctive and Circumvent, the listed winners Biz Bar and Market Day and the smart Sanbuch, The Betchworth Kid and Tobosa. Standing at East Burrow Farm, Devon. **2010 fee:** £2,500.

TRADE FAIR 2000 *Zafonic – Danefair (Danehill)* **Racing record:** Won the Group 3 Criterion Stakes, the Group 3 Minstrel Stakes and two listed events. **Stud record:** His first runners appeared in 2009 and totalled 13 individual winners. Standing at Tweenhills Stud. **2010 fee:** £3,000.

TRANS ISLAND 1995 *Selkirk – Khubza (Green Desert)* **Racing record:** Won 6 races including the Group 2 Prix du Rond-Point and the Group 3 Diomed Stakes. **Stud record:** His best winners include the smart sprinter Bond City and the smart listed 7f winner Kalahari Gold. Standing at Arctic Tack Stud, Ireland. **2010 fee:** €3,000.

VAL ROYAL 1996 *Royal Academy – Vadlava (Bikala)* **Racing record:** Won the Grade 1 Breeders Cup Mile, the Group 2 Prix Guillaume d'Ornano and the Grade 2 Del Mar Derby. Died 2008.

VERGLAS 1994 *Highest Honor – Rahaam (Secreto)* **Racing record:** Won 3 races including the Group 3 6f Coventry Stakes. **Stud record:**

Sire of the Group 1 French 2,000 Guineas winner Silver Frost, the Group 1 Prix Jean Prat winner Stormy River, the US dual Grade 2 winner Blackdoun, the Group 3 winners Love Lockdown, Ozone Bere, Spirited One and Wilside, and numerous listed winners including the smart Glass Harmonium. Standing at the Irish National Stud. **2010 fee:** €10,000.

WAR CHANT 1997 *Danzig – Hollywood Wildcat (Kris S)* **Racing record:** Won 5 races including the Grade 1 Breeders Cup Mile. **Stud record:** Sire of the 2-y-o Group 1 National Stakes winner Kingsfort, the US Grade 2 winners Brilliant and War Kill, Group 3 Nell Gwyn Stakes winner Karen's Caper, the US Grade 3 winners Ballymore Lady, Chamberlaine Bridge, Chattahoochee War and En Roblar & Sea Chanter, Irish Group 3 winner Norman Invader and the French Group 3 winner Asperity. Standing at Three Chimneys Farm, Kentucky. **2010 fee:** $12,500.

WHIPPER 2001 *Miesque's Son – Myth To Reality (Sadler's Wells)* **Racing record:** Won the Prix Morny and the Prix Maurice de Gheest. **Stud record:** His first runners in 2009 included the Group 3 winner Dolled Up and the Group 2 Rockfel Stakes second Atasari. Standing at Ballylinch Stud, Ireland. **2010 fee:** €10,000.

WITH APPROVAL *Caro – Passing Mood (Buckpasser)* **Racing record:** Raced in Canada where he won the Triple Crown (Queen's Plate, Breeders Stakes and Prince Of Wales's Stakes). **Stud record:** His best winners include the Group/Grade 2 winners Allende, Dust Me Off, Just Approval, T H Approval, Talkin Man and Lasting Approval, the US Grade 3 winners Mission Approved, OK By Me, Ray's Approval, Silverfoot, Tasteyville, Thesaurus, Van Minister and Zanetti and the smart English winners Lonesome Dude and Frosty Welcome. Standing at Lanwades Stud, Newmarket. **2010 fee:** £4,500.

XAAR 1995 *Zafonic – Monroe (Sir Ivor)* **Racing record:** Won 5 races including Prix Cabourg, Prix de la Salamandre, Dewhurst Stakes, Craven Stakes. **Stud record:** Balthazaar's Gift, Criterium de Maisons-Laffite, Hungerford Stakes, Wake Up Maggie, Chartwell Fillies Stakes, Oak Tree Stakes. Standing at Darley Japan. **2010 fee:** 1m yen.

ZAFEEN 2000 *Zafonic – Shy Lady (Kaldoun)* **Racing record:** Won the Group 1 St James's Palace Stakes and the Group 2 Mill Reef Stakes and second in the 2,000 Guineas. **Stud record:** His first runners appeared in 2009 and he had a number of winners but no stakes horses. Standing at Haras Du Petit Tellier. **2010 fee:** €4000.

ZAMINDAR 1994 *Gone West – Zaizafon (The Minstrel)* **Racing record:** Won the Group 3 Prix de Cabourg at 2 yrs and was placed in the Prix Morny and the Prix de la Salamandre. **Stud record:** Has sired a number of very good fillies, notably the outstanding Zarkava (five Group 1 wins including the Prix de l'Arc de Triomphe), Darjina (three Group 1 wins), the Group 1 Prix Saint-Alary winner Coquerelle and the Group 1 French 1,000 Guineas winner Zenda. He also has the Group 2 winners Crossharbour and Modern Look. Standing at Banstead Manor Stud, Newmarket. **2010 fee:** £15,000.

Stallions index

Stallions appear under the reference number of their offspring.

Acclamation 52, 198, 269, 285, 422, 581, 786, 794, 815, 875, 1153, 1310, 1447
Act One 1649
Ad Valorem 97, 374, 424, 838, 1012, 1179, 1384, 1488, 1654
Afleet Alex 445
Alhaarth 191, 291, 471, 538, 578, 1564, 1568, 1603
Anabaa 643, 1158, 1425
Antonius Pius 261, 402, 842
Aptitude 857, 1368
Araafa 75, 236, 316, 442, 564, 579, 912, 923, 1213, 1218, 1306, 1318, 1404, 1427, 1433, 1528, 1550
Arch 64, 73, 1095, 1141, 1357, 1529, 1608
Artie Schiller 671
Auction House 214
Aussie Rules 220, 296, 324, 359, 421, 698, 858, 981, 1237, 1314, 1320
Avonbridge 323, 525, 762, 805, 854, 900, 975, 1088, 1175
Awesome Again 1638
Azamour 392, 459, 658, 941, 956, 1345, 1348, 1601

Bachelor Duke 45, 293, 1045, 1302
Bahamian Bounty 102, 217, 263, 266, 390, 461, 549, 589, 697, 816, 833, 1082, 1114, 1198, 1557
Bahri 764, 1372
Balmont 1052, 1374, 1572
Barathea 149, 177, 531, 704, 752, 765, 881, 1029, 1346, 1440, 1574
Beat Hollow 16, 256, 298, 326, 411, 500, 873, 1035, 1121, 1389, 1548, 1602
Bellamy Road 1168
Bernardini 607, 680, 681, 684, 1140, 1199, 1351
Bernstein 1463
Bertolini 10, 22, 187, 476, 530, 788, 928, 1076, 1110, 1190, 1303, 1462, 1467
Byron 301, 753, 768, 820, 1353

Cacique 772, 910, 911, 930, 1172, 1644, 1647, 1648
Cadeaux Genereux 20, 71, 185, 197, 200, 204, 259, 262, 363,
377, 426, 675, 720, 745, 821, 982, 1033, 1176, 1474
Camacho 372, 560, 1019, 1062, 1373, 1588
Cape Cross 39, 93, 94, 103, 112, 175, 275, 383, 444, 451, 473, 477, 480, 494, 496, 598, 600, 603, 612, 621, 649, 714, 726, 755, 926, 937, 943, 960, 964, 999, 1002, 1100, 1200, 1321, 1375, 1446, 1449, 1470, 1562, 1580
Captain Rio 412, 739, 770, 862
Chevalier 844
Chineur 488, 582, 1123, 1582
Choisir 65, 219, 381, 388, 436, 775, 812, 826, 853, 921, 1053
Clodovil 265, 501, 804, 913, 1075
Compton Place 32, 76, 428, 438, 506, 536, 555, 569, 574, 575, 718, 771, 1032, 1086, 1222, 1436, 1438
Congaree 144
Country Reel 400

D'Wildcat 138
Dalakhani 140, 491, 522, 604, 624, 712, 878, 1332, 1352, 1450, 1531, 1581
Danbird 380
Danehill Dancer 87, 99, 237, 365, 420, 492, 636, 686, 715, 729, 759, 777, 801, 879, 888, 909, 918, 984, 1001, 1125, 1192, 1201, 1203, 1205, 1216, 1228, 1238, 1246, 1250, 1274, 1280, 1289, 1298, 1323, 1361, 1362, 1386, 1391, 1430, 1476, 1479, 1481, 1482, 1485, 1497, 1519, 1520, 1539, 1541
Dansili 6, 118, 195, 205, 209, 244, 248, 249, 255, 258, 497, 504, 505, 548, 550, 623, 656, 691, 708, 806, 893, 998, 1101, 1113, 1127, 1134, 1136, 1293, 1296, 1330, 1343, 1397, 1489, 1494, 1498, 1530, 1533, 1534, 1589, 1617, 1646
Deploy 1466
Deportivo 407
Desert Style 41, 1068, 1206, 1556, 1610
Diamond Green 123, 304, 355, 389, 449, 590, 696, 780, 824, 865, 1083
Diktat 186, 264, 328, 347, 417, 587, 593, 955, 1081, 1188
Distorted Humor 510, 628
Dixie Union 235, 986, 1226,
1245
Dr Fong 74, 542, 779, 789, 1016, 1087, 1102, 1119, 1434, 1464
Dubai Destination 344, 368, 484, 495, 627, 800, 962, 1050, 1195, 1300, 1316, 1322, 1344, 1354
Dubawi 108, 282, 345, 354, 362, 364, 371, 469, 475, 716, 744, 757, 802, 839, 940, 1105, 1173, 1223, 1326, 1385, 1431, 1616, 1618, 1623, 1625
Dynaformer 632, 634, 646, 871, 953, 1129, 1598

E Dubai 580
El Prado 116, 932, 1049, 1633
Elnadim 409, 1452
Elusive City 210, 222, 281, 403, 404, 551, 785, 834, 1116, 1160, 1480
Elusive Quality 339, 393, 633, 635, 663, 669, 1540, 1565, 1569, 1634
Empire Maker 241, 257, 876, 1509
Encosta De Lago 122, 472, 566, 577, 583, 746, 863, 887, 922, 968, 1065, 1067, 1108, 1139, 1486, 1560, 1587
Eurosilver 822
Exceed And Excel 48, 109, 168, 184, 299, 707, 747, 803, 1038, 1094, 1124, 1133, 1319, 1622

Fasliyev 313, 391, 790, 1024
First Samurai 1282
Footstepsinthesand 67, 348, 571, 591, 1064, 1242, 1287, 1304, 1358, 1369
Forest Wildcat 1048
Forestry 443, 897, 1566

Galileo 18, 28, 92, 95, 137, 139, 141, 142, 147, 154, 155, 157, 161, 163, 215, 230, 239, 240, 252, 253, 338, 640, 642, 661, 674, 676, 682, 683, 732, 740, 885, 917, 945, 1181, 1207, 1211, 1219, 1220, 1231, 1247, 1248, 1253, 1254, 1256, 1260, 1262, 1263, 1266, 1270, 1271, 1281, 1285, 1288, 1292, 1294, 1299, 1325, 1342, 1413, 1505, 1507, 1515, 1621, 1624, 1626, 1639
George Washington 778
Giant's Causeway 51, 148, 613, 665, 750, 929, 1212, 1272, 1543
Gone West 159, 1107
Good Reward 622, 767

STALLIONS INDEX 345

Green Desert 23, 114, 160, 260, 307, 366, 453, 493, 654, 927, 934, 996, 1006, 1194, 1336, 1456, 1547, 1631

Haafhd 15, 68, 466, 706, 733, 868, 872, 905, 977, 1007, 1147, 1393, 1437, 1558, 1576, 1577, 1600, 1650
Halling 89, 468, 539, 728, 847, 938, 954, 990, 991, 1347, 1387
Harlan's Holiday 1448
Hawk Wing 36, 827
Hennessy 662, 766
Henny Hughes 335, 874, 1117
Hernando 42, 47, 167, 1280
High Chaparral 127, 227, 349, 382, 399, 405, 563, 783, 860, 1377, 1400, 1487, 1537, 1559
Holy Roman Emperor 58, 59, 80, 121, 132, 276, 315, 336, 489, 678, 782, 792, 807, 859, 948, 970, 1089, 1251, 1252, 1257, 1259, 1278, 1283, 1284, 1309, 1371, 1442, 1443, 1477, 1627, 1630
Hurricane Run 34, 70, 88, 146, 164, 228, 233, 245, 250, 303, 427, 457, 486, 520, 561, 668, 760, 773, 813, 817, 915, 950, 992, 1009, 1011, 1026, 1041, 1071, 1163, 1170, 1258, 1269, 1527

Iceman 120, 182, 188, 346, 529, 644, 1078, 1150, 1191, 1217, 1409, 1422, 1493, 1551
Iffraaj 1, 57, 106, 413, 456, 553, 556, 557, 572, 573, 584, 647, 769, 791, 793, 861, 935, 1056, 1079, 1106, 1415, 1444, 1468, 1472, 1599
Imperial Dancer 297, 302
Indesatchel 273, 419, 434, 559, 738, 1014
Indian Haven 135, 840, 1619
Intikhab 54, 60, 431, 446, 447, 867, 1561, 1612
Invincible Spirit 3, 100, 133, 143, 145, 151, 156, 165, 172, 179, 199, 267, 330, 357, 394, 482, 515, 567, 601, 609, 630, 694, 695, 722, 723, 724, 787, 819, 841, 946, 997, 1031, 1096, 1128, 1130, 1146, 1183, 1210, 1214, 1341, 1350, 1378, 1410, 1412, 1593, 1628, 1640
Ishiguru 69, 225, 397, 1060, 1407
Ivan Denisovich 478, 568, 1013

Johannesburg 126, 270, 870, 1061, 1109, 1236, 1240, 1429

Kheleyf 2, 8, 113, 211, 283, 308, 386, 545, 651, 717, 837, 849, 1092, 1126, 1441, 1542
King's Best 321, 369, 490, 1324, 1333, 1469, 1525, 1645
Kingmambo 105, 111, 117, 356, 464, 474, 503, 606, 615, 936, 1046, 1104, 1241, 1267, 1268, 1273, 1276, 1295, 1297
Kirkwall 543
Kodiac 432, 711, 796, 830, 846, 852, 899, 1308, 1312, 1313, 1475
Kyllachy 278, 311, 395, 429, 441, 485, 540, 565, 641, 810, 848, 914, 974, 1030, 1132, 1202, 1233, 1414, 1597

Langfuhr 1355
Le Vie Dei Colori 378, 398, 1652, 1653
Lemon Drop Kid 96, 350, 1185
Librettist 84, 294, 524, 798, 919, 1545, 1592
Lord Of England 532
Lucky Story 1151, 1189

Majestic Missile 286, 385, 408, 814, 1651
Malibu Moon 1366
Maria's Mon 243, 329, 1359, 1573, 1575
Marju 101, 320, 353, 440, 512, 576, 597, 735, 748, 797, 1221, 1335, 1383, 1418
Medaglia d'Oro 192, 448, 596, 692, 1460
Medicean 44, 50, 53, 66, 107, 169, 305, 319, 360, 373, 376, 552, 614, 620, 659, 719, 734, 741, 743, 754, 781, 836, 877, 884, 958, 987, 1028, 1039, 1059, 1080, 1103, 1115, 1143, 1184, 1224, 1331, 1340, 1379, 1394, 1428, 1453, 1513, 1585, 1620, 1632
Mind Games 1112, 1435
Mingun 231
Mizzen Mast 322
Monsieur Bond 226, 1174, 1549
Monsun 610, 959, 1499, 1586
Montjeu 234, 487, 638, 655, 677, 693, 845, 856, 880, 896, 961, 1010, 1182, 1208, 1227, 1261, 1277, 1279, 1290, 1334, 1408, 1492, 1496, 1522
More Than Ready 332, 1159, 1165, 1426, 1594
Motivator 77, 79, 104, 119, 279, 361, 379, 425, 452, 483, 535, 605, 666, 673, 924, 978, 1042, 1234, 1406, 1419, 1473, 1491, 1536
Mr Greeley 25, 511, 713, 756,

903, 976, 995, 1118, 1138, 1232, 1424, 1495, 1578, 1584, 1609
Muhtathir 414, 454, 650
Mujadil 271, 289, 317, 667, 758, 763, 1396, 1591

Namid 894, 972, 1338
Nayef 12, 508, 705, 942, 1356, 1454, 1570, 1571
Needwood Blade 1311
Night Shift 14, 516
Norse Dancer 19, 55, 61, 533, 544, 546, 1022, 1023
North Light 247
Noverre 208, 292, 351, 352, 375, 528, 541, 689, 703, 908, 1015, 1025, 1036, 1054, 1055, 1063, 1072, 1111, 1327, 1432, 1552
Numerous 430

Oasis Dream 11, 13, 27, 56, 183, 190, 201, 207, 254, 331, 340, 367, 401, 458, 460, 537, 670, 687, 699, 710, 904, 906, 907, 931, 963, 988, 1037, 1043, 1044, 1084, 1135, 1137, 1144, 1145, 1169, 1171, 1187, 1286, 1367, 1490, 1508, 1517, 1567, 1635, 1643
Officer 124
One Cool Cat 423, 439, 586
Oratorio 46, 82, 170, 288, 310, 774, 795, 811, 882, 920, 1017, 1074, 1085, 1099, 1131, 1235, 1317, 1364, 1478, 1604
Orientate 396, 1307
Orpen 685, 1027

Pastoral Pursuits 125, 129, 173, 218, 761, 1180, 1301, 1445
Peintre Celebre 1155
Phoenix Reach 24, 35, 721
Piccolo 287, 547, 902, 1484, 1553
Pivotal 7, 43, 110, 171, 202, 280, 295, 450, 507, 558, 608, 645, 709, 730, 731, 843, 883, 886, 949, 967, 1142, 1225, 1229, 1239, 1328, 1363, 1382, 1399, 1405, 1421, 1502, 1503, 1506, 1510, 1516, 1518, 1523, 1606
Pleasantly Perfect 1655
Proclamation 284, 406, 415, 526, 1152, 1315, 1563

Rahy 203, 518, 828
Rainbow Quest 21, 1097, 1416, 1546
Rakti 1073
Red Ransom 26, 189, 196, 221, 238, 290, 327, 465, 498, 514, 519, 592, 727, 891, 989, 994, 1122, 1156, 1349, 1471, 1514,

346 TWO YEAR OLDS OF 2010

1554, 1596, 1605
Redback 62, 128, 384, 410, 850, 889, 1020
Redoute's Choice 509, 660, 895, 933, 1583
Reel Buddy 9
Refuse To Bend 176, 181, 223, 272, 435, 1021, 1058, 1091, 1360, 1398
Rock Hard Ten 585, 619
Rockport Harbor 5
Roman Ruler 1439
Royal Academy 829
Royal Applause 31, 91, 212, 274, 314, 325, 463, 534, 818, 864, 866, 901, 1000, 1034, 1090, 1178, 1193, 1370, 1459, 1465, 1483, 1613, 1637, 1642

Sadler's Wells 166, 232, 318, 333, 343, 527, 653, 672, 688, 702, 916, 1243, 1265, 1402, 1500, 1501, 1636
Sakhee 63, 81, 799, 898, 966, 1149
Seeking The Gold 72
Selkirk 341, 521, 523, 629, 701, 947, 973, 993, 1008, 1215, 1401, 1403, 1423, 1504
Shamardal 98, 150, 180, 416, 470, 479, 502, 588, 616, 625, 648, 657, 725, 751, 855, 892, 969, 983, 1003, 1004, 1057, 1120, 1167, 1209, 1339, 1376, 1451, 1458, 1511, 1526, 1590, 1611

Shirocco 37, 38, 49, 136, 224, 246, 387, 517, 570, 617, 664, 823, 944, 951, 1051, 1337, 1365, 1381, 1390, 1395
Silver Train 1230, 1455
Singspiel 33, 40, 83, 86, 131, 178, 229, 268, 300, 462, 599, 626, 639, 939, 985, 1154, 1420, 1579
Sinndar 242
Sky Mesa 594
Sleeping Indian 90, 213, 277, 825, 831, 952, 980, 1018
Smart Strike 134, 358, 437, 679, 1275, 1521
Smarty Jones 513, 1047
Songandaprayer 206, 1204
Soviet Star 30
Speightstown 334, 618, 637, 925
Statue Of Liberty 851
Storm Cat 251, 611, 631, 1249, 1255, 1264, 1291, 1535
Storming Home 1077
Stormy Atlantic 306, 890, 979
Street Cry 193, 194, 370, 602, 652, 690, 742, 957, 1005, 1098, 1524, 1532, 1614, 1629
Striking Ambition 418, 1538

Tagula 808
Tale Of The Cat 776, 832, 1555
Tapit 595
Thunder Gulch 4
Tiger Hill 78, 130, 174, 467, 499, 749, 965, 1186, 1196, 1329, 1411, 1461, 1595

Titus Livius 1162
Tobougg 17, 85, 481, 737, 971, 1157, 1457
Touch Gold 835
Trade Fair 309
Trans Island 1066

Val Royal 152, 869, 1040, 1164, 1166, 1197
Verglas 115, 312, 337, 342, 562, 736, 1069, 1070, 1177, 1244, 1388, 1392, 1512, 1544

Westerner 1615
Where Or When 700
Whipper 153, 158, 162, 554, 809, 1082, 1305, 1607
With Approval 29, 433, 1417

Xaar 1161

Zafeen 455, 1148
Zamindar 216, 784, 1641

Racing Trends

The following tables focus on those two-year-old races that seem to produce winners that improve the following year as three-year-olds. This type of analysis can enable us to select some of the best of this year's classic generation.

In last year's book the selected races highlighted Lahaleeb (Grade 1 E.P. Taylor Stakes and Group 3 Musidora Stakes), Mastercraftsman (Group 1 Irish 2,000 Guineas, Group 1 St James's Palace Stakes and Group 3 Diamond Stakes), Rainbow View (Group 1 Matron Stakes), Serious Attitude (Group 3 Summer Stakes) and the Listed winner Ashram.

Previous selections include the classic winners George Washington, Haafhd, King Of Kings, Pennekamp, Mister Baileys, Refuse To Bend, Rock Of Gibraltar, Rodrigo de Triano and Zafonic (all 2,000 Guineas), Finsceal Beo (English & Irish 1,000 Guineas), Bosra Sham, Cape Verdi, Harayir, Natagora, Russian Rhythm, Sayyedati (1,000 Guineas), Gossamer and Marling (Irish 1,000 Guineas), Dubawi (Irish 2,000 Guineas), Culture Vulture (French 1,000 Guineas), American Post (French 2,000 Guineas), Shamardal (French 2,000 Guineas and French Derby), Authorized, Dr Devious, High Chaparral, Motivator, New Approach and Sir Percy (Derby), Lammtarra and Sinndar (Derby and 'Arc'), Alamshar (Irish Derby and the 'Arc'), Desert King, (Irish 2,000 Guineas and Irish Derby), Reams Of Verse (Oaks), Celtic Swing (French Derby), Rule Of Law, Brian Boru, Silver Patriarch and Bob's Return (St Leger), Aussie Rules (French 2,000 Guineas) along with the Prix de l'Arc de Triomphe winner Sakhee and a multitude of other top-class winners.

In the tables, the figure in the third column indicates the number of wins recorded as a three-year-old, with GW signifying a Group race winner at that age.

The horses listed above are the winners of the featured races in 2009. Anyone looking for horses to follow in the Group and Classic events of this season might well want to bear them in mind. I feel that those in bold text are particularly worthy of close scrutiny.

Ameer	**Music Show**
Azmeel	Silver Rock
Beethoven	Sir Parky
Free Judgement	**Siyouni**
Hibaayeb	**Special Duty**
Kingsfort	**St Nicholas Abbey**
Lady of the Desert	Take It To The Max

Lowther Stakes		
York, 6 furlongs, August.		
1991	Culture Vulture	2 GW
1992	Niche	2 GW
1993	Velvet Moon	1
1994	Harayir	4 GW
1995	Dance Sequence	0
1996	Bianca Nera	0
1997	Cape Verdi	1 GW
1998	Bint Allayl	NR
1999	Jemima	0
2000	Enthused	0
2001	Queen's Logic	1 GW
2002	Russian Rhythm	3 GW
2003	Carry On Katie	0
2004	Soar	0
2005	Flashy Wings	0
2006	Silk Blossom	0
2007	Nahoodh	1 GW
2008	Infamous Angel	0
2009	Lady of the Desert	

Despite a few disappointing years, this race often has a big say in the following season's Group 1 events for fillies. For example Harayir, Cape Verdi and Russian Rhythm won the English 1,000 Guineas whilst Culture Vulture and Al Bahathri took the respective French and Irish versions. Add the top-class sprinters Habibti and Polonia (both winners prior to 1991) and the Falmouth Stakes win for Nahoodh and it's clear this race is an important pointer. Lady Of The Desert hails from the same family as the Arc winner Dylan Thomas, but she's much more likely to stick to six furlongs herself. Although beaten in the Cheveley Park Stakes by Special Duty, she can win another nice race this season.

TWO YEAR OLDS OF 2010

Dewhurst Stakes
Newmarket, 7 furlongs, October.

1991	Dr Devious	2 GW
1992	Zafonic	1 GW
1993	Grand Lodge	1 GW
1994	Pennekamp	2 GW
1995	Alhaarth	1 GW
1996	In Command	0
1997	Xaar	1 GW
1998	Mujahid	0
1999	Distant Music	1 GW
2000	Tobougg	0
2001	Rock Of Gibraltar	5 GW
2002	Tout Seul	0
2003	Milk It Mick	0
2004	Shamardal	3 GW
2005	Sir Percy	1 GW
2006	Teofilo	NR
2007	New Approach	3 GW
2008	Intense Focus	0
2009	Beethoven	

The Dewhurst Stakes remains our premier race for two-year-old colts. Rock of Gibraltar was a real star of course, but other outstanding colts in this line up include Shamardal, Zafonic, Dr Devious, Grand Lodge and Sir Percy. New Approach can now be added to that illustrious list, with 3 Group 1 wins to his name in 2008 (the Derby, Champion Stakes and Irish Champion). Beethoven was a 33-1 winner of this race last year and although he's very smart and tough (he ran no less than eleven times as a 2-y-o) and he might well add another nice win to his tally, it's hard to see him troubling the best of his contemporaries this season.

Zetland Stakes
Newmarket, 10 furlongs, October/November.

1991	Bonny Scot	2 GW
1992	Bob's Return	3 GW
1993	Double Trigger	1 GW
1994	Double Eclipse	1
1995	Gentilhomme	0
1996	Silver Patriarch	2 GW
1997	Trigger Happy	0
1998	Adnaan	1
1999	Monte Carlo	0
2000	Worthily	0
2001	Alexandra Three D	2 GW
2002	Forest Magic	NR
2003	Fun And Games	NR
2004	Ayam Zaman	0
2005	Under The Rainbow	0
2006	Empire Day	NR
2007	Twice Over	2 GW
2008	Heliodor	1
2009	Take It To The Max	

As one can see from the list, previous winners include the St Leger and Coronation Cup winner Silver Patriarch, the good four-year-olds Double Eclipse and Rock Hopper, Bob's Return (also a St Leger hero) and the Ascot Gold Cup winner Double Trigger – surely the most notable of them all. Despite being a very smart 3-y-o, Twice Over is another that improved again at four and took the Champion Stakes for Henry Cecil. Take It To The Max might struggle to emulate those notable performers, but he can win more races.

Cheveley Park Stakes
Newmarket, 6 furlongs, October.

1991	Marling	3 GW
1992	Sayyedati	2 GW
1993	Prophecy	0
1994	Gay Gallanta	0
1995	Blue Duster	1
1996	Pas de Reponse	2 GW
1997	Embassy	NR
1998	Wannabe Grand	1
1999	Seazun	0
2000	Regal Rose	NR
2001	Queen's Logic	1 GW
2002	Airwave	1 GW
2003	Carry On Katie	0
2004	Magical Romance	0
2005	Donna Blini	1
2006	Indian Ink	1 GW
2007	Natagora	2 GW
2008	Serious Attitude	1 GW
2009	Special Duty	

A number of these fillies have gone on to further Group race success. Indian Ink saved her best day for Royal Ascot having previously been fifth in the 1,000 Guineas. Natagora raised the profile of this race even further when winning the 1,000 Guineas and Serious Attitude returned to sprinting for another Group race success after a stab at a Guineas glory floundered through lack of stamina.

Special Duty certainly appears to be well named and further success in Group One events at around a mile beckons.

Washington Singer Stakes Newbury, 7 furlongs, August.		
1991	Rodrigo de Triano	4 GW
1992	Tenby	2 GW
1993	Colonel Collins	0
1994	Lammtarra	3 GW
1995	Mons	0
1996	State Fair	0
1997	Bahr	2 GW
1998	Valentine Girl	0
1999	Mana-Mou-Bay	0
2000	Prizeman	0
2001	Funfair Wane	1
2002	Muqbil	1 GW
2003	Haafhd	3 GW
2004	Kings Quay	0
2005	Innocent Air	1
2006	Dubai's Touch	2
2007	Sharp Nephew	1
2008	Cry of Freedom	0
2009	Azmeel	

As can be seen from the table, this race can often provide us with Group race or Classic pointers and in that regard Lammtarra, Rodrigo de Triano and Haafhd were outstanding. After winning this race impressively Azmeel disappointed on his only subsequent start, over a mile. He should certainly stay that distance though and it's not hard to see him winning again for trainer John Gosden this season,

Veuve Clicquot Vintage Stakes Goodwood, 7 furlongs, July.		
1991	Dr Devious	2 GW
1992	Maroof	1
1993	Mister Baileys	1 GW
1994	Eltish	0
1995	Alhaarth	1 GW
1996	Putra	0
1997	Central Park	2 GW
1998	Aljabr	1 GW
1999	Ekraar	3 GW
2000	No Excuse Needed	1 GW
2001	Naheef	1 GW
2002	Dublin	1
2003	Lucky Story	0
2004	Shamardal	3 GW
2005	Sir Percy	1 GW
2006	Strategic Prince	0
2007	Rio De La Plata	0
2008	Orizaba	0
2009	Xtension	

All in all, this race is very informative in terms of sorting out future stars, with the classic winners Sir Percy, Shamardal, Don't Forget Me, Dr Devious and Mister Baileys and the King George winner Petoski standing out. Aljabr, Central Park, Ekraar and No Excuse Needed were all high-class colts too. An inexpensive yearling purchase, Xtension was a credit to his handler last year and he'll not be too far away in the better races at around a mile this season.

National Stakes, Curragh, 7f, September.		
1991	El Prado	0
1992	Fatherland	0
1993	Manntari	1
1994	Definite Article	1
1995	Danehill Dancer	1 GW
1996	Desert King	3 GW
1997	King Of Kings	1 GW
1998	Mus-If	0
1999	Sinndar	5 GW
2000	Beckett	1
2001	Hawk Wing	1 GW
2002	Refuse To Bend	3 GW
2003	One Cool Cat	1 GW
2004	Dubawi	2 GW
2005	George Washington	2 GW
2006	Teofilo	NR
2007	New Approach	3 GW
2008	Mastercraftsman	3 GW
2009	Kingsfort	

As one can see by the list of recent winners, this race is as important as any for figuring out the following year's top performers. For instance New Approach was outstanding when winning the Derby, the Champion Stakes and the Irish Champion, and despite Mastercraftsman being amongst an excellent crop of three-year-olds that included his stable companion Rip Van Winkle and the outstanding Sea The Stars last year, he still managed a couple of Group One wins. Kingsfort only ran twice as a two-year-old and he won them both, showing bags of promise for the future, which will be in the hands of Godolphin. Sadly he got an injury just as the season was about to start, but given a full recovery he'll surely win more races.

Racing Post Trophy Doncaster, 8 furlongs, October.		
1991	Seattle Rhyme	0
1992	Armiger	1 GW
1993	King's Theatre	2 GW
1994	Celtic Swing	2 GW
1995	Beauchamp King	1 GW
1996	Medaaly	0
1997	Saratoga Springs	1 GW
1998	Commander Collins	0
1999	Aristotle	0
2000	Dilshaan	1 GW
2001	High Chapparal	5 GW
2002	Brian Boru	1 GW
2003	American Post	3 GW
2004	Motivator	2 GW
2005	Palace Episode	0
2006	Authorized	3 GW
2007	Ibn Khaldun	0
2008	Crowded House	0
2009	St Nicholas Abbey	

Some notable performers have won this race, including one of my own favourites the French Derby winner Celtic Swing, the outstanding colt High Chapparal and the Derby heroes Motivator and Authorized (both by Montjeu – also the sire of St Nicholas Abbey). The Derby would seem the obvious aim for this colt this year, but don't be surprised if he wins another Group One over a mile on the way there.

Fillies Conditions Race Newbury, 7 furlongs, September.		
1991	Freewheel	1
1992	Sueboog	1 GW
1993	Balanchine	2 GW
1994	Musetta	1
1995	Wild Rumour	0
1996	Etoile	0
1997	Amabel	NR
1998	Fragrant Oasis	1
1999	Veil Of Avalon	1
2000	Palatial	1
2001	Fraulein	2 GW
2002	L'Ancresse	1
2003	Silk Fan	1
2004	Shanghai Lily	0
2005	Mostaqeleh	0
2006	Darrfonah	1
2007	Rosa Grace	1
2008	Lassarina	0
2009	Silver Rock	

The brilliant fillies Balanchine and Milligram stand out in this group and although the race has thrown up a few disappointments of late, both Fraulein and L'Ancresse came up with excellent performances over the Atlantic, with the former taking Canada's Grade 1 E P Taylor Stakes and Ballydoyle's L'Ancresse only just getting touched off in the Breeders Cup Filly & Mare Turf. Silver Rock disappointed after winning this when unplaced in the Rockfel Stakes. A daughter of Rock Of Gibraltar, she should be suited by distances at around a mile this year.

Haynes, Hanson and Clark Stakes Newbury, 8 furlongs, September.		
1991	Zinaad	1
1992	Pembroke	1
1993	King's Theatre	2 GW
1994	Munwar	2 GW
1995	Mick's Love	1
1996	King Sound	1
1997	Duck Row	0
1998	Boatman	0
1999	Ethmaar	0
2000	Nayef	4 GW
2001	Fight Your Corner	1 GW
2002	Saturn	0
2003	Elshadi	0
2004	Merchant	NR
2005	Winged Cupid	NR
2006	Teslin	2
2007	Centennial	2 GW
2008	Taameer	0
2009	Ameer	

The high-class horses Rainbow Quest, Unfuwain, King's Theatre and Nayef have all won this race and indeed Shergar won it in 1980, but it's been a while since those glory days. Centennial, a son of Dalakhani, managed two Group race wins in 2008. After winning this race Ameer went on to finish third of four in the Prix Thomas Bryon, a result which suggests he's likely to be a smart 3-y-o, if not a high-class one.

Meon Valley Stud Fillies' Mile
Ascot, 8 furlongs, September.

1991	Midnight Air	0
1992	Ivanka	0
1993	Fairy Heights	0
1994	Aqaarid	1 GW
1995	Bosra Sham	3 GW
1996	Reams of Verse	2 GW
1997	Glorosia	0
1998	Sunspangled	0
1999	Teggiano	0
2000	Crystal Music	0
2001	Gossamer	1 GW
2002	Soviet Song	0
2003	Red Bloom	1 GW
2004	Playful Act	1 GW
2005	Nannina	1 GW
2006	Simply Perfect	1 GW
2007	Listen	0
2008	Rainbow View	1 GW
2009	Hibaayeb	

Diminuendo (in 1987), Bosra Sham, Reams of Verse, Gossamer and Soviet Song stand out amongst recent winners of this race, although the latter had to wait until after her 4-y-o career before reaching her full potential. Rainbow View was campaigned in eight Group/Grade One events last season and eventually came good in the Matron Stakes over a mile in Ireland. Hibaayeb, now with Godolphin, has every chance of improving further this year, particularly as she's by Singspiel. Her dam was best at around a mile though, so one couldn't guarantee she'd get the twelve furlongs of the Oaks.

Somerville Tattersall Stakes
Newmarket, 7 furlongs, September/October.

1991	Tertian	0
1992	Nominator	0
1993	Grand Lodge	1 GW
1994	Annus Mirabilis	1
1995	Even Top	1 GW
1996	Grapeshot	1
1997	Haami	1
1998	Enrique	1 GW
1999	Scarteen Fox	0
2000	King Charlemagne	3 GW
2001	Where Or When	2 GW
2002	Governor Brown	NR
2003	Milk It Mick	0
2004	Diktatorial	0
2005	Aussie Rules	2 GW
2006	Thousand Words	0
2007	River Proud	1
2008	Ashram	2
2009	Sir Parky	

The bare figures in this table don't really tell the whole story, for there are some very good horses here. The Group winners speak for themselves but Milk It Mick, Opening Verse and Annus Mirabilis all went on to win good races abroad and Haami was certainly a smart colt too. Aussie Rules won the French 2,000 Guineas and a Grade 1 event in the USA and both River Proud and Ashram won listed races in their 3-y-o season. Sir Parky is a useful colt and may emulate the latter pair at around a mile.

Killavullan Stakes.
Leopardstown, 7 furlongs October.

1991	Misako-Togo	3
1992	Asema	3 GW
1993	Broadmara	0
1994	Kill The Crab	2 GW
1995	Aylesbury	0
1996	Shell Ginger	0
1997	Kincara Palace	1
1998	Athlumney Lady	0
1999	Monashee Mountain	2 GW
2000	Perigee Moon	0
2001	Stonemason	0
2002	New South Wales	1
2003	Grey Swallow	2 GW
2004	Footstepsinthesand	1 GW
2005	Frost Giant	1 GW
2006	Confuchias	1 GW
2007	Jupiter Pluvius	0
2008	Rayeni	1
2009	Free Judgement	

During the period researched, seven of the winners subsequently went on to Group success as three-year-olds, most notably the Irish Derby winner Grey Swallow and the English 2,000 Guineas winner Footstepsinthesand. Unbeaten in both his two-year-old starts, Rayeni trained on to win a listed event at the back-end of his 3-y-o career after suffering a setback earlier in the year. After winning this race, Free

Judgement went on to contest the Dewhurst and was unplaced but acquitted himself quite well. He's already shown he stays a mile (he won his maiden over that distance at Dundalk) and as his dam was a sprint stakes winner in Canada, I'd say he'll be kept at distances around a mile and that he can win again.

Rockfel Stakes, 7 furlongs, Newmarket		
1991	Musicale	1 GW
1992	Yawl	0
1993	Relatively Special	0
1994	Germane	0
1995	Bint Salsabil	1
1996	Moonlight Paradise	0
1997	Name Of Love	NR
1998	Hula Angel	1 GW
1999	Lahan	1 GW
2000	Sayedah	0
2001	Distant Valley	0
2002	Luvah Girl	1 in USA
2003	Cairns	0
2004	Maids Causeway	1 GW
2005	Speciosa	1 GW
2006	Finsceal Beo	2 GW
2007	Kitty Matcham	0
2008	Lahaleeb	2 GW
2009	Music Show	

Three Newmarket 1,000 Guineas winners have hailed from the winners of this race in the last 10 years – Lahan, Speciosa and Finsceal Beo. For good measure Maids Causeway won the Coronation Stakes and Hula Angel won the Irish 1,000 Guineas (a race Finsceal Beo also added to her tally). After winning the Group 3 Fred Darling Stakes (Dubai Duty Free) on her reappearance at three, Lahaleeb was second in the Irish 1,000 and at the end of the season she took the Grade 1 E P Taylor Stakes in Canada. Her stable companion and last year's winner of this event, Music Show, won three of her four races as a 2-y-o. She's likely to stay a mile and despite her lowly price tag (16,000 euros at a breeze up sale in Ireland) she has every chance of enhancing her record this season.

Prix Jean-Luc Lagardere – formerly the Grand Criterium, Longchamp, 7 furlongs (1 mile before 2001)		
2001	Rock Of Gibraltar	5 GW
2002	Hold That Tiger	0
2003	American Post	3 GW
2004	Oratorio	2 GW
2005	Horatio Nelson	0
2006	Holy Roman Emperor	NR
2007	Rio de la Plata	0
2008	Naaqoos	0
2009	Siyouni	

The last four winners have all failed to win as three-year-olds, but sadly they include Horatio Nelson who had to be put down after an injury in the Derby. A winner of four of his six races last season, the Aga Khan owned Siyouni looks like adding to his Group race tally this season, probably at distances of around a mile.

Beresford Stakes, Curragh, 1m		
1991	El Prado	0
1992	Frenchpark	0
1993	Sheridan	0
1994	Burden Of Proof	1
1995	Ahkaam	0
1996	Johan Cruyff	1 GW
1997	Saratoga Springs	1 GW
1998	Festival Hall	0
1999	Lermontov	0
2000	Turnberry Isle	0
2001	Castle Gandolfo	1
2002	Alamshar	3 GW
2003	Azamour	2 GW
2004	Albert Hall	0
2005	Septimus	1 GW
2006	Eagle Mountain	1 GW
2007	Curtain Call	1
2008	Sea The Stars	6 GW
2009	St Nicholas Abbey	

What more can you say about Sea The Stars that hasn't already been said. Suffice to say he might just have been the perfect racehorse. His trainer John Oxx must be very fond of this race because he also trained Alamshar and Azamour and they both went on to win the King George. Among the others, Frenchpark was a Grade 1 winner in the USA at 4 yrs, Eagle Mountain also went on to win as a 4-y-o in a Group 1 event (in Hong Kong) and Curtain Call won a Group 3 event at that age. St Nicholas Abbey won the Racing Post Trophy after taking the Beresford and he must rank among the leading candidates for further Group One success this season.

Horse Index

Name	Page	Name	Page	Name	Page
A Word Apart (IRE)	1610	Apezine (USA)	631	Black Moth (IRE)	1096
Abacist (IRE)	41	Apparel (IRE)	444	Blackleyf (IRE)	386
Abbakham (IRE)	491	Appealing (IRE)	1403	Blake Dean	847
Abjer (FR)	178	Approve (IRE)	710	Bless You	217
Above All	705	Apticanti	857	Blessed Biata (USA)	713
Above Standard (IRE)	855	Arabian Heights	1404	Blink Of An Eye	76
Above The Stars	547	Arabian Star (IRE)	260	Bloodsweatandtears	1029
Achaemenes	599	Aramid (IRE)	858	Blue Cannon (IRE)	1377
Aciano (IRE)	1093	Ardlui (IRE)	215	Blue Dazzler (IRE)	1352
Acoustic Cheer (USA)	1608	Armoire	166	Blue Deer (IRE)	266
Acts Out Loud (USA)	1609	Around The Clock (USA)	1351	Blue Tiger's Eye (IRE)	605
Ad Vitam (IRE)	1012	Arowana (IRE)	711	Blue Vinney	1563
Adaeze (IRE)	1369	Artemisia (IRE)	600	Boogie Shoes	928
Addock And Egg	380	Asheerah	1376	Boogie Star	1157
Adlington	548	Aspantau (IRE)	1560	Bountiful Guest	263
Adorable Choice (IRE)	381	Astragal	1167	Bradbury (IRE)	128
Afkar (IRE)	179	Astromagick	1546	Brandy Snap (IRE)	766
Agadir Summer	1446	Astroverdi	1547	Bravestofthebrave (USA)	633
Agbalat	926	Atia	1370	Brazilian Breeze (IRE)	1378
Aiken	629	Atraaf (IRE)	1561	Brazza Di Mare (IRE)	1097
Ajabny Alzain (IRE)	1447	Attracted To You (IRE)	760	Breathless Storm (USA)	1535
Ajeeb (USA)	1448	Audacious	1491	Breton Star	1453
Akrias (USA)	350	Auld Burns	761	Brevity (USA)	1098
Akser (IRE)	1559	Aussie Dollar	6	Brick Dust (IRE)	352
Aktaaf	1558	Avonmore Star	762	Bridal Belle	550
Al Birrwaz	1449	Awaroa (IRE)	1562	Bride Unbridled (IRE)	228
Al Mayasah (IRE)	1451	Back For Tea (IRE)	384	Brinmore	1030
Alaskan Spirit	432	Bahamian Sunset	549	Broken Belle (IRE)	913
Albaasil (IRE)	1489	Bahceli (IRE)	763	Brown Butterfly	1379
Albaraka	1401	Bahia Emerald (IRE)	1198	Brown Panther	387
Albert Bridge	42	Baisse	227	Buckland (IRE)	1099
Aldwick Bay (IRE)	759	Bakoura	493	Buddy Miracle	9
Alemaratiya	1450	Ballista (IRE)	385	Buille Cliste (IRE)	134
Alexander Pope (IRE)	1246	Ballroom (USA)	1249	Bumbling Bertie	10
Alheera (IRE)	706	Banimpire (IRE)	132	Bunce (IRE)	767
Alhoralhora	585	Baraaya	712	Burj Hatta (USA)	606
Aljana (IRE)	707	Barachiel	7	Burn The Floor (IRE)	135
Alkimos (IRE)	349	Barking (IRE)	764	Buthelezi (USA)	634
All Honesty	1028	Barney Rebel (IRE)	859	Buttonhole	1492
All My Heart	1402	Bary	351	Byrony (IRE)	768
All The Evil (IRE)	1094	Bash On (IRE)	127	Cadore (IRE)	303
Alltherightmoves (IRE)	972	Basilica	1148	Cae Shen (IRE)	769
Allumeuse (USA)	5	Battle Ensign (IRE)	601	Café Electric	1405
Already Basking (CAN)	332	Bawrich	1548	Canada Fleet (CAN)	445
Alshazah	1147	Beach Patrol (IRE)	261	Canaveral	1100
Amallna	927	Beart (IRE)	133	Canna (IRE)	860
Amazing Beauty (IRE)	1247	Beauchamp Zorro	216	Canukeepasecret	1435
Amen (IRE)	1248	Bedevilment (USA)	602	Capal Liath (IRE)	861
Amjaad	708	Bedjat	74	Cape Classic (IRE)	714
Amore Et Labore	1013	Bendigedig	1014	Cape Gooseberry	480
Amun Ra (USA)	580	Better Self	433	Cape Of Good Grace (IRE)	1321
Ana Emarati (USA)	443	Beyond Reason (IRE)	603	Cape Rambler	218
Aneedah	630	Biaraafa (IRE)	75	Cape To Rio (IRE)	770
Angel Fisa (IRE)	382	Bilko Pak (IRE)	765	Captain Bellamy (USA)	1168
Angle Knight (USA)	1095	Bint Elnadim (IRE)	1452	Captain Bertie (IRE)	862
Ankh (IRE)	383	Bint Nas (IRE)	265	Captain Sharpe	481
Anoint	709	Bint Yazmouna	262	Card Trick (IRE)	1250
Another Whisper (IRE)	856	Biographical (USA)	632	Caresse	167
Ansaab	1375	Birdwatcher (IRE)	982	Carousel	43
Anton Dolin (IRE)	492	Bishops Moon	1427	Carsulae (IRE)	353
Anya Amasova	1156	Black Aura (IRE)	604	Casamento	751
Apace (IRE)	1490	Black Cadillac (IRE)	8	Cassini Flight (USA)	1199

Name	No.	Name	No.	Name	No.
Casual Glimpse	771	Damson Vodka	2	Ducal	1409
Catherineofaragon (IRE)	1251	Danadana (IRE)	354	Duja Allayl (USA)	1455
Catopuma (USA)	635	Dance For Livvy (IRE)	846	Duke Of Florence (IRE)	781
Celestial Flyer (IRE)	1052	Dance Secretary (IRE)	1323	Dumbarton (IRE)	1497
Census (IRE)	772	Dance To The Stars	1408	Dunmore Boy (IRE)	553
Certral	1	Danceyourselfdizzy (IRE)	777	Durante Alighieri	230
Chabelle	136	Dancing On Turf (IRE)	140	Dustland Fairytale (IRE)	1055
Chain Lightning	773	Dancing Rain (IRE)	715	Dysios (IRE)	357
Chasing Pirates	697	Danish Pastry	1201	Eagle Rock (IRE)	1537
Chatterer (IRE)	1564	Danzig's Grandchild (USA)	1158	Early Applause	866
Chef	523	Darajaat	1565	Easy Ticket (IRE)	211
Chesnut Coffee	1454	Dare To Bare (IRE)	1353	Eaves Lane (IRE)	554
Chewdeh (USA)	494	Darika (IRE)	752	Ebony Song (USA)	1204
Chilled	1493	Dark And Dangerous (IRE)	1648	Echo Ridge (IRE)	46
Chilworth Lad	264	Darsan (IRE)	1599	Edmaaj (IRE)	867
Chinook Wind (IRE)	863	Date With Destiny (IRE)	778	Eight Keys	1149
Chiswick Bey (IRE)	551	Dawn Gale (IRE)	1170	Ekhraaj (USA)	932
Chosen Character (IRE)	388	Days Of Summer (IRE)	45	Ektibaas	868
Circus Master	540	Dazzling Dream (IRE)	1380	El Djebena	1410
Ciste Naisiunta (IRE)	137	De Rigueur	1496	El Muqbil (IRE)	1103
Cisteoir (USA)	138	Dean Swift	1101	El Viento (FR)	555
Claiomh Solais (IRE)	139	Defence Of Duress (IRE)	1536	El Wasmi	183
Clara Zetkin	210	Defer	1202	Elan	1498
Clarke Lane (USA)	929	Deity	1203	Eland Ally	1538
Classic Gem (IRE)	389	Delphi Dream	1171	Elas Diamond	1205
Classic Voice (IRE)	774	Deny	1495	Elfaaten (USA)	1566
Classical Air	495	Desert Law (IRE)	11	Elfine (IRE)	482
Clinical	1406	Destiny Of Dreams	344	Elizabeth Coffee	753
Clondinerry (IRE)	1053	Devastation	638	Elrasheed	498
Club Oceanic	1200	Deveze (IRE)	914	Elvira Delight (IRE)	1206
Coachlight	496	Dffar (USA)	180	Elwazeer (USA)	1567
Cobbs Quay	636	Dffra (IRE)	181	Elysian Heights (IRE)	1207
Coconut Ice	390	Diamond Geezah (IRE)	865	Elzaam (AUS)	933
Codemaster	219	Diamond Noir (IRE)	1084	Embezzle	318
Coeus	1407	Diamond Run	915	Emkanaat	934
Cold Secret	529	Dictate	1550	Emotional Dream	1381
Colebrooke	983	Dinkum Diamond (IRE)	220	Emperor Hadrian (IRE)	1252
Colonel Percy (IRE)	984	Diplomasi	182	Emperor's Princess (FR)	782
Commended	864	Director's Dream (IRE)	1649	Empress Charlotte	80
Commercial (IRE)	1308	Disco Dancing	229	Enabling (IRE)	783
Communicator	77	Discoteca	12	Enchanted Forest (IRE)	1253
Compassion	78	Disturbia (IRE)	1354	Encore Un Fois	869
Comrade Bond	1549	Divine Rule (IRE)	1172	Encore Une Annee	47
Conjuror's Bluff	1186	Divinite Green	304	Encore View	13
Control Chief	44	Do The Bosanova (IRE)	141	End Or Beginning	333
Copex	1436	Dolcezza (IRE)	1102	Energizing	784
Corsican Run (IRE)	552	Dominant (IRE)	930	Enjoy Today (USA)	1104
Cosmic Love (IRE)	1054	Dordogne (IRE)	985	Enlightening (IRE)	785
Countess Ellen (IRE)	391	Double Dice	1069	Entikaal	1613
Countrywide Flame	1437	Dr Darcey	779	Epic Storm (IRE)	1208
Court Dress (USA)	637	Dr Green (IRE)	780	Eraadaat (IRE)	447
Crafty Roberto	446	Dragon Storm (USA)	607	Escape The Heat	268
Creekside	1322	Dreams of Dawn	267	Eskimo (IRE)	1254
Crème Anglaise	79	Dresden (IRE)	355	Estilaam (IRE)	1568
Crew Cut (IRE)	581	Dress Up	1015	Estithmaar (IRE)	1382
Cruiser	1187	Dressing Room (USA)	986	Eternal Youth (IRE)	1612
Crystal Etoile	1494	Droxford (USA)	1307	Eucharist (IRE)	786
Cuban Piece (IRE)	392	Drummer Boy	1650	Evening Dress	987
Cuban Quality (USA)	393	Dubai Affair	1173	Excelebration (IRE)	168
Cuban Spirit (IRE)	394	Dubai Celebration	1300	Exchange	717
Cult Classic (IRE)	775	Dubai Metro	931	Experimentalist	1174
Cupani	497	Dubai Prince (IRE)	1611	Expose	718
Custom House (IRE)	776	Dubai Queen (USA)	356	Extra Power (IRE)	269
Da Ponte	524	Dubarshi	345	Ezzles (USA)	334
Daffydowndilly	1169	Dubawi Dancer	716	Face The Problem (IRE)	870
Damascus Symphony	129	Dubawi Star	1326	Factum (USA)	1255

HORSE INDEX

Failasoof (USA)	871	Garde Cotiere (USA)	1212	Highest	646
Fairy Familiar (USA)	358	Garmoosha (USA)	936	Highland Colori	398
Falkland Flyer (IRE)	270	Gatewood	642	Highly Composed	1478
Fallen From Grace	639	Gawaarib (USA)	643	Hill Of Content (IRE)	1615
Fancourt	1188	Gay Gallivanter	644	His Excellency (IRE)	1324
Fanlight	1209	Geblah (IRE)	1456	Hisaabaat (IRE)	1625
Fantasy Fry	1175	Geesala (USA)	1440	History Repeating	83
Faraway Mountain (IRE)	1619	Gemma's Pearl (IRE)	1383	Ho Ya Mal (IRE)	1458
Farhh	608	General Synod	787	Hobbesian War	1539
Farlow (IRE)	48	Gentle Lord	397	Hollow Tree	16
Fastada (IRE)	1371	George Woolf	1078	Holy Mackerel (IRE)	275
Favart (IRE)	609	Georgina Bailey	1079	Honeymead (IRE)	558
Favorite Girl (GER)	49	Glenavon	1356	Hoofprintsinthesnow	1358
Fettuccine (IRE)	1210	Glendaragh (IRE)	1384	Hooray	1412
Field Of Miracles (IRE)	640	Glitter Bug (IRE)	988	Hoppy's Flyer (FR)	400
Fifth Commandment	1309	Global Dance (IRE)	232	Hortensia (IRE)	276
Fifth Dimension	1310	Go Maggie Go (IRE)	1441	Hot Ticket (IRE)	1504
Fifth Estate	1311	Gobooll	724	Humdrum	789
Fifth In Line (IRE)	1312	Gold Pendant (USA)	448	Hurricane Guest	1071
Figaro	719	Gold Tobougg	1457	Hurricane Havoc (IRE)	146
Fighter Jet	1085	Golden City (IRE)	1601	Hursley Hope (IRE)	531
Fimias	359	Golden Delicious	1176	Ibsaar	727
Fiorente (IRE)	1499	Golden Hinde	989	Ice Magic	1551
Fire Fighter (IRE)	1411	Golden Shine	274	Icebuster	1150
Firebeam	720	Golden Taurus (IRE)	918	Il Battista	1080
First Battalion (IRE)	1500	Goldenveil (IRE)	556	Illandrane (IRE)	451
First Sea Lord (IRE)	1256	Good Morning Dubai (IRE)	1105	Imeall Na Speire (USA)	147
Firstknight	395	Good Timin	212	Imperator Augustus (USA)	1259
Flaming Arrow (IRE)	1501	Gospel Music	1602	In Babylon (GER)	401
Flash Forward	1600	Govenor General (IRE)	1213	In Spirit Bar (IRE)	3
Flash of Intuition (IRE)	231	Gradam Ceoil (USA)	144	Inagh River	790
Flavia Tatiana (IRE)	1257	Great Huzzar (IRE)	1476	Incitement	452
Flea Cheoil (IRE)	142	Green Future (USA)	1357	Indian Ballard (IRE)	1086
Fleet Captain	1438	Grey Speedfit (IRE)	1070	Indian Mist (IRE)	937
Fleeting Tiger	499	Grumeti	81	Indian Narjes	277
Fleiscin (IRE)	143	Guards Chapel	361	Indieslad	434
Flic Flac (IRE)	1616	Guided Missile (IRE)	14	Indigo Way	1108
Flo Motion (IRE)	916	Guisho (IRE)	1106	Inexcused (IRE)	754
Flodden (USA)	335	Gulbarg	362	Inimitable Romanee (USA)	1359
Florestan Match	50	Gunmaker's Choice (USA)	1159	Insidious	966
Flying Phoenix	721	Gypsy Legend	1016	Instance	1214
Focal	1502	Haamaat (IRE)	725	Intercept (IRE)	647
Fog Cutter (IRE)	271	Hakeeka	726	Intrusion	559
Foghorn Leghorn	305	Halifax (IRE)	990	Invigilator	483
Follow My Dream	641	Hamasat	645	Invincible Don (IRE)	694
Folly Drove	1372	Handassa	1385	Ippios	363
For The Reason (IRE)	1428	Handel's Messiah	82	Irie Ute	1018
Forjaat (IRE)	935	Handicraft (IRE)	991	Irtidaa (USA)	1569
Formidable Girl (USA)	1439	Happy Today (USA)	1107	Isaba	502
Forty Proof (IRE)	1031	Harangue (IRE)	1614	Island Commander (USA)	148
Four Nations (USA)	1355	Harry Luck (IRE)	221	Isolate	1177
Foxtrot Hotel (IRE)	1651	Haylaman (IRE)	449	Istishaara (USA)	503
Franciscan	360	Haymana (IRE)	1503	Ithoughtitwasover (IRE)	992
Frankish Dynasty (GER)	336	Head Space (IRE)	145	Jaaryah (IRE)	938
Freedom	1258	Heartbreak	557	Jack Smudge	586
Freedom Trail	530	Heaven Knows Why	450	Jackaroo (IRE)	1260
Frozen Frontier (IRE)	1475	Heavenly Song	1017	Jadhwah	1570
Full Pelt (USA)	396	Height Of Summer (IRE)	1603	Jambo Bibi (IRE)	791
Fury	722	Here To Eternity (USA)	306	Jamesway (IRE)	560
Futyaan	872	Herminella	1189	Jan Smuts (IRE)	1109
Gainsboroughs Best (IRE)	723	Hflah (USA)	610	Janet's Pearl (IRE)	435
Galiando	1211	Hidden Valley	15	Janicellaine (IRE)	873
Galivant (IRE)	917	High Award (IRE)	1477	Jasmine Flower	278
Galloping Queen (IRE)	272	High On The Hog (IRE)	501	Jawhar (IRE)	728
Galtymore Lad	273	High Table (IRE)	399	Jibouti	184
Gamesmanship	500	Highcliffe	788	Jiwen (USA)	939

Name	No.	Name	No.	Name	No.
Joe Eile (IRE)	1056	Levitate	1506	Marie Du Plessis	997
Joe Strummer (IRE)	84	Lexington Bay (IRE)	563	Marie Jeanne	655
Johnny Castle	648	Liberty Cap (USA)	652	Marked Card (IRE)	308
Jollywood (IRE)	792	Libranno	798	Marlinka	320
Joviality	649	Light Well (IRE)	653	Martine's Spirit (IRE)	695
Juhd (IRE)	1571	Lilac Song (IRE)	1604	Mashaaref	943
Julius Geezer (IRE)	402	Lindoras Grace	1507	Master Of Hounds (USA)	1268
Just Incredible (IRE)	1262	Lion Court (IRE)	1415	Master Perfect	368
Justification	1261	Lisa Gherardini (IRE)	149	Maunby Rumba	849
Justinian	650	Little Curtsey	1178	Mayfair Lady	1462
Justlookdonttouch (IRE)	1505	Little Hot Shot (IRE)	1110	Mayhab	185
Kadoodd (IRE)	279	Local Singer (IRE)	281	Measuring Time	800
Kalahaag	793	Long Journey Home (IRE)	1330	Mediplomat	169
Kalgoolie	698	Long Live The King (IRE)	1263	Meejanah	186
Kalkan Bay	1301	Longhunter	1387	Mega Mount (IRE)	52
Kalleidoscope	280	Look Twice	1459	Meinaawi (USA)	1463
Kasanka (IRE)	1325	Look Who's Kool	1087	Melodize	1191
Kawssaj	940	Looking Lovely (IRE)	1264	Memen (IRE)	337
Kayalar (IRE)	1327	Loose Quality (USA)	1540	Memorabilia	998
Kelinni	1360	Lordofthehouse (IRE)	729	Memory (IRE)	801
Kepler's Law	1413	Louis Girl	564	Memory Lane	1417
Key West	651	Louis The Pious	1443	Memphis Tennessee (IRE)	1269
Khor Sheed	364	Louise Mary (IRE)	994	Mereli (IRE)	755
Kilbirnie	1328	Lovat Lane	975	Merlin's Oak (IRE)	1057
King Bling (IRE)	1019	Love Me Only (IRE)	1265	Mettal	86
King Ferdinand	17	Love Nest	506	Mi Regalo	20
King Of Aquitaine (IRE)	1442	Luckbealadytonight (IRE)	995	Midas Moment	1192
King Of Jazz (IRE)	794	Lucy Limelites	319	Midnight Caller	656
King Torus (IRE)	795	Ludicrous (IRE)	730	Midnight Mirage (FR)	283
Kingarrick	973	Luminance (IRE)	1216	Midnight Music (IRE)	1618
Kings Fortune	85	Lupa Montana (USA)	51	Midnight Rider (IRE)	1605
Kinlochrannoch	848	Luxurious (IRE)	1266	Midnight Show (IRE)	1058
Kirthill (IRE)	365	Mabsam	453	Mijhaar	944
Kissable (IRE)	1386	Machaputo (IRE)	1480	Milldown Magic	1151
Kissing Clara (IRE)	1160	Madany (IRE)	875	Millennium Star	405
Kodiac Star (IRE)	1313	Madeira Man (IRE)	1388	Ministry	120
Kojak (IRE)	796	Mafroodh	507	Minkie Moon (IRE)	1361
Konsal (USA)	611	Maggie R (USA)	1416	Minsk (IRE)	1332
Konstantin (IRE)	1572	Magic Minstrel	19	Mirror Lad	406
Korabushka	1215	Magic Word (USA)	1267	Mishtaag	187
Korngold	504	Maher (USA)	1460	Miskkhitaam (USA)	510
Kristollini	1190	Mahoyogin (IRE)	235	Miss Boops (IRE)	1429
Krypton Factor	1414	Maid Of Ice	1217	Miss Clairton	1418
Kucharova (IRE)	1479	Majestic Dubawi	282	Miss Diagnosis (IRE)	53
Kyncraighe (IRE)	974	Major Conquest (IRE)	919	Miss Dutee	802
Kyzyl Kum	366	Major Dude	799	Miss Elegance	1112
L'Ami Louis (IRE)	222	Majounes Dream	1508	Miss Exhibionist	309
Laajooj (IRE)	941	Make A Dance (USA)	876	Miss Nimbus (USA)	4
Labba	1329	Make Light (USA)	1509	Miss Thea	1574
Lady Chloe	1552	Makyaal (IRE)	508	Miss Topsy Turvy (IRE)	511
Lady Fashion	367	Malakeh (IRE)	307	Miss Villefranche	87
Lady Intrigue (IRE)	561	Malanos (IRE)	532	Missy O'Gwaun (IRE)	1333
Ladt Magdalena	233	Malayan Mist (IRE)	1617	Mist (IRE)	1270
Lady Kildare (IRE)	1302	Malibu Beach (IRE)	150	Mixed Emotions (IRE)	803
Lady Rosamunde	1573	Malpas Missile	404	Mohedian Lady (IRE)	88
Lady Woodcote	967	Malthouse (GER)	996	Mokalif	89
Ladyanne	1020	Manaaber (IRE)	877	Moment Of Time	21
Lamasaas (IRE)	874	Mancunian (IRE)	119	Montefino (IRE)	657
Las Verglas Star (IRE)	562	Manieree (IRE)	1331	Montegonian (USA)	1575
Lastarria (IRE)	612	Mantoba	1111	Moon Over Water (IRE)	945
Late Telegraph (IRE)	234	Map Of Heaven	731	Moone's My Name	54
Later (IRE)	797	Maqaasid	654	Moonlight Mystery	1606
Lay Time	18	Maqaraat (IRE)	878	Moonlight Rhapsody (IRE)	879
Lejaam	505	Maraheb	509	Moons Of Jupiter	1271
Lenjawi Pride	403	Marhaba	942	Moonscape	1510
Les Landes (IRE)	1314	Marhaba Malyoon (IRE)	1461	Moorland Boy	1315

HORSE INDEX

More Than A Lot (IRE)	756	Novel Dancer	806	Planet Waves (IRE)	189
Morermaloke	1114	Noverton	541	Play Music	284
Moriarty (IRE)	804	Nuba (IRE)	1622	Plea	666
Mortitia	1113	Nucals Star (IRE)	1482	Plenty Power	285
Mother Jones	213	Numeral (IRE)	807	Poinsettia (IRE)	1281
Motivado	1419	Nutshell	484	Pope Leo (IRE)	1513
Mount Crystal	880	Nuzool (IRE)	514	Poplin	373
Mountain Glow	1218	Obligada (IRE)	1389	Posh Cracker (USA)	1061
Mountain Woman (IRE)	1334	Obsession (IRE)	1221	Power Punch (IRE)	884
Mr Mojito (IRE)	1481	October (USA)	1273	Precocious Kid (IRE)	1607
Mr Optimistic	565	Odin (IRE)	533	Premier Clarets (IRE)	568
Mrs Dee Bee (IRE)	881	Offbeat Safaris (IRE)	1652	President Lincoln (USA)	1282
Mrs Greeley	976	Old Master Expert	91	Press Release	409
Mrs Neat	1021	Old Navy	664	Presto Volante (IRE)	1364
Mubtadi	1464	Olfa	1623	Primadona (IRE)	1626
Muhandis (IRE)	454	Oliver's Gold	1362	Prince Freddie	1554
Mujarah (IRE)	512	Ollianna	408	Prince Of Burma (IRE)	667
Mujrayaat (IRE)	946	Olympiad (IRE)	1624	Princess Icicle	346
Mulaqen	1576	Omid	371	Princess Izzy	1555
Mullingar	757	Omnipotent (IRE)	808	Pritzker Prize	1445
Munaaseb	455	On Alert	1466	Profondo Rosso (IRE)	1514
Munaawib	1577	On The High Tops (IRE)	1542	Proper Charlie	1033
Mundana (IRE)	369	One Flag Please	457	Proudie	321
Mungo Park	993	Oneladyowner	214	Provide (IRE)	1627
Muntasib	1578	Opera Box	1579	Pure Luck (IRE)	92
Muqtarrib (IRE)	1115	Opera Dance	1023	Pure Science (IRE)	885
Murbeh (IRE)	1116	Oracle (IRE)	1274	Purification (IRE)	668
Murjaan	188	Oratouch (IRE)	170	Pursuitofexcellence (IRE)	1515
Musawama (IRE)	658	Orientalist	977	Qenaa	1000
Musharakaat (IRE)	456	Our Play (IRE)	882	Quadrant (IRE)	1120
Music In My Heart	1219	Outrider (IRE)	1275	Qubuh (IRE)	1628
Music In The Rain (IRE)	151	Overeasy (IRE)	1088	Queen Myrine (IRE)	811
Mutawel Al Gaiba	1465	Pabusar	56	Queen O' The Desert (IRE)	23
Mutayaser	1511	Paco Belle (IRE)	809	Queen Of Cash (IRE)	1179
Muzdahi (USA)	513	Paid Up Front	542	Queen Of Spain (IRE)	1283
My Mate Al	407	Pale Moon Rising (IRE)	1276	Queen's Journal (USA)	615
My Single Malt (IRE)	1541	Palindramic (IRE)	582	Questioning (IRE)	669
My Son Max	805	Palitana (USA)	665	Quixotic	1516
Naaseh	1620	Palm Pilot (IRE)	458	Qushchi	968
Nafedah (USA)	1117	Pandoro De Lago (IRE)	566	Raahin (IRE)	1517
Nahrain	947	Papas Fritas	1119	Raasekha	886
Najoum (USA)	613	Paradise Place	1222	Rafella (IRE)	57
Namibian (IRE)	999	Paradise Way	339	Ragsah (IRE)	616
Nantucket Bay (USA)	1272	Partout Le Magasin	1161	Rainbow Red	1223
Naqash (IRE)	659	Parvana (IRE)	732	Rasheed	670
Naqshabban (USA)	370	Passion Planet	1059	Rave (IRE)	920
Narjawa (IRE)	1335	Pausanias	810	Ravindra	238
Nashaat	660	Pawnee	1277	Raw Spirit	617
Nasharra (IRE)	1444	Peahen	1060	Rawaki (IRE)	24
Natalisa (IRE)	1336	Perfect Mission	22	Real Sense (IRE)	239
Nathaniel (IRE)	661	Peters Spirit (IRE)	567	Reasons Unknown (IRE)	1062
Nella Sofia	587	Petronius Maximus (IRE)	1278	Reckless Reward (IRE)	812
Nessina (USA)	662	Piave (IRE)	310	Red Calima (IRE)	1337
Neutrafa (IRE)	236	Piccarello	1553	Red Copper	93
New Hampshire (IRE)	663	Piceno (IRE)	372	Red Eyes	1121
Neytiri	90	Piece D'Or (IRE)	1512	Red Largo (IRE)	887
Night And Dance	237	Pierides (USA)	614	Red Lite (IRE)	1122
Night Of Fantasy (IRE)	1220	Pink Diva (IRE)	1543	Red Lover	459
Ninth Parallel (USA)	1118	Pintrada	130	Red Marling (IRE)	888
No Heretic	338	Pippa's Gift	1193	Red Mercury	286
No Larking (IRE)	223	Pirate Chest (IRE)	1279	Red Oleander	1421
No Peace	1072	Pirateer (IRE)	1280	Red Presence (IRE)	410
Noonenose	1032	Pivot Bridge	883	Red Remanso	889
Norse Blues	1022	Pivotman	1363	Red Riverman	733
Norse Wing	55	Pizzarra	588	Red Spades	311
Notable Graduate (IRE)	1621	Pizzetti (IRE)	1420	Red Zeus	1162

Name	No.	Name	No.	Name	No.
Redskin Dancer	1338	Sanadaat	1631	Sky Diamond (IRE)	590
Reflect (IRE)	813	Sapphire (IRE)	1632	Sleek Gold	1127
Regal Heiress	1518	Sapphire Girl	569	Sleeping Wolf	825
Regal Rocket (IRE)	814	Saqil (USA)	1633	Slim Shadey	1164
Regal Salute	1224	Sar Poot (IRE)	1468	Sluggsy Morant	226
Regal Tramp (USA)	1629	Saucy Buck (IRE)	289	Smart Red	293
Remotelinx (IRE)	921	Scarborough Lily	1589	Smart Violetta (IRE)	437
Rerouted (USA)	890	Scented	734	Snow Cannon	312
Retainer (IRE)	815	Schism	224	Snow Legend (IRE)	415
Retreat Content (IRE)	1316	Schoolmaster	673	Snow Ridge	1422
Rex Romanorum (IRE)	1284	Sciampin	172	Snow Watch (IRE)	1392
Rhodesian Moon (IRE)	58	Scot Lane	1081	Snowy Peak	1225
Rhythm Of Light	411	Scottish Lake	1303	So Choosy	826
Rich Tapestry (IRE)	1630	Scottish Star	543	Soie De Chine	1423
Right Said Fred (IRE)	59	Screenprint	98	Solar Event	155
Rimth	340	Scribe (IRE)	1290	Sole Bay	536
Ringstead Bay (FR)	60	Sea The Flames (IRE)	1582	Sole Danser (IRE)	893
Riochas (IRE)	152	Seal Rock	225	Song Of The Siren	29
Rishikesh	94	Searing Heat (USA)	241	Sovereign Street	438
Rising Wind (IRE)	1390	Seattle Dawn	323	Soviet Spring	30
Riverdale (IRE)	436	Seattle Drive (IRE)	535	Spanish Fleet	675
Riviera Stars	95	Secret Gold (IRE)	1124	Spanish Pride (IRE)	516
Roayh (USA)	618	Seeking Glory	1469	Spartan Spirit (IRE)	1183
Robin Hood USA (USA)	25	Sergeant Ablett (IRE)	1001	Spasha	1003
Roche Des Vents	816	Sergeant Troy (IRE)	324	Specific Gravity (FR)	244
Rocky Rebel	61	Set Me Free (IRE)	375	Speed Dancer	544
Roderic O'Connor (IRE)	1285	Set To Music (IRE)	99	Spey Song (IRE)	131
Roi Du Boeuf (IRE)	817	Shadow Of The Sun	290	Splice (USA)	1226
Rojo Boy	26	Shafgaan	190	Squires Gate (IRE)	894
Roman Eagle (IRE)	948	Shaman Dancer (GER)	27	St Augustine (IRE)	121
Romany Stone (IRE)	949	Shaqira	1583	St Oswald	325
Rosa Midnight (USA)	96	Shaqraa	1584	Stage Attraction (IRE)	31
Rosamunde Ffrench	287	Sharestan (IRE)	1339	Star Blossom (USA)	622
Rose Bonheur	1391	Sharp Relief (IRE)	1181	Star Commander	1556
Rose Bush (IRE)	171	Sheer Courage (IRE)	819	Star Ferry	313
Rose Willow (USA)	671	Sheila's Star	1163	Star Now	294
Rosina Grey	1152	Shewalksinbeauty (IRE)	820	Star Of Dance (IRE)	1519
Rougette	891	Shim Sham (IRE)	1125	Star Today	1128
Rowan Spirit (IRE)	412	Shirataki (IRE)	1002	Star Value (IRE)	1520
Royal City	1040	Shirocco Vice (IRE)	570	Starbound (IRE)	739
Royal Exchange	818	Shop Local (IRE)	153	Stars In Your Eyes	676
Royal Liaison	97	Shostakovic (IRE)	1024	Starstudded (IRE)	740
Royal Opera	1153	Shropshire (IRE)	892	State Opera	1004
Royal Peculiar	240	Shuhra (IRE)	735	State Senator (USA)	1424
Royalorien	1034	Sidera (IRE)	620	Stella Point (IRE)	295
Ruby Alexander (IRE)	62	Signs In The Sand	621	Stentorian (IRE)	1005
Ruby Brook	63	Sikeeb (USA)	191	Stilettoesinthemud	591
Rudolf Valentino	1286	Silca Conegliano (IRE)	291	Storm Runner (IRE)	1073
Ruling (IRE)	1287	Silent Ninja	1182	Stormy Thunder	1590
Rumooz	1580	Silenzio	821	Strategic Bid	341
Run Rabbit Run	950	Silk Bounty	589	Strength And Stay (IRE)	978
Rusoom	1581	Silly Billy	1025	Strewth (IRE)	122
Rutland Boy	1467	Silver Shine (IRE)	736	Strictly Rhythm	827
Ryton Runner (IRE)	672	Silver Show (IRE)	292	Striking Veil (USA)	1521
Sacred Sound (IRE)	288	Silverware (USA)	822	Strong Suit (USA)	828
Sadafiya	460	Singe The Turf (IRE)	154	Style Squad (USA)	1129
Sagramor	1180	Sinnfonia (IRE)	242	Stylish One (IRE)	156
Sahafh (USA)	619	Sir Rocky (IRE)	823	Sud Pacifique (USA)	1227
Sailing North (USA)	322	Sirius Superstar	28	Sugar Beet	326
Salmon Rose (IRE)	413	Sisindu (IRE)	1126	Suhaili	951
Salvationist	515	Sister Red (IRE)	824	Sukhothai	243
Sam Lord's Castle (IRE)	1288	Sixty Eight Guns (IRE)	1063	Sultah (USA)	895
Samanda (IRE)	374	Sizzle (FR)	414	Summer Jasmine	485
Sammy Any Two (IRE)	534	Skeleton (IRE)	737	Sun Queen (USA)	1291
Samuel Morse (IRE)	1289	Skip Alone	674	Sunpearl	32
Sanaabek (IRE)	1123	Sky Booster	738	Super (IRE)	829

HORSE INDEX

Supreme Seductress (IRE)	896
Sweet Cecily (IRE)	830
Sweet Diamond (IRE)	696
Sweetie Time	100
Swimsuit	952
Swiss Dream	537
Sylvestris (IRE)	64
Tafaneen (USA)	953
Tafjeer (USA)	1634
Tahitian Princess (IRE)	439
Takeaway	831
Talbot Green	1194
Talbyah (USA)	897
Tale Untold (USA)	832
Talk Talk (IRE)	1131
Talkative Guest	1074
Talkhees (IRE)	1130
Tamareen (IRE)	461
Tameen	517
Tanassuq (USA)	518
Tanfeer	623
Tanfeeth	462
Tarjeyh (IRE)	1585
Tarkeeba (USA)	954
Tarkhees	1393
Tartan Jura	1006
Tasfeya	1007
Tasheyaat	898
Tashqeel	1394
Tawseef (IRE)	1586
Tazaamun (IRE)	1395
Tees And Cees (IRE)	833
Tell The Wind (IRE)	1396
Temple Meads	1089
Tenba (IRE)	545
Tenby Lady (USA)	1425
Tenuous Link (IRE)	1635
Teo's Sister (IRE)	157
Thawaabet	1397
The Guru of Gloom (IRE)	1195
The High Man	1340
The Long Game	1132
The Mongoose	1522
The Reaper (IRE)	1064
The Resistance (IRE)	1065
The Sydney Arms (IRE)	834
Thekrayaat (IRE)	519
Thirty Pieces (IRE)	65
Thunda	979
Tiberius Claudius (IRE)	1075
Tiger Webb	245
Time For Applause	463
Time To Work (IRE)	34
Timothy T	173
Tinkertown (IRE)	342
To The Spring	741
Tobar Na Gaoise (IRE)	158
Together (IRE)	1292
Tokum (IRE)	1228
Tom Bowler	440
Tom Sawyer	1293
Toms River Tess (IRE)	899
Toolain (IRE)	955
Toparichi	1557
Totheendoftheearth	1026
Touch Of Red (USA)	835
Touques (IRE)	624
Trade Commissioner (IRE)	677
Traffic's Sister (USA)	1165
Train Of Thought (IRE)	1636
Trans City (IRE)	1066
Treasured (IRE)	327
Trend	101
Triple Charm	1229
Triple Eight (IRE)	1637
Trojan Nights (USA)	742
Tropical Spirit (IRE)	1341
Tsarina Louise	592
Tugboat (IRE)	1342
Tullius (IRE)	1653
Tuscan Blue	836
Tweenie (IRE)	837
Twin Soul (IRE)	33
Twinkled	102
Twist Of Silver (USA)	1230
Unbeatable	1035
Uncut Stone (IRE)	1638
Unex El Greco	678
Unex Goya (IRE)	743
Union City Blues (IRE)	1067
Unique Style (IRE)	1068
Universe	103
Up In Time	1036
Utley (USA)	679
Val O'Hara (IRE)	1654
Valdaw	1166
Valeo Si Vales (IRE)	1317
Valera (IRE)	838
Valley Tiger	1196
Velesgo (IRE)	1343
Veloce (IRE)	520
Velvet Underground (IRE)	1133
Vencedor (IRE)	159
Ventura Sands (IRE)	571
Venus Empress	1090
Vestitas (IRE)	160
Vienna Woods (IRE)	850
Viking Rose (IRE)	546
Viking Storm	486
Vita Lika	1134
Viva Diva	1041
Voodoo Prince	464
Waiter's Dream	1135
Walking On Water (IRE)	1639
Waltzing Cat (USA)	1426
War In Babylon (IRE)	487
War Is War (IRE)	1231
Warm Welcome	104
Warneford	1136
Water Ice	416
Waterborne	328
Watered Silk	1587
Watneya	744
Wave Of Applause	1483
Web Of Dreams (IRE)	1137
Welsh Dancer	839
West Leake Bridge (IRE)	900
West Leake Melody	901
Western Aristocrat (USA)	1232
Westhaven (IRE)	538
What About Now	922
What Is The Stars (IRE)	161
Whiplash Willie	35
Whipless (IRE)	162
Whistle On By	902
Whitby Jet (IRE)	1591
Why (IRE)	1294
Wilaya (USA)	680
Wild Coco (GER)	246
Wild Hysteria (IRE)	1544
Winged Diva (IRE)	36
Wiqaaya (IRE)	465
With A Flower	37
Witzend (IRE)	1304
Wolf Slayer	417
Wonder Of Wonders (USA)	1295
Wong Again	923
Wootton Bassett	572
Ya Hafed	466
Yair Hill (IRE)	521
Yakamoz	174
Yarooh (USA)	192
Yashila (IRE)	840
Yasmeena (USA)	903
Yojimbo (IRE)	296
Young Sahib (USA)	1138
Zafaraan	314
Zafarana	467
Zaidan (USA)	193
Zanazzi (USA)	681
Zarafshan (IRE)	468
Zebedee	841
Zenella	441
Zippy Zitter (IRE)	163
Zoffany (IRE)	1296
Zoowraa	956
Zykina	1523

Unnamed 38-40, 66-73, 105-118, 123-126, 164-165, 175-177, 194-209, 247-259, 297-302, 315-317, 329-331, 343, 347-348, 376-379, 418-431, 442, 469-479, 488-490, 522, 525-528, 539, 573-579, 583-584, 593-598, 625-628, 682-693, 699-704, 745-750, 758, 842-845, 851-854, 904-912, 924-925, 957-965, 969-971, 980-981, 1008-1011, 1027, 1037-1039, 1042-1051, 1076-1077, 1082-1083, 1091-1092, 1139-1146, 1154-1155, 1184-1185, 1197, 1233-1245, 1297-1299, 1305-1306, 1318-1320, 1344-1350, 1365-1368, 1373-1374, 1398-1400, 1430-1434, 1470-1474, 1484-1488, 1524-1534, 1545, 1588, 1592-1598, 1640-1647, 1655

Dams index

Dams appear under the reference number of their offspring.

Aberdovey	186
Abide	1042
Achieve	904
Acts Of Grace	505
Adaala	1376
Adees Dancer	716
Adoration	1275
Aethra	988
Affair Of State	294
Affaire Royal	288
Affianced	154
Affirmed Crown	842
Agata	194
Agnetha	491
Ahdaaf	454
Aileen's Gift	297
Akarita	439
Akrmina	625
Al Dhahab	23
Al Joudha	1028
Alasha	1344
Alaya	1345
Alba Stella	1402
Albahja	938
Alborada	1401
Alegria	540
Alexander Eliott	62
Alexander Phantom	432
Alexandrine	670
Alhufoof	1484
Alinga	281
Aljafliyah	573
All Embracing	131
All Quiet	821
All Too Beautiful	1295
Alla Prima	224
Alleluia	1342
Alluring Park	620
Almaaseh	920
Almurooj	898
Alpine Park	122
Alshakr	1393
Altana	147
Alter Ego	433
Alvarita	42
Always Awesome	957
Am I	669
Amaryllis	37
Amathia	88
Amazed	185
Ameerat	940
Amenixa	1403
Amonita	1212
Amorette	697
Amsicora	2
Anazah	1591
Anbella	195
Ancient Secret	385
Anestasia	1227
Angara	1522
Angel Isa	382
Angel Of The Gwaun	1333
Angel Wing	55
Angel's Camp	418
Anna Frid	1640
Anna Karenina	1115
Annabelle Ja	798
Annaourna	83
Annex	1579
Antediluvian	847
Anyaas	705
Apache Star	676
Aquarelle	216
Arabesque	682
Arabian Spell	358
Arabica	743
Arabis	919
Ardbrae Lady	1260
Aricia	13
Aristocratic Lady	1232
Art Eyes	1169
Artful	500
Artistic Blue	1108
Arutua	104
Asaafeer	1130
Ascoli	372
Asheyana	345
Aspen Leaves	868
Aspired	408
Astrocharm	1546
Ataboa	1469
Atamana	737
Athlumney Lady	1221
Atlantic Frost	5
Attraction	638
Auspicious	1379
Australian Dreams	66
Autumn Pearl	56
Autumnal	1139
Averami	24
Ayun	498
Bahr	947
Baileys First	1079
Baileys On Line	123
Bakhoor	307
Bali Breeze	349
Bali Royal	711
Ball Chairman	1323
Balladonia	572
Ballet	779
Ballette	683
Ballymore Celebre	130
Balmy	905
Bank On Her	832
Baraka	1276
Barakat	1556
Baralinka	320
Barboukh	536
Barnabas	3
Barnacla	1151
Basking	332
Bay Tree	1008
Bayalika	1134
Baywood	1652
Beading	1078
Beautiful Noise	571
Beautifulballerina	643
Beauty Bright	1270
Because	105
Bedazzle	602
Bella Chica	213
Belle de Cadix	875
Belle Et Deluree	836
Beraysim	956
Berenica	1588
Berkeley Lodge	833
Best Side	227
Bethesda	861
Bezzaaf	1449
Bianca Nera	75
Bible Box	1602
Binavicar	652
Bint Zamayem	1128
Birdie	92
Birthday Present	410
Black Belt Shopper	912
Black Opal	38
Blaenavon	12
Blessing	100
Blodwen	485
Blue Crystal	1093
Blue Lightning	1590
Blue Sirocco	555
Blue Symphony	1328
Blueberry Walk	568
Bluebird Day	1425
Blush Damask	247
Blushing Barada	1377
Bobbydazzle	808
Bold Classic	1539
Bold Desire	767
Bolero Again	823
Bollicina	858
Bolsena	417
Bolshaya	790
Bon Vivant	831
Bonheur	781
Border Minstral	67
Bordighera	729
Borgia	1511
Born To Glamour	1441
Bourbon Blues	1460
Bourbonella	726
Bradamante	1470
Branston Jewel	274
Brave Madam	860
Brazilian Bride	1378
Bread Of Heaven	745
Break Point	699
Brecon	1197
Breezy Louise	226
Briery	279
Brighella	974
Bright Bank	1216
Bright Spells	1365
Brightest	28

DAMS INDEX 361

Briolette	1503	Cherokee Stream	1086	Dabaweyaa	742
Brocatelle	1463	Cheviot Indian	1162	Dabiliya	315
Bronntanas	133	Chic	1498	Daftara	834
Bronwen	969	Chica Roca	1628	Daganya	1321
Brush Strokes	280	Child Prodigy	1067	Dali's Grey	376
Bunditten	1233	Child Star	543	Dame Alicia	694
Bunood	493	Choice House	1109	Damjanich	461
Burnin' Memories	381	Choirgirl	120	Dance Away	305
Burqa	1576	Chorist	719	Dance Lively	70
Burren Rose	1609	Christmas Player	96	Dance Sequence	529
Bush Baby	707	Chrysalis	1370	Dance Solo	843
Bush Cat	605	City Gambler	1040	Dance Time	135
Bywayofthestars	234	Clare Hills	68	Dance Troupe	164
Cal Norma's Lady	1592	Clarice Orsini	403	Dancing Feather	982
Call Collect	1308	Class	396	Dancing Steps	846
Camaret	558	Claxon	495	Dancingintheclouds	1408
Cambara	1021	Clear Impression	469	Danehill's Dream	486
Camlet	1524	Clear Vision	1154	Danielli	873
Canouan	604	Clepsydra	248	Danish Gem	1084
Capannacce	1210	Cleveland Browni	835	Danzante	329
Cape Charlotte	218	Clincher Club	574	Danzelline	145
Cape Columbine	554	Clog Dance	876	Daqtora	881
Cape Trafalgar	1081	Cloud Hill	1326	Darariyna	752
Capilla Bonita	1366	Cloudy Bay	1122	Dardshi	452
Capistrano Day	1471	Cochin	1367	Dark Indian	152
Cappa Blanca	1054	Collada	769	Darling	916
Cappella	57	Colorado Dancer	616	Dashiba	538
Capriole	1234	Colorspin	1261	Dawn Chorus	223
Cara Fantasy	511	Colza	244	Dawn Raid	1375
Carabine	581	Coming Home	1111	Dawnus	1387
Carafe	655	Compton Girl	582	Dazzling Dancer	1380
Carefree Cheetah	1138	Confetti	1422	Dear Catch	1373
Carenage	167	Congressional	106	Dedicated Lady	863
Caribbean Escape	1082	Conspiracy	521	Delight Of Dawn	1166
Carinae	367	Contiguous	1525	Delphic Way	1171
Cash Run	1279	Cool Clarity	1636	Delphinium	1615
Cashel Queen	600	Cool Question	1414	Delta	685
Cashew	484	Coolrain Lady	1599	Desert Alchemy	1088
Cassandra Go	1343	Coralita	1259	Desert Beauty	1514
Cassis	1199	Cordelia	1065	Desert Bloom	1499
Castara Beach	552	Corndavon	1356	Desert Design	8
Castelletto	1235	Corrine	420	Desert Frolic	1611
Castilian Queen	267	Counting Blessings	852	Desert Gold	1153
Catch	298	Country Maiden	192	Desert Royalty	1305
Catherinofaragon	723	Courting	722	Desiraka	1155
Caumshinaun	1624	Coveted	7	Deveron	180
Cayman Sunset	1293	Coy	1502	Dhelaal	1570
Ceanothus	668	Coyote	107	Di Moi Oui	166
Cedar Sea	1456	Cozy Maria	841	Diabaig	1303
Cefira	1031	Cozzy Corner	953	Diamonaka	405
Ceirseach	143	Crackle	761	Diamond Line	330
Celestial Princess	1029	Cradle Brief	69	Diamond Lodge	818
Cellars Shiraz	1359	Crafty Example	1290	Didina	662
Celtic Heroine	949	Craigmill	1	Dietrich	1254
Centifolia	171	Crinkle	1076	Digger Girl	539
Centre Court	569	Crofters Ceilidh	980	Diliza	799
Champagne Toni	812	Crossmolina	1043	Dimelight	533
Changeable	53	Crumpetsfortea	564	Dinka Raja	1430
Changing Partners	52	Crystal Ballet	134	Diplomats Daughter	1542
Chantilly	849	Crystal Gazing	757	Dipterous	795
Charlene Lacy	560	Crystal Music	684	Disco Ball	229
Charlie Girl	419	Crystal Star	1494	Disco Volante	999
Charlotte O'Fraise	80	Cuca Vela	386	Distinctive Look	240
Chater	658	Culture Queen	1454	Divi	671
Chaturanga	1287	Cumulate	416	Divine Dixie	613
Cheal Rose	1009	Curriculum	871	Divinite	304
Cheeky Madam	146	Cut Short	1098	Dixie Belle	1431
Chelsea Rose	196	Cute Cait	1258	Dixiehunt	1307

Name	#	Name	#	Name	#
Djebel Amour	1540	Eurostorm	1317	Forever Fine	586
Doctor's Glory	1406	Eve	504	Forty Carats	448
Dollar Bird	1099	Evensong	237	Forum Floozie	599
Dolydille	1001	Everlasting Love	383	Fountain Of Peace	1291
Donna Giovanna	313	Excellent	1340	Four Legs Good	1014
Donnelly's Hollow	482	Exchanging Glances	1459	Frangy	360
Donyana	1157	Exclusive	1496	Frappe	708
Dorelia	340	Exclusive Approval	724	Free Lance	1480
Doula	1247	Exorcet	14	Frenzy	814
Dowhatjen	264	Express Logic	198	Friendlier	678
Downtown Blues	663	Exultate Jubilate	725	Frizzante	1513
Drama Class	1504	Ezilla	163	Frond	316
Drawing A Blank	124	Face The Storm	796	Fur Will Fly	958
Dream Genie	421	Factice	869	Gabriella	1195
Dream Rose	1538	Fair Settlement	1448	Galapagar	788
Dream Time	736	Fairy Of The Night	630	Gallivant	644
Dress To Thrill	1626	Fallen Star	639	Gamra	777
Dubai Diamond	437	Famcred	1083	Garanciere	39
Dubai Surprise	108	Fame At Last	1641	Gates Of Eden	1479
Duchy Of Cornwall	583	Fancy Rose	1037	Gemini Gold	1362
Dundrummin'	335	Fantastic Account	1396	Geminini	959
Duty Paid	542	Fantastic Belle	336	Generous Gesture	1016
Dynacam	1526	Fanzine	631	Generous Lady	1601
Early Evening	866	Far Shores	906	Gentle Peace	1072
East Cape	1455	Farfala	1182	Genuine Charm	1630
Easy Mover	1563	Farrfesheena	109	Ghazal	706
Easy Option	603	Fashion	101	Gibraltar Bay	1301
Easy Sunshine	1184	Fashion Cat	25	Gift Of Spring	456
Easy To Love	1446	Fashion Guide	775	Gilah	1648
Ego	523	Favorite	49	Gilded Edge	1252
Ekleel	470	Feeling Blue	525	Gillipops	1020
Ela Athena	1205	Felicita	815	Gipsy Moth	468
Elanaaka	782	Felicity	642	Gladstone Street	424
Elbaaha	611	Fey Rouge	286	Glatisant	665
Election Special	820	Fictitious	806	Glimpse	771
Elegant Times	1044	Fiddle-Dee-Dee	1069	Glinting Desert	739
Element Of Truth	193	Fidelio's Miracle	50	Glorious	1395
Elite Guest	984	Fig Tree Drive	566	Glory Oatway	902
Eliza	1289	Figlette	1071	Gloved Hand	71
Ellen	946	Fille De Joie	746	Gold Bar	1512
Elutrah	1568	Film Buff	530	Gold Queen	1110
Eman's Joy	422	Fin	339	Gold Strike	1038
Emerald Peace	1198	Final Favour	1075	Golden Cat	635
Eminencia	341	Fine And Mellow	178	Golden Flyer	1203
Emly Express	48	Finty	488	Gonbarda	608
Emma's Star	398	Firebelly	720	Gonfilia	621
Emplane	249	Firecrest	1411	Good Girl	1187
Encore My Love	506	Fireman's Ball	619	Goodie Twosues	77
Encouragement	1056	Five Fields	907	Graceful Air	935
Endless Peace	1612	Fiveofive	1545	Gracility	1439
Entente Cordiale	1206	Fizzy Treat	125	Gracious	172
Entrap	188	Flames	1582	Grade A Star	1313
Eoz	1354	Flanders	941	Grand Design	1445
Epping	215	Flash Of Gold	1491	Grand Lili	1053
Erstwhile	191	Flawlessly	778	Grand Slam Maria	794
Es Que	930	Fleet Lady	628	Grandalea	1363
Escouades	423	Fleeting Rainbow	499	Granted	864
Eshaadeh	654	Floppie	1174	Great Hope	156
Esloob	1580	Flora Burn	277	Greek Symphony	151
Esteemed Lady	827	Flower Market	1462	Green Castle	992
Esterlina	889	Flying Finish	575	Green Lassy	1398
Eswarah	936	Follow A Dream	641	Green Room	986
Et Dona	324	Follow Flanders	217	Grizel	1642
Eternal Beauty	197	Foodbroker Fancy	1201	Guana Bay	299
Eternelle	47	Foofaraw	870	Guermantes	848
Eternity Ring	514	Footlight Fantasy	1175	Guignol	853
Etizaaz	943	For Evva Silca	1562	Gulchina	61
Eurolink Café	1549	Foreplay	1605	Hachiyah	471

Half Glance	250	Intrigued	338	Kiftsgate Rose	520
Halland Park Lass	1253	Intriguing	561	Kilbride	698
Halo River	1578	Inya Lake	214	Kimola	162
Hammiya	1583	Irina	576	Kind	252
Handaza	1346	Iris May	994	Kiralik	548
Hannda	1214	Irish Question	140	Kirk Wynd	33
Happy Flight	1384	Irresistible	1493	Kirtle	365
Harda Arda	960	Irtahal	1569	Kismah	1561
Harryana	1089	Isis	200	Kiswahili	1355
Hataana	357	Island Destiny	1172	Kitty O'Shea	1386
Haute Volta	760	Island Escape	148	Kitza	1248
Hawait Al Barr	377	Israar	1467	Koniya	1035
Hawala	686	Ithaca	1527	Kushnarenkovo	1046
Hazariya	1347	Itnab	503	Kylemore	1183
Hazimah	1567	Itqaan	1581	L'Acajou	776
Heat Lightning	1140	Ivy League Star	1604	L'Ancresse	653
Heat Of The Night	306	Iwunder	1552	L-Way First	803
Heavenly Whisper	856	Jabali	1560	La Caprice	914
Heckle	1472	Jade Chequer	362	La Cucaracha	903
Helen Sharp	481	Jaish	494	La Persiana	968
Hellenic	1505	Jalissa	549	La Reine Mambo	1141
Helwa	828	Jamrah	1428	La Sky	253
Hendrina	531	Janayen	1124	La Tintoretta	921
Herminoe	1189	Jasmick	1180	Labrusca	1476
Hesperia	16	Jasmine Pearl	384	Lac Dessert	1485
Hi Katriona	1024	Jathaabeh	944	Ladeena	1329
Hidden Charm	1637	Jaya	1208	Lady Angola	867
Hidden Hope	110	Jaywick	266	Lady Express	913
Hideaway	1263	Jazz Princess	175	Lady Georgia	1407
High Walden	251	Jellett	756	Lady Gregory	1064
Highbrook	63	Jeritza	650	Lady High Havens	1593
Hill Welcome	290	Jessica's Dream	1271	Lady In Waiting	201
Hit The Sky	1269	Jewell In The Sky	590	Lady Joshua	211
Hoh Dancer	347	Jinskeys Gift	1181	Lady Kris	1190
Hollow Haze	436	Jorghinia	1106	Lady Luck	1610
Holly's Kid	1061	Josie Doocey	759	Lady Miletrian	1432
Holy Nola	425	Joyful Green	783	Lady Of Talent	126
Honey Gold	159	Jude	688	Lady Ragazza	1352
Honour Bright	199	Judhoor	895	Lady Scarlett	1654
Hopeful Sign	1426	June Moon	713	Lady Zonda	990
Houdini's Honey	1236	Juno Madonna	1250	Ladylishandra	1070
Housekeeper	837	Justice System	804	Lalindi	451
Humouresque	741	Kahira	160	Lanark Belle	865
Hureya	509	Kalagold	522	Landela	689
Hymn Of Love	1608	Kalimanta	242	Landinium	1167
Hypnotize	1412	Kamarinskaya	111	Landmark	640
Ibtikar	1228	Kanisfluh	1478	Largo	1650
Ice Dream	401	Kanun	312	Las Flores	629
Icing	700	Kardelle	1121	Last Impression	409
Imagine	1297	Karla June	112	Latest Chapter	1170
Imperial Bailiwick	592	Kassana	1325	Latina	1553
In My Life	1010	Kassiopeia	260	Legend Maker	1267
In The Highlands	1013	Katch Me Katie	1059	Leonica	91
In The Limelight	319	Kathy Jet	545	Liege	797
In The Woods	1000	Katiykha	1327	Light Jig	1509
Inaaq	1558	Kawn	728	Lighthouse	426
Incense	292	Keepers Dawn	1045	Lightsabre	1209
Inchberry	800	Kelang	174	Lightwood Lady	1026
Independence	444	Kelly Nicole	342	Lila	1515
Indian Belle	937	Kelsey Rose	308	Lily Valley	283
Indiana Blues	1022	Key Academy	993	Line Ahead	556
Indienne	179	Key To Coolcullen	161	Lines Of Beauty	1507
Ink Pot	1447	Khamseh	1278	Lingering	1388
Inner Strength	399	Khasayl	1117	Lisfannon	1015
Innocent Air	687	Khatela	567	Lisieux Orchid	624
Inseparable	966	Khubza	1322	Little Doll	1622
Insight	231	Khulood	507	Lizzysue	414
Intaaj	361	Kicking Bird	1220	Lloc	20

Lobby Card	979	May Kiersey	1482	Mosquera	727
Local Spirit	86	May Light	1436	Most Remarkable	618
Lochangel	1017	Maybe In May	1594	Mostaqeleh	932
Locharia	1119	Maycocks Bay	94	Mount Street	1306
Lochridge	46	Mayenne	695	Mountain Law	1147
Lochsong	19	Mazuna	1420	Mouramara	1348
Locorotondo	1062	Me	593	Mouwadh	1577
Londonnetdotcom	673	Mellow Jazz	747	Moving Diamonds	220
Lonesome Me	375	Mellow Park	1371	Mowazana	446
Look Here's Carol	1091	Melrose Morning	594	Mrs Brown	1438
Lords Guest	690	Meranie Girl	844	Mubkera	1500
Lorien Hill	1034	Merle	931	Much Faster	1490
Louve Royale	51	Mermaid Island	1281	Mureefa	176
Love For Ever	672	Mexican Hawk	1218	Muschana	1619
Love Knot	696	Mezzanine	1094	Musical Horizon	1643
Love Me Tender	459	Mezzogiorno	951	Musical Treat	614
Love Me True	1264	Mia Mambo	1451	Musicanti	857
Love Medicine	939	Midnight Air	656	My Dubai	626
Love Quest	952	Midnight Mist	1618	My Funny Valentine	1116
Love Sonnet	1012	Midnight Partner	908	My Lass	1200
Luana	991	Midpoint	483	My Mariam	368
Luanshya	380	Mille Couleurs	371	My Renee	132
Lucina	732	Millie's Choice	1158	Mystery Hill	1487
Lucky For Me	584	Milly Of The Vally	1039	Mythie	296
Lulu Island	1123	Mimiteh	1161	Myths And Verses	738
Luminda	411	Min Asl Wafi	1105	Naayla	1318
Lynnwood Chase	1185	Mini Driver	922	Naazeq	392
Macadamia	480	Minkova	1361	Nadeszhda	1575
Madame Anne Peters	1047	Mint Royale	438	Nadwah	918
Madeleine's Blush	400	Misaayef	770	Naharnook	524
Maganda	1286	Misplace	1574	Najah	517
Magical Romance	1101	Miss Ahabaa	934	Najayeb	1649
Magicalmysterykate	1142	Miss Amadeus	900	Najiya	121
Magnificent Bell	562	Miss Bellbird	1564	Najmati	961
Magnificent Style	661	Miss Corniche	87	Naked Poser	1353
Maids Causeway	610	Miss Demure	740	Nando's Dream	1211
Mail Express	369	Miss Hawai	987	Nandy's Cavern	1126
Majestic Sakeena	1528	Miss Honorine	1519	Nantyglo	1196
Majinskaya	153	Miss Intimate	754	Naomi Wildman	1551
Majorata	532	Miss Lacey	359	Naraina	850
Majoune	1508	Miss McGuire	309	Narmina	1335
Makhsusah	1404	Miss Megs	851	Nasharaat	427
Making Waves	1483	Miss Meltemi	467	Nasheed	1397
Maltage	996	Miss Prim	455	Nasij	462
Mambo In Freeport	933	Miss Prism	1417	National Swagger	137
Mamonta	1461	Miss Riviera Golf	95	Natural Skill	766
Manayer	1631	Miss Shaan	763	Nausicaa	801
Mandolin	534	Misskinta	1063	Navajo Love Song	1550
Manger Square	142	Misterah	1565	Navajo Rainbow	1585
Mania	1112	Misty Heights	1617	Nawaji	1319
Mansiya	303	Mocca	733	Neath	1644
Manuka Magic	1572	Model Queen	472	Nebraas	1399
Maraami	501	Modesta	254	Needlecraft	877
Maramba	1136	Mokaraba	519	Nemea	1118
Marannatha	1450	Molomo	265	Neutrina	236
Mare Aux Fees	1011	Mona Em	31	Never A Doubt	891
Maria Bonita	784	Mona Lisa	1262	Never Gone	1048
Mariah's Storm	1265	Monevassia	1251	New Assembly	787
Marienbad	615	Mono Star	785	Nidhaal	460
Marieval	445	Monturani	657	Night Club	553
Maristax	1457	Mood Swings	819	Night Frolic	649
Mariyba	755	Moon Drop	58	Night Haven	190
Market Slide	1621	Moon Flower	879	Night Symphonie	587
Marling	888	Moon Goddess	1510	Nirvana	1177
Masaader	465	Moon's Whisper	645	No Frills	1049
Maugwenna	285	Moonmaiden	300	No Hard Feelings	1019
Mauri Moon	1606	Morina	1466	No Matter What	679
Mawaakeb	623	Mosaique Bleue	1486	Noble Desert	565

DAMS INDEX

Name	№	Name	№	Name	№
Noble Lady	1409	Phariseek	1625	Queen's Cape	978
Noble Peregrine	1464	Pharoah's Delight	45	Queen's Logic	1104
Noble View	1032	Photogenic	648	Queen's Wharf	753
Noddle Soup	1002	Pickle	964	Query	1434
Noelani	1336	Pilgrim Spirit	1090	Quest For Eternity	1330
Nomistakeaboutit	1005	Pina Colada	1481	Quevada	311
Non Dimenticar Me	1488	Pink Stone	1433	Quick Feet	874
Norfolk Lavender	1571	Pious	709	Quickfire	1529
North East Bay	413	Piper's Ash	182	Quickstyx	744
Not Before Time	21	Pippa's Dancer	1193	Quiet Mouse	1256
Notjustaprettyface	1613	Pirie	1125	Quiet Waters	845
Noushkey	962	Pitcroy	1554	Quiff	1530
Nouveau Riche	791	Pitrizza	1392	Quintrell	541
Ntombi	634	Pivot d'Amour	764	Quinzey	651
Nufoos	1007	Pizzicato	588	Quite Elusive	1120
Nutmeg	1547	Playgirl	1176	Rachelle	103
Nuzooa	1634	Playing Footsie	822	Rada	40
Nymphs Echo	1237	Plenty Of Grace	203	Rada's Daughter	901
Oak Tree Miss	4	Plenty Of Light	1351	Radiate	1150
Oblique	1389	Plume Rouge	1442	Raghida	878
Off Message	458	Plymsole	893	Rah Wa	1050
On A Soapbox	1006	Pocketbrook	580	Rahcak	585
One Of The Family	1194	Point Perfect	173	Rain Flower	715
Opalescent	1651	Polish Descent	1239	Rainbow End	1114
Opera Comica	748	Polished Gem	1632	Rainbow Goddess	1219
Opera Glass	36	Polished Up	85	Rainbow Queen	1223
Opera Ridge	859	Polite Reply	1616	Raindancing	809
Optaria	1023	Politesse	714	Ramona	150
Orange Sunset	924	Polly Perkins	473	Raphimix	813
Oriental Queen	977	Pongee	373	Rasana	177
Orinoco	1360	Pooka's Daughter	762	Rasmalai	721
Ouija Board	464	Portmeirion	1186	Rave Reviews	636
Our Little Secret	1435	Post Modern	84	Ravish	170
Our Queen Of Kings	202	Praia Grande	60	Raze	187
Our Sheila	428	Prancing	204	Reach For The Moon	1241
Out Of Thanks	388	Preach	1282	Reading Habit	79
Oyster Bay	72	Prealpina	855	Ream Three	370
Painted Moon	98	Prends Ca	1018	Reams Of Verse	257
Palace Affair	1173	Preseli	1334	Rebelline	885
Palisade	1368	Presently	1374	Recite	165
Panic Stations	102	Presently Blessed	374	Record Time	212
Pantita	210	Pretty As Can Be	730	Red Affair	1338
Paris Glory	334	Pretty Meadow	1240	Red Azalea	1277
Park Approach	271	Pretty Poppy	1300	Red Bloom	527
Park Romance	1238	Pretty Sharp	1143	Red Camellia	1492
Parvenue	1266	Prevail	350	Red Conquest	93
Passata	1311	Pride Of My Heart	337	Red Feather	1391
Passiflora	1222	Priere	601	Red Fuschia	824
Pastorale	627	Princess Electra	222	Red Garland	734
Pay The Bank	1559	Princess Ellen	391	Red Heaven	450
Peace	1080	Princess Killeen	817	Red Peony	1421
Peace In The Park	310	Princess Kris	622	Red Ryding Hood	429
Pearly Brooks	774	Princess Manila	364	Red Shoe	882
Pearly Gates	1052	Private Seductress	896	Reddening	352
Pedicure	1074	Promptly	73	Redrightreturning	1452
Pendulum	805	Protectress	255	Reem Al Barari	513
Peneia	884	Puce	230	Reem Dubai	617
Penza	1332	Pudding Lane	975	Reematna	577
Peony	674	Purepleasureseeker	1160	Regal Rose	1518
Perfect Partner	263	Putuna	10	Regency Rose	1224
Perfect Solution	701	Puzzling	442	Regrette Rien	1600
Perfectly Clear	1655	Qasirah	955	Remote Romance	239
Perle d'Irlande	758	Qhazeenah	948	Request	666
Persian Fortune	526	Quandary	256	Requested Pleasure	1213
Persian Jasmine	963	Quantum Lady	717	Resistance Heroine	262
Pescia	1501	Quarter Moon	1273	Return	1645
Petite Spectre	149	Queen Cleopatra	1298	Revival	1217
Phantom Ring	289	Queen Isabella	1589	Rhapsodize	1191

Riberac	985	Sauterne	205	Sinndiya	1349
Ridotto	1458	Save The Table	792	Sister Sylvia	477
Right Answer	273	Savieres	807	Ski For Gold	492
Right Key	1390	Sayedati Eljamilah	712	Sky Bird	1429
Ring Of Love	1033	Scandalette	997	Slewvera	811
Ringarooma	1030	Scarlett Rose	1242	Slieve	772
Ringmoor Down	1369	Schonbein	449	Slip Ashore	261
Rise	366	Schust Madame	563	Slip Dance	1541
River Belle	550	Science Fiction	90	Smart 'n Noble	333
Road Harbour	1324	Scootie Utie	595	Snippets	276
Robe Chinoise	1423	Scottish Stage	1497	Snow Princess	1225
Rock Dove	1025	Scribonia	139	So Admirable	664
Rock Salt	189	Se La Vie	228	So Glam So Hip	378
Romantic Myth	557	Sea Angel	475	So Precious	355
Ros The Boss	508	Sea Picture	1097	So Well Red	1337
Rosacara	973	Seattle Ribbon	535	Soar	1506
Roselyn	894	Second Prayer	404	Soft Touch	397
Rosie's Posy	839	Secret Garden	1285	Solaia	646
Rosina Mae	1152	Secret Justice	412	Soliza	1473
Rosy Outlook	546	Seed Al Maha	476	Solo De Lune	232
Rouge Noir	272	Sensational Mover	430	Something Blue	1132
Rouwaki	890	Sentimental Value	998	Sonachan	181
Roxy	826	Set Fair	1320	Sonorous	899
Royal Consort	415	Shadow Song	1292	Sontime	434
Royal Mistress	97	Shahaamah	1623	Sound Asleep	910
Royals Special	1383	Shaieef	406	Sound Of Sleat	825
Rubies From Burma	915	Shaken And Stirred	1465	Source Of Life	1092
Ruby Rocket	967	Shanghai Lily	1405	Soviet Moon	1531
Rule Britannia	466	Sharesha	1339	Spa	1003
Rumansy	1633	Shariyfa	981	Space Time	928
Rumplestiltskin	1294	Sharp Catch	647	Spanish Falls	1415
Runs In The Family	854	Sharp Point	1316	Spanish Gold	17
Russian Countess	972	Sharp Secret	22	Spanish Lady	516
Russian Dance	1215	Shastye	1243	Sparkle Of Stones	1517
Russian Lullaby	393	Shawanni	892	Sparky's Song	275
Russian Rhythm	1523	Shbakni	301	Special Moment	1192
Saada One	351	She's Classy	578	Speciale	887
Sachet	773	Sheboygan	1058	Specifically	883
Sadika	862	Sheena's Gold	596	Spectacular Show	6
Safeen	1095	Sheer Spirit	1331	Speed Cop	11
Sahara Rose	44	Shemaka	1520	Speed Of Sound	544
Sahara Silk	589	Shersha	1596	Speirbhean	157
Sahool	1586	Shesasmartlady	394	Spinning Queen	677
Saibhreas	1073	Shimna	983	Spinning Ruby	667
Sail With The Wind	1310	Shining Creek	1068	Spinning Top	789
Saintly Persuasion	1584	Shining Desert	1475	Spirito Libro	1418
Sakhya	314	Shirley Moon	1427	Spitting Image	463
Salvia	515	Shirley Valentine	258	Splendeur	1614
Sanctify	1257	Shiva	235	Splendid	1314
Sanpala	113	Shivaree	1440	Spotlight	496
Santa Isobel	35	Show Off	718	Spring Easy	1304
Santisima Trinidad	675	Shy Lady	1107	Spring Snowdrop	1358
Santorini	1188	Siena Gold	363	Spring Will	30
Saoire	1543	Sigonella	1244	Spurned	15
Saphire	768	Sil Sila	942	Square Pants	1245
Sarabah	346	Silent Heir	1144	Square The Circle	27
Sarah Georgina	1135	Silk And Scarlet	1268	St Clair Ridge	144
Sarah Stokes	291	Silk Fan	1537	Star Express	114
Sarayir	897	Silken Cat	681	Star Tulip	32
Saree	474	Silky Dawn	323	Starchy	158
Sassari	435	Silver Bandana	65	Starlight Dreams	1283
Sassy Bird	970	Silver Bracelet	1595	Starry Dreamer	1255
Sateen	141	Silver Pursuit	82	Starship	1246
Satin Bell	326	Silver Rhapsody	1416	Starstone	1385
Satin Doll	225	Silver Star	322	State Crystal	880
Satin Rose	786	Simianna	1113	Stormy Channel	911
Saturday's Child	1357	Simonaventura	128	Street Scene	1165
Saudia	1272	Singing Diva	909	String Quartet	1573

Name	No.	Name	No.	Name	No.
Strings	1004	Tetravella	81	Vale View	765
Strut	321	Thaminah	1566	Valencia	1534
Stylish	1129	Tharwa	431	Valentine Band	241
Stylist	233	The Manx Touch	54	Valjarv	344
Subtle Affair	1055	The Stick	591	Valley Lights	1607
Succession	243	The Strand	810	Vampire Queen	1468
Succumb	1202	There With Me	1444	Varenka	659
Suitably Discreet	1638	Thermopylae	490	Vas Y Carla	1041
Sukuma	9	Thesky'sthelimit	1168	Vayavaig	749
Sulaalah	660	Thicket	1148	Velvet Moon	945
Sulitelma	29	Think	206	Velvet Slipper	1027
Sulk	1495	Third Party	1437	Velvet Waters	89
Summer Dreams	1603	Thiscatsforcaryl	1204	Venturi	295
Summer Night	1424	Thorntoun Piccolo	1145	Verbal Intrigue	219
Summer Shower	691	Thousand Thrills	692	Verbania	793
Summer Trysting	1635	Three Owls	487	Verbose	1646
Summerhill Parkes	528	Tidal Chorus	282	Very Nice	208
Summertime Parkes	1149	Tikitano	780	Very Racy	1364
Sumora	995	Time Away	155	Via Milano	1309
Sun Seasons	1410	Time Saved	18	Victoria Cross	633
Sun Shower	168	Tina Heights	1413	Victoria Lodge	551
Sunset	348	Tipperary Honor	838	Victoria's Secret	402
Super Supreme	829	Tiriana	1620	Victory Spirit	1555
Supereva	43	Tokyo Rose	816	Villarrica	612
Superlove	1315	Top Of The Form	478	Vino Veritas	1164
Superstar Leo	731	Top Row	704	Vintage Escape	269
Surrender To Me	1312	Topatori	1557	Violet Ballerina	259
Susi Wong	923	Topkamp	1597	Virginia Waters	1249
Susun Kelapa	325	Totality	1085	Virtuous	1516
Swain's Gold	976	Treacle	989	Viscaria	570
Sweet Angeline	1077	Treasure The Lady	1639	Viscountess Brave	34
Sweet Gypsy Rose	702	Treble Heights	387	Walayef	1382
Sweet Pea	497	Treble Seven	184	Waldmark	693
Swindling	547	Tree Chopper	270	Walesiana	927
Swiss Lake	537	Trick	318	Walk On Quest	317
Sybella	1131	Tricoteuse	1381	Walkamia	1231
Syrian Queen	129	Triennial	207	Wannabe	1280
Ta Rib	447	Trillion Wing	1159	Wannabe Grand	1453
Taalluf	1133	Triple Edition	443	Wansdyke Lass	287
Tadkiyra	1288	Triple Gold	950	Warrior Queen	1299
Tafseer	489	Triple Joy	1229	Warrior Wings	1179
Tahirah	1474	Triple Sharp	278	Warsaw Girl	116
Tahrir	886	Trishay	41	Wasnah	518
Takarna	268	Trois Heures Apres	353	Waterfall One	328
Takarouna	327	Tropical Lady	1341	Waterfowl Creek	559
Takesmybreathaway	1535	Truly Bewitched	579	Way To The Stars	26
Talented	1532	Truly Generous	1146	Web Of Intrigue	1137
Tamise	1419	Tshusick	1096	Wedding Cake	1102
Tanaghum	512	Tussah	1587	Wedding Gift	751
Tanzania	680	Twist Of Faith	1230	Wedding Party	395
Tara Gold	221	Tychy	1178	Week End	453
Tara's Girl	840	Tyranny	1296	Well Dressed	637
Tarascon	1477	Ugo Fire	1400	Welsh Diva	872
Tarfshi	926	Ulfah	1394	Welsh Valley	74
Tariysha	1103	Uliana	1627	Wendylina	183
Tarneem	1100	Ultra Finesse	1536	West One	441
Tarocchi	1533	Ulysses Daughter	1060	Western Sal	971
Tashawak	510	Unbridled Treasure	138	Where's Carol	1087
Tawaaded	1226	Undercover	389	Where's Charlotte	1066
Tee Cee	802	Unique Pose	1629	Whipped Queen	1653
Teide Lady	703	Unreal	597	White Queen	502
Tell It	632	Up And About	115	White Wisteria	1544
Teller	457	Up At Dawn	1036	Whole Grain	1443
Tembladora	440	Upskittled	169	Wijdan	735
Tender Is Thenight	59	Urgele	609	Wild Side	246
Tenpence	1548	Vadahilla	606	Willowbridge	1284
Teodora	1302	Vagary	136	Wimple	479
Terri's Charmer	925	Valdara	917	Windmill	78

Winds Of March	117	Wrong Bride	302	Zarabaya	99
Winds Of Time	750	Wrong Key	1489	Zarannda	293
Windsharp	607	Wunders Dream	598	Zarara	954
Winesong	119	Wyola	710	Zarawa	379
Wink	76	Ya Hajar	1127	Zayn Zen	965
Winter Ice	390	Yaqootah	830	Zeeba	354
Withorwithoutyou	127	Yaselda	1163	Zibilene	1274
Wivenhoe	1051	Yashmak	1521	Ziffany	1207
Wonder Lady Anne L	929	Yes Dear	407	Zither	118
Wonderful Desert	245	Young And Daring	238	Zoena	1372
Woodland Orchid	1057	Zabadani	1156	Zomaradah	356
Woodlass	209	Zacchera	284	Zorleni	1647
Woodmaven	64	Zalaiyma	1350	Zuppardo Ardo	1598
Wosaita	343	Zante	331		